ITINERARIUM ITALICUM

STUDIES
IN MEDIEVAL AND
REFORMATION THOUGHT

EDITED BY

HEIKO A. OBERMAN, Tübingen

IN COOPERATION WITH

E. JANE DEMPSEY DOUGLASS, Claremont, California
LEIF GRANE, Copenhagen
GUILLAUME H. M. POSTHUMUS MEYJES, Leiden
ANTON G. WEILER, Nijmegen

VOLUME XIV

ITINERARIUM ITALICUM

LEIDEN
E. J. BRILL
1975

ITINERARIUM ITALICUM

THE PROFILE OF THE ITALIAN RENAISSANCE IN THE MIRROR OF ITS EUROPEAN TRANSFORMATIONS

Dedicated to Paul Oskar Kristeller
on the occasion of his 70th birthday

EDITED BY

HEIKO A. OBERMAN

WITH

THOMAS A. BRADY, JR.

LEIDEN
E. J. BRILL
1975

ISBN 90 04 04259 8

TABLE OF CONTENTS

ACKNOWLEDGEMENTS

In a Festschrift the contributions themselves are the most eloquent acknowledgement conceivable. Shown by agreement and dissent alike they express respect and, in this case, admiration for the recipient.

But secondly, a more than formal expression of gratitude is due to the contributors themselves. The traditional Festschrift is a collection of *varia sparsa*, and this does not lay an inordinate claim on time and thought. This time, however, the contributors were invited to write a chapter in a carefully plotted book, to lay aside their own projects, and to adjust their writing plans, which are already pushed to the margins of their lives by the increasingly complex structure of the modern university. The fact that six leading scholars in their field were prepared to accept our invitation bespeaks their sense of indebtedness to Paul Oskar Kristeller. The sacrifices made in undertaking and completing the task of contributing to this Festschrift in the *via moderna* deserve our explicit and special expression of esteem. Ms. Katherine Gingrich Brady transformed the receiving end of the Oregon Trail into a true communications center between Leiden, Tübingen and Eugene. Finally, we owe a word of thanks to Mr. F. C. Wieder, Jr., and the direction of Brill Publishers, Leiden, for their efforts to have this book ready for presentation on the eve of May 22, 1975.

THOMAS A. BRADY, Jr.
University of Oregon

HEIKO A. OBERMAN
Universität Tübingen

QUOSCUNQUE TULIT FOECUNDA VETUSTAS

Ad Lectorem

HEIKO A. OBERMAN

Universität Tübingen

I

It is not decorative considerations but rather *decorum* in the sense recaptured during the Renaissance which justifies the place of the following poetic verses by Giovanni Pico della Mirandola at the beginning of these introductory pages:

> Hanc studiis servire suis sophia alta coegit
>   Iudicio cunctis anteferenda meo.
> . . . quoscunque tulit foecunda vetustas,
>   Sive ea Graia fuit sive Latina fuit.
> Hoc studium semper nobis preciosius, idque
>   Quod fuit, una mihi nunc quoque cura manet.
> Est cura abstrusas rerum cognoscere causas,
>   Cum veri hoc unum sit sapientis opus,
> Et modo pugnantes pacis sub foedera sectas
>   Ducere et ancipites dissolvisse dolos,
> Et modo quae brevior quisquam collegit in arctum
>   Effusa in plures explicuisse modos.[1]

The fecundity of classical antiquity, by no coincidence elementarily related to the idea of 'Renaissance' and probably its most eloquent common denominator, bespeaks a bewildering wealth of inquiries, insights and interpretations in modern scholarship. Against the background of this overpowering fecundity which has lent wings to the imagination of so many generations of scholars, we can readily see the significance of a recurring theme in the work of Paul Oskar Kristeller. It was this theme which allowed him to conclude sometimes his articles and often his numerous guest-lectures after a characteristically sober and descriptive presentation

---

[1] "Joannis Pici Mirandulae Concordiaeque Comitis Carmina," ed. Paul Oskar Kristeller, *Giovanni Pico della Mirandola and His Sources* (in *L'Opera e il pensiero di Giovanni Pico della Mirandola nella storia dell'umanesimo*), I: *Relazioni* (Firenze, 1965), 35-142; 91f. This collection of poems is preserved in the Bayerische Staatsbibliothek Munich, cod. lat. Monac. 485, dated "Quarto idus Julii MDLX", fol. 53v-66. *Ibid.*, 116.

with what one must call a zealous appeal: ". . . humanism has been studied by scholars from different historical disciplines, who have been working at cross purposes . . . I believe that the best hope for bringing the problem of humanism closer to a satisfactory solution . . . lies in an attempt to coordinate and integrate the results attained by students in various historical disciplines who have been concerned with the problem. . . . We must try to coordinate and integrate the various opinions, not by making compromises between them, but by examining and sifting them, and by recognizing how much each of them is supported by historical evidence . . ." [2]

There is no need to stretch the text in applying Pico's *Carmen* line for line to the scholarly program of Kristeller. Living and thinking this side of the Enlightenment, most of us may feel inclined to replace or rather translate *sophia alta* with 'the historical record'— since these two concepts share the unusual combination of untouchable authority and factual elusiveness. But the parallels between Pico and Kristeller prevail in the single-mindedness of their one concern to overcome the confusion of the warring schools and to respect the diversity of moods and ideas expressed in the sources. Yet, both know about the dangers lurking in the tempting attempt to unravel the abstruse secrets (Milton!) of final causality—which when transposed to the modern field of Renaissance studies may stand for the isolation and promotion of one concept or force as the ultimate concern of humanism as such.

Another and final parallel is to be seen in that 'covenant of peace' which Pico envisioned and aspired to, but which did not materialize. The very fecundity of the classics proved to be more than could be harvested in an unseasonable climate by the generations to come. Above all, the *concordia vetustatis*, the unified vision of antiquity, would prove to be a fiction, a *fable convenue*,[3] unable to withstand the test from those very fields of scholarly endeavor it had given birth to—philology and history. With Pico we divine more than discern that the reason why this attempt could not succeed lies partly in the

---

[2] "Studies on Renaissance Humanism during the last Twenty Years," *Studies in the Renaissance*, IX (1962), 7-30; 9, 21. Granted the external limitations of a short 'Forschungsbericht' this article can still be regarded as the best introduction for a new student both to the state of Renaissance scholarship and to the basic views of the author.

[3] Cf. Heinz Liebing, "Perspektivische Verzeichnungen. Über die Haltbarkeit der *fable convenue* in der Kirchengeschichte," *Zeitschrift für Kirchengeschichte*, LXXIX (1968), 289-307.

unfathomable *sophia alta*, but partly also in her recipient, the equally elusive *sapiens*. This 'wise man', soon on the crossroads between the Faustian wizard and the career-oriented 'wise guy' of the "Humanistik",[4] is no longer the *humanista* of the Italian student slang of the Quattrocento.[5] Instead he is a very particular representative of the program implied in the terms *studia humanitatis* and *studia humaniora*.[6] Pico's openness for knowledge wherever encountered— quoscunque (!) tulit foecunda vetustas—and his quest for an even more inclusive synthesis than the one envisaged in Ficino's Platonism [7] has continued to fascinate Kristeller since it provides contemporary thought with one of the most lasting challenges of Renaissance philosophy: ". . . we must liberate ourselves from the narrow limitations of a single school, and be ready to learn from all schools and thinkers of the past since each of them had its own share in that immense truth whose totality could not be grasped by any one of them . . . In working towards this end, Pico's faith that truth is universal because every tradition may contain a part of it should serve us in this difficult task as a guiding principle, and as a source of inspiration." [8]

Yet, this high praise does not tempt Kristeller to find in Pico della Mirandola *the* model of Italian humanism. As he insists, this model can only be found in the humanities, the home territory of the humanists, and not by indiscriminately choosing one of the many fields on which humanism exerted a powerful, but only *indirect* influence. In this sense Kristeller's conclusion is to be understood: ". . . Renaissance humanism as such was not Christian or pagan, Catholic or Protestant, scientific or antiscientific, civic or despotic,

---

[4] This German designation introduced by Josef Engel in his comprehensive survey of the period, I prefer to reserve for the affectations and social trappings of a humanism which has become 'reçu' in a post-medieval society—or at least one that liked to regard itself as such. Cf. "Von der spätmittelalterlichen respublica christiana zum Mächte-Europa der Neuzeit," in *Handbuch der europäischen Geschichte*, Theodor Schieder, ed., III: *Die Entstehung des neuzeitlichen Europa*, Josef Engel, ed. (Stuttgart, 1971), 58-77; esp. 60ff.

[5] Paul Oskar Kristeller, *Renaissance Thought*, I (New York, 1961), 9.

[6] *Ibid.*, 110. Lefèvre d'Etaples uses the term "artes humanae" at the beginning of the sixteenth century: *Libellus de constitutione et utilitate artium humanarum* (Parisiis, c. 1504). Eugene F. Rice, Jr., lists and documents further synonyms for the non-professional "educational program [expressed] in a vocabulary shaped by humanistic values . . ." current in the circle around him. See *The Prefatory Epistles of Jacques Lefèvre d'Étaples and Related Texts* (New York, 1972), XIII.

[7] *Giovanni Pico della Mirandola and His Sources, op. cit.*, 67.

[8] *Ibid.*, 84.

Platonist or Aristotelian, Stoic or Epicurean, optimistic or pessimistic, active or contemplative, although it is easy to find for any of
these attitudes, and for many others, a certain number of humanists
who favored them. What they all have in common, is something
else: a scholarly, literary, and educational ideal based on the study of
classical antiquity." [9]

Besides the innumerable manuscripts catalogued, texts edited,
documents interpreted and secondary sources reviewed and annotated,
it is this basic thesis that will continue to be associated with the name
of Kristeller. It is this thesis which will force posterity to pause,
ponder, and probe. This future has begun; posterity is already there.
Kristeller is well aware of this; and its challenge does not come
unexpectedly or find him unprepared: "This theory has been criticized as being too prosaic and as tending to debunk Renaissance
humanism. . . . [But] the task of a historical theory, as that of a
scientific hypothesis, is not its appeal, but rather its truth and objective validity. A historical theory is to me the more convincing the
larger is the number of documents and established facts for which it
is able to account, and the fewer are the known facts which it seems
to contradict. As of now, I am convinced that a vastly larger number
of facts known about Renaissance humanism can be explained in this
way than by any of the attempts that have been made to identify
Renaissance humanism with a given set of philosophical or theological opinions." [10]

II

At the beginning of this introduction we placed a quotation from
Pico della Mirandola. If it had not been a text which allows us to
draw attention with few words to something so characteristic for the
Septuagenarian, the most natural choice would have been to borrow
words from Marsilio Ficino, in particular from the *Theologia Platonica*. It is after all the interpretation of the philosophy of Ficino which
spans Kristeller's years of scholarship and simultaneously marks the
itinerarium scholaris which came close to being a total *translatio studii*, the
forced emigration by a whole generation of true *humanistae*. In the

---

[9] "Studies on Renaissance Humanism," *art. cit.*, 7-23; 22. Cf. most recently
Kristeller's "The Role of Religion in Renaissance Humanism and Platonism,"
in *The Pursuit of Holiness in Late Medieval and Renaissance Religion*, Charles Trinkaus,
ed., Studies in Medieval and Reformation Thought, X (Leiden, 1974), 367-370.
[10] "Studies on Renaissance Humanism," *art. cit.*, 22.

fall of 1931, soon after completing his dissertation on Marlowe, Kristeller, as a young German scholar, began his work on Ficino in Freiburg.

At that time he was forced to interrupt his studies and leave his native country for Italy, living first in Pisa then in Florence and Rome where on August 25, 1937 he finished what he had intended to be his Habilitationsschrift. In February 1939 followed the next stage of his trek, this time from Italy to the United States. In 1943 the English version of the German Ficino manuscript was published by the Columbia University Press. After the war, in 1953, Sansoni published the most elaborately documented version in Florence. But this *itinerarium* did not come full circle until thirty-five years later when *Die Philosophie des Marsilio Ficino* was published in Germany by Vittorio Klostermann.[11]

Usually an historian so steeped in a theme, with such a grasp of a certain range of sources and with such obvious empathy as Kristeller feels for the Platonic Academy, is inclined to chart his field from the perspective thus gained. As a matter of fact, Ficino is presented as the key for our understanding of the intellectual climate of Florence in the late Quattrocento.[12] But again, as we noticed with Pico, the significance of Ficino and his program of Christian Platonism as a *philosophia perennis*—which permeates and conditions sixteenth-century thought to an impressive extent—has not led Kristeller to narrow the horizon of his field. Just as the 'Renaissance' is for him the whole period reaching from the middle of the fourteenth through the sixteenth century, so 'humanism' is understood in the extensive-descriptive sense indicated above, and thus withstands the predelic-tions, favorite sons, and 'Steckenpferde' of his colleagues ... or himself. It is not by chance that Kristeller likens his thesis—or as he prefers to say, his 'theory of humanism'—to a scientific hypothesis, since the Neoplatonic quest for comprehensiveness and universality is firmly harnassed here by a scientific code which bases proof on analytical tests and factual observations.[13]

---

[11] "... jetzt [schließt sich] der Kreis nach echt neuplatonischer Weise, und das, was zuerst gedacht und geschrieben wurde, wird nun zuletzt doch noch gedruckt." *Die Philosophie des Marsilio Ficino* (Frankfurt am Main, 1972), VII.

[12] "Das geistige Bild von Florenz im späten Quattrocento, wie wir es aus Alberti, Verrocchio und Botticelli, aus Pulci, Poliziano und Lorenzo, aus Landino und aus Pico kennen, wäre ohne das Werk Ficinos nicht vollständig und nicht zu verstehen." *Ibid.*, XI.

[13] For the most important preceding stage of this conceptual clarification, see

The designation 'extensive'—or 'comprehensive' for that matter—calls for one more clarification. Whereas Kristeller in his earlier writings warns especially against the legacy of Romanticism and its misreading of the Renaissance, of which his German background must have made him particularly aware, a second theme has become increasingly prominent in his work; namely, the relation between the Renaissance and the Middle Ages. In this context Kristeller explicitly warns against the interpretation of humanism "as the new philosophy of the Renaissance, which arose in opposition to scholasticism, the old philosophy of the Middle Ages." [14] It can safely be said that few scholars in the field have been both so well equipped and so successful in establishing clearly the limits within which the claim by Renaissance authors to represent a new beginning over against 'the Dark Ages' can be accepted. Due to his own work on Ficino Kristeller is understandably more oriented towards Thomism than to Scotism, which seems for him to comprise Nominalism as well. But in this very way he has given the continuity of Renaissance philosophy with medieval thought the attention it so much deserves.

Yet here the restriction of the designation 'extensive' becomes relevant: it is the humanism of the Renaissance period which provides the subject matter for Kristeller's theory of humanism. With all his empathy for Thomas Aquinas, he cannot regard a reference to 'the (Christian) humanism of Aquinas' as more than an *aperçu* which necessarily adds to the confusion about the precise meaning of the term 'humanism'.[15] Here again, we see how the scientific application

Augustin Renaudet: Chapter IV, "Autour d'une définition de l'humanisme," in *Humanisme et Renaissance: Dante, Pétrarque, Standonck, Érasme, Lefèvre d'Étaples, Marguerite de Navarre, Rabelais, Guichardin, Giordano Bruno* (Geneva, 1958), 32-53.

[14] *Renaissance Thought*, I, *op. cit.*, 99. Cf. earlier P. O. Kristeller and J. H. Randall, Jr., "The Study of the Philosophies of the Renaissance," *Journal of the History of Ideas*, II (1941), 449-496.

[15] "Non seulement le terme et l'idée d'humanisme chrétien ou même d'humanisme tout court ne se trouvent pas dans les écrits de saint Thomas et de ses contemporains; il y a de plus la difficulté que le mot 'humanisme' a acquis de nos jours des acceptions si vagues et si variées que son emploi prête à de grandes confusions, si l'on ne tente de le circonscrire grâce à une définition bien rigoureuse. L'humanisme de la Renaissance dont il nous faudra parler n'était peut-être ni vrai ni integral; on peut discuter en quel sens et dans quelle mesure il était chrétien; mais il a eu une signification bien précise dans l'histoire de l'érudition et de la littérature, ..." *Le thomisme et la pensée italienne de la Renaissance* (Montreal and Paris, 1967), 23f. The "Pièces Justificatives" which—though half the volume—have not yet drawn the attention deserved, are at once a contribution to Renaissance thought and to late medieval scholasticism: Battista Spagnoli, O.C. (†1516), *Opus aureum in Thomistas*, and Vincentius Bandellus de Castronovo, O.P. (†1506),

of the theory of humanism serves to prune away the foliage and even the fruits on the tree of humanism which tend to conceal its basic shape. When we are impatient with this sober view of humanism and are inclined to disassociate ourselves from this basis, we run the risk of proving to be more platonizing than the chief student of this movement. When we insist on looking for the so-called 'spirit' of humanism we may well find ourselves in pursuit of the abstruse truths not made accessible by the *sophia ulta*!

Both by the very force of this theory and by his application of it, the name of Paul Oskar Kristeller stands for the whole field of Renaissance studies to an extent which has always been exceptional, but which has become increasingly rare in this era of specialization in the humanities.

III

This controlled comprehensiveness by one who has thoroughly engrossed himself in all the *studia humanitatis* is itself cause for a Festschrift. Our prevailing motive, however, is not only the appropriate celebration of a man of whom it can safely be said that even his opponents are his students and that among his critics are found no detractors. Rather, this celebration has been given the shape of a presentation of the various forms of the dissemination of the Italian Renaissance and implicitly therein is a scientific test of Kristeller's theory of humanism.[16]

Since the era of Festschriften with their large number of often technical and detailed contributions is drawing to a close, it seemed

---

Opusculum Fratris Vincentii de Castronovo Ordinis Praedicatorum . . . quod beatitudo hominis in actu intellectus et non voluntatis essentialiter consistit. For the English version of the introductory part see *Medieval Aspects of Renaissance Learning: Three Essays by Paul Oskar Kristeller*, ed. and trans. Edward P. Mahoney, Duke Monographs in Medieval and Renaissance Studies, I (Durham, 1974), 29-91.

[16] This line of inquiry directed at learning the cause through its effects was proposed and carried out by Paul Oskar Kristeller himself, now fifteen years ago. See his "The European Diffusion of Italian Humanism," based on a paper read before the Modern Language Association of America in Philadelphia on December 27, 1960. Reprinted from *Italica*, XXXIX (1962), 1-20, in *Renaissance Thought*, II (New York, 1965), 69-88. In this context it is understandably the historians of Italian literature who are especially addressed: ". . . it is important for the student of Italian humanism to know which of its many aspects were influential in other European countries. The historians of Italian literature who usually follow a scholarly tradition established in nineteenth-century Italy might do well to pay greater attention to certain aspects of Italian literature that seem to be peripheral from that traditional point of view, but that were extremely important for the international diffusion of Italian civilization." *Ibid.*, 88.

appropriate to choose that form of Festschrift which represents an effort to draw together the present state of scholarship through a small number of large essays, written by an international company of scholars who could seize this opportunity to provide a European chart of the spread of humanism in its changing manifestations. The title chosen is a fortunate combination of an allusion to Kristeller's magnum opus ITER ITALICUM [17] and a reference to that itinerary which in all its windings and complexities is to appear on the map intended in this enterprise.

The chapter arrangement according to countries and the chance to reflect within these chapters the generally acknowledged "Phasenverschiebung" of the evolvement and reception of humanism allow for a *conspectus* of the profile of European humanism which transcends the boundaries of national schools of scholarship, while still allowing for the diverse conceptions characteristic of the present state of scholarship.

Two major restrictions have to be made at the outset. What is presented here is not *the* European chart of the spread of humanism. It cannot be such without chapters dedicated at least to humanism in Spain and Portugal, in Bohemia, Poland, Hungary, and Scandinavia—and above all to the spread of humanism within that conglomerate of states and principalities we have good reason to call Italy. Yet no apologies are necessary for presenting a partial picture comprising five countries. Like the torso in a classical statue, this allows us to surmise the shape of the parts absent. An encyclopedic history of humanism is highly desirable and will have to be undertaken by an international company of scholars, with the provision that all national traditions of Renaissance scholarship are tapped according to their different degrees of maturity.

A second restriction helps to alleviate the disadvantages implied in the first. A chapter arrangement by countries does not do justice to the international dimensions of humanist aspirations. Very often local pride and chauvinism—often in one and the same person—are interwoven with strains of international or, better yet, supra-national awareness, a pride in belonging to the *docti* and their Republic of Letters without boundaries and borders.

Hence the authors of the two parts of the Italian chapter cannot but

---

[17] *Iter Italicum: A Finding List of Uncatalogued or Incompletely Catalogued Humanistic Manuscripts of the Renaissance in Italian and other Libraries,* 2 vols. (London and Leiden, 1965 and 1967).

cross and recross the Alps in pursuing lines of communication and traditions of thought which extend to Spain and the city-states of Zürich and Geneva. Similarly, the chapters dedicated to France, the Low Countries, England and Germany cannot but deal at the same time with the Renaissance in Italy, in view of the fact that the long-treasured thesis of the indigenous origins of humanism is now in full-fledged retreat. This retreat may well prove to be too hasty. The cultural vitality and sensitivity expressed in arts and letters, especially at the Burgundian and Vienna courts as well as in Scotland and in Italy itself, coincide or even precede the early phases of Italian influence. We may have to think in terms of an initial thrust towards what one may call 'vernacular humanism' which stands in the service of a national pride in autochthonous sources and skills. This is soon overlaid and dwarfed by the substantial Italian claim to a classical heritage with more fertile roots and above all with less divisive sources. At least in the way these were read, they gave expression and support to the quest for concord and peace—at once so thoroughly missed, and so programmatically proclaimed. As the following chapters document, in our day the humanist call 'ad fontes' has become so automatically identified with the return to the sources of classical antiquity that we find it difficult to give vernacular humanism its justified though limited place.[18]

The evidence in favor of Italian export rather than indigenous developments as fundamentally decisive for the beginnings and growth of humanism North of the Alps is so overwhelming, that this side of the debate does not deserve to be reopened. Much more fruitful is that other side which concerns the coexistence of national and supra-national ingredients in early European humanism. By no means always peaceful, this coexistence has to stand the immense tension between *imitation* and *emulation*, between ready acceptance of Italian superiority in view of its proximity to classical antiquity and the desire to equal and even surpass the Italian masters in skills,

---

[18] I would like to call attention to the delightful epistular debate between Ms. E. Marcu and Mr. C. Reedijk about the merits, or rather the absence of such, of the Latin, consciously non-vernacular 'ideology' of Erasmus *cum suis* as the major cause of the failure of European humanism to shed the shackles of an elitist movement. Notwithstanding the force of Reedijk's arguments, this may well yield new appreciation for the early efforts to use the vernacular as national and hence potentially more popular vehicle for the rediscovered *studia humanitatis*. See *Bibliothèque d'Humanisme et Renaissance*, XXXII (1970), 454f.; XXXIII (1971), 419-425.

knowledge, and wisdom. It is this oscillation, this back and forth between competitive emulation and affirmation of imitation as the proper attitude in the Republic of Letters, which underlies both the chapter arrangement according to countries *and* the constant gaze beyond these boundaries which characterizes all these chapters.

In order to read this 'map' as a comparative chart, it is important to realize that the chapters are written by different kinds of historians, who along with their individual preferences bring very different professional priorities to bear on their subject matter. Although all are concerned with the history of Western civilization, there is a difference of approach and outlook between the historian of ideas and of literature, as well as between the institutional historian and the neo-Latinist. Even among the historians of ideas, there is a wide range allowing one to highlight the Stoic and Augustinian traditions; another to stress Catholic reform before it issued into the Counterreformation; and yet another, the Reformation in its interaction with humanism. Since no structural harmony should be 'planned into' a book dedicated to a period and movement too rich (fecunditas!) for the organizing grasp of a single orthopraxy or orthodoxy, the one common point of reference which remains is the joint search for the several forms and stages of the reception of Renaissance humanism.

IV

In our effort to characterize the contribution of Paul Oskar Kristeller to the field of Renaissance studies we referred to his 'sober' theory of humanism. It is the scientific factor in this theory—*n'en déplaise* Kristeller's own reservations, best likened to Ockham's famous razor—which encourages a non-romantic definition of humanism. His theory is so fashioned as to be able to take into account the sum-total of observed and documented phenomena. This definition has met with opposition,[19] partly due to the fact that it has been misunderstood, which in turn has provided Kristeller with the occasion to restate his point of departure.[20] We have already

---

[19] For a recent example see James E. Biechler in *Theological Studies*, XXXV (1974), 758.

[20] "I never meant to say that humanism made no contribution to philosophy or theology. I did not even say that the moralists among the humanists were not philosophers; I merely said that they were not professional or technical philosophers. The humanist profession as a whole was a scholarly and literary profession, and those members of the profession who were interested in philosophy

indicated the extent to which the 'sum-total' theory of humanism seems to offer us the necessary remedy against the confusion and arbitrariness in the use of the term 'humanism', ranging from the humanism of the Church Fathers to Marxist humanism, and all the more dangerous when operating in the field of Renaissance studies itself.

But the ships of interpretation are pulling at their anchors fastened to the rock bottom of the 'sum-total' theory. In his excellent study of Renaissance anthropology and the relation of man to God and world during the successive stages of Italian humanism, Charles Trinkaus has succeeded in keeping the anchor chains intact.[21] At the same time, one cannot avoid the impression that he could achieve this only by putting them under considerable strain. While deeply indebted to the methods and results of Kristeller's scholarship, Hanna Gray has shown that eloquence is to be regarded as the integrating force in the *studia humanitatis* and therefore is the impetus behind the often non-professional concern with grammar, rhetoric, poetry, history and moral philosophy: "Before the word 'humanist' gained general currency, the humanists were referring to themselves and to their colleagues by other names—sometimes 'philosophers' often 'poets'. Most frequently, however, they called themselves 'orators' . . . they wished to be known as men of eloquence." [22]

What concerns us here is not so much the question of the professional status of the early humanists. The importance of this question cannot be doubted since the humanists' new professionalism is based on the ideal of 'amateur'-scholarship in the original sense of that word. Time and again we find this self-image proudly implied in their caricature of 'professional' scholasticism. Rather, the salient point for us is the awareness that eloquence was not a goal in itself but was geared towards the ideal of the *dicendi faciendique magister*, the consonance of scholarly erudition and moral integrity. The prefaces to humanist editions, as well as the usual first lines of praise in their letters, amply document this ideal.

combined philosophy with scholarship and literature, as at other times philosophy may have been combined with theology or with the sciences." "The Role of Religion in Renaissance Humanism and Platonism," *art. cit.*, 369.

[21] Charles Trinkaus, *In Our Image and Likeness: Humanity and Divinity in Italian Humanist Thought*, 2 vols. (Chicago, 1970), XVIIff.; cf. my review in *Speculum*, XLVII (1972), 808-814.

[22] Hanna H. Gray, "Renaissance Humanism: The Pursuit of Eloquence," *Journal of the History of Ideas*, XXIV (1963); republished in *Renaissance Essays*, Paul Oskar Kristeller and Philip P. Wiener, eds. (New York, 1968), 199-216; 202.

This vision of man, which has implications for the education of princes and children, as well as for political action, receives an ever changing content—in that sense it would be erroneous to speak in terms of *the* humanist educational ideal or to declare civic humanism *the* political program of humanism. But in unraveling the webs of communication between Italian humanism and northern Europe we cannot but be confronted with the question how to explain the ground swell of excitement. For a number of early 'outposts' North of the Alps, from Rudolph Agricola to Conrad Celtis, this impulse and motivation does not seem to be derived from a professional occupation with the *studia humanitatis* but from the manifold uses of eloquence. What Hans Baron has described as the Florentine ideal of republican liberty in the circle around Bruni, Palmieri and Alberti [23] could merge in the North with the late medieval 'Stadtbewußtsein' into a coalition of humanism and public service. At least until the beginning of the thirties of the sixteenth century [24] the cities, and especially the imperial cities, could play a major political role in implementation of the reformation of Church and society.[25] But many other forms of use will be presented to us in the following chapters. The question is therefore how to control by scientific means the concept 'humanism' while at the same time capturing the content of such an elusive entity as 'excitement'.

V

Against this background, the chapter by William Bouwsma on "The Two Faces of Humanism" takes on special significance for us. To exploit an image coined by Bouwsma for our purposes, we can say that Kristeller has reshaped the vague and all too elastic designation 'humanism' into a "definable piece of ground", "a battlefield" on which issues are fought out. The respect for the borderlines of this battlefield is the presupposition for following Bouwsma on the changing scenes of the altercation between 'Stoicism' and 'Augustinianism'. This trek is risky not only because of the difficulty in defining these two concepts, but also because the tension between them is not

---

[23] *The Crisis of the Early Italian Renaissance* (Princeton, 1955); and especially his *Humanistic and Political Literature in Florence and Venice at the Beginning of the Quattrocento* (Cambridge, Mass., 1955).

[24] Cf. Thomas A. Brady, Jr., "Jacob Sturm of Strasbourg and the Lutherans at the Diet of Augsburg, 1530," *Church History*, XLII (1973), 1-20; 20.

[25] Cf. Bernd Moeller, *Reichsstadt und Reformation* (Gütersloh, 1962) trans. *Imperial Cities and the Reformation* (Philadelphia, 1972).

always explicit or consciously exhibited by the participants. Never-theless, it is not often that an historian of ideas has been able to take so many contradictory pieces of evidence into account in telling the story of the struggle for the right use of the *studia humanitatis*.

Bouwsma's point of departure is the awareness of the absurdity in thinking that if a man is questioned at length—and profoundly!—he will confess to being either a Platonist or an Aristotelian. Those ancient sources that had the greatest influence in Renaissance humanism, however, were not Hellenic but Hellenistic, dating therefore not from the fourth century B.C.E. but from the third century C.E. Originating from the rhetorical tradition at about the same time, Stoicism and Augustinianism confronted the humanist with life options by presenting alternative views of cosmos, man and history. Both could provide a moral philosophy; both offered a new style for life in the spreading towns with their—to the untrained rural ear— incessant noise and frequent urban disorder. Stoicism could contribute the needed personal endurance; Augustinianism the essential public action. Both were valiant efforts to survive in a threatening or at least unpredictable world.

The Renaissance discovery of Stoicism, often associated with the names of Cicero and Seneca, [26] is matched by a new encounter with St. Augustine. Though the term 'Augustinianism' with its mystifying elasticity has proved to be a confusing rather than a clarifying designation in medieval studies, the Augustinian Renaissance of the Quattrocento can be given a more definable content because of Gregory of Rimini's recovery of the authentic Augustine and Petrarch's promulgation of the 'new' Augustine.[27]

While interpreting the tensions and debates among humanists in the light of these two frames of mind and thought, Bouwsma leaves the reader not with two parties but with an inner dialectic which pervades the writings of the major humanists from Petrarch to Erasmus and Calvin. What he has achieved is a presentation of the suspenseful story of the quest for the right use of the *studia humanitatis*,[28]

---

[26] Cf. Charles B. Schmitt, *Cicero Scepticus: A Study of the Influence of the Academica in the Renaissance* (The Hague, 1972).

[27] See my "'Tuus sum, salvum me fac.' Augustinréveil zwischen Renaissance und Reformation," in *Scientia Augustiniana. Studien über Augustinus, den Augustinismus und den Augustinerorden. Festschrift Adolar Zumkeller OSA*, Cornelius Petrus Mayer and Willigis Eckermann, eds. (Würzburg, 1975), 349-394.

[28] Cf. his complementary article "Renaissance and Reformation: An Essay in their Affinities and Connections," in *Luther and the Dawn of the Modern Era*,

which proves not to be an external battle with scholasticism and the 'Dark Ages' but an internal one fought on the battlefield of Renaissance humanism itself.

In "Italian Reactions to Erasmian Humanism" Myron Gilmore shows the often neglected counterpart to the Italian export of humanism when he relates the impact of Erasmus South of the Alps. But much more than a description of the interaction between Italy and the North, he presents a profile of the *princeps humanistarum* under the threefold avalanche of criticism as a 'northern Barbarian', as the spiritual father of Martin Luther and hence the harbinger of heresy, and as the lame sceptic without sufficient courage to join forces with the Wittenberg Reformation. Defeated by the Council of Trent's canonization of the *Vulgate* and censured by the placing of several of his works on the *Index*, Erasmus is nevertheless shown to have served the cause of Catholic reform and to have contributed to the decree *De sacris imaginibus* drafted by the very Council that had sought to distance itself from him.

Over against Augustin Renaudet, who saw in Erasmus the advocate of a 'third Church', Gilmore underscores the basic loyalty of Erasmus to the Church of Rome. In addition to Erasmus's statement that he counts himself fortunate not to have allied himself with Luther we recall his words: "Ista dissidii nomina detestor. Christianus sum et Christianos agnosco; Erasmistas non feram, Reuchlinistas non novi." [29] Here the humanist search for *pax* and *concordia* has found ecclesiological expression in the abhorrence of intramural rifts and tensions. The *alta sophia*, which is brought down to earth by Erasmus in the *philosophia Christi*, no longer transcends the Church as it did with Pico, but the Church herself now transcends the members and their factions: "quoscunque tulit foecunda ecclesia!" Since this vision does not allow for any 'second Church', Gilmore's argument against Renaudet's 'third Church' is fully convincing. The emerging shape of 'Nicodem-

---

Heiko A. Oberman, ed., Studies in the History of Christian Thought, VIII (Leiden, 1974), 127-149.

[29] 'Ad Lectorem' appended to Martens's enlarged edition of the *Colloquiorum Formulae*, c. Nov. 1519; *Opus Epistolarum Des. Erasmi Roterodami*, eds. P. S. Allen and H. M. Allen, IV (1519-1521), (Oxonii, 1922), 121, 13-15. Quoted and discussed by S. Dresden, *Humanistische Wijsheidsidealen*, Mededelingen der Koninklijke Nederlandse Akademie van Wetenschappen, Afd. Letterkunde, Nieuwe Reeks 29, 7 (Amsterdam, 1966), 40f. (246f.).

ism' in the late twenties of the sixteenth century [30] suggests the proximity to and perhaps even the parentage of Erasmus. Yet it is exactly this group which does not want to change allegiances or form a 'third Church' because of their firm belief in the one *ecclesia spiritualis*.

Sem Dresden's essay on the reception of the Italian Renaissance in France shows up a pattern, which with minor variations and without a set chronological rhythm, pertains to all countries. We can summarize this with three words: imitation, emulation and transformation. He offers a broad perspective on Renaissance humanism, Renaissance Platonism and Renaissance art in their development to Rabelais; to Margaret of Navarre and Montaigne; and to mannerism and baroque in the visual arts. We use the designation 'essay' advisedly, not only because the canvas painted upon is large and the preceding scholarship meager in comparison, but also because of a personal style, which allows suggestive observations but is less given to formulating hard and fast theses. Awe for the complexity of the theme is a constant safeguard against the pitfall of simplification. The conclusions seemingly whispered in our ear thus prove all the more convincing.

Three points stand out in a characterization of French humanism: the French *double* imitation of both classical and Italian examples; the intensity of French competitive emulation in its effort to equal and surpass the Italian model in both Greek and Latin; and finally, the significance of a royal court in centralist France which could make the enrichment of the vernacular an affair of state. But again, many observations made by Dresden pertain also to Italian humanism or more generally to humanism per se, such as: the specific function of the written word as the real presence of the author which later develops into a pretence of this presence; the *ars poetica* as the vehicle for a newly discovered charisma of originality, intimately related to the creation of a design in the visual arts. Behind this design lies a high regard for the 'artificial', which carries none of the modern negative overtones based on our sense of difference between nature and culture.

Notwithstanding the impressionistic character of an essay, the

---

[30] See Carlo Ginzburg, *Il nicodemismo. Simulazione e dissimulazione religiosa nell'Europa del '500* (Torino, 1970), 29ff.; cf. the review by M. E. Welti in *Bibliothèque d'Humanisme et Renaissance*, XXXIII (1971), 235f.

totality of the insights presented conveys the thesis that the *studia humanitatis* represents not merely a series of new fields of professional endeavor but as Dresden puts it: "certain forms of study inevitably produced a certain type of man". In English the word "certain" may sound more definite than it has been intended. But pervading all the sources touched upon is a common psychological makeup of man, at once both creator and creature, probing for a new reality which is not to be created but to be reconstituted. The humanist's double glance, oriented toward the future by looking at the past, is reflected in a mixture of nostalgia and aspirations. This in turn leads to inner resistance against or at least dissatisfaction with the status quo.

The chapter on humanism in the Low Countries had to be construed along very different lines. Jozef IJsewijn had to contend here with the overpowering presence of Erasmus which has obscured the historical beginnings of humanism, both due to his own propaganda and to the inescapable attraction he has held for later scholarship. Thanks to the way Myron Gilmore dedicated himself to the portrayal of Erasmus, IJsewijn could concentrate on laying the first foundations for a serious investigation of the reception of the Renaissance in the Low Countries.[31] For that reason a special bibliography of sources and studies has been appended which will henceforth provide the basis for modern research. This detailed account draws out of the sphere of semi-anonymity a large number of major and minor intermediaries: Joannes de Meerhout, Anthonius Haneron, Wessel Gansfoort, and above all, Rudolph Agricola. For all of them their interest in humanism is due to the recognition of the service it provides for the study of the Holy Scriptures. IJsewijn formulates this as the *transitus humanismi ad christianismum* to which Erasmus also turned—or rather returned—after the Italian experiment and his encounter with John Colet in England.[32] In pondering the evidence presented one cannot but come to the conclusion that we may have to reconsider R. R. Post's view in his rich, final monograph where he advances the thesis of the relative irrelevance of the *Devotio Moderna* for humanism.[33] The debate about 'paganism'

---

[31] Cf. the descriptions and literature in the careful "catalogus", *Erasmus en Leuven*, 'Woord vooraf' by J. K. Steppe (Leuven, 1969), 143-232.

[32] Cf. C. Reedijk, *The Poems of Desiderius Erasmus* (Leiden, 1956), 54ff.

[33] *The Modern Devotion. Confrontation with Reformation and Humanism*, Studies in Medieval and Reformation Thought, III (Leiden, 1968), 673, 675.

In the Italian Renaissance which is associated with the names of Burckhardt, Pastor and Toffanin is apparently slow to die out. From the perspective of early Netherlandish humanism it is indeed hard to avoid the impression that such an Italian 'paganism' did exist. Whatever other points of contact and even shared motivations may have to be recognized, at least the pious shiver which characterized this strand of humanism in its encounter with Italian secular tendencies can be traced back to the *Devotio Moderna*.

It is important to realize that as much as the discontinuity with the Middle Ages so vividly expressed by early humanism cannot stand the test of modern scholarship, so the sense of avulsion from Italian frivolous poetry (Erasmus contra Poggio's *Facetiae*!) provides more of an insight into psychology and ethics in the Low Countries than a reliable yardstick for modern interpretation. As IJsewijn shows, by putting the humanities to the use of piety and scriptural exegesis this *transitus* is a real transformation. The designation 'pagan' stands here for the protest against regarding rhetoric and poetry as ends in themselves. Whereas in France this protest recedes after the days of Budé, it would continue to mark Netherlandish humanism even in its later stages.

A very different picture emerges on the English scene. Without the mediation of a *Devotio Moderna*, it is the pre-Reformation system of primary and secondary schools which provides the social structure for the introduction and transmission of humanism. In Denys Hay's presentation of the reception of humanism in fifteenth century England the shifts and changes in Italian humanism and their effect on 'Great Britain'—as James VI, King of Scotland and England, and the author prefer to call the temporarily United Kingdom—are seen in close conjunction. In contrast to the standard work of Roberto Weiss [34] the economic, political and particularly the social backgrounds are given special attention.

For Hay the point of departure is the far-reaching range of similarities throughout the fourteenth century between Britain and the rest of Europe, including Italy. This encompasses a shared experience

---

[34] *Humanism in England During the Fifteenth Century* (Oxford, 1967³, 1941). Cf. his pages dedicated to England and "the slight influence of humanism in Wales, Scotland, Ireland", "Learning and Education in Western Europe from 1470 to 1520," in *The New Cambridge Modern History*, I: *The Renaissance 1493-1520*, G. R. Potter, ed. (Cambridge, 1957), 106-111.

of religion, society and culture. All the more striking therefore are the new and independent directions which the arts and literature take in Italy. Thus, the factors less weighed by Weiss are presented by Hay not so much as 'causes', but as foils for the uniqueness of the beginnings of the Italian Renaissance.

Accordingly the period of 'pre-humanism' is presented as characterized by unique individuals, by such personalities as Petrarch and Boccaccio, succeeded in the following decisive stages by Coluccio Salutati and Leonardo Bruni.

Since the education and instruction of laymen for public service was at the nucleus of the humanist program in England, it is this particular role of the *studia humanitatis* which stands at the center of Hay's narration. The increasing control of royal administration by the laity explains the interest in an Italian educational model which is able to satisfy the need for secular officials. This is the essential stage before the emergence of what we have called 'Humanistik' and what is described by Hay less solemnly and therefore more eloquently as 'keeping up with the humanist Jones.' When we look at the fourteenth-century origins and the fifteenth-century spread of endowed schools, we see that in England just as on the Continent their establishment is due to the devout motivations of their benefactors. But in England the schools themselves serve political and social needs at the very time when these same institutions in the Low Countries seem to prepare for the growth of 'the inner man', if not for the independent and critical reading of the Scriptures.

As the role of John Colet in Erasmus's development from *poeta* to *theologus* documents, such contrasts can be easily overstated. But the fact remains that at a time when the humanist in Deventer, Louvain, Nuremberg and Wittenberg is associated with the mastery of the three 'biblical', or at least the two classical languages, in England, as Hay points out, he is recognized by his command of Latin. One wonders whether we are here close to solving the mystery of the different roads speculative continental and pragmatic English philosophy would travel in the next century. While we may see here proof for a more secular orientation or even find an example of English common sense in taking the relevance of Latin for public office into account, the English lettered gentleman showed a closer resemblance to the 'pre-cabalist' Italian humanist of the Quattrocento than to his French or German counterpart.

A chapter on the course of German humanism has to contend with a special set of problems. The difficulty here is due not so much to the lack of preliminary work as it is to the lag between nineteenth and twentieth century scholarship, with the latter's tendency towards a more descriptive and less romantic approach to humanism. Furthermore, the unclarity of national and cultural boundaries has made the effort to define the German character of the movement exceedingly hazardous. Finally, the tendency to view Renaissance humanism as the born opponent of the German Reformation has obscured their cohesion. The severance of these two aspects of one field has often received institutional implementation by being assigned to two different university chairs.

Conscious of these drawbacks, Lewis Spitz presses these disadvantages into the service of progress in the field by making a careful survey of the present state of scholarship the substance of his narrative. In this way geographical or confessional myopia can be indicated while simultaneously drawing together into a comprehensive picture elements of truth and well understood aspects of documents. The stages in the growth of humanism in Germany, as in France, include a beginning in the conciliar epoch, an interlude at the secular and episcopal courts and a flowering in the urban centers . . . and finally also in the schools and universities. The main phenomenon of humanism, however, is its gradual transition and, to this extent, continuity in three respects: with late medieval scholasticism, notwithstanding the dramatic Reuchlin affair; within humanism itself unperturbed by the challenge of the Reformation throughout the sixteenth century until its *terminus ad quem*, the Thirty Years' War; and with the Reformation movement, notwithstanding the dispute between Erasmus and Luther.[35]

Whereas Spitz seemingly remains on the safe ground of indicating and describing recent source editions, monographs, and articles, all three continuity-theses he presents are 'kühn' and challenging. At the center of his arguments stands the effort to overcome the solidly entrenched tradition of the irreconcilable opposition between the reformer Luther and the humanist Melanchthon. Notwithstanding

---

[35] Special attention should be called to a substantial and rich article by Heinz Liebing not yet sufficiently 'received.' In short compass he discusses the limits of continuity and the ways in which humanism bifurcated under the onslaught of the confessional issue: "Die Ausgänge des Europäischen Humanismus," *Geist und Geschichte der Reformation. Festgabe Hanns Rückert*, Heinz Liebing and Klaus Scholder, eds. (Berlin, 1966), 357-376; 373f.

this emphasis on continuity and gradual transformation, the Italian inspiration and challenge is seen in all phases to evoke the response of both imitation and emulation. Perhaps a shade less oriented towards the life of private devotion and more inclined to speculate about structural reform of town, Church and even cosmos, German humanism runs a course hardly different from that in the Low Countries. At both sides of a border which would not be officially (!) acknowledged until 1648, the *studia humanitatis* proves to have excited and captured the leading minds for much the same reasons. They are willing to immerse themselves in these new studies because of their use in fusing erudition and integrity, the constituent elements of *humanitas*.

Provided we clearly avoid the present tendency to use the term Petrarchism in the sense of a gentleman's cultivation of 'Humanistik', then it can be said that within the borders of the former Holy Roman Empire that aspect of the Petrarchan heritage emerged as the dominant factor which we find expressed in a letter to Boccaccio: "Vitam mihi alienis dictis ac monitis ornare, fateor, est animus, non stilum . . ." [36]

Glancing back once more to the different uses and applications of the humanist program North of the Alps, the theory of Kristeller may seem to be too sober to fill Petrarch's ideal *vita* with 'life' and too technical to account for the excitement and enthusiasm with which Italian humanism swayed the more perceptive northern minds.

Yet it is exactly the multiformity of style and content with which this *vita* is filled that forces us to look for the common denominator underlying all these forms of expression. The ships of interpretation are straining their anchor chains—but they can only do so safely in the awareness that these are well-fastened. The theory of humanism advanced by Paul Oskar Kristeller, and the manifold expressions with which he has instilled life in it provide for that rock bottom solidity which can withstand the shifting tides and winds of Renaissance research.

"Augustus", Montegrotto, Italy   March 1975

---

[36] *Epistolae Familiares* XXII.2.

ITALY

THE TWO FACES OF HUMANISM

Stoicism and Augustinianism in Renaissance Thought

WILLIAM J. BOUWSMA

University of California, Berkeley

Recent emphasis, stemming primarily from the work of P. O. Kristeller, on the central importance of rhetoric for Renaissance humanism, has enabled us to understand the underlying unity of a singularly complex movement; and it has proved singularly fruitful for Renaissance scholarship. At the same time, since this approach depends on the identification of a kind of lowest common denominator for humanism, it may also have the unintended effect of reducing our perception of its rich variety and thus of limiting our grasp of its historical significance. I should like, accordingly, to begin with Kristeller's fundamental insight, but then to suggest that rhetoric, for reasons closely connected with the circumstances under which the rhetorical tradition was appropriated in the age of the Renaissance, was also the vehicle of a set of basic intellectual conflicts crucial to the development of European culture in the early modern period. For there were divisions within Renaissance humanism which, since they were perennial, seem hardly incidental to the movement and which can perhaps be explained more persuasively than by the familiar suggestion that, as "mere rhetoricians," humanists felt comfortable in invoking any set of ideas that seemed immediately useful for their purposes, a notion that is in any case psychologically not altogether persuasive. The humanists were not inclined, I think, to invoke simply *any* set of ideas but tended rather to be divided by a fairly constant set of issues.

From this point of view humanism was a single movement in much the sense that a battlefield is a definable piece of ground. The humanists, to be sure, were often engaged in a conscious struggle with the schoolmen, but this was an external conflict in which the opposing sides were more or less clearly separated. But the struggle within humanism which I shall discuss here, though related to that external struggle, was subtler, more confused, and more difficult, though possibly of greater significance for the future of European culture. Often scarcely recognized by the humanists themselves, more frequently latent than overt for even the most acutely self-conscious among them, and never fully resolved, this internal struggle also helps to explain the adaptability of Renaissance humanism to changing needs, and hence its singular durability.

The two ideological poles between which Renaissance humanism oscillated may be roughly labeled "Stoicism" and "Augustinianism." Both terms present great difficulties, and neither, as an impulse in Renaissance intellectual culture, is yet susceptible to authoritative treatment. I will employ them here in a rather general sense, to designate antithetical visions of human existence, though both are rooted in concrete movements of thought that invite more precise analysis. But any effort to deal with the ideological significance of Renaissance humanism must now grapple with their confrontation.

I. STOICISM AND AUGUSTINIANISM: THE ANCIENT HERITAGE

It seems curious that historians have been so slow, until quite recently, to recognize the importance of the opposition between these impulses in humanist thought.[1] One reason for this, perhaps, has been the persistent notion that Renaissance culture was centrally preoccupied with the recovery of an authentic classicism; and the classical world of thought has been ultimately brought into focus through the issues raised by ancient philosophy. Thus it has been assumed that the two greatest philosophers of classical antiquity, Plato and Aristotle, must represent, however distantly, the essential options available to the thinkers of the Renaissance. This approach to the Renaissance problem may still be encountered in the familiar notion of a medieval and Aristotelian scholasticism confronted by a Platonic humanism.

Whether because or in spite of its neatness, almost everything in this formula is misleading, if not wrong. In the first place it is wrong in fact. Medieval philosophy, even in the thirteenth century,

---

[1] For example the *Grande Antologia Filosofica*, though it includes a section on Renaissance Epicureanism, gives no special treatment to either Stoicism or Augustinianism; and Eugenio Garin's distinguished *L'umanesimo italiano: filosofia e vita civile nel rinascimento* (Bari, 1952) has much on Platonism but little directly on Stoicism or Augustinianism. On the other hand both receive substantial recognition in Charles Trinkaus, *In Our Image and Likeness: Humanity and Divinity in Italian Humanist Thought* (Chicago, 1970), to which I am heavily indebted. The chief difference between his treatment of the subject and my own is one of emphasis; Trinkaus seems to me primarily concerned with the humanist effort to harmonize Stoic and Augustinian impulses (cf. I, xx-xxi).

was by no means entirely Aristotelian, and on the other hand the
culture of Renaissance humanism probably owed at least as much
to Aristotle as to Plato. But it is equally wrong in principle, for it
seeks to comprehend the eclectic and non-systematic culture of the
Renaissance in overtly systematic terms. It seems to be based on the
quaint but durable notion that every man must, in his deepest instincts,
be either a Platonist or an Aristotelian. In fact the conflict between
Plato and Aristotle is, for the understanding of the Renaissance,
a false scent, especially if we are primarily concerned with the tensions
within humanism. Neither Plato nor Aristotle was closely connected
with the rhetorical tradition, for whose ancient sources we must look
instead to the Sophists and the less overtly philosophical pronouncements of the Latin orators. Furthermore, though Renaissance thinkers
(including some humanists) sometimes disputed the relative merits
of Plato and Aristotle, this rather academic debate was not a major
or a regular concern of humanism; hence it can hardly be expected
to illuminate its central concerns. More seriously, when compared
with the humanists of the Renaissance Plato and Aristotle seem more
to resemble than to differ from one another, not only because both
were systematic philosophers but also because, however serious
their disagreements, they came out of the same cultural world.
By the later fifteenth century this was commonly observed by the
humanists themselves, and Raphael, in an early representation of
the division of labor, celebrated their complementarity by placing
Plato and Aristotle side by side in the Stanza della Segnatura. Finally,
the attempt to understand the polarities of Renaissance culture in
terms of Plato and Aristotle seems to be based on the common but
mistaken identification of antique thought with classical hellenism.
It ignores the rich variety of the ancient heritage, and above all the
significant fact that the earliest and probably the most influential
ancient sources on which Renaissance humanism was nourished were
not hellenic but hellenistic.

Thus although it is useful, both for the longer historical perspec-
tives the exercise affords and for the deeper resonances it releases,
to associate the impulses at work in Renaissance humanism with
the various resources of the western cultural tradition, we must
locate these resources first of all in the hellenistic rather than the
hellenic world of thought. Stoicism and Augustinianism both meet
this requirement, but they are also closer to Renaissance humanism
in other respects. Both were bound up with the ancient rhetorical

tradition, Stoicism through the ethical teachings of the Latin orators and essayists particularly beloved by the humanists, Augustinianism through the rhetorical powers of Augustine himself and, more profoundly, the subtle rhetorical quality of his mature theology.[2] Furthermore the tension between Stoicism and Augustinianism was a perennial element in the career of Renaissance humanism, and indeed persisted well beyond what is conventionally taken as the end of the Renaissance; the ambiguous confrontation between the two impulses is still as central for Antoine Adam's distinguished Zaharoff Lecture on the thought of seventeenth-century France as it is in Charles Trinkaus's rich studies of fourteenth and fifteenth-century Italian humanism.[3] Finally, Stoicism and Augustinianism represented, far better than Plato and Aristotle, genuine alternatives for the Renaissance humanist to ponder.

Nevertheless it must be admitted that neither Stoicism nor Augustinianism is easy to define with precision, and here may be another reason for our slowness to grasp their importance. In the case of Stoicism the difficulty arises from the singular complexity of the problem of isolating a pure body of thought from the tangled bundle of hellenistic ideas that were the common property of Stoics, Epicureans, Cynics, Neoplatonists, later Peripatetics, Gnostics, hellenized Jews, Christians, and other groups in later antiquity.[4]

---

[2] For the ambiguous connections between Stoicism and rhetoric there is much in George Kennedy, *The Art of Rhetoric in the Roman World, 300 B.C.—A.D. 300* (Princeton, 1972); see also Jerrold E. Seigel, *Rhetoric and Philosophy in Renaissance Humanism: Ciceronian Elements in Early Quattrocento Thought and their Historical Setting* (Princeton, 1968), esp. ch. 1, and Nancy S. Struever, *The Language of History in the Renaissance: Rhetoric and Historical Consciousness in Florentine Humanism* (Princeton, 1970), esp. ch. 1. For the rhetorical element in Augustine, I have had fundamental guidance from Peter Brown, *Augustine of Hippo: a Biography* (Berkeley, 1967); see also Marcia Colish, *The Mirror of Language: a Study in the Medieval Theory of Knowledge* (New Haven, 1968). Henri Irénée Marrou, *Saint Augustin et la fin de la culture antique*, 4th ed. (Paris, 1958), also remains basic. For the importance of Cicero and Stoicism in Augustine, see also Maurice Testard, *Saint Augustin et Cicéron: Cicéron dans la formation et dans l'œuvre de Saint Augustin* (Paris, 1958).

[3] Adam, *Sur le problème religieux dans la première moitié du XVIIIe siècle* (Oxford, 1959); Trinkaus, *op. cit.*

[4] On this problem cf. Raymond Klibansky, *The Continuity of the Platonic Tradition in the Middle Ages* (London, 1939), 36. For one recent effort to sort out this mixture, see Andreas Graeser, *Plotinus and the Stoics: a Preliminary Study* (Leiden, 1972), a title whose modesty suggests the difficulty of the problem. Moses Hadas, *Hellenistic Culture: Fusion and Diffusion* (New York, 1959), is generally useful on the subject, in spite of its tendency to exaggerate semitic elements in the hellenistic bundle.

Stoicism was itself eclectic in its sources and syncretist in its aims. It combined an Aristotelian (and perhaps pre-Socratic) materialism with Socratic ethical theory, the hint of an Asiatic passion for right-eousness with, in its later stages, the severe moralism of Rome. Its sense of the unity and harmony of nature and its emphasis on the structural and dynamic affinities of macrocosm and microcosm readily fused with Babylonian astrology. Stoicism embraced the allegorical principle by which every philosophical and religious position in the hellenistic world could be perceived as a legitimate insight into the nature of things, and it popularized the notion that the various schools of ancient philosophy constituted, all to-gether, a single Great Tradition of consistent, developing, and overlapping wisdom. Seneca himself, with Cicero the major source of Europe's early knowledge of Stoic teaching, frequently borrowed from non-Stoic sources. In addition Stoicism had a history. In its later, Roman form its physical, metaphysical, and epistemological foundations receded into the background, though these dimensions of its influence continued to work more subtly; and the absolutism of its ethical demand was modified. It is thus hardly remarkable that Renaissance humanists were often far from clear about the precise lineaments of Stoicism, nor is it surprising that modern scholars who are not technical historians of philosophy more often refer to than try to define Stoic philosophy. Stoicism, for the humanist, was sometimes a fairly particular set of beliefs, but it was also the particular form in which the pervasive and common assumptions of hellenistic paganism presented themselves most attractively and forcefully to the Renaissance.

The definition of Augustinianism is at least equally difficult, partly because Augustine himself was a product of the same philo-sophically confused culture that produced Stoicism (with the difference that several additional centuries had made the spiritual atmosphere even more turgid), partly for other reasons. His *Confessions*, not to mention the remarkable eclecticism of the pagan culture reflected in his other works, provide in themselves a sufficient explanation for his vision of ancient philosophy as "the city of confusion." [5] In addition Augustine was a singularly complex and unsystematic thinker who presents many different faces to his readers. He has been compared to a turbulent stream into whose rushing waters an

---

[5] *De Civitate Dei*, XVIII, 51; cf. XVIII, 41.

abundance of silt has been washed, with the result that, although its waters are opaque, it deposits much rich nourishment along its banks for the support of a wide variety of life. A recent work, proceeding systematically, has identified some eleven distinct and in some respects incompatible types of "Augustinianism". [6] Like a river, the mind of Augustine was in constant movement. His voluminous writings were evolved out of his rich and varied experience, the changing circumstances of his external life, and above all his inner development. His thought can therefore be apprehended fully only as a set of tendencies rather than a system; its coherence is biographical rather than structural. His successive works constantly combined and recombined old and new elements in his thought, in a constant struggle to discover where he stood and where he was moving. He saw this himself. "I am the sort of man," he wrote in a letter, "who writes because he has made progress, and who makes progress— by writing." [7] And he knew that he had, in some important respects, changed his mind; hence, late in his life, he felt compelled to correct, in his *Retractions*, the errors committed in his earlier works.

Nevertheless the direction of Augustine's movement is reasonably clear, and this may suggest that a useful and legitimate definition of Augustinianism, as a particular impulse in European thought, may be sought in the tendencies of his maturity or even, more profoundly, in the vision he presents of a mind engaged in a certain kind of movement. That movement can be generally described as a slow, steady, though incomplete advance from a hellenistic understanding of Christianity, which sought to reconcile the Gospel with the commonplaces of later antique culture, toward an increasingly biblical understanding of Christianity. For it is now generally recognized that Augustine's conversion did not lead to an immediate break with his hellenistic heritage; for some time (like many, perhaps the majority, of the Christians of his age), he understood his new faith as a better statement of what he had previously believed. Christianity, from this standpoint, brought the Great Tradition of ancient philosophy to its culmination. Only gradually, particularly under the influence of the Pauline Epistles, did he become aware of the

---

[6] Eugene Teselle, *Augustine the Theologian* (London, 1970), 347-348.

[7] Ep. 143, quoted by Brown, 353. For the general point, in addition to Brown and Teselle, I am much indebted to F. Edward Cranz, "The Development of Augustine's Ideas on Society before the Donatist Controversy," *Harvard Theological Review*, 47 (1954), 255-316, and R. A. Markus, *Saeculum: History and Society in the Theology of St. Augustine* (Cambridge, 1970).

ıı ıısiıııı ıwiıliıı ılıiı ıııiıııııı ıııı1 ıııı ıı ıııııııııııı ılıııı. Thuu
Augustinianism, like Stoicism, may be seen to have had, for the
Renaissance, both a more precise and a more general significance.
It can be taken to represent, at the same time, a set of propositions
antithetical to those brought into focus by Stoicism, and the process
by which some thinkers were freeing themselves from the old
assumptions of hellenistic culture and moving toward a more specifically Christian vision of man and the human condition.

The notion of the compatibility and even the affinity between
Stoicism and Christianity goes back to the yearning of early Christian
converts for some bridge between the old world of thought and
the new. Stoic elements in the expression (if not the thought) of
the Apostle Paul tended to obscure their radical differences, and
the apocryphal correspondence between Paul and Seneca confused
the issue further.[8] The affinities, indeed, might seem immediately
impressive, as they did in the Renaissance. The Stoics were com-
mendably pious; they spoke much about the gods and even about
God, praising his wisdom, his power, and his love for mankind.
Their emphasis on divine providence and its ultimate benevolence
seemed a particular point of contact with Christianity, and the idea
of a single providential order led in turn to an ostensibly Christian
ethic of absolute obedience and acceptance of the divine will. The
Stoics displayed a singular moral seriousness; and their emphasis
on virtue, through their famous contrast between the things that are
within and those that are not within human control, recognized its
inwardness; they acknowledged the problem of sin and stressed man's
moral responsibility. They preached the brotherhood of man as well
as the universal fatherhood of God, and they had much to say about
the immortality of the soul.

But at a deeper level Stoicism and Augustinian Christianity were
in radical opposition. The issue between them, in its most direct
terms, was the difference between the biblical understanding of
creation, which makes both man and the physical universe separate
from and utterly dependent on God, and the hellenistic principle
of immanence which makes the universe eternal, by one means or
another deifies the natural order, and by seeing a spark of divinity
in man tends to make him something more than a creature of God.[9]

---

[8] For this apocryphal correspondence, *Epistolae Senecae ad Paulum et Pauli ad
Senecam 'quae vocantur'*, ed. C. W. Barlow (Rome, 1938).

[9] For an excellent introduction to the fundamental importance of this issue,

This fundamental difference has massive implications, and from it we may derive the major issues on which Stoicism and Augustinianism would be in potential opposition within Renaissance humanism. The anthropological differences between the two positions were of particular importance. The Stoic view of man attributed to him a divine spark or seed, identified with reason, which gave man access to the divine order of the universe, from which the existence, the nature, and the will of God could be known. Stoicism therefore pointed to natural theology; and since reason was seen as a universal human attribute, which meant that all men have some natural understanding of God, Stoic anthropology virtually required a religious syncretism. As the distinctive quality of man, reason also gave him his specifically human identity; a man was most fully human, best realized the ends of his existence, and became perfect, through the absolute sovereignty of reason over the other dimensions of the human personality. Virtue consisted, accordingly, in following the dictates of reason, to which the rebellious body and its passions were to be reduced by the will. But the will was not perceived as an independent faculty; it was the faithful and mechanical servant of reason, and therefore Stoicism rested on the assumption that to know the good is to do the good. Through rational illumination and rational control man was capable of reaching perfection. The body presented problems, but these could be solved through a disciplined *apatheia*, a cultivated indifference to physical needs and impulses, to the affections, and to external conditions. But since only man's reason was divine, immortality was reserved for the soul. Conversely Stoicism had a typically hellenistic contempt for the body.

Augustinianism contradicted this view at every point. Seeing man in every part of his being as a creature of God, it could not regard his reason (however wonderful) as divine and thus naturally capable of knowing the will of God. Such knowledge was available to man only in the Scriptures, particular revelations from God himself, which spoke not to mankind as a general category but to the individual. And because neither reason nor any other human faculty was intrinsically superior to the rest, Augustinianism tended to replace the monarchy of reason in the human personality with a kind of corporate democracy. The primary organ in Augustinian

see *Creation: the Impact of an Idea*, ed. Daniel O'Connor and Francis Oakley (New York, 1969).

anthropology is not so much that which is highest as that which is central; it is literally the heart (*cor*), whose quality determines the quality of the whole. And that this quality is not a function of rational enlightenment is seen as a matter of common experience. The will is not, after all, an obedient servant of the reason; it has energies and impulses of its own, and man is a far more mysterious animal than the philosophers are inclined to admit. Human wickedness thus presents a much more serious problem than the Stoics dream of, and the notion that man in his fallen condition can rely on his own powers to achieve virtue is utterly implausible. Nor, in any event, is there virtue in withdrawal from engagement with the non-rational and external dimensions of existence. The physical body and the emotional constitution of man were created by God along with man's intellectual powers, and their needs too have dignity and are at least equally worthy of satisfaction. For the same reason immortality cannot be limited to the soul; man must be saved, since God made him so, as a whole.

The contrasts are equally significant in respect to the position of man in society. Although the self-centeredness in the Stoic ideal of individual existence was often uneasily and joylessly combined with a Roman concern for civic duty, the Stoics generally left the impression that social existence was a distraction from the good life, which could be satisfactorily pursued only by withdrawal from the world of men. Despite his recognition of the basic equality of man, the Stoic was also persuaded that the good life based on the contemplation of eternal verities was possible only for a few select souls; he was therefore contemptuous of the vulgar crowd. By contrast the mature Augustine, though still yearning for a contemplative life, insisted unequivocally on the obligations of the individual to society, obligations at once of duty, prudence and love; and at the same time the conception of the blessed life opened up by his less intellectual vision of man was not for the few but accessible to all.

Stoicism, again, had little use for history. Its conception of a rational and unchanging law of nature underlying all things led to a peculiarly rigid notion of cyclical recurrence that denied all significance to discrete events, which in any case belonged to the uncontrollable outer world irrelevant to the good life, just as it precluded the idea of a direction and goal for history. Its cultural values were not the products of particular experience in the world of time and matter but eternal, perennially valid, and so perennially recoverable. Thus its only remedy for present discontents was a nostalgic return to a better past. But Augustine vigorously rejected the eternal round of the ancients. He brooded over the mystery of time as a creature and vehicle of God's will and proclaimed that history was guided to its appointed end by God himself and therefore, expressing his wisdom, must be fraught with a mysterious significance.

But underlying all these particular contrasts was a fundamental difference over the order of the universe. For the Stoics a single cosmic order, rational and divine, pervaded all things, at once static and, through a divine impulse to achieve perfection planted in everything, dynamic, its principles operative alike in physical nature, in human society, and in the human personality. The existence of this order determined all human and social development; and the end of man, either individually or collectively, could not be freely chosen but consisted in subjective acceptance and conformity to destiny. The perfection of that order meant that whatever is right, however uncomfortable or tragic for mankind; at the heart of Stoicism is that familiar cosmic optimism which signifies, for the actual experience of men, the deepest pessimism. Against all this Augustinianism, though by no means denying in principle the ultimate order of the universe, rejected its intelligibility and thus its coherence and its practical significance for man. The result was to free both man and society from their old bondage to cosmic principles, and to open up a secular vision of human existence and a wide range of pragmatic accommodations to the exigencies of life impossible in the Stoic religious universe. In this sense Augustinianism provided a charter for human freedom and a release for the diverse possibilities of human creativity.[10]

II. Stoicism and Augustinianism: The Medieval Heritage

I do not mean to imply that either Stoicism or Augustinianism presented itself to the Renaissance humanist with even the limited coherence of this short sketch, which is introduced here only to suggest the antithetical impulses in the two movements for the clarification of what follows. Earlier (and indeed much of later) humanism was afflicted with the same kind of ideological confusion

---

[10] The classic work of Charles Norris Cochrane, *Christianity and Classical Culture* (Oxford, 1940), is particularly useful on this fundamental difference.

that prevailed in the hellenistic world, and Stoic and Augustinian impulses were persistently intermingled and fragmentary. Their operation on the Renaissance mind also depended on the manner in which they were transmitted, their reception on the needs of a changing historical situation.

Obviously neither tradition was a complete novelty in the Renaissance. This is clearest in the case of Augustine, although it is essential to recognize that the diversities and ambiguities in his thought require us to treat medieval Augustinianism with some precision. The earlier Middle Ages seems to have been attracted chiefly to the more hellenistic aspects of Augustinianism and generally resisted (though without altogether rejecting) the full implications of his theology of justification. It was largely oblivious to his secularism or to the problem of his personal development. And with the revival of Aristotle in the thirteenth century, the influence of Augustine (and indeed of the Fathers in general) suffered some decline. A strong loyalty to Augustine persisted among the Franciscans and above all among the Augustinian Hermits, whose claims to ancient origin were regarded with some reserve and who therefore needed to demonstrate their close affinities with their alleged founder.[11] But Thomas, put off by Augustine's Platonism and troubled by the possibility that Augustine had changed his mind, recommended that his earlier writings be approached with caution; and Albertus Magnus rejected his authority in philosophy, though respecting it in theology.[12] This more selective treatment of Augustine may well have prepared the way, by its recognition, however negatively, of his development, for the more personal Augustinianism of the Renaissance. At the same time the relative eclipse of Augustinianism made it possible for Renaissance Augustinianism to present itself as something of a novelty.

The decline of Augustinianism is vividly illustrated by the *Divine Comedy*, from which, in spite of deeper traces of Augustinian influence in Dante's thought, Augustine as a personality is strikingly absent. He does not appear among the representatives of sacred

---

[11] Damasus Trapp, "Augustinian Theology of the 14th Century: Notes on Editions, Marginalia, Opinions, and Book Lore," *Augustiniana*, VI (1956), 189.

[12] M. D. Chenu, *Toward Understanding St. Thomas*, tr. Albert M. Landry and Dominic Hughes (Chicago, 1964), 43, 54, 142 (I cite the English edition rather than the French original, *Introduction à l'étude de Saint Thomas d'Aquin* [Paris, 1950], because of its richer documentation); Henri-Irénée Marrou, *Saint Augustin et l'augustinisme* (Paris, 1955), 161-162.

wisdom in Paradise, introduced by Saint Thomas in what may be interpreted as Dante's basic philosophical and theological bibliography,[13] nor does he appear in the next group of cantos which deal with the theological virtues. He is not assigned to answer any of Dante's questions, or to explain to him any of the mysteries of Christian doctrine and human destiny. Indeed he can scarcely be said to *appear* at all; Saint Bernard merely mentions him in the course of explaining the order in which the souls of the blessed are grouped around Christ. And even at this point, although he is introduced in the estimable company of Saint Francis and Saint Benedict, both of whom do play didactic roles in other cantos, he seems of only historical interest, as marking off a phase in the evolution of the church.[14] For Dante Augustine has almost literally disappeared. It is hardly surprising that Dante was unimpressed by the *Confessions*.[15]

Medieval Stoicism has received far less attention than medieval Augustinianism, possibly for the same reasons that account for the neglect of Stoicism in the Renaissance. But in spite of the absence of systematic study of this subject, it is not difficult to demonstrate the importance of a Stoic element in medieval thought, sometimes at the deepest level.[16] Cicero and Seneca (along with Boethius who, as a transmitter, may have been at least as important for Stoicism as for Neoplatonism and for Aristotle) were favorite philosophical authorities during the entire Middle Ages; and, in contrast to Augustine's, their influence was not decreasing in the thirteenth century. Roger Bacon defended Seneca's "elegance of statement about the virtues which are commonly required for honesty of life and the community of human society";[17] the *Romance of the Rose*

---

[13] Canto X.

[14] Canto XXXII.

[15] He cites the *Confessions* from time to time in the *Convivio* but appears to regard it as no more than a conventional work of moral guidance.

[16] This has been noted by Nicola Abbagnano, "Italian Renaissance Humanism," *Cahiers d'histoire mondiale*, XI (1963), 269; cf. Charles B. Schmitt, *Cicero Scepticus: a Study of the Influence of the Academica in the Renaissance* (The Hague, 1972), 33-34, on the importance (and neglect by modern scholars) of Cicero for the Middle Ages. Hans Baron, "Cicero and the Roman Civic Spirit in the Middle Ages and the Early Renaissance," *John Rylands Library Bulletin*, XXII (1938), 72-97, has useful remarks on the medieval, as contrasted with the Renaissance, image of Cicero.

[17] Quoted by John Mundy, *Europe in the High Middle Ages 1150-1309* (London, 1973), 478, noting the prominence of Seneca in Bacon's *Opus maius*.

is full of Stoic precepts; [18] Thomas made heavy use of Cicero, [19] and Dante cited Cicero many times, often linking his authority with Aristotle's.[20] But this parallelism chiefly suggests the ambiguous place of Stoic influences in European thought, and their presence is often most powerful when it is not explicit. We may discern it in medieval preoccupation with the systematic and unitary order of the cosmos, which probably owes more, at least directly, to Stoicism and other hellenistic influences than to the great hellenic philosophers, and in the intellectual vision of man so often conveyed by the Ciceronian commonplace that the erect stature of the human body had been decreed by nature so that men "might be able to behold the sky and so gain a knowledge of the gods." [21] We may see it again in medieval interest in the religious truths available to all mankind through reason alone, so important for missionary strategy; [22] or, at another level, in the distinction between the things belonging to man and those in the domain of fortune,[23] or in medieval debates over the character of true nobility, which so regularly invoked Stoic belief in the natural equality of man.[24]

The Stoic element in Renaissance humanism may thus represent more actual continuity with the Middle Ages than does Renaissance knowledge of Augustine. At any rate it is not clear, before the assimilation by later Renaissance humanists of Marcus Aurelius and the chief Stoic (or Stoicizing) Greek writers, Epictetus and Plutarch, that Renaissance thinkers knew significantly more about the Stoics than their medieval predecessors had known. But the men of the Renaissance had far more of Augustine. During the Middle Ages

---

[18] Cf. the passages on fortune in the translation of Charles Dahlberg (Princeton, 1971), 87, 102-104, 121-122.

[19] For his use of the Senecan notion of seeds of virtue and knowledge, see also the passages listed by Maryanne C. Horowitz, "Pierre Charron's View of the Source of Wisdom," *Journal of the History of Philosophy*, IX (1971), 454 n. 44. Professor Horowitz is working on a general study of the career of Stoicism from antiquity to the later Renaissance.

[20] Esp. in the *Convivio*; cf. Inferno, IV, 141, where Cicero appears in the company of "Seneca morale."

[21] *De natura deorum*, ed. H. Rackham (Cambridge, Mass., and London, 1957), 257-259. For medieval use of the image, cf. R. W. Southern, *Medieval Humanism and Other Studies* (New York, 1970), 37-41.

[22] Cf., for example, Marsilius of Padua, *Defensor pacis*, I, v, 10.

[23] See, for example, *Romance of the Rose*, 110, and the Knight's and Monk's tales in Chaucer's *Canterbury Tales*.

[24] Cf. *Romance of the Rose*, 308-312, and the passages collected in Mundy, 265-269. Johan Huizinga, *Waning of the Middle Ages*, tr. F. Hopman (New York, 1959), 64-67, directs attention to the importance of this motif in medieval literature.

Augustine had been known, even to many of those who venerated him most deeply, chiefly through the *Decretum* of Yves of Chartres with its 425 extracts from Augustine, through Peter Lombard's *Book of Sentences*, so overwhelmingly based on Augustine, or through Robert Kilwardby's *tabulae* and *capitulationes*. Even Bonaventura knew Augustine at least partly from sources of this kind; he cited one of Augustine's early works eleven times, but ten of his citations were to the same text, presumably garnered from one or another of the compendia available to him.[25] But the fourteenth century saw a concerted effort, particularly among his followers in the Augustinian Order, to recover the whole corpus of Augustine's works and, in a manner that would be characteristic of Renaissance scholarship, to develop a systematic acquaintance with his whole thought, not from the standard medieval proof-texts but from the direct study of his entire writings. For the first time a careful attempt was made to identify the exact location, by title, chapter, and verse, of quotations from Augustine, and to verify their accuracy. The great figure in this enterprise was Gregory of Rimini (d. 1358), who has been called the first modern Augustinian. Gregory not only knew the writings and followed the doctrines of Augustine more closely than any previous scholar; he also restored long-neglected works to circulation, in a movement that would result in the critical rejection of the substantial body of apocrypha from the Augustinian corpus and eventually culminate in the great critical editions of Augustine in the sixteenth and seventeenth centuries.[26] Already in the later fifteenth century a single series of sermons by the Augustinian friar Johann Staupitz contained 163 citations from 24 separate works of Augustine.[27]

But, neither Stoicism nor Augustinianism was, in the Renaissance, primarily a function of the availability and transmission of literary sources. They were rather responses to the deep and changing needs of Renaissance society and culture. These needs had been created by the growing complexity of European life in the later Middle Ages, and above all by the development of towns and the new vision

---

[25] Chenu, 47-48, 52 nn. 3 and 4, 152.

[26] Trapp, 150-151,181, describing Gregory as the "first Augustinian of Augustine" to distinguish him from the more equivocal Augustine of the Middle Ages.

[27] David Curtis Steinmetz, *Misericordia Dei: the Theology of Johannes von Staupitz in its Late Medieval Setting*, Studies in Medieval and Reformation Thought, IV (Leiden, 1968), 155.

of human existence towns increasingly evoked. For towns produced a set of conditions that made parts of Europe more and more like the hellenistic world in which both the Stoics and Augustine had been reared: the constant menace of famine and pestilence, urban disorders and endemic warfare in the countryside, incessant conflict among individuals, families, and social groups, a growing social mobility that left a substantial proportion of the urban population rootless and insecure, above all the terrible anxieties of a life in which the familiar conventions of a close and traditional human community had given way to a relentless struggle for survival in a totally unpredictable and threatening world.

It was this situation to which scholastic culture seemed irrelevant, and which conversely Stoicism and Augustinianism sought, in their different ways, to interpret and remedy; and the needs of this grim predicament primarily explain why men sought and read Stoic and Augustinian writings. Paradoxically Stoicism, though pagan in a Christian culture, proved the more traditional and conservative of the two prescriptions; Augustinianism, though it appealed to the most authoritative of the Latin fathers, was at least potentially the more novel. But the conservatism of the Stoic adaptation to a new situation—certainly an element in its attraction—was disguised by the graceful and unsystematic form of the sources in which it was chiefly available: dialogues, personal letters, pensées, essays filled with memorable sayings and concrete examples.[28] Stoicism could therefore present itself as an alternative to scholastic habits of thought.

III. The Stoic Element in Humanist Thought

Stoicism addressed itself to the problems of modern Europe, as to those of later antiquity, by reaffirming the divine, harmonious, and intelligible order of nature and drawing appropriate conclusions, practical as well as theoretical. The Stoicism of the Renaissance, perhaps especially when it was least aware of its Stoic inspiration, was based, like ancient Stoicism, on natural philosophy and cosmology, a point of some importance in view of the common supposition that Renaissance thinkers only drew isolated, practical ethical precepts from Stoic sources. Valla's Epicurean (in this case made, perhaps deliberately, to sound like a Stoic) declared nature

---

[28] The point is made by Trinkaus, I, 307.

virtually identical with God.[29] Vives from time to time elaborated on the meaning of this proposition. The universe, he wrote, was governed "by the divine intelligence which commands and forbids according to reason." [30] Calvin, for all his concern to maintain the distinction between God and nature, drew on the same conception. "This skillful ordering of the universe," he argued, "is for us a sort of mirror in which we can contemplate God, who is otherwise invisible." [31] For Charron nature was "the equity and universal reason which lights in us, which contains and incubates in itself the seeds of all virtue, probity, justice." [32]

And man is also a part of this rational order of nature. Montaigne found this humbling: "We are neither superior nor inferior to the rest. All that is under heaven, says the sage, is subject to one law and one fate. . . . Man must be forced and lined up within the barriers of this organization." [33] Others saw in it some justification for glorifying man. "This is the order of nature," wrote Vives, "that wisdom be the rule of the whole, that all creatures obey man, that in man the body abides by the orders of the soul, and that the soul itself comply with the will of God." [34] Another way to coordinate man with the universe was the notion of man as microcosm in Pomponazzi and even Calvin.[35] Calvin was willing, too, to acknowledge the influence of the rational order of the heavens on the human body.[36]

Implicit in these passages, and sometimes more than implicit,

---

[29] *De vero falsoque bono*, ed. Maristella de Panizza Lorch (Bari, 1970), 18. See the discussion of this discourse in Trinkaus, I, 110-113.

[30] Quoted in Carlos G. Noreña, *Juan Luis Vives* (The Hague, 1970), 216.

[31] *Institutes*, I, v, 1. For a balanced view of Calvin's Stoicism, which is sometimes exaggerated, see Charles Partee, "Calvin and Determinism," forthcoming in *Christian Scholar's Review*. I will make no distinction in these pages between men of humanist backgrounds such as Zwingli, Melanchthon, and Calvin, who became Protestants, and other humanists. However conventional, such a distinction seems to me to rest on assumptions that cannot be justified in the light of recent scholarship. This is an obvious inference from Kristeller's fundamental contributions to our understanding of humanism, and the fact that we have been so slow to draw it is perhaps chiefly attributable to the over-specialization that artificially separates students of the Renaissance from those of the Reformation.

[32] Quoted by Horowitz, 453, from *De la sagesse*; Charron cites Seneca.

[33] "Apologie de Raimond Sebond," *Essaies*, ed. Maurice Rat (Paris, 1958), II, 140-141. I follow here the translation of E. J. Trechman (Oxford, 1935).

[34] Quoted by Noreña, 201-202.

[35] See the passage from *De fato* in Trinkaus, II, 547; for Calvin, *Institutes*, I, v, 3.

[36] *Calvin's Commentary on Seneca's De Clementia*, ed. Ford Lewis Battles and André Malan Hugo (Leiden, 1969), 103 n. 69, citing *Contre de l'astrologie judiciaire* (1549).

is the assumption that this divinely-ordered universe is accessible to the human understanding, that man's perception of the rational order of the universe tells him a good deal about the nature and will of God, and that man's reason is thus the link between himself and God. This conception of nature leads us accordingly to the notion of man as essentially an intellectual being. As Aeneas Sylvius declared, the mind is "the most precious of all human endowments;" [37] and Petrarch's definition of man as a rational animal is enthusiastically developed, in the *Secretum*, by Augustinus: "When you find a man so governed by Reason that all his conduct is regulated by her, all his appetites subject to her alone, a man who has so mastered every motion of his spirit by Reason's curb that he knows it is she alone who distinguishes him from the savagery of the brute, and that it is only by submission to her guidance that he deserves the name of man at all . . . . when you have found such a man, then you may say that he has some true and fruitful idea of what the definition of man is." [38] As this passage suggests, this view of man requires the sovereignty of reason within the personality. For Pomponazzi human freedom depended on the subservience of will to intellect,[39] and for Calvin this had been the situation of Adam in Paradise, the consequence of his creation in God's image: "In the mind [of Adam] perfect intelligence flourished and reigned, uprightness attended as its companion, and all the senses were prepared and molded for due obedience to reason; and in the body there was a suitable correspondence with this internal order." Before the fall, apparently, Adam had been a model of Stoic perfection.[40] "The understanding," he wrote more generally, "is, as it were, the leader and governor of the soul" and the instructor of the will.[41]

---

[37] *De liberorum educatione*, tr. William Harrison Woodward, in *Vittorino da Feltre and Other Humanist Educators* (New York, 1970), 140.

[38] *Secretum*, 460. My references to this work are to the edition in Francesco Petrarca, *Opere*, ed. Giovanni Ponte (Milan, 1968), but I have generally followed the translation by William H. Draper (London, 1911). For the confrontation between Stoicism and Augustinianism in Petrarch, see Klaus Heitmann, *Fortuna und Virtus: eine Studie zu Petrarcas Lebensweisheit* (Cologne, 1958); and for his Augustinianism, Pietro Paolo Gerosa, *L'umanesimo agostiniano del Petrarca* (Turin, 1927).

[39] See Trinkaus, II, 544, for a passage from *De fato* in which Pomponazzi expresses his disagreement with the more Augustinian notion of the will as mistress of the intellect.

[40] *Commentary on Genesis* 1:26. I quote in the translation of John King (Edinburgh, 1847).

[41] *Institutes*, I, xv, 7.

On the other hand this elevation of reason was often likely to be accompanied by a denigration of other dimensions of the personality, especially the passions and the body with which they were regularly associated, which threatened to challenge the sovereignty of reason. From this standpoint the body and the rational soul could be seen as radically opposed. Petrarch claimed to have learned from his own body only "that man is a vile, wretched animal unless he redeems the ignobility of the body with the nobility of the soul." He saw his soul as imprisoned in and weighed down by the body, the one "an immortal gift, the other corruptible and destined to pass away." [42] With Vives attack on the body achieved an almost pathological intensity.[43] But happily the rational soul, however threatened by the body and the affections, was in the end clearly superior to them. As Lipsius remarked, "For although the soul is infected and somewhat corrupted by the filth of the body and the contagion of sense, it nevertheless retains some vestiges of its origin and is not without certain bright sparks of the pure fiery nature from whence it came forth." [44]

Reason, in any case, because of its access to the divine order of the universe, is a legitimate source of religious insight, a point exploited at some length by Calvin, who quoted Cicero that "there is no nation so barbarous, no race so savage that they have not a deep-seated conviction that there is a God." In sound Stoic fashion Calvin found the order of the heavens, but also the wonders of the human body, a natural witness to the greatness of God. "The natural order was," he declared, "that the frame of the universe should be the school in which we were to learn piety, and from it pass over to eternal life and perfect felicity." [45] Because the religious insights from nature are the common possession of mankind, it must also be true that all peoples may be expected to reveal some knowledge of God; and this belief contributed heavily to the study of the classics.

---

[42] *Epistolae familiares*, XI, 1 and XXI, 15, in *Le famigliari*, ed. Vittorio Rossi (Florence, 1937), II, 23, IV, 94; I use the translations in David Thompson, *Petrarch: an Anthology* (New York, 1971). Cf. Augustinus on soul and body in *Secretum*, 468, 498.

[43] Cf. the remarkable passage in Noreña, 202. For Vives's hatred of sex, see also pp. 209-211.

[44] *De constantia libri duo* (Antwerp, 1605), 7.

[45] *Institutes*, I, iii, 1; I, xiv, 21; I, v, 2; II, vi, 1. Egil Grislis, "Calvin's Use of Cicero in the Institutes I:1—A Case Study in Theological Method," *Archiv für Reformationsgeschichte*, LXII (1971), 5-37, shows how closely Calvin follows *De natura deorum*.

Petrarch, thinking of himself as following Augustine, was deeply impressed by Cicero's Stoic arguments for the providential order of the world, phrased, as he thought, "almost in a Catholic manner." [46] Aeneas Sylvius maintained that Socrates had taught the Christian way of salvation and recommended "the poets and other authors of antiquity" because they were "saturated with the same faith" as the fathers of the church.[47] Erasmus saw various values in classical education, among others the fact that Plato "draws the reader to true knowledge by similes." [48] His follower Zwingli placed a number of the ancients among the elect.[49] Through all of this we may discern traces of the hellenistic idea of a great tradition of developing and coherent wisdom, with its corollary that, properly understood, all schools of philosophy are in agreement and that philosophy itself is consistent with and complementary to Christian truth. Thus Bruni had argued for the essential agreement of all the philosophers,[50] a conception of which Pico's *Theses* was a kind of *reductio ad absurdum.*

But rational knowledge was also a resource in a more practical sense. From an understanding of the general rationality of nature, man could discover the rational laws of his own nature and, by following them, variously perfect himself. Augustinus advised Franciscus "to order your life by your nature," [51] and this principle was basic to much humanist thought about education. Alberti's Uncle Lionardo recommended that a child be formed by encouraging the best elements in his nature, on the general principle that "excellence is nothing but nature itself, complete and well-formed." [52] Erasmus made the point broadly: "All living things strive to develop according to their proper nature. What is the proper nature of man? Surely it is to live the life of reason, for reason is the peculiar pre-

---

[46] *Invectiva contra eum qui Maledixit Italiae*, in Thompson, 230-231; *Secretum*, 470; *De sui ipsius et multorum ignorantia*, tr. Hans Nachod, in *The Renaissance Philosophy of Man*, ed. Ernst Cassirer, et al. (Chicago, 1948), 83-85.

[47] *Op. cit.*, 141-142.

[48] Quoted by Charles Partee, "The Revitalization of the Concept of 'Christian Philosophy' in Renaissance Humanism," *Christian Scholar's Review*, 3 (1974), 364.

[49] *An Exposition of the Faith*, tr. G. W. Bromiley, *Zwingli and Bullinger*, Library of Christian Classics, XXIV (London, 1953), 275-276.

[50] Seigel discusses this, 104-106.

[51] *Secretum*, 494.

[52] *I libri della famiglia*, ed. Cecil Grayson, in *Opere volgari*, I (Bari, 1960), 63; I use the translation of Reneé Neu Watkins, *The Family in Renaissance Florence* (Columbia, S. C., 1969), 75-76.

rogative of man." [53] Calvin, who in his youth had identified the injunction to follow nature as Stoic doctrine,[54] did not hesitate in his maturity, like Boccaccio and Valla, to exploit the principle as an argument against celibacy.[55] Charron repeated the general point: "the doctrine of all the sages imports that to live well is to live according to nature." [56]

But clearly the formation men most required in a brutal and disorderly world was training in morality, and it was in this area that Stoic doctrine seemed most relevant to contemporary needs, most immediately prescriptive. The rational order of nature was to be the foundation for the orderly behavior of men; this was its practical function. Stoic moralists were attractive, then, because of their emphasis on the supreme value of virtue, sometimes, as Augustinus tells Franciscus, because it is the only basis for human happiness, sometimes, as Petrarch wrote elsewhere, because virtue, "as the philosophers say," is "its own reward, its own guide, its own end and aim." [57] Pomponazzi, who had clearer reasons, agreed that virtue could have no higher reward than itself and praised it as the most precious quality in life; [58] and Calvin recognized the peculiar emphasis of the Stoics on virtue.[59] Guarino applied the conception directly to education, seeing "learning and training in virtue" as the peculiar pursuit of man and therefore central to *humanitas*.[60]

This concern with virtue reflects also the persistence of the intellectual conception of man so closely bound up with the rational order of the Stoic universe. This is apparent in two ways. In the first place Stoic virtue is acquired through the intellect; it is a product of philosophy, absorbed from books. Thus Erasmus believed that even small children could absorb it through beginning their education by reading ancient fables. He particularly recommended the story of Circe, with its lesson "that men who will not yield to the guidance

---

[53] *De pueris instituendis*, in *Desiderius Erasmus concerning the Aim and Method of Education*, ed. William H. Woodward (New York, 1964), 192-193.

[54] *Comm. Seneca*, 280-281.

[55] *Institutes*, IV, xiii, 3, 21.

[56] Quoted by Horowitz, 452-453.

[57] *Secretum*, 442; *Epist. fam.*, XXI, 15, in IV, 95.

[58] See his argument in *De immortalitate animae*, tr. William Henry Hay II, *Renaissance Philosophy of Man*, 359-377; discussed by Trinkaus, I, 539-541.

[59] *Comm. Seneca*, 112-113.

[60] *De ordine docendi et studendi*, in Woodward, *Vittorino da Feltre*, 177.

of reason, but follow the enticements of the senses, are no more than brute beasts." "Could a Stoic philosopher," he asked rhetorically, "preach a graver truth?" [61] But in the second place, as this passage also suggests, the practice of this Stoic virtue depended on the sovereignty of reason and its powers of control over the disorderly impulses arising out of other aspects of the personality. Alberti's Uncle Lionardo made the point clearly. "Good ways of living," he declared, "eventually overcome and correct every appetite that runs counter to reason and every imperfection of the mind." [62] Vives identified this ethics of rational control with the teaching of Christ:

> Our mind is a victim of its own darkness; our passions, stirred by sin, have covered the eyes of reason with a thick layer of dust. We need a clear insight, serene and undisturbed. . . . All the precepts of moral philosophy can be found in the teachings of Christ. In his doctrine, and in his words, man will find the remedy to all moral diseases, the ways and means to tame our passions under the guidance and the power of reason. Once this order has been secured man will learn proper behavior in his relations with himself, with God, and with his neighbor; he will act rightfully not only in the privacy of his home but also in his social and political life. [63]

And in this emphasis on rational control we may perhaps discern an important clue to the attraction of Stoic ethical doctrine for the age of the Renaissance. It presented itself as an antidote for a terrible fear of the consequences of the loss of self-control. Montaigne suggested this in his ruminations over the perils of drunkenness, which may cause man to spill out the secrets on which his survival and dignity depend. "The worst state of man," Montaigne concluded, "is when he loses the knowledge and control of himself." [64] And the ability of men to control their lower impulses with the help of philosophy gave some hope for a better and more orderly world. So it seemed to Aeneas Sylvius: "Respect towards women, affection for children and for home; pity for the distressed, justice towards all, self-control in anger, restraint in indulgence, forbearance in success, contentment, courage, duty—these are some of the virtues to which philosophy will lead you." [65]

The Stoic model for the order of society, like its model for the

---

[61] *De pueris instituendis*, Woodward, 212.
[62] *Della famiglia*, 64.
[63] Quoted by Noreña, 207.
[64] "De l'yvrongnerie," *Essaies*, II, 10.
[65] *De liberorum educatione*, Woodward. 157.

order of the individual personality, was also derived from the order of the cosmos. An authentic and durable social order that would properly reflect the stability of the cosmos had thus to meet two basic requirements. It had to be a single order, and it had to be governed by reason. This meant in practice that the human world must be organized as a universal empire, and that it must be ruled by the wise, by men who are themselves fully rational and in touch with the rational principles of the cosmos.

Thus the Stoic type of humanist tended, from Petrarch in some moods to Lipsius in the waning Renaissance, to admire imperial Rome. The conquest of the Roman Empire, Petrarch once remarked, had been "actuated by perfect justice and good will as regards men," however defective it may have been in regard to God.[66] Castiglione's Ottaviano Fregoso found an earlier example of the universal model to admire; he praised Aristotle for "directing Alexander to that most glorious aim—which was the desire to make the world into one single universal country, and have all men living as one people in friendship and in mutual concord under one government and one law that might shine equally on all like the light of the sun." [67] Erasmus decried any attachment to a particular community; he had succeeded himself, he said, in feeling at home everywhere.[68] Lipsius similarly attacked love of country as an expression of the lower demands of the body and of custom rather than nature, which commands us to regard the whole world as our true fatherland.[69]

But the sovereignty of reason in the cosmos also required that the world be governed by the wise. All political disorder, Erasmus argued, was the result of stupidity; hence, he declared, "You cannot be a prince if you are not a philosopher." [70] Vives saw the ruler as simply a sage with public authority.[71] There was some discrepancy between this ideal and political actuality, but it could be remedied; since it was rarely possible to elevate sages into kings, it was necessary to convert kings, by education, into sages. This was the

---

[66] *De vita solitaria*, II, ix, tr. Jacob Zeitlin, *The Life of Solitude* (Urbana, 1924), 250-251.

[67] *The Book of the Courtier*, tr. Charles S. Singleton (New York, 1959), 332.

[68] Letter to Servatius Roger, 8 July 1514, *Opus Epistolarum Erasmi*, ed. P. S. and H. M. Allen (Oxford, 1906-1958), I, 567-569.

[69] *De constantia*, 15-19.

[70] The adage *Aut fatuum aut regem nasci oportere*, in Margaret Mann Phillips, *The Adages of Erasmus* (Cambridge, 1964), 219; *Institutio principis Christiani*, tr. Lester K. Born (New York, 1968), 150.

[71] Noreña, 213.

aim of Erasmus's *Institutio principis Christiani*, and Rabelais presented Grangousier as a model philosopher-king. Properly educated, the ruler might be made to excel all other men in wisdom and therefore in virtue, and his central duty was then to instruct his subjects in virtue.[72] But always, in this conception of kingship, the Stoicizing humanist kept in mind the ultimate source of wisdom and virtue. The philosophy of the prince, for Erasmus, was the kind that "frees the mind from the false opinions and the ignoble passions of the masses, and following the eternal pattern laid up in heaven points the way to good government." [73] It is not (too much has been made of the point) just a practical moral wisdom, despite its disclaimer of metaphysics, but an application to human affairs of the general principles of order in the cosmos. "As the sun to the sky," Erasmus wrote, in what was no mere figure but the reflection of a whole world of thought, "so is the prince to the people; the sun is the eye of the world, the prince the eye of the multitude. As the mind is to the body, so is the prince to the state; the mind knows, the body obeys." [74]

The idealism in this conception of government generally makes it appear singularly unsuited to the actualities of political life, but in at least one respect it helped to meet genuine practical needs. By its conception of a rational law of nature, it assisted in the rationalization of law and social relations. The problem is suggested by Salutati's confrontation between law and medicine, in which the latter offers a kind of diagnosis of the human scene: here, without the stability of some eternal principle, all things would belong "to the realm of the accidental." Law, "based upon eternal and universal justice," placed government upon a more secure foundation than the whims of the ruler or the accidents of custom.[75] It seems likely that the Stoic conception of a natural law governing all human intercourse and authenticating all particular laws gave some impetus, perhaps most powerful when the cosmic vibrations in the conception were least felt, to the systematic codification of the chaos of existing legislation, to the general rule of law, and to more equal justice. Yet we may sense something equivocal,

---

[72] *Gargantua*, I, ch. xlv; cf. Erasmus on the philosopher-king in the adage cited above, Phillips, 217, and Castiglione, *Courtier*, 307.

[73] From the dedication of the *Institutio principis Christiani*, tr. Born, 134.

[74] From the adage cited above, Phillips, 219.

[75] See the discussion of Salutati's *De nobilitate legum et medicinae* in Garin, 36-38.

however opportune, even here. This is apparent in the impersonal rationality in the Stoic idea of social virtue based on law, which corresponded to the increasing legalism and impersonality of the new urban scene. It tended to base social order not on the unreliable vagaries of personal ties, personal loyalties, and personal affection, but on abstract and general social relationships: in a word, on duty rather than on love. The social thought of Stoic humanism thus reflected and probably helped to promote the rationalization of society on which large-scale organization in the modern world depended. But it also made the human world a colder place.

On the other hand the Stoic conception of social improvement was diametrically opposed to the actual direction in which European society was moving. Its ideal, like Seneca's, was nostalgic. As the retrospective prefix in the familiar Renaissance vocabulary of amelioration attests—*renascentium, reformatio, restoratio, restitutio, renovatio,* etc.—it could only look backward for a better world. Petrarch chose deliberately to live in spirit in the ancient past; one of the participants in an Erasmian colloquy deplored the disappearance of "that old time equality, abolished by modern tyranny," [76] which he also associated with the Apostles; Castiglione thought men in antiquity "of greater worth than now." [77] Even the improvement Renaissance writers occasionally celebrated was regularly conceived as the recovery of past excellence, and hope for the future usually was made to depend on some notion of revival. Petrarch found strength in the greatness of Rome. "What inspiration," he exclaimed, "is not to be derived from the memory of the past and from the grandeur of a name once revered through the world!" [78] Lorenzo de Medici's motto in a tournament of 1468 was *le tems revient.*[79] Machiavelli's chief ground for hope, when he deplored the decadence of contemporary Italy, was that "this land seems born to raise up dead things, as she has in poetry, in painting, and in sculpture." [80] Giles of Viterbo applied the conception to ecclesiastical renewal: "We are not innovators. We are simply trying, in accordance with the

---

[76] "Inns," *The Colloquies of Erasmus,* tr. Craig R. Thompson (Chicago, 1965), 150.

[77] *Courtier,* 82.

[78] *Epistolae variae,* XLVIII, tr. Thompson.

[79] Harry Levin, *The Myth of the Golden Age in the Renaissance* (Bloomington, 1969), 38.

[80] From the concluding reflections in the *Arte della guerra,* in Machiavelli, *The Chief Works and Others,* tr. Allan Gilbert (Durham, 1965), II, 726.

will of God, or living back in the choice ancient laws whose observance has lapsed." [81]

All of this suggests the lack of a sense of the positive significance
of change in Stoic humanism. Since excellence was associated with
the divine origins of all things, change could only mean deterioration;
and improvement necessarily implied the recovery of what was
essentially timeless. The static character of this ideal was reflected
in its vision of the good society which, once it had achieved perfection,
could not be permitted to change. So Erasmus hoped that the conflicting interests of human society might "achieve an eternal truce"
in which proper authority and degrees of status would be respected
by all.[82] One of the essential duties of the Erasmian ruler is to resist
all innovation.[83] The central virtue in the Stoic ideal of society is
thus peace, which is not simply the absence of war but ultimately
dependent on the correspondence of social organization to the
unchanging principles of universal order. This is a dimension of
the humanist peace movement that it is well to remember in assessing
the significance of the pacifism of Petrarch, the emphasis on peace
in the circle of Erasmus, or Lipsius's peculiar admiration for the
pax romana. Peace, too, for the Stoic humanist, required the strong
rule of a single "head". And again Stoicism can be seen to supply,
at least in theory, a remedy for one of the most glaring defects of
Renaissance Europe.

One service performed by Stoic humanism was, then, to supply
a foundation for personal and social order in the very nature of
things. But this was only one, and perhaps not the major, dimension
of its significance. For there was a crucial ambiguity in its moral
thought, and indeed in its understanding of virtue, which pointed
not to the improvement of the conditions of life but rather to acceptance of the necessary and irremovable discomforts of existence.
If the rationality of the universe could be regarded as a resource
for a better order, it could also be taken to imply that in some sense
the structure of the universe is already perfect and so beyond improvement. From this standpoint Stoicism became a strategy by
which, through a combination of enlightenment and disciplined
accommodation, the individual could come to terms with the humanly

---

[81] Quoted by John W. O'Malley, *Giles of Viterbo on Church and Reform* (Leiden,
1968), 141.

[82] From the adage *Festina lente*, in Phillips, 183-184.

[83] *Institutio principis Christiani*, 211.

pessimistic implications of a cosmic optimism. It was a strategy of protection for the isolated self in a thoroughly unsatisfactory world. Virtue, in this light, was the ultimate resource by which the ego could minimize its vulnerability to adversity. And this represented a very different kind of adaptation to the changing patterns of European life.

This application of Stoicism was based on the crucial Stoic distinction between those external elements of existence, generally identified with fortune, that are not absolutely within the control of the individual, and the inner world that belongs entirely to himself, the realms, respectively, of necessity and freedom. The inner world alone is the area in which the highest dimension of the personality, man's reason, can exercise total sovereignty, and therefore in which alone man can realize his highest potentialities and attain the ends of his existence; thus it is also the only realm in which he can hope to achieve total happiness. For this is where man discovers the laws governing the universe. As Salutati declared, "They inhere in our minds as of nature. Thus we know them with such certainty that they cannot escape us and that it is not necessary to seek them among external facts. For, as you see, they inhabit our most intimate selves." [84] Lipsius outlined the ideal: "I am guarded and fenced against all external things and settled within myself, indifferent to all cares but one, which is that I may bring in subjection this broken and distressed mind of mine to right reason and God and subdue all human and earthly things to my mind." [85]

The ideal had various implications, notable among them the definition of virtue as that self-sufficiency which, by freeing the individual from all dependence on things external to himself, makes him invulnerable to fortune and so supplies him with inner freedom, the only freedom to which man can aspire. This is the burden of Augustinus's injunction to Franciscus in the *Secretum*: "Learn to live in want and in abundance, to command and to obey, without desiring, with those ideas of yours, to shake off the yoke of fortune that presses even on kings. You will only be free from this yoke when, caring not a straw for human passions, you bend your neck wholly to the rule of virtue. Then you will be free, wanting nothing, then you will be independent; in a word, then you will be a king,

---

[84] Quoted by Garin, 37.
[85] *De constantia*, 46.

truly powerful and perfectly happy," [86] Virtue in this way was
the power to raise the mind above all the external accidents of
existence in order to dwell securely in the realm of the eternal.
It enabled man to identify himself subjectively with the divine
order of the universe, and accordingly a special kind of numinous
awe surrounded it, of a sort that could hardly adhere to the more
practical virtues of social existence. So this species of virtue meant
at once identification with higher and separation from lower things,
especially from all those dimensions of existence that distracted or
troubled the mind and threatened the self-sufficiency of the discrete
individual. Franciscus confessed to Augustinus that his dependence
on others was, in his life, "the bitterest cup of all;" [87] and Petrarch,
who periodically longed for a Stoic repose, reproached Cicero for
betraying his own best convictions by giving up the "peaceful
ease" of his old age to return to public service.[88] The Stoic impulse
in Renaissance humanism favoring such contemplative withdrawal
would find regular expression among later writers, from Salutati
to Montaigne.[89]

In view of the importance of the city as a stimulus to Renaissance
moral reflection, it is also of some interest that it was, for Petrarch,
a peculiar threat to his inner freedom; and he gave vivid articulation
to the historical implications of these Stoic sentiments. "I think of
liberty even while in bonds," he wrote, "of the country while in
cities, of repose amidst labors, and finally . . . of ease while I am busy."
A pattern of concrete associations emerges here. The modern world,
with its greed, bustle, and conflict, means bondage to demanding
work in the city; but against this is the vision of freedom, simplicity,
and solitary repose in an idealized rural world. We may find here,
therefore, some hint of the social realities underlying this discussion.[90]

A more positive dimension of this emphasis in Stoic humanism
was its contribution to that inwardness which, with its genuine
affinity to one aspect of Augustinianism, deepened consciences and

---

[86] *Secretum*, 494.

[87] *Secretum*, 514.

[88] *Ep. fam.*, XXIV, 3, tr. M. E. Cosenza, *Petrarch's Letters to Classical Authors*
(Chicago, 1910), 1-4.

[89] For Salutati, cf. Seigel, 70-76; for Montaigne, see for example "De la solitude," *Essaies*, I, esp. 276. For a typical debate on the subject cf. Alberti, *Della
famiglia*, 179-185.

[90] *Ep. fam.*, XVII, 10, in III, 263; cf. his dismal vision of urban life, with
special reference to Avignon, in *Secretum*, 516-518.

provided one source for the moral sensitivity of the Catholic as
well as the Protestant Reformation. Inwardness pointed to the
role of conscience in the moral life, the inner voice which is concerned rather with motives than with outward acts and results.
The young Calvin recognized this element in Stoicism. "Nothing is
great for the Stoics," he wrote, "which is not also good and inwardly
sound;" and he attacked "*monsters of men, dripping with inner vices,*
yet putting forth the outward appearance and mask of uprightness."
In his maturity he noted that men can discover some ideas of God
within themselves and denounced the indolence of those who refused
this inward search.[91] Montaigne's habitual self-examination also
owed much to Stoicism. "For many years now," he declared, "my
thoughts have had no other aim but myself, I have studied and
examined myself only, and if I study any other things, it is to apply
them immediately to, or rather within myself." Only by looking
within, rather than at his deeds, could he discover his "essence,"
for here resided his "virtue." [92] The Stoic pursuit of truth within
would also leave a fundamental mark on the thought of Descartes.

And from this source also came the remedy for the disagreeable
agitation of mind resulting from the trials of modern life. The
Stoic humanist recognized that perturbation of mind was a response
to external stimuli; but he also saw that, since it was in the mind,
it was potentially subject to rational control. Augustinus criticized
Franciscus for his distractability and called on him to concentrate
his attention, with the clear implication that this was within his
power.[93] Philosophy, then, could quiet the wars of the self and
induce a genuine and reliable tranquility of mind, as Pico argued.[94]
Vives identified this belief with the Gospel: "The immediate and
direct goal of Christianity is to calm down the storm of human
passions, thus to provide the soul with a joyful serenity which
makes us similar to God and to the angels." [95] It was in this sense
that, for Pirckheimer, philosophy "(in Cicero's words) heals souls,
dispels needless care, and banishes all fear." [96] Calvin recognized

---

[91] *Comm. Seneca,* 348-349, 52-53; *Institutes,* I, v, 3.

[92] "De l'exercitation," *Essaies,* II, 50; "Des cannibales," I, 241.

[93] *Secretum,* 472.

[94] *Oration on the Dignity of Man,* tr. Elizabeth Livermore Forbes, in *Renaissance Philosophy of Man,* 231.

[95] Noreña, 207.

[96] Quoted by Hans Rupprich, "Willibald Pirckheimer: Beiträge zu einer Wesenserfassung," *Schweizer Beiträge zur Allgemeinen Geschichte,* XV (1957), 85.

the attractions of this Stoic teaching "Peace, quiet, leisure especially serve pleasure and usefulness," he wrote, and identified Stoic tranquility with what "the theologians almost always call 'peace'." [97] Lipsius emphasized the intellectuality of the conception, the opposition it posited between reason and the affections. "Constancy," he declared, "is a proper and immovable strength of mind which is neither elevated nor depressed by external or casual accidents." [98]

At times the Stoic remedy for the evils of modern life found concrete application. Augustinus saw in it a better antidote for the problems of Franciscus than flight to the country; Stoic discipline would make it possible for him to live happily even in the city. "A soul serene and tranquil in itself," he observed, "fears not the coming of any shadow from without and is deaf to all the thunder of the world;" and he cited Seneca and Cicero to make the point that if "the tumult of your mind should once learn to calm itself down, believe me this din and bustle around you, though it will strike upon your senses, will not touch your soul." [99] Lipsius turned to Stoic doctrine specifically as consolation for the disruption of his personal life by the wars in the Low Countries, which had forced him to flee from place to place.[100] Stoicism was thus a doctrine of consolation not only for adversity in general; it was called forth by the particular troubles of the contemporary world, the chronic annoyances and indignities of urban life, and the acute dangers of war.

But it was also a regular and conscious feature of the Stoic prescription for human trouble that it was available only to the few; in practice Stoic humanism consistently rejected the implications of that vision of human brotherhood which had been one of the most genial features of ancient Stoicism. The aristocratic impulses in Renaissance society therefore found support in the powerful analogy between the order of the universe, the order of the human personality, and the social order, which suggested that society too must consist of both a higher rational principle and a lower, duller and less reliable component to which the higher force, personified by an elite, was in the nature of things superior. The blessedness to which the Stoic

---

[97] *Comm. Seneca*, 84-85, 40-41.
[98] *De constantia*, 6.
[99] *Secretum*, 522, 516.
[100] *De constantia*, 2.

aspired was available only to a select few capable of the rational enlightenment and self-discipline of the wise; the masses were condemned to the external and turbulent life of the body, the passions, the senses. And one of the marks of the Stoic humanist was his constant, rather nervous concern to differentiate himself from the vulgar crowd and to reassure himself, somewhat in the manner at times discerned in the Protestant elect, of his spiritual superiority.

From this standpoint one's opponents, whoever they might be, could represent the mob. Petrarch seems variously to have identified the crowd with the enemies of the poetic way to truth (presumably the schoolmen), with vulnerability to the blandishments of the more disreputable rhetoricians, and with popular piety, as well as (more conventionally) with "the rank scum that pursues the mechanic arts."[101] Aeneas Sylvius, as Pius II, associated it with disrespect for the pope, in a passage that also invokes the Stoic longing for repose. "Some," he wrote of his enemies in Siena, "as is the way of the populace, even hurled abuse at him, and the ruling party actually hated him. The way of the world is certainly absurd with nothing about it fixed or stable." "Eloquence, like wisdom, like nobleness of life," he had written earlier, "is a gift of the minority." [102] Pico feared that access to philosophy by the commonalty would contaminate it.[103] Erasmus made separation from the crowd one of his "General Rules of True Christianity": "This rule is that the mind of him who pants after Christ should disagree first with the deeds of the crowd, then with their opinions;" the mark of the philosopher is his contempt for "those things which the common herd goggles at" and his ability "to think quite differently from the opinions of the majority." That this was not altogether metaphorical is suggested by his indignation at Luther for "making public even to cobblers what is usually treated among the learned as mysterious and secret." [104] Calvin, too, was impressed by the dangers of the

---

[101] *Ep. fam.*, XIII, 6, in III, 72; *Secretum*, 442-444, 476-478, 512.

[102] *Memoirs of a Renaissance Pope: the Commentaries of Pius II*, tr. Florence A. Gragg (New York, 1959), 58; *De liberorum educatione*, 148.

[103] Cf. *Oration*, 250. For the esoteric notion of communication based on this view, see Edgar Wind, *Pagan Mysteries in the Renaissance* (New Haven, 1958), 24-30.

[104] *Enchiridion militis Christiani*, tr. Ford Lewis Battles, in *Advocates of Reform*, ed. Matthew Spinka, Library of Christian Classics, XIV (London, 1953), 349 and cf. 350, 357; adage *Aut fatuum aut regem nasci oportere*, Phillips, 217; letter to Jodocus Jonas, 10 May 1521, Allen, IV, 487-488.

crowd. "These are the unchanging epithets of the mob: *factious,
discordant, unruly*, and not groundlessly applied!" he commented
in connection with Seneca; and he proceeded to illustrate the point
copiously from Roman history.[105] For Montaigne dissociation from
the crowd was an essential condition of intellectual freedom.[106]
The general ideal of the intellectual life in this tradition was well
expressed by Charles de Bouelles: "The wise man who knows the
secrets of nature is himself secret and spiritual. He lives alone,
far from the common herd. Placed high above other men, he is
unique, free, absolute, tranquil, pacific, immobile, simple, collected,
one. He is perfect, consummated, happy. . . ." [107]

IV. THE AUGUSTINIAN STRAIN IN THE RENAISSANCE

Stoicism, then, had both attractions and weaknesses as the basis
for accommodation to the conditions of Renaissance life, and these
were not unrelated to one another. It identified the major problems
of modern existence, often vividly and concretely, as the schoolmen did not. It reaffirmed in a new form a traditional vision of
universal order which seemed an attractive prescription for the
practical evils of a singularly disorderly society. It affirmed personal
responsibility, its inwardness corresponded to the growing inwardness of later medieval piety, and it promised consolation for the
tribulations of existence. But the structure of assumptions that
enabled Stoic humanism to perform these services was not altogether
adequate to the changing needs of a new society. Its conception
of a universal order was singularly contradicted by the concrete
world of familiar experience, and its idealism, however plausible
in theory, ran the risk of seeming as irrelevant to life as the great
systems of the schoolmen. Its intellectual vision of man was hardly
adequate to a world in which men constantly encountered each
other not as disembodied minds but as integral personalities whose
bodies could not be ignored, whose passions were vividly and often
positively as well as dangerously in evidence, and whose actions
were profoundly unpredictable. The Stoic idea of freedom was too
elevated to have much general application, and also severely limited

---

[105] *Comm. Seneca*, 24-25.
[106] "De la coustume et de ne changer aisément une loy receüe," *Essaies*, I, 125.
[107] *Metaphysicum introductorium*, E1ʳ, quoted by Augustin Renaudet, *Préréforme
et l'humanisme à Paris pendant les premières guerres d'Italie*, rev. ed. (Paris, 1953),
420 n. 2.

by the large area of determinism in Stoic thought. And Stoicism appeared often to ignore or to reason away rather than to engage with and solve the practical problems of life; its disapproval of cities, of political particularity and individual eccentricity, of change, demonstrated the high-mindeness of its adherents, but it did not cause these awkward realities to go away. And it was scarcely helpful, especially since even the Stoic had no remedy for the misery of the overwhelming majority of mankind, to deny that suffering was real because it belonged to the lower world of appearances, or to direct the attention of wretched men from mutable to eternal things, or to insist that the world ought to be one and to be ruled by the wise. Like ancient Stoicism, therefore, the Stoic humanism of the Renaissance was ultimately hopeless. It is thus hardly surprising that, like the Stoicism of the hellenistic world, it was contested, within humanism itself, by another and very different vision of man, his potentialities, and his place in the universe. The great patron of this vision was Saint Augustine.

Here too Petrarch's *Secretum*, which I have frequently exploited to illustrate the Stoic elements in humanist thought, is singularly instructive. For, despite the ambiguities of this work, which foreshadow the perennial tension between the Stoic and Augustinian impulses in the Renaissance, it makes one clear point. It calls back to life the great Latin father who had virtually disappeared from Dante's intellectual universe, and it recalls him, however dimly realized, as a person. The personal appearance of Augustine in Petrarch's world of thought, only a generation after the completion of the *Divine Comedy*, may thus be taken as a kind of watershed between medieval and Renaissance culture. But it also suggests the crucial polarities within humanism itself.

For although Petrarch often makes Augustine into an ancient sage, a spokesman for the commonplaces of hellenistic moral thought who repeatedly quotes Cicero, Seneca, and other Latin writers, the Scriptures hardly at all, and although the Franciscus of the dialogues often seems more truly Augustinian than Augustine himself, the work gives eloquent testimony to the need of an anguished man of the fourteenth century not only for abstract wisdom but for a direct encounter with another human being in the past whose spiritual experience, as an individual, might be a source of nourishment for himself. Petrarch's Augustinus, however equivocal, is in the end not Truth itself, for a direct encounter with truth, Petrarch suggests, is more than man can bear.[108] He is a man, himself an individual, who performs the role of one man with another. He listens and reacts to the confession of Franciscus, argues with him, not always successfully, and compels him to look more deeply and honestly into himself.

This humanization of Augustine, however incomplete, was a notable achievement. Because Augustine was a Christian, a saint, and still the most venerated source of religious wisdom in the West outside of Scripture itself, he provided the ultimate test for a typically Renaissance impulse, which Petrarch applied more successfully to such pagan worthies as Cicero or Seneca, and even to Aristotle. That he could manage it at all with Augustine testifies to the intensity of a new vision of existence even in its earliest stages. A fresh breeze had begun to blow in the old European atmosphere.

The uses of Augustine in the Renaissance did not always reflect this new awareness of his personality. He continued, with some regularity, to be cited in the old way as a guarantor of the highest truths. The later fifteenth-century Roman humanist Benedetto Morandi, for example, thought it "not only wicked but foolhardy" to oppose him; [109] and Melanchthon generally thought (though he did not always adhere to this opinion) that agreement with Augustine was virtually identical with Christian orthodoxy.[110] But it became increasingly common to praise him for his eloquence,[111] a human competence in which Renaissance rhetoricians might aspire to emulate him, or to call attention to dimensions of his personality or his earthly life, a tendency not confined to humanists. Gerson described his own mother as a "Saint Monica",[112] and Vives observed that "if Augustine lived now, he would be considered a pedant or a petty orator." [113] And it became possible to take issue with Augustine, at least by implication; Poggio testifies to this in his attack on the presumption of Valla in implying that "the blessed Augustine also (such is the pride of this man, or rather of this brute) would have fallen into error about fate, the Trinity, and divine providence." [114]

---

[108] Secretum, 434.
[109] Quoted by Trinkaus, I, 287.
[110] Peter Fraenkel, Testimonia Patrum: the Function of the Patristic Argument in the Theology of Philip Melanchthon (Geneva, 1961), 94-96.
[111] Cf. Trinkaus, II, 562, 568, 631.
[112] James L. Connolly, John Gerson, Reformer and Mystic (Louvain, 1928), 22.
[113] In his commentary on De civitate Dei, quoted by Noreña, 135.
[114] Quoted by Salvatore I. Camporeale, Lorenzo Valla, umanesimo e teologia (Florence, 1972), 34.

So thoroughgoing an Augustinian as Staupitz thought that Augustine "had no idea of the depths of the mystery of the Incarnation." [115]

But the humanization of Augustinianism has a larger significance for our purposes. It directs us to a crucial difference between Stoic and Augustinian humanism and helps to explain the very different order in which it is necessary, in the following pages, to analyze the latter. With Stoicism we must begin with the cosmos, and this in turn implies a certain view of man. But with Augustinianism we must begin with man, and from here we reach a certain view of the cosmos.[116] In Augustinian humanism the nature and experience of man himself limit what can be known about the larger universes to which man belongs and how he can accommodate to them.

Thus Augustinian humanism saw man, not as a system of objectively distinguishable, discrete faculties reflecting ontological distinctions in the cosmos, but as a mysterious and organic unity. This conception, despite every tendency in his thought to the contrary, is repeatedly apparent in Petrarch, in the *Secretum* and elsewhere, and it explains Melanchthon's indifference to the value of distinguishing the various faculties of the human personality.[117] One result was a marked retreat from the traditional sense of opposition between soul and body. Bruni found support for the notion of their interdependence in Aristotle,[118] and Valla, as Maffeo Vegio, vigorously rejected the possibility of distinguishing the pleasures of the soul from those of the body; [119] Pomponazzi's notorious refutation of the soul's immortality must be understood against this background. A corollary of this position is that the soul cannot be seen as a higher faculty in man, a spark of divinity which is intrinsically immune from sin and can only be corrupted from below. Petrarch confessed that, in the end, his troubles came rather from his soul than his body; [120] and Calvin was only applying this insight in his

---

[115] From the sermon "Eternal Predestination and its Execution in Time," in Heiko A. Oberman, *Forerunners of the Reformation* (New York, 1966), 179.

[116] Trinkaus, I, 104, notes a similar contrast between the cosmological and rational emphasis of scholastic and the anthropological emphasis of humanist thought, a point with some bearing on the historical significance of Stoicism.

[117] Cf. *Loci communes theologici*, tr. Lowell J. Satre, in *Melanchthon and Bucer*, ed. Wilhelm Pauck, Library of Christian Classics, XIX (London, 1969), 23-24.

[118] Cf. Hans Baron, "Franciscan Poverty and Civic Wealth in Humanistic Thought," *Speculum*, XIII (1938), 21, quoting Bruni's commentary on the *Economics* of Aristotle.

[119] *De vero bono*, 76.

[120] *Secretum*, 516.

insistence that the fall of Adam had its origin in deeper regions of the personality. "They childishly err," he wrote against a hellenistic understanding of Christianity, "who regard original sin as consisting only in lust and in the disorderly motion of the appetites, whereas it seizes upon the very seat of reason and upon the whole heart." [121] It follows, therefore, that the distinctive quality of man cannot be his reason. Valla identified it with his immortality,[122] Calvin with his capacity to know and worship God.[123] It also follows that the abstract knowledge grasped by reason is not sufficient to make men virtuous and therefore blessed, a point made with considerable emphasis by Petrarch in praising oratory above philosophy; thus Aristotle suffered as a moralist in comparison with Cicero, whom Petrarch now exploited in his less Stoic mood.[124] Since to know the good could no longer be identified with doing the good, it might also now be necessary to make a choice between knowledge and virtue, and the Augustinian humanist regularly came out on the side of virtue.

Despite their underlying belief in the integral unity of the personality, the Augustinian humanists accepted and argued in terms of the old vocabulary of the faculties; but the faculties they chose to emphasize implied a very different conception of the organization of man from that of the Stoics. They spoke above all of the will. Petrarch recognized clearly that Augustine's own conversion had been a function of his will rather than his intellect,[125] and Calvin was similarly Augustinian in recognizing the crucial importance of the will in the economy of salvation.[126] But the essential point in this conception of the will was its separation from and its elevation above reason. "It is safer," Petrarch declared, "to strive for a good and pious will than for a capable and clear intellect. . . . It is better to will the good than to know the truth." [127] Melanchthon was developing the implications of this view in saying that "knowledge serves the will. . . . For the will in man corresponds to the place of a despot in a republic. Just as the senate is subject to the despot, so is knowledge to the will, with the consequence that although

---

[121] *Comm. Genesis* 3:6.
[122] Trinkaus, I, 153, 155.
[123] *Institutes*, I, iii, 3.
[124] *De ignorantia*, 104 and more generally.
[125] *Secretum*, 448-450.
[126] As in *Institutes*, II, v, 15.
[127] *De ignorantia*, 70.

knowledge gives warning, yet the will casts knowledge out and is borne along by its own affection." [128] One consequence was a new degree of freedom for the will, always severely restricted by the Stoic conception of the will as the automatic servant of reason. Salutati recognized this with particular clarity. Nothing, he wrote, could "even reach the intellect without the consent or command of the will," and once knowledge had penetrated the intellect, the will could freely follow or disregard it.[129] Valla saw in the freedom of the will the only conception of the matter consistent with the evident reality of sin, which would be impossible, and man would be deprived of responsibility and moral dignity, if reason in fact ruled will.[130]

The will, in this view, is seen to take its direction not from reason but from the affections, which are in turn not merely the disorderly impulses of the treacherous body but expressions of the energy and quality of the heart, that mysterious organ which is the center of the personality, the source of its unity and its ultimate worth. The affections, therefore, are intrinsically neither good nor evil but the essential resources of the personality; and since they make possible man's beatitude and glory as well as his depravity, they are, in Augustinian humanism, treated with particular respect. Thus even when Augustinus recommended Franciscus to meditate on the eternal verities, he called on him to invest his thought with affect, as a necessary sign that he has not meditated in vain.[131] Valla was especially emphatic about the positive quality of the passions, a primary consideration both in his perception of the particular importance of oratorical as opposed to philosophical communication and in the understanding of Christianity. "Can a man move his listeners to anger or mercy if he has not himself first felt these passions?" he asked. "It cannot be," he continued; "So he will not be able to kindle the love of divine things in the minds of others who is himself cold to that love." [132] For Valla religious experience was not intellectual but affective; the love of God is to be understood as man's ultimate pleasure. Calvin was working out the same line of thought in arguing, against the schools, that "the assent which we give to the divine word ... is more of the heart than the brain, and more of the affec-

---

[128] *Loci communes*, 23-24.

[129] Quoted by Trinkaus, I, 64.

[130] Cf. Giorgio Radetti, "La religione di Lorenzo Valla," *Medioevo e rinascimento: studi in onore di Bruno Nardi* (Florence, 1955), II, 617-618.

[131] *Secretum*, 462.

[132] *De vero bono*, 91; cf. Trinkaus, I, 115-116, 127, 138.

tions than the understanding . . . . faith is absolutely inseparable from a devout affection." [133] Prayer, he observed in the Geneva Confession, "is nothing but hypocrisy and fantasy unless it proceed from the interior affections of the heart;" [134] and because of its power to rouse the heart he vigorously supported congregational singing.[135] Melanchthon remarked on the irrepressible power of the affections: "When an affection has begun to rage and seethe, it cannot be kept from breaking forth." [136] Against the scholastic view of the affections as a "weakness of nature," he argued that, on the contrary, "the heart and its affections must be the highest and most powerful part of man." Thus he saw that the consequence of control over the affections (if such control were truly possible) would be not rationality but insincerity, the presentation not of a higher and rational self to the world but of an inauthentic self.[137] We may find in this psychological discussion, therefore, a shrewd contribution to Renaissance concern, another reflection of social disruption, with the problems of friendship and hypocrisy.

This sense of the power and positive value of the passions was frequently the basis of an explicit attack on the Stoic ideal of *apatheia*, a point on which Stoicism seemed peculiarly unconvincing. Salutati doubted that "any mortal ever attained to such perfection besides Christ." [138] Brandolini denied that Stoic virtue could be truly divine because of its rejection of feeling, "for whoever lack affects necessarily lack virtues." [139] Erasmus denounced Stoic apathy in the *Praise of Folly*,[140] as did the young Calvin, citing Augustine; the older Calvin also attacked "the foolish description given by the ancient Stoics of 'the great-souled man' " and also denounced "new Stoics who count it depraved not only to groan and weep but also to be sad and care-ridden." We, he declared, citing Christ's tears, "have nothing to do with this iron-hearted philosophy." [141]

This same vision of man relieved the body of its old responsibility for evil and dignified its needs. Calvin particularly emphasized the

[133] *Institutes*, III, ii, 8; cf. 33, 36.
[134] Article 13, in *Calvin: Theological Treatises*, ed. J. K. S. Reid, Library of Christian Classics, XXII (London, 1954), 29.
[135] *Comm. Genesis* 4:21.
[136] *Loci communes*, 30; cf. Calvin, *Institutes*, II, vii, 10.
[137] *Loci communes*, 29, 28.
[138] Quoted by Struever, 59; cf. Seigel, 72-73.
[139] Quoted by Trinkaus, I, 317-318.
[140] *Opera*, ed. J. Leclerc (Leiden, 1703-1705), IV, 430.
[141] *Comm. Seneca*, 360-361; *Institutes*, III, viii, 9.

error of associating sin primarily with the body; this mistake tended to make men "easily forgive themselves the most shocking vices as no sins at all." He traced the growth of this error historically, from the philosophers of antiquity, "till at length man was commonly thought to be corrupted only in his sensual part, and to have a perfectly unblemished reason and a will also largely unimpaired." [142] Such a view required a fresh understanding of the Pauline meaning of "flesh". It had to be construed, not narrowly as the physical body, but more broadly as those tendencies that alienated every part of man from God.[143] Melanchthon thought that "flesh" must especially signify reason, the site of unbelief.[144]

At the same time the impulses of the body could be viewed more tolerantly. Augustinus waived, for Franciscus, the strict Stoic doctrine regarding man's physical needs in favor of the golden mean,[145] and Calvin argued that "God certainly did not intend that man should be slenderly and sparingly sustained; but rather . . . he promises a liberal abundance, which should leave nothing wanting to a sweet and pleasant life." [146] He insisted on the legitimacy of pleasure, at least in moderation; severity on this score would lead to "the very dangerous error of fettering consciences more tightly than does the word of the Lord." Calvin was thinking of the monks, but the point applied equally to Stoic moralism.[147] It applied especially to sex, so often the special worry of traditional moralists because of its association with the body. Civic humanism had long applauded the family as the source of new citizens, and Valla had suggested a positive view of sex because it gave pleasure. But the sense, among the Augustinian humanists, of the integrity of the personality also provided a deeper foundation for the value of the sexual bond. As Bucer declared, "There is no true marriage without a true assent of hearts between those who make the agreement," and marriage is accordingly "a contract not only of body and of goods but also of the soul." [148] Calvin praised marriage, attributing disapproval of

---

[142] *The Necessity of Reforming the Church*, in *Calvin: Theological Treatises*, 198; *Institutes*, II, ii, 4.

[143] For Calvin see, among other places, *Comm. Genesis* 6:3 and *Comm. Romans* 8:10; for Melanchthon, *Loci communes*, 31, 37-38.

[144] *Loci communes*, 144.

[145] *Secretum*, 490; cf. Baron, "Franciscan Poverty," 7.

[146] *Comm. Genesis* 1:30.

[147] *Institutes*, III, x, 1.

[148] *De regno Christi*, in *Melanchthon and Bucer*, 322.

it to "immoderate affection for virginity." [149] A higher estimate of the body and of sex led also to some perception of the dignity of women. [150]

This better view of the body had even wider ramifications. It was related to Renaissance debate over the value of the active life, for the alleged inferiority of activity to contemplation assumed the inferiority to the mind of the body, which does the active business of the world. It also had deep theological significance, for it re-directed attention from the immortality of the soul to the resurrection of the body; the more Augustinian humanist was likely to emphasize the central importance of the resurrection. Thus, although Petrarch often spoke of the soul, he had also learned "the hope of resurrection, and that this very body after death will be reassumed, indeed agile, shining, and inviolable, with much glory in the resurrection." [151] Calvin saw with particular clarity (and here his relation to Pomponazzi is evident) that "the life of the soul without hope of resurrection will be a mere dream." [152] And this Augustinian anthropology also posed the question of human freedom and man's need for grace in a new way. If it freed the will from obedience to reason, it per-ceived that this only meant the bondage of the will to the affections of the heart. And this meant that man can only be saved by grace, not by knowledge; for knowledge can at best reach only the mind, but grace alone can change the heart. [153]

It thus precluded the natural theology towards which Stoic humanism tended; its theology regularly opposed the folly of the cross to the rational wisdom of the philosophers. [154] Augustinus thus urged on Franciscus the irrelevance to his own deepest needs of that knowledge of nature on whose religious significance the Stoic set so much store. [155] In reply to his own more Stoic vision of the order of the universe, Calvin insisted on the actual inability of men, as the vain and contradictory speculations of the philosophers clearly demonstrated, to discover religious truths from nature. [156]

---

[149] *Institutes*, IV, xii, 27.
[150] For Calvin, cf. *Comm. Genesis*, 131; for Melanchthon, see Fraenkel, 293.
[151] Quoted by Trinkaus, I, 190-191.
[152] *Comm. Matthew* 22:23, in *A Harmony of the Gospels Matthew, Mark and Luke*, tr. A. W. Morrison (Grand Rapids, 1972), III, 29.
[153] Cf. Melanchthon's formulation, *Loci communes*, 27.
[154] Cf. Trinkaus, I, 55, on Salutati.
[155] *Secretum*, 476.
[156] *Institutes*, I, v, 4; cf. 12.

Valla had argued that philosophy was the mother of heresy.[157] The Augustinian humanist was clear that, however valuable they might be for other purposes, the classics, based on reason alone, were valueless for Christianity. There was, Petrarch suggested, a qualitative difference between knowledge and faith, which he saw as something like the difference between seeing and listening: the difference, that is to say, between learning by means of one's own natural powers and learning directly, and so with peculiar certainty, from God.[158] Thus an Augustinian anthropology was fundamental to the new emphasis among humanists on the Bible, on the "school of the Gospel," which Budé contrasted with the Stoa as well as the Academy and the "subtle debates of the Peripatetics." [159]

Ultimate truth, then, is mysterious, beyond rational comprehension, and therefore first planted in the heart by grace, not discovered by the mind. "It is not man's part to investigate the celestial mystery through his own powers," Petrarch declared after emphasizing the gulf between God the creator and man his creature; [160] and Petrarch's sense of the incalculability of the world was carried by Salutati to a more general skepticism. "Every truth which is grasped by reason," Salutati wrote, "can be made doubtful by a contrary reason;" consequently man's rational knowledge cannot be absolute but, at best, is "a kind of reasonable uncertainty." [161] Valla humanized knowledge by representing truth as a matter not of objective certainty but of believing and feeling "concerning things as they themselves are." [162] And this notion of truth was hardly appropriate to the kind of conviction required by the Gospel. Accordingly philosophy, when it approached religious questions, was, for Melanchthon, a "chaos of carnal dreams;" the sacred mysteries, he insisted should be adored, not investigated.[163] Calvin, since "human reason neither approaches, nor strives, nor takes straight aim" toward religious truth, suggested that a skeptical agnosticism was the best posture for men without revelation: "Here man's discernment is so over-

---

[157] See passages from the *Elegantiae*, in Camporeale, 7.
[158] Cf. passage from *De otio* in Trinkaus, I, 39; cf. Calvin, *Institutes*, III, ii, 14.
[159] From *De transitu Hellenismi ad Christianismum*, quoted by Josef Bohatec, *Budé und Calvin: Studien zur Gedankenwelt des französischen Frühhumanismus* (Graz, 1950), 70.
[160] Quoted by Trinkaus, I, 36.
[161] Quoted by Seigel, 74.
[162] Quoted by Trinkaus, I, 162.
[163] *Loci communes*, 99, 21.

whelmed and so fails that the first attempt almost always in the school of the Lord is to renounce it." [164] This skepticism is obviously fundamental to the humanist case for the superiority of rhetoric to philosophy; like Scripture, rhetoric recognized the weakness of reason and spoke to the heart.

The Augustinian humanist recognized a very different tendency in Stoicism and occasionally displayed some insight into the affinities of Stoicism with medieval intellectuality. Valla sometimes used "Stoicism" to represent philosophy in general, by which he meant both ancient and medieval philosophy; [165] and Brandolini pointed to the rational (and for him specious) methodology which the Stoics shared with "almost all the philosophers and theologians of our time." [166] Calvin noted the "Stoic paradoxes and scholastic subtleties" in Seneca.[167] Here, then, is another area in which the tensions between Stoic and Augustinian humanism were threatening to break out into the open.

But all this was evidently the reflection of a more general insistence, within Augustinian humanism, on man's absolute dependence on his creator, which contrasted sharply with the Stoic tendency to emphasize man's sufficiency. This sense of human dependence is especially apparent in the Augustinian attitude to virtue, the supreme good of the Stoic. Valla thought the Stoic ideal of the sage a contradiction in terms, if only because the triumph of virtue implied constant struggle; Stoic serenity was therefore unattainable.[168] Brandolini doubted that virtue could overcome suffering.[169] The examples of ancient virtue adduced as models by the Stoic humanist thus required some analysis. It might be remarked in general, as Petrarch and Erasmus did, that "true" virtue could not be attributed to any pagan, since his actions were obviously not done in the love of Christ.[170] Valla went beyond such generality to suggest that

---

[164] *Institutes*, II, ii, 18; III, ii, 34.
[165] Seigel, 152.
[166] Quoted by Trinkaus, I, 299.
[167] *Comm. Seneca*, 336-337.
[168] *De vero bono*, 108.
[169] Trinkaus, I, 169.
[170] For Petrarch see the passage from *De otio*, quoted by Trinkaus in "The Religious Thought of the Italian Humanists and the Reformers: Anticipation or Autonomy?" *The Pursuit of Holiness in Late Medieval and Renaissance Religion: Papers from the University of Michigan Conference*, ed. Charles Trinkaus and Heiko A. Oberman, Studies in Medieval and Reformation Thought, X (Leiden, 1974), 352; for Erasmus, *Erasmus and the Seamless Coat of Jesus*, tr. Raymond Himelick Lafayette, Ind., 1971), 58.

pagan virtue was vitiated by its concern for glory,[171] a point the young Calvin also emphasized. "Remove ambition," he wrote, "and you will have no haughty spirits, neither Platos, nor Catos, nor Scaevolas, nor Scipios, nor Fabriciuses." He saw the Roman Empire as "a great robbery", a notion also bearing on the Stoic ideal of a universal state.[172] Melanchthon viewed the virtues that enabled Alexander to conquer an empire simply as evidence that he loved glory more than pleasure.[173] These humanists did not deny the practical value of the alleged virtues of the pagans, but they insisted on distinguishing between the restraint of human nature and its purification, which only grace could accomplish. From this standpoint the Stoic ideal was shallow and therefore, in the end, unreliable. Christianity, as Melanchthon remarked, was not primarily concerned with virtue, and the pursuit of instruction on this topic in the Scriptures "is more philosophical than Christian." [174]

In fact a deeper knowledge of the self revealed that, like his knowledge of God, man's virtue and happiness also come entirely from God. To realize this was the goal of self-knowledge. Such knowledge, Calvin declared, "will strip us of all confidence in our own ability, deprive us of all occasion for boasting, and lead us to submission;" [175] and Petrarch's own spiritual biography may be understood as a prolonged search for this kind of knowledge. It taught man, for example, the precise opposite of Stoic wisdom. Against the Stoic notion that blessedness can be founded only on the things that are man's own, Petrarch argued directly that in fact the only things that are a man's own are his sins; thus "in what is in one's own power" there is chiefly "matter of shame and fear." [176] There is an obvious connection between this interest in self-knowledge and the Pauline teaching on the moral law as the tutor of mankind, a conception again quite at odds with the Stoic notion of the function of law. If Petrarch's self-knowledge brought him to despair, he could take hope if only "the Almighty Pity put forth his strong right hand and guide my vessel rightly ere it be too late, and bring me to shore." God was the only source of his virtues (these are clearly not his own), of his blessedness, of his very existence: "In what state could I

---

[171] *De vero bono*, 2.
[172] *Comm. Seneca*, 94-95, 32-35.
[173] *Loci communes*, 27-28.
[174] *Ibid.*, 22.
[175] *Institutes*, II, i, 2.
[176] Trinkaus, I, 45-46, quoting *De otio*.

better die than in loving, praising, and remembering him, without whose constant love I should be nothing, or damned, which is less than nothing? And if his love for me should cease, my damnation would have no end." [177] Peace itself, the essence of Stoic beatitude, could only be the consequence, not of "some human virtue", Brandolini contended, but of grace.[178]

But there are, for the general development of European culture, even broader implications in the sense, within Augustinian humanism, of man's intellectual limitations. It pointed to the general secularization of modern life, for it implied the futility of searching for the principles of human order in the divine order of the cosmos, which lay beyond human comprehension. Man was accordingly now seen to inhabit not a single universal order governed throughout by uniform principles but a multiplicity of orders: for example, an earthly as well as a heavenly city, which might be seen to operate in quite different ways. On earth, unless God had chosen to reveal his will about its arrangements unequivocally in Scripture, man was left to the uncertain and shifting insights of a humbler kind of reason, to work out whatever arrangements best suited his needs. Hence a sort of earthy practicality was inherent in this way of looking at the human condition.

Indeed it is likely that the sharp Augustinian distinction between creation and Creator, since it denied the eternity of the universe, also promoted that secularization of the cosmos implicit in the Copernican revolution. If human order no longer depended on the intelligible order of the cosmos, the motive for discerning any such order was seriously weakened; conversely much of the resistance to Copernicanism stemmed from a concern, so strong in Stoic humanism, to protect a universal order that supplied mankind with general guidance for its earthly arrangements. Galileo relied heavily on Augustine to support his argument that the proper concern of religion is how one goes to heaven, not how heaven goes.[179]

If Machiavelli is the most famous example of the secularizing tendency in the Renaissance, he also had predecessors among earlier humanists of an Augustinian tendency. But the secularism implicit in Augustinian humanism achieved its clearest articulation in figures

---

[177] *Secretum*, 466-468; *Ep. fam.* XXII, 10, in IV, 127.
[178] Quoted by Trinkaus, I, 318.
[179] In his letter to the Grand Duchess Christina, in Galileo Galilei, *Opere*, ed. Antonio Favaro (Florence, 1890-1909), V, 307-348.

connected with the Reformation, not because Protestantism originated the secular impulse, but because, since Stoic arguments had been a major resource to support the old order, they now required a more direct attack. Calvin, distinguished with particular clarity between the heavenly and earthly realms and the kinds of knowledge appropriate to each:

> There is one understanding of earthly things; another of heavenly ones. I call those things earthly which do not pertain to God and his kingdom, to true justice, or to the blessedness of the future life, and are in some sense confined within the limits of it. Heavenly things are the pure knowledge of God, the nature of true righteousness, and the mysteries of the heavenly kingdom. The first class includes government, domestic economy, all the mechanical skills and the liberal arts. In the second are the knowledge of God and of his will, and the rule by which we conform our lives to it.

He was emphatic about the separation between the two, whose correspondence had been so long cited in support of the ecclesiastical hierarchy. There was no basis, he declared, "to philosophize subtly over a comparison of the heavenly and earthly hierarchies," thus challenging not only the Neoplatonism of Dionysius but also the fundamental principles of Stoic world order.[180] By the same token he had no use for idealistic prescriptions for earthly order; he dismissed utopia as "a foolish fantasy the Jews had." [181] For Melanchthon "the civil and external dispensation of things has nothing to do with the Spirit's righteousness, no more than do plowing a field, building, or cobbling shoes." [182] This was not to deny the utility of humbler things but rather to assert that they worked best when it was recognized that they belong to a sphere of their own.

The pragmatic secularism to which Augustinian humanism pointed opposed the political idealism of Stoic humanism in all its dimensions: its belief in the universal principles needed to validate all government, its universalism, its insistence on the rule of the wise, its indifference to changing circumstance, its pacifism. Bruni gave concrete expression to the secularist mood in his own acceptance, without setting them in a larger framework of objective justification, of the common political values of Florence. "I confess that I am

---

[180] *Institutes*, II, ii, 13; IV, vi, 10.
[181] *Contre les Anabaptistes*, quoted by Michael Walzer, *The Revolution of the Saints: a Study in the Origins of Radical Politics* (Cambridge, Mass., 1965), 47.
[182] *Loci communes*, 129.

moved by what men think good," he wrote in his *Florentine Histories*, "to extend one's borders, to increase one's power, to extol the splendor and glory of the city, to look after its utility and security." [183] Here is the Machiavellian principle that the affairs of this world should be based on the dynamic interplay of earthly interests whose sordid realities are honestly faced; in short, the eternal reason of the Stoics must, for the practical good of men on earth, give way to reason of state.

This signified that laws and institutions must be accommodated to the variety of the human condition, and thus the desirability of many states with various kinds of government. This, rather than a universal empire, was, for Calvin, what God had intended. "If you fix your eye not on one city alone," he wrote, "but look round and glance at the world as a whole, or at least cast your sight upon regions farther off, divine providence has wisely arranged that various countries should be ruled by various kinds of government. For as elements cohere only in unequal proportion, so countries are best held together according to their own particular inequality." By the same token civil laws are not primarily the reflection of eternal law but should vary according to practical circumstance. "Every nation," Calvin declared, "is left free to make such laws as it forsees to be profitable for itself." [184] Melanchthon carried this relativism to extremes, finding in it the most likely guarantor of earthly order:

> Indeed, the political art covers external action in life, concerning possessions, contracts, and such like, and these are not the same among all nations. Laws arc of one kind among the Persians, of another in Athens, or in Rome. Accordingly a Christian dresses differently in one part of the world than in another, reckons days differently in one place than he does in another. Whatever the policy of the place, that he uses; as Ezra judges cases according to Persian law when in Persia, so in Jerusalem he judges according to Jewish law. These things do not belong to the Gospel, anymore than do clothes or the spacing of days. This distinction between the Gospel and political affairs is conducive to maintaining tranquility and increasing reverence for the magistrates.[185]

---

[183] Quoted by Donald J. Wilcox, *The Development of Florentine Humanist Historiography in the Fifteenth Century* (Cambridge, Mass., 1969), 88-89.

[184] *Institutes*, IV, xx, 8; IV, xx, 15. For Calvin's rejection of universal empire, see also IV, vi, 8.

[185] From his commentary on Aristotle's *Politics*, quoted by Quirinus Breen, *Christianity and Humanism: Studies in the History of Ideas* (Grand Rapids, 1968), 84.

Augustinian humanism was thus closely related, as Stoic humanism was not, to the political realities of contemporary Europe.

In the same way Augustinian humanism attacked the spiritual elitism of the Stoic tradition, both in its loftier forms and in its application to government; and it was thus more sympathetic to those populist movements that found religious expression in the dignity of lay piety, political expression in the challenge of republicanism to despotism. For it was obvious that if rational insight into cosmic order could not supply the principles of either religious or political life, neither the church nor civil society could be governed by sages. This conviction had deep roots in Italian humanism. Charles Trinkaus has presented at least one group of humanists as lay theologians who were concerned to assert the religious competence of ordinary men by their emphasis on Christianity as a religion of grace accessible to all.[186] Valla contrasted the exclusiveness of Stoicism with the popularity of Epicureanism,[187] and he rested his case for eloquence against philosophy largely on the fact that it employed the language of ordinary men rather than the specialized vocabulary of an elite who "teach us by an exquisite sort of reasoning both to inquire what illiterates and rustics do better than philosophers transmit." [188] There is a hint of this attitude even in Castiglione, who was willing to leave the evaluation of his *Courtier* to public opinion "because more often than not the many, even without perfect knowledge, know by natural instinct the certain savor of good and bad, and, without being able to give any reason for it, enjoy and love one thing and detest another." [189] Augustinian humanism denied any privileged position to a philosophically enlightened class. Calvin attacked the monks on the basis of the equality of all callings before God and broke with traditional humanist elitism by praising the manual as well as the liberal arts.[190] For the church this tendency would culminate in the priesthood of all believers. Melanchthon minimized the specialized competence of the clergy,[191] and Calvin insisted on the popular election of ministers "so as not to diminish any part of the common right and liberty of

---

[186] The point is made in connection with Petrarch, I, 147; cf. Seigel, 75, on Salutati.

[187] *De vero bono*, 110.

[188] Quoted by Trinkaus, I, 152.

[189] *Courtier*, 7.

[190] *Institutes*, IV, xiii, 11; II, ii, 14.

[191] *Loci communes*, 146.

the church." [192] For civil society this implies now and the rejection

of theocracy, and a fully secular government. "Just as Socrates, at
the beginning of the *Republic*, sent poets out of the state," Melanchthon asserted, "so we would not eject the theologians from the state
but we would remove them from the governing group of the commonwealth," [193] a principle also applied in the Italian republics.
Calvin's preference for a republic over other forms of government is
well known. "This is the most desirable kind of liberty," he wrote,
"that we should not be compelled to obey every person who may be
tyrannically put over our heads, but which allows of election, so
that no one should rule except he be approved of us." [194] This
position did not preclude social hierarchy, but it meant that differences in status among men could only be seen as an accident of
history; they are not rooted in the order of the universe, and accordingly social structures can be modified as needs change.

So the willingness to accommodate human institutions to the
varieties of circumstance also implied a willingness to acknowledge
the significance of change in human affairs. "Now we know," Calvin
declared, "that external order admits, and even requires, various
changes according to the varying conditions of the times." [195] The
historicism of the Renaissance, to which recent scholarship has given
much attention, was distinctly not a function of the Stoic tendencies
in humanism, which could only view mutability with alarm, but rather
of the Augustinian tradition, in which God's purposes were understood to work themselves out in time. Thus for Salutati God "foresaw
all that was and will be in time entirely without time and from
eternity, and not only did he infallibly foresee and wish that they
occur in their time, but also that through contingency they should be
produced and be." [196] Contingency was no longer a threat to order
but the fulfillment of a divine plan, and discrete events thus acquired
meaning. This repudiation of Stoic stasis opened the way to the
feeling for anachronism that we encounter not only in Valla's analysis
of the Donation of Constantine and Guicciardini's attack on Machiavelli's rather Stoic application of the repetition of analogous situations
but also in a more general relativism that left its mark on Calvin's

---

[192] *Institutes*, IV, iii, 15.
[193] Quoted in Breen, 83-84.
[194] *Comm. Deuteronomy* 1:16, quoted by David Little, *Religion, Order, and Law:
a Study in Pre-Revolutionary England* (New York, 1969), 73.
[195] *Institutes*, IV, vii, 15.
[196] Quoted by Trinkaus. I, 196.

understanding of church history and on his exegetical methods. He saw the rise of episcopacy, for example, as a practical response to the problem of dissension in the early church, an "arrangement introduced by human agreement to meet the needs of the times;" and he noted that there are "many passages of Scripture whose meaning depends on their [historical] context." [197] For Calvin fallen man seems to confront God in history rather than in nature.

At the same time these tendencies in Augustinian humanism also suggest the repudiation of the Stoic vision of peace as the ideal toward which man naturally aspires. This too was an expression of the greater realism in the Augustinian tradition; it had no conflict in principle with the acceptance by Renaissance society of warfare as a normal activity of mankind.[198] Within the Renaissance republic conflict had been institutionalized by constitutional provisions for checks and balances among competing social interests; [199] the Stoic ideal, on the contrary, would have sought to eliminate conflict by submitting all interests to the adjudication of reason, settling for nothing less than final solutions to human problems. And the restlessness of human society was paralleled, in the vision of Augustinian humanism, by the inescapable restlessness of individual existence. The Augustinian conception of man as passion and will implied that he could only realize himself fully in activity, which inevitably meant that life must be fraught with conflict, an external struggle with other men, but also an inner struggle with destructive impulses in the self that can never be fully overcome. For Valla virtue was only ideally a goal; practically it was an arduous way.[200] And the Calvinist saint, unlike the Stoic sage, could by no means expect a life of repose; on the contrary he must prepare himself "for a hard, toilsome, and unquiet life, crammed with numerous and various calamities .... in this life we are to seek and hope for nothing but struggle." [201] The ideal of earthly peace, from Calvin's standpoint, was a diabolical stratagem in which the struggle with sin was left in abeyance and God's will went undone. Here too it was

---

[197] *Institutes*, IV, iv, 2; IV, xvi, 23. Cf. *Comm. Genesis* 2:3.

[198] Cf. J. R. Hale, "War and Public Opinion in Renaissance Italy," *Italian Renaissance Studies: a Tribute to the Late Cecilia M. Ady*, ed. E. F. Jacob (London, 1960), 94-122.

[199] For Calvin's Renaissance attitude to checks and balances, cf. *Institutes*, IV, iv, 12; IV, xi, 6.

[200] Cf. Trinkaus, I, 161.

[201] *Institutes*, III, viii, 1; IV, ix, 1.

apparent that Stoicism tended to confuse earthly with heavenly things.

Yet, far less equivocally than Stoic humanism, the vision of Augustinian humanism was social; and, based on the affective life of the whole man, its conception of social existence was animated not by abstract duty but by love. Augustinus reproved the anti-social sentiments of Franciscus by pointing out that life in society is not only the common lot of mankind but even the most blessed life on earth: "Those whom one counts most happy, and for whom numbers of others live their lives, bear witness by the constancy of their vigils and their toils that they themselves are living for others." [202] Salutati found in charity, understood in an Augustinian sense as a gift of divine grace, a way to reconcile—that there should have been a problem here testifies to the strength of the contrary Stoic impulse— his religious values with his love of Florence and his other attachments to the world. Love alone, he wrote, "fosters the family, expands the city, guards the kingdom, and preserves by its power this very creation of the entire world." [203] Thus Stoic withdrawal was countered by Augustinian engagement, which offered not the austere satisfactions of Stoic contemplation but the warmer and more practical consolations of a love applied to the needs of suffering mankind. Zwingli was writing in this tradition in describing the moral ends of education. "From early boyhood," he declared, "the young man ought to exercise himself only in righteousness, fidelity, and constancy: for with virtues such as these he may serve the Christian community, the common good, the state, and individuals. Only the weak are concerned to find a quiet life: the most like to God are those who study to be of profit to all even to their own hurt." [204] Calvin, who was explicit that man is by nature a social animal, saw in the limitations of individual knowledge a device by which God sought to insure human community. "God," he wrote, "has never so blessed his servants that they each possessed full and perfect knowledge of every part of their subject. It is clear that his purpose in so limiting our knowledge was first that we should be kept humble, and also that we should continue to have dealings with our fellows." Because of the needs of social existence he early rejected Stoic contempt for reputation; conscience was by itself an insufficient guide for human

---

[202] *Secretum*, 514.
[203] Quoted by Trinkaus, I, 74-75.
[204] *Of the Education of Youth*, in *Zwingli and Bullinger*, 113.

conduct, he argued, because, strictly a private and individual faculty, it was likely, operating in a social void, to cut man off from his neighbor. For Calvin the struggles of the Christian life were above all required by loving service to the human community.[205] Augustinian humanism sought to meet the crisis of community in the age of the Renaissance not by protecting the individual from destructive involvement with the social world but by full engagement, if possible out of love, in meeting its deepest and most desperate needs.

V. STOIC AND AUGUSTINIAN HUMANISM: FROM AMBIGUITY TO DIALECTIC

At least two general conclusions emerge from this contrast between Stoic and Augustinian humanism. The first comes out of the fact that we can illustrate either with examples drawn indiscriminately from anywhere in the entire period of our concern, and this suggests that the tension between them found no general resolution in the age of the Renaissance and Reformation. But it is equally striking that we have often cited the same figures on both sides. Neither pure Stoics nor pure Augustinians are easy to find among the humanists, though individual figures may tend more to one position than the other. Erasmus, for example, seems more Stoic than Augustinian; Valla appears more Augustinian than Stoic. A closer study of individuals may reveal more personal development, from one position to another, than has been possible to show here. Petrarch, Erasmus, and Calvin may especially invite such treatment. But the general ambivalence of humanists makes clear the central importance for the movement of the tension between the two positions. It was literally in the hearts of the humanists themselves. At the same time this ambiguity also reveals that Stoicism and Augustinianism do not represent distinguishable factions within a larger movement but ideal polarities that help us to understand its significance as a whole.

Yet I suggest that we can discern in this confrontation, if not a clear resolution, at least some instructive patterns of development. The humanism of the earlier Renaissance uneasily blended Stoic and Augustinian impulses which it neither distinguished clearly nor, in many cases, was capable of identifying with their sources. Its Augustinianism consisted of a bundle of personal insights that had, indeed, legitimate affinities with Augustine himself, as Petrarch

---

[205] *Institutes*, II, ii, 13; *Comm. Romans*, Epistle; *Comm. Seneca*, 250-251.

vaguely conced; but its Stoicism was singularly confused. What to a
Stoicism may have meant to Valla, his Cato Sacco, who probably is
intended to represent the contemporary understanding of Stoicism,
offers little more than a set of clichés about the misery of man and
the malevolence of nature, hardly a legitimate Stoic idea; it is chiefly
his emphasis on virtue that stamps him as a "Stoic". Conversely
there is more genuine Stoicism in Maffeo Vegio, Valla's Epicurean,
who defends the rational order of nature.[206] This seems to suggest
that earlier Renaissance humanism, until the middle decades of the
quattrocento, was profoundly confused about the variety in hellenistic
thought, and confused as well about the gulf between antique paganism and the biblical world of ideas represented by the mature
Augustine. Its historical sense was not yet adequate to sort out basic
polarities.

But there were also resources within the Petrarchan tradition
for overcoming this confusion. They are suggested by Petrarch's
recall of Augustine in the *Secretum* as a vital personality whose
personal experience and peculiar mode of thought can be apprehended
in all their particularity by the philological imagination. Petrarch
himself gave a large impetus to the novel tendency of Renaissance
humanism to associate schools of thought with individual personalities, to dissolve the identity of ancient philosophy as a whole with a
perennial wisdom and thus up to a point with Christianity itself, to
sort out one school from another, and so to see every set of ideas,
individually identified, as a product of the human mind at work under
the limitations of historical circumstance. On this basis Petrarch
was compelled to recognize (quoting Augustine) that no ancient
philosopher, not Aristotle or even Plato, could be fully trusted for
the truth; and he laid down an important principle for clarifying the
understanding of the ancient philosophers, whom he characteristically
insisted on regarding as men. "Far be it from me," he wrote, "to
espouse the genius of a single man in its totality because of one or
two well-formulated phrases. Philosophers must not be judged from
isolated words but from their uninterrupted coherence and con-
sistency ... He who wants to be safe in praising the entire man
must see, examine, and estimate the entire man." [207]

We can begin to discern something of the implications of this
principle in Salutati. "To harmonize Aristotle with Cicero and Seneca,

[206] This is well brought out by Trinkaus, I, 107-109, 365 n. 21.
[207] *De ignorantia*, 101, 87.

that is the Peripatetics with the Stoics, is," he observed, "a great deal more difficult than you think." [208] But the point had a larger resonance; it tended to dissolve not only the bonds that hellenistic syncretism had forged among the various schools of philosophy but also those between philosophic and Christian wisdom. It may also be observed that this impulse to sort out one strand of thought from another came not from the Stoic strain in the European inheritance, which was itself permeated by an opposite motive, but from an Augustinian recognition of the conflict between the pagan (and clearly human) and the Christian worlds of thought. In the early Renaissance this impulse was most fully developed by Valla, who recognized the eclectic confusion in Stoicism itself and thus significantly reduced its authority.[209] Valla defended eclecticism, but he did so playfully, in full awareness of its philosophical deficiencies, and on behalf of the rhetorician rather than the philosopher. His treatment of Stoicism and Epicureanism was designed primarily to demonstrate the peculiar identity of Christianity, not its affinities with the rational systems of antiquity. And his own philological acumen provided the instrument for a further development of the historical sensitivity that made it increasingly difficult for the Renaissance humanist to persist in the confusions of the earlier stages of the humanist movement.

We encounter evidence of greater sophistication about ancient philosophy and its bearing on Christianity in various places after Valla, some of them unexpected. Later humanists increasingly perceived the differences rather than the agreements among the various schools of antiquity.[210] Savonarola, who as a Dominican could hardly have been expected to look kindly on Plato, protested against the effort to make either Plato or—more surprisingly—Aristotle into a Christian. "It is to be wished that Plato should be Plato, Aristotle Aristotle, and not that they should be Christian. . . . Let philosophers be philosophers and Christians Christians." [211] Erasmus, at other moments something of a Platonist, similarly protested the notion that Plato (or any other pagan writer) could have written under the inspiration of the Holy Spirit. He also denied

---

[208] Quoted by Seigel, 105.

[209] *De vero bono*, 14-15.

[210] Paul Oskar Kristeller, *The Philosophy of Marsilio Ficino* (New York, 1943), 23.

[211] Quoted by D. P. Walker, *The Ancient Theology: Studies in Platonism from the Fifteenth to the Eighteenth Century* (Ithaca, 1972), 46.

the authenticity of the letters between Seneca and Paul, on which some part of the affinity between Stoicism and the Gospel was thought to depend; and he insisted, though venerating him still, that Seneca be read as a pagan who, if this were not clearly recognized, might otherwise mislead the Christian reader.[212] Here Erasmus displayed a concern for the individuality of the historical personality that was also reflected in the first volume of his edition of Augustine, in which he began with the *Confessions* and *Retractions*, on the ground, so alien from medieval thought, that it is necessary, in order to comprehend a writer, to have some preliminary knowledge of his biography and the general scope of his work.[213]

But the perception of differences did not automatically lead to the elimination of pagan elements from what was taken as the Christian tradition. Sometimes, as with Pico, it resulted in a more self-conscious and enthusiastic acceptance of the syncretist principle, which was given new life in the Neoplatonism of the later Italian Renaissance. And while Neoplatonism continued to reflect impulses central to the Stoicism of the earlier Renaissance, Stoicism itself remained attractive, with the possible difference that it could now be appropriated more consciously and deliberately. Traversari was attracted to the Stoic notion of virtue because he believed that it reinforced monastic life,[214] and Pico supported the Gospel with precepts from Seneca.[215] Pomponazzi underwent a late conversion from Aristotelianism to Stoicism, Stoic elements in the thought of Machiavelli were prominent enough to stimulate refutation by Guicciardini (himself not untouched by Stoicism), Erasmus and above all Vives were heavily influenced by the Stoics, and Clichetove's ideal for the priesthood resurrects something of the Stoic conception of the sage.[216] Meanwhile in Italy, Augustinianism, or at least the kind of Augustinianism that had attracted the earlier Renaissance, seems to have undergone some decline. Augustine was of major

---

[212] André Hugo discusses these matters in his introduction to Calvin's *Comm. Seneca*, 57-59.

[213] Quoted by Luchesius Smits, *Saint Augustin dans l'œuvre de Jean Calvin* (Louvain, 1957), I, 42.

[214] See Charles L. Stinger, "Humanism and Reform in the Early Quattrocento: the Patristic Scholarship of Ambrogio Traversari (1386-1439)," Stanford Doctoral Dissertation (1971), 116.

[215] Noted by Jean Dagens, *Bérulle et les origines de la restauration catholique (1575-1611)* (Paris, 1952), 54.

[216] Jean-Pierre Massaut, *Josse Clichtove, l'humanisme et la réforme du clergé* (Liège and Paris, 1968), II, esp. 125-134.

importance for Ficino, as he was for Giles of Viterbo, but chiefly because he seemed helpful to reconcile Platonism with Christianity. He was also more generally important to support the notion of a perennially valid "ancient theology," one of the less "Augustinian" uses to which he could have been put.[217] The reasons for this shift must be sought in the growing insecurity and disorder of later fifteenth-century Italy, which at once increased the attractions of Stoic consolation and Stoic emphasis on order and control, and at the same time decreased opportunities for the individual activity and social engagement called for by the mature Augustine.

But not all of Europe felt similarly damaged, and the Protestant Reformation stimulated some humanists to resume the debate between Augustinianism and Stoicism. The link between this tendency in Protestantism and Renaissance humanism may be discerned in the high degree of philological and historical sophistication in the thought of the Reformers. Melanchthon was peculiarly sensitive to the infiltration of Christian doctrine by Greek philosophy, and he traced the process from the Fathers (with the partial exception of Augustine) to the contemporary schoolmen. Though, like most subsequent historians of medieval philosophy, he discerned in it first a Platonic and then an Aristotelian phase, the essential elements of his indictment apply equally to the central assumptions of Stoicism: to its emphasis on the power of reason and accordingly on the self-sufficiency of man, especially man's ability to procure his own salvation.[218] On the other hand he humanized Augustine, whom he could perhaps admire precisely because Augustine had been aware of his own fallibility, recognized his mistakes, and changed his mind. Melanchthon recognized the relation between Augustine's opinions and the concrete historical circumstances that had produced them. Augustine was for Melanchthon, as Petrarch had tried to see him, not the personification of reason, but a person.[219]

The same point can be made even more strongly about Calvin. Augustine had helped him, even as a youth, to recognize the vanity in ancient disputes about the supreme good.[220] And his instincts for distinguishing between the philosophical residues in the thought

[217] Kristeller, *Ficino*, 15, and "Augustine and the Early Renaissance," *Studies in Renaissance Thought and Letters* (Rome, 1956), 355-372; O'Malley, 58-61; Trinkaus, II, 465; Walker, *passim*.

[218] *Loci communes*, 19-20, 22-23.

[219] *Ibid.*, 22; Fraenkel, 19, 302.

[220] *Comm. Seneca*, 24-25.

of Augustine and the biblical dimensions of his thought were un
usually sound. He paid small attention to Augustine's earlier, more
philosophical compositions, though he otherwise drew massively
on the works of Augustine; he disliked his allegorizing and his
more speculative flights; and he thought him "excessively addicted
to the philosophy of Plato," so that (for example) he had misunderstood the Johannine *logos*.[221] But if Augustine did not interest him
as a philosopher, Calvin was profoundly impressed by him as a theologian—and as a person. His respect for Augustine as a historical
personality compelled him to insist on absolute fidelity—again we
hear the authentic Renaissance note—to the intentions, and so to the
full context, of any pronouncement of Augustine. "If I pervert his
words into any other sense than Saint Augustine intended in writing
them," he declared against his opponents, "may they not only attack
me as usual but also spit in my face." [222] His sensitivity to what was
authentically Augustinian made him particularly effective in sorting
out genuine from pseudo-Augustinian writings, an exercise in which
he made some improvement over Erasmus. He exploited his knowledge of Augustine's changes of mind against his Catholic enemies
who still, apparently, thought an Augustinian pronouncement from
any period in the saint's life equally representative of his views.[223]
But above all Augustine was for Calvin a model of the open, developing spiritual life, of the mind in movement which we have seen as
perhaps the central feature in Augustine's significance for the Renaissance. In the 1543 edition of the *Institutes* he included the quint-
essentially Augustinian motto: "Ie me confesse estre du reng de ceux
qui escrivent en profitant, et profitent en escrivant." [224]

Although this study is not generally concerned with the problem
of the connections between Renaissance humanism and the Reformation, it may thus be of some help in explaining why some humanists,
but not others, turned to Protestantism. Humanists of more Stoic
tendencies, like Erasmus, seem to have been less likely to become
Protestants than those of the more Augustinian kind. But the more
Augustinian humanist might end up in either the Protestant or Catholic camp.

For Augustine was also an important figure, though in a more

---

[221] Smits, I, 146, 265-270; *Comm. John* 1:3.
[222] *Institutes*, IV, xix, 12.
[223] Smits, I, 191-194, 145, 252.
[224] Quoted by Smits, 63; cf. the passage quoted, p. 8 above.

complex way, in the Catholic Reformation. The reaffirmation of
the authority of tradition at Trent guaranteed to the Fathers collectively an essential place, linking the apostolic to the medieval
church, in the historical continuity of the faith; and Augustine
shared in a general patristic flowering. He received extensive treatment in Bellarmine's *De scriptoribus ecclesiasticis*; [225] and his works
went through numerous printings in Catholic countries, culminating
with the authoritative Benedictine edition of Saint Maur (1679-1700).[226]
But Augustine had many uses. The thought of the mature Augustine
was of fundamental importance for the circle of Bérulle, who, in the
tradition of Augustinian humanism, opposed it to Stoic tendencies in
Catholic thought.[227] The significance of this species of Augustinianism
for the Catholic world is evident in the deep influence of Augustine
at Louvain, where it found expression in the works of Baius and
Jansen, and in the controversy *De auxiliis*. Since Thomist theology
was so deeply rooted in Augustine, the growing influence of Thomism
also operated to keep Augustine alive as a theologian of grace. But
the condemnations of Baius and of Jansenism and the inconclusiveness
of the dispute *De auxiliis* indicate the reserve of ecclesiastical authority toward this kind of Augustinianism; and meanwhile the Platonic
Augustine of the Florentine Platonists, who could be invoked
to support the old mixture of philosophy with Christianity, was still
very much alive. Some of the opponents of Jansenism also exploited
the authority of Augustine to support a heavily moralistic and rather
arid scholasticism from which Augustine himself seems strikingly
absent.[228]

At the same time Stoicism was becoming stronger than ever in
later sixteenth-century Europe, once more presenting itself both as
a source of personal consolation and a force for order in a period
when religious wars were creating general anarchy, when the challenge
to ecclesiastical authority threatened to produce a deeper kind of
disorder, when the ruling classes were made profoundly insecure by

---

[225] Augustine is given almost twice as much space as any other writer.

[226] See Henri-Jean Martin, *Livre pouvoirs et société à Paris au XVIIe siècle (1598-
1701)* (Geneva, 1969), I, 113-116, 494; II, 601, 609.

[227] Dagens, 55 and *passim*. For Augustine in seventeenth-century France
see, more generally, Nigel Abercrombie, *Saint Augustine and French Classical
Thought* (Oxford, 1938).

[228] The literature on seventeenth-century Augustinianism is massive, but see
especially J. Orcibal, *Jean Duvergier de Hauranne, abbé de Saint-Cyran, et son temps*
(Paris, 1947), and Henri de Lubac, *Augustinisme et théologie moderne* (Paris, 1965).

what they discerned an the danger of mass uprising from below, and
when all the world seemed in the grip of unrestrained passion. Under
these conditions both the moral disciplines and the larger theories
of control advanced by the Stoics once more appeared singularly
attractive, and Stoicism reinforced the more general impulse of the
Catholic Reformation to discipline every dimension of life.[229] This
period saw, with Lipsius, the first fully systematic presentation of
Stoicism; Lipsius was perhaps the first modern European to recognize
clearly, though earlier Stoic expression often gave inadvertent
testimony to it, that the heart of Stoicism is not its ethics but its
philosophy of nature.[230]

Lipsius, and to a lesser extent Charron and Du Vair, therefore
mark the beginning of a new phase in the influence of Stoicism. Since
it was now an increasingly articulated system, it was more successful
than the eclectic bits and pieces gleaned from Seneca and Cicero,
not only in establishing the cosmic foundations of order but also
in promoting the peace of the contemplative life. Lipsius recognized
a number of Christian objections to Stoicism in his *De constantia*,
but it is significant that the ideal of *apatheia* was not among them;
indeed, his own ideal of constancy explicitly includes freedom from
hope and fear.[231] And the recovery of a more consistent Stoic anthropology, in which reason was seen as the essential faculty of
man and thus capable of imposing order on the passions and finally
on society, was supplemented in this movement by a renewal of the
effort of Stoic humanism to join philosophical with Christian wisdom.
Neostoic writers even assimilated Augustine, whom they often
quoted.[232]

On the other hand Stoic doctrine was also popular, among
Protestants as well as Catholics, in a more secular form. It is worth
remembering that even those Augustinian humanists who had rejected
the mixture of philosophy with religion recognized the value of
rational insight for the humbler business of this world; and it was

---

[229] Cf. John Bossy, "The Counter-Reformation and the People of Catholic
Europe," *Past and Present*, 47 (May, 1970), 51-70.

[230] Jason Lewis Saunders, *Justus Lipsius: the Philosophy of Renaissance Stoicism*
(New York, 1955), 67. In general, see also Julien Eymard d'Angers, "Le Stoïcisme
en France dans la première moitié du XVIIᵉ siècle," *Études Franciscaines*, II (1951),
287-299, 389-410.

[231] *De constantia*, 9.

[232] Noted by Abercrombie, 6; Lipsius described Augustine as "nostrorum
scriptorum apex" (*Manductio ad Stoicam philosophiam*, I, iv).

therefore entirely consistent with a fundamentally Augustinian position to draw on isolated Stoic maxims for their relevance to practical situations. Calvin himself continued to exploit Seneca for his sermons and elsewhere.[233] In this form Stoicism nourished the secularization of morality and the discovery of principles of social order independent of religion. This species of Stoicism was responsible for the attempt by such figures as Charron and Grotius, in a time when religious passion was a source of general disturbance, to base ethics on the laws of nature. Eventually this would lead to the notion that the principles of human behavior might be based solely on the knowledge of human nature.[234]

In this secularized form Stoicism could be reconciled with Augustinianism. The two could be seen to complement each other, as law is complemented by grace, or the earthly by the heavenly city. But such a reconciliation, which depended on the deracination of Stoicism, was obviously a reconciliation on Augustinian terms. And Stoicism had a peculiar facility for growing new roots; thus the tension between the two old antagonists was never fully resolved.

---

[233] The point is made by Hugo, introduction to Calvin's *Comm. Seneca*, 36-40.

[234] On this point, in addition to Léontine Zanta, *La Renaissance du Stoïcisme au XVIe siècle* (Paris, 1914), see Anthony Levi, *French Moralists: the Theory of the Passions, 1585 to 1649* (Oxford, 1964).

ITALIAN REACTIONS TO ERASMIAN HUMANISM

MYRON P. GILMORE

Harvard University

I. Interaction between Italy and the North

The sixteenth century saw the triumph of the Italian Renaissance in northern Europe. Increasing numbers of students from France, Germany, England, the Netherlands, and Spain flocked to the Italian centers. Kings and princes formed the style of their courts and built their palaces and chateaux on Italian models. New universities in Louvain, Paris, Alcalá, and Vienna bore witness to the prestige of the *studia humanitatis*. The reception of Italian arts, letters, and scholarship, particularly as they reflected a deeper and wider knowledge of classical antiquity, transformed the cultural inheritance of the Middle Ages and introduced one of the most significant revolutions in the intellectual history of the western world.

The figure of Desiderius Erasmus dominated the development of the ideals of humanism in the north. The movement associated with his name has traditionally been called Christian humanism—justifiably so inasmuch as it was oriented toward the return *ad fontes* of the Christian church and the removal of the abuses which had accumulated over the centuries in the slow growth of a vast ecclesiastical establishment. Unjustifiably, however, is it called Christian humanism if the intent is to contrast the northern movement with a "pagan" humanism in Italy. Recent scholarship has emphasized the fact that it is difficult, if not impossible, to find a humanist of the fifteenth or sixteenth centuries who was not a Christian. The conclusion of Lucien Febvre in 1947 that the sixteenth was a century "qui veut croire" is valid for Italy as well as the north.[1] How is it possible to say in a general sense that Erasmus was more or less Christian than Lorenzo Valla? From the time of Petrarch onward humanist scholars had been extending the knowledge of Greek and Roman antiquity, translating Greek texts, improving medieval translations, and writing commentaries. With the invention of

---

[1] Lucien Febvre, *Le problème de l'incroyance au XVIe siècle: la religion de Rabelais*, L'Évolution de l'humanité, 53 (Paris, 1947), 491-501.

printing practically the whole corpus of ancient literature was made available in new editions before the end of the sixteenth century. The greatly enlarged knowledge of Greco-Roman civilization gave a new dimension to the debate which was as old as Christianity on the compatibility of the classical heritage with Christian revelation. Augustine had proposed the metaphor of using the gold and silver vessels which the Israelites brought with them out of Egypt, but Jerome had dreamed of being beaten at the gates of heaven for being a Ciceronian rather than a Christian. It was a question not only of reconciling Greek philosophy, especially Plato and Aristotle, with Christian theology in which it had already been largely assimilated, but also of defining the role of classical mythology. Could such myths as Hercules at the crossroads and Cupid and Psyche be allegorized in the service of Christian truth? Was it possible that the virtuous pagan had been saved? Was there a *prisca theologia* which went back to the Hermetic corpus, to Moses, Zoroaster, and Plato and was this an anticipation of the truths of revealed religion? Answers to these and other questions had varied over the centuries, sometimes allowing a larger and sometimes a narrower assimilation of classical culture in a Christian synthesis. In fifteenth-century Italy many painters, poets, scholars, and philosophers held the most comprehensive views on the compatibility of the classical with the Christian world. No doubt some were so seduced by the literary and artistic masterpieces of antiquity that they seemed to wish to escape from their own time and recreate a golden age of antiquity. Yet even these are not to be thought of as pagans but as Christians occupying one end of a spectrum which allowed for many variations.

In the North most of the humanists were in the middle or at other the end of the spectrum, that is, they accepted the predominance of the Christian tradition and were less disposed to allow any real synthesis between it and the classical world. Erasmus himself dedicated his scholarly life primarily to the *restitutio* of Christianity. His discovery of Valla's *In Novum Testamentum ... Annotationes*, the manuscript of which he found in the summer of 1504 and which he published in the spring of 1505, confirmed his ambition to apply the new philological methods to the editing of the basic texts of Christianity. The result was the *New Testament* of 1516, containing the first published Greek edition, a new Latin translation, and an extensive commentary. This work was dedicated to Pope Leo X, commending him for his efforts for the restoration of Christian piety. Erasmus proclaimed with ironic modesty that while men of wealth were contributing ivory, marble, gems, and gold to the building of St. Peter's, his own contribution would be the restoration of the fundamental sources of the Christian religion.[2] The *New Testament* was followed by the *Paraphrases* and was both preceded and followed by the editions of the Church Fathers, Greek as well as Latin, including Ambrose, Augustine, and Jerome, and Cyprian, Gregory of Nazianzus, and Origen. Interspersed with these were the editions of classical authors and the literary works, the *Enchiridion militis Christiani*, *Moriae encomium*, *Institutio principis Christiani*, *Querula pacis*, *Ecclesiastes*, and many homiletic and polemical works. There can be no question of the centrality of the Christian tradition in the vast *opera* which fill eleven volumes in the Leiden edition of 1703. Although Erasmus had assimilated fully the classical scholarship of the Italian Renaissance, the message he gave to the world was summarized in his formulation of the *philosophia Christi*. In spite of this greater emphasis on Christianity which he shared with most of his northern contemporaries but which differentiates him in general from the Italian humanists, he sometimes went very far in what might be called an Italianate direction in asserting the perfect compatibility of the best classical morality with revealed Christianity. Although in the *Ciceronianus* he condemned not only the rigid adherence to Cicero's vocabulary and style, but also the "paganizing" tendencies of the Italian humanists, it did not escape his Italian critics that he had permitted his characters in the colloquy *Convivium religiosum* to maintain that the virtuous pagans are divinely inspired, that there are more saints than exist in the Christian calendar, and that one can even utter the apostrophe, "Sancte Socrate, ora pro nobis!"

Erasmus had reached the height of his reputation in 1517. He corresponded with friends and admirers from Poland to Portugal and from the Scandinavian countries to Italy. His letters are perhaps our most valuable source for the intellectual history of the period. His friendship and favor were sought by ruling monarchs and by highly placed churchmen. Although he had never accepted an academic appointment except briefly in Cambridge, England, he was by now in receipt of a good income, derived, for the most part, from presents in money or in kind bestowed on him by the grateful

---

[2] P. S. and H. M. Allen, eds., *Opus epistolarum Des. Erasmi Roterodami*, 12 vols. (Oxford, 1906-1958), No. 384 (hereafter cited as Allen, with number of letter, or, when relevant, l. or ll. indicating line or lines).

recipients of his dedications.[3] In the spring of this *annus mirabilis* he wrote letters both to a friend and to Pope Leo saying that he foresaw the dawn of a golden age. Christian piety which had fallen into decay was about to be restored, scholarly learning (i.e. the study of the classics) which had been neglected and corrupted was now flourishing and peace had been brought about among the European sovereigns.[4] Six months after the expression of these hopes Martin Luther made his historic protest against indulgences, and the next four years saw the rapid development of his revolutionary program, culminating in the *Three Treatises* of 1520, followed by the final excommunication of 1521, and the ban of the Empire decreed by the Diet of Worms on his refusal to retract. Erasmus had earlier regarded Luther with qualified approval and even intervened at a critical moment with Frederick of Saxony to urge him to give his protection to the cause of an innocent man.[5] However, by the time the movement had reached revolutionary proportions, Erasmus found many aspects of Luther's program unacceptable. He disapproved of the discussion by an ignorant public of theological questions which should be settled by experts in a council. He deplored the abolition of most of the sacraments, the confiscation of property, and the secularization of monasteries. He found Luther's uncompromising personality antipathetic. Consequently in the early years of the Reformation he hesitated while the supporters of both Rome and Wittenberg urged him to declare himself. When Luther was in hiding in the Wartburg and the news of his death had been spread abroad, Albrecht Dürer was among those who recorded in his diary an apostrophe to Erasmus, "Ride forth you knight of Christ. Defend the truth and win a martyr's crown." [6]

Erasmus did not ride forth, but he did make one more attempt to heal the breach by publishing in 1524 the colloquy *Inquisitio de fide*. In this his purpose was to demonstrate how much of the Christian faith was shared in common by Rome and Luther. In the dialogue a Lutheran is interrogated and is found to accept not only fundamental positions from Scripture but also the Apostles' Creed and the Nicene Creed. If agreement is so far established, asks Erasmus,

---

[3] Jean Hoyoux, "Les Moyens d'existence d'Erasme," *Bibliothèque d'humanisme et renaissance*, V (1944), 1-59.

[4] Allen, 541, 566.

[5] Allen, 939.

[6] Quoted in Roland Bainton, *Erasmus of Christendom* (New York, 1969), 167.

how can Luther be regarded as a heretic? This approach was acceptable to neither side, and within six months Erasmus published, at
the urging of the Pope and on the original suggestion of Henry VIII,
the *De libero arbitrio*, the treatise on the freedom of the will which
marked his definite repudiation of Luther and the Reformation. From
his residence at Basel in the twenties he no longer wrote to friends
of the imminence of a golden age but on the contrary declared that
he was living in the worst century since the beginning of the Christian
era.[7]

It was in this period of his life that Erasmus had to meet the
attacks of the first and most prominent of his Italian critics. His
achievements in literature and scholarship had brought a reputation
unrivalled in the history of European literature unless perhaps by
Petrarch and Voltaire. The first impact of the Reformation stimulated
a re-examination of his famous works in the Roman Curia and elsewhere among Italian humanists. He was attacked first on religious
grounds, but subsequently as an anti-Ciceronian and a northern
barbarian. So began in Italy a reaction to northern humanism inaugurating a period in which the intellectual currents, which in the
fifteenth century had predominantly flowed from Italy to the north,
now moved in both directions as they had in the trecento, the age
of Petrarch and Boccaccio.

II. Erasmus as the Precursor of Luther

The attack most resented was thought by Erasmus to be by
one who had formerly been a close friend. Girolamo Aleandro
was born in 1480 in a village near Treviso in the Veneto.[8] His ancestry
had been noble, but his father was in very moderate economic
circumstances and practiced medicine. His early education was
acquired in his native town and in Venice where he frequented
a series of humanist masters. He early demonstrated a remarkable
capacity for languages and before he was twenty had mastered
not only Greek and Latin but also Hebrew. In 1503 he joined the
household of Aldo Manuzio and for five years was closely associated
with the Aldine press, then one of the most active intellectual centers

---

[7] Allen, 1239.

[8] On Aleandro, see Giuseppe Alberigo, "Aleandro, Girolamo," in *Dizionario
biografico degli Italiani*, II (Rome, 1960), 128-135; and Jules Paquier, *L'humanisme
et la réforme: Jérôme Aléandre, de sa naissance à la fin de son séjour à Brindes, 1480-1529*
(Paris, 1900).

in Europe, engaged in publishing practically the entire corpus of
Greek literature. The so-called Aldine Academy consisted of a group
of learned men, some refugee Greeks and other western scholars,
who conversed and wrote in the Greek language and dedicated
themselves to disseminating the heritage of ancient Greece. Erasmus,
arriving at the beginning of 1508 to work on the second edition of
his *Adages*, was warmly welcomed by Aldo and formed a close
intimacy with Aleandro, some twelve years younger than himself.
They shared a room in the Aldine household and Erasmus owed to
Aleandro some useful suggestions for the *Adages*. In return Erasmus
gave to the younger scholar letters of recommendation to his Paris
friends when Aleandro determined to go north to seek his fortune
in April of 1508.

He arrived in Paris in June, and by the end of the summer he
was giving lectures at the University to large and enthusiastic
audiences, using the Greek publications which he had ordered
from the Aldine press. Although there had been a few predecessors,
he had the honor of inaugurating the serious teaching of Greek
in France. In 1510 he left Paris because of the plague and accepted an
appointment at Orleans. In 1512 and 1513 he was occupied with his
scholarship and also was charged by King Louis XII with the defense
of the Council of Pisa. In 1513, seeking a more lucrative employment,
he became secretary of the Bishop of Paris and in the following
year took a similar post with the Prince Bishop of Liège, and subsequent Cardinal, Erard de la Marck. The service of the Bishop took
him to Rome, where he rose rapidly in favor at the Court of Leo X.
Cardinal Giulio de' Medici, the Pope's cousin, made him his secretary,
and he presently succeeded to the librarianship of the Vatican.

In 1520 he was given the difficult and critical mission of carrying
to Germany the papal bull *Exsurge Domine*, the condemnation of
Luther, and supervising its enforcement. At the Diet of Worms in
1521 he made the critical oration in favor of condemnation and urged
the emperor and the princes to publish the Edict of Worms, putting
Luther under the ban of the Empire. A year later Aleandro was in
the Netherlands presiding over the suppression of heresy, and there
in Brussels met with Erasmus and tried to persuade him to write
against Luther. Although their meeting was outwardly cordial, it is
clear from what Erasmus wrote to other correspondents immediately
after this meeting that he already felt that Aleandro was secretly
spreading lies about the Erasmian influence on Luther and the

Erasmian authorship of certain Lutheran works. In this letter Erasmus described Aleandro as "natura excelsus, ferox, irritabilis, cui nihil neque lucri neque gloriae satis est." [9]

Aleandro returned to Rome and his positions in the curia under the new Pope Adrian VI. However great his own hostility towards Erasmus, he was compelled as a papal advisor to participate in the drawing up of the brief which the pope sent to Erasmus on December 1, confirming the orthodoxy of his writings and inviting him to come to Rome to take part in the campaign against Luther.[10] Ten years later after the crisis in their relationship Aleandro wrote in one of his last letters to Erasmus that he had indeed prepared the draft of the papal brief and that he had proposed many more phrases in praise of Erasmus than the pope had included.[11]

On June 6, 1526, Erasmus, writing to Willibald Pirckheimer, told him that a certain Jew at Rome, known to Pirckheimer, had brought out part of a book against Erasmus. Erasmus always considered, without justification, that Aleandro was of Jewish ancestry. In the letter he listed some of the charges contained in this manuscript, that, although so many thousands of men had been killed in Germany, Erasmus alone remained who had taught the Germans, and that even the Lutherans, although most impious, had written against him because they could not bear the impiety of one who had denied the virginity of the Virgin Mary and the divinity of Christ and held other outrageous doctrines.[12]

In the succeeding years in letters to some of his closest friends Erasmus made repeated references to this manuscript *Racha*. He always made it clear that he considered Aleandro the author but he rarely mentioned him by name. It is as if he felt a certain reticence about expressing his bitterness at what he considered a monstrously unjust attack from one whom he might have supposed to be an ally.[13]

---

[9] Allen, 1268.

[10] Allen, 1324.

[11] Allen, 2638, ll. 34-44.

[12] Allen, 1717, ll. 33-41: "Romae verpus quidam, quem nosti, qui misere invidet omnibus doctis Germaniae, exhibit libri partem olim in me scripti, nisi quod adiecit quaedam ex hoc temporum statu furiose. Nomen suum dissimulat. Inter cetera dicit se mirari quod in Germania tot hominum millibus coesis, ego supersim, qui sic docuerim Germaniam. Deinde dicit Lutheranos, quamquam impiissimos, ideo scribere in me, quod impietatem meam ferre non possint, qui Virgini Mariae dextraxerim suam virginitatem Christo suam divinitatem, aliaque his furiosora."

[13] For the various references to this work in Erasmus's letters, see Eugenio

The manuscript is known as *Racha*, because one of the principal points of the author's critique of Erasmus is his alleged misunderstanding of the Hebrew word *Racha*, which occurs in Matthew 5:22 and on which Erasmus had commented in his *Annotations*. Although a general idea of *Racha*'s content could be reconstructed from Erasmus's references to it, the work itself was long supposed to be lost. In 1948, however, Professor Eugenio Massa discovered 19 folio pages of it in the Bibliothèque Nationale in Paris.[14]

A large part of the nineteen folios of the Paris Ms. is devoted to philological questions. The analysis of the Hebrew term *Racha* occupies more than a third of the text. The author contends that the correct form is *Recha* and defines its meaning as "carentia bonorum." [15] There are in Hebrew philosophy three kinds of wisdom and three kinds of folly. Of the latter, *stultitia*, the first, destroys the foundation of all things, the second those benefits which can be achieved by human industry, and the third the gifts of divine grace and favor. The first and the third species of folly are named after seers whose names are Avel and Nabal, while the second type which pertains to human studies is frequently called *Recha* by the prophets.[16]

There are other criticisms of Erasmus on philological grounds; The author indicts him for changing the beginning of the Gospel of St. John from "In principio erat verbum" to "In principio erat sermo." [17] He also charges that Erasmus has understood neither the orthography nor the etymology of Gohenna, on which he claims that Erasmus's note contains as many lies as words.[18]

Interspersed somewhat inconsistently among these rather pedantic

---

Massa, "Interno ad Erasmo: Una polemica che si credeva perduta," in *Classical, Mediaeval and Renaissance Studies in Honor of Berthold Louis Ullman*, ed. Charles Henderson, Jr., 2 vols., Storia e letteratura, 93-94 (Rome, 1964), II, 435-454.

[14] *Ibid.*, 436-437. Professor Massa has concluded that the author of the *Racha* is not Aleandro but Egidio of Viterbo. See his article, "Egidio da Viterbo e la metodologia del sapere nel Cinquecento," *Pensée humaniste et tradition chrétienne aux XVe et XVIe siècles* (Paris, 1950), 185-239. This conclusion was not accepted by Augustin Renaudet. Professor Massa has promised an edition of the *Racha*.

[15] Parisiensis Latinus, 3461, fol. 8v (hereafter cited as Par. Lat.).

[16] Par. Lat., 3461, fols. 8r-8v: "Porro tres stultitiae species: ita constitutae sunt ut prima tollat rerum omnium fundamentum; secunda ea quae assequi possumus industria humana; tertia gratiam amicitiam divinam. Prima et tertia stultitiae species a vatibus dictae sunt quorum nomina sunt Avel et Nabal ut supra demonstravimus. Medium genus quod ad humana studia pertinet solet crebro apud profetas Recha nuncupari."

[17] Par. Lat., 3461, fol. 5r.

[18] Par. Lat., 3461, fol. 15r.

[illegible] of those who, like Erasmus and his followers, reduce all celestial and divine things to lowly grammatical
analysis. The understanding of the divinely inspired words of Christ
and the Evangelists is not to be compared with the interpretation
of the vocabulary of Plautus or the scholia of Aristophanes.[19] There is
in this argument an indication of the revolt against humanist grammarians which was taken up by many critics later in the sixteenth
century.

Finally there are the sweeping charges of heresy. The Saxon and
German heretics have been armed as from a Trojan horse. Erasmus
has denied the divinity of Christ and defended the Arians.[20] The *Racha*
marvels that the world bears these things. How comes it that this
scoffer has not been removed by God? He first of all after John Hus
has stirred the waters of the deep, set the flood in motion, and brought
forth the tempest. He has given birth to the Carlstadts, Melanchthons,
and the whole race of monsters.[21]

Erasmus was particularly sensitive to the charge that he was
responsible for the religious revolution. Although the *Racha* was
never published, it circulated in manuscript copies, and Erasmus
answered it in letters to friends, denouncing his anonymous opponent
but always claiming that he knew who the author was. In addition
to his letters however he included a more formal reply in his *Annotationes in Novum Testamentum*, beginning with the edition of 1527.[22]
Furthermore, he did protest directly to Clement VII in a letter of
April 3, 1528, that he had learned from the books of Alberto Pio of
Carpi and from that of Girolamo Aleandro that there were some
who accused him to His Holiness of either favoring Luther secretly
or at any rate allowing him an opportunity to present his cause.
These charges he emphatically denies, citing his two *Hyperaspistes*
against Luther. He asserts that he has not up to then responded to
either book, as he did not wish to harm any third person who might
be involved and hesitated to rekindle a blaze which was already
dying.[23] Considering that Erasmus was usually only too ready to

---

[19] Par. Lat., 3461, fols. 2r, 14r.
[20] Par. Lat., 3461, fol. 6r.
[21] Par. Lat., 3461, fol. 18r.
[22] Cf. Massa, *op. cit.* The relevant passage of which Professor Massa discovered
the significance is the note on Matthew 10:27, in Erasmus, *Opera omnia*, 10 vols.
(Leiden, 1703), VI, cols. 56-57 (hereafter cited *LB* with volume and column
numbers).
[23] Allen, 1987.

answer, and at great length, any attack on his scholarship or his ideas, it is curious that he did not make a more formal public reply to the charges of Aleandro. Perhaps he was moved by the recollection of their life together in Venice at the Aldine academy when their friendship had been so close. Perhaps he feared the harm that Aleandro could do him in the Roman curia. The violence of his vocabulary in the letters to his intimates would support the latter rather than the former of these possibilities. Their personalities led them to irreconcilable views on the causes of the Lutheran revolution. Aleandro could not understand, as Erasmus could, the religious impulses behind Luther and in consequence felt that the remedy was the imposition of more institutional discipline. In any case this polemic, unpublished on one side and half concealed on the other, remains as testimony of one of the most complex and ambiguous relationships of Erasmus's career.

If Erasmus had doubts about the wisdom of writing against Aleandro, he clearly had none about refuting the charges of the author of the second book mentioned in the letter to Clement VII, Alberto Pio, Prince of Carpi.

The Pio family had possessed themselves of the little signory of Carpi in the fourteenth century and for services to the House of Savoy were allowed to call themselves Pio di Sabaudia. In the course of time they received an investiture from the emperor Sigismund. Since they did not follow the rule of primogeniture, there was in almost every generation a struggle among brothers for the small inheritance. Alberto was born in 1475, and his father died two years later, leaving him in the guardianship of his uncle Marco and his maternal uncle, Giovanni Pico della Mirandola. Pico supervised his nephew's education and engaged as his tutor, Aldo Manuzio, who instructed him in the classical languages. Alberto formed a close attachment to his tutor which led ultimately to his taking a prominent part in the foundation of the Aldine press in Venice for which he furnished subsidies. In the meantime he was educated at Ferrara and Padua, attended the lectures of Pomponazzi, and found close friends in Bembo and Ariosto.

After his uncle's death he came into conflict with his cousin Giberto, and the inheritance was at first shared and then finally confirmed to Alberto by a brief of the emperor Maximilian. Alberto then embarked on a diplomatic career, serving first as the agent of the Gonzaga of Mantua at the court of France and subsequently in the pay of Louis XII. He was one of the negotiators of the League of Cambrai in 1508 and carried the terms of the treaty to the emperor. Maximilian was much impressed with his abilities and after the defeat of the French in 1512 Alberto became the orator or diplomatic agent of the emperor at the papal court. For the next decade he played a considerable role in European affairs. At Rome he was a prominent figure and close friend of Leo X. At Carpi he was a Renaissance prince, rebuilding palace and churches and collecting a library and works of art. All came to an end in 1520, when Alberto left the allegiance of the new emperor Charles V and switched to being the agent of the king of France. Charles confiscated his principality, and his efforts to regain it, aided by the support of three popes, were futile. In the Sack of Rome he shared the captivity of Clement VII and afterwards fled with his family to France, where he was warmly welcomed by Francis I. Provided with honors and an income and established in a palatial house in the quarter of St. Germain, he devoted his remaining years to an analysis of the works of Erasmus. He died in January 1531, leaving unfinished his indictment of Erasmus which was prepared for the press by his young Italian secretary, Francesco Florido Sabino, and published two months later.[24]

Erasmus had already heard reports as early as August 1524 and repeated the following spring that Alberto Pio was talking against him in the Roman curia, accusing him of heresy and declaring that he was neither a philosopher nor a theologian and that there was no sound doctrine in him.[25]

On October 10, 1525, he wrote to Alberto a flattering and conciliatory letter, in which he protested his orthodoxy and declared that he had never tried to be a philosopher or a theologian. As for having been the occasion of Luther's revolt, at the very beginning he urged his friends to have nothing to do with the movement. He preferred to be exposed to the attacks of both parties than to raise a finger in aid of a faction not recognized by the Roman church. As for the accusation that Luther was inspired by his books, Luther himself denies it absolutely.[26]

---

[24] On Alberto Pio, see Hans Semper, F. Otto Schulze, and W. Barth, eds., *Carpi: Ein Fürstensitz der Renaissance* (Dresden, 1882); Allen, vol. VI, p. 200; and Myron P. Gilmore, "Erasmus and Alberto Pio, Prince of Carpi," in *Action and Conviction in Early Modern Europe*, eds. T. K. Rabb and J. E. Seigel (Princeton, 1969), 299-318.

[25] Cf. Allen, 1479, l. 130 note, and 1576, ll. 38-41.

[26] Allen, 1634.

Alberto replied to this with a *Responsio paraenetica* which reached Erasmus in the summer of 1526 at the same time as the anonymous tract which he attributed to Aleandro.[27] Alberto, although interspersing his criticisms with compliments and reservations, reiterated the charge that Erasmus had been an important source of Luther's ideas, and particularly indicted the *Praise of Folly* and the *Paraphrases*. Erasmus wrote to Thomas More that he thought Alberto had not read his books, but had taken his criticisms from the chatter of the theologians with whom he associated. For, says Erasmus, as a layman, he aspires to be considered a theologian and is marvelously complacent over the fact that he is an Aristotelian.[28]

Erasmus did not immediately reply to this *Responsio*, and he moved to do so only after news had reached him that Alberto was preparing the work for publication. He then wrote to Alberto at the end of December, 1528, with the rather thin excuse that, although he had prepared a reply, he had not sent it because he was unsure where Alberto was in the troubles that preceded and followed the Sack of Rome in 1527. Now he has heard that Alberto is in the service of the king of France and is preparing to publish his attack on Erasmus. He warns him not to do so, or, if he does, to mitigate his charges against Erasmus.[29] But it was too late; the book was already in press and appeared in Paris on January 7, 1529. It reached Erasmus by February 9, and he immediately composed a reply in his usual sharp, polemical style, although he still addressed Alberto as "clarissimus ac doctissimus." He expands on the arguments which had been the subject of his original letter. It was finished in four days and published in March by Froben in an edition of forty quarto pages.[30] On receiving it, Alberto devoted the remaining months of his life in Paris to composing a massive refutation and defense. As we have seen he died in January of 1531, and his secretary brought out in March the folio volume *Alberti Pii Carporum illustrissimi et viri longe doctissimi praeter prefationem et operis conclusionem tres et viginti libri in locos lucubrationum variarum D. Erasmi Roterodami quos censet ab eo recognoscendos et retractandos*. This work is the most comprehensive attack on Erasmus's religious position and the most complete presentation of the thesis that Erasmus was responsible for Luther. It allows us to study in

---

[27] Allen, 1744, l. 130.
[28] Allen, 1804, ll. 249-256.
[29] Allen, 2080.
[30] Allen, 1634, introduction.

detail the reaction to northern humanism of a l hmr one important segment of Italian opinion during Erasmus's own lifetime.

The book appeared with a preface of the publisher Jodocus Badius Ascensius eulogizing the piety of the late Count of Carpi, who did not cease till the last day his labors for the Catholic faith. Badius says Alberto wrote the work for two reasons, the first to prove clearly what he had written in the paraenetic epistle to Erasmus, that there were many things published by him which were harmful both to the dignity of the church and to the catholic faith, the second that by a benign warning and modest instruction he should induce Erasmus to retract those passages in so many of his works which were suspect and offensive.[31]

Alberto's *magnum opus* contains, after the publisher's preface, a short poem by Francesco Florido in the form of a dialogue between the book and the reader, in which the book pays tribute to its author and mourns that it was left in unfinished condition by his death. This is followed by the text of Erasmus's original letter of October 10, 1525, with Alberto's *Responsio paraenetica* dated at Rome May 15, 1526, but not printed until January 7, 1529. This occupies the first 46 folios. Then comes Erasmus's hastily written reply printed with the marginal notes of Alberto, so that the reader has the impression of a spoken dialogue between the opponents. For example, when Erasmus complains that his private letter to Alberto was published, Alberto replies in the margin that Erasmus brought about the publication himself and is pleased with it because of its elegance.[32] Alberto asserts that he has not twisted the sense of material reprehended by all.[33] He denies that he has ever circulated cheap slanders about Erasmus at Rome, such as calling him "Porrophagus" or "Err-asmus."[34] When Erasmus complains that he hates revision, Alberto sharply notes that he had rightly stated that there are some who edit their books before they are written and write them before they are conceived.[35] Erasmus admits that he has written and done certain things which he would not have done had he known the

---

[31] Alberto Pio, *Alberti Pii Carporum illustrissimi et viri longe doctissimi praeter prefationem et operis conclusionem tres et viginti libri in locos lucubrationum variarum D. Erasmi Roterodami quos censet ab eo recognoscendos et retractandos* (Paris, 1531), Preface (hereafter cited as *XXIII Libri*, with number of folio).

[32] *XXIII Libri*, fol. XLVII^r.

[33] *XXIII Libri*, fol. XLVIII^r.

[34] *XXIII Libri*, fol. XLVIII^v.

[35] *XXIII Libri*, fol. XLIX^r.

outcome.[36] Then, says Alberto, why is he not now ready to recant? [37] On the great question of the relationship between Luther and Erasmus, when Erasmus exclaims that no one has ever been able to show a single dogma wherein he agrees with Luther, the reply is that naturally it does not suit Luther's pride to admit that he received his dogmas from Erasmus.[38] Elsewhere Alberto notes that many know that Erasmus did declare Luther to be a good and blameless man sent by a divine plan to cleanse the sins of the world.[39] When Erasmus protests that he has always given authority to the constitutions of the church, the reply is that he has written against the sacraments of penance and matrimony.[40] When Erasmus reflects that human institutions always deteriorate, Alberto replies that this is patently false, and refers to the example of the coming of Christ when such institutions were everywhere brought up from a worse state to a better.[41] Erasmus asks desperately, who has ever heard from him that the pope should be controlled, cardinals removed, and bishops made equal and the reply is that in everything he has ever written, whether sacred or profane, whether serious or light, Erasmus has always ridiculed ceremonies, priests, monks, institutions, and theologians.[42]

In this last comment Alberto seems more sweeping and severe than in the rest of the notes. In most of the dialogue he observes at least a modicum of correctness, on certain points agrees that the charges have no validity or interest and even permits himself to make some compliments. The interest of these marginalia, however, is that they show a stage in the composition of Alberto's final *magnum opus* against Erasmus. Erasmus's printed reply to the *Epistola paraenetica* was probably in Alberto's hands by the end of February, 1529. He later said that it was printed before he saw it. The marginal notes were very probably the result of his reactions on a first reading but many of them announced the themes of the larger work on which Alberto concentrated for the remaining months of his life. These themes had indeed already been present in the *Paraenetica*; they included the condemnation of the *Moria* and the *Paraphrases* and

---

[36] *XXIII Libri*, fol. XLIX^v.
[37] *XXIII Libri*, fol. XLIX^v.
[38] *XXIII Libri*, fol. XLIX^v.
[39] *XXIII Libri*, fol. L^r.
[40] *XXIII Libri*, fol. LI^r.
[41] *XXIII Libri*, fol. LI^v.
[42] *XXIII Libri*, fol. LV^r.

perhaps, above all, of the Erasmian doctrine that the spirit is more
important than the letter, which seemed to include an attack on the
sacraments and on many of the most fundamental institutions of
the church. It is clear from his whole approach that Alberto had no
understanding of the Erasmian sense of humor.

After all this prefatory material which counts as Book I, the
XXIII Libri begin on folio LXVI^v of the posthumously published
treatise. Alberto commences with a philosophical reflection on
the unexpected in human affairs. Neither he nor Erasmus when
they first corresponded could have expected to get into such a great
controversy. Erasmus had begun by charging that Alberto spoke
against his ideas and declared him responsible for the Lutheran
revolution, for which the blame was actually to be put on incompetent
theologians, priests, and monks. Alberto declares that he replied as humanly as possible, expressly admitting how great had been his opinion of
Erasmus, but criticizing the Moria and also the fact that Erasmus had
remained silent at the beginning of the controversy. After two years
without reply came the far longer epistle—printed before Alberto
saw it. In spite of some polite expressions it violently accused Alberto
of stupidity, negligence, and malice. To the charge that Alberto had
not read Erasmus's books, he replies frankly that at the time he had
not read many, but he cautions Erasmus not to think that all that he
writes is worth reading. Some ten years before the beginning of
their controversy, Alberto had been through the Adages, which he
judged most useful to humane studies. Then the Moria, which at
first he found lively and elegant but which then so excited his bile
that it deterred him from reading anything else of Erasmus. He had
also read the work on Confession and the Diatribe on the Freedom of
the Will and the New Testament with some of the Paraphrases. In
addition he had read some of the censures of Stunica and Erasmus's
replies. After he received Erasmus's reply he asserted that he had
tried to get as many of his books as possible. In composing his
present work he maintains that he has not been moved by a zeal
for controversy. He knows how great Erasmus is and how powerful
his eloquence.[43]

After this introduction which counts as Book II, the first book
being the reprint of Erasmus's reply to the Paraenetica, Alberto
enters upon the particular issues of his indictment. Book III opens

---

[43] XXIII Libri, fols. LXVI^v-LXXI^r.

the attack with an analysis of the *Praise of Folly* which Alberto considers the beginning of Erasmus's downfall. He marvels that Erasmus
can write so sarcastically against grammarians after all the help he
had from them during the period of his residence with Aldo at
Venice. He deplores the attacks on the other professions, poets,
jurisconsults, philosophers, and mathematicians. But worst of all
is the treatment of theologians, where Erasmus shows his ignorance
of scholastic theology and especially of Aquinas, Bonaventura, and
Albertus Magnus. Monasticism, the power of the popes, the efficacy
of good works, the cult of the Virgin and saints, and even some of
the canonical scriptures are satirized or called in doubt by Erasmus. In
the sweeping conclusion to this book Alberto finds the same views
expressed in a variety of Erasmus's works, including the *Enchiridion*,
Ratio verae theologiae, *Christiani matrimonii institutio*, and the *Colloquia*.[44]

The subsequent books are much more specific in subject matter.
The method followed by Alberto is to quote extensively from a
number of Erasmus's works on a given topic and then reply in an
almost scholastic style of argument. He does show that he has read
widely in the Erasmian *corpus*, citing not only the better known
works, but also the notes to the editions of Jerome, Hilary, and
other Church Fathers.

In Book IV on fasting and dietary prohibitions, Alberto accuses
Erasmus of recommending modifications in fast days for reasons of
health and also of complaining that the dietary regulations of Christians were now more severe than those of the Jews. According to
Alberto, Erasmus maintains that such regulations were never in-
stituted by Christ, and that they are furthermore in many cases
injurious to health. Therefore, Christians ought not to have to obey
them. Alberto attempts to refute this argument from Scripture and
from the Fathers.[45]

In the next book, on monasticism, the main argument turns on the
historical question whether the institution is the same as it was in the
primitive Church and especially in the time of St. Jerome. Alberto
maintains that monasticism is even older than Christianity and was
known in such sects as the Essenes. In Alberto's opinion, Erasmus
cannot escape the charge of condemning monasticism by pretending
that he blames the abuses but not the institution itself.[46]

---

[44] *XXIII Libri*, fols. LXXIII-LXXIV^r.
[45] *XXIII Libri*, fols. LXXXIV^r-XCIII^v.
[46] *XXIII Libri*, fols. XCIII^v-CIII^v.

Book VI—one of the longest—is devoted to "ceremonies and animal rites." Alberto charges that Erasmus has never accurately defined ceremonies and has lumped together in a general condemnation many diverse regulations, such as prescribed prayers and rules for vestments on certain occasions. Alberto pleads that ceremonies are an outward and visible sign aiding "viatores" in their passage through life.[47]

In Book VII Alberto especially attacks Erasmus for the passages in the colloquy *The Godly Feast* which describe the magnificence of the tomb of St. Thomas at Canterbury and the marble church of the Certosa at Pavia. Erasmus had maintained that the money spent for these elaborate structures might better have been devoted to the poor, but Alberto defends such expenditure *ad maiorem gloriam dei* and reminds Erasmus that the poor are always with us.[48]

Book VIII is concerned with the justification of images and the veneration of saints. Alberto expressed horror at the fact that in the *Enchiridion* Erasmus had pointed out that praying to the statues of patron saints and lighting candles to them was not very different from the practices of the ancient pagans, when they pledged a sacrifice to Hercules or Aesculapius. Also, in the *Annotations* on the New Testament, Erasmus had permitted himself to say that "today it has been discovered that a wooden statue may be adored by the same adoration as is given to the Holy Trinity."[49]

On the basis of these texts, Alberto accused Erasmus of making no distinction between heathen idolatry and the Christian veneration of saints. The pagans worshipped corporeal objects as actual gods, whereas the statue of a saint is always the *simulacrum* of a *numen* which it represents. Christian art must be symbolic.[50]

Book IX continues the discussion of the cult of saints and the veneration of relics. Alberto cites with horror the passage in the *Enchiridion* in which Erasmus derides the invocation of St. Christopher, St. Barbara and St. Roch in the hope of receiving particular favors. Alberto strongly defends the veneration of saints and their relics, the cult of the Virgin, and the institution of canonization. In the middle of folio CLXXI^r there is a note stating that up to this point the whole text had been reviewed and corrected by Alberto himself.

---

[47] *XXIII Libri*, fols. CIII^v-CXX^r.
[48] *XXIII Libri*, fols. CXX^v-CXXXIII^v.
[49] *LB*, VI, col. 1015 D-E.
[50] *XXIII Libri*, fols. CXXXIII^v-CXLVII^r.

Premature death prevented his continuing this task, but the remainder of the manuscript, entirely written by him, has been faithfully reviewed by his secretaries.[51]

Book X on theological innovations and scholastic theology is devoted to Alberto's plea for the necessary connection between philosophy and theology. He denounces Erasmus's treatment of St. Thomas and Duns Scotus as complete fools in the *Enchiridion* and the *Praise of Folly*. He points out that St. Augustine would not have been able to write on the Trinity without an understanding of philosophy.[52]

In Book XI Alberto registers his shock that Erasmus ever declares his preference for one book of the Bible over another, as *Isaiah* over *Judith* or *Matthew* over the *Apocalypse*. In doubting the authorship of the *Epistle to the Hebrews*, Alberto considers that Erasmus detracts from the majesty of Scripture, which is entirely divinely inspired. The issue here turns on the validity of the application of humanist scholarship to the sacred texts.[53]

The mystery of the Trinity is defended and the doctrine of Arius refuted in Book XII. Carried away by his conviction, Alberto announces that in the nine hundred years since he was condemned, Arius has not found a greater defender than Erasmus. He scorns the statement of Erasmus in the notes in the edition of Jerome that the followers of Arius constituted a "schism" or "faction" rather than a heresy.[54]

Book XIII is on the authority and function of priests and bishops. Here again Alberto finds that Erasmus errs on the historical question. According to Erasmus, bishops were in the beginning simple priests with pastoral functions, and now they have jurisdictions, keys, and powers. Alberto accused Erasmus of denigrating priests and bishops in more than six hundred places in his works and also of failing to understand the history of tithes and the exemption of the priesthood from the payment of tribute.[55]

The subject of Book XIV is the primacy of St. Peter, the power of the pope, and the titles and honor due to other prelates. Alberto finds that there are many places in Erasmus's works in which he

---

[51] *XXIII Libri*, fols. CLXVII^r-CLXXII^v.
[52] *XXIII Libri*, fols. CLXXII^v-CLXXVI^v.
[53] *XXIII Libri*, fols. CLXXVII^r-CLXXXI^v.
[54] *XXIII Libri*, fols. CLXXXI^v-CLXXXVI^r.
[55] *XXIII Libri*, fols. CLXXXVI^r-CXCIV^r.

casts doubt on the Petrine theory, especially in the passage in the *Methodus verae theologiae*, where Erasmus says that the power of the keys was granted to the whole *corpus* of Christian people. On this account Alberto concludes that the *Methodus* ought to have been entitled a manual *against* true theology.[56]

Book XV is on ecclesiastical constitutions and laws and human traditions. In it Erasmus is accused of not making a sufficient distinction between those institutions or practices of the church which are provisions of divine law and those which are human ordinances, conducive to the observance of divine precepts.[57]

Book XVI discusses the vow of chastity and the observance of other vows made to God. Alberto condemns Erasmus's remark that it would aid the cause of matrimony if the church were to decree that a vow of chastity is void unless undertaken with the express authority of a prelate. In Alberto's opinion, Erasmus does not understand the difference between simple and solemn vows, since a dispensation may be granted in the case of the former but not the latter.[58] In Book XVII Alberto takes up virginity and celibacy. Erasmus had raised the question when matrimony became a sacrament, suggesting that if Jerome had known that matrimony was one of the seven sacraments of the church, perhaps he would have extolled virginity less enthusiastically and spoken more reverently of matrimony. Alberto repudiates this argument as illogical.[59] Book XVIII continues the argument on the history of the sacrament of matrimony.[60]

Book XIX is devoted to another sacrament, confession, and the discussion is again centered on the historical question whether secret and private confession was known in the time of Jerome. Alberto is much offended by Erasmus's treatment of confession in the colloquy, *The Confession of a Soldier*.[61]

In Book XX Alberto comes to the great question of faith and works. He considers that Erasmus has over-emphasized the role of faith in proclaiming that no one can participate in the efficacy of Christ's grace unless he has faith in Christ. Alberto replies with the example of Saul, who had not faith but, on the contrary, perse-

---

[56] *XXIII Libri*, fols. CXLIV^r-CCVI^r.
[57] *XXIII Libri*, fols. CCVI^r-CCX^v.
[58] *XXIII Libri*, fols. CCX^v-CCXVI^v.
[59] *XXIII Libri*, fols. CCXVI^v-CCXXIV^v.
[60] *XXIII Libri*, fols. CCXXIV^v-CCXXVII^r.
[61] *XXIII Libri*, fols. CCXXVIII^v-CCXXX^r.

cuted the Christians and yet received divine grace. Matthew was
called to be an apostle before he had faith. Alberto's own formulation
was very similar to that arrived at in the defined dogma of the Council
of Trent on justification, some seventeen years later. He is clear that
no work by itself is sufficient to eternal salvation unless he who does
it has grace. He admits that faith is greater than works, as gold is
more valuable than silver, but points out that he who prefers gold to
silver does not for that reason say that silver is to be despised.[62]

Book XXI discusses the question of the just war. Here Alberto
condemns Erasmus's pacifism but also finds that he is inconsistent,
especially in his views on war against the Turks.[63] In Book XXII on
oaths, Alberto argues that Erasmus limits unjustifiably the occasions
on which a Christian may take an oath in the name of the Lord.[64]

Book XXIII curiously takes up the subject of lying. Alberto
accuses Erasmus of following Plato in the belief that the guardians
of the Republic may indulge in deceit, and of holding the conviction
that the common people cannot be led by truth. Erasmus has cited the
examples of Abraham and Ruth in the Old Testament to show that a
lie is sometimes justified. Alberto completely rejects this argument:
for him any lie whatever is depraved.[65]

As a conclusion to this long examination of the *loci* of heresy
in the whole corpus of Erasmus's works, Alberto adds a twenty-fourth
book, in which he summarizes his charges and calls on Erasmus to
recant.[66] However arrogant Alberto's tone in parts of the *XXIII
Libri*, by the time he reaches these final pages he professes modesty
and humility. He is thankful he has accomplished the task he set
himself. Even if he has done less than he ought, yet his attempt
and his zeal cannot be reprehended. It is human to err, and those
who write much are bound to do so. Alberto hopes that Erasmus
will accept the criticisms he presents, which are offered only as an
aid to piety. He submits to the judgment of the church and the
professors of sacred theology. In closing, he gives his best wishes to
Erasmus and prays that he may continue to be an influence for the
good.[67]

The conclusion is dated on Holy Saturday, 1530, indicating that

---

[62] *XXIII Libri*, fols. CCXXX^r-CCXXXIX^v.
[63] *XXIII Libri*, fols. CCXXXIX^v-CCXLIIII^v.
[64] *XXIII Libri*, fols. CCXLIIII^v-CCXLVIII^r.
[65] *XXIII Libri*, fols. CCXLVIII^r-CCLI^r.
[66] *XXIII Libri*, fols. CCLI^r-CCLII^r.
[67] *XXIII Libri*, fol. CCLII^r.

Alberto had finished a draft of the whole work almost a year before his death.

Although the tone of the work is often sharply polemical, it rests on a very solid command of the sources of church history and doctrine and on a remarkably close reading of the Erasmian texts. Alberto's charges are sometimes unjustified, notably on the question of faith and works, where he endeavors to make Erasmus's position equivalent to that of Luther, but it must also be said that there are inconsistencies and exaggerations in Erasmus's works, which Alberto exposed. The *XXIII Libri* contain the most severe and comprehensive attack directed against Erasmus in his lifetime, and his reaction shows that he felt he had received some wounds.

His opponent had died before the book appeared, but Erasmus was not deterred from continuing the controversy and, indeed, more passionately and at greater length than ever. He charges that Alberto had ingeniously escaped through death, leaving his sting behind. He admits that "it is odious to write against the dead, but, what is to be done if the dead write against you and indict you in the tribune of the whole world for things which it is impious to close one's eyes to?" [68] He then attacks Alberto for his hypocrisy in having assumed the Franciscan habit only three days before his death, an act which provided Erasmus with the material for the colloquy *The Seraphic Funeral*, and which now impels him to go so far as practically to maintain that Alberto's motive was to make it more difficult to refute his charges without blaming the whole Franciscan order. [69]

Erasmus begins with general charges that Alberto has misunderstood and perverted the Erasmian texts on which he depended, used materials provided for him by others (including Aleandro and the Spaniard Sepulveda), and descended to calumnies, lies, insults, and stupid jokes. He then proceeds to answer *seriatim* the marginal comments of Alberto on his *Responsio* to the *Epistola paraenetica*. Some of his sharpest replies indicate how far they were divided. On the decline of human institutions, Erasmus asserts that even those things which Christ restored with so much zeal have decayed. On the question whether Luther was sent by God as a corrective to a decadent Christianity, Erasmus scoffs at Alberto for doubting

---

[68] *LB*, IX, col. 1123.
[69] *LB*, IX, *loc. cit.*

that this is the case and cites Biblical and patristic examples when God had afflicted his people in order to bring them to amendment.[70]

After dealing with all of the marginalia Erasmus takes up the body of the *XXIII Libri* and endeavors to refute in turn the charges in each of the books. He examines all the topics of their earlier exchanges and generally follows the organization of Alberto's attack. Thus he begins with the defense of the *Moria*, and goes on to his views on monasticism, feast days, ceremonies, decoration of churches, the cult of saints, the veneration of relics, the Virgin, scholastic theology, Scripture versus tradition, the Trinity, the authority of priests and bishops, the primacy of Peter, vows, celibacy, matrimony, confession, faith and works, the right of war, oaths, and mendacity.[71] This wide range of topics which included most of the great debates of the period of the Reformation could not of course be treated exhaustively even in a long apologia and individual subjects are very unevenly handled. Perhaps the liveliest chapter is the defense of the *Moria*, in which Erasmus takes obvious pleasure in demonstrating that Alberto has not understood the intent of the speeches put into the mouth of Folly. On some other topics, such as the question of images, Erasmus's reply was uncharacteristically brief, partly perhaps because he was in substantial agreement with most of Alberto's distinctions and felt that it was hardly worth a long rebuttal to show that he had been misrepresented. He states simply that he had pointed out the dangers of superstition among uneducated people and distinguished between the veneration of saints and the adoration of God.[72]

The peroration of Erasmus's *Apologia* is a culminating and passionate condemnation of the Prince of Carpi:

> Gladly do I welcome his prayer that in the future I utter only what is proper, but I in turn pray for Pio that he may find in the Lord a more equitable and clement judge than he has been toward me . . . . Now the vulgar summon me to recant. But what am I to recant?—the propositions that Pio has formulated?—that *I* wished theologians done away with, that *I* despoil priests of their possessions, that *I* condemn the institution of monasticism, that *I* abrogate the authority of Scripture, that *I* condemn the ceremonies and constitutions of the church, protect the doctrine of the Arians, revive that of Priscillan and the Epicureans, and many other charges more absurd than these?

---

[70] *LB*, IX, col. 1128.
[71] *LB*, IX, cols. 1136-1196.
[72] *LB*, IX, col. 1160 D & E.

Never have I thought in the way that he has interpreted, and up to now he has proved none of those things to which he has so often, so strongly and so bitterly objected. It would be a new kind of recantation if, yielding to men who are delirious with the vice of slandering, I were to become my own accuser. Nay, rather, let them recant who furnish us with an example of the devil, openly and shamelessly fastening libels of this kind on the undeserving and, through such sordid actions, either seek fame or promise themselves vindication and victory, as if Christ were dead and had no care of His Church.[73]

In their attacks on Erasmus and indeed on the whole movement of northern humanism of which he was the chief representative, Girolamo Aleandro and Alberto Pio appear as the first figures of the Counterreformation. They had both been intimately associated with Aldo Manuzio and his press, Aleandro for three years resident in the master's house as a favorite and Alberto in an even closer relationship as former pupil and financial patron who received the dedication of the Aldine edition of Aristotle and other productions. But Venice in the early years of the sixteenth century was not only distinguished because of the achievement of the Aldine press in making available in the original most of the great classics of Greek literature. There were evidences of a revivification of Christian spirituality which a few years later led to the conversion of two young Venetian aristocrats, Vincenzo Quirini and Tommaso Giustiniani, who decided to enter the Camaldolese Order, the first as a hermit and the second as a coenobite. This decision surprised and shocked their contemporaries, but it bore fruit in 1513 in the reform program which they presented to Pope Leo X for the consideration of the Fifth Lateran Council in 1513.[74] Many of the provisions of this program would have been acceptable to Erasmus—condemnation of ignorance among both clergy and laity, and of superstition, necessity for the Bible in the vernacular, reform of monasticism, reorganization of the religious orders, and revision of the canon law. It is a paradox that these two powerful figures, Aleandro and Alberto Pio seem not to have been touched by this reform movement; they never understood the Erasmian emphasis on the importance of the spirit rather than the letter. From their controversy with Erasmus emerged two contrasting views on the causes of the Reformation. They

[73] LB, IX, col. 1196 B-D; cited by Gilmore, "Erasmus and Alberto Pio, Prince of Carpi," Action and Conviction in Early Modern Europe, 315.

[74] See Hubert Jedin, A History of the Council of Trent, trans. Ernest Graf, O.S.B., I (London, 1957), 128.

asserted that the humanist program had led to religious revolution by its application of philology to the Scriptures, by its rejection of scholastic philosophy and theology, and by its questioning of established ecclesiastical institutions and doctrines. Erasmus replied that the Lutheran protest was occasioned by abuses, immoral monks, ignorant priests, worldly prelates, and sophistic theologians. Both of these partial and erroneous views were to enjoy a long continued fortune in polemical historiography. The fact that they were already formulated by 1530 foreshadowed the official condemnation of Erasmus and the victory of the Counterreformation over the cause of Catholic Reform.

The doctrinal program of Alberto's XXIII Books against Erasmus was on the whole accepted by the Council of Trent. The predominant Italian view in the sixteenth century was that Erasmus was a heretic and responsible for Luther. His works were put en bloc on the *Index librorum prohibitorum* of Paul IV and remained with some discrimination on subsequent editions of the Index. This was the official judgement of Rome but it must be remembered that in Italy as in other countries the Erasmian influence was as many-sided as the Erasmian achievement. Although the Counterreformation condemned Erasmus there were aspects of the Catholic reform movement which, if not the direct result of a positive reaction to Erasmus's works, were at least perfectly consonant with his ideas.

III. Erasmus and the Counterreformation

From the time of his first visit to England in 1499 and his association with John Colet, Erasmus had realized the possibilities of biblical scholarship. His discovery of Lorenzo Valla's *Annotationes in Novum Instrumentum* in 1504 confirmed his ambition to devote himself to the edition and translation which he produced in 1516. In the years before and after this edition there were many humanist translations into the vernacular languages and learned commentaries as well as other editions like the *Complutensian Polyglot* of Cardinal Ximenes in Spain. In this situation the Tridentine fathers were confronted with the necessity of asking whether the Latin *Vulgate* was indeed the work of St. Jerome, and how far it could be accepted as in accordance with the original texts. The decree which emerged from commission and was voted on 8 April 1546 affirmed that "haec ipsa vetus et vulgata editio, quae circumferuntur sacrorum librorum, quaenam [illegible]"[75] This [illegible] among members of the Council and authorities at Rome. Alessandro Farnese for the Cardinals' Commission in Rome wrote that the decree was unacceptable since no provision had been made for revision. "It would have been better," he declared, "to leave out the chapter on the authenticity of the *Vulgate*, but since it has been drawn up, we must look for ways and means to tone it down." Many were shocked that there was no mention of the original languages in which the Bible was written. One Roman agent of the Cardinal Legate Cervini wrote, "You have given no small scandal! People in Rome are surprised and dismayed that you speak of the 'ancient, familiar edition,' without describing it more particularly; but the worst is that there is not a single word in the decree on the necessity of revision."[76]

The Papal Legates and Seripando, General of the Augustinian Order, answered the criticisms from Rome, explaining that the decree had been intended to declare the Latin *Vulgate* free of dogmatic *error* without denying that the text was in many places corrupt and that revision in the light of the Hebrew and Greek texts was necessary. Seripando in particular pressed for the appointment of a scholarly commission. No action was taken on this recommendation at the Fourth Session, and Seripando was likewise disappointed when, at the opening of the last period of the Council fifteen years later in 1561, he urged another decree on revision.[77] Thus it seemed that the humanist cause of applying philology to the improvement and understanding of the basic text of Christianity had suffered a defeat. Yet the very fact that men like Cervini and Seripando had pressed for revision of the *Vulgate* was an indication of the strength of the program for which Erasmus had been the principal spokesman. Subsequent pontiffs appointed commissions to undertake the scholarly preparation of a new edition of the *Vulgate* and, although the project made small progress under Pius IV and Pius V, it was prosecuted in earnest under Sixtus V who appointed a group of serious scholars in 1586. Unfortunately the pope became impatient with the slowness

---

[75] Text in Denziger, *Enchiridion Symbolorum* (Freiburg i. B., 1967), 365.

[76] *Concilium Tridentinum. Diariorum, actorum, epistularum, tractatuum nova collectio*, ed. by the Görres-Gesellschaft (Freiburg i. B., 1901 ff.), X (1916), 506, for Farnese's letter, and p. 468 for Cervini's. See Hubert Jedin, *A History of the Council of Trent*, II (1961), 92-98; *idem*, *Papal Legate at the Council of Trent: Cardinal Seripando*, trans. Frederic C. Eckhoff (St. Louis and London, 1947), 283-300.

[77] Jedin, *History of the Council of Trent*, II, 97-98.

of the work and undertook himself to bring the revision to a conclusion, publishing in 1589 the *Sistine Vulgate* with many unjustifiable
emendations of his own, and leaving out of account several thousand
recommendations made by his own commission. These errors were
corrected under Clement VIII with the participation of the great
Jesuit scholar, Robert Bellarmine, and in 1592 appeared the Clemen-
tine revision of the *Sistine Vulgate*.[78] In a longer perspective therefore
it can be said that humanist textual criticism of the *Bible* had its
victories in the Catholic as well as in the Protestant world.

The indirect influence of Erasmus can be traced in another area
of Tridentine debate—the problem of the validity of images in Christian worship. In the *Moria*, in several of the *Colloquies*, and in some
portions of the *Annotationes in Novum Testamentum*, Erasmus had
satirized the superstitions by which the ignorant invoked particular
saints and in fact committed idolatry by considering that the image
itself had a kind of magical power. These passages caused Alberto
Pio to attack Erasmus as an iconoclast.[79] In fact, however, Erasmus in
all of his major pronouncements on the subject was careful to distinguish between the idolatry of antiquity in which the pagans had
believed the *numen* of their gods and goddesses existed in their very
images and the Christian veneration of the images of saints which
was, or should be, purely symbolic. He recognized that there were
abuses which it was the duty of the clergy to correct. He further
recognized the value for moral and religious instruction of statues
and frescoes in churches and chapels.[80] In a letter to Sadoleto written
in March, 1531, he replies to a query of Sadoleto, saying that he has
never anywhere condemned the true veneration of saints in images
and pictures. "But," he declares, "I have condemned superstition
and I define as an example of superstition a soldier about to go into
mercenary service who genuflects before an image of St. Barbara
and recites a few little prayers very like magic in her honor and
promises himself that he will return unharmed. Pictures and symbols
I have never wished demolished although I want nothing seen in

---

[78] *The New Catholic Encyclopedia*, vol. II, pp. 450-451, s.v. Bible.

[79] *XXIII Libri*, fols. CXXXIIIᵛ-CXXXVIIʳ.

[80] On Erasmus's views on the arts in general and images in particular, see
Rachel Giese, "Erasmus and the Fine Arts," *Journal of Modern History*, VII (1935),
257-279; Erwin Panofsky, "Erasmus and Painting," *Journal of the Warburg and
Courtauld Institutes*, XXXII (1969), 200-227; and also Myron P. Gilmore, "Erasmus on Images and the Decrees of the Council of Trent," in *Essays Presented
to George Kaftal* (Florence, 1975).

churches which is not worthy of the place. . . . Any trace of superstition which creeps in through images must be eliminated but
their utility must be preserved." [81] Also in one of his last works,
De amabile ecclesiae concordia, published in 1533, Erasmus emphasized
the representative and symbolic character of Christian art.

> In my opinion, [he says] those who have raged against the images
> of saints have been stimulated to their bigotry however immodest
> not quite without justification. . . . For idolatry is a horrible crime,
> that is, the cult of simulacra, and though long since removed from
> civilized habits, there yet remains the danger that the unwary may fall
> into the snares of demons. But, since sculpture and painting were
> formerly considered among the liberal arts as silent poetry, they may
> sometimes stir human emotions more than a man, however eloquent,
> can do with words. . . . Therefore anyone who is persuaded that no
> honor should be given to the images of the saints since they have no
> sensation should be allowed to enjoy his belief, but let him not object
> to those who, without superstition, so venerate images through the
> love of those whom they represent, that they resemble the new bride,
> who, through love for her absent husband, kisses the ring or chaplet
> which he left or sent. Such devotion cannot be unpleasing to God,
> which springs not from superstition but from overflowing affection.[82]

The whole question of the justification of images which had
been dormant in the western church since the Carolingian period
when the echoes of the iconoclastic controversy in Byzantium
reached the west, was re-opened by Luther and his followers. Luther
himself displayed relative moderation and on his return from the
Wartburg restrained Carlstadt from the breaking of images and the
desecration of churches in Wittenberg. Zwingli and the Swiss reformers were far more radical in this respect as in others. Erasmus
deplored the destruction in Zurich and fled from Basel when the
Reformation triumphed there in 1529. Calvin, whose Institutio
christianae religionis was published in the first edition in 1536 a few
months before Erasmus's death, devoted only a relatively short
comment to the explanation of the second commandment but gave
an incisive condemnation of all images as forbidden by Scripture.[83]
In the subsequent editions this text was much expanded, until in

---

[81]   Allen, 2443, ll. 191-241.
[82]   LB, V, col. 501.
[83]   Ioannis Calvini opera quae supersunt omnia, eds. Johann Wilhelm Baum, Eduard
Cunitz, and Eduard Reuss, 59 vols., Corpus Reformatorum, vols. XXIX-XCVII
(Braunschweig and Berlin, 1863-1900), I, cols. 32-34 (hereafter cited as Calvini opera).

the edition of 1550 it became a treatise *contra imagines* occupying some ten quarto pages in the *Corpus reformatorum* edition. Calvin deals systematically with all the arguments used by the opponents of iconoclasm. A favorite text familiar to all the defenders of images in the west was the dictum of Gregory the Great that statues are the books of the illiterate. Characteristically Calvin pronounced: "So says Gregory but the spirit of God speaks in a completely different sense, and, if Gregory had studied longer in that school, he would never have spoken thus." [84]

Calvin's followers—Theodore Beza in Switzerland, John Knox in Scotland, the Puritan ministers in England—accepted these views and wherever Calvinism spread, images, crucifixes, and frescoes were destroyed.

By the summer of 1561 the gains of the Huguenot party in France had become so considerable as to threaten the outbreak of civil war. In the period after the Treaty of Cateau-Cambrésis and the death of Henry II, many nobles had become protectors of Protestant communities. The political struggle for the control of the royal power during the reigns of two young and weak kings, Francis II and Charles IX, was intensified by the ideological conflict. In this situation the Queen Mother Catharine de Medici, whose aim it was to preserve at all costs the position and prestige of the monarchy, attempted a policy of reconciliation with a considerable degree of tolerance towards the religion *prétendue reformée*. Like some other sixteenth century sovereigns she had very little understanding of the depth of religious conviction that divided her subjects; her hope was that by initiating a dialogue some formula could be found which would preserve the unity of the kingdom and the power of the monarchy. Advised by Admiral Coligny and by the Chancellor de L'Hôpital, she took the radical step of inviting Calvin to send a Protestant delegation to Paris to discuss with representative Catholic theologians and prelates the principal points in dispute. Calvin himself did not come because of uncertainty about the adequacy of measures for security which could be provided in the French capital, but he did decide to send his principal lieutenants. So it came about that there opened on September 9, 1561, at Poissy one of the most extraordinary confrontations of the sixteenth century, when distinguished Protestants like Theodore Beza and Peter Martyr Vermigli met the highest

---

[84] *Institutio*, ed. Geneva, 1550, in *Ibid.*, II, col. 386.

ranks of the French clergy, the Cardinal of Tournon and the Cardinal of Lorraine, in the presence of many bishops, members of Parlement, officers of the crown, and Catharine, her children, and the court.

There came also from Italy the former Papal Legate, Hippolito d'Este, and in his train the new General of the Jesuit Order, Lainez. The chief orators were to be Beza and the Cardinal of Lorraine.

Beza's eloquent address explaining Protestant belief shocked his hearers when he reached the point of denying the real presence, either as transubstantiation or as consubstantiation. This assertion so horrified the assembly that a further exchange of views on other points no longer seemed possible, although Catharine and de L'Hôpital managed to keep a few representatives from each side in negotiations at St. Germain until October 18, when the colloquy was formally closed. The French bishops did produce a series of reform proposals which came to nothing in expectation that the correction of abuses with which they dealt would be taken up by the resumption of the Council of Trent.[85]

Catharine, however, did not give up hope, and after the publication of the Edict of January 13, which gave to the Huguenots a larger degree of toleration than they had previously enjoyed, she assembled at St. Germain a small group consisting of Beza and three colleagues and representatives of the French episcopate and the Faculty of Theology of the University of Paris. She selected the subject of images as one on which she hoped there would be a possibility of agreement.

Participants in this conference had the advantage of a much more detailed and accurate knowledge of the iconoclastic controversy in the Byzantine empire than was available in the earlier Reformation debates on the subject. Neither Luther, Zwingli, Erasmus, nor Calvin before the 1550 edition of the *Institute* show more than a vague knowledge of the eighth-century conflict and the decrees of the various councils. Alberto Pio makes brief reference to it but does not reveal his source. All the western authors in the first decades of the century depended chiefly on the *Letters* of Gregory the Great in taking a position pro or contra images.

---

[85] On the colloquy of Poissy, see the letters of Theodore Beza to Calvin, in *La correspondance de Théodore de Bèze*, eds. Fernand Aubert, Henri Meylan, Alain Dufour, 7 vols., Travaux d'humanisme et renaissance, vols. 40, 49, 61, 74, 96, 113, 136 (Geneva, 1960-1973), II, passim; Lucien Romier, *Catholiques et protestants à la cour de Charles IX* (Paris, 1924), 211-222; and Donald Nugent, *Ecumenism in the Age of the Reformation: The Colloquy of Poissy* (Cambridge, Mass., 1974).

In 1540, however, a learned French bishop, Jean du Tillet, published a series of manuscripts found in the monastery of St. Hilaire at Poitou. First he published in Greek, dedicated to Cardinal Tournon, the canons of the first seven ecumenical councils through the Second Nicea, in which Constantine and his mother Irene had reversed the stand of the previous emperors forbidding the use of images, but affirming that they were not to be adored by *latria*, the form of worship which was reserved for God alone.[86] In the following year he published a Latin translation by Gentian Hervet of these Greek canons, together with extensive quotations from the Greek fathers and a preface by Photius, the Patriarch of Constantinople.[87]

Finally, Bishop Tillet published in 1549 the *Libri Carolini*, a capitulary in the name of Charlemagne, written, as now seems to established, by Theodulph of Orleans in response to a very garbled version of the decrees of the Second Council of Nicea, which had been sent to the pope and by him forwarded to the court of France. This document set out in four books the considerations which should govern the church's doctrine on images. The argument of these books was against image worship because it was supposed, on the basis of the garbled version of Second Nicea, that the Byzantine court had restored a kind of idolatry and the actual subtleties of the Byzantine theologians were not understood. Whether it was because of the pro-iconoclastic arguments, or because of the example of secular interference in a question of ecclesiastical doctrine, the *Libri Carolini* were put on the *Index Librorum prohibitorum*, first in Louvain, secondly by Paul IV, and finally on the *Tridentine Index* of Paul V, where they remained until 1900. In the sixteenth century they were widely attributed to an heretical author, and it was perhaps for this reason that Du Tillet published them under the pseudonym of Elias Phili (interpreted as Elias for John as it was a denomination of John the Baptist, and Phili as an abbreviation of the Greek word for the French *tilleul*, the linden tree from which the family took its name.[88] Calvin cites the *Libri Carolini* as an argument against

---

[86] *Kanones* τῶν Ἀπόστολων καὶ τῶν Ἁγίων Συνόδων (Paris, 1540).

[87] *Canones Sanctorum Apostolorum Conciliorum Generatium et Particularium Sanctorum* (Paris, 1541).

[88] Hubert Bastgen, "Das Capitulare Karls d. Gr. über die Bilder oder die sogenannten *Libri Carolini*," *Neues Archiv der Gesellschaft für ältere deutsche Geschichtskunde*, XXXVII (1911), 16-17. For a fuller discussion of the circumstances of composition, contents, and subsequent editions of the *Libri Carolini*, see Bastgen's other studies in the same journal, vols. XXXVI, pp. 631-636, and

image worship in the 1550 Geneva edition of the *Institutio* and in every subsequent edition for the remainder of his life.

Thus by 1562, when the Council of Trent was summoned to continue its sessions, the historical and doctrinal material available for a debate on iconoclasm was vastly greater than it had been thirty years earlier when Alberto attacked Erasmus. During the discussions at Poissy and St. Germain, a document, presumably prepared by a radical of the Faculty of Theology at Paris, was presented in an extreme attempt to conciliate the Protestants. This document recommended the elimination of all images and allowed only the crucifix which must be placed on the altar. Although Catharine favored this solution at least as a basis of discussion, the uncompromising Beza refused to accept the crucifix. The presumed author of the proposal, Claude d'Espence, a member of the Faculty of Theology was censured by the Faculty and a retraction demanded. D'Espence was a protégé of the Cardinal of Lorraine who had already twice accompanied the Cardinal to sessions of the Council of Trent. He formally denied that he had been the author of the proposal and refused to make a retraction, contenting himself but not his opponents with a declaration that on the matter of images he followed the Fathers and that he never found in the works of Ambrose, Augustine, Jerome, or Gregory that they used the words, "honor, cherish, venerate or adore," of images except that of the Cross.[89]

Although the conference of St. Germain came to an unresolved conclusion, it did not disperse without leaving one document of considerable importance. This was a declaration or *sententia* of the delegates of the Faculty of Theology, who had repudiated the proposed concession and drew up on February 11, 1562, their version of what the true doctrine on images ought to be.

The first paragraph declares:

> The making and keeping of images of Jesus Christ and placing them in churches and oratories is in no way repugnant to the command of God. If images are venerated and honored in such a way that the

---

XXXVII, pp. 15-51, 455-533. For the most recent presentation of the authorship of Theodulph of Orleans, see Ann Freeman, "Theodulph of Orleans and the Libri Carolini," *Speculum*, XXXII (1957), 663-705.

[89] On this conference and the role of D'Espence, see Pierre Feret, *La Faculté de théologie de Paris et ses docteurs les plus célèbres. Époque moderne*, 5 vols. (Paris, 1900-1907), I, 237-240; and Nugent, *Ecumenism*, 190-203.

honor which is given to them is referred to that which they represent, this, by the tradition and custom of the church, is neither idolatry nor superstition, nor is it repugnant to Sacred Scripture which prohibits idolatry alone.

Citation from the Fathers and further examples support this conclusion.

The second paragraph is devoted to abuses:

We do not deny that some abuses against the doctrine and intent of the church can enter into this practice. It would be a plainly intolerable abuse of this kind if any divinity or virtue was thought to exist in the images themselves on account of which they ought to be venerated or honored ... and it is plainly an abuse to seek one image rather than another or to venerate one more than another because it is made of more precious material, or has a more beautiful exterior or is more recent or more ancient. ... And it is also no small abuse if any images are painted or depicted in a shameless or lascivious way which is not suited to the chastity or integrity of the saints whom they represent.

The final paragraph prescribes the necessity of instructing the people so that these abuses may be eliminated.[90]

Although I have found no evidence of direct filiation between Erasmus and the authors of the declaration of St. Germain, it must be remembered that Erasmus's works were widely circulated in Paris in the twenties and thirties, and he had often repeated his ideas on images, emphasizing the same distinctions as are described by the Paris theologians. The very phraseology of the definition of superstition and the condemnation of the abuse of invoking one image rather than another because of its greater material or artistic value were parallelled in several of Erasmus's many discussions of the subject, perhaps most clearly in the *De amabile ecclesiae concordia* of 1533.[91]

Ten months after the failure of the negotiations at St. Germain, the Cardinal of Lorraine with the French delegation arrived at the Council of Trent to participate in the closing sessions. They brought with them the declaration on images of the Paris theologians. Hubert Jedin has shown in detail how the French Cardinal maneuvered the reluctant papal legate Cardinal Morone into including a decree on images in the final agenda of the council. He has also shown how the commission which composed the text of the decree was dominated by the French and, finally, by printing parallel passages has proven

---

[90] The *sententia* is published in *Concilium Tridentinum*, XIII (1938), 581-583.
[91] *LB*, V, cols. 501-502.

that the decree adopted in the congregation session on December 3, 1563, was based on the document of St. Germain.[92]

The text incorporates the conclusions on the legitimacy of images, on the definition of idolatry and superstition, and on the exclusion of lewd or immoral portrayals from the representation of sacred themes, ideas that are to be found many times repeated in the works of Erasmus. These conclusions may have been arrived at independently by the Paris theologians through a study of the same sources that had convinced Erasmus, or they may have been derived from considering the new material on the Byzantine controversies available since the death of Erasmus. Nevertheless we are at least justified in saying that Erasmus gave wide publicity to the ideas and even to the very language which formed the basis for the Tridentine decree on images.

In the case of the *Vulgate*, the Erasmians who had supported the cause of a scholarly revision at the Council had suffered a momentary defeat, although the pressure for applying the results of humanistic theology to the sacred texts continued and finally resulted in action. On the question of images, however, the very language which Erasmus had used was enshrined in a decree of the Council that ironically put some of his works on the *Index*. In view of the later effect of the decree *de sacris imaginibus* on the visual arts in the service of the church, this must be counted not the least important of the uses to which the many-sided legacy of Erasmus was applied.

One of the most prominent aspects of the Catholic reform movement in Italy was the campaign for the reform of the monastic orders. As early as 1510 and 1512 the noble Venetians, Quirini and Giustiniani, had left the secular life for the Camaldolese order. The Fifth Lateran Council considered programs of reform, and in the subsequent decades came the new orders of Capuchins, Somaschi, the Theatines, Barnabites and finally the Jesuits. Most of this creative activity was generated from the traditions of Italian spirituality and was hardly a reaction to either northern humanism or to Protestantism.[93] Can it be said that Erasmus's views on monasticism had any influence in Italy?

---

[92] Hubert Jedin, "Entstehung und Tragweite des Trienter Dekrets über die Bilderverehrung," *Theologische Quartalschrift*, CXVI (1935), 143-148, 404-429. The parallel passages are printed on pp. 181-186.

[93] On monastic reform in Italy, see H. O. Evennett, "The New Orders," in *The New Cambridge Modern History*, ed. G. R. Elton, II (Cambridge, 1958), chap. ix.

Among the commonest accusations brought against Erasmus's
orthodoxy was the charge that he did not believe in the institution
of monasticism and that his works were full of satirical portraits
of monks. It was true that he had himself left the monastery at
Steyn, although finally with a papal dispensation. It was also true
that in the *Moria* and in the *Colloquies* there were many disparaging
pictures of monks.

The subject of monasticism was particularly emphasized by
Alberto Pio in his attack on Erasmus, and the latter replied at greater
length than he did to most of Alberto's charges. He maintains that
Alberto is wrong to cite his descriptions of monastic life in the age
of Jerome as if his intent was to condemn the later development
of monastic institutions. He was simply pointing out the difference
as an historian. Furthermore Jerome in his *Epistles* did not hesitate
to condemn those who had lapsed from their monastic vows. Similarly in all that Erasmus has written about monks he has been careful
to distinguish between the institution and the individual: "Institutum
nusquam improbo, mores plurimorum non probo." [94] In support
of his cause he might have cited the letter to Jodocus Jonas of 13
June 1514 in which he gives an affecting portrait of the lives of John
Colet and a Franciscan, John Vitrier. The latter is presented as a
model of the monastic career.[95]

In a curious publication which appeared in Basel four years after
the death of Erasmus, there are some indications that there was
Italian support for the position that he had condemned only abuses
in monasticism and not the institution itself. This work, a dialogue,
was entitled *In Des. Erasmis Roterodami funus dialogus lepidissimus.*
Its author was Ortensio Lando, a prolific writer and translator of
More's *Utopia* into Italian.[96] There are two interlocutors, Arnoldus,
a German and his friend Anianus, an Italian. Arnoldus has just
returned from Germany, and on their meeting Anianus pressingly
inquires for news of Erasmus. Arnoldus first equivocates and says
that Erasmus is freed from all his troubles but then breaks down

---

[94] *LB*, IX, cols. 1147-1152.
[95] Allen, 1211, ll. 13-243.
[96] On Lando and the *Funus*, see Paul Grendler, *Critics of the Italian World,
1530-1630* (Madison, Wis., 1969), 21-48; and Conor Fahy, "Per la vita di Ortensio
Lando," *Giornale storico della letteratura italiana*, CXLII (1965), 243-258; also
Myron P. Gilmore, "Anti-Erasmianism in Italy: The Dialogue of Ortensio
Lando on Erasmus' Funeral," *The Journal of Medieval and Renaissance Studies*, IV
(1974), 1-14.

and admits that he is dead. Thereupon Anianus begs for a full account, saying that he did not know enough about Erasmus and has read him only with diffidence because of the rumor that Luther whom Rome has condemned drew much from this source. Arnoldus categorically denies this allegation and launches into a panegyric of Erasmus's virtues which is so extravagant as to create the suspicion that it is ironic. Even more than by the deplored death of so great a man, however, Arnoldus says he is afflicted by the behavior of the monks who no sooner heard the news than they mounted a drunken celebration with a parody of the requiem and the eulogy. Even worse, according to Arnoldus's account when the funeral was over and all had left the monks returned and defiled the corpse, cutting out the golden tongue and the lynx-like eyes, chopping off the beautiful hands and limbs, and throwing the remains into the sewer, chanting the while:

> Lude nunc nos si potes, Erasme,
> Lacera nos si potes, O transfuga,
> Morde nunc nos, si vales, lucifuga,
> Transfige nos, si licet, Erasme.[97]

When Anianus inquires why there is such bitter hatred on the part of the monks, his friend tells him that Erasmus wrote a great deal against monks and they have not forgiven him for the attacks. But Anianus replies that Erasmus really wrote against bad monks and condemned them for their abuses so that those who had strayed from the true path might return to it.[98] Arnoldus does not accept this suggestion but affirms again that all the monks were so depraved that they would take no criticism, especially from one as saintly as Erasmus. Anianus rather hesitantly suggests that Arnoldus may be exaggerating to which the latter replies indignantly by mentioning a number of learned Italians who can testify to the saintly qualities of Erasmus's soul. This is matched by Anianus who produces a list of names of those in Italy who he says hate rather than love Erasmus. Arnoldus dismisses this argument and proceeds to a still more extravagant encomium of Erasmus in which he reports a vision of Erasmus in heaven surrounded by angels holding his works on the Scripture and the Fathers, receiving a martyr's palm before the heavenly throne, and interceding for his enemies that they may

---

[97] *Funus*, fol. 18v.
[98] *Funus*, fol. 20r-v.

no longer be punished.[99] This speech, together with the earlier one on the funeral and the desecration of the grave, are so exaggerated that they may well be intended as parodies of both the extreme pro-Erasmian and the extreme anti-Erasmian views.[100]

Anianus now asserts himself to advise Arnoldus to cease weeping, "Erasmus must not be given that place to which you have assigned him." He dismisses the feeble protests of Arnoldus and the latter contents himself with a final request that Anianus will beware of the German monks. This elicits from Anianus a renewed defence of monasticism, "which he says may appear degenerate but which sometimes lights a small fire which will burst out in a great flame of virtue." [101] He cites examples of "good" monks in the current Italian scene and among others lists the brothers Zancho, learned canons of the Lateran, Seripando, the Augustinian who became General of his order, and among Benedictines Isidore Clario, who was occupied with a new edition of the *Vulgate*, and Gregorio Cortese, the monastic reformer and future cardinal. These individuals had in common the fact that they had received a humanistic education and wrote secular works in Latin and Greek as well as contributions to theology, church history, or law: they combined learning and piety.[102]

In a dialogue which was in part devoted to satirizing the extremes of adulation and denigration which the name of Erasmus evoked, it may seem surprising to find at the conclusion this testimony of the influence of the Erasmian ideal of monasticism in Italy, but it seems clear that the author found it possible to separate the various parts of the Erasmian legacy. He could thus reject Erasmian theology, and, although answering ambiguously the question how far Erasmus had brought souls back to Christ, he could register the influence and the efficacy of Erasmus's ideal of monasticism in the developing Counterreformation.

Finally in considering Erasmus and the Counterreformation, what can be said of an Erasmian influence on the most important of the new orders created by the Catholic Church—the Society of Jesus? Although its founder was a Spaniard and its recruitment

---

[99] *Funus*, fols. 27r-31v.

[100] I owe this suggestion to Professor Conor Fahy of Birkbeck College, University of London.

[101] *Funus*, fol. 37r.

[102] *Funus*, fols. 37r-41r. Cf. Gilmore, "Anti-Erasmianism in Italy," 12-14.

international, the order was established in Rome; its members
played a role of critical importance at the Council of Trent, and
its colleges and educational curriculum were first developed in
Italian centers.

The relationship between the *Enchiridion* and the *Spiritual Exercises*
is filled with ambiguity. Ignatius de Loyola was certainly in Alcalá
in 1526 and 1527, when the influence of the *Enchiridion* and other
works of Erasmus was at its height: he was friendly with the Eguía
family who published Erasmus's books. It is also asserted by Jesuit
authorities that the teaching in the *Exercises* on the use of means
in view of our last end is taken from a page of the *Enchiridion*.[103]
On the other hand there are the anecdotes that Loyola's confessor
advised him to read the *Enchiridion* and that he refused, or, in another
version, that he read part of it and then stopped because "his spiritual
ardor was cooled." [104] He left Alcalá after two inquiries into his
orthodoxy and went first to Salamanca and then to Paris, where in
1528 the works of Erasmus were examined by the Sorbonne and
the French translator and follower of Erasmus, Louis de Berquin,
was condemned to the stake. In the next year he probably journeyed
to Brussels to see the Spanish Erasmian, Luis Vives, who was teaching
there. Of this interview he apparently retained a negative impression.[105]
The fact that the *Enchiridion* and the *Spiritual Exercises* are alike
in being methodical manuals for entering into Christian spirituality
and that they are both Christocentric has perhaps led many students
to exaggerate the influence of the first on the second. There was
nothing new about a methodical approach to spiritual experience,
and both may be said to be indebted to medieval precedent and
especially to the pietistic tradition in the Netherlands.

It is nevertheless true that the years of the formation and approval
of the order do show some points of contact between Erasmian
humanism and Loyolan spirituality. At the end of December, 1536,
when the little band of Loyola's Paris disciples was journeying to
meet him in Venice, they arrived at Basel and, as pilgrim scholars,
paid their homage at the tomb of Erasmus in the Cathedral. This
was the moment when Cardinal Contarini, whose theology may be

---

[103] Joseph de Guibert, S. J., *The Jesuits, Their Spiritual Doctrine and Practice*,
trans. W. J. Young, S. J. (Chicago, 1964), 159.

[104] Marcel Bataillon, *Erasme et l'Espagne; recherches sur l'histoire spirituelle*
(Paris, 1937), 229-230; and Guibert, *op. cit.*, 165, n. 36.

[105] De Guibert, *The Jesuits*, 164-165; and esp. Ricardo Garcia-Villoslada,
Loyola y Erasmo: Dos almas, dos epocas (Madrid, 1965), 217-233.

considered at least in part "Erasmian," was supporting Ignatius in his effort to get approval of the Order, and Pope Paul III had named several Erasmians to the commission that produced the *Consilium de emendanda ecclesiae*.[106]

After the organization of the Order and the drawing up of its constitutions, the attitude of Loyola towards both Erasmus and Vives hardened. In 1548 there were added to the *Exercises* the *Regulae ad orthodoxe sentiendum* which included exhortations to many observances and ceremonies which Erasmus had made light of as having more to do with the outer man than with the inner spirit.[107] Furthermore in 1555 instructions were sent to all the Jesuit colleges to destroy certain books as unsuitable for young scholars but to put aside those of Erasmus and Vives for further decision. Eventually even the grammatical works of Erasmus were removed from the Jesuit schools and were replaced with those by Jesuit authors, although the forbidden books continued to find a place in the catalogues of some of the Jesuit schools.[108]

Yet in spite of the prohibitions of the *Index* and the directives of the Jesuit Generals there were some areas of Jesuit thought with which Erasmus might have found himself in substantial agreement. The Jesuit theologians became the most extreme defenders in the Roman communion of the doctrine of the freedom of the will, and, although the Erasmus of the *Diatribe De libero arbitrio* and the first and second *Hyperaspistes* would not have felt himself at home with all their theological arguments, this was still the position on which he had taken his stand. If he could have lived to see the controversy between Jesuits and Jansenists in the seventeenth century, he would probably have sided with the Jesuits, however much he deplored the style in which the debate was conducted.

The second area is that of education, both primary and secondary. In spite of the prohibition of Erasmian grammatical and pedagogic books, the essential characteristics of Erasmus's educational system survived in the Jesuit schools as they did also in the Protestant schools in northern Europe. Both communions came to accept

---

[106] Richard Douglas, *Jacopo Sadoleto, Humanist Reformer* (Cambridge, Mass., 1958), 124; and Ricardo Garcia-Villoslada, "La Muerte de Erasmo," in *Miscellanea Giovanni Mercati*, 5 vols. (Rome, 1946), IV, 496. The visit to Erasmus's tomb is described by one of the participants, Simon Rodriguez, in *De origine et progressu Societatis Jesu*, ed. P. Boero (Rome, 1869).

[107] Bataillon, *Erasme et l'Espagne*, 768-769.

[108] Garcia-Villoslada, *Loyola y Erasmo*, 233-277.

the humanist emphasis on the importance of the knowledge of the classical languages and literatures. Indeed it may be suggested that in the Jesuit schools with their cult of the spoken Latin and their re-enactment of classical drama, the spirit of Erasmian pedagogy survived more than in Protestant Europe. No doubt Erasmus would have been unhappy with the rigidities of dogmatic orthodoxy imposed by the Jesuits and the Council of Trent, but in a European Christendom divided by religious war, the history of education shows that at least an important part of the Erasmian legacy was not lost in the ideological struggle.

IV. ERASMUS AND THE EVANGELICALS AND RADICALS

The indictment of Erasmus as the precursor of Luther and the man really responsible for the religious revolution, made in its most complete form by Alberto Pio, was publicly accepted by the Counterreformation Church. Alberto had exclaimed that either "Luther Erasmized or Erasmus Lutherized," and this fallacious identification came to prevail over any more discriminating judgment of Erasmus's religious position. Although Paul III had been willing to offer Erasmus a cardinal's hat, Paul IV put all his works on the *Index*. Even, however, when the Counterreformation had triumphed over the earlier cause of Catholic reform, there were some members of the hierarchy like Cardinals Seripando, Madruzzo, and Pole who remained to a greater or lesser degree representatives of an Erasmian influence; and, as we have seen, without being attached directly to Erasmus's name, that influence made itself felt in the continuing tradition of humanistic philology applied to the sacred texts, in the definition of the church's doctrine on images, and in the areas of monastic reform and education.

In another sector of Italian intellectual and religious life in the sixteenth century, the impact of Erasmus's religious message was direct and of great importance, although difficult to trace.

This message was in large part transmitted through Spain. The University of Alcalá, founded by Cardinal Ximenes de Cisneros, had applied the program of humanism to its curriculum and to the study of Christian texts. Among its professors and students were the first enthusiastic supporters of Erasmus in Spain. His influence began to grow relatively late in his career. The *Querula pacis* (1517) was translated into Spanish in 1520, but the widespread popularity

of Erasmus in Spain began only after the condemnation of Luther
and the involvement of Erasmus in controversy with him.[109]

In 1524-1525 the University printer of Alcalá brought out some
of Erasmus's most important works as re-issues in Latin. These
included the *Paraphrases on the Gospel and Epistles*, the *Exomologesis*,
and the *Enchiridion*. It is significant that the *Colloquies* and the *Moria*
were not among these first reprints, so that the image of Erasmus
which came to be dominant in Spain in the third decade of the
century was less the ironic satirist of abuses and follies in contemporary life than the serious and devout apostle of the *philosophia
Christi*.[110]

Many of these works were soon translated into the vernacular,
and among them the most significant was the *Enchiridion*. This
manual of Christian piety, first published in 1503, appealed directly
to those currents in the Spanish religious life which emphasized the
possibility of direct religious experience and of receiving the grace
of God without the intervention of ceremonies and sacraments. In
the fifth rule Erasmus expands on this thesis: "I think there are far
too many who count up how many times they attend mass and rely
almost entirely on this for their salvation," and, "No veneration
of Mary is more beautiful than the imitation of her humility." And
in conclusion, "Advance from the body to the spirit, from the
visible world to the invisible, from things sensible to things intelligible, from things compound to things simple." [111] Alfonso Fer-
nandez, the Archdeacon of Alcor, who was responsible for the
translation, wrote triumphantly to Erasmus that, whereas formerly
the *Enchiridion* had been read by the few who were skilled in Latin,
"there is now hardly anyone who does not have in hand the Spanish
version in the imperial court, in cities, in churches, in monasteries,
and even in inns." [112]

Among the younger generation of Spanish students who came
into contact with Erasmian evangelism were the brothers, Alfonso
and Juan de Valdés. Born of a noble family and in part self-taught in
the classical languages, they were both precocious students, and Alfonso, while still a young man, became a devoted disciple of Erasmus.

He had entered the imperial service when he was only nineteen

---

[109] Cf. Bataillon, *Erasme et l'Espagne*, chaps. 1-3.

[110] *Ibid.*, 173-177.

[111] *Enchiridion militis Christiani*, trans. John P. Dolan (New York, 1964), 65,
66, 71.

[112] Allen, 1904.

and was present at the coronation of the emperor at Aix la Chapelle
and at the Diet of Worms in the following year. By 1526 he had
become the emperor's principal Latin secretary. In the summer
of the next year after the Sack of Rome he produced, in the style
of an Erasmian colloquy, a dialogue between Lactantius and an
Archdeacon, absolving the emperor of blame for the sack and interpreting it as a judgment of God on the papacy for the policies of
Clement VII and the evil abuses in the church. This occasioned an
attack on Alfonso by Baldassare Castiglione, the papal nuncio in
Spain, perhaps stimulated against Valdés by the jealousy of a rival
secretary at the court. The attack was dismissed by the Inquisitor
General, but Alfonso remained suspect in the eyes of the powerful
Dominicans. He wrote a second dialogue between Mercury and
Charon in 1529, defending the imperial policies against the intrigues
of Francis I of France. After 1529 he left Spain with the imperial
court for the coronation at Bologna and subsequently conferred
with Melanchthon on the Augsburg Confession, which he afterwards translated into Italian at the emperor's request. He died of
the plague in Vienna in 1532, still faithful to the Erasmian ideals
which he had tried to realize in the service of Charles V.[113]

His brother Juan's relationship to Erasmus's thought is far more
complicated. Although the brothers are spoken of as twins, it is
probable that Juan was some years younger than Alfonso. Little
is known of his early years in the family house in Cuenca. In 1523,
when he was probably about fourteen, he entered the household of
the Marques Villena at Escalona. There he came under the influence
of an *alumbrado*, Pedro Ruiz de Alcaraz, who had a profound effect
on his spiritual orientation. After the arrest of Alcaraz by the Inquisition in 1524, Juan left Escalona, and the next secure date in
his biography is December, 1527, when he is enrolled at the University of Alcalá. There he entered the arts faculty and especially
took Greek and studied the New Testament under Francisco de
Vergara. In January, 1529, the University printer Miguel de Eguiá
brought out the *Dialogo de Doctrina Christiana*.[114]

---

[113] On Alfonso de Valdés, see Jose C. Nieto, *Juan de Valdés and the Origins
of the Spanish and Italian Reformation*, Travaux d'humanisme et renaissance, 108
(Geneva, 1970), 171-175; and John Edward Longhurst, *Alfonso de Valdés and
the Sack of Rome* (Albuquerque, N.M., 1952), 1-16.

[114] On Juan de Valdés, see Bataillon, *Erasme et l'Espagne*, 368-390 and passim;
John Edward Longhurst, *Erasmus and the Spanish Inquisition: The Case of Juan
de Valdés* (Albuquerque, N.M., 1950); and esp. Nieto, *Juan de Valdés*.

This dialogue is also modelled on the Erasmian *Colloquies*. There are three characters: Antronio, an ignorant parish priest; Eusebio, a monk who seems to represent the author himself; and Pedro de Alva, Archbishop of Granada, an historical personage. Eusebio has heard Antronio giving instruction to the children of his parish and, appalled at his ignorance, has proposed that they seek the wisdom of the Archbishop about how the elements of Christianity should be imparted. In a monastery garden in Granada they put their question to the Archbishop who expounds the basic tenets of Christianity. He begins with the Apostles' Creed and continues with the ten commandments, the seven sins, the seven virtues, the seven gifts of the Holy Spirit, the five commandments of the church, and the Lord's prayer. At the end there is a brief summary of the Bible and selections from St. Matthew.[115]

Besides being cast in the form of an Erasmian colloquy, this dialogue has passages borrowed directly from Erasmus, the most important of which is the description of the creed, which is taken from Erasmus's colloquy *Inquisitio de fide* of 1524. These facts have led to its being interpreted as an essentially extended application of the exposition in the *Enchiridion* of the Pauline doctrines on the importance of the spirit above the letter and the membership of all Christians in the body of Christ. It was seen as a synthesis between Erasmian spiritualism and the native, Spanish mystical and quietist tradition with which Valdés had come into contact at Escalona.

In 1970, however, Professor José Nieto argued that the Erasmian influence had been much exaggerated. He pointed out that the spiritualism of Alcaraz and of Valdés was theocentric, insisting on the absolute incapacity of the human soul to be justified without a free gift of divine grace, whereas Erasmus in the *Enchiridion* and elsewhere had emphasized what the individual could do to participate in the process of regeneration. Erasmus, for example, at the beginning of the *Enchiridion*, exclaims, "The human mind has never strongly commanded itself anything it has failed to accomplish!" Such confidence in human reason, even understood as spirit, is at the opposite pole from the theocentric mysticism which Nieto finds in Alcaraz and in Valdés.[116]

---

[115] The only known copy of this dialogue was discovered and edited in facsimile by Marcel Bataillon (Coimbra, 1925). On its interpretation, see Bataillon, *Erasme et l'Espagne*, 374-390; Longhurst, *Erasmus and the Spanish Inquisition*, 79-94; and Nieto, *Juan de Valdés*, 114-141.

[116] Nieto, *Juan de Valdés*, 111.

If this argument be accepted, it is still necessary to explain why Valdés should have given such an Erasmian coloring to his *Dialogo*, borrowing actual passages from Erasmus and recommending the reading of his works. This difficulty Professor Nieto ingeniously answers by suggesting that Valdés purposely introduced the Erasmianism in his *Dialogo* in order to win the support of the powerful Erasmians at Alcalá against the Inquisition. His former master, Alcaraz, had been arrested and his doctrines already condemned. If Valdés appeared as a simple follower of Alcaraz, he would certainly be in most immediate danger, but if he seemed to be joining the Erasmian movement just at that time at the peak of its popularity he might avoid condemnation.[117]

If these were indeed his motives, Valdés was speedily disillusioned. Almost immediately after the publication of his *Dialogo*, the Inquisitor General Alonso Manrique appointed a commission of theologians from the University of Alcalá to examine the work for heresy. This commission was dominated by the influential, pro-Erasmian party and Juan was acquitted.[118]

The decision, however, gave him only a brief respite from persecution. By 1531 the fears aroused by the increasing progress of the Reformation in Germany and Switzerland and the attacks against the influence of Erasmus had caused the Inquisition to take up again the question of the *Dialogo*, and this time Juan could no longer count on highly placed support. The process before the Inquisition which involved both Juan's and his brother's *Dialogos* dragged on through 1531 and before the final verdict Juan fled to Italy.[119] Although the record of the trial is lost, it is clear that the dialogue was condemned as heretical, and it was later put on every Spanish list of forbidden books. So complete was the destruction that it was only in 1925 that Bataillon found a copy in the National Library in Lisbon and published a facsimile.

By August of 1531 Juan had reached Rome, where he established relations with the Spanish humanist, Sepulveda, and, probably through the influence of his brother, was subsequently appointed as an imperial secretary and papal chamberlain. In 1533 he was briefly offered the position of archivist in the city of Naples but returned to Rome and remained there until the death of Clement VII in 1534.

---

[117] *Ibid.*, 137.
[118] Longhurst, *Erasmus and the Spanish Inquisition*, 35-45.
[119] *Ibid.*, 47-51.

He then moved again to Naples and settled there, creating a center for religious instruction and conversation until his death in 1541.[120]

During the six years of his residence in Naples at a villa in the district of Chiaia, Valdés gathered about him an extraordinary circle of friends and disciples. Many were aristocratic women like his close friends Giulia Gonzaga and Vittoria Colonna. Others were ecclesiastics like Bernardo Ochino, General of the Capuchin Order, Peter Martyr Vermigli, and Pietro Carnesecchi. But in addition to influencing individuals who were highly placed in secular or religious life, he worked also to reach the common people.[121]

The literary and religious works composed during the Neapolitan period were all posthumously published. They included *The Christian Alphabet*, a dialogue with Giulia Gonzaga, the *Dialogo* on the Spanish Language, and the translations and commentaries on Scripture. The interpretation of Christianity presented in these works is consonant with the spirituality of the *Dialogo de doctrina Christiana* but more explicit on such subjects as justification by faith and Christian liberty. Consider, for example, the passage toward the end of the *Alfabeto Christiano*, where Giulia begs Valdés to tell her "in two words about Christian liberty." Valdés replies,

> You know, Signora, that Christian liberty is a thing which, however much it is reasoned about, and however good the conduct be, can never be understood if it be not experienced; so that you will know so much of it as you experience it in your soul, and no more. . . . But at all events I wish to say this: that it appears according to what St. Paul says: "though I be free from all, yet have I made myself the servant unto all, that I might gain them all for Christ"; the liberty of the Christian is in the conscience, for the real and perfect Christian is free from the tyranny of the law, from sin and from death, and is absolute lord of his affections and appetites. And on the other part he is the servant of all as to the outward man, because he is subject to serve the necessities of the body, to keep the flesh subject, and to serve his neighbors according to his power, either with his faculties, if gifted with them, or with good doctrine, if this be added, and with the example of a good and holy life. So that such a Christian person is free as regards the spirit, acknowledging no other superior than God, and as to the body, he is subject to everybody in the world for Christ's sake.[122]

---

[120] Nieto, *Juan de Valdés*.

[121] *Ibid.*, 147, n. 44. For a list of the disciples of Valdés at Naples, see *Spiritual and Anabaptist Writers*, eds. George H. Williams and Angel M. Mergal, The Library of Christian Classics, XXV (Philadelphia and London, 1957), 304-305.

[122] Juan de Valdés, *Alfabeto Christiano*, ed. and trans. Benjamin Wiffen (London, 1861), 192.

Valdés died at a moment when the Counterreformation was beginning to triumph in Italy over the cause of Catholic reform. The failure of the Colloquies of Worms and Regensburg, the approval of the Jesuit order, the establishment of the Inquisition, and the summoning of the Council of Trent mark a decisive change in the posture of Rome towards protestantism. The heritage of Valdés was ambiguous and his disciples took different directions. Ochino and Peter Martyr Vermigli fled Italy and embraced the protestant cause. Carnesecchi was burned as a heretic in 1567, Giulia Gonzaga died in 1561, believing herself in the Catholic communion as Valdés had done; but Pius V said at the time of the Carnesecchi trial that if she had still been living she would have been burned at the stake.[123]

The research of Professor Nieto has presented a Valdés whose theology was not influenced by medieval mysticism, by Erasmus, or by contact with the sources of the northern Reformation. Instead, he derived his basic themes from the *alumbrado* Alcaraz. These were stated in the *Dialogo de doctrina Christiana* and further developed in his later works.[124] If this interpretation be accepted, there remains no contrast between an earlier "Erasmian" Valdés and the later reformer, some of whose doctrines are so close to protestantism. The borrowings from Erasmus in the *De doctrina* are to be understood as an effort to escape the danger of persecution for embracing the ideas of Alcaraz who was already in the prison of the Inquisition. Therefore the influence of Erasmus on the Valdesian movement is better described as one of form than of content. The tone not only of the earlier *Dialogo* but also of the conversation between Valdés and Giulia Gonzaga is reminiscent of the *Colloquies*. The emphasis on persuasion and the effort to create an atmosphere of mutual understanding rather than dogmatic assertion runs through the Erasmian program from the *Enchiridion* to the *Paraclesis*, the *Colloquies* and finally the *Ecclesiastes*. Although Valdés did not find in Erasmus his theocentric theology, he did find in Erasmian humanism a congenial mode of expounding it.

Certain other sectors of Italian religious life in the sixteenth century were more directly influenced by aspects of Erasmus's scholarship and the *philosophia Christi*.

Michael Servetus was another Spaniard who, like Alfonso de Valdés, came to Italy in 1529 in the train of the emperor for the

---

[123] Nieto, *Juan de Valdés*, 167, n. 122.
[124] *Ibid.*, 333.

historic meeting at Bologna. He had been born probably in 1511, and at the age of fourteen he was attached to the service of Juan de Quintana, a highly placed Franciscan, who was sympathetic to the general interest in the works of Erasmus which prevailed at Alcalá and other centers of Spain in the twenties. Under Quintana's tutelage he presumably studied the liberal arts and the classical languages. He was then sent by his patron to the University of Toulouse, a great center of legal studies, to study the civil and canon law. After two years there he interrupted his legal career to go to Italy with Quintana who now had become confessor to the emperor. At Bologna the young Servetus was a witness to the pageantry of the meeting between pope and emperor. Like Valdés, he was disgusted by the submission of Charles V to Clement VII which involved the observance of the traditional custom of kissing the pope's slipper. In his *Restitutio christianismi* (an Erasmian title) of 1553 he wrote, looking back,

> With these very eyes we have seen him (the Pope) borne in pomp on the necks of princes, making with his hand the sign of the cross, and adored in the open streets by all the people on bended knee, so that those who were able to kiss his feet or slippers, counted themselves more fortunate than the rest, and declared that they had obtained many indulgences, and that on this account the infernal pains would be remitted for many years. O vilest of beasts, most brazen of harlots! [125]

This revulsion seems to combine the kind of reaction which Erasmus had felt in 1506, when he witnessed Pope Julius II's triumphal entry into conquered Bologna, with the denunciations of papal power characteristic of the spiritual Franciscans.

Shortly after the imperial coronation Servetus made his way to Basel, where he took up residence with the principal reformer of that city, Oecolampadius, and brought out in 1531 the *De erroribus trinitatis*.

His doubts about the Trinity had been stimulated by his biblical studies in which he had probably used the *Complutensian Polyglot*, which had been printed under the supervision of Cardinal Ximenes de Cisneros in 1516 and published in 1522. It has been plausibly argued that he did not use the *Novum Instrumentum* of Erasmus, since in his text and translation Erasmus had omitted the so-called Johan-

---

[125] For the preceding paragraph, see Roland H. Bainton, *Hunted Heretic: The Life and Death of Michael Servetus, 1511-1553* (Boston, 1953), 3-20. The quotation from the *Restitutio* is from the edition of Vienne, 1553, p. 462.

nine comma, I John 5·8, "There are three that bear record in heaven,
the Father, the Word and the Holy Spirit, and these three are One,"
on the grounds that there was no authority in the Greek manuscripts
for this addition. If Servetus had used the Erasmian version, he would
undoubtedly have relied on this argument. However it is clear that
he did use the Erasmian edition of St. Hilary of 1523, in the preface
to which Erasmus had cast doubts about the possibility of a philosophical explanation of the Trinity.[126] Had Alberto Pio lived to see
the *De erroribus trinitatis*, printed in the very same year as his attack
on Erasmus, he would have welcomed it as sustaining his charge
that Erasmus was a supporter of the Arians, regardless of the fact
that Servetus and other anti-Trinitarians drew on many other sources
besides Erasmus in the history of Christian apologetics.

On numerous other subjects besides the Trinity, Erasmus provided
material for the radical and evangelic movements in Italy as well as
in the north. His emphasis on the importance of the spirit rather than
the letter, and on what could be accomplished by the human will, his
appeal for a return to the purity of the primitive church, his denuncia-
tion of war in secular society and of abuses in the institutional church,
and his inclination toward toleration, found assent in whole or in
part among radical anabaptists and catholic evangelists.[127]

V. ERASMUS AND THE CICERONIANS

Erasmus published in Basel in March 1528 the *Ciceronianus*, and
this witty and penetrating dialogue alienated many of the lesser
Italian humanists by its attack on their Latin style as well as their
religious opinions.

The dialogue opens with the meeting between Bulephorus, who
represents Erasmus, and Hypologus with their old friend Nosoponus
who is pining away because of his passion for Cicero. He has removed
all books not by Cicero from his library and filled his house with
images of the great orator. The first part of the dialogue presents a
satiric picture of the difficulties and inconsistencies of attempting a
complete imitation of Cicero's vocabulary and style. The discussion
of what vocabulary and idioms are permitted and what forbidden by

---

[126] Bainton, *Hunted Heretic*, 34-35.
[127] On Erasmus's relation to evangelicals and radicals, see George H. Williams,
The Radical Reformation (Philadelphia, 1962), 8-26; and Delio Cantimori, *Eretici
italiani del Cinquecento* (Florence, 1939), 42-49, 196-201.

this canon gives occasion for a display of Erasmus's command of the Latin language.[128]

Bulephorus becomes more serious in his objections when he raises the question of the relationship of language and history. When Nosoponus is persuaded to agree that language must be relevant to contemporary life, Bulephorus then asks how it can be maintained that the situation of the present century is at all like that in which Cicero lived:

> What effrontery then would he have who should insist that we speak on all occasions as Cicero did. Let him bring back to us first Rome as it was; let him give us the senate and the senate house, the Conscript Fathers, the knights, the people in tribes and centuries; let him give back the college of augurs and soothsayers, the chief priests, the flamens and the vestals, the aediles, praetors, tribunes of the people, consuls, dictators, ... Wherever I turn I see things changed, I stand on another stage, I behold a different play, nay, even, another world.[129]

Bulephorus (that is, Erasmus) goes on to illustrate the same point from his own experiences years before in Rome. He recounts that Phaedrus (Tommaso Inghirami), papal secretary and orator, had been invited to preach a sermon on the death of Christ before Julius II and the papal court. He gave an elaborate rhetorical performance with many compliments to the pope whom he addressed as Jupiter Optimus Maximus. The sermon was filled with classical figures of speech and reference to classical history and mythology but totally failed to convey the Christian significance of the subject.[130]

The interlocutors conclude that the imitation of Cicero is thus not only inappropriate at the present day because of the movement of history but is also positively harmful in deflecting men from the Christian religion. "It is paganism," says Bulephorus,

> which influences our ears and minds. We are Christians only in name. The body is baptized in sacred water, but the mind is unwashed; the

---

[128] Text of the *Ciceronianus* in *LB*, I, cols. 974-1026; and English translation by Iorza Scott, in *Controversies over the Imitation of Cicero as a Model for Style and Some Phases of their Influence on the Schools of the Renaissance*, Teachers College, Columbia University, Contributions to Education, No. 35 (New York, 1910), Part II, 19-30.

[129] Scott, *Controversies*, 61-62; see also Myron P. Gilmore, "Fides et eruditio: Erasmus and the Study of History," in *Humanists and Jurists* (Cambridge, Mass., 1963), 87-114.

[130] Scott, *Controversies*, 62-65.

forehead is signed with the cross, the mind curses the cross; we profess Jesus with our mouths, we wear Jupiter Optimus Maximus and Romulus in our hearts.[131]

Bulephorus confesses that he has in the past himself been afflicted by the disease of Ciceronianism but has been healed by reason. He exhorts his friends to consider the meaning of the title of Ciceronian and whether it can be justly applied to anyone but Cicero himself. This leads to a survey of ancient and modern authors, and finally to an account of the revival of learning and scholarship from the time of Petrarch to Erasmus's contemporaries. This is naturally concentrated first on Italy and subsequently on the important figures of northern humanism. Erasmus has here provided in a surprisingly complete and discriminating outline one of the first accounts of the significance of the Italian Renaissance.[132]

In the conclusion, Bulephorus rejects the exaggeration of the Ciceronians: he would give to Cicero the first place in the curriculum but not have him slavishly imitated. And,

> He who is so much of a Ciceronian that he is not quite a Christian is not even a Ciceronian because he does not speak fittingly, does not know the subject thoroughly, does not feel deeply those things of which he speaks, ... the liberal arts, philosophy and oratory are learned to the end that we may know Christ, that we may celebrate the glory of Christ.
> This is the whole scope of learning and eloquence. And we must learn this, viz., that we may imitate what is essential in Cicero which does not lie in words or in the surface of speech but in facts and ideas, in power of mind and judgment.[133]

With this we return to the message of the *Enchiridion* and the *Paraclesis*. Bulephorus's cure by the application of reason is accepted by his companions, and Nosoponus declares that he feels only some remnants of that long familiar illness.

The *Ciceronianus* evoked responses not only in Italy but all over Europe. The most violent came from France. The first was from the pen of Julius Caesar Scaliger, an Italian adventurer who had come into France in the service of a Della Rovere who was Bishop of Agen. He had studied at Padua and Bologna and, on reading the *Ciceronianus*, thought he might use the occasion to bring himself to public notice

---

[131] *Ibid.*, 73.
[132] *Ibid.*, 94-118.
[133] *Ibid.*, 129.

and wrote hastily the *Pro Marco Tullio Cicerone contra Desid. Erasmum Roterodamum*. He sent it to the University of Paris, but this copy was lost, and he did not succeed in having it published until 1531. Erasmus took no notice of it and persisted in thinking that it was the work of his enemies, Aleandro or Beda. When he was informed that Erasmus did not think him the author of the *Oratio*, Scaliger composed a second *Oratio*, more scurrilous than the first. This however was published after Erasmus's death.[134]

A second indictment of Erasmus for the *Ciceronianus* came in France from the young Etienne Dolet at Lyons. Dolet had studied in Italy at Padua and come completely under the influence of the Italian Ciceronians. His master there, Simon de Villeneuve, had been the successor of Longolius, one of the principal targets of criticism in the *Ciceronianus*. Dolet composed and published in 1535 a *Dialogus de Ciceroniana imitatione pro C. Longolio*. The interlocutors in this dialogue are Thomas More and Simon de Villeneuve, and the latter is made to be the mouthpiece of the most abusive criticism of Erasmus. As in the case of Scaliger, Erasmus took no public notice of this attack but again supposed it came from the pen of Aleandro.[135]

In Italy among the leading "Ciceronians" Pietro Bembo and Jacopo Sadoleto were sufficiently admirers and friends of Erasmus that they did not join the attack. Most of those who entered the controversy in defense of Cicero were lesser men of letters, eager to make a reputation by attacking the great name of Erasmus. Such a one was Ortensio Lando, the author of the satiric *Erasmi Funus* of 1540, who brought out in 1534 two small dialogues, *Cicero relegatus* and *Cicero revocatus*. In the first a group of friends decided on the banishment of Cicero because of his faults. When in the second the decree is announced in Rome, there is a great outcry and the previous accusations are refuted so at the end Cicero is returned with triumph.[136]

Another anti-Erasmian who rose to the defense of Rome and Italy against the "barbarian" north was Petrus Cursius, the Roman academician and poet who published in 1534 a *Defensio pro Italia ad Erasmum Roterodamum* dedicated to Pope Paul III. Rather than an attack on the *Ciceronianus* this work was directed against the alleged slighting

---

[134] See the account in Augustin Renaudet, *Erasme et l'Italie*, Travaux d'humanisme et renaissance, 15 (Geneva, 1954), 205-206, 232, 233.

[135] *Ibid.*, 234; Scott, *Controversies*, 63-97; Richard Copley Christie, *Etienne Dolet, Martyr of the Renaissance* (London, 1899), 195-228.

[136] Scott, *Controversies*, 98-99.

remarks made by Erasmus on the warlike capacities of the Tullian people in his Adage "Myconius calvus."[137] In a letter to his young Portuguese friend, Damian de Goes,[138] and in a *Responsio* dedicated to John Choler,[139] Erasmus replied somewhat disingenuously, basing his defense on the contention that the word "bellax" was pejorative and therefore that to say that it was rare to find an Italian *bellax* was a compliment rather than an insult.

Among the most interesting of the Italian defenders of Erasmus in the Ciceronian controversy is Francesco Florido Sabino, the former secretary of Alberto Pio, who had corrected and published the *XXIII Libri contra Erasmum*. After the death of Alberto in 1531, he had returned to Italy and become a professor of Latin at Bologna. During this period he became tutor to two members of the Farnese family. On the publication of Dolet's *Dialogue* Florido wrote a bitter attack on it, filled with personal abuse against the author as well as a refutation of the charges brought against Erasmus.[140] Florido alleged that Dolet stole a large part of his material from other scholars, also that he was ignorant of Latin, and, most important, that he was irreligious and did not believe in the immortality of the soul, which is in fact the charge on which Dolet was burned in Paris in 1546.[141] Dolet immediately replied to this attack with a pamphlet entitled *de imitatione Ciceroniana adversus Floridum Sabinum*, published in 1540, in which he charged Florido with having appropriated one of his dialogues from his former patron, the Prince of Carpi. Florido responded with still another repetitive polemic in the following year.[142]

It may seem somewhat surprising that Florido, who had seemed so convinced of the justice of Alberto Pio's accusations against Erasmus when he published the *XXIII Libri* in 1531, should now have come so enthusiastically to his defense only a few years later. Some explanation is provided by Florido himself in the *Lectiones succisivae*, where

---

[137] See Margaret Mann Phillips, *The Adages of Erasmus* (Cambridge, 1964), 160-161; and also Allen, XI, pp. 113, 114.

[138] Allen, 3019.

[139] Allen, 3032, ll. 33-101.

[140] On Francesco Florido, see Christie, *Etienne Dolet*, 281-286; Remigio Sabbadini, "Vita e opere di Francesco Florido Sabino," *Giornale storico della letteratura italiana*, VIII (1886), 333-363. The text of Florido's reply is printed in his *Opera* (Basel, 1540), "Lectiones succissivae," Bk. I, chaps. 2-3, and Bk. III, chap. 4.

[141] Christie, *Etienne Dolet*, 283.

[142] *Ibid.*, 284-286; cf. also Scott, *Controversies*, 88-97.

there is a chapter entitled, "Quid Erasmo sit in literis tribuendum?"[143] He begins by recounting that Erasmus owed his great success to his mastery of Greek and Latin. However, after he wrote the *Moria* he was charged with being suspect in the matter of religion. He admits that some Germans have called him "ἄθεος" because of his addiction to Lucian and that he was subjected to more attacks on the same ground after the publication of the *Novum Instrumentum* and its *Annotationes*. Florido lists the principal controversies with Lefèvre d'Etaples, Edward Lee, Latomus, Stunica, Sutor, and Beda: all this as a background to the account of the controversy with Alberto in which Florido presents Erasmus as calumniating the Prince of Carpi who he maintains had always preserved the decorum of scholarly discussion. He refutes the suggestion that Alberto had been furnished material by the Paris theologians or by any assistant other than himself. But then Florido significantly says that he will not linger longer on "these and other matters which are theological" but turn to another type of men who persecute Erasmus with inexpiable hatred and still continue to persecute him. They are in fact "those who seek to be called Ciceronians and attack Erasmus because of his *Dialogue* written against them."[144]

On this theme Florido recalls here and elsewhere that he has always praised the glory of Erasmus. Whatever happens to others the works of Erasmus will be immortal unless "per totius literaturae naufragium ex manibus doctorum." He has the merit of having restored literature and is erudite in both Greek and Latin.[145] In spite of this enthusiasm, Florido does admit that he is not afraid to dissent from the judgments Erasmus has made on other authors.[146]

Florido wrote the *Lectiones succisivae* before the Church had officially condemned Erasmus, but, because of his former close association with Alberto Pio, he was well aware of what the grounds for such a condemnation might be. It is interesting that by 1539 or 1540, when he was writing the *Lectiones*, Erasmus is described only as having gone "beyond decorum" in his controversy with Alberto and as having been called "scepticus" by the Germans. Florido thus moderated his earlier view of Erasmus as the precursor of Luther and recorded at the same time his conviction of Erasmus's immortal glory in literature.

---

[143] Florido, *Opera*, "Lectiones succissivae," Bk. III, chap. 4.
[144] *Ibid.*, 264, 274.
[145] *Ibid.*, 136, 235, 260, 265.
[146] *Ibid.*, 136.

The juxtaposition of these opinions provide a particularly example
of the fact that it was possible, within four years of the death of
Erasmus, for an Italian to compartmentalize the significance of
Erasmus.

VI. The Divided Legacy

The diversity of the judgments on Erasmus is a measure of the way
in which sixteenth-century Italy reacted to northern humanism. The
character of Erasmus's religious thought permitted interpretations
which extended over a whole spectrum of new or revived formula-
tions of Christianity. Likewise his indictment of the Ciceronians on
grounds that they denied history as well as Christianity evoked
responses which ranged all the way from agreement to passionate
condemnation of the northern barbarian who had dared to criticize
or condemn the greatest exponents of the neo-Latin literature which,
in Italian eyes, was the living symbol of continuity with the glories
of Rome.

Erasmus dominated the intellectual and literary interests of his
generation as have few other figures in the history of European
literature except perhaps Petrarch and Voltaire. The fortune of such
eponymous heroes is full of ironies and contradictions. They may
have some who profess to be their followers whom they would have
disowned if they could have had the gift of foresight. On the other
hand, elements of their thought often survive in the works of those
who officially condemn and repudiate the master.

Such was the fate of Erasmus in sixteenth-century Italy. The whole
program of the Counterreformation was shaped by the attack on
Erasmus in the third decade of the century (Aleandro and Alberto
Pio). Yet there are elements of Tridentine catholicism in which the
Erasmian influence can be traced (revision of the Vulgate, the decree
on images, the varieties of monastic reform, doctrines on the freedom
of the will). A large number of Catholic evangelists were directly or
indirectly inspired by Erasmus (Contarini, Sadoleto, Pole, Seripando).
The Valdesian school was Erasmian in the style of its religious
discourse if not in its theology (Juan de Valdés, Giulia Gonzaga,
Vittoria Colonna). And heretics as diverse as Ochino, Peter Martyr
Vermigli, Celio Curione, and Servetus could claim they owed something to Erasmus. Recent scholarship may be said to have found
more elements of Erasmian thought in the Counterreformation than
had previously been supposed and less direct influence on the move-

ment associated with Juan de Valdés. On the issue of Ciceronianism in both its secular and religious implications the Italian humanists were divided, but many, like Francesco Florido Sabino, were able to separate the literary achievements of Erasmus from the religious consequences of his work.

Are we to conclude from the variety of judgments and misjudgments pronounced on Erasmus by his Italian enemies and disciples that he had himself no consistent position in the great struggle which severed the Christian community in his generation? The older biographies for the most part agree that this was the case, but recent scholars have emphasized the fact that the Erasmian message remained unchanged from the *Enchiridion* (1503) to the *De praeparatione ad mortem* (1534).[147]

In 1954 Augustin Renaudet described the final position of Erasmus in the religious revolution of his time as the advocacy of a "third church." [148] This church would be intermediary between Wittenberg and Rome: it would consist of the Roman church purified of its abuses, restored to primitive simplicity, and therefore more acceptable to the reformers. Renaudet based this theory on the words addressed by Erasmus to Luther in the *First Hyperaspistes* of 1526, where he says, "Fero igitur hanc ecclesiam donec videro meliorem." [149] "I shall bear this church until I shall have seen a better." There is no doubt that Erasmus spent most of his life formulating a program for a "better" church and, taken in isolation, this declaration might be interpreted, as Renaudet has, to mean that he expected to see one realized. In the context of the whole paragraph in which the sentence occurs, however, what Erasmus is doing is affirming his loyalty to the Church of Rome with all its recognized abuses. Luther had described Erasmus as navigating unharmed between Scylla and Charybdis. Erasmus, addressing Luther, replies that

> I hardly know how to respond unless you declare which church you call Charybdis and which Scylla. I have never withdrawn from the Catholic Church. And I have been so far from enrolling in your church that, although a man otherwise most unfortunate in most of my associations, I count myself fortunate in this respect that I have refrained from joining you. I know that in this church which you

---

[147] Roland H. Bainton, "Continuity of Thought of Erasmus," *American Council of Learned Societies*, XIX, 5 (May, 1968); and the same author's *Erasmus of Christendom*.

[148] Renaudet, *Erasme et l'Italie*, 200-251.

[149] *LB*, X, 1258 A.

call papistic there are many men who displease me. But I see such men also in your church. More easily, however, are borne those evils to which one has become accustomed. Therefore I bear this church until I shall have seen a better, and it is compelled to put up with me until I am better. Nor is he an unfortunate navigator who holds a mean course between two evils.[150]

Although this statement admits that there are evils on both sides, it is perfectly clear that Erasmus can live with those on the side of the Roman Church but not with those on the side of Luther. The reference to seeing a better church—in the future perfect—expresses a pious hope which Erasmus before 1517 might have expected to be realized, but now, in 1526, the tone is one of resigned acceptance of Rome and repudiation of Luther. This declaration, made ten years before his death, Erasmus never changed although the experience of that decade could only confirm his judgment of the mixture of corruption and error in the church to which he gave his allegiance.[151]

---

[150] *LB*, X, 1257 F-1258 A: "Porro quod mihi videor, ut dicis inter *Scyllam* et *Charybdim* navigare, vix habeo quod respondeam, nisi tu declares, utram ecclesiam *Charybdim* aut *Scyllam* appelles. Ab Ecclesia Catholica nunquam defeci. Tuae Ecclesiae adeo nunquam fuit animus dare nomen, ut homo plurimis alioqui nominibus infelicissimus, hoc certe nomine videar mihi felix, quod constanter a vestro foedere abstinuerim. Scio in hac Ecclesia, quam vos Papisticam vocatis, esse multos qui mihi displicent: sed tales video et in tua Ecclesia. Levius autem feruntur mala quibus assueveris. Fero igitur hanc Ecclesiam donec videro meliorem: et eadem me ferre cogitur, donec ipse fiam melior. Nec infeliciter navigat, qui inter duo diversa mala medium cursum tenet."

[151] Two articles by Dr. Sylvana Seidel Menchi containing important contributions to the subjects of the influence of Erasmus in Italy reached me after this study had gone to press: "Spiritualismo radicale nelle opere di Ortensio Lando attorno al 1550," *Archiv für Reformationsgeschichte*, LXV (1974), 210-276; and "Alcuni atteggiamenti della cultura italiana di fronte a Erasmo," *Eresia e Riforma nell' Italia del cinquecento*, Biblioteca del Corpus Reformatorum Italicorum (Florence and Chicago, 1974), 71-133.

FRANCE

THE PROFILE OF THE RECEPTION OF THE ITALIAN RENAISSANCE IN FRANCE

SEM DRESDEN

University of Leiden

I. RECEPTION AS HISTORICAL PROBLEM

Any investigation into *the* profile of *the* reception of *the* Renaissance is surely a hopeless task. The difficulties involved have been so frequently and so accurately described that the undertaking now seems virtually impossible. Its sole justification lies in what we may call the challenge. And a challenge it is, especially when we think of the number of detailed studies devoted to so many aspects of the topic. Nor is this all: precisely because such important and interesting details have come to light, it appears increasingly difficult to impose any order on the mass of seemingly unconnected data, let alone to discover any unity deserving the name "Renaissance." No one can take into account all the things he ought to know if he is to say anything at all significant about what the Renaissance in Italy actually was.

Rezeptionsgeschichte also entails difficulties of its own. The transmission of cultural "products" (and by this I mean everything connected with ideas, works of art, philosophical and political theories, or religious doctrines) presents a problem very different from that of an arbitrary, material object which passes from hand to hand. Such an object undergoes little or no change as it moves from one person to the next. If the same were true of culture, such a derivative form of culture would be unworthy of the name. The essential characteristic of cultural transmission is that whatever is transmitted changes. It remains the same in certain respects, yet it can no longer be called the same. T. S. Eliot's words about tradition may be referred to culture in general: "It cannot be inherited, and if you want it you must obtain it by great labour." [1] This entails adaptation, assimilation, and thus alteration. The greater the enthusiasm and devotion with which these cultural products are "inherited," the more radical the changes they undergo. Consequently all that Italian culture brought to France

---

[1] *Selected Essays*, 6th ed. (London, 1946), 14.

looks and sounds different there, although the original forms are still recognizable. Nor is there any question of influence in a single direction only, of the giver simply giving and the receiver merely receiving. The receiver is subjected to influences willingly and in the manner of his own choosing, but he can at the same time very well influence the giver, resulting in an exchange which is hard to describe but which should never be obscured or, as happens all too often, oversimplified.

However difficult it may be to know what the Italian Renaissance represented and how it was "received" in France, this is far from being the whole of the problem. Laying aside such recurring questions as when the Renaissance began and ended, its connections with humanism, the survival of scholasticism despite the founding of the Collège de France, and many others, there still remain a number of factors which make the already complex matter of the reception of the Renaissance in France still more complex. As contrasted with what we may justly call the age of Renaissance and humanism in Italy, the situation in France appears far more confused and the influences more varied. Despite the inevitable reservations which must be advanced and dealt with, we may regard Italian humanism and the Renaissance during the fifteenth century as a self-contained whole which developed on its own accord, more or less independently of the outside world. The spread of Italian humanism into the outside world, of course, was a very different sort of affair, as the Renaissance outside Italy was no longer exclusively a matter of Italian influences but was also shaped by such major factors as the prestige of Erasmus and the Reformation. For this reason, if we endeavor to trace the lines of cultural transmission and to describe the alteration of cultural products from one country to another, we must take into account the inevitable influence of third parties. In most cases—but not in all, and this makes the complication still greater—French humanism was indeed based on Italian models; but it was also affected by facts and ideas which, if only for chronological reasons, had nothing to do with these models.

Shall I magnify the confusion still more? Obviously the French sixteenth century, the traditional century of its Renaissance and humanism, followed the Italian fifteenth century; but, due to the numerous and intensive contemporary contacts between the two countries, the Italian sixteenth century also exerted a direct influence upon France. Ficino's Platonism did not spread into France much before the work of Castiglione did, though it could have done so.

And so there developed a double influence: Platonism spread directly through a number of channels, but it also spread indirectly through such works as *Il Cortegiano*. Petrarch's influence was felt in France partly through his own works and partly through those of his later Italian imitators, who were considerably closer in time to their own French disciples. Amid this tangle of events, the chronology of which threatens to ensnare every observer, and through these influences which affected each man differently, no universally valid line of development can be discerned.

Perhaps every attempt at cultural history suffers from this defect, imputable to the many details which have now come to light. What one scholar may regard as purely accidental may be central for another, who is perfectly entitled to proceed as he does and who literally cannot "see" things in any other way. Of course everyone hopes to do justice not necessarily to all, but at least to the majority of, the data. But what is a "datum"? Are all the sources of the same kind and did they remain the same in their influence within French culture? Florentine Platonism undoubtedly had a great influence in France. But then we immediately think of ideas in the work of Maurice Scève, Margaret of Navarre, and so on. What happened seems to be a trifle but is in fact of the utmost importance: ideas which originated in philosophical tracts were carried into a work of literature and started to serve the function of literature. There is no need to go into the subtle problems which this raises; suffice here to say that they exist and cannot be dismissed. And in this case we are at least dealing with written works on both sides. If we consider that Platonism also affected the visual arts, the complexity of the matter increases still more.

Where is the conductor of cultural history who knows how to organize the instruments (his numerous data and "facts") and make them play in such a way that a harmonious whole develops—a whole which is prescribed for him and which he can follow? One thing is sure: he will never succeed in enumerating all the facts one after the other: from Ficino and Bembo to the "école lyonnaise"; from Pomponazzi to Montaigne via Gianfrancesco Pico della Mirandola; from Leonardo, Michelangelo, and Raphael to the "école de Fontainebleau," the mannerists and the baroque artists via Giulio Romano. Where will be put Jean Lemaire de Belges, Marot, Gaguin, Fichet, Lefèvre d'Étaples, Briçonnet and so many others? What strikes us most about this sort of enumeration is the quantity of omissions, the total lack of details. The day when we can present an all-inclusive synthesis has not yet dawned and will only arrive after still more extensive and still more detailed research has been done. But, despite all the objections that arise, despite all our doubts about whether, in present circumstances, that day ever will dawn, I shall try both to keep away from crude generalizations and to avoid losing myself in details.

What then? I can see only one path, however difficult it may be to tread. I shall confine myself to the vague outlines of the profile. If we study certain texts or documents, we can obtain some insight into what they contain. This can then be compared with what other texts say about similar subjects. My path is made of texts and, at first, as I pore over them, I can see no farther. I cannot get a view of where the path is leading. But the surprising thing about texts, and perhaps about all cultural products, is that they contain the view, as it were, within themselves. Textual details reveal wide prospects, but of course these prospects pertain to one particular text and are, to begin with at least, only valid so far as this particular text is concerned. So I read one text to see how it resembles and how it differs from another. I can only do this with regard to a few points, but this has the advantage of keeping me away from excessive abstraction. Initially I shall refrain from broaching general problems and do the only thing a cultural historian can do: read and watch.

II. Antiquity and Respect: French Humanism and the Classical Heritage

This well-known passage was written by Niccolò Machiavelli to Francesco Vettori:

> Venuta la sera, mi ritorno in casa ed entro nel mio scrittorio; e in su l'uscio mi spoglio quella veste cotidiana, piena di fango e di loto, e mi metto panni reali e curiali; e rivestito condecentemente entro nelle antique corti degli antiqui uomini dove, da loro ricevuto amore- volmente, mi pasco di quel cibo, che *solum* è mio, e che io nacqui per lui; dove io non mi vergogno parlare con loro e domandarli della ragione delle loro azioni: e quelli per loro umanità rispondono; e non sento per quattro ore di tempo alcuna noia, sdimentico ogni affanno, non temo la povertà, non mi sbigottisce la morte: tutto mi transferisco in loro.[2]

---

[2] N. Machiavelli to Francesco Vettori, 10 December 1513, in *Opere di Niccolò Machiavelli*, ed. Mario Bonfantini, 2nd ed. (Milan and Naples, 1966), 23.

Although Machiavelli was hardly a humanist in the true sense of the word—he took a limited interest in ancient texts—his lines reveal an attitude that we can call humanistic, a frame of mind which can be found, in different forms and perhaps to different degrees, in the writings of other figures. There is nothing very surprising about the special position of ancient writers in Machiavelli's mentality. Everyone knows that the period of humanism and the Renaissance saw the rediscovery of Antiquity; but what did Antiquity mean? The humanists, drawing few esthetic or historical distinctions, declared that Antiquity was everything old. They admired and identified themselves with anything written in Greek or Latin before the medieval era, including numerous fathers of the church and other Christian writers. The "Antiquity" of the humanists was thus highly heterogeneous, comprising works widely different in purpose, content, and form, covering a period from many centuries before to several hundred years after Christ—all became objects of study and veneration.

Here I am not concerned with the study of the ancients, the hunt for manuscripts, or the development of interest in ancient monuments,[3] but rather with the nature of this veneration and it transformations. Before he met with the ancients, Machiavelli dressed himself up, making each evening into a formal, official occasion. One reason for this was doubtless that, for him, the ancients truly were old. They stood at a distance and were somehow utterly different from their modern admirers, never actually belonging to the everyday life of the present. Machiavelli's own behavior was obviously based on personal motives, connected partly with his experiences as an exile; yet his entire attitude toward the ancients is both characteristic and indicative. Unlike most medieval thinkers and writers (who tended to be far better educated in classical culture than used to be believed), the men of the Renaissance examined the classical heritage on its own terms. Whereas during the Middle Ages ancient literature was exploited for contemporary ends, the fifteenth century saw the study of Antiquity as an end in itself. This attitude naturally made possible a superior understanding and a purer judgment of Antiquity, but something was also lost: the living presence of the ancients, the

---

[3] Every study of humanism or the Renaissance naturally discusses the significance of Antiquity more or less extensively. On classical manuscripts, the reader is referred to the well-known, indispensable works of R. R. Bolgar and, of course, of P. O. Kristeller. For "antiquities," see Roberto Weiss, *The Renaissance Discovery of Classical Antiquity*, 2nd ed. (Oxford, 1973).

uncontrollable desire to use the cultural heritage spontaneously and
freely. Machiavelli made each contact, each encounter, into an
altogether extraordinary event. Even imitation, about which I shall
say more in due course, contained elements of distance as well as of
proximity. In the translations on which Ficino expended so much
energy, we are struck not only by his desire to make important texts
known but also by the fact that precisely this desire shows that, the
texts were recognized as being monuments of a culture different from
Ficino's own. It would of course be easy to illustrate other features
of this reverence for the ancients in fifteenth-century Italy, but it
seems to me that it is this particular aspect which became increasingly
influential and obtained an ever greater significance in the course of
time, especially in France.

This is hardly surprising; intense veneration relaxes in the long run.
For, however many years the respectful distance has been maintained,
it ends by becoming familiar, by being regarded as normal, and
consequently by losing its intensity. Apart from these general
considerations, there were also some concrete facts which propelled
the veneration of the ancients in another direction. One of these was
the appearance of Erasmus and the influence of his writings. Even
without dwelling on his own personal form of reverence for classical
Antiquity, it must be said that his books had an immense significance
for future developments.

As was so frequently the case, Erasmus set the fashion in this
domain, too. Principally with his *Adagia*, but also with his *Colloquia*,
both of which were expanded over the years, he presented the *docti* of
his time—and anyone else who needed it—with a vast supply of
ancient culture to which they could help themselves. This was
merely one aspect of an idea which inspired him throughout his life.
He wished, with a precise religious purpose, to encourage an accurate and responsible revival of the ancients. To this end, education
in the broadest sense of the word, from the pupil's very first lessons
up to the university level, was to be radically reformed; and pedagogy,
to which Erasmus, like so many other humanists, understandably
devoted a great deal of attention, was to be basically altered. I do not
propose to describe Erasmus's ideas on this matter, but simply to
point out that in many respects he accomplished his aim—perhaps not
so successfully as he might have done, but more than enough to
create a different cultural climate. In countless tracts, manuals, and
textbooks, Erasmus, explicitly or implicitly, displayed his great respect

for the ancients—a respect he wished to transmit to the young. The
more he succeeded, the younger the men who inherited his respect,
the more common did this reverence become. It was not that the
original passion for the ancients, so typical of Petrarch and many
Italian writers of the fifteenth century, disappeared. It may have lost
some of its force, but above all its nature was changed. The respect
ceased to be out of the ordinary. It ceased, in other words, to be
outside everyday life and became a part of it. The respect became
customary in the literal sense of the word and was consequently put to
the most varied uses.

We all know that Rabelais was an *érasmisant* par excellence.[4] In a
letter to "Bernardo Salignaco," who is generally accepted to have
been Erasmus, Rabelais tells how he owes his true education to the
great humanist,

> qui me tibi de facie ignotum, nomine etiam ignobilem, sic educasti,
> sic castissimis divinae tuae doctrinae uberibus usque aluisti, ut quidquid
> sum et valeo, tibi id uni acceptum, ni feram, hominum omnium qui
> sunt aut aliis erunt in annis ingratissimus sim.

And he signed with the traditional but none the less significant
words: "Tuus quatenus suus."[5] There can be no doubt about his
sincerity or about the humanistic veneration which Rabelais felt.
All the sources that have been examined so far point in the same
direction: Rabelais possessed a great knowledge of classical Antiquity.
He repeatedly quoted ancient writers as authorities, especially texts
on medicine and natural philosophy.[6] But he also made use of every
sort of expedient, such as the anthologies which had been supplied by
Erasmus and others, and he did so in a book of an altogether exceptional kind, within an entirely individual structure. This gives a
curious twist to the current admiration for the ancients.

In the "Prologue" of *Gargantua*, written by "M. Alcofribas,
Abstracteur de Quinte Essence" (Rabelais's mouthpiece), there are
several remarks which continue to inspire detailed commentaries and
the significance of which has not yet been fully clarified.[7] This is all

---

[4] Cf. Raymond Lebègue, "Rabelais, the last of the French Erasmians," *Journal
of the Warburg and Courtauld Institutes*, XII (1949), 91-100; Verdun Louis Saulnier,
Le dessein de Rabelais (Paris, 1957), 8ff., 201ff.; and various studies in *Colloquia
Erasmiana Turonensia*, I (Paris, 1972).

[5] In *Œuvres complètes*, ed. Jacques Boulenger (Paris, 1934), 979.

[6] See the various introductions to editions by Abel Lefranc and others.

[7] Leo Spitzer, "Ancora sul prologo al primo libro del 'Gargantua' di Rabelais,"
Studi francesi, No. 27 (Sept.-Dec., 1965), 423-434; Floyd Gray, "Ambiguity and

the more surprising, because there earlier seemed to be less doubt about them. For, following the most venerable models, Rabelais speaks at length about the topos *Sileni Alcibiadis*, in which the external appearance of a phenomenon tells us nothing of its true content. We see this when we come across a dog (the most philosophical of animals, according to Plato in the second book of the *Republic*) trying to suck the marrow out of a bone. He cracks the outside in order to reach the inside—and this is what the author feels should happen to his own work. The reader must not take it at its face value, but "à plus hault sens interpreter ce que par adventure cuidiez dict en gayeté de cueur."

Thus far the interpretation meets with no difficulties. Marshalling a quantity of arguments and appealing, as did all the humanists, to the authority of ancient writers, Rabelais demands only to be read in the traditional manner. He wishes his work to be regarded as an allegory in which the true significance is on another level, more profound or more elevated than the meaning that appears at first sight. Only then will the reader encounter a "doctrine plus absconce, laquelle vous révélera de très haultz sacremens et mystères horrificques, tant en ce que concerne nostre religion que aussi l'estat politicq et vie oeconomicque." [8] Of course, these vertiginous heights and unfathomable depths of horror arouse suspicion. This is still more evident in the context, but the reader does not need to dwell on either the one or the other. Only when he reads on does he run into difficulties, and he is then required to discover an essential reality which has nothing to do with the absurdity, ugliness, and vulgarity of external appearances. And then he reads to his horror (or rather to his amusement!), that he should not think that Homer ever dreamt of the allegories which Plutarch, Heraclides, and imitators such as Poliziano borrowed from his work. Thus allegories must be excluded—and most of all from the work of Rabelais. Although much has been said about a *volte-face*, there is no need to see any contradiction in these paragraphs.[9] In the long tradition of exegetical allegorization, we must simply distinguish between the various types of allegory, some of which are acceptable and others of which are not. Rabelais supposedly intended first one

Point of View in the Prologue of *Gargantua*," *Romanic Review*, LVI (1965), 12-21; Wolfgang Raible, "Der Prolog zu *Gargantua* und der Pantagruelismus," *Romanische Forschungen*, LXXVIII (1966), 253-279.

[8] *Œuvres complètes*, 26, 27.

[9] M. A. Screech, in Rabelais, *Le Tiers livre*, Textes littéraires français, 102 (Geneva, 1964), 15.

category and then the other. But that seems too subtle to me, and, buuldan, it appears to contradict the whole purpose of the work. From start to finish Rabelais intended that the reader should have nothing to guide him. One of the comic aspects of the book resides in the helplessness of the reader when he wants to know for certain what he should believe in and what not, what is intended seriously and what is merely meant to amuse. These customary distinctions cannot be made in *Gargantua* or in Rabelais's other books. The borders which appear to be closely marked in normal life, between what is serious and what is not, dissolve.

Consequently the respect for the ancients, which cannot ever be denied Rabelais, is located within a whole which, if not satirical, is at least parodical and mocking in tone. In a sense we can speak of a mirthful admiration. Machiavelli invited the ancients to a stately, solemn meeting, a formal feast for which only "panni reali e curiali" were suitable. Rabelais also dressed himself up, but in his own way: his was a feast of abandon, where anything could happen and where the most revered figures wore fools' caps. His admiration was expressed in the genial laugh of the giants who, not unlike Erasmus's *Stultitia*, disguised their earnestness in fun.

It can also be said that the tone of Rabelais's amazing work is not uniform. There are passages which are clearly intended more seriously, and some of them concern ancient writers. Take the eighth chapter of *Pantagruel*, Gargantua's letter to his son. In this manifesto of humanist pedagogy, as it was traditionally understood, Rabelais was undoubtedly being serious. This is proved by the paternal, somewhat solemn words intended to stimulate the students to give the very best of themselves, and it might even be possible to see in this letter a "hymne d'allégresse et de reconnaissance." [10] But are these lines in conflict with the rest of the text? Without detracting in any way from its impressive and unquestionably noble form and content, I would like to point out that the letter is far from being a "foreign body," a *Fremdkörper*, in the general structure of the book. It is wrong to isolate this chapter from the work as a whole and to present it as a virtually independent piece, as happens all too frequently in selections and anthologies. In the first place, we must never forget that a giant is writing to his no less colossal son. This could explain the abundance of knowledge to be stored and the truly gigantic series of

---

[10] Jean Plattard, *Montaigne et son temps* (Paris, 1933), 161.

demands on body and mind; but it also suggests an unreality which may be satirical elsewhere but which is probably not so here. This seems to me to be emphasized by the setting: Gargantua is king of Utopia, and the reference at the end "De Utopie, ce dix septiesme jour du moys de mars" should not be overlooked. Equally indicative is the passage at the beginning of the chapter (not at the beginning of the letter—this may be why it has attracted so little attention). Here, too, there are only a couple of lines devoted mainly to Pantagruel's mental capacities: "Il avait l'entendement à double rebras et capacité de mémoire à la mesure de douze oyres et botes d'olif." [11] But it is odd to speak of an understanding of double dimensions and odder yet to speak of a memory whose capacity can be compared to twelve empty skins and casks of oil. Or is it so odd? For this is what makes the letter, however individual its tone, fit into the work.

In Rabelais's case we are dealing with a very particular kind of respect for ancient culture, and so it is not only necessary but also relatively easy to devote our attention to this theme. In most other major writers of the sixteenth century, we do indeed find individual versions of this respect (otherwise they would not be great writers); but the difference is rarely great enough to merit more than a single comment. The great enthusiasm that the poets of the Brigade, and later of the Pléiade (thanks in part to the teaching of Dorat) felt for Antiquity and displayed in their works is well enough known. Its most striking aspect is naturally the type of the interest they showed. To give some idea of this we could pick passages from the poems of Ronsard, Du Bellay, or others; but, from the century of commentaries and theoretical speculations, when rhetoric, with its carefully elaborated flourishes and precepts, was still a living force, a commentary can serve our purpose just as well.

After Ronsard's first volumes of verse, Marc-Antoine de Muret started writing an apology, a commentary on Ronsard's *Amours*, which was published in 1553. "N'avons-nous pas veu," he said in the foreword,

> l'indocte arrogance de quelques acrestez mignons s'esmouvoir telle-
> ment au premier de ses escrits, qu'il sembloit que sa gloire encores
> naissante deust estre esteinte par leurs efforts? L'un le reprenoit de se
> trop louër, l'autre d'escrire trop obscurement, l'autre d'estre trop
> audacieux à faire de nouveaux mots; ne sachans pas que ceste coustume

---

[11] *Oeuvres complètes*, 224.

de se louër luy est commune avecques tous les plus excellens Poëtes qui jamais furent; que l'obscurité qu'ils pretendent n'est que une confession de leur ignorance; et que, sans l'invention des nouveaux mots les autres langues sentissent encores une toute telle pauvreté, que nous la sentons en la nostre.[12]

I shall pass over some of the charges against Ronsard which Muret challenged or invalidated by stating the real aims of the new poetry. I shall discuss neither the self-exaltation, which was to be peculiar to this school, nor the hermetic style, which appears to have aroused protests from the outset. The only point of interest is that these and other attacks were parried by Muret with an appeal to tradition and the authority of the ancients. Still more important, however, is the fact that the poets of the Pléiade, of whom this commentary by a member is just as characteristic as Du Bellay's *Deffence* written several years earlier, never hesitated to make a radical distinction between the true audience they desired and chance readers. Those who dared to criticize Ronsard were simply accused of "indocte arrogance." But more remarkable than their supposed arrogance is their illiteracy, or rather their ignorance of what letters should be and should do. There was an implicit appeal to competence: only those were competent to judge poetry who possessed the knowledge of things, and this knowledge could only be acquired through the study of rules and ideas developed by the ancient writers in their rhetorical tracts. This entailed a line of demarcation which had never before been so clearly drawn in France.

The difference vis-à-vis the past is obvious: the question is whether there was a difference between these concepts and those *currently* held in Italy. Perhaps we could say that the Italian fifteenth century was indeed fettered by rules which dominated the various domains of art, but that these were less cumbersome and less "academic" than those which developed during the sixteenth century. The French sixteenth century, then, had to adapt itself to what was current in Italy; and when we think of the numerous exchanges of this period, we must admit that this is what we should have expected. The difference between the Italian and the French Renaissance consisted largely in the emphases and the preferences with which the rules were used and in the prestige acquired by the *docti*.

---

[12] In Pierre de Nolhac, *Ronsard et l'humanisme* (Paris, 1922), 95. Cf. Isidore Silver, in *Lumières de la Pléiade*, De Pétrarque à Descartes, No. 11 (Paris, 1966), 33-48.

It seems to me that the French were more successful than others in this field. There were several reasons for this: the desire for organization which led to the formation of "académies" in various artistic domains, based admittedly on an Italian model [13] but more official and with a more solid foundation; and a tendency towards centralization which encouraged academicism in the worst sense of the word but which also created the climate in which the literary classicism of the seventeenth century could develop. It was not by chance that the Académie française, whose statutes were finally approved in 1637, was the first of a long series of similar bodies that we regard as public institutions. Men of letters and learning acquired an official status. They were to apply and enforce their code in various fields, especially as regarded the significance of the ancients. Anyone who failed to follow suit was *indocte* and consequently of no importance. This later development was the result of a tendency which had always existed and was perhaps more marked in France than elsewhere: we can already sense it in the words of Muret.

How great the powers of centralization were to be is shown by what befell another observation by this same commentator. For Muret defended the neologisms that Ronsard had distributed so lavishly in his verse. Admittedly he suggested certain modifications and, in later editions, Ronsard took them to heart. But it is none the less interesting that, many years later, in 1714, Fénelon should have raised the same objection, and should have done so in a letter to the Académie: "[Ronsard] parlait français en grec, malgré les Français mêmes," he wrote.[14] After Malherbe and others, maintaining a classical code that rejected neologisms and sustained the purity of the language, he turned against the Pléiade on this point; and so powerful was this code in France, so influential is it still, that I wonder whether I am not mistaken, or am not myself influenced by classical concepts, when I refer to the neologisms that Ronsard "distributed so lavishly in his verse." So far as he was concerned there was no question of overabundance for its own sake; he wanted to show his respect for the classics, and, rather than keep them at a distance, he wished to introduce them into his own work.

Aside from being a personal preference, this was also a matter of considerable general, not to say national, interest. It is significant that

---

[13] Cf. Frances A. Yates, *The French Academies of the Sixteenth Century*, Studies of the Warburg Institute, 15 (London, 1947).
[14] *Éducation des filles* . . . (Paris, 1929), 270.

Muret should speak of the "pauvreté" that characterized the French language and that would continue unless it were ended by the introduction of neologisms taken from Latin and Greek. The duty of enriching the national language was by no means new: even in the title of his work, *La Deffence et Illustration de la Langue Françoyse*, Du Bellay had heralded the new school by referring to its task. Others had done so before him, and the whole question of enrichment had originated, needless to say, in Italy. There is no point in repeating what has already been said about this.[15] The only problem concerns the difference between the French products and the Italian models. I speak of models deliberately, for the French theorists were faced here, as elsewhere, with a process of double imitation. They looked not only to ancient Rome and Greece but also to Italy; and this, of course, was one of the most important differences between them and the Italians of the fifteenth century. There is also the question of what we can at best call a cultural inferiority complex. Let me give an example. Centuries earlier, when he had to translate Greek philosophical terms into Latin, Seneca had complained: "Quanta verborum nobis paupertas [cf. *pauvreté*], immo egestas sit, numquam magis quam hodierno die intellexi. Mille res inciderunt, cum forte de Platone loqueremur, quae nomina desiderarent nec haberent..."[16]

We find similar words in those Italian writers who studied the Latin classics and in those Frenchmen who were confronted both by the ancients and the Italians. It is, as I noted, a cultural complex which may have originated from the secret power that a foreign language seems to possess when one actually wants to translate it. However this may be, in most cases there soon developed a spirit of competition, of *aemulatio*, a desire to do just as well in one's own language and ultimately to alter it in such a way as to be able to compete on an equal footing. The Romans had done so with regard to Greek, the Italians with regard to Latin, and the French with regard to Greek, Latin, and Italian. In a sense they started at a greater disadvantage than anyone else, and it may well be that in their case the cultural complex was at its most acute. It was thus in France that the competitive spirit was at its strongest and that it assumed forms and dimensions that were far less visible in Italy. Together with the

---

[15] Cf. Paul Oskar Kristeller, *Renaissance Thought*, II: *Papers on Humanism and the Arts* (New York, 1965), 14, 28, 84, 119ff.; F. Brunot, *Histoire de la langue française*, II, 4th ed. (Paris, 1947), 1ff.

[16] *Epistolae ad Lucilium*, VI, 58, 1. Cf. I, 9, 1, and VI, 58, 7.

development of a royal court, the enrichment of the French language became an affair of state in the modern sense of the word; and national feeling (which had undoubtedly always been present) played a far greater part in France than elsewhere. Both in the domain of politics and in that of culture, the competitive spirit turned into a barely concealed form of rivalry. The mutual envy, which frequently developed in humanist circles, was exacerbated over the years by nationalist prejudice. A phenomenon that had existed in Italy but had there been confined to individual rancor or to small principalities, acquired a far wider significance in France owing to the forces of centralization. The *translatio studii* and the *translatio imperii*, which had been known for centuries and had often been combined, now assumed a nationalistic hue in countries such as France and Germany, and reverence for the ancients blended with a not altogether justified feeling of self-esteem.

Just as Ronsard spoke Greek in French and wanted to make his language the same as that of the ancients, so he enriched his poems with every sort of device borrowed from the ancient heritage. A problem thus arose which is of the greatest importance for the manner in which Greek mythology was manipulated and admired. In Ronsard's work we can find much that can be classified as occasional verses. As official court poet he had to write poetry for every kind of festivity or *entrée*; and in these poems he no longer appears to have taken the mythological elements seriously, treating them as little more than embellishments never intended to serve other than a decorative purpose. Like the mannerists in the plastic arts, Ronsard often makes it appear that an ironic distance from the ancients should be observed.[17] Italian models can be found for this, but I shall leave to one side the question of tradition and precursors. Why should it be just here that Ronsard displays a form of irony, since there is such heartfelt and profound veneration in the Pindaric odes? The answer is that in the Pindaric odes and some other poems the poet expressed his inner self, while his occasional verses depend on an external event, a commission, an occasion. I do not propose to examine Goethe's idea that all poems can be called *Gelegenheitspoesie*, nor am I in a position to gauge the profundity or sincerity of feelings. Such a psychological approximation is always difficult, as it cannot be applied to the vast

---

[17] Marcel Raymond explains this very well in *Lumières de la Pléiade*, 391ff., and esp. 406ff.

majority of sixteenth-century poets and is contrary to what was then expected of their poetry. The mythological embellishments that Ronsard provided in early and later poems, in "personal" and occasional verses, are not decorations in the modern sense. On the contrary, it was impossible to omit them without actually affecting the essence of the poem. Nowadays decoration is something that can be used as an accompaniment but can equally well be omitted. In the sixteenth century the situation was entirely different: *decorum*, the "fitness to purpose," was an essential part of the theme.[18]

I shall return to this theme below. At this point we can affirm that our perception of the mythological ornamentation in Ronsard's poetry is obscured by the fact that *decorum* has since come to mean something like "decorative" as we understand the word today. This happened to such an extent that in the eighteenth century poetry became a desirable social pastime, while theorists tended to regard it as a useless and senseless expression of matters that could be conveyed far more naturally and directly in prose. The time of the "poète en prose" had begun. If we want to grasp the essence of Renaissance poetry, we must therefore overlook this development and the effect that it has had on our poetic sensibility. *Decorum*, perhaps the most fundamental category of rhetoric and of what is now termed esthetics, will then appear as essential to the structure of the poem. If we ask ourselves about the degree of irony or seriousness of a poem of this period, we must proceed along completely different lines; and we will see that the veneration expressed in the French Renaissance poem for Antiquity cannot be fitted into modern categories or be split into personal feelings and traditional images. In the thought and feeling of the time there is no place for such distinctions. If we were to follow in the tradition of the nineteenth-century biographers and pass from the poem to the poet, our chances of obtaining a satisfactory result would be virtually nil. Neither in the Italian nor in the French Renaissance can we take a psychological approach to the poet or to the poetic expression of personal feelings.

That there was no interest or no potential interest in the sixteenth century for what we would call psychology, however, is a conclusion which is far from being generally true, as we can see from the work of

---

[18] There is more about this, though in connection with a slightly later period, in Rosemond T. M. Tuve, *Elizabethan and Metaphysical Imagery: Renaissance poetic and twentieth-century Critics*, 2nd ed. (Chicago, 1954), *passim*.

Montaigne. Montaigne may have been an exceptional figure, and the *Essais* may well be one of the most amazing works ever written; but the fact remains that he lived and wrote in the sixteenth century, and his work became the great model for certain forms of introspection and psychological analysis. His period has been called "le moment historique de Montaigne," [19] although we might wonder what this actually means and whether cultural history is not full of such moments—that of Petrarch, that of Descartes, that of Rousseau.

I shall limit myself initially to a very definite point: the way in which Montaigne read and admired the ancient writers. During the first months of 1571, in his thirty-eighth year, Montaigne withdrew to his castle or, more precisely, to his tower where he settled into a chamber lined with books, which "libertati suae tranquillitatique et otio dicavit." [20] It was a chamber like Machiavelli's, but the circumstances were utterly different, and the man devoting himself to reading and writing a very different man from Machiavelli. Each evening, Machiavelli celebrated a solemn feast by reading the ancients who lay outside the normal world of everyday life. The room in the Collège de Coqueret, where Ronsard worked until two o'clock in the morning, and Baïf awoke when Ronsard went to sleep, resembled a cloister in which the culture of the ancients was studied with enthusiastic devotion: the monks were simply young scholars. Montaigne, however, did not dress himself up, and still less was he impelled by youthful enthusiasm. Admiration for every product of Antiquity had become an everyday occurrence. The exceptional quality of the matter had vanished, and the veneration had literally become a part of Montaigne's normal existence.

It was chiefly because of Montaigne's own personality that the nature of the veneration changed, and not because Montaigne made a different choice from what Antiquity had to offer than the other humanists had done. Each obviously had his personal preferences. For all his veneration (although it is hard to apply this term to Montaigne) for Socrates, he had less feeling for Plato and Renaissance Neoplatonism than had other authors of the sixteenth century. There is no doubt that Montaigne preferred historians and moralists such as Plutarch (whom he read in Amyot's translation), and philosophers such as Seneca and Cicero, and, of course, Pliny, a source of countless

---

[19] The title of a chapter on Montaigne in Léon Brunschvicg, *Le progrès de la conscience dans la philosophie occidentale*, 2 vols. (Paris, 1927), I, 118ff.

[20] *Les Essais de Michel de Montaigne*, ed. F. Strowski, I (Bordeaux, 1906), ix.

marvellous stories and anecdotes. No objection can be made to this, and it is as true of Montaigne as of anyone else that the choice characterizes the chooser. I am personally inclined to believe that it was not what Montaigne read so much as the manner in which he read that was distinctive. There is no doubt that however much Montaigne admired a writer, he never read him from beginning to end: "Je feuillette les livres, je ne les estudie pas..." His veneration cannot be compared to that of a modern scholar, whose insight into the purpose of a writer depends on an overall perspective of his work. But still less can Montaigne be compared to Machiavelli, for whom the ancients were endowed with a kind of intangibility. Montaigne used the authors whom he read. They became a property he employed as he thought fit, and he remained true to his dictum "Ce qui m'en demeure, c'est chose que je ne reconnois plus estre d'autruy..." [21]

It was partly because of this change that a modern scholar wrote: "In Montaignes Umgang mit den Büchern fehlt das Passionierte, Kultische, Andachtsvolle. Er lässt sich von ihnen nicht beherrschen." [22] This is certainly true. In Montaigne we find neither the sense of cult (which we encounter to a limited extent in Machiavelli and which probably pervaded Coqueret) nor the truly devoted reverence for the book. And to talk of passion in connection with Montaigne seems to be nothing short of farcical. The fact remains nonetheless that Montaigne read with a definite purpose, and it is by no means unlikely that he pursued his special, highly personal purpose with passion. It would be wrong, of course, to think of passion here as having all the faults and virtues displayed by the romantic poets. Yet it remains possible to pursue an aim with dogged determination, and, without denying or underestimating Montaigne's nonchalance and "dilettantisme," we can still say that for him reading served a totally absorbing purpose: the purpose of living or realizing the art of living. "Mon mestier et mon art, c'est vivre," [23] he said tersely and forcefully; and he repeated it in one form or another on numerous occasions. It is curious to observe that the *ars*, in his sense an art or a skill, fulfilled its purpose within this life: it was self-fulfilment. The "art" which is life led to perfect life. Montaigne, who did not have much time for Roman or other *rhetores*, paid little heed, I think, to the

---

[21] Livre II, essai 27. In the edition by Jean Plattard, 6 vols. (Paris, 1931), at vol. IV, p. 75. All subsequent quotations are from this edition.

[22] Hugo Friedrich, *Montaigne* (Bern, 1949), 58.

[23] II, 6 (vol. III, p. 71).

significance held by *ars* in theoretical writings about rhetoric.[24] He was content with the fact that each *ars* set up rules for a certain purpose. That this purpose had nothing to do with the life of the *auctores*, and was restricted to an entirely independent problem, must have been indifferent to him. His own purpose was confined to life, to *his* life; it *was* his life.

We cannot escape the fact that there is something paradoxical about this attitude. We begin with a book which attacks the writing of books: "Quel que je soye, je le veux estre ailleurs qu'en papier. Mon art et mon industrie ont esté employez à me faire valoir moy-mesmes; mes estudes, à m'apprendre à faire, non pas à escrire. J'ay mis tous mes efforts à former ma vie." [25] It looks paradoxical to modern eyes that we can deal, in this day and age, only with Montaigne's work as it stands and not in the least with his life as he lived it. Not for a second shall I deny that we are confronted with an extremely complex problem, even if it is clarified (if not solved) by the words Montaigne wrote on the first page of his *Essais*: "Je suis moy-mesmes la matiere de mon livre..." [26] Whether we can still speak of a paradox, as happens so frequently nowadays,[27] and whether Montaigne himself saw the paradoxical side of his undertaking, are entirely different questions, which, for the time being, do not need to be raised. My only concern is to establish that Montaigne's knowledge of ancient writers does not fall far behind that of others of his contemporaries, and that his admiration for Antiquity was no less consistent or sustained. But in his case knowledge and veneration were of such an entirely different kind and were aimed at such a curious goal that they can, indeed, be called paradoxical. The ancients were not kept at a solemn distance; they were absorbed and controlled by the life of the reader, which we then see emerging from his writing. And so Montaigne may well have put into practice something that had existed potentially in Italian humanism from the start. Despite the distance maintained, despite the desire to study the ancients on their own terms and to regard them as intangible, many humanists also used

---

[24] For a broader exposition of the term *ars*, see Paul Oskar Kristeller, "The Modern System of the Arts," *Journal of the History of Ideas*, XII (1951), 496-527, and XIII (1952), 17-46.

[25] II, 37 (vol. IV, p. 264).

[26] "Au Lecteur" (vol. I, p. 1).

[27] Alfred Glauser, *Montaigne paradoxal* (Paris, 1972), goes fairly far in this respect.

their reading matter for their own ends; but never was that done so intensively and so "systematically" as by Montaigne.

III. THE PRESENCE OF ANTIQUITY IN THE FRENCH RENAISSANCE

No one will deny that the ancients were obviously *present* during the Renaissance of the fifteenth and sixteenth centuries, or that respect for ancient culture was directly connected with this phenomenon. But the problem is to establish the form and the manner of their presence. Was it, for example, no more than a metaphor? To answer this question we should perhaps start by establishing what the presence of the ancients *was not* for the vast majority of humanists. Even in Italy, where people lived, as it were, among the ruins of ancient Rome, interest in the concrete remains was by no means particularly pronounced in all circles. A great deal happened, of course, between Brunelleschi and Raphael.[28] Most of the buildings and images literally had to be "uncovered," and we cannot overlook the development of archeology begun by the first antiquarians. Yet most of those whom we regard as great humanists often paid very little attention to this new activity. It is in vain that we look for this, the most direct and most concrete presence of the ancients, in Salutati, Valla, Ficino or Pico della Mirandola, or later in Erasmus. There are various reasons, of which I shall simply give one that is particularly evident in France.

Quite apart from the fact that people had to learn to *see* this form of presence, there is no doubt that this new visual activity was hindered by habits of thought from which it was hard to break away. The French who visited Rome did indeed see the ruins, but all they observed in this spectacle of former greatness was decay. They frequently "moralized" in a medieval fashion about the majestic remains which were the expression and the symbol of earthly transience. *Roma pagana* and the fate which befell it were contrasted with the specific immortality of *Roma aeterna*. This idea appeared in the Middle Ages in the famous poem by Hildebert of Lavardin, to give just one example. And Joachim du Bellay did more or less the same thing centuries later. In *Antiquitez de Rome*, which, according to his own words, contains "une generale description de sa grandeur et comme une deploration de sa ruïne," [29] he expressed his grief over the

---

[28] Cf. Weiss, *The Renaissance Discovery*; and Arnaldo Momigliano, "Ancient History and the Antiquarian," *Journal of the Warburg and Courtauld Institutes*, XIII (1950), 285-315.

[29] *Œuvres poétiques*, II (Paris, 1910), 1.

decline of a once so mighty city. But for him *aeternitas* lay elsewhere, and precisely because of that the actual seeing of the ruins presented to him severe problems. Take the tercets of the fifth sonnet:

> Le corps de Rome en cendre est devallé,
> Et son esprit rejoindre s'est allé
> Au grand esprit de ceste masse ronde.
> Mais ses escripts, qui son loz le plus beau
> Malgré le temps arrachent du tumbeau,
> Font son idole errer parmy le monde.

Admittedly there is no religious note in these lines, but the eternity of texts is contrasted with the palpable disintegration of physical buildings. Written texts are free from "tempus edax," as so many other poems pointed out, and so they know neither old age nor decrepitude. I feel that this emphasis on the significance of the written word is a salient characteristic of humanism, or at any rate of humanism in France, where people naturally had fewer chances to see the ancient ruins with their own eyes. Although Budé's *De Asse* is of great numismatic value, although Montaigne did indeed show a tourist-like interest in archeology on his famous journey, the fact remains that the interest in written sources was substantially greater and, in the course of time, acquired an exclusive importance. Even in the eighteenth century, Président de Brosses complained that, though he had descended into Herculaneum and Pompeii as into a cavern, he found no new manuscripts.[30] The same reaction was quite common as late as the nineteenth century: "humanism" was still the domain of men of letters and philologists. It was a long time before archeology acquired the position which it enjoys today as one of the most interesting and exciting aspects of the presence of the ancients.

But what can the presence of the ancients have meant if it was limited to texts? As we have seen, Machiavelli spoke to the writers he read. He asked them to account for what they had done, and they evidently complied. At first sight there is nothing surprising about this. It can be seen as little more than a metaphor which, by definition, is not to be taken literally. And, indeed, there is no room for surprise —but whether for this reason or another is an entirely different matter. What Machiavelli described was quite usual and had often been said before him in almost identical terms. Petrarch concluded his *Familiari* with a number of letters addressed to ancient writers. Time which

---

[30] Cf. *Le Président De Brosses en Italie* . . . (Paris, 1858), 428.

had passed, which was over and could no longer be reached or recaptured, appears not to have existed for him. He addressed himself to Cicero, Quintilian, and others as though they were contemporaries with whom he could have a discussion and who were still alive despite their death.

Is this, too, a metaphor? Is it simply another remarkable attitude toward the past and the absent? It would be all too simple to dismiss the problem in this way. We should at least look for the significance of such an attitude and for its consequences, especially when we see that many men had similar experiences and emphasized their importance in strikingly similar terms. Erasmus was one of them. When he published a work by Cicero, the reader was informed in the "Foreword":

> Geri videtur quod legis, nec secus afflat animum tuum quidam orationis ἐνθουσιασμός, quam si ex vivo ipsius pectore felicissimo illo ore manantem audires . . .
> Quid enim felicius quam cum eloquentissimis simul ac sanctissimis viris, quoties lubitum est, confabulari? neque minus habere perspectum illorum, qui ante tot annos vixerunt, ingenium, mores, cogitationes, studia, facta, quam si multis annis egisses cum illis consuetudinem.[31]

Erasmus tells us that Cicero is dead and absent, but once he has admitted this, he goes on to emphasize Cicero's living presence. *Audire, confabulari* and other words, or *familialiter vivere* in the same passage, show that the dialogue is actually taking place between the living. Thus far Erasmus is doing what others had done before him, although he is perhaps still more emphatic and radical in his abolition of the time separating him from Cicero. But we find something quite different in a few lines of the *Paraclesis*, a text added to his edition of the New Testament and which, to my mind, is of paramount importance. I refer to the last lines of the tract, lines which are accentuated precisely because they appear at the end:

> Si quis ostendat Christi pedibus impressum vestigium, quam procumbimus Christiani, quam adoramus. At cur non potius vivam illius et spirantem imaginem in hisce veneramur libris? . . . Ligneam aut saxeam statuam amore Christi gemmis auroque decoramus. Quin haec potius auro gemmisque et si quid his pretiosius insigniuntur, quae tanto praesentius Christum nobis referunt quam ulla imaguncula? Siquidem illa, quid aliud quam corporis figuram exprimit—si tamen

---

[31] *Opus Epistolarum Des. Erasmi Roterodami*, eds. P. S. and H. M. Allen, 12 vols. (Oxford, 1906-1958), No. 1390, ll. 92-101.

> illius quicquam exprimit—at hae tibi sacrosanctae mentis illius vivam referunt imaginem, ipsumque Christum loquentem . . . denique totum ita praesentem reddunt, ut minus visurus sis, si coram oculis conspicias.[32]

I need say nothing about *vivus, spirans* and similar terms. What is more interesting is the comparative *praesentius*: an expression such as "more present" points to an impossible reality; it says exactly what Erasmus meant. For him the presence of Christ in the Book was richer, more significant, even more visible than if we were actually to see his body on earth. I shall not analyze the spiritualization which takes place in this passage and is characteristic of Erasmus (and of some forms of humanism). I simply want to stress that it would be absurd to regard these lines as expressing a metaphor which is not meant literally— this is simply out of the question when Erasmus thinks about Christ and the *philosophia Christi*. For Erasmus and for many others, the written word made the absent far more present than they could ever be in reality.

Unless I am mistaken, little of this is to be found in French humanism. I cannot say why this is or why it should be. Is there any point in suggesting the existence of a typically French mentality or some innate rational tendency? These are clichés, or they serve as a *passepartout* which is used whenever people are at a loss for explanations. No one can say what "typically French" really means. Even if rationalism did play an important part at an early stage, even if it did help to condition thought and literature, there are many forms of reason, and few of them have any decisive or preponderant significance in the Renaissance. I am inclined to believe that, in the fifteenth century and even in the days of Erasmus and Luther, the written word served a different function and was regarded differently from how it later came to be regarded. When the Italian humanists sat before the written word of a newly discovered manuscript, it was something of a monument, an excavated image. It came from Antiquity (or so they thought) and was indeed the living presence of an ancient writer. In the case of a printed edition, however, this was felt far less acutely or not at all. But even here we must remember that the written word appeared in a strictly orally-oriented culture. For centuries men had read aloud, and although they did so far less by the fifteenth century, an element of the oral tradition survived. In short, for a long time reading presupposed not only the presence of a

---

[32] *Ausgewählte Werke*, eds. Hajo Holborn and Annemarie Holborn, 2nd ed. (Munich, 1964), 148-149.

reader, but also of others. Reading was like a conversation. Consequently, there undoubtedly remained a Platonic and Christian preference for the spoken word, which seemed to be a more natural and
direct reflection of man's innermost concerns.[33] This alone was
reason enough to hear the spoken word in the written word and to
find the speaking presence of an absent writer in it.

But why did the force of this habit gradually dwindle? It is quite
likely that the spread of printing had something to do with it. At
first—and Erasmus, as we saw, is an obvious example of this—it had
hardly any effect on the idea of the speaking author in the printed
book. But as the years went by some far-reaching changes must have
occurred. The book stood as a book, in other words it replaced the
writer and accentuated his absence. Fewer and fewer conversations
with ancient authors took place, and what had previously been regarded as a presence came more and more to be regarded as the
pretence of a presence: books were read *as if* the authors were there.
Must I add that there was no radical split? Neither Petrarch nor
Erasmus lost sight of the text; on the other hand, nobody denied the
past existence of the author. The point is that the manner of reading
changed; the conversation with the living and present author was
replaced, to a certain extent, by a conversation with the text. That appears to have been the case in sixteenth-century France and has more
or less remained so ever since. Nowadays we are really faced with a
metaphor, which only gives an approximate, figurative indication of
how a text is dealt with, but this originated from a clear and concrete
attitude towards the text. Although we are still familiar with, and
even experience, the same metaphor, although the text still pretends
to be present, there are nevertheless certain elements in the humanist
way of reading which strike us as odd. What actually happened to the
text?

IV. Reading, Books, and Language: French Humanism and the Written Word

A central question concerns the manner of reading and, more
particularly, interpreting literary texts. We can only gain an idea of
this when the readers of a certain period give an account of their
experiences, turning from readers into writers. Their writings can be

---

[33] According to some recent studies by the French philosopher Derrida,
this was the most important and fatal prejudice of metaphysics and consequently
of European thought in general.

theoretical—instructions for interpretation, for example—or, as new literary creations, they can shed light on how other, earlier works were read. I shall not spend too much time on the first category, which is the most accessible to us. There would be no point in giving detailed accounts of the countless *arts poétiques* in Italy and France or the important contemporary monographs devoted mainly to epic and tragedy. In view of the mass of modern studies on this topic, it would be superfluous even to give a list of names.[34] Of far greater interest, precisely because they are less in fashion now (although there is no lack of them!) are the literary works which reveal both how the authors read and how they thought people ought to read. This alone is a reason for dwelling on them. This sort of literature is not merely a part of the literary production of this period; it constitutes nearly the whole of Renaissance literature. The reason for this is clear, though it must be sought in the distant past, and I shall content myself with a single suggestion.

When discussing *decorum* I referred to the importance of ancient rhetoric. Its importance must be stressed once again. Not only did the rhetorical texts and instructions have a colossal influence on the way of writing, but also on the manner of thinking which characterized the Renaissance and humanism.[35] The influence went so deep and spread so far that it can be found everywhere and is therefore especially difficult to trace: in literature, in the visual arts, in theories of logic, in dramaturgy, and in many other fields. The presence of rhetoric is pervasive, whether we look at Italy, France, or, of course, England. Nowadays this is puzzling in more than one respect. To begin with, we are puzzled by the fact that a system of instructions and rules could exercise so obvious and so great a power, especially since this system was designed primarily for orators. Even if we disregard the development of rhetoric since Antiquity, it should be pointed out that in this respect, too, we can see how the importance and the diffusion of the spoken word was replaced by the written one.

---

[34] August Buck, *Italienische Dichtungen vom Mittelalter bis zum Ausgang der Renaissance*, Beihefte zur Zeitschrift für romanische Philologie, 94 (Tübingen, 1952); Bernard Weinberg, *A History of Literary Criticism in the Italian Renaissance*, 2 vols. (Chicago, 1961); Baxter Hathaway, *The Age of Criticism: The late Renaissance in Italy* (Ithaca, N.Y., 1962).

[35] Buck, *Italienische Dichtungen*; Weinberg, *History of Literary Criticism*; Paul Oskar Kristeller, *Renaissance Thought: The Classic, Scholastic, and Humanist Strains* (New York, 1961), 11ff.; Grahame Castor, *Pléiade Poetics: A Study in Sixteenth-Century Thought and Terminology* (Cambridge, 1964).

It is in these rhetorical tracts, both ancient and modern, that we find the virtually prescribed manner of reading and interpreting. Precisely because *imitatio* was from the beginning regarded as one of the basic principles, it makes little difference whether we quote an ancient text or an *ars poetica* of the French or Italian Renaissance. Their relationship is one of continuous imitation. I shall therefore select my examples at random, though I should first emphasize that the humanists based themselves almost entirely on a tract wrongly attributed to Cicero, the *Rhetorica ad Herennium*, and on the works of Quintilian. At one point in Quintilian's *Institutiones Oratoriae*, the various qualities of listening and reading are compared with one another. Among the advantages of reading is the fact that critical judgment can be exercised more easily, for, unlike the listener, the reader is not obliged to follow the flow of the speaker's words. He can, and indeed must, reread. What follows is particularly important, especially the way in which Quintilian illustrates with an image: "Repetamus autem et retractemus, et ut cibos mansos ac prope liquefactos demittimus, quo facilius digerantur, ita lectio non cruda, sed multa iteratione mollita et velut confecta, memoriae imitationique tradatur." [36] The written word must be chewed like a piece of food and be liquified, which is the true way of making sure that it remains in the memory and can be used for imitation. Is this a mere metaphor? If so, it is one that had an enormous success. Centuries later, Petrarch expressed himself in almost identical terms in his famous letter to Giovanni da Certaldo. That by then other traditions had presumably entered into play along with the purely rhetorical one, is a point on which I shall not dwell.[37] This qualification did not apply, in any case, to Machiavelli, whose words we may recall, any more than it did to Du Bellay, who laid more emphasis than anyone else did on this curious form of "eating." Both men are in a strictly rhetorical tradition, and nowhere is the need for this *ruminatio* presented with more vigor —we might almost say youthful aggression—than in the *Deffence*. How did the Romans manage to enrich their language, asks Du Bellay, and make it the equal of Greek? "Immitant les meilleurs aucteurs Grecs, se transformant en eux, les devorant, et apres les avoir bien digerez, les convertissant en sang et nourriture ...." [38] Although

---

[36] X, i, 19.
[37] Cf. S. Dresden, "Het herkauwen van teksten," in *Forum der Letteren*, 3/4 (1971), which is due to appear in an expanded form in French.
[38] Ed. Chamard (Paris, 1948), 42.

the images almost tumble over one another, they all lead in the same direction and can be regarded as synonymous. The words "eat," "devour," and the expression to "convert to the reader's flesh and blood" (*convertere* is a conventional term in this context) undoubtedly mean one and the same thing. What then has happened to the text? Simply what Montaigne so calmly stated: What I remember no longer belongs to the author but to me.[39] The reader has absorbed the text. If we now reread the words of Du Bellay, he seems to say that the Roman readers transformed themselves into their Greek models. May I again recall Machiavelli and his words, "tutto mi transferisco in loro"? This can only mean that the readers are absorbed by their models, thus reaching the extreme opposite to what Du Bellay suggests.

I can see no solution to this contradiction, but perhaps we should not take the metaphor too seriously. There is no reason to do so, and the fact remains that the doctrine of imitation, with which these images of *ruminatio* are intimately connected, moves between the two poles. Du Bellay thus probably meant to refer to both images at once. At any rate, reading was intended to bring a certain change to the text, which is hardly surprising in view of the rhetorical tradition. For centuries the *paraphrasis* had always been one of the obligatory exercises for understanding the contents of a text. Judging by the definitions given by the ancients and continually repeated by, among many others, Erasmus during the Renaissance, the purpose was to retain the sense of the words, while changing the words themselves. Consequently, or so the humanists thought, the essential was retained and only the adventitious altered. *Imitatio* thus acquired a very different meaning and turned easily into *aemulatio*. Within the rigid framework of rhetorical literary tradition, the reader, and above all the creator, was to compete with the text which he read. He endeavored to reach the same level, to attain the same degree of perfection, as his model.

Precisely because of the paraphrastic alterations, the product of the writing reader was never quite like the original text. "Simile non idem," said Petrarch, and the doctrine was repeated and elaborated in countless later works.[40] The man who wishes to produce a work of

---

[39] Cf. note 21 above.

[40] Cf. the correspondence between Bembo and Gianfrancesco Pico della Mirandola, and Erasmus's *Ciceronianus*. An interesting study on earlier views is A. Reiff, *Interpretatio, Imitatio, Aemulatio* (Würzburg, 1959).

art must work like a bee (a simile which had been used since Seneca),[41] otherwise he will never get beyond mimicry—a defect to be found in the French theorists, who revived the standard theories of imitation and added very little that was new. Ronsard, who took relatively little interest in theoretical problems, displayed a singular lack of interest in this topic. Can we assume that he recognized the need for imitation, just as everyone else did? Undoubtedly so, but it was equally true that an entirely different theory played an important role in the circle of the Pléiade, a theory which seems to us far more modern and which was to come into its own in the age of Romanticism. It is as though a relatively elaborate doctrine of "fureur poétique," of genius and divine inspiration, was to become the exact opposite of rhetorical imitation.[42] But this view is an anachronistic misconception. The amazing part of it all is that, for these poets, inspiration was expressed *within* rhetoric, and originality (a virtually unknown concept, for which the word *naïveté* tended to be used) was an aspect of imitation.

Nowhere did this relationship appear so clearly as in the manner of handling quotations. The quotation is obviously connected with and is, in a sense, the consequence of paraphrase. In the paraphrase, the words of a text are replaced, while the meaning is retained. A form of quotation develops when a few words of the text remain, while others and, ultimately, the sense of the whole text, are altered. As we know, humanist literature—poetry, philosophical tracts, and every other type of literature—was full of quotations. What was the point of this practice? Initially, we must consider the admiration of the humanists for venerable, ancient models, and then the authority with which they tried to clothe their own writings by recalling what ancient writers had said on the subject. This appeal to the ancients makes it likely that, in the beginning at least, quotations also had another source. In order to clarify this, I shall choose an example not from the ancients, but from a source in every way comparable to the ancient ones. Speaking of Origen, whom he greatly admired, Erasmus wrote: "totus huius sermo sacrorum Voluminum sententiis ceu gemmulis emblematibus distinctus est, sed adeo commode et in loco insertis ut nihilo secius

---

[41] *Ad Lucilium*, XI, 84. Cf. Jürgen von Stackelberg, "Das Bienengleichnis," *Romanische Forschungen*, LXVIII (1956).

[42] Castor, *Pléiade Poetics*; Henri Franchet, *Le Poète et son oeuvre d'après Ronsard*, Bibliothèque littéraire de la Renaissance, series 2, vol. 7 (Paris, 1923).

currat oratio. Dicas esse non ascita sed ibi nata, nec aliunde quaesita
sed sua sponte praesto esse." [43]

We can say, without exaggerating, that Origen knew the Bible by
heart, and that biblical texts thus flowed quite naturally from his pen.
They cannot be considered quotations in the modern sense of the
term, quotations which can be verified. Their presence in a new text
is such that they belong completely to it and emanate from it ("ibi
nata"). What Erasmus says of Origen can be applied to many medieval
writers—Bernard of Clairvaux is a particularly splendid example—and
to some humanist writers with regard to the ancients. The humanists,
too, appropriated texts to the extent that they no longer knew whether
they were quoting or not, at least in our sense of the term "quote."
This point may well be more important than it has so far seemed,
because all of the other reasons leading to the practice of quotation
(and which may still be justified) may in fact stem from this one source.

The consequences were numerous, most important of which was
that the humanist system of quotation rested on a completely different
basis than our own system; and not only quotation, but also imitation
in general, including plagiarism, stood in an entirely different light.[44]
Humanistic quotations show how much things have changed, in the
reading of texts as well as in the character of the audience. By quoting
so much and with such evident satisfaction, the writers of the Renaissance did not simply want to exhibit their knowledge, to embellish
their own work with borrowed glory, or to expand it with the authority of others. For they relied on the learning of their reading public, so
that their skill, their *ars*, should not be displayed in vain. They did not
have to specify when they were quoting, paraphrasing, or making
allusions, because they assumed that their readers were just as well
educated as they themselves were and therefore quite capable of
recognizing the quotations. The writers' art was to manipulate the
sources so well that the borrowed products fitted organically (think of
the term *ruminare*) into their new contexts. Quotations thus served to
make old literature new. They belonged to the ancients but also to the

---

[43] *Opera omnia*, 10 vols. (Leiden, 1703-1706), VIII, 438 A-B. The terminology
is reminiscent of Valla: "Et sicut gemma aureo inclusa annulo non deornamento,
sed ornamento est, ita noster sermo accedens aliorum sermoni vernaculo contulit
splendorem, non sustulit." *Prosatori latini del Quattrocento*, a cura di Eugenio
Garin, La letteratura italiana, storia e testi, 13 (Milan and Naples, 1952), 596.

[44] Michael Metschies, *Zitat und Zitierkunst in Montaignes Essais*, Kölner romanistische Arbeiten, new series, 37 (Geneva and Paris, 1966), who gives a brief,
general survey.

poetry of Ronsard and to the poems of Montaigne, where they took up
a new place of their own.[45] Once more the temporal distance was
overcome.

In this important area of humanistic reading and writing, the
French authors did not deviate from the custom established in Italy;
nor could they have done so, because the established methods were a
major, even a truly essential, element in the humanistic "attitude".
This remained true, despite the rise of various differences of opinion
about who should be imitated and how. Rabelais, for example,
naturally quoted different authors than Montaigne did; and, given the
structure of his work, Rabelais was probably in a better position than
any other writer of the fifteenth or sixteenth century to make his
quotations sound relatively modern. He turned them into parodies,
pastiches, which we regard as purely ironical; [46] and his puns rest
partly on quotations which have been slightly distorted, retaining the
same sound but assuming a completely different, ridiculous or bawdy,
meaning.

Nothing similar is to be found in Montaigne. His relativism
develops on another level and does not depend on quotations. The
most remarkable aspect of his writings is that so many quotations
should appear in so independent and wayward a work. Once more,
however, our surprise arises from an anachronistic attitude. Like
every other humanist, Montaigne, as we see from his very first *Essais*,
was concerned to compile extracts and interesting passages from the
ancient writers he had read.[47] We have already shown how he appro-

---

[45] Admittedly E. Löfstedt, "Reminiscence and Imitation," *Eranos*, XLVII
(1949), 148, says that "an expression, a phrase, a thought, which in the original
place is natural, clear and well motivated, usually becomes somewhat peculiar,
a trifle hazy or less suitable in the context, when borrowed or imitated by another
author, especially if this author is not a very great artist." But the terms have been
so carefully chosen and the last words reveal such a great restriction that I do
not feel that I have gone too far.

[46] Cf. Jean Milly, *Les pastiches de Proust* (Paris, 1970); and idem, "Les pastiches
de Proust," in *Le Français Moderne* (January-April, 1967). I mention these studies
which deal with an entirely different writer because they deal at length with the
general problem of the pastiche. Besides, it would be wrong to think that the
habit of pastiche has disappeared (i.e., after Romanticism). On the contrary, it
has had a strong revival in modern literature (since Joyce's *Ulysses* and various
works by Thomas Mann). I hope to go into this at greater length in a different
context.

[47] In his edition of the *Essais* (Paris, 1962), Samuel de Sacy wrote (p. xii):
"Montaigne, comme tant d'autres en son temps, compilait, compilait,
compilait . . . ." The quotations are regarded as the infrastructure of the entire
work.

priated them. He regarded quotations in the modern sense of the word as "un ridicule fruict de la science," [48] tokens of the bookish knowledge he despised. But he rejected book-learning only to the degree that it replaced personal meditation about the proper manner of living or failed to be assimilated and become part of the reader. This does not mean that Montaigne was against the custom of basing oneself on books: he, too, accepted the precept.

All of this leads us to think of a kind of secondary literature, by which phrase is meant neither a qualitative judgment nor a body of literature about literature. On the contrary, I mean literary works that developed out of already existing works. In a certain sense, Renaissance literature was conditioned by the works available to its writers. It developed out of them and wanted to be, in its own way, what the original was. This was true, up to a point, from the very beginning; but sixteenth-century writers were more conscious of the situation, and its theoretical basis had been further developed in France and further yet in Italy. In addition, the specifically humanistic form of imitation was no longer limited to classical models and was extended to the great modern masters, who were to be equalled, if not surpassed, by their pupils. The new works were no longer conceivable without the old ones. In fact, there was no longer acknowledged an essential difference between old and new. A kind of timelessness of art was accepted, implicitly or explicitly, by everyone.

It is a striking fact that humanists and other Renaissance writers should have been so engrossed in texts. The curious presence of books and the great reverence for the written word (even if it seemed to be spoken) are aspects of a life spent in the midst of books and language. Examples are so numerous that we can choose them at random. Petrarch said repeatedly that he lived for letters, for reading and writing. The same idea is found in Erasmus's first *epistolae* and also in Pico della Mirandola. The French humanists differed little in this respect from their Italian predecessors, nor did the later Italians, quite apart from individual variations.

A still more interesting consequence of this bookish life was that the vast majority of humanists, whether in Italy or elsewhere, whether of the fifteenth or the sixteenth century, tended to regard their books as their children. We still recognize this metaphor and need not be sur-

---

[48] III, 12 (vol. VI, p. 167).

prined by it. At that time, however, it was conceived in a far more concrete manner. What to us may seem a pun, such as "libri-liberi," is to be found in the writings of Ficino,[49] as well as those of Erasmus, and it is characteristic of the whole of humanism. Nor does spiritual fatherhood appear in this context alone; it also occurs in connection with pupils. The teacher is literally a spiritual father, who must be regarded as still more important than the natural father. Humanistic pedagogy, one of the most popular subjects in the literature of the time, acquired a special dimension through this concept; and no one hesitated to accept one of its most remarkable consequences: the pupil formed by his "father" became like a book written by his father. Ficino wrote in one of his letters: "liber est discipulus carens anima, discipulus est liber vivens." [50]

The idea of spiritual fatherhood was far from original with Ficino. The fact that the Torah had for centuries been regarded as the spiritual father of the faithful can hardly have influenced Ficino, but he was certainly aware of the importance of the tradition passed from father to son in the Hermetic writings. In any case, his translations and commentaries set the fashion for later generations, who were to use similar expressions. The idea of the "Vermenschlichung des Buches" [51] persisted everywhere, although, as time went by, the echo of these words and expressions faded in France and finally blended with the metaphor as we know it today.

Not only was the idea of the pupil as a book taken seriously and literally at the time, but the cult of the book had also other effects. Each person, and each nature as a whole, was regarded as a book. In this respect, too, humanism contributed nothing new: I need hardly recall the biblical tradition which was so devoutly cultivated during the Middle Ages. Suffice here to quote Alanus de Insulis: "Omnis mundi creatura / Quasi liber et pictura / Nobis est in speculum. . . ." What strikes us in some humanistic writers (and had, incidentally, already taken place some time before) is a radicalization whereby the "quasi" was driven into the background. Another concept, considered far more disquieting, was now coupled with this orthodox theory. Cabalistic views, which always claimed to be interpretations of the

---

[49] *Opera omnia* (Basel, 1561), I, 883.

[50] *Ibid.*, 659.

[51] Walter Rüegg, in his introduction to *Geistige Väter des Abendlandes. Eine Sammlung von hundert Buchtiteln antiker Autoren*, ed. Gerda Finsterer-Stuber (Stuttgart, 1960), viii.

Torah, entered humanist thought once and for all with Pico della Mirandola. The speculations about the Book, now deserving to be written with a capital letter, became of immense importance. Although not necessarily connected with Hermetic and Platonic doctrines, such ideas were all predicated, despite their variations, on the pre-existence of the Torah as a book. The Book existed before the creation of the world. Not only was it the absolute model for creation, it actually produced the creation.

These were fascinating notions, which endured in European culture all during the Renaissance and long thereafter, in theology as well as in literature. Fifteenth and sixteenth-century Italy and France saw many contributors to this tradition: Lazzarelli, Egidio da Viterbo, Symphorien Champier, Guillaume Postel, and the two brothers Le Fèvre de la Boderie.[52] None of these men attained the significance or the influence of a Pico or a Reuchlin, a fact that may well imply more than a difference of quality, at least in so far as France is concerned. Erasmus was little influenced by Cabalistic fantasies, which were contrary to his natural inclinations; and he was apprehensive about a judaizing influence upon the faith. Most, but not all, of the reformers steered clear of the Cabala for another reason: for them the Bible was the only Book. Finally, the influence of the Paduan philosophers and the development of scientific thought in France hindered the rapid spread of Cabalistic notions. Although it is perfectly possible to encounter them unexpectedly in every sort of book, the general line moved in another direction. The cult of the Book could barely retain its hold against the mathematical world view that was coming into being. It had to content itself with an underground existence until the nineteenth century, when it reappeared with full force in French symbolism.

We can undoubtedly refer to magical and mystical notions in the Book—strong words, perhaps, but surely justified when speaking of certain lofty theories which contributed to the climate of the Renaissance. It may therefore be well to produce an antidote. That Rabelais should have produced it is not surprising, while the fact that he should have taken an interest in the "book" as such also proves the importance and influence of the ideas connected with it. Pantagruel is travelling with his friends to the oracle of the Dive Bouteille in order to discover

---

[52] François Secret, *Le Zôhar chez les kabbalistes chrétiens de la Renaissance*, Etudes juives, No. 10 (Paris and The Hague, 1964); idem, *Les Kabbalistes chrétiens de la Renaissance* (Paris, 1964).

whether Panurge was right to trust it. In the *Cinquiesme Livre*, whose
authenticity has not been established, the author describes in the
usual satirical manner the ceremonies of this superhuman revelation.
The priestess Bacbuc interprets the oracles, but in her own way.
Philosophers and others feed people through their ears while "icy nous
réallement incorporons nos préceptions par la bouche"—a form of
ruminatio, incidentally. She then picks up an object which at first looks
like a book ("comme ung bréviaire"), but is no more than "ung
vénéré, vray et naturel flacon, plain de vin. ..." If Panurge wants to
understand what he "reads," he must remember above all that Bacbuc
never said to him: "Lisez ce chappitre, voyez ceste glose," but
"Vuidez, tastez ce chappitre, avallez ceste belle glose." [53] Panurge could
hardly complain about the authenticity of this particular manner of
reading! Not only is fun poked at the age-old passion for commentaries,
which still dominated humanism, but, by adding to this yet another
long tradition which regarded mystical inspiration as a *sobria ebrietas*,
Rabelais makes the Book itself seem ridiculous.[54] Supernatural wisdom
is imbibed, because the book is a bottle. Or rather, the book turns
into a bottle, because it had been said for centuries that the mystical
experience entails an intoxication of a very special sort. In those days
it was no metaphor. It has become for Rabelais an image which he
perpetuated and appeared to take seriously in his own fashion, that is,
within the framework of a parody. The cult of the Book thus endured
and grew.

Even less than in Rabelais, do we expect to find the cult of the book
in Montaigne. Yet, although it takes a very special form, the cult is not
only present but may be regarded perhaps as the basis of his entire
scheme. Not that he paid any attention to a pre-existing Book, though
he was well acquainted with such notions. It was his own book that
assumed a special function for him. His true purpose may have been
"de se faire connaître," but he adds elsewhere that the study of himself
was his "metaphisique" and his "phisique." [55] The surprising part is
that he wanted not only to cultivate himself, but to do so at very close
quarters indeed: "Le monde regarde tousjours vis à vis; moy, je

[53] Chapitre XLV. Here and for *ruminatio* in general, one should recall Ezechiel
2, and Revelation 5:1ff.

[54] Cf. *Rabelais-Nuchtere dronkenschap*, Mededelingen der Kon. Nederl. Akademie
v. Wetenschappen, Afd. Letterkunde, XXXV, 4 (1972), which will appear in an
expanded French version. Cf. Florence M. Weinberg, *The Wine and the Will:
Rabelais's Bacchic Christianity* (Detroit, 1972).

[55] III, 13 (vol. VI, p. 191).

replie ma veue au dedans, je la plante, je l'amuse là." [56] His book had nothing supernatural about it. On the contrary, it remained especially close to an individual human life, and, so far as Montaigne himself was concerned, there is no doubt that, if the *Essais* were not his life *realiter*, they became his life *idealiter*. I shall pass by the many statements he makes to this effect, wishing only to show that, in Montaigne's case, too, we can speak of a special place occupied by the book. Admittedly the place is nearly at the opposite extreme to that accorded it in other views, but it is no less the result of a radical ambition.

It is obvious that attitudes toward the Book were closely connected with the function attributed to language; and it is well known that language was central to humanist thought. It is thus all the more surprising that, until relatively recently, little attention was paid to the linguistic theories of the Renaissance.[57] Such studies have on the whole, been confined to analyses of rhetorical theories, *artes poeticae*, and the like—subjects very wide in themselves and of unquestionably great importance. I have little to add on this topic, because the difference between France and Italy on this score was not very great. Both countries were dominated for many years by a concept best described as linguistic theology. Its historical roots, of course, go back a long way, and, in its relation to the idea of the world as Book, it comes down to the notion that every phenomenon can and must be read (i.e., interpreted). Human language is a reflection of the writing of the world. The man who has "read" well not only possesses the reflection of the object, he possesses the object itself.

Some fascinating pages have recently been devoted to this "prose du monde." [58] Their author has perhaps attributed too much importance to the subject, for he gives the impression that this theory was the only one which had reason to exist and could have existed in this era. Be that as it may, it is certain that the idea of a primeval language was extremely important and assumed an almost religious significance; for, once unity was rediscovered and due honor was accorded to it, the existing confusion of tongues could come to an end. This end

---

[56] II, 27 (vol. IV, pp. 84-85).

[57] Cf. P. A. Verburg, *Taal en functionaliteit* (Dissertation, Amsterdam, 1951), and above all Karl Otto Apel, *Die Idee der Sprache in der Tradition des Humanismus von Dante bis Vico*, Archiv für Begriffsgeschichte, 8 (Bonn, 1963).

[58] Michel Foucault, *Les mots et les choses. Une archéologie des sciences humaines*, Bibliothèque des sciences humaines (Paris, 1966), 32ff. But see Claude Gilbert Dubois, *Mythe et langage au seizième siècle* (Paris, 1970).

would be nothing less than the ideal beginning described in Genesis 11:1: "Erat terra labii unius, et sermonum eorundem." That Hebrew should have received a preferential position is hardly surprising. Postel and many others, both before and after him, made their contributions to this development.[59] At the same time, however, it was possible to discern some very different tendencies. Besides Cabalistic and other speculations, there developed the first theories that we would call properly linguistic; but they stemmed from authors such as Fauchet, who remain fairly obscure. To various degrees, then, all these elements are to be found in France, but the French endeavored to combine the incompatible and hence never attained the heights aimed at by a writer such as Giordano Bruno, in his *De gl'Heroici Furori*.

What we have said about language in general can be applied more particularly to the requirements and the function of the poetic image, or what nowadays can at best be called the symbol. At the time of the Renaissance we can find, on the one hand, statements by men who keep strictly within a given technical framework, who might limit themselves to a (usually) brief analysis of what a metaphor is or should be, and who finally substantiate their theory with a quantity of examples and attempt to impose it with more or less force. On the other hand, however, "iconology" also found its place in Platonizing philosophy and the Hermetic writings. Here we find every sort of combination, and here, too, the French failed to distinguish themselves by making contributions.

If we are unable to speak of symbolization in previous centuries without risking a confusion of terms, it is nevertheless incontestable that allegorization was the great fashion. But this word hardly does justice to the phenemonon. Following the ancient allegory of the Stoics and the typological interpretation of the Scriptures, allegorization determined to a large extent the train of thought of medieval writers and theologians.[60] To this single observation I will merely add that, in this domain at least, there is no difference between the Middle

---

[59] See William J. Bouwsma, *Concordia Mundi: The Career and Thought of Guillaume Postel* (Cambridge, Mass., 1957), 104ff.

[60] Cf. Jean Pépin, *Mythe et allégorie. Les origines grecques et les contestations judéo-chrétiennes*, Philosophie de l'esprit (Paris, 1958); and Henri de Lubac, *Exégèse médiévale. Les quatre sens de l'Ecriture*, 2 parts in 4 vols., Théologie, Nos. 41, 42, 59 (Paris, 1959-1964). For the plastic arts, see E. H. Gombrich, *Symbolic Images: Studies in the Art of the Renaissance* (London, 1972). One of the most important humanist texts in this field is Salutati's *De Laboribus Herculis*.

Ages and the Renaissance. All we can say is that the humanists, for instance with Salutati, went still further and tended to declare the allegory, which had previously been mainly theological, suitable for the plastic arts. Even Erasmus, the founder of modern philology, did not fail to emphasize the necessity of allegorization.

Let me illustrate what I mean with a few examples, although I am well aware that the terminology which does not always distinguish between image, metaphor, allegory and symbol, does not make the matter any easier. I shall therefore begin with something which at first sight appears to be of a completely different nature. From the earliest times, men's attention had been attracted by certain obscure, not to say incomprehensible, passages in the Scriptures. Why should they be there? Many thinkers had tried to find a satisfactory answer. Some said that even in the Holy Scriptures not everything ought to be revealed to everyone; others that these obscurities were intended as a test and a challenge to the believer; and still others that ultimately inexpressible secrets were being concealed. As we know, the problem of the *claritas Scripturae* had been dealt with extensively by St. Augustine and remained of fundamental importance through the Reformation.[61] But that is less relevant. Combined with what I shall call the elitist concept and with ideas which were derived mainly from Horace, these notions found expression in the poetic convictions cherished by men such as the poets of the Pléiade. As the spiritual aristocrat that he was, the poet expressed himself in such a way that he chose his public and made it a matter of principle not to speak to all and sundry. He was an initiate addressing other initiates.

The *obscuritas* of what the poet said was of great importance. But for this there were other reasons and other motives. Obscurity suggests profundity, and it is important that St. Augustine had devoted so much attention to the *mira profunditas*. It is no mere coincidence that the ancients, or pseudo-ancient Hermetic tracts which, thanks partly to Ficino, had become so fashionable, laid continual emphasis on secrecy and on the impossibility of knowing and appreciating fully the inner depths of the secret and mysterious truth. The theme recurred in Neoplatonic texts,[62] writings which most humanists read avidly, which they "imitated" in their turn, and which became so

---

[61] Cf. Cornelius Augustijn, "Hyperaspistes I, Erasmus en Luther's leer van de Claritas Scripturae," *Erasmiana* (= *Vox Theologica*, April, 1969), 93ff.

[62] Peter Crome, *Symbol und Unzulänglichkeit der Sprache — Iamblichos, Plotin, Prophyrios, Proklos*, Humanistische Bibliothek, series I, 5 (Munich, 1970).

influential among the creative artists, because the best means of expressing the inexpressible is the poetic image. Without giving excessive importance to the inexpressible, Maurice Scève, with his *Délie*, is probably the best example of this sort of Hermetic-Platonic literature in western Europe. His poetry is also "exemplary" in the sense that he endeavored to convey a certain "knowledge," a profound Truth, by the appropriate means: similes, images, and metaphors.[63]

We can, of course, advance some other, still more obvious, reasons for *obscuritas*. In addition to *profunditas*, which led to obscurity and incomprehensibility, some authors may also have felt a sense of incapacity, reluctance, or fear. I shall leave aside incapacity. So far as fear was concerned, it was normally of a social nature: an author, usually of prose, might be frightened of expressing his ideas openly, because they were contrary to the official, predominant notions of a given period. Obscurity would then be employed as a form of self-preservation. One of the most intriguing texts in the French Renaissance, *Cymbalum Mundi* by Bonaventure des Périers, can indeed be "interpreted" in this way; but the four dialogues of this tiny work have been so submerged by commentaries (which, incidentally, are most necessary) that no single explanation can claim to be the right one, let alone the definitive one. There are too many problems of a social, religious, and literary nature, not to mention the fact that Des Périers may well have been influenced by Hermetic notions.[64] This only helps to show how complex the matter is. In the case of Scève, where there were probably no such social considerations, the obscurity is easier to fathom. Just like other poets of this period, he may have spoken in what were riddles for most men, whose ignorance prevented them from understanding his meaning. To the initiates and the connoisseurs, he revealed the profound truths contained in his mysteries, and his obscurity became transparent, even illuminating. And that is where the true significance of allegorizing writing and reading probably lies.

The remarkable thing is that, in sixteenth-century France, various tendencies which are to be found elsewhere are here developed to the extreme. The secrecy which needs "unravelling" is to be discerned just as often as allegorization in theology and philosophy, especially

---

[63] Hans Staub, *Le curieux désir: Scève et Peletier du Mans, poètes de la connaissance*, Travaux d'humanisme et renaissance, 94 (Geneva, 1967).

[64] Lucien Febvre, *Origène et des Périers ou l'énigme du Cymbalum mundi* (Paris, 1942); also in *Bibliothèque d'humanisme et renaissance*, II (1941).

in the prevailing fashion of *emblemata*. In the French Renaissance some writers went farther than writers did in other parts of Europe, while others abstained almost completely from notions such as those connected with linguistic theology. I do not regard this latter phenomenon as "typically French," and I would prefer to confine myself to the definite differences between individual thinkers and artists, although this may seem so banal that nobody will bother to disagree. I am well aware that it allows no great scope for elucidation, but are we any better off if we examine the cultural development of this period, which was so similar in Italy and France?

V. MANNERISM AND HUMANISM IN THE FRENCH RENAISSANCE

What had been taking place in Europe, particularly in western Europe, since the beginning of the sixteenth century is often described as a *crisis*; and for many it is a crisis which foreshadowed the situation of modern man in modern times. However doubtful this may be, the fact remains that there are enormous differences between the art and the thought of the two periods. This is especially obvious in the visual arts, and I would like to dwell on them for a moment. It would distort the French Renaissance unforgivably if we did not include sculpture, painting, and architecture. The chateaux on the Loire were not only concrete manifestations of the influence of Italian thought and Italian art in France, they also provided a model for the imaginary Abbaye de Thélème, which Rabelais described with such evident predilection. It is generally known how very much the literature of the Pléiade was inspired by the much abused Horatian adage, *ut pictura poesis*,[65] and we know of a great many cases of mutual contact and exchanges among various artists.

Although there are more sufficient reasons to devote some attention to the visual arts, we must realize that the problems connected with them are numerous and complex. Very soon after the "discovery" of the Renaissance, the term "baroque" assumed a definite place in art history. This place was located in the sixteenth century, especially the later part, with whose stylistic pecularities the term is identified. In French studies, relatively little heed was paid to this point, especially in the domain of literary history. Here the word "baroque" was introduced only after the Second World War and was then used to

---

[65] Rensselaer W. Lee, "Ut pictura poesis," *The Art Bulletin*, XXII (1940); John R. Spencer, "Ut rhetorica pictura," *Journal of the Warburg and Courtauld Institutes*, XX (1957), 26-45.

excess, while naturally the connection with the visual arts was immediately accentuated. Yet literary baroque arrived relatively late, in France at least, and it has even been said that the whole of seventeenth-century classicism was, in fact, baroque.

It is nonetheless clear to everyone that, despite chronological differences in the visual arts, music, and literature, baroque was not confined to national frontiers. We speak of an internationalism, which can be partially explained by the numerous journeys of connoisseurs and artists who found commissions and work outside their own country, but this does not make it easier to distinguish with any degree of accuracy between the various forms and phases of Italian influence in France.

The distinctions which must necessarily be made in order to do justice to the artistic situation become ever subtler. At the very moment when French scholars started to use the term baroque systematically, there appeared from the domain of art history the phenomenon known as Mannerism, a term used to describe the anticlassicism which succeeded the High Renaissance, in other words, the period after the death of Raphael and the Sack of Rome. It has justifiably been claimed that the Italian Renaissance affected France at the same time as Mannerism, not to say in a mannerist form; yet even in Mannerism we can find a number of phases and some pre-baroque elements. Rabelais's *Pantagruel* has been called baroque, but then so have some important passages from Racine's tragedies. Montaigne was declared a baroque artist twenty-five years ago, and many scholars now regard him as a mannerist. Finally, Ronsard, to mention just one other name, suffered a similar fate.[66]

This is not the place to investigate the chronological phases of the history of the visual arts. [67] Still less shall I deal with the especially delicate problem entailed by the "wechselseitige Erhellung der Künste." [68] I shall also try to maintain my distance from those who wish to see a radical change of mentality and a deep rift between the

---

[66] V. L. Saulnier, in Rabelais, *Pantagruel* (Paris, 1946), xl; L. Spitzer, "The 'récit de Théramène,' " in his *Linguistics and Literary History* (Princeton, 1948), 87ff.; M. Raymond on Ronsard, in the introduction to *La Poésie française et le Maniérisme* (Geneva and Paris, 1971), and his article cited in note 17 above.

[67] For recent views, see the volume *Renaissance, Maniérisme, Baroque* (Paris, 1972). See also *Manierismo, Barocco, Rococo* (Rome, 1962).

[68] The most cautious approach to this subject is in the work by Raymond, cited in note 66 above.

Renaissance and Mannerism.[69] Even if we limit ourselves to single facts, works, and ideas, too many difficulties still remain. There are plenty of facts: for example, the presence in France of Italian artists, such as Rosso and Primaticcio, and their significance for the so-called *école de Fontainebleau*. Some doubts still remain, however, about the precise nature and extent of their significance and about their ideas. I want only to concentrate on the term *maniera*, so essential for Mannerism. According to the most reliable investigations,[70] the approximate meaning of the word is "style," and, rather than coming from the visual arts, it was a term (following medieval French precedents) for what can best be called the art of living. Vasari, as we know, made excessive use of the term in the mid-sixteenth century to characterize the works of all sorts of artists.

We can now establish two facts: first, that a transposition took place from one domain to another; and, secondly, that we are dealing with a frequently recurring cultural-historical phenomenon. Let us start with the second. Vasari appears to support the thesis of a break between Mannerism and all that preceded it. At the same time, however, it is clear that there was no such break. On the contrary, there was continuity, for this same Mannerism was an accomplishment which included and went beyond what Leonardo, Raphael, and especially Michelangelo had done. Perhaps we can speak of a break and continuity simultaneously; an important artist is always different from all others, but, in the sixteenth century, this uniqueness did not appear as a denial of the past—nor does it today, at least not nearly so much as some would like to believe. The new artist finds his "originality" in the adaptation and assimilation of what is already present but, in his hands, assumes a new form. Thus, all we should see in Mannerism is a *forme seconde*, that is, a fairly common trait of the art of that era (and perhaps of all art). While we can refer to exaggeration and hyperboles, to distortion and irrationalism, and to discontinuity and paradox in Mannerism, all these qualities are in fact con-

---

[69] The most extreme example is to be found in Gustav René Hocke, *Die Welt als Labyrinth* (Hamburg, 1957); and *Manierismus in der Literatur* (Hamburg, 1959). Arnold Hauser, in *Mannerism* (London, 1965), goes slightly less far, though the word "crisis" is to be found in his subtitle. See, on the other hand, the far more disciplined analysis by John K. G. Shearmann, in *Mannerism* (London, 1967); and the observations by E. H. Gombrich in *Norm and Form* (London, 1966), 99ff.

[70] J. Shearmann, "*Maniera* as an aesthetic Ideal," in *Renaissance Art*, ed. C. Gilbert (New York, 1970), 181ff.

ditioned by unstated, or unconscious, starting points which assume the "equilibrium" of the Renaissance and classicism. Admittedly they are not valid for all works of this period. They may apply to the architecture of Giulio Romano, for example, but hardly to the French chateaux; and they throw little or no light on the *maniera* as a function in itself, or on how this style actually worked.

In the course of time, especially because of the fascinating effect of Michelangelo's personality and work, the artist's self-awareness increased immeasurably. I do not mean his social status and prestige (though these should not be underestimated), but an attitude toward art itself. The artist was asking himself more and more frequently what the concept of art was to mean, and of what his talent actually consisted. As concerns the first point, I allude only to the numerous tracts which emphasized *disegno*, the inner notion that underlay every concrete work and was purer, "more real," and richer than the work itself could be. Vasari, Lomazzo, and Zuccari, not to mention their fifteenth-century precursors, discussed it extensively.[71] It is the *maniera* which executes the *disegno*, that is to say, which realizes it in a work. The great question which every artist asked himself was how the *maniera* could do this and just what its power was. Mannerism and, if one will, the entire French Renaissance wanted to show what an artist could do. Let us accept for a moment the erroneous distinction between form and content: the mannerist preferred the possibilities offered him by form. He took pride in showing his talent in achievements which appeared to make the impossible possible. It is no mere coincidence that just in this period appeared the figure of the *virtuoso*. The artist wanted to display his unlimited, godlike skill; and he wanted (perhaps a little too often) to make the public comprehend the immense difficulties he had created for himself and had then overcome. This was the artistic *virtus* which was to amaze the connoisseurs.

French poetry, with its countless *concetti*, *pointes*, and other figures, should provide many examples of mannerist virtuosity, but the best example is Rabelais. He is always called a virtuoso of language, for reasons which every reader can appreciate after reading a few pages; but he hardly mentions virtuosity itself. It seems to me that his (mannerist? baroque?) virtuosity consists in the quest for realization of all language's potential for the creation of an impossible universe. He literally knew how to carry the reader into a world where giants

---

[71] Erwin Panofsky, *Idea*, 2nd ed. (Berlin, 1960).

consort with normal people and are sometimes giants no more, a
realm where our everyday, familiar world becomes a topsy-turvy
universe.[72] It is all very amusing and intended for entertainment, but
it also contains a gruesome element. Take the episode of the peasant.
The author, who suddenly appears in the story as a friend of Pantagruel, meets a peasant in the giant's mouth, where the peasant is
planting cabbages. Here, says the author, speaking in his own name,
"et qui vous fais ces tant véritables contes," we are in a new world.
Although the peasant has never been far from home, he knows that
there is another world over the mountains, and the author sets off on
a voyage of discovery over the rocks (read: teeth).[73] And what if *our*
world lay in the mouth of a giant? However loud and unconcerned
Rabelais's laugh (about which so much has been written), it would be
wrong not to perceive an undertone of burlesque in it. The exploration
of possibilities, which is virtuosity, also leads to restlessness and
insecurity.

If, some years ago, there were many reasons for regarding Montaigne
as a baroque artist, there are now just as many and just as sound
ones for seeing him as a mannerist. Of the often over-subtle arguments
which have led to this state of affairs, I shall say nothing. To indicate
the difficulties, which arise inevitably when we try to arrange everything in categories, it suffices to mention Montaigne's negative
attitude toward *maniera* and to point out the lack of a clear idea of it in
his work. It is true that Montaigne is regarded by many as a skeptic
par excellence; and it is also true that expressions of doubt appear
frequently in his work. It is perfectly legitimate to move from doubt
to disquiet, and thus to Mannerism, but not to move from doubt to
despair—and nothing in Montaigne's writings entitles us to regard
him as having done so. According to some scholars, Montaigne, the
representative of a late form of Mannerism, illustrates the despondency
and fundamental uncertainty reflected in the spiritual disruption of
Mannerism.[74] But even with the best will in the world, I find it
impossible to detect such an attitude in his work, and I am actually

---

[72] Hauser, *Mannerism*, 50, finds this nearly everywhere.

[73] Cf. Erich Auerbach's excellent analysis in *Mimesis* (Bern, 1946), 250ff.

[74] Cf. Hauser, *Mannerism*, 49ff. and 325ff.; M. Recksiek, *Montaignes Verhältnis
zu Klassik und Manierismus* (Bonn, 1966); and R. A. Sayce, in the volume *Renaissance,
Maniérisme, Baroque*, 43ff. and esp. 137ff. Montaigne had previously also been
labelled "baroque" by Sayce, in *French Studies*, VIII (1954), 1ff.; and by Imbrie
Buffum, *Studies in the Baroque from Montaigne to Rotrou*, Yale Romanic Studies,
2nd series, 4 (New Haven, 1957).

inclined to say the opposite. Montaigne may maintain that only
maihin in prudent certainty, and he may note with a certain satisfaction
that he himself "ne voit le tout de rien," but none of this amounts to
despair. If anything, the reverse is true: Montaigne lived in perfect
tranquillity with this radical uncertainty. It is, to repeat his much-
quoted words, "un doux et mol chevet." [75] Besides his skepticism,
some other typically mannerist traits may be found in Montaigne, but
they are all counterbalanced by the absence of the *maniera* itself. If we
accept that *maniera* is really a manner of acting and being, a certain
style, and that mannerists paid great, not to say exclusive, homage to
this concept, then Montaigne was not a mannerist. He made it quite
clear, that literary style was of no interest to him and rather to be
avoided than practiced with excessive devotion: "Comme à faire,
à dire aussi je suy tout simplement ma forme naturelle...." And
elsewhere we find the famous words, "que le Gascon y arrive, si le
François n'y peut aller! ... Le parler que j'ayme, c'est un parler
simple et naïf, tel sur le papier qu'à la bouche ...." [76] He wrote "sans
contention et artifice," as he asserted in his "Foreword." In short,
Montaigne pleaded repeatedly for simplicity and naturalness in writing
and in living. In this alone did he want to display his virtuosity.

I do not deny that there is something paradoxical about this:
Montaigne's sole ambition was to *conquer naturalness*. But perhaps it
only seems paradoxical to us; and the paradox existed hardly, or not at
all, for the artists of the sixteenth century. It may be objected that
some scholars have taken an excessive interest in the part played by
artificiality in Mannerism and have classified Montaigne as a mannerist, while he was in fact a supremely natural artist. The main error
probably resides in paying insufficient attention to the difference
between nature on the one side and art or artificiality on the other.
Admittedly, the boundary was different then from what it is now. With
slight oversimplification we can say that despite, or maybe because of,
a certain vagueness of terms, there exists for us a sharp division
between art and nature. In the days of Montaigne, they merged with
each other and could not be separated. For centuries the problem of
the relationship between τέχνη and φύσις, between *ars* and *natura*,

---

[75] III, 13 (vol. VI, p. 192). We should bear in mind, incidentally, that this
chevet was intended "à reposer une teste *bien faicte*"!

[76] II, 27 (vol. IV, p. 57); I, 26 (vol. II, p. 45). Speaking of Platonic authors,
he writes: "Je naturaliserois l'art autant comme ils artialisent la nature." III, 5
(vol. V, p. 130).

had played an important part in rhetoric. That was no less true in the Italian and French Renaissance, and everywhere the dividing lines were drawn in such a way as to amaze us.[77] We call natural all that is spontaneous, or which flows directly from man's innermost self and is produced without any artificial surgery. So obvious is this to us, that we can hardly imagine how it could ever have been possible to refer to anything else, let alone to anything artificial, as being natural. Yet people did so for centuries and certainly continued to do so at the time of the triumph of humanism. The result was not only that less of a distinction was made between nature and culture than we make today, but even the artificial was regarded as a part of nature, while nature fulfilled itself in *ars* which became a second nature. On the one hand, nature and the universe could be regarded in their totality as the consequence of *ars*, and, on the other hand, every *ars* could be regarded as a type of nature. The former idea is extremely ancient and has been familiar to European thought ever since Plato. The view of the universe as the consequence of the activity of a *Deus artifex* was also known to medieval thinkers, and in the Renaissance an artist such as Michelangelo could be called *divino*, because he imitated the activity of God, like a god on earth.[78] It was this, not something unfavorable, in any way connected with modern artificiality, that people had in mind when, as happened more and more frequently in Mannerism, they emphasized a quality described as *artifizioso*.

I cannot go very deeply into the various consequences of this development. That natural grottoes should be built, that architects contrived to pretend that art was nature and nature art, that sculptors endeavored (with *contrapposto* and *linea serpentina*) to create unnatural and "impossible" postures, that poets and others should have made such extensive and enthusiastic use of figures like the oxymoron, which have been rightly called *contrapposti verbali*—all this was just as common in France as it had been and still was in Italy. Over the years, and probably more in seventeenth-century France than elsewhere, it was almost inevitable that Mannerism should degenerate into a collection of external, "learnable" *trucs* or devices, which could be applied by anybody to every material and fitted to any subject. It is in this light that *préciosité*—though not in all its manifestations—should

---

[77] Cf. the article by Kristeller on the *artes*, cited in note 24 above. A specific example in the visual arts is Palissy. Cf. E. Kris, "Der Stil 'rustique,' " *Jahrbuch der kunsthistorischen Sammlungen in Wien*, new series, I (1926).

[78] Of course this was closely connected with the incipient cult of genius.

be seen. Salons and academies turned the *maniera* into a foil. The first indication of this tendency can be seen in Philippe Desportes. It gained strength among those who inherited his ideas and his style; and, in a sense, it was enforced by the objections that Malherbe raised about his work. Artificiality, which had previously been one of many aspects of Mannerism and was only intended as such, now assumed its modern meaning, while, with the metaphysical poets in seventeenth-century England, Mannerism came into its own once more with a final and glorious flourish.

The word "game" is often used in connection with mannerists, *précieux* and *metaphysicals*. It is said that they were striving exclusively for effect, that the primary, if not the only, purpose of their work was to astound the public by the performance of improbable feats. To deny this would be to contradict the numerous contemporary statements concerning the significance of the *meraviglie* in every possible domain, yet we can hardly stop at this desire to "épater le bourgeois." That it existed is undoubtedly true, but people were not addressing themselves, as they were during the nineteenth century, to a bourgeoisie that had no notion of art, but rather to *connoisseurs* and *doctes*, who could appreciate exactly what the artist was about. Thus, the mannerist's attempt to *épater* was a far more difficult undertaking: the display of artistic ability and new potentialities contained in, and advancing beyond, what had already been accomplished. So far as we are concerned, this implies an activity which we can call a "game" or, in other words (which can be equally misleading), an "exercise" or an "experiment." These terms suggest a lack of sincerity and seriousness, but I am convinced that such considerations will lead us nowhere in our examination of the Italian and French Renaissance. Sincerity and seriousness are categories typical of the nineteenth and twentieth centuries and cannot be applied to humanist thought. To illustrate this we need only refer to Ignatius Loyola's *Spiritual Exercises*, which are and remain exercises, but lack neither devout sincerity nor seriousness. Broadly speaking, we can say that the word "exercise" had an entirely different meaning then: the exercise was simply the work itself. To practice meant to work, and the work produced was an exercise. At the same time, the practicing, exercising work contained a form of experimentation which, in its turn, brought to the fore possibilities that could be tested.

That this was the case in ancient rhetoric or, to take a completely different example, in the monastic ἄσκησις (which originally meant "exercise"), is easy to prove. It can equally well be illustrated in various domains of the High Renaissance in the fifteenth century. What took place in the sixteenth century can perhaps best be described as auto-nomization. In art, and especially in the visual arts, the element of exercise can be discerned with relative ease; and it becomes still clearer and acquires still greater emphasis in theoretical writings. Nowhere, however, is it so evident or so fundamental as in the work of Montaigne. His *Essais* are basically exercises. Little needs to be said about the originality of the form in which Montaigne chose to express himself; [79] even the title, which gave rise to a new literary genre, first in England and then throughout the world, was really new.[80] True humanist that he was, Montaigne practiced. Like many mannerists, he regarded this as an end in itself. But, unlike others, he managed to produce from his practice or exercise a work which again became himself. He wanted no differences among living, writing, and working. He practiced by writing and worked on himself; and he really came to life in his work and in his work alone. Even if the work of other artists can be said to have stood outside their lives, this never happened to Montaigne. Only after his death did his work assume a place of its own. A writer or other artist practices by working at his subject until he has completed it. He then goes on to another exercise, to another task. In Montaigne's case, practice or exercise consisted in a continual examination of himself, of his life, of who and what he was. His book should not be called a work, for in a sense it is a continuous activity, the humanist's life of exercise and experimentation.

In Mannerism there was obviously great interest, not to say passion, for the *meraviglie*, for the bizarre and the exceptional. Both in nature and in art, people had an experienced and receptive eye for all that seemed unusual and incredible. This gave rise to, among other things, the collections of curios which were so common in the sixteenth century, and which contained every freak of nature. Works of art were intended to make the spectator marvel. Artists seemed to make it a point of honor to create impediments and difficulties for them-

---

[79] Peter M. Schon, *Vorformen des Essays in Antike und Humanismus. Ein Beitrag zur Entstehungsgeschichte der Essais von Montaigne*, Mainzer romanistische Arbeiten, 1 (Wiesbaden, 1954); Wolfgang E. Träger, *Aufbau und Gedankenführung in Montaignes Essays*, Studia romanica, 1 (Heidelberg, 1961).

[80] Andreas Blinkenberg, in *Mélanges linguistiques et de littérature offerts à Mario Roques*, I (Baden-Baden and Paris, 1950), 3ff.; A. M. Boase, in *Studies in French Literature presented to H. W. Lawton*, ed. J. C. Ireson (Manchester, 1968), 67ff.

selves. There was almost a cult of the obstacle, of difficulty for its own sake. But this is not all. Just as important as the power of the obstacle was the ultimate triumph, and, more especially, the way in which it was achieved. The practice or exercise of experimenting with unknown difficulties was all the more intense and marvellous, the greater, more controlled, and more easily elegant the results obtained. Even if the speed of execution was not a goal in itself, it was nevertheless an indispensable element and a most laudable quality in the artist. Alberti stressed this point as early as the fifteenth century; nearly a hundred years later, Vasari referred to it repeatedly; and, according to Francesco de Hollanda, Michelangelo held an analogous view, regarding it a godlike gift to be able to work "con grande ligeireza e destrezza." [81]

This speed, an aspect of the artist's *virtù*, should never obscure the ultimate goal of art, the fulfillment; but the fulfillment entailed a difficulty and an effort, which seemed to be overcome playfully, spontaneously, and gracefully. New elements were thus added to the artistic experiment, and their importance is perhaps at its most obvious when the experiments failed. In France one of the most interesting examples is the poetry of Jean-Antoine de Baïf. With great perseverance, but also with a tendency towards "academicism" in the worst sense of the word, he wrote a number of "vers mesurés" in which he systematically applied ancient meter to French verse. His readers no doubt marvelled at such an undertaking; they respected the great difficulty, too, and perhaps even admired the "impossibility" of the task. But the task was so impossible that all that remains is the difficulty of accomplishing it. There was no question of finding a solution, let alone an elegant one.

Artistic elegance in the sixteenth century was closely connected with, and probably originated from, what, in the art of living, was called *sprezzatura*. So much has already been said about the immeasurable influence of Castiglione's *Cortegiano* that I need not discuss it.[82] All that matters here is that this elusive elegance did not repose only in natural qualities; it also had to be acquired through study and labor. Admittedly, nothing of this latter aspect was to appear in the final

[81] In *Vier Gespräche über die Malerei*, ed. and tr. Joaquin de Vasconcellos, Quellenschriften für Kunstgeschichte, N.S., 9 (Vienna, 1899), 121.

[82] Despite certain outdated interpretations, Eduard Bourciez's *Les moeurs polies et la littérature de cour sous Henri II* (Paris, 1886), still has a great deal to offer. See also Samuel H. Monk, "A grace beyond the reach of art," *Journal of the History of Ideas*, V (1944), 131-150.

result, the life of the courtier or of the ideal man, but that does not mean that these elements were lacking or had never been present. This *art de vivre* contained much that is characteristic of every *ars*, and here, too, we see the curious combination of nature and culture that Rabelais demanded for the inhabitants of his "utopia" in the Abbaye de Thélème. He was of the opinion that everyone should do as he thought best, "parce que gens liberes, bien nez, bien instruictz, conversans en compagnies honnestes ont par nature un instinct et aguillon qui tousjours les poulse à faictz vertueux. . . ." This can lead to considerable misunderstanding, especially when "plein consentement à la nature" [83] is also mentioned in the same connection; and, indeed, it frequently is in Rabelais. Nevertheless, this passage shows us the extent to which nature and culture were intertwined. The Thelemites are of noble descent and possess a natural instinct for what is good, but they need a good education, too. Thus the combination, which for many men of the sixteenth century was not a combination but a primordial unity, was absolutely essential, if they were to experience the *sprezzatura* of the true man.

It is probably symptomatic that words such as *honnête* and *vertueux* should have been used, and we can conclude that, so far as Rabelais and many others were concerned, *sprezzatura* had an essentially moral meaning. This was also true, admittedly, of most Italians, but in Italy, especially among artists, the attitude was so blended with artistic preoccupations that it is hardly possible to distinguish between the moral and the artistic. The moralizing element in Rabelais, on the other hand, is far more visible and can therefore be more easily examined. Of course, the moralizing remains within the structure of a parody, which raises other problems; but in the Thélème episode the satirical note is a little less marked. Be that as it may, it is as though *virtù* were gradually approaching what we now know as *vertu*. And even if we might hesitate to say this too definitely about Rabelais, or even about Ronsard, in later authors, such as d'Aubigné, or baroque poets, such as Sponde and Chassignet, *vertu* assumes the meaning it has had ever since, and *virtù* is more or less forgotten.

Something similar happened in Montaigne. In his own way, in theory and in practice, he carried on the idea of *sprezzatura*. But it is indicative that he should speak of *honnêteté*, and that it was he who laid the foundation for the seventeenth-century cultural ideal of the

---

[83] *L'Abbaye de Thélème*, ed. Raoul Morçay (Geneva and Paris, 1949), 23 and xix.

honnête homme. I would like to add the hypothesis that, precisely because of Montaigne and the moralization of *sprezzatura*, a more clearly delineated form of rationalization appeared. This had already appeared much earlier, having been mentioned in Dolce's theories of art and, more generally, by Petrarch. But we can hardly regard as fortuitous the fact that the elusive grace, which seems, by nature, to defy every definition, is now definitely called a *je ne sais quoi*. Seventeenth-century reason admitted defeat and acknowledged its own powerlessness on this point, and this, in its turn, led to a violent revival of grace and elusiveness during the eighteenth century. The acknowledgement may well have taken place, it may well have played an important part in French classicism, but the fact remains, as the verb *savoir* suggests, that it is impossible to discuss reasonably the miracle that grace has always been.

VI. The Place of Man: Humanism, Platonism, and Religion

The forms of respect for ancient authors and artists, the way in which they were present in the Renaissance, and the manner in which their works were read belong to the formal characteristics of the period. This is truer yet of Mannerism and its specific concern with the manner and style with which possibilities could be tested. If it seems nearly impossible to draw a line or establish consistent differences between Italian and French humanism, it becomes harder still to make any general distinctions, when we ask the question "what?" rather than "how?" It may be true that nearly every French artist of the sixteenth century had some kind of contact with Italian culture and underwent some Italian influence, but the consequences of such contacts and influences were not predictable. What may be said of one artist cannot be applied to another. We must therefore accept the virtual impossibility of speaking of a single humanistic attitude toward religion, love, morals, or any other subject.

An especially good example of this unpredictability is presented by Renaissance Platonism. There is hardly a textbook which fails to point out that French Platonism derived from Italy. The statement, though largely true, requires one necessary qualification: other channels carried Platonic ideas throughout French medieval culture, both in the literary and in the religious domains. It is important to stress in each case that this Platonism had sometimes much, sometimes little, and sometimes hardly anything at all to do with Plato. The great distinction of having propagated Platonism once and for all as

an independent philosophical current must doubtless belong to
Ficino. In his translations, however, and especially in his commentaries, he rarely draws a line between Platonism and Neoplatonism.
To draw such a line was no easy task, because, long before Ficino's
day, Platonism had been made a potent cultural system by such
figures as Dionysius the Areopagite, St. Augustine, Boethius, Calci-
dius, Macrobius, and Proclus. For most Renaissance thinkers, it was
their Neoplatonism, their interpretations, and their commentaries
which constituted true Platonism. Then, too, there had occurred
during the first centuries after Christ a fusion of Platonism with the
Hermetic writings, which were thought by the humanists to teach,
but in different ways, what Plato had taught. If we add to this the
presence of Cabalistic and Arabic influences, it appears clear that even
Florentine Platonism was an amalgamation of what we would
consider very disparate parts. At that time, however, it was considered
to be a valuable unity, which might absorb, or at least strike contacts
with, Aristotle and the numerous forms of Aristotelianism.[84] This
amalgamation appeared in French culture during the first half of the
sixteenth century and was chiefly propagated by the circle around
Margaret of Navarre. The current derived from a mutilated Plato,
whose later dialogues tended to be neglected, but it still bore the
name of Platonism.[85] Its representatives included translators, such as
Antoine Héroët and Louis le Roy, and commentators, such as Pontus
de Tyard. Enthusiasm was widespread, and so were protests. Lefèvre
d'Étaples, for example, turned against the new fashion fairly early
on and appealed to the authority of—Ficino.[86] His own concern was
to maintain the purity of the Scriptures; and he would admit the

---

[84] As an introduction to the extensive literature on this subject, see R. T.
Wallis, *Neoplatonism* (London, 1972). On Renaissance Neoplatonism, I refer
the reader to Eugenio Garin, "Aristotelismo e Platonismo del Rinascimento,"
La Rinascita, II (1939); and Nesca A. Robb, *Neoplatonism of the Italian Renaissance*,
2nd ed. (New York, 1968).

[85] See the old article by Abel Lefranc, in his *Grands Ecrivains de la Renaissance*
(Paris, 1914); Jean Festugière, *La philosophie de l'amour de Marsile Ficin et son
influence sur la littérature française au XVIe siècle*, Études de philosophie médiévale,
31 (Paris, 1941); Robert V. Merrill and Robert J. Clements, *Platonism in French
Renaissance Poetry*, New York University Studies in Romance Languages and
Literature, 1 (New York, 1957); various articles by Albert Marie Schmidt, in his
Études sur le XVIe siècle (Paris, 1967); and the debatable study by H. Weber,
in the volume *Lumières de la Pléiade*.

[86] Cf. J. Dagens, "Humanisme et évangélisme chez Lefèvre d'Étaples," in
Courants religieux et humanisme à la fin du XVe et au début du XVIe siècle (*Colloque
de Strasbourg, 9-11 mai 1957*) (Paris, 1959), 130ff.

authority of no heathen philosopher, but Dionysius (himself an ardent Platonist) ????? ?? ????. Lefèvre thought, however, that the greatest danger came from the Neoplatonists, whom he put in their place, he said, by copying Ficino!

Platonism, to be further discussed below, here merely increases the confusion. If we still want to talk of unity despite the many forms of Platonism (magical, mystical, and Hermetic), the concept becomes especially difficult with respect to French literature. Petrarchism affected France at almost the same time as Platonism. The former flourished, for various reasons, at Lyons, where Scève, Pernette du Guillet, and, in a very original way, Louise Labé were active. One of their sources was the work of Leone Ebreo. Should their poems be called Platonic or Petrarchan? A vast amount has been written on this subject and, as is so often the case, we hardly know which interpretation to choose.[87] On the one hand, we would certainly be going too far if we drew a sharp distinction, especially in view of the fact that the fifteenth and sixteenth-century Petrarchans had assimilated platonizing ideas (as had Petrarch himself, probably via the medieval *trobar clus* and the troubadours). On the other hand, we cannot deny that the ideas of Petrarchist poetry differ in many respects from Plato's own views, for example, on the subjects of beauty and love. It is precisely the attitude toward love which might provide a solution to the problem. Love as a cosmic force, as it appears in Plato's *Symposium*, is also to be found in Ficino. We find the same concept in French poetry, particularly in what was known as "poésie scientifique." It is also found in characteristic form in the *discours* of Panurge in Rabelais's *Tiers Livre* (chaps. 3 and 4): Panurge "loue les debteurs et emprunteurs." Like love, debts and loans hold the world together.[88] In neither case is the term "Petrarchism" appropriate. A different problem is raised by *amor platonicus*, an expression created by Ficino with the meaning of, first and foremost, cosmic love. It is probably with Pico della Mirandola and his commentary on Benivieni's poems that we first find the modern concept of Platonic love, even though Pico expresses it in quite unmodern terms.[89] The connection with

---

[87] In contrast to the work by Merrill, cited in note 85 above, V. L. Saulnier sees a clear difference between them. See his "Étude sur Pernette du Guillet," *Bibliothèque d'humanisme et renaissance*, IV (1944), 7-119.

[88] For a general survey, see Robert Marichal, in the volume *François Rabelais*, Travaux d'humanisme et renaissance, 7 (Geneva and Lille, 1953), 182ff.

[89] Cf. P. O. Kristeller, *Studies in Renaissance Thought and Letters*, Storia e lette-

Petrarchism began around the same time. It is my view that, in the works of the great French poets, such as Scève (at least in his *Délie*), Du Bellay, and Ronsard, the concept of cosmic love plays a relatively minor role, and that the significance of Platonic love, as well as the identity of Platonism and Petrarchism, can be accepted all the more readily.

Petrarchism had a precarious career in France. After a first period of infatuation at Lyons and among the Pléiade, French poets suddenly reacted against all that seemed artificial and unnatural, forced, or hypocritical. It is all too easy to see in this reaction a healthy outburst of the true *esprit gaulois*. We can detect a form of sensuality and natural directness in those same poets who had somewhat earlier been "petrarchizers," but their reaction, too, was somewhat bookish. We can go still further: when the fashion changed (whatever that may mean) and Petrarchism, together with Mannerism, once again became powerful in France, Ronsard did not withdraw—at least not voluntarily. The *Sonnets pour Hélène* are proof enough of that. In terminology, style, and a certain attitude toward life, Platonizing Petrarchism was important for *préciosité* in the seventeenth century; but, unlike what happened in contemporary England, its literary significance in France was relatively limited.

Platonism itself underwent a corresponding transformation. It had, on the one hand, spread into every cultural domain. In England, for example, it turned into a sort of religious philosophy among the Cambridge Platonists; while everywhere it became part of more or less secret doctrines, embryonic forms of theosophy, if not theosophy itself. On the other hand, magical Platonism disappeared from astronomy and cosmology to the advantage of a scientific development we may call a "mathematicization" of the world view. A writer such as Montaigne showed very little interest in either Platonism or Petrarchism. If we overlook his admiration for the dialogue form and for Socrates (whose personal δαίμων, incidentally, he totally ignored), he felt nothing for the "fantastiques elevations Espagnoles et Petrarchistes." As for the ideal of love, I shall simply quote his sober observation, more characteristic of its author than of the spiritual climate of the era: "Mon page faict l'amour et l'entend. Lisez luy Leon Hébreu et Ficin: on parle de luy, de ses pensées et de ses actions, et si, il n'y entend rien." [90]

---

ratura, 54 (Rome, 1956), 119ff.; idem, *Renaissance Thought*, II, 96ff.; and Edward F. Meylan, in *Humanisme et Renaissance*, 1938, 418ff.

[90] II, 10 (vol. III, p. 116); III, 5 (vol. V, p. 130).

It is nearly impossible to separate Platonism and literary Petrarchism from the religious currents of the time. This is still truer of Erasmianism; and, with *évangélisme*, Reformation, Counterreformation, and the ideas of the *libertins spirituels*, we find ourselves at the heart of the religious problem. Far more than in Italy or anywhere else during the fifteenth century, the French Renaissance was shaped by a potent complex of religious factors, whose effects varied from artist to artist. To this we must add political and social considerations, as well as personal ambitions. It was quite possible for an individual to change both his political and his religious attitude in the course of time. To plot any direct line through this confusion is not so much impractical as it is dangerous. Where do we find a typical and pure Erasmianism? What exactly is meant in this period by Catholic orthodoxy? Which elements in the work of Margaret of Navarre can be attributed to Luther, to Erasmus, to the *évangéliques*, to Platonism, or to political and social circumstances?

These questions are easily asked and have been asked frequently. Before looking for answers, which are usually contradictory, it might be well to wonder about the value of the questions themselves. During the entire Renaissance, we observe a very curious phenomenon called the *docta religio* or *prisca theologia*.[91] In ancient times—that is to say, in the Graeco-Roman period and more especially during the first centuries after Christ—there had existed a conviction that all religions were essentially one, each, in its own manner, professing the same principle. During those centuries, furthermore, philosophy, especially Platonic philosophy, differed very little from religion and theology, so that the unity went still further than we might assume. Thinkers such as Ficino and Pico della Mirandola continued these apparently incompatible ideas with enthusiasm, with the result that there developed what we now regard as a medley of heterogeneous and irreconcilable ideas. They did not see it this way, for they were convinced that they could discover the basic unity of religion and its earliest sources.

The vast majority of scholars never doubted that this primeval Truth was in full accord with the Catholic faith and was to be fulfilled within it. Their arguments mostly came down to what had been said

---

[91] Cf. P. O. Kristeller, *Renaissance Concepts of Man* (New York, 1972); D. P. Walker, *The Ancient Theology: Studies in Platonism from the Fifteenth to the Eighteenth Century* (Ithaca, N. Y., 1972).

by Lazzarelli, one who stretched the limits of orthodoxy especially far.
What he actually said is not so important as his method of arguing:

> In primis . . . Hermes . . . de hac re occulte praecipit etc. . . . . Habraam
> quoque in libro qui Sepher Izira appellatur, docet etc. . . . . Plato quoque
> sic in Phoedro dicitur etc. . . . secundum Philonis interpretationem
> etc. . . . Sed longe ante omnes dominus noster Jesus Christus verus
> messias et verbis praecipit, et opere adimplevit.[92]

We find similar arguments in other writers. One might prefer Brahma
and Enoch or Moses, another the gymnosophists and Poimander, but
nearly all mention Plato, Philo, and, of course, Christ. That some
writers looked on this group of ideas with suspicion is just as typical
as is the unbridled passion of others for these same ideas.

The same thing happened in France. Perhaps people were a little
more cautious about orthodoxy there, despite the audacity of a man
such as Guillaume Postel, and a sense of chauvinism also played a part.
Besides Zoroaster and others who appear in Italian writings, there
are frequent references to the importance of the Druids (whom
Ficino also mentions). The Druids were seen as the forefathers of
the French and were supposed to have made an important contribution to primeval religious wisdom. This honor they shared with
several other groups, including, according to the French, especially
the Jews. Thanks undoubtedly to Reuchlin's work, the hidden wisdom
of the Cabala assumed a still greater significance than it had had for
Pico.[93] Even Ramus, the master logician, continued the tradition of
the *docta religio*.

It is not my contention that, because of these complications, it is
pointless to try to distinguish between Platonic and Catholic or
Protestant elements in the religious views of individuals. Such a
position is precluded by the opposition to Platonic ideas which we
encounter so surprisingly in Lefèvre. I point out only that this
complicates the picture still more and makes it particularly difficult to
talk about *syncretism*. This concept is, in my opinion, a modern
anachronism, which stems from and accentuates the indisputable need
for certain historical and religious distinctions. But it is just these
distinctions which are absent from the *docta religio*. Some scholars
contrive to retain the individuality of the component strands better
than others, but ultimately justice is done to none of them. Scholars
lump together religious ideas which had little or nothing to do with

---

[92] In *Testi Umanistici sul' Ermetismo* (Rome, 1955), 68.
[93] See the works by Secret, cited in note 52 above.

another and could not be united. Thus, too, an injunction is close to a fundamental view of the humanists: that unity had existed in the distant past, that it must be revived, and that its revival would produce a renewal of religious faith.

We have already seen that Erasmus was totally unreceptive to what we may call the excrescences of the *docta religio*, and we can assume that this whole intellectual current was entirely alien to him. Still less can he be called a Platonizing thinker, though his admiration for Socrates and his various statements about friendship may have had a Platonic origin. Be that as it may, he cannot be fitted into the framework of the tradition of the *prisca theologia*. Yet traces of it can indeed be found in his work, though they are limited in scope and far more soberly clad than in other writers. These same vestiges affected French culture.[94] Ever since his youth, Erasmus had defended emphatically the value of ancient culture, sometimes, perhaps, as a value in itself, but normally as a propaedeutic for the true and accurate knowledge of the Scriptures. The strange thing is that he consciously made some statements which resemble, and which may be connected with, the type of argumentation peculiar to the *docta religio*.

In his first work, the *De contemptu mundi*, we find the striking observation that monks alone enjoy the true *voluptas*, a view he elaborated in the last colloquy (the *Epicureus*). In both works he draws a comparison which is presumably intended to shock, and which sounds almost blasphemous to us. But this "identification" becomes more understandable, even reassuring, when we consider that Erasmus was simply employing commonly used expressions of the time. It seems less shocking when he places the *ethnici*, especially Cicero, higher than many thinkers of his own time; but it again has a suspect sound when, in one of the colloquies, a speaker can hardly keep from exclaiming, "O sancte Socrates, ora pro nobis." This seems a direct parody of a Catholic prayer, and scholars have often regarded it as such. Yet I need hardly point out that, despite the dangerous

---

[94] For his influence in general, see Will Grayburn Moore, *La Réforme allemande et la littérature française. Recherches sur la notoriété de Luther en France*, Publications de la Faculté des Lettres de l'Université de Strasbourg, 52 (Strasbourg, 1930); Margaret Mann, *Erasme et les débuts de la Réforme française*, Bibliothèque littéraire de la Renaissance, N.S., 22 (Paris, 1934); Margaret Mann Phillips, "Erasmus in France in the later Sixteenth Century," *Journal of the Warburg and Courtauld Institutes*, XXXIV (1971), 246-261; A. Renaudet, "Le message humaniste et chrétien d'Erasme," in *Sodalitas Erasmiana*, I (Naples, 1950); Emile V. Telle, " 'Essai' chez Erasme, Essay chez Montaigne," *Bibliothèque d'humanisme et renaissance*, XXXI (1970), 333-350.

"game" that is here being played, this interpretation is incorrect — it flies in the face of everything Erasmus ever wrote.

We must nonetheless admit that Erasmus's French enemies also considered him an atheist, who undermined the mysteries of the Catholic religion and cunningly turned them to ridicule. The most widely read author in Europe enjoyed the most widespread influence. We can repeat here what was noted of Platonism: in one form or another, Erasmus is to be found everywhere, among the Catholics who wanted to absorb him no less than among the Protestants, skeptics, and rationalists, not to mention the circles of mystics and atheists (such as there were). Although his attitude toward Luther changed and cannot be stated in a few lines, during the first years of his influence in France he was mentioned in the same breath with the Reformation. Louis de Berquin translated both Erasmus and Luther and confused them in a very curious way. Worshipped and reviled, Erasmus was subjected to excessive admiration and excessive abuse, neither of which diminished after the Council of Trent. Meanwhile, many of the ideas he had expressed so casually merged with those advanced by an *évangélique* such as Lefèvre d'Etaples who, together with such disciples as Farel and Roussel, did not stand that far from Luther. Despite frequent differences of opinion, they all passionately desired a renewal of religious life, which was to entail, above all, an interiorization, pure evangelical charity, and a profound spiritual peace. Lefèvre was more of a mystic than was the critical Erasmus. Neither of them left the church, but, through their activity and their influence, they both contributed to a general indifference toward the cult and any, too closely defined dogma. In his own way, each was involved in that amalgamation of religious ideas called *prisca theologia*.

We might be tempted to think that certain "rationalistic" elements in Erasmian thought could easily be combined with the Italian influence, which contributed to the formation of a critical philosophy in which religion played a secondary role or lost all significance. As we know, such views are upheld in many studies with an abundance of examples, and are contradicted on no less valid grounds in just as many others.[95] Two philosophers from Padua, Pomponazzi and

---

[95] J. Roger Charbonnel, *La pensée italienne au XVIe siècle et le courant libertin* (Paris, 1919); Henri Busson, *Le rationalisme dans la littérature française de la Renaissance, 1533-1601*, new ed. rev., *De Pétrarque à Descartes*, 1 (Paris, 1957), pronounces himself in the very first pages against Lucien Febvre, *Le problème de l'incroyance au XVIe siècle: la religion de Rabelais*, L'Évolution de l'humanité,

Cremonini, supposedly exerted an "atheistic" influence clearly visible in Des Périers and especially in Montaigne. According to others, this view is either exaggerated or basically incorrect. After the fashion of the beginning of this century for calling many Renaissance writers all but veiled atheists, a reaction set in. Closer examination has made it clear, once and for all, that many irreverent and seemingly blasphemous quips used by Rabelais were current in Franciscan houses and, in any case, tell us nothing about his own convictions.[96]

As for "la religion de Montaigne," the subject seems inexhaustible.[97] If we were to accept all the studies at the same time, we would be confronted by an orthodox Catholic whose beliefs are above suspicion, by a thinker who asserted his rationalistic convictions while accepting Catholicism, by a skeptic who actually took no interest in religion, by an atheist who never dared declare himself, and by an atheist "qui s'ignorait." The selection is large. Fortunately, I do not have to make a choice, and in some respects there is no choice to be made. Atheism, in the modern or the eighteenth-century sense of the word, can hardly have developed then, and, even if it had, we would be hard put to recognize it. Freer, broader views certainly existed, and it is quite possible that people could only express them in a veiled form, or that they preferred to keep silent about them. But is was naturally a "speaking silence." [98] How else could we know about it?

It is also true that, in his daily life and, especially in the diary he kept during his journey to Italy, Montaigne gave the impression of being a good Catholic, while in his *Essais* we find precious little about religion. But what was a good Catholic in those days? That true religiosity meant something different than what it came to mean after the emotional outburst of Romanticism, seems incontestable. Nor

---

No. 53 (Paris, 1942), who had attacked Busson's thesis. See also P. O. Kristeller, "The Myth of Renaissance Atheism and the French Tradition of Free Thought," *Journal of the History of Philosophy*, VI (1968), 233-243.

[96] Etienne Gilson, *Les Idées et les lettres* (Liège, 1932), 197ff. A more general work is Alban John Krailsheimer, *Rabelais and the Franciscans* (Oxford, 1963).

[97] Especially Maturin Dréano, *La pensée religieuse de Montaigne* (Paris, 1936); Clément Sclafert, *L'âme religieuse de Montaigne* (Paris, 1951).

[98] See various articles in the volume *Courants religieux et humanisme*. Saulnier has on several occasions referred to an evolution of *évangélisme* toward what he calls *hésychisme*, an urge or compulsion to be silent. Cf. his "L'Évangélisme de Pierre du Val et le problème des libertins spirituels," *Bibliothèque d'humanisme et renaissance*, XIV (1952), 205-218; and "Le silence de Rabelais," in *François Rabelais*, 233ff. On the subject in general, see Carlo Ginzburg, *Il nicodemismo. Simulazione e dissimulazione religiosa nell'Europa del '500*, Biblioteca di cultura storica, 107 (Turin, 1970).

should we ever forget that, where the Renaissance is concerned, in religious matters personal devotion and what I shall call the psyche of the religious individual were very different from what they are today. Despite the mystical sects which laid emphasis on intense personal experience, and which consequently have such an appeal for us, in the vast majority of cases, there were established codes of religious experience and expression. People adapted themselves to such codes quite naturally, but this naturalness often has something artificial and false about it to our eyes. The fault, therefore, resides in ourselves, who have failed to understand this type of faith, and not in the religion of the humanists.

It is in the context of faith and religion that I propose to deal with the place of man. An obstinate and erroneous tradition has it that the humanistic view of man was free of religious considerations, that the humanists could therefore see man in himself, in his full worth and dignity, and that this was the main difference between humanism and Renaissance on the one side and the Middle Ages on the other. Quite apart from the danger entailed by such generalizations as *the* Middle Ages, this traditional approach leads to the most extraordinary and implausible conclusions. If we admit that man occupied a central position in humanist thought, this was no less true in medieval theology and philosophy. It could hardly have been otherwise, for no one was prepared to doubt the words of *Genesis* in which God declares that he created man "ad imaginem et similitudinem nostram." [99] Consequently, the most we can say is that the Renaissance concentrated on man in a different manner than before, and that this certainly never involved a complete break with the past. Thus, on the one hand, there were no radical differences between the Middle Ages and the Renaissance, as is all too often supposed, and, on the other, during the Renaissance (or after it?) the situation became far more complicated than many scholars like to believe. As we know, during the sixteenth century, the century of humanism and Renaissance in France, the development of astronomy discredited the theory of geocentricism

---

[99] For the Middle Ages, see Robert Javelet, *Image et ressemblance au douzième siècle. De saint Anselme à Alain de Lille*, 2 vols. (Paris, 1967); and esp. Eugenio Garin, "La 'dignitas hominis' e la letteratura patristica," *La Rinascita*, I (1938), 102ff.; Giovanni di Napoli, " 'Contemptus Mundi' e 'Dignitas hominis' nel Rinascimento," *Rivista di filosofia neoscolastica*, 1956, 9ff.; and the important studies in Charles Trinkaus, *In Our Image and Likeness: Humanity and Divinity in Italian Humanist Thought*, 2 vols. (Chicago and London, 1970).

and thus the central position of man in the cosmos. A number of scholars see this as one of the main causes of Mannerism, in far too broad a sense of the word, that is, in the sense of a violent crisis of and a reaction against the High Renaissance of the fifteenth century. The Renaissance thus becomes a crisis of the High Renaissance. I have no intention of entering this labyrinth of opinions, but shall simply concern myself with the place occupied by man in the work of certain authors.

It must be admitted that one misunderstanding looms up after the other. It is customary to begin with Pico's *De hominis dignitate* and to find there a confirmation of the central position of man and the exaltation of human possibilities. The title alone seems to justify this —but the title was in fact provided to the *Oratio* much later and by others, and it therefore proves nothing. In the first pages of the tract, man is indeed extolled as the *magnum miraculum*, and an appeal is made to the usual, heterogeneous authorities: Arabs, Persians, Hermes-Trismegistus, David, Moses, and Plato are all named in one breath. This alone should prove that Pico in no way intended to advance something entirely new; and, besides, he speaks of Adam before the Fall, implying that the great possibilities and the complete freedom implied in God's words clearly have a completely different meaning for man as he is. It is thus neither strange nor paradoxical that Pico should be far less enthusiastic about man in other parts of his work.[100] Admittedly, man as a microcosm was to keep his place as *vinculum et nodus mundi*, but this view had been defended far earlier, and with just as much vigor, in strictly orthodox circles.

Similar views are presented slightly less clamorously by Ficino. We even encounter such epithets for man as "Deus in terra." [101] This phrase appears to be the proof of a great change since the Middle Ages. Who would have dared to express himself in such a way before Ficino? It is well known that some men had no hesitations on this

---

[100] Particularly Engelbert Monnerjahn, *Giovanni Pico della Mirandola. Ein Beitrag zur philosophischen Theologie der italienischen Humanismus*, Veröffentlichungen des Instituts für Europäische Geschichte Mainz, 20 (Wiesbaden, 1960); Giovanni di Napoli, *Giovanni Pico della Mirandola e la problematica dottrinale de suo tempo*, Collectio philosophica Lateranensis, 8 (Rome, Paris, and Tournai, 1965); and the studies in the volumes *L'Opera e il pensiero di Giovanni Pico della Mirandola nella storia dell'Umanesimo, Convegno internazionale (Mirandola: 15-18 settembre 1963)*, 2 vols. (Florence, 1965).

[101] Cf. the numerous studies by Kristeller. For the doctrine of immortality in general, see Giovanni di Napoli, *L'immortalità dell'anima nel Rinascimento* (Turin, 1953).

score in earlier times, and that it was not so daring after all—but this is irrelevant. Ficino uses these words; what does he mean by them? What does the word *homo* mean for him? The question seems slightly foolish, for Ficino can have had nothing else in mind than what we should have expected: man is man. When Ficino gives "definitions" such as "homo est animus," however, the whole perspective changes. There is no longer any question of bold, typically humanist terminology, or even of heterodoxy. Ficino is simply saying in a novel form what the Catholic faith had always maintained. In so far as he is an *animus* on earth, man is godlike, and this concept is to be found without much difficulty in numerous theological and monastic treatises.

These mystical attitudes towards man played a part in France, especially in the poems of Margaret of Navarre. Combined with elements taken from *évangélisme* and Lutheranism, her mysticism was in many respects similar to that of Ficino. Perhaps she went even farther towards a universal interiorization of human existence. Neither matter nor body have any purpose in her poetry. Man has become all soul, a soul which at times is unlike anything else and rests in God. Even human language becomes an obstacle to the true love of God: in a play such as the *Comédie de Mont de Marsan*, the author's mouthpiece, "la ravie de l'Amour de Dieu," sings what she has to say. And what she wants to "say" is simply "pure amour": "Je ne sçay rien sinon aimer."

It may be surprising to hear such notes in the Renaissance. They seem diametrically opposed to the fashionable views of scholars who would like the importance and beauty of the human body to have been the center of attention—in contrast with the Middle Ages. The proof of this is supposedly to be found in the visual arts. Unqualified as I am, I shall not go into this aspect. I shall simply point out that the puzzling element (for us, at least) resides in the fact that both phenomena, the exaltation of the soul and of the body, appear at the same time and sometimes even in the work of the same person. The intense power of the body has seldom been depicted more vigorously than by Michelangelo. But, just like his uncompleted statues, his poems express a passionate desire of the soul to escape from the body and to flee elsewhere. And should we not place the *Heptaméron* beside Margaret's mystical writings? It is a volume of short stories in which, in addition to Platonism, sensuality and physical love occupy important places. It is certainly not distinguished by prudishness (but what is prudishness in the sixteenth century?). The stories have often been described as bawdy and are completely different from her other writings. It is this combination which puzzles us, indeed, which defeats us, but which clearly presented no problem at the time.[102]

Mystical attitudes towards man, in which the body no longer has any function, are hardly to be found in Rabelais. If anything, the opposite is true: it is the body which is described with obvious relish, along with everything that can be called bodily in the basest sense of the word. Urine, feces, sexuality, the pleasure of eating and drinking, and everything else we can expect from "realism" are to be encountered frequently—indeed, so frequently and to such excess (they always refer to giants) that all these descriptions sound highly unreal. I let aside this "unreality" and note here only that this, we might almost say gigantic, human being has been called typical of the Renaissance. But he is no more typical, indeed probably less so, than the little shepherdess who wanders through the work of Margaret of Navarre in various forms as *ravie*. And maybe we should also keep in mind that Rabelais was a member of Margaret's circle.

Montaigne's attitude towards man is a chapter apart, and this, if any, is the moment to establish how impossible it is to reduce humanism and the Renaissance to a single factor. It is not surprising that there are so many attitudes toward this one subject, *i.e.*, man. What is odd is that Montaigne seems to have held them all at the same time. On the other hand, it is natural that this should happen in the work of a writer who never missed a chance of expressing mobility, diversity, conflicting or fluctuating opinions, and extreme doubt. In the first *essai* of the first book, we read the famous and characteristic words: "Certes, c'est un subject merveilleusement vain, divers et ondoyant, que l'homme." [103] What can we add to that? "Divers" and "ondoyant" could suggest a "mannerist" attitude towards man; "merveilleusement" could take its place among the *meraviglie*. It could also at least be suggested that Montaigne was no mannerist in his attitude to nature, but that he was so in this particular use of term. This might be acceptable, but why should *merveilleusement* not make us think of Pico's *miraculum*? The most interesting point is this: in Montaigne man becomes a *vanum miraculum*. His wonderful qualities are no bigger

---

[102] Lucien Febvre, *Autour de l'Heptaméron: Amour sacré, amour profane* (Paris, 1944).

[103] I, 1 (vol. I, p. 6). Of the numerous studies on this subject, I mention only Donald M. Frame, *Montaigne's Discovery of Man* (New York, 1955).

and no smaller, but they have changed completely. The wonder has now become the fundamental *vanitas* of the human existence, which does not know or recognize any mystical ascent to God. This does not mean that the continuous process of "testing" has been stopped or even impeded. On the contrary, precisely because one aspect after the other has been declared vain, and a vanity fair has come into being, there remain countless possibilities for unprejudiced inquiry. Skepticism can kill interest as much as it can stimulate it and give rise to enthusiasm. Unless I am mistaken, Montaigne was enthusiastically engaged in revealing the vanity of man everywhere, and in demonstrating it in his various exercises. And it would seem that, in Montaigne's view, which brought out the relativity and basic uncertainty of opinions and of the world itself, man had no firm point of support. But perhaps not. Montaigne was certain of one thing. He said so on several occasions over the years and repeated it in the last essay of the last book and again in the last lines: "C'est une absolue perfection, et comme divine, de sçavoyr jouyr loiallement de son estre." Can we thus find the idea of perfection in the writings of this relativist? Absolute perfection even? More than that, it is almost godlike perfection. Although there is no similarity to Pico's mystical rapture or to the perpetuation of the human soul which Ficino ascribes to man, Montaigne does refer to deification. The essential difference is that he makes no distinction between body and soul, and that the man who honestly and fully appreciates the fact that he is what he is, comes close to a godlike perfection. But, according to Montaigne, human existence is in constant motion and must be fashioned and adapted. Being, living, comes through writing and testing.

The manner in which this happens in Montaigne is more characteristic than the fact itself. For there is hardly a Renaissance writer who did not concentrate in one way or another on the terms *humanitas* and *studia humanitatis*. It may even be that the interest in these subjects constituted a certain unity in the midst of such diversity, a unity which might cover humanism but not *the* Renaissance. In this sense Pico or Ficino or Margaret of Navarre, who can doubtless be called Renaissance writers (with a few humanist traits), cannot be regarded specifically as humanists. But opinions on the subject are divided, and I shall confine myself to certain observations which confirm the impressions of a general similarity between Italy and France and of individual differences among the great minds.

It is certain that, for many humanists, *humanitas* primarily implied

immortality on earth. In a sense, it was posterity that won to insure the
perpetuation of the individual. In the letter to his son Pantagruel,
Gargantua brings this out one more time. This has, of course, been
seen as a sign of religious indifference. According to the Catholic
faith, immortality should come about in heaven alone. I myself fail to
see why the one should preclude the other, and why both views cannot
exist together or even through one another. It may be objected that
this earthly perpetuation of the invididual also appears from his works,
such as the books regarded as children. But even if this is so, the same
answer can be advanced. What is probably of far greater importance is
the unbridled desire for fame which characterized some humanists.
Led by Cicero and other ancient writers, but also by their own impulses,
they strove for a reputation which was to embrace the entire world of
letters and prevail forever after. We can easily find examples of this in
Italy, as we can in the poetry of Ronsard. But, at the same time, we
must also bear in mind that there was no lack of protests against this
cult of *gloria*, and that they were still more numerous and violent in
such prominent humanists as Erasmus, than were the traits of vanity
and touchiness. It is still more interesting to note that we find both phenomena in Petrarch. In short, we cannot confine humanistic *humanitas* to
this "perpetuation" alone, although it is an important part of it.

There is every reason to begin by drawing a close connection
between *humanitas* and *studia humanitatis*, so close a connection that
the one was impossible without the other, and certain forms of study
inevitably produced a certain type of man.[104] These studies were more
or less what we still call the humanities, and the word humanist
(*humanista*) had originally no other meaning than the teacher who
concerned himself with these studies. The *studia* included a number of
closely circumscribed disciplines, including grammar and rhetoric;
and here humanism, in the broader sense of the word, began. It
started but did not end, for, in the cycle of the humanities, the study of
morals also had a place of its own, and, unless I am mistaken, this was
more than theoretical.[105] Still less than rhetoric, for example, was the

---

[104] Cf. esp. August Buck, *Die humanistische Tradition in der Romania* (Bad
Homburg v. d. H., Zurich, and Berlin, 1968); and Gregor Müller, *Bildung und
Erziehung im Humanismus der italienischen Renaissance: Grundlagen, Motive, Quellen*
(Wiesbaden, 1969).

[105] Klaus Heitmann, *Fortuna und Virtus. Eine Studie zu Petrarcas Lebensweisheit*,
Studi italiani, I (Cologne and Graz, 1958), is an interesting study which gives
a good account of the development of and the attitudes toward morals, beginning
with Petrarch.

study of morals limited to theoretical expositions. It had to be put into practice; it had to be lived; and it had to acquire its true sense and fulfillment in the life which the humanists led. Hence the numerous explanations of and commentaries on Aristotelian ethics, and the countless analyses of *fortitudo, temperantia, prudentia,* and the like; hence also the special interest in pedagogy which I noted above. Pedagogy was to bring about in the life of every man what had already been stipulated by the moral doctrine: spiritual fulfillment. To this the power of *virtus* contributed enormously. In fifteenth-century Italy, many, if not all, humanist circles had devoted their attention to it. Sometimes we hear notes typical of Stoicism, at others notes typical of Epicureanism; but rarely, or never, are they unaccompanied by a sense of religion. The fact is that, on the whole, the primary meaning of *virtus* was the spiritual force contained within the individual, which gave him the chance to arm himself against, and to resist the inconstancy of, life and power of *fortuna.* Some attributed greater, others less, power to this *fatum.* Everyone agreed that the acquisition and preservation of *virtus* demanded a colossal effort, and in allegorical conceits *virtus* was often placed on the peak of a steep and unscalable mountain.

The same happened in France, where Rabelais, too, demanded of his heroes a certain contempt for the "choses fortuites." No one had a good word for *fortuna,* although it did have a certain attraction for Montaigne. In order to see to what extent the same concept can change and yet retain its customary function, let us hear Montaigne on the subject of *vertu:* "[Elle] n'est pas... plantée à la teste d'un mont coupé, rabotteux et inaccessible. Ceux qui l'ont approchée, la tiennent au rebours, logée dans une belle plaine fertile et fleurissant ... si peut on y arriver ... par des routes ombrageuses gazonnées et doux fleurantes...." [106] There is no hint of Stoicism. Every form of spasmodic resistance to the surrounding world, every defence against all that comes under the laws of Destiny, fades away and makes way for the sweet enjoyment of *vertu.*

But even this *vertu* requires an effort and cannot be considered a natural gift. Every humanist believed that *humanitas* must be won. What must be acquired, and how, were other questions, but for no one was *humanitas* a simple, given fact. It could be that, too, of course, for sometimes there is mentioned "tua nativa humanitas." In Erasmus's correspondence, for example, this expression is intended to put the

---

[106] I, 16 (vol. II, p. 30).

correspondent in a good humor. At times, however, we find phrases such as "inducere humanitatem feritatemque deponere" in Petrarch and "ad suscipiendam et ad ingrediendam humanitatem" in Ermolao Barbaro. Even Erasmus seems to have been devoted to such concepts, especially in his pedagogical writings. One example will suffice. In *De pueris* he argues that trees are born as trees and horses as horses, to which he adds the astonishing words: "at homines, mihi crede, non nascuntur sed finguntur." [107] Men are not born as men, they are made into men over the course of time, through themselves and through others. A newborn bear is said to be a formless mass ("massa informis") which the mother licks into shape with her tongue; but no animal is so formless as the human mind is at birth. The mind is first formed through study and by teachers, who are its spiritual—that is to say, its real—fathers.

It is perfectly possible to see this notion as a doctrine of human perfectibility. But to say that it constitutes a form of optimism after medieval pessimism is to say too much. In any event, it is important to note that this humanistic *humanitas* involves a kind of "éducation permanente." The forming of the mind never ends. It can be carried to great heights, and the end comes only with the end of (spiritual) life itself. This means that the humanists could never have conceived of a man whose possibilities had no limits. They were well aware, and they wanted to make others aware, of the enormous powers enjoyed by man as a creative being; but they also recognized the limitations imposed on every creature. Man, in the humanist view, was both a *creator* of almost godly stature and a powerless *creatura*. It would thus be wrong to regard the humanism of the fifteenth and sixteenth centuries primarily, much less exclusively, as Promethean (the myth of Prometheus, incidentally, was of little importance at the time). The figure of Faust does, indeed, stem from this period, but the Faustian element in Renaissance culture has been vastly exaggerated and only assumed its more extreme form much later. In short, a distinction between humanist *humanitas* and Christian *humilitas* cannot be made.[108] Both appear in various forms, and, even when Pico exhibits an occasional tendency to angelify man, he does no less than what many monks, defenders par excellence of humility, had done before him.

What characterized *humanitas* in both France and Italy was precisely

---

[107] Ed. Jean Margolin (Geneva, 1966), 389.

[108] For *humilitas-curiositas* (related to *humanitas*) in religious writings, see Heiko A. Oberman, *Contra vanam curiositatem* (Zurich, 1974).

mediocritas. This implied both the central place of man in the cosmos and the need for a central faculty within the human mind. Human qualities should be developed to the full, but all the faculties should be fitted together into a perfect order. This harmony was the general meaning of *humanitas*. *Concinnitas*, which Leon Battista Alberti discussed at length in his theories on art, was also a quality of what we would call the human psyche. The harmony obviously assumed a different color or sound in every case, but this did not preclude the possibility of pure concord everywhere. One writer might lay emphasis on the *vita contemplativa*, another on "civic humanism," but all acknowledged the need for and value of both and endeavored to do justice to both at the same time.

The best French example of this harmonious balance is to be found in Rabelais. This may seem surprising, if we think only of the immensity or the exuberance, which appear to be the exact opposite of the ideal I refer to; but, even if we do not look for deeper purposes in his work and confine ourselves to what we read, there is more to Rabelais than excess. What is odd is the very fact that superabundance should exist in his work and at the same time be controlled. It is attuned to, and finds its place in, a "doctrine" of *mediocritas*. Traditionally it is called *pantagruélisme*, and here, too, some scholars have traced an evolution in Rabelais's thought.[109] At the start, they assert, there was little but eating, drinking, and making merry. Later, however, in the foreword to *Le Quart Livre*, we find the famous definition: "Une certaine gayeté d'esprit conficte en mespris des choses fortuites." The distance between the two concepts, apparently unbridgeable, can actually be filled by earlier statements in *Le Tiers Livre*, such as: "une forme specifique ... moienant laquelle jamais en maulvaise partie prendront (les pantagruélistes) choses quelconques ils cognoistront sourdre de bon, franc et loyal couraige." It is nonetheless true that the gluttony and excessive, but always pleasurable, drinking can easily be found in the later books; while honesty and open-heartedness are already present in the description of Thélème. I do not doubt that there is development in Rabelais; but it is certainly not linear, and I must stress that, in all forms of *pantagruélisme*, we find a combination of epicurean joy and contemplativeness, of love of action and stoical aloofness. They blend with one another and can hardly be comprehended separately. So far as Rabelais's ideal of man

---

[109] For example, Saulnier in his edition of *Pantagruel*, xx ff.

is intentional, one is not absolutely against Croce the critic. All traditional, readers have seen nothing in Rabelais's work except the "abysme de science," which is man. It has been regarded as a splendid example of the typically humanistic thirst for learning and the desire to devour and know everything. It is all too easy to forget, however, the advice Pantagruel receives from his father in the same letter: "Et veux que de brief tu essaye combien tu as proffité."

Humanitas requires both terms of the antinomy, that is to say, it requires harmonious mediation between apparently conflicting qualities. Because Rabelais was describing giants, everything had to be on a colossal scale, and the tension between the various qualities had to be heightened as much as possible. This may appear to contrast with Montaigne, but was his concept of *essayer* really so very different from Gargantua's? I doubt it. In any case—and this view may have been more widespread in France than in Italy—he was also convinced that man must know his place in the middle and be content with it. For Montaigne the intermediate position went hand-in-hand with a form of *humilitas*, which, already present in Erasmus, had now become more skeptical. Man is "ni ange ni bête," but it is easier for him to degenerate into bestiality than to join the heavenly choir. Human reason leads to uncertainty, and man must spend his life with this fact. He can do so, and do so well, if he adapts himself and lives in harmony with what he actually is. Indeed, awareness of imperfection, and the peace that comes from it, resembles an almost godlike perfection. Further, in the same passage of the last *essai*, Montaigne dedicates the last years of his life to Apollo, "protecteur de santé et sagesse, mais gaye et sociale." It is the adjectives which interest me. Montaigne, who wanted every man to retreat regularly and permanently into a spiritual "arrière-boutique," and who, writing in his tower chamber, worked on his own life and appears to have been interested in it alone, this aloof, contemplative Montaigne also demanded a "sagesse sociale." Not only in these words, but also in many others, we can see the humanistic equilibrium which Montaigne, too, wanted to acquire, and which could be sustained only by constant effort.

Montaigne's wisdom was not only social, it was also "gaye." What we find in various Italian pedagogues (especially in Vittorino da Feltre) can also be found in Rabelais and Montaigne. *Concinnitas* clearly meant a good mood in the spiritual sense, too. According to another, older concept, still held to be true, the right mixture of bodily *humores* produced a good humor. True *humanitas*, therefore, was cheerful and enjoyed, with controlled pleasure, what it was and what it could acquire.

How this ideal developed is briefly told. We find in all humanists two, interdependent suppositions, sometimes explicit and sometimes implicit: the rôle of the *bonae litterae*; and the need for free time. *Otium*, not to be confused with a holiday or a leisurely form of idleness, serves the purpose for which man was born: to become man. This is his true, if not his only, task, but a task which reappears each day and monopolizes man's entire being all day long. His free time is fully occupied by this essential purpose.

It is perfectly possible to discern in this uninterrupted search for *humanitas* a kind of *basso continuo*, which, despite national variations, pervaded European humanism. The good-humored and gay harmony was an ideal not only of the fifteenth but also the sixteenth century, in France and Italy as well as in Spain, England, and other countries. We must therefore be content with harmony as a general concept, interpreted differently in every instance, but never absent. The search for perfect harmony can be seen, for example in the "construction" of ideal cities to which such importance was attached, especially in Italy. The French were slightly less interested, but (under the influence of Thomas More, no doubt) the number of Utopias grew. Descriptions of states where complete order reigned in every domain and, thanks to human common sense, a total transparence of structure existed, were in fashion. Such states were projected as images of the future or set in a golden age of the past. They frequently found a literary vehicle in the festive dream-world of the pastoral. In each one was expressed the cultural ideal which dominated the Renaissance and humanism: a perfect order of complete clarity, lying within the range of human possibilities. Man's duty was to realize it.

At first sight, this ideal seems to contradict the notions of those historians who wish to see the late Renaissance and Mannerism or the baroque—in other words, the sixteenth century—as an age character-ized by the fear of death, melancholy, a profound unease, and a violent feeling of crisis. I have already mentioned the exaggerations which have contributed to this attitude and shall not dwell further on them, because, though I do not want to deny the existence of the phenomena, I cannot regard them as having been uniquely characteristic of that age. Melancholy and a religiously inclined mood of nostalgia, no doubt, with or without Platonic ideas, exercised a strong influence on the poetry of the period. The significance of the fear of death and of the

countless *artes moriendi* (for dying well was also an art) can hardly be
overestimated. But when has this not been so? These sensibilities of
fear, melancholy, and crisis, which some have emphasized so much
with regard to the sixteenth century, can be applied with equal force to
the Middle Ages, to the modern era, and, indeed, to every cultural
epoch. We cannot dismiss such views as simply wrong, for in a sense
they are true; but it is also true that this type of analysis can be applied
not only to the Renaissance and Mannerism, but to all "isms."

If forced to reject one view and accept another, I would inevitably
be obliged to see Renaissance culture as having been basically paradoxical. The position is not new, and the choice of it would be an
indirect justification of all the theories about crisis and disruption.[110]
For many scholars, the desire for paradox and, even more, the inevitability of paradoxical works in the sixteenth century, symbolizes the
entire culture. Even though we cannot accept this view unreservedly,
we must say something about it. We ought to bear in mind that many
sixteenth-century paradoxes appear paradoxical only to us. We have
already seen a good example of this in the "puzzling" connection
between nature and culture. As a general rule, I should observe that
it is very easy to use such epithets as "paradoxical," and that we should
do so only with great care, especially because such terms were rarely
used in the period itself.

Despite every sort of literary "game" the writers played with such
obvious relish, despite the artistic need to make the impossible possible
(every work of art is surely a miracle), we very seldom read about the
positive value of the paradox. Perhaps the best example is Erasmus's
Stultitiae Laus, which he undoubtedly intended to be a serious game.
A serious game already suggests, at least to us, a paradoxical scheme.
Did it do so in the sixteenth century? Probably not. Erasmus, for
example, accuses his opponents—especially Luther—of using *paradoxa*.
Did he use them himself for fun or to copy Lucian? The *Laus*, of
course, is a *declamatio*, in which paradoxes are legitimate (or so it seems
to us). But the distinction between play and seriousness was different
then. Let us look at the end of the *Stultitiae Laus*, to which insufficient
attention has been paid. The Erasmian paradox is *aufgehoben*, that is to
say, raised and at the same time abolished, in the Pauline words about
the *stultitia crucis* and by the Platonic theory that even heavenly bliss

---

[110] This happens most systematically and thoroughly in Rosalie L. Colie,
Paradoxia epidemica: The Renaissance Tradition of Paradox (Princeton, 1966); and
see Barbara C. Bowen, *The Age of Bluff: Paradox and Ambiguity in Rabelais and
Montaigne*, Illinois Studies in Language and Literature, 62 (Urbana, Ill., 1972).

is no more than a form of folly: "Atque haec est Moriae pars, quae non aufertur commutatione vitae, sed perficitur." If we still insist on calling this a paradox, we must admit that there is no longer any question of its representing a modern, exclusively playful attitude. We are now faced with a fundamental matter (and one which has always been so) which presents itself in the form of a mystical rapture, reminding us of Pico and of Margaret of Navarre's *ravie*. If we continue to view this in terms of a crisis, then we should do so primarily in the sense of a possibility of and a need for choice, decision, and solution.

What we have written about Erasmus can be repeated about Rabelais, Montaigne, and all those others whose works give us an impression of "impossibility." If we still wish to insist on this paradoxical crisis with its paradoxical elements, we must start from one, incontestable point: we can talk of "impossible" works only because they are *works*. They appear to *have been* possible, for they were indeed produced. This brings me back to the essential function of the experiment, which is an investigation into human possibilities, an account of which is given in the work. Brunelleschi's cupola of the Duomo in Florence, the paintings of Uccello, the works of Leonardo and of countless mannerists are just as good examples of experiment as are the works of Petrarch, who has been called, not incorrectly, an "essayeur d'idées," and, of course, Montaigne. Already in Salutati, writing around 1400, we can read: "Fateor ... me non semper explorata scribere sed scribendo potius explorare." [111]

Salutati declared a principle which remained valid for the entire Renaissance and expressed the dynamism of the era to the full. People were constantly seeking new possibilities which were contained in the old ideas and the old art but which had not yet been fully elaborated or completed—which remained to be perfected. This was the object of all those who practiced the *bonae litterae* in Italy and in France. They formed a community of their own, across national boundaries, an ideal *respublica*, whose aim was the acquisition of *humanitas* in life and in art. This they all shared, beyond all their many differences. These differences among them were not primarily due to national peculiarities. The *docti*, the humanists, formed a unity (or they wished to form one) which distinguished them from all those who could or would not join their community, unity which affirmed the possibility of reviving

---

[111] *De laboribus Herculis*, ed. B. L. Ullman, 2 vols. (Zurich, 1951), II, 548-549.

the unity of the world. Italian and French humanists desired to reconcile opposites, through their lives and through their thought, and to combine them in a harmonious whole. Unease or rather restlessness was neither unknown nor concealed, but its most important aspect was its positive significance for any dynamic investigation. As with Pico and Ficino, humanist restlessness strove for *concordia* and *pax*. *Concordia discors* it may have been, but above all it was unity—unity in the world and, before all else, unity in the human mind and the life of man on earth.

THE LOW COUNTRIES

THE COMING OF HUMANISM TO THE LOW COUNTRIES *

JOZEF IJSEWIJN

University of Leuven

I. Preconditions and Phases of Early Netherlandish Humanism

For students of humanism the so-called "Low Countries" cover a much larger geographical area than the modern states of Holland and Belgium. The humanism of the Netherlands developed throughout the whole territory bordered on the West and North by the Channel and the North Sea, on the East by a line running roughly from Emden through Münster, Wesel, Cologne and the Rhine down to the Abbey of Sponheim in the Hunsrück, and on the South by a line from Trier to Cambrai and Boulogne in northern France. Beyond these boundaries, close cultural links connected the Alsatian towns and Basel with the Low Countries, easily reached by the Rhine route. Finally, Paris and Orléans—later on also Bourges—in France and Heidelberg and Erfurt in Germany were centers of academic life and learning, through which much of the Italian humanist message was conveyed to the Netherlands and to which many of the northern humanists flocked.

This area never formed a political unity, though a great many of its counties and duchies came under the dukes of Burgundy during the course of the fifteenth century and passed into the Hapsburg empire after the collapse of the Burgundian power (1477). Nor was there a cultural unity, except in matters concerning the Church and higher education. The people spoke Frisian dialects in the extreme North, Dutch and Low German ones in most of the Netherlands, Westphalia and the Rhineland, and French dialects in the Walloon

* The author thanks the following for their valuable help and advice in the preparation of this study: his wife, Mrs. Jacqueline IJsewijn-Jacobs; his assistant, Dr. Gilbert Tournoy; his colleagues, Willem Lourdaux (Louvain) and Dieter Wuttke (Göttingen); Dr. Ernest Persoons of the Rijksarchief, Brussels; H. Wouters, director of the town library of Maastricht; and the directors and staffs of many libraries all over Europe, who in the course of years kindly provided photostats or copies of rare editions and manuscripts.

[Editors' Note: English versions are provided for the Latin texts quoted in this study except where the texts are quoted principally for style rather than content. Ms. Linda Vadimski, M.A. candidate in classics at the University of Oregon, prepared the translations.]

and Artesian provinces of the South. French was also the language of the Burgundian court at Brussels and Mechlin and of a considerable part of the nobility. Latin, in its late mediaeval and scholastic form, was the common language in the Church, the school, and many sectors of public and intellectual life. Because humanism in Italy was first and foremost a renewal of Latin and the whole cultural life connected with Latin, the leading position of this language in the intellectual milieux of the Low Countries obviously opened a channel through which humanism could flow from the South to the North. During the fifteenth century, however, this channel was obstructed—as we shall see—by many a shoal and wreck, making rather difficult sailing for the first heralds of humanism.

A most dangerous shoal was formed by the completely different approaches to Latin by the humanist *oratores et poetae* on the one side, and the mass of professional users of this language, such as professors of theology, law, and medicine, on the other. Humanism awakened in the towns of the Veneto and Tuscany when some individuals were captured again by the spell of classical Latin and the formal beauty and richness of ancient literature as compared with the writings of the waning Middle Ages. These men wearied of the mediaeval school Latin and became averse to the contemporary philosophical and theological disputes held in an abstruse jargon.

Very often this attitude of the humanists and their wholesale condemnation of the scholastic world has been misunderstood by modern scholars, who are interested either in merely scientific research on classical texts or in the great social, philosophical or religious debates of the early Reformation period. But the profound and, we might say, romantic love of the humanists for the literary charms of classical Latin and Greek, which awoke with Petrarch and his forerunners, such as Lovato and Mussato, can only be assessed at its true value if one is sensitive to the fascinating appeal of classical Latin—once compared to a charming and immortal mermaid by the great scholar, Karl Vossler[1]—and to the music of its sounds or the divine harmony of its phrase. This sensitivity requires, in order to develop, not only extensive reading of the ancient authors in their original language for the sole sake of textual beauty and charm, but also a sustained practice of writing Latin and even Greek, as the humanists themselves did. The ancients already knew the truth

---

[1] Karl Vossler, *Geist und Kultur in der Sprache* (Heidelberg, 1925), 57.

of the principle, "Poetam non potest nonne nini qui verum prodest struere," as it was formulated by the great stylist, St. Jerome.[2] The nearly total abolition of Latin composition from the modern educational curriculum, together with the widely prevailing custom of consulting authors—often in translation—rather than reading them for pleasure, makes it almost impossible for the modern scholar to do justice to the humanists' attitude. In this respect he resembles somewhat the antihumanists of the later Middle Ages.

In the Low Countries during the fifteenth century, Latin was either a field of research for philosophical linguists (the so-called *modistae*) or simply a tool of communication for academic or international use. The eternal beauty of classical Latin was largely ignored or neglected, and even the particular qualities of mediaeval Latin during its great age in the twelfth century were rapidly decaying, as one can easily see by the extremely low level on which poetry and prose was being produced for literary purposes. Verse-makers, such as Laurentius *physicus* at Nijmegen, Henricus de Oesterwijck at Louvain, Arnoldus Buderick at Rooklooster near Brussels, or even Thomas a Kempis and Dionysius the Carthusian, and chroniclers, such as Willem van Berchen, Edmund van Dynter, or Cornelius of Zandvliet, prove beyond a doubt that the sense of beautiful and harmonious Latin was completely lost by their time. The early humanists were right when they spoke of "tenebrae," of a "dark age," for, so far as Latin literature is concerned, their age was very dark indeed, and it was to take several generations before Latin was restored to its ancient splendour. Many among the humanists made the error of extending the charge of shabbiness to the whole period between the end of Roman civilisation and their own day. This attitude, however, should not be generalised. The German arch-humanist Celtis edited mediaeval poets, such as Hroswitha of Gandersheim, and Walter de Châtillon's epic, *Alexandreis*, was printed more often in humanist than in modern times.

Before passing to a more detailed survey of the initial stages of humanism in the Low Countries, we should point out some of the fundamental differences between Italy, the homeland of humanism, and the late mediaeval Netherlands. The renaissance of classical Latin in Italy was an essential part and the main weapon of a campaign to restore, at least in the cultural field, the greatest glory of the

---

[2] Hier., *epist.* 66, 9.

peninsula, namely, the Roman empire. This seemed possible because of the unmatched beauty of classical Latin, which was resuscitated by the newly discovered Roman and Greek literature, and the improved teaching of the language. By a happy chance of history, the early stage of this campaign of restoration was conducted by genial men, such as Petrarch and Boccaccio, who from the very beginning put humanist activity on a very high level. The next generation also produced many writers and philologists capable of maintaining the same high level in science and literature, making the fifteenth century one of the really great ages of Italian culture.

In the Netherlands we find a quite different situation. Here a nostalgia for the Roman past, at least in the Italian manner, was inconceivable. It was thinkable, however, that some people would aspire to literary performances comparable to the great classical works, but precisely this aspiration was lacking during the fourteenth century, and practically also during the fifteenth, among the northern latinists: scholastic theologians and philosophers, such as Heimericus de Campo, Henricus van Zomeren, Dionysius the Carthusian, and Petrus Crockaert; pious writers of devotional works, such as Thomas a Kempis, Wessel Gansfort, and Petrus Dorlandus; and canonists, lawyers, and chroniclers, such as Edmund van Dynter, Willem van Berchen, Anianus Coussere, and Werner Rolevinck. Whereas in Italy of the Trecento the dominating personalities were poets and literary men, their greatest contemporaries in the Netherlands were the mystic, Joannes Ruusbroec (b. Ruisbroek near Brussels, 1293; d. monastery of Groenendaal, 2 December 1381), in the South and the founder of the Modern Devotion, Geert Groote (b. Deventer, October 1340; d. 20 August 1384), in the North. This fact was to have lasting consequences for the period during which humanism penetrated the Low Countries and even for the character of humanism itself in the northern context.

There were other differences between Italy and the Netherlands. In Italy, humanism developed among learned urban magistrates, in the universities, and at princely or episcopal courts. Moreover, Latin and the vernacular could be considered and were taken as two forms of the same language and literature, which could be cultivated together. The greatest authors were all bilingual writers, and among them we find many of the very important figures in public life. Italy was also in close contact with the Greek world, and Greek scholars could be met everywhere.

In the Netherlands, the main centres of learning until the end of the fifteenth century were monasteries, where studies only flourished if an abbot or prior were interested in them. Adwerth (now Aduard), near Groningen, and Sponheim are typical cases. There were only two universities in the region, Cologne and (from 1425) Louvain, and they were dominated by scholastic theologians. During the second half of the sixteenth century, the historian and professor at Louvain, Johannes Molanus, noted that the Faculty of Arts there had been extremely slow to abandon its mediaeval Latin style.[3] Greek professors never came so far north, and even in Paris such teachers happened to be available before 1500 only rarely and for short terms. Until 1500 it was impossible to print Greek in the Netherlands, since no printer had a Greek font at his disposal, and it even happened that Gothic fonts were substituted.[4]

In the towns and at the noble courts, literary life flourished in the vernacular. At the time of Petrarch's visit to the Netherlands (1333), the chief poet was Jan van Boendale (b. Tervuren, 1279; d. Antwerp, ca. 1347/50), the town clerk of Antwerp, who wrote exclusively in Dutch. Not until 1509/12 would a humanist and Latin poet, Petrus Aegidius (Gillis, b. 1486) become town clerk at Antwerp, and then it was an exceptional event, for which Erasmus wrote a colloquy in which the Muses flee from barbarous Louvain to the new Parnassus at Antwerp.[5] During the first quarter of the fifteenth century, Dirc Potter (ca. 1370-1428) was a famous court poet in Holland. Although he probably wrote his main poem (*Der minnen loep*) during a journey to Rome (1410-11), and though one of his sources was Ovid's *Metamorphoses*, the work appears purely mediaeval and shows no influence from humanist writings. The second half of the fifteenth century witnessed the flourishing of the *cameren van Rhetorica*, which also cultivated literature in the vernacular. Finally, the Burgundian court

---

[3] P. F. X. De Ram, *Joannis Molani . . . Historiae Lovaniensium libri XIV*, 2 vols., Publications de la Commission Royale d'Histoire de Belgique, Collection de chroniques belges inédites (Brussels, 1861), I, 588.

[4] Marcel A. Nauwelaerts, *Latijnse school en onderwijs te 's-Hertogenbosch tot 1629*, Bijdragen tot de geschiedenis van het Zuiden van Nederland, II, 30 (Tilburg, 1974), 240. Even at Paris in 1516, the famous printer J. Badius could not satisfy Erasmus, who had to go to Basel to J. Froben to have printed his *Novum Testamentum*. Cf. *Imprimeurs et libraires parisiens du XVIe siècle*, ouvrage publié d'après les manuscrits de Philippe Renouard (Paris, 1964ff.), II (1969), 17-18.

[5] "Epithalamium Petri Aegidii," in *Opera Omnia Desiderii Erasmi Roterodami*, I, 3: *Colloquia*, eds. Léon-E. Halkin, Franz Bierlaire, René Hoven (Amsterdam, 1972), 411-416, here at 412-413.

stimulated literature in French by such writers as Jean Lemaire de Belges, Georges Chastellain, Jean Miélot, and Jean Mo[u]linet. Classical and Italian humanist writers were read in French translations. A wandering Latin poet, Stephanus Surigonus of Milan, tried in vain to obtain a post as Latin poet at the court of Charles the Rash. It can hardly have been chance that Anthonius Haneron, a successful professor of Latin at the University of Louvain and celebrated afterwards as the first herald of humanism, abruptly stopped writing from the moment he entered Burgundian service as tutor to Charles the Rash. Compare his evolution with the careers of such men as Guarino da Verona, Pier Paolo Vergerio, Giovanni da Ravenna, and many other Italian pedagogues!

This situation changed only at the very end of the fifteenth century, when literary life in Latin strengthened at some town schools, such as those of Bruges, Ghent, Deventer, and Münster. It is no wonder, then, that a man such as Rudolph Agricola (d. 1485) felt himself in exile among the barbarians when, after his return from Ferrara, he entered the service of the town of Groningen. At nearly the same time, the court at Brussels became a little bit more attractive to humanists, that is, since the succession of the house of Hapsburg to the Burgundian inheritance. No earlier than the sixteenth century, however, do we find keen interest in humanist affairs and even maecenases among the patricians of the towns of the Low Countries, such as the Antwerp banking family of Gaspar Schets, with whom Erasmus was on friendly terms and whose descendants became the great protectors of Latin poets and philologists in the time of Christopher Plantin. Erasmus was keenly aware how indispensable for the *litterae humaniores* were the aid and protection of the patriciate. In his letter to Anna of Borselen, Lady of Veere, written from Paris on 27 January 1500/01, he openly invokes her help for his studies, adding a list of Greek and Roman princes who fostered poets and concluding with the contemporary example of Lorenzo de' Medici, protector of Angelo Poliziano, "seculi nostri delicias." [6]

Let us now cast a glance at those men who were the first to bring the new love of classical Latin to the Low Countries. Some of them were natives of the Netherlands who went to Italy for study or other reasons. As a matter of fact, the peninsula had always attracted a

---

[6] P. S. Allen and H. M. Allen, eds. *Opus epistolarum Des. Erasmi Roterodami*, 12 vols. (Oxford, 1906-58), ep. 145, I, 342-346, here at 344, l. 81. Hereafter cited as Allen, with epistle number, volume, page(s), and line(s).

great number of persons from the North: prelates and others in the
service of the church, and in particular of the Roman Curia, such as
Anselmus Fabri of Breda, *litterarum cancellariae apostolicae corrector*
(1414-1446), who participated in the negotiations about the creation
of a faculty of theology at Louvain, and Nicholas of Cusa; and students or even professors of theology, canon law, or other sciences,
such as the Dominican, Dominicus de Flandria (d. Florence, 16 July
1479), who taught at Bologna, Pisa, and Florence, where he was in
touch with Alemanno Rinuccini. There were also numerous merchants
and even prostitutes, as we learn from the *Epitaphium Nichinae
Flandrensis scorti egregii* of Antonio Beccadelli (in his *Hermaphroditus*)
and from the first short novel of F. Molza, where one finds a "Teo-
dorica Fiamminga." [7] More important from a cultural point of view
were the copyists of manuscripts, of whom Theodoricus Nicolai
Werken de Abbenbroek (Holland) may serve as an example. In 1445
he travelled to Italy in the train of the Englishman, Thomas Gray, for
whom he copied several works by classical and contemporary authors.
During the second half of the fifteenth century, these copyists were
followed by printers, of whom the best known is Gerardus de Lisa
of Ghent, who settled in Treviso and took an active part in the
humanist life of this and other towns of the Veneto. Another such
man is Arnaldus de Lishout or de Bruxella, whom we know as a copyist
of manuscripts in the service of the king of Naples at least since 1455
and as a printer of at least fourteen books published at Naples between
15 June 1472 and 9 May 1477. From Holland came a certain Henricus
de Haarlem (d. 1496), who established his printing shop at Siena.

Not all these persons, of course, came under the spell of the new
learning which had been developing in some schools and at the most
important courts of northern and central Italy from the Trecento
onwards. Some of them did, however, and came home full of new
ideals and with plenty of books, from which still others would draw
in turn inspiring readings and humanist impulses. But it is also true
that their young enthusiasm often was killed in the bud by the icy
cold with which the North generally greeted the innovations of the
South until far into the fifteenth century. Only during the second

---

[7] On this novel by Molza is based that of Matteo Bandello narrated by Arnaldo
da Bruggia (IV, 7). Matteo Bandello, *Tutte le Opere*, ed. Francesco Flora, 2 vols.,
3rd ed. (Milan, 1952), II, 691-694. Cf. Letterio di Francia, "Alla scoperta del
vero Bandello, III," *Giornale storico della letteratura Italiana*, LXXXI (1923),
1-75, here at 37-38.

half of that century did the prestige of Italy increase, and by 1500 a stay in Italy had become a "must" for anyone who wished to be taken for a man of learning. The first reason for going to Italy which Erasmus mentions in his letter to Anna of Borselen is precisely "so that from the fame of the place, our small learning may acquire some authority." [8]

The efforts of local enthusiasts would have needed much more time to produce appreciable results had they not been complemented by the visits of a number of Italians. If many Netherlanders crossed the Alps southward, an equally large number of Italians moved in the opposite direction. Bruges, and later Antwerp, attracted merchants and shipping agents, some of whom had literary aspirations, such as the novelist, Francesco Tedaldi, who arrived in Bruges for the first time in 1465 as an agent of Antonio de Lutiano and returned after 1484 to stay until his death. Several of these Italians established themselves well in Flanders and became important cultural and political figures, such as members of the Adorno family of Genoa and the Marcatelli of Venice. In the context of humanism, it must be stressed that, from the sixties of the fifteenth century onward there arrived from time to time Spanish scholars as well. Juan Luis Vives remains the most famous, though a late, example. Already in 1464, Jacobus Publicius Rufus, a teacher of eloquence, arrived at Louvain; and, less than twenty years later, Flavius Gulielmus Raimundus Mithridates, a converted Spanish Jew from Vich, came to Louvain in search of Rudolph Agricola and to teach ancient and oriental languages. In his tracks were to follow, early in the next century, Matthaeus Adrianus, first professor of Hebrew in the Collegium Trilingue of Louvain, and Vives—both Spanish Jews.

An important centre at which Italians could be found was Louvain. Very soon after the foundation of the university (1425), Italians, such as Antonio Columbella de Recaneto (1434-41) and Lodovico de Garsiis (1435-38), were to be found there as professors of theology or canon law. It would be a mistake, however, to see in all these men "the first heralds of the Renascence," as Professor H. de Vocht was inclined to do. In fact, there is a fair chance that they were strongly opposed to the new Latin of the humanists. We are on better ground when we take as such heralds the wandering poets and orators who visited Louvain during the second half of the fifteenth

---

[8] Allen, ep. 145, I, 344, ll. 105-106: "quo scilicet ex loci celebritate doctrinulae nostrae nonnihil auctoritatis acquiratur."

century. The very first of them seems to have been "D Joannes Leonardus De Bovis [De Bonis? Delbene?], Siculus, orator," who was inscribed on the roll on 28 July 1464 but left no other trace of his visit.

A third important line along which Italians came to the Low Countries was through various diplomatic and ecclesiastical missions. Thus Enea Silvio Piccolomini and Ermolao Barbaro visited Brabant and Flanders, and Cardinal Branda Castiglioni the Rhineland and Liège. The possible cultural consequences of such missions may be illustrated by the case of Herbenus of Maastricht. In 1468 the papal legate, Onufrio, brought the humanist poet, Angelus de Curibus Sabinis, to Liège and Maastricht in order to write an epic on some military operations of the moment. To gather the necessary information, Angelus secured the aid of Matthaeus Herbenus, who afterwards accompanied Onufrio to Italy, where he entered the service of Niccolò Perotti and became one of the very first Netherlandish humanist grammarians and historians.

Finally, one should not forget the mutual exchange of information through correspondence. The letters of Poggio Bracciolini to the dean of Utrecht [9] and the correspondence between Ermolao Barbaro and Arnoldus Bostius of Ghent or Adam Jordaens of Louvain bear eloquent testimony to the fundamental importance of this kind of contact, which enabled placebound monks and others to participate in the progress of learning.[10]

We have arrived at the starting point of a systematic survey of early humanism in the Low Countries. Let us stress the very provisional character of this survey. There are, in fact, almost no critical editions of even the most important works of the early humanists of the Netherlands. No systematic inventory of all surviving texts has ever been made; and recent discoveries, such as the correspondence of Joannes de Veris and the anonymous *Collatio de laudibus facultatum Lovaniensium* compel us to revise many previous opinions. We shall try, therefore, to gather here what is known and to formulate conclusions in a very tentative and conditional way.

So far as we can now establish, it may be possible to discern

---

[9] *Poggii Epistolae*, ed. Thomas De Tonellis, 3 vols. (Florence, 1832-61), III, 45-46 (Book X, ep. 23); reprinted in Poggius Bracciolini, *Opera Omnia*, con una premessa di Riccardo Fubini, III (Turin, 1964).

[10] Ermolao Barbaro, *Epistolae, orationes et carmina*, ed. Vittore Branca, 2 vols., Nuova Collezione di Testi Umanistici o Rari, 5-6 (Florence, 1943). The letters of A. Jordaens are lost.

roughly three periods in the beginnings of humanism in the Low Countries. The first brings us to the early sixties of the fifteenth century; and in this period we know little more than the names of some individuals who showed interest in ancient and humanistic literature. The next two decades, until about 1485, is really the time of epoch-making pioneers; when Rudolph Agricola and his friends, on the one side, and the Italian wandering poets, on the other, were laying some solid foundations on which the men of the end of the fifteenth and the early sixteenth centuries would be able safely to build. The Collegium Trilingue of Louvain, founded in 1517, was the symbolic crown on their work. But the founding of the Collegium did not mean that humanism had by that time overcome all opposition or even that its adepts had become a majority. On the contrary, humanism was soon to be blamed as one of the causes of Lutheranism. Among those causes the Louvain theologian, Eustachius de Zichenis (Zichem), in his *Erasmi Roterodami Canonis Quinti Interpretatio* enumerated three: the neglect of vernacular and scholastic studies ("neglecta studia vulgaria et scholastica"); the passions of ignoble citizens ("mali civium affectus"); and the cultivation of the humanist disciplines ("humaniorum litterarum cultus"). One should thus not be deluded about the state of humanism in the Low Countries around 1517 by some contemporary encomiastic literature, such as Eobanus Hessus's *Hodoeporicon*, in which he describes his visit to Erasmus at Louvain in 1518:

> 373 As the sun was touching the western waves,
> We enter, silently admiring all
> 375 The city's ornaments . . . ye gods, what marvels! But I tarry less
> With such ephemera than because the city nourishes
> And adds honour to, as is just, the university and studies.
> The town excels also in men, and not only in such
> As tend Latin teachings and the word-rich figures of
> the Roman tongue,
> 380 Nor only such as tend the Hellenic lamps,
> But also such as ponder Hebrew with toil, imitating,
> In every fine part of the school, Athens of old . . . .[11]

---

[11] A part of Eobanus Hessus's "Hodoeporicon" has been reprinted by Jozef IJsewijn, "Bij het Begin van een Erasmus-jaar," *Onze Alma Mater*, XXIII (1969), 52-62, here at 53:

> 373 Iam sol Hesperias afflabat proximus undas,
> Ingredimur tacito mirantes omnia visu
> 375 Ornamenta urbis . . . dii qualia! Sed neque tantum
> Ista caduca moror, quantum quia principe floret

On the basis of these verses, one might think of Louvain as a rival of the Florence of the Medici or the Rome of Leo X. They represent, in fact, wishful thinking, or they are specimens of rhetorical exaggeration, so common in humanist poetry. The truth was that the basis had now been laid on which the next generations could build the culminating points of Netherlandish humanism—the work of Lipsius at Louvain and of Dousa, Heinsius, and many others at Leiden. But that is the story of the period from 1550 until 1650!

II. THE FIRST CONTACTS WITH ITALIAN HUMANISM (ca. 1330-ca. 1465)

It is impossible to speak of a real humanist current in the Low Countries during this first period. Humanist interests are only to be found among a few individuals, and this humanism is often very superficial and even quite incidental.

The first noteworthy "incident" is the famous friendship between Petrarch and Ludovicus Sanctus (Heyligen?) of Beringen, whom the great Italian poet called his "Socrates." Sanctus came to Avignon about the year 1429 and met Petrarch in the house of the Colonna. He was to remain there for several decades, as he did not follow his friend to Italy. A study by Professor Billanovich has shed light on the literary activities of Sanctus at Avignon. We now know of two manuscripts which belonged to him: one (Ravenna, Class. 261), which he bought on 6 March 1330, contains texts of Cicero's *De Inventione* and the *Rhetorica ad Herrenium*; and the second (Milan, Ambros. F. 138 sup.) was composed for him and contains a remarkable collection of Roman historians, among them Valerius Maximus, Iustinus, Florus, and Sallust. The first manuscript bears many (meagre, it is true) traces of study by Sanctus, the second almost none.

We may assume that Petrarch's enthusiasm for humanist studies stimulated Sanctus to some degree; but it is equally clear that no comparison between the two friends is possible. Petrarch profoundly revolutionized Italian and European culture. The man of Beringen lay in oblivion until 1905, when modern scholarship finally revealed the true name of Petrarch's "Socrates." Petrarch became one of the great names of Western literature and a renewer of Latin style.

> Gymnasio studiisque adhibet, quem debet, honorem,
> Excellitque viris, non qui Latialia solum
> Dogmata Romanaeque loquacia schemata linguae,
> 380 Nec tantum ad Graias possint vigilare lucernas,
> Verum etiam Haebraeo student in pulvere et omni
> Parte schola celebri veteres imitentur Athaenas . . . .

Sanctus wrote hardly anything, and the few pages discovered in the early twentieth century are sufficient proof that his style always remained purely mediaeval. The cultural background and education of the northern musician clearly was stronger than all the enthusiasm of the Tuscan poet and philologist for the great past of Rome. In this respect, Sanctus is a prototype for many other Netherlanders who came into contact with Petrarch or his work and borrowed from it only what was mediaeval or what could be interpreted as such. After all, it was Petrarch who unearthed Cicero's *Pro Archia* at Liège, where no one was intellectually prepared to catch the cultural importance and uniqueness of this praise of poetry.[12]

These observations are fully confirmed by a glance at the Petrarchan heritage in the Low Countries during the fifty or so years after his death, and at the rare men who, in one way or another, came into closer contact with the developing Italian humanism. An even better confirmation is afforded by a comparison of Latin prose and poetry written between the Rhine and the North Sea with the productions of Florence, Padua, and other Italian cities.

Concerning Petrarch's influence in the Netherlands, I can only repeat the statements made by Professor Sottili for Germany in his introduction to the catalogue of Petrarchan manuscripts in the Federal Republic.[13] Direct traces of Petrarch's visit to the Rhineland and Liège are nowhere to be found. The literary tradition, however, moved in two directions. In the northern tradition, as shown by the manuscripts produced in monasteries, Petrarch was known and read almost exclusively as a moral philosopher, not to be distinguished from a St. Augustine, a St. Bernard, or other pious writers. Again and again we find the *De Remediis utriusque fortunae*, the *De Vita solitaria*, the *De otio religiosorum*, the *Psalmi poenitentiales*, and the Griseldis story. The latter was not read as an example of a humanist adaptation of a vernacular work—as Petrarch himself had intended— but as a moralizing and allegorical story on the Christian soul, which could be read to nuns and monks in their religious communities. In this monastic tradition, Petrarch's works were copied along with

---

[12] Marc Dykmans, "Les premiers rapports de Pétrarque avec les Pays-Bas," *Bulletin de l'Institut Historique Belge de Rome*, XX (1939), 51-122, here at 56-60.

[13] Agostino Sottili, "I codici del Petrarca nella Germania Occidentale, I-VII," *Italia Medioevale e Umanistica*, X (1967), 411-491; XI (1968), 345-448; XII (1969), 335-476; XIII (1970), 281-467; XIV (1971), 313-402; XV (1972), 361-423; to be continued; the introduction is in vol. X (1967), 411-421. Hereafter cited as Sottili, "I codici," *IMU*, with volume, year and page.

treatises by Augustine, Gerson, Henricus Echer of Kalkar, and a host of less well known mediaeval theologians. It is clear that in this context one should not speak of humanism or humanist influences. Petrarch's moral works could be read in a purely mediaeval perspective; and the author's own connections with the Augustinians and Carthusians certainly favoured this interpretation, because these religious orders played a preponderant role in the diffusion of these works.

The *De Remediis* achieved the greatest success in this monastic Petrarchism. It was, among other things, the only "humanist" work to be found in the library of the Arts Faculty at Louvain as late as 1447, having been purchased for the faculty on 10 November 1446.[14] This work was often used by local moralists, who paraphrased or used it extensively for their own purposes. One such man was Arnoldus Geilhoven of Rotterdam (d. 31 August 1442), a monk at Groenendaal near Brussels, who studied in Italy for several years and knew Petrarch's works very well, even the Latin poetry. In his own works, Arnoldus sometimes copied almost verbatim from Petrarch, without being for that any more of a humanist than were his fellow monks. Another writer, Adrianus Monet Hollandinus (d. Geertruidenberg, 19 December 1411), imitated Petrarch in his own *De Remediis utriusque fortunae*. Although a sixteenth-century historian said of him that he was "humanis litteris nobiliter doctus," [15] I find it hard to consider his work a specimen of humanist literature— as one can do unhesitatingly with young Erasmus's compendium of Valla's *Elegantiae linguae Latinae*. An epitome of his work, together with Petrarch's own *De remediis*, was written at Monterberg in 1469 by Matthaeus of Mechlin, physician to the duke of Cleves.

The second way along which Petrarch came to the North was the academic one, through works being copied or bought by students attending Italian universities. Although the number of such manuscripts is much smaller than those of the first class, they are highly interesting because of their completely different composition. Here we often find Petrarch's poetical works, especially the *Bucolicum carmen*, together with pieces from the schools or circles of Guarino,

---

[14] Henry de Vocht, *History of the Foundation and Rise of the Collegium Trilingue Lovaniense 1517-1550*, 4 vols. (Louvain, 1951-55), I, 109. Hereafter cited as De Vocht, *HCT*, with volume and page.

[15] Petrus Sutor, *De vita Cartusiana* (Paris, 1522), lib. II, cap. 7, also quoted in Theodorus Petreius, *Bibliotheca Cartusiana* (Cologne, 1609), 3.

Poggio, Bruni, and others. Nothing can be so instructive as to compare in Sottili's catalogue of the manuscripts of Petrarch now in
Trier the one of Italian origin (No. 186) with the others.[16]

Petrarch's usual epithet of "poeta" or "poeta laureatus" was
probably propagated by these university students. It is difficult to
say if this always means "humanist poet," as opposed to the old-
style "versificator," but it cannot be doubted that this distinction
was known in the Netherlands by the sixties of the fifteenth century.
An interesting document in this respect is the anonymous *Collatio
de laudibus facultatum* of Louvain, in which Petrarch is introduced as
the "poetarum maximus." The Latin of this speech, held by a young
professor of canon law, displays an awkward but unmistakable
intent to imitate the humanist style. If my hypothesis is correct,
namely, that the *Collatio* was held in 1435 by Johannes Snavel, it
can be taken for granted that "poeta" here really means "humanist."
Snavel had arrived quite recently in Louvain from Padua, where he
must have been in close contact with Johannes von Eych, later bishop
of Eichstätt but at that time a student in Padua and deeply interested
in Petrarch. Men such as Snavel may have diffused the term "poeta,"
which afterwards was applied to him by even the most scholastic
writers, such as Dionysius the Carthusian, and by the traditional
chroniclers. A passage from the writings of one such man may round
out this survey of Petrarch's heritage in the Low Countries before
1450, because it illustrates well what was known and how it was
transmitted. The passage is found at the year 1341, date of Petrarch's
coronation, in the work of Cornelius Menghers of Zandvliet (d. ca.
1461/62), one of the last of the great chroniclers of Liège. He writes:

> Further, there are available many noteworthy works by Francesco
> Petrarca, in prose and in verse, all revealing his divine art. Indeed,
> we have his most famous work, cast in heroic verse, which he entitled
> *Africa* and in which are narrated the mighty deeds of the first Scipio
> Africanus. There is also a bucolic poem that is everywhere renowned;
> and also a book of letters written in verse to his friends. His Boccaccio
> writes of these things.[17]

---

[16] Sottili, "I codici," *IMU*, XIV (1971), 313-402, here at 369.

[17] *Chronicon Cornelii Zantfliet*, in *Veterum scriptorum et monumentorum . . . amplis-
sima collectio*, eds. Edmond Martène and Ursin Durand, V (Paris, 1724), col. 229:
"Porro Francisci Petrarchae multa patent opera metrica et prosaïca memoratu
dignissima, certum de celesti eius ingenio testimonium hinc inde ferentia. Stat
equidem poetica sua nobilissima, quam Africam titulavit, primi Scipionis Africani
narrans magnalia heroico carmine scripta. Stat et Bucolicum carmen iam ubique
sua celebritate cognitum. Stat et liber epistolarum ad amicos metrico stilo scrip-
tarum . . . . Haec de eo suus scribit Boccacius."

This is clearly second-hand information, borrowed from D̶u̶ ̶ ̶ ̶ ̶ ̶,̶ ̶w̶h̶o̶ ̶t̶h̶e̶r̶e̶f̶o̶r̶e̶ ̶w̶a̶s̶ known at Liège about the middle of the fifteenth century.

Besides Petrarch's "Socrates," we know of one more Netherlander of the fourteenth century who had humanistic interests, one Radulphus or Rolandus de Rivo (Roelof van der Beek; b. Breda, before 1350; d. Tongeren, 3 November 1403). He was in Italy already by 1362 and returned twice in later years. He was a learned man and a prolific writer on grammar, history, and ecclesiastical problems; and of vital importance to our purpose is his testimony about his own studies in Rome around 1380: "Simon, archbishop of Thebes in Beotia [Simon Atumanus] of blessed memory..., who arrived at Rome and lived there in 1380, taught me from Greek whatever in my books I emended of the errors of the grammarians." [18] One hundred years later, Engelbertus Schut of Leiden still knew this text, perhaps through some tradition at Windesheim (of which De Rivo had been a counsellor), and he transmitted the additional information that "hunc... magister Anthonius Haneron imitatus [est]." [19] To this point, which is important for the beginnings of humanist teaching of grammar at Louvain, I shall return when treating Haneron.

Before looking for other specific traces of humanism in the Low Countries during the period under concern, let us first broaden our view and ask ourselves what kind of original Latin literature was produced there, and by whom. The answers will prove to be of fundamental importance for the study of early "humanist" literature. Apart from mere scholarly writings on theology and law, or encyclopaedic works such as those written by Heimericus de Campo between 1435 and 1460, prose was nearly limited to devotional treatises and historical chronicles. Good examples of the latter are the writings of Cornelius Menghers and of Edmund van Dynter (d. 1449), who wrote a *Chronica ducum Lotharingiae et Brabantiae* which one has only to put beside Bruni's Florentine history in order to appreciate

---

[18] "Recolende memorie Simon archiepiscopus Thebarum Baeotie..., qui pervenit et permansit Rome anno 1380, quidquid in libris meis de grammaticorum erroribus emendavi ex Greco edocuit." Cunibert Mohlberg, *Radulph de Rivo, der letzte Vertreter der altrömischen Liturgie*, 2 vols., Recueil de Travaux publiés par les membres des Conférences d'Histoire et de philologie de l'Université de Louvain, 29, 42 (Louvain, 1911-15), I, 20, 22. Cf. Giuseppe Di Stefano, *La découverte de Plutarque en Occident. Aspects de la vie intellectuelle en Avignon au XIVe siècle*, Memoria dell'Accademia delle Scienze di Torino. Classe di Scienze Morali, Storiche e Filologiche, series 4, No. 18 (Turin, 1968), 30-31.

[19] Anthonius Haneron, *Diasynthetica* (Gouda, 1481), praefatio, fol. a1r-v.

the difference between the two worlds. It would take several more decades before humanist *historiae* would be written in the Netherlands. During the second half of the fifteenth century, Willem van Berchen (*fl.* 1460/85) in Nijmegen, Adrianus de But in Ter Duinen Abbey, the Westphalian Werner Rolevinck (1425-1502) at Cologne, and many others continued the mediaeval historical traditions without any trace of humanist style. The devotional literature is still more significant. It may suffice here to single out two typical figures. The first is Gerlacus Petri (b. Deventer, 1378; d. Windesheim, 18 November 1411), author of an ascetic handbook (*Breviloquium*) and the famous *Ignitum cum Deo soliloquium*, the greatest mystical treatise of the Modern Devotion. Precisely through the Modern Devotion and the Windesheim movement, works of this kind were to have a lasting impact on literature in the Netherlands and largely to prevent the development of a humanist literature of Italian character. There would be many *soliloquia* with God or Christ, but almost never one with "Laura" or "Neaera!"

Gerlacus never went to Italy, but the second writer we want to look at, Arnoldus Geilhoven, studied at Padua and was familiar with relatives and students of Petrarch. In this way he became acquainted with Pier Paolo Vergerio and his *De ingenuis moribus*. Returned to Brabant, Geilhoven became a truly prolific writer. Although one of his works, the *Vaticanus*, contains a "Speculum philosophorum et poetarum," and though his *Sompnium doctrinale* assigns a proper place to "Poetica" among the Arts, Geilhoven was not (as N. Mann has convincingly shown) a man deeply touched by humanism. He belongs rather to the mass of pious, late mediaeval writers, whose influence never died in the Low Countries until the Reformation and even much later. It is typical that a great work of Geilhoven, his *Gnotosolitos sive Speculum conscientiae*, was one of the very first and largest books printed by the first printers at Brussels, the Brethren of the Common Life (1475). This work fits perfectly the dominating features of the literary landscape of the fifteenth century: Wessel Gansfort (*Tractatus de Oratione, Scala Meditationis*); Dionysius the Carthusian (*De quattuor novissimis*); Thomas a Kempis (*Imitatio Christi*); Jacobus de Gruitrode (*Lavacrum conscientiae*); Petrus Dorlandus (*Viola animae*); Johannes Mauburnus (*Rosetum exercitiorum spiritualium*); and many others. To this literature Erasmus returned after his youthful experiments as an Italianising humanist, and several of Vives's shorter works belong to the same genre. If representative-

ness means quantity, the Latin literature originating from the Modern
Devotion or from Christian meditation in general by far surpasses
that which owes its characteristics to Italian humanism. It is true,
nonetheless, that, toward the end of the fifteenth century, the devotional literature began to adopt humanist linguistic dress, an evolution
which was completed in Erasmus and Vives and to which I shall
return.

What we have said about prose is valid also for poetry. There
is even an interesting parallel with the story of Petrarch's influence,
albeit at a later date: just as Petrarch proved most successful as a
traditional moralist, so one of the greatest successes in poetry was
the work of a man who in Italy was far overshadowed by his less
puritan Brethren of Apollo, the Carmelite, Baptista Mantuanus. In
the North, his eclogues ousted Virgil's and his *Parthenicae* were
favourite readings. This is easily understood, since the content of
this poetry was similar to what the men of the Netherlands themselves
wrote. Perhaps the most important Latin poet during the early
fifteenth century was the Augustinian, Arnoldus Buderick (d. 1444)
of Rooklooster priory near Brussels. Besides *Odae de laude Dei*, he
wrote a long, mystic poem (*Contemplativa metrica*), which continued
the living traditions of the monasteries in the forest south of Brussels
(Zoniënwoud) ever since the time of Ruusbroec. Other poets are
less well known. An enigmatic case is that of a certain Jan de Wilde
(1360-1417), a priest of Ghent, about whom authors of biographical
articles continue to repeat a notice to be found in the *Annales Flandriae*
of Jacobus Meyer (1491-1552): Jan de Wilde was a "poeta et orator
eloquentissimus" and author of many "carmina lyrica," which (at
least according to Franciscus Sweertius's *Athenae Belgicae*) Jodocus
Badius published at Paris nearly a hundred years later. One searches
for him in vain among Badius's editions, and the whole story remains
as obscure as it is unlikely. Be that as it may, Latin poetry in the Low
Countries, even after a more or less successful adoption of humanist
language and style, remained firm on its religious track until well into
the sixteenth century.

Apart from this pious versification, one finds only some didactic
and encomiastic poetry, most of which achieved only ephemeral
notoriety. A contemporary of Petrarch at Louvain, Johannes Caligator or Coussemaecker (b. 1320), composed a versified *Principis
speculum* for the duke of Brabant, but of it we know only a few verses
quoted by the sixteenth-century historian, Molanus. Thanks to

Professor Kristeller's *Iter Italicum*, another text, the *Laus Brabantiae* of Henricus Custodis of Oesterwijck, has emerged from oblivion. Written in or about 1430, it is, so far as we know, the oldest specimen of Latin poetry written by a member of the University of Louvain, where Henricus was a professor of medicine. Nothing could be more mediaeval in style and content than this praise of Brabant, as the following sample amply proves:

> Ter tres litterulas vox dat "Brabantia" gratis,
> Plenas misteriis per ter tria nomina pulchris.
> Littera B grata dat significare beata.
> Multa beatorum genitrix Brabantia Florum;
> Sanctos et sanctas genuit Brabantia plantas;
> Mater Amelberga quinorum sancta proborum,
> Ymmo beatorum merito splendet puerorum:
> Gudila, Reynildis, Ermelindis, Pharaildis
> Et Cameracensis sanctus presul Emebertus
> Ex Amelberga venerunt matre beata,
> Que Karlemanni ducis extitit optima nata.[20]

Since the *Laus urbis* belongs to a very popular genre, it is appropriate to make some comparisons between Italy and the Netherlands through a few other examples. Henricus was a contemporary of the Florentine, Leonardo Bruni, whose *Laus Florentiae* is a model of humanist elegance in classical prose.[21] If one should want to compare verses, the fluent distichs of the Sicilian, Marrasius, on the fountain Gaia in Siena will leave no doubt as to the conclusions to be drawn.[22] About two decades after Henricus, another verse-maker wrote a similar poem of praise. He was the physician, Laurentius, member of the court of Arnold of Egmond, duke of Guelders, who celebrated Nijmegen in verses which are perhaps more barbarous still than those of Oesterwijck. This Laurentius *physicus* wrote around 1450 and should therefore be compared with poets such as Landino, Filelfo, Strozza, and the like, but between them yawns an unbridge-

---

[20] Jozef IJsewijn, "Henricus de Oesterwijck, the First Latin Poet of the University of Louvain (ca. 1430)," *Humanistica Lovaniensia*, XVIII (1969), 7-23, here at 15. This journal is hereafter cited as *HL*, with volume and page.

[21] Leonardo Bruni, *Laudatio urbis Florentinae*, in Hans Baron, *From Petrarch to Leonardo Bruni: Studies in Humanistic and Political Literature* (Chicago, 1968), 232-263.

[22] Antonio Altamura, "I carmi latini di Giovanni Marrasio," *Bollettino del Centro di Studi filologici e linguistici Siciliani*, II (1954), 204-244; separately printed as the third volume in the *Biblioteca del Centro . . . Siciliani*, the poem on the fountain Gaia at pp. 26-27. The same text in *Poeti latini del Quattrocento*, ed. Francesco Arnaldi, Lucia Gualdo Rosa, Liliana Monti Sabia (Naples, 1964), 114-116.

nble nbvon, Only twenty five years later, Agricola wrote his own
"Praise of Pavia" in classical verses, but he did it while in Italy.[23]
One had to wait until 1498 before there would be written in the
Lowlands a *Laus urbis* which displayed some classical qualities: the
praise of Roermond by the Westphalian, Hermannus Busschius,[24]
a pupil of the same Agricola and of Pomponio Leto in Rome.

With this panorama of Netherlandish literature in mind, let us
now collect whatever traces of humanist concern we are able to find
between the time of Petrarch's death and the middle of the fifteenth
century. We do have, as a matter of fact, some Italian testimonies to
the state of humanism in the Netherlands, written about 1450/51,
which are worth being tested against local evidence. Enea Silvio
Piccolomini, in his *Tractatus de liberorum educatione* (1450), made the
following statement about the reception of Italian humanism in
Germany, which certainly applies as well to the Netherlands (then
a part of "Germania"):

> Soon a crowd of those fellows who want to seem to be more than
> theologians would taunt me about speaking of the poets and recom-
> mending their writings. "Why do you bring us poets from Italy,"
> they will say, "and why are you so eager to corrupt the pious character
> of Germany with the effete licentiousness of poets? ... Get out of
> here, and take those poets with you." Nor do they criticize the poets
> justly, these fellows whose teaching rests on glosses rather than on
> texts, and who believe that nothing in the civil law is more distin-
> guished than the *Novels*. To whom we respond: "If all men in Germany
> agree with them, we will gladly depart, rather than stay here among
> such ignorance or blindness. Even in these regions, however, there
> are learned men who greatly respect poets and orators—nor are they
> moved by the arguments of such opponents.[25]

[23] *Rodolphi Agricolae Phrisii De inventione dialectica*, ed. Alardus Amstelredamus
(Cologne, 1539; reprint, Nieuwkoop, 1967), II, 309-310: "In laudem Papiae."

[24] Cf. Hermann Joseph Liessem, *Hermann van dem Bussche. Sein Leben und seine
Schriften*, (Cologne, 1884-1908; reprint, Nieuwkoop, 1965), 4-5.

[25] *De Liberorum Educatione*, trans. Joel Stanislaus Nelson, Studies in Medieval
and Renaissance Latin Language and Literature, 12 (Washington, D.C., 1940),
172-174: "Locuturo autem mihi de poetis eorumque lectiones suasuro, mox
turba illorum insultabit, qui videri magis quam esse theologi volunt. 'Quid tu
nobis ex Italia poetas adducis, inquient, sanctosque Germanie mores enervata
poetarum lascivia corrumpere properas? ... Abi tu procul a nobis atque poetas
tecum referto.' Neque ab his juriste quidam discrepant, quorum doctrina non in
textibus sed in glossis heret, quique nihil ornatius in iure civili reperiri censent
Autenticorum libris. Quibus pauca respondentes dicimus: 'si omnes, qui sunt
homines in Germanis, cum his sentiant, libentius migrabimus, quam cum tanta
ignorantia aut cecitate morabimur. Sed sunt etiam his in regionibus viri docti,
qui poetas et oratores magnopere colunt nec argumentis moventur adversa-
riorum."

Another most interesting witness is Poggio, who, on the last day of December, 1451, wrote the following letter from Rome to the dean of the cathedral of Utrecht, Willem van Heze:

A learned man, dean Jacob of Borselen, recently came to me and showed me certain documents in your name, one listing the orations of Cicero which you possess, the other those works of Cicero and others which you wish to have. From which I understood that you devote not a little attention to our *studia humanitatis*. I marveled that a man so avid for eloquence and the liberal arts should be found so far from Italy, the country to which such studies seem to be natural. Everywhere on earth are born outstanding natures, suitable to all kinds of instruction, just as fertile fields are cultivated if men wish to devote attention and care to them . . . .

As to the orations of Marcus Tullius, however, I see that you lack many of them, which I will send to you in a sealed scroll. I will also comment on the works of Cicero that you require and that may be available here. Truly, those books are rarely available, and one who wants them needs to have them copied. If you entrust this commission to someone, I will take care to see if copies can be had.

One thing especially I ask of you, that, as you write that you have the fifth oration against Catiline, which begins: "If anything with prayers among the immortal Gods," etc., you would arrange to have it transcribed as soon as possible and sent to me, since I am very anxious to see it. We do not have it. And I am amazed that a fifth oration has been found, because Cicero himself wrote that he had composed four orations against Catiline. But I think that either there was another oration, or that it was written by someone else. However that may be, I shall be much obliged if you see to it that I have a copy as soon as possible.[26]

---

[26] *Poggii Epistolae*, III, 45-46 (Book X, ep. 23): "Venit ad me nuper vir prudens Jacobus ex Borsalia decanus, et nomine tuo certas mihi cedulas ostendit, quarum in altera orationes continentur Ciceronis, quas habes, in altera scribis tibi orationes et volumina quaedam deesse tum ipsius Ciceronis operum, tum aliorum, quae cupis habere. Ex quibus intellexi te non parvam operam nostris humanitatis studiis impendisse. Miratus sum tam studiosum eloquentiae et optimarum artium virum tam longe ab Italia, cuius haec studia vernacula esse videntur, reperiri. Sed ubique terrarum egregia nascuntur ingenia atque ad omne genus doctrinae apta, si tamquam agri frugiferi excolantur et si operam et curam illis homines impendere velint . . . . Verum ut ad orationes Marci Tullii veniam, video te multis ex iis, quas habemus, orationibus carere, quas tibi descriptas in cedula mittam praesentibus interclusa. Similiter in ea adnotabo opera Ciceronis, quae requiris, quae quidem apud nos reperiantur. Verum ista raro venalia sunt, et si quis ea cupit, necesse est ut faciat describi. In quo dabo operam, si cui eam rem commiseris ut exemplaria haberi possint.

Unum te maxime rogo ut, cum scribas te habere quintam Orationem contra Catilinam, quae incipit: 'Si quid praecibus apud Deos immortales' etc., des operam ut quamprimum illam transcribi atque ad me mitti, quoniam summopere illam videre cupio. Non est enim apud nos. Et miror, cum ipse Cicero scripserit se

The evidence of these humanists, who both knew the North from personal visits, is clear: Italian humanism met with strong opposition, but there were a few adepts of it, sometimes to the amazement of the Italians themselves. Let us find these "rari nantes in gurgite vasto."

A first group may have been made up of copyists of manuscripts, in so far as they were not professional craftsmen who transcribed in the service of some other person, such as the man mentioned above, Theodorus Nicolai Werken of Abbenbroek. It is not always possible to distinguish such persons from students who attended the lessons of Italian masters. Most probably a student was Henricus de Brugis, who in 1451 copied for Guarino da Verona a manuscript (now Ms. Vindob. 259) containing the De immortalitate animae of Aeneas of Gaza and an Epitome Lactantii. A student also may have been the Jacobus Witte de Flandria necnon de Biervliet, who in the first years of the fifteenth century copied some works by Giovanni Conversino (d. 1408), a manuscript now in the Biblioteca Marciana of Venice (Cod. lat. XIV, 224 [4341]). Unfortunately, our list of such names is short, either because they were very rare exceptions or because the scattered materials have never been collected in a systematic, easily available survey.[27] Moreover, too little is known about those persons whom we find named in the colophons of their manuscripts. What sort of person was Petrus Swilden of the diocese of Liège, who copied Petrarch and classical texts in Italy (Bologna?) in 1458? Who was Radulphus de Zeelandia, who transcribed the Griseldis story in Brussels in 1436? And who was this enigmatical Arnoldus de Gheel Buscoducensis, who collected humanist manuscripts (Petrarch, Bruni) from 1429 onward and seems to have

---

tantum quatuor orationes contra Catilinam edidisse, quintam reperiri. Sed existimo aut aliam esse orationem aut ab alio quam a Cicerone compositam. Sed quaecumque ea sit, gratissimum mihi feceris si curabis ut illam quamprimum tua diligentia possim videre."

[27] In the excellent catalogues of manuscripts in the Vatican Library, I found, i.a.: Henricus Scyedam [Schiedam] (Vat. lat. 1939, fol. 267^v); Petrus de Middelburch (Vat. lat. 358, fol. 356^v; Vat. lat. 1742, fol. 371^v); Johannes Jedenville de Rupe [La Roche] in Ardenna (Vat. lat. 1895, fol. 163^v); and Johannes Hornsen Monasteriensis. About this last scribe, see José Ruysschaert, "Miniaturistes 'romains' sous Pie II," in Enea Silvio Piccolomini—Papa Pio II. Atti del convegno per il quinto centenario della morte e altri scritti raccolti da Domenico Maffei (Siena, 1968), 245-282, at 253 n. 44. About scribes from the Lowlands in Italy during the Renaissance, see in general Paul Liebaert, Artistes flamands en Italie pendant la Renaissance (Rome, Brussels, and Paris, 1913), 69-74; and the enlarged version by the same author, "Miniatori e scribi tedeschi," in Atti del X Congresso internazionale di storia dell'arte in Roma (Rome, 1922).

followed contemporary literature very closely? In any case we find him copying, about 1450, the *Vita Petrarcae* by Manetti, written only a decade earlier. It cannot be proved that he belonged to the Premonstratensian abbey of Park, just outside the Geldenaken Gate of Louvain; but, if he did work there, he may have been one of the men behind the shaping of the abbey's library, which was rich in humanist literature. There Erasmus discovered the *Adnotationes in Novum Testamentum* by Valla, and it held a copy of the *Elegantiae linguae Latinae* as well.

Still less is known of Hugo Victor, who copied Petrarch's *Familiarium Rerum Libri XXIV* at Bruges in 1456, or of Johannes Robini (Robijns?) de Campis, writer at Liège (St. Jacques?) of a most interesting codex (Darmstadt 1996), in which we find humanist works of several kinds: treatises on letter-writing by Barzizza and Haneron, four orations by Petrus Marcellus, a wealth of translations from the Greek by Jacobus Angelus de Scarperia (Plutarch's *Moralia*) and Bruni (Aristotle's *Ethics*), Demosthenes's *De Corona*, Xenophon's *Hieron*, and Basil's *De legendis libris gentilium*. Such a manuscript cannot but point to men deeply interested in the *humanitatis studia*.

These mere names raise more questions than we can answer; and one wonders if the presence of several men from northwest Flanders and Zeeland indicates that humanism took root in Bruges —a port with a strong Italian community—at an even earlier date than that which we now assume, the sixties of the Quattrocento. Once more the cases are too isolated from their historical context to permit the drawing of conclusions.

Besides these students and copyists and sometimes hardly distinguishable from them, we find collectors of classical and humanistic works. Such men are not numerous, but some of them were truly important persons. Apart from Arnoldus de Gheel, mentioned above, and the dean of Utrecht to whom Poggio wrote concerning the fifth "Catilinarian" of Cicero, a few others are known. About 1420 Jan de Wilde (1389-1419), alderman of the Brugse Vrije (the Jurisdiction of Bruges) collected manuscripts, not only of mediaeval literature but also of classical authors: *i.a.* two Italian manuscripts containing works by Cicero, a Valerius Maximus, and Seneca's tragedies, richly decorated with miniatures and de Wilde's coat of arms. Another collector was Anthonius Haneron, professor at Louvain during the 1430s, who is discussed at length below (p. 218), in the section on the teaching of Latin. He merits a very special mention, because it was for him that Joris van Houdelem (now: Oedelem), another copyist of Bruges, produced in 1439 a Sallust, which, except for the two middle quires (fols. 72-89v), was written in the *humanistica* and therefore seems to have been the first book ever written in the Netherlands in the new script. It is appropriate here to mention that, in the margins of the anonymous *Collatio de laudibus facultatum Lovaniensium* (which we tentatively date to 1435), there are a few corrections also written in a *humanistica*. These two cases perhaps permit the conclusion that it was due to professors of Louvain that the use of the new script was first tried during the late 1430s.

It also happened that wealthy students had their books made by wandering Italian scribes. There is a fine example at Cologne, where a manuscript containing Petrarch's *Bucolicum carmen* and *Epystola ad Italiam*, together with Lactantius's *De Ave Phoenice*, bears the subscription: "Scripsit Milo de Carraria [Milone dei Carraresi from Padua] apud Agrippinam Coloniam anno a nativitate Domini MCCCCXLIV *ad instantiam nobilis adolescentis Aymo de Poypone*." [28]

It is clear from all of this that "Germania" contained some persons of humanistic inclinations; but their rarity explains, at the same time, why Poggio was rather astonished to find such a person at Utrecht. In order to study the situation in more depth, we need to know whether any humanist literature was being produced in the Netherlands during this period and what was the state of the teaching of classical languages. The answer to the first question is short: we know of no humanist authors—no poets, no dramatists, no "orators." Other names could be added to those of the Latin writers of the late fourteenth and early fifteenth century already mentioned, but the picture would not be changed thereby. Take, for example, a colleague of Geilhoven, Henricus Pomerius of Brussels (1382-1469), prior at Groenendaal and Zevenborre. He wrote several devout works, such as a dialogue *Inter animam et hominem de Passione Domini*; but he is now best remembered as the author of three books on the origins of Groenendaal (*De origine monasterii Viridis-vallis*), including a life of Ruusbroec composed between 1414 and 1421. He writes a literary but clearly mediaeval Latin, and the spirit of the work is purely monastic. A comparison between his life of Ruusbroec and a specimen of roughly contemporary, humanistic hagiography, such as Leon

---

[28] Cologne, Historisches Archiv der Stadt Köln, Ms. W Kf 348. Cf. Sottili, "I codici," *IMU*, XI (1968), 345-448, at 409-410.

Battista Alberti's *Vita S. Potiti*,[29] is truly instructive, as both style and mood are totally different. Other works of this era, including the *Chronicon universale ab origine mundi usque ad annum 1457* by the Benedictine abbot, Anianus Coussere (d. Oudenburg, 1462), are less well known, but they would offer few surprises. The only known work in which one traces with certainty a still awkward imitation of humanist Latin style is the anonymous *Collatio de laudibus facultatum Lovaniensium*. If, however, Johannes Snavel was the author of this piece, his speech was an ephemeral incident, the result of recent impressions brought home from Italy and not to be sustained. So far as we can ascertain, he devoted the remainder of his life to canon law and the study of his masters, Giovanni da Imola and Francesco Zabarella.

The matter of the teaching of Latin is more complicated. Except for a few Latin schools, chiefly Zwolle and Deventer, reliable information for the fifteenth century is extremely scarce. Moreover, the Latin courses given in the University of Louvain by Anthonius Haneron and Carolus Viruli still have not been edited and analysed in depth.

As a rule one can assume that all the schools used the traditional textbooks: Donatus, Alexander de Villa Dei's *Doctrinale*, and Priscian. Much evidence attests the importance accorded the *Doctrinale* by Netherlandish scholars, and the percentage of Netherlanders among its fifteenth-century commentators is strikingly high. An early but eloquent example is the *Grammaticale*, a versified adaption written in 1405 by Godefridus de Traiecto (Utrecht, or rather Maastricht?), who was at that time established in the convent of St. Barbara at Tienen. The second printed edition of the *Doctrinale* (Treviso, 1472) was produced by Gerardus de Lisa from Ghent, who taught Latin in Italy. Commentaries on the work continued to multiply during the last two decades of the century as well as early in the next one; some were strongly mediaeval (philosophical) in concept, such as Gerardus of Zutphen's *Glosa notabilis* (Cologne, 1489) and the *Opus Minus* (Antwerp, 1493) of Willem Zenders of Weert, and met with strong opposition from the early humanists. Some of the latter tried to adapt the *Doctrinale* to the new principles and add

---

[29] *Opusculi inediti di Leon Battista Alberti*: *Musca—Vita S. Potiti*, ed. Cecil Grayson, Nuova Collezione di Testi Umanistici Inediti o Rari, 10 (Florence, 1954).

linguistic comments: J. Synthen, a colleague of Hegius, his successor, Hermannus Torrentinus, and Kempo of Texel at Zwolle; Timannus Kemenerus at Münster; Badius at Paris; and the inmates of Lily College at Louvain, whose work finally led to the famous grammar of Despauterius.

These attempts to modernize Alexander were occuring at a time when new Italian grammars and handbooks of style—Valla, Dati, Perotti—were becoming available in the Low Countries. They were not, however, the first efforts by local scholars to improve the teaching of Latin. Two centres seem to have been important in this respect, the priory of Korsendonk near Turnhout and the Faculty of Arts at Louvain. The establishment of Korsendonk's proper contribution and possible contacts with Italy requires further study. We know for certain that already from its very beginning (1393), this Augustinian community had a lively interest in grammar and literature: Godefridus de Traiecto went from Korsendonk to Tienen; Subprior Joannes de Palude (d. 1418) is said to have written a *Brevis summa circa rhetoricam*; and, above all, here worked Joannes de Meerhout (*fl.* 1440s-1476). Manuscripts at Brussels and Vienna preserve many works by this man: commentaries on Virgil and Horace, work on Latin grammar and vocabulary, a mnemotechnical treatise, and even a *Tractatus de greca grammatica* (Vienna, Österreichische Nationalbibliothek, series nova, cod. 12702, fols. 128ʳ-130ᵛ). De Meerhout's work urgently needs investigation, because there is a fair chance that he was one of the very first humanists in the Low Countries. Especially the treatise on Greek grammar, if it proves to be connected with the humanist revival of Greek studies, could overturn all we know about the earliest Greek scholarship in the Netherlands.

We know more about Louvain, though here, too, modern scholarship has greatly neglected what the age of Erasmus had forgotten. Until the end of the fifteenth century, the name of one great forerunner was alive: among the poems of Jodocus Beissel, we find the following epitaph of Anthonius Haneron (b. Steenvoorde, ca. 1400; d. Bruges, 10 December 1490):

> Fleeing this age of iron, old Anthonius Haneron
> Strips off the mortal husk of his soul, seeking the stars.
> He was the first to bring the Muses' arts to the Netherlands,
> And worthily he educated Duke Charles.
> He was a provost of the Church

And spoke with authority to ambassadors
And in the courts. Death vainly claims him for its own.
Only the inessential dies completely. The man's fame stands
As a wonderful testimony: it fears the reaping goddess not at all.[30]

The man who is here said to have been the first to bring the arts of the Muses to the Netherlands—an accomplishment attributed by Erasmus to Agricola [31]—is remembered today merely as a famous diplomat of the Burgundian dukes. Thus his biographers forget his successful activity as professor of Latin in the University of Louvain during the years 1430-1437. Several facts witness to his success there. His writings were used by students until the end of the century, more than fifty years after he had left the university. Moreover, when Hugo van Rimen from Haarlem stood for the post of "professor eloquentiae" in 1453, the decisive argument which he advanced to the academic council on 18 July was that he was a student of Haneron.

What were the peculiar qualities of Haneron's teaching? A master of arts and doctor of canon law of the University of Paris, Haneron taught Latin in the Faculty of Arts at Louvain from 1430 until 1438/39. He wrote for students a number of handbooks: a *Diasynthetica*, or syntax; a *De brevibus epistolis*, a kind of *ars dictaminis*; and short treatises on style, the most important of which was *De coloribus verborum sententiarumque cum figuris grammaticalibus*. Four features of Haneron's works are quite striking. First, he uses a simple, straightforward Latin. He says of himself: "I shall describe the rules in plain words, so that the thing may more easily be grasped by everyone." [32] It would be wrong to call this humanist Latin, as the vocabulary still contains many mediaevalisms, but in other respects one can agree with Beissel that Haneron paved the way for humanism.

---

[30] Iudocus Beisselius, *Rosacea augustissime cristifere Marie corona* (Antwerp, ca. 1498, fol. [e.vi.]ʳ (I use the copy in the Plantin-Moretus Museum, Antwerp):

"Ferrea secla senex fugitans Anthonius Haenron
　Hic anime exuvias occulit astra petens.
Pieridum primus Belgis hic intulit artes
　Instituit Karolum dignus et ipse ducem.
Prefuit et templis, regum legatis et aulis
　Intonuit. Frustra hunc mors putat esse suum.
Solus iners moritur totus. Stat pulchra superstes
　Fama viri: occantem non timet illa deam."

[31] In the letter to J. Botzheim (Allen, I, 2), Erasmus writes: "Rodolphus Agricola primus omnium aurulam quandam melioris literaturae nobis invexit ex Italia."

[32] Anthonius Haneron, *Diasynthetica* (Cologne, ca. 1475/77), fol. a.1ᵛ: "Plano sermone quo res omnis cognitu sit facilior, precepta complectar."

Secondly, Haneron's sources are almost exclusively classical: Cicero (including *Ad Herennium*), Terence, Virgil, Augustine, and sometimes Priscian. He mentions Alexander de Villa Dei once in his *Syntax* but more often elsewhere. His dependence on Radulphus de Rivo, attested by Schut, needs careful investigation, for it might connect him with an interesting prehumanist of the Netherlands. Thirdly, his teaching is linguistic and stylistic, without many philosophical reflexions or interpretations. He clearly avoids the methods of the *modistae*. Finally, Haneron uses vernacular (Dutch) forms to explain Latin ones and, in this way, put into practice an important rule of language teaching, which Rudolph Agricola would defend, fifty years later, in his theoretical treatise, *De formando studio*.[33]

These features show us a teacher who, almost *avant la lettre*, applied, within his limited possibilities, some of the essential rules of humanist pedagogy: to teach Latin from the ancient sources and on a level adapted to the capacities of the young students' minds. Even if Erasmus and Vives never mentioned Haneron's name, their methods were largely the same, though they had better tools at their disposal with which to work them out in practice. It is worthwhile, therefore, to read what Haneron tells us about the study of Latin:

> To learn grammar first is by all means necessary to anyone who wants to acquire other arts. For, how can anyone who is ignorant of Latin know aught of theology, civil law, or any of the other disciplines? How can one understand Latin at all, if he doesn't understand Latin idioms, the meaning and use of words, and the rules of syntax? Finally, how do you think that one ignorant of grammar could be an expert in rhetoric, especially as Latinity and purity of speech are of great importance to a properly rhetorical oration?[34]

While Haneron was still a professor at Louvain, another man began his career in the same university and the same faculty. He was Carolus Viruli, of whom more will be said below. Suffice here to say that he was for the greater part of a century the central person in the university in matters of Latin teaching and the fostering of

---

[33] R. Agricola, *De inventione dialectica* (reprint, 1967), II, 193-201, at 196.

[34] A. Haneron, *Diasynthetica* (Cologne, ca. 1475/77), fol. a.1r: "Nempe grammaticam prescisse necesse est eum, qui velit artes reliquas adipisci. Quo enim pacto quis vel theologie, vel civilis iuris vel cuiuslibet artium aliarum habuerit noticiam, qui latinam linguam non norit? Quomodo latinum intelligeret, qui latinum non intelligat ydeoma, significancias verborum modosque, congruam denique nexionem? Qua deinceps ratione quempiam expertem grammatice, expertum rhetorice fore credideris, presertim cum ad rhetoricam orationem latinitas nonnichil attineat et puritas sermonis?"

humanism. Both Erasmus and Vives remembered him, the latter
with far more justice than the former.

   To complete this section on the first traces of humanism and the
study of Latin, we must notice one last author of an *ars dictaminis*
and examine the founding of a chair of eloquence in the University
of Louvain. In 1454, Engelbertus Schut of Leiden wrote a *De Arte
Dictandi* in 1540 hexameters, which is worthy of Alexander de Villa
Dei. This is a very puzzling work. Its form clearly imitates the *Doctrinale* and similar versified handbooks. The contents reveal beyond
doubt a close connection with Haneron's *De brevibus epistolis*, which
Schut sometimes followed verbatim. Worth noting is the still un-
noticed fact that Schut, in his edition (Gouda, 1481) of Haneron's
syntax, added summaries in verse to each chapter. Schut's own work
contains a strong representation of classical authors: Hesiod, Demosthenes, Seneca, Varro, Aristotle, and Quintilian are each quoted
once; Horace, Virgil, and especially Cicero many times. The passage
"De vetustis" (vv. 1469-1500) merits a complete reproduction:

> If you wish to speak well, use ancient words,
> Such as poets, speaking learnedly, used to employ.
> They could illustrate all things with words.
> But you will choose those words which all are able to
> Know. The best are the newer of the old ones.
> The older ones are to be preferred to the new.
> Wine which everyone in the past took into his mouth
> Cannot decently be given to others.
> Thus, what flows randomly from everyman's mouth
> Are names thought unworthy of a famous rhetorician.
> "Custom is the surest teacher of speaking,"
> As the distinguished orator, Quintilian, avers.
> Each has his own expertise: the rhetorician knows rhetoric well,
> The best orator is acquainted with every word.
> That which may be hidden from others is for your daily use.
> An orator comprehends every manner of speech;
> There are some words avoided by everyone;
> What these stories mean, scarcely anyone, I think, knows.
> An orator ought not to use such words,
> For he who does not know these himself, cannot speak clearly, can he?
> Whoever is a good orator, will want to use lucid words.
> Speaking most aptly, Anthonius begins:
> "I would not dare to touch those who are said to be poets.
> They seem to me to have spoken in no known tongue."
> He reckoned he must avoid obscurities of words.
> He himself is accustomed to deny that he knows any poets
> Or orators, so that he might be so much the more praised,

For, having no teacher, he could be held to be a natural talent,
~~Read the proper writings~~, looking for the lucidity of good ones.
Poetic metres decorate us in a wondrous way,
So that each thinks that we sustain the true art of speaking.
Thus I say: "Reor, o Soboles"; vulgarly: "Puto, Fili." [35]

The place of honour here given to the ancients and the argument
from Quintilian would not be out of place in any humanist treatise.
The last part of the passage, however, needs further investigation.
Who is Anthonius of line 1490? Is he Haneron? If so, the next verses
would shed unexpected light on discussions about humanism in
the milieu of Haneron, the University of Louvain. For it must be
clear then that "poetas" (v. 1491) and "oratores" (v. 1495) mean
here "humanists" and that Haneron strove for simplicity of speech
(v. 1493), a fact confirmed by his own writings, but that, at the same

---

[35] Engelbertus Schut, *De arte dictandi* (Gouda, Gerardus Leeu, ca. 1480), fols.
[c.7ᵛ-c.8ʳ] (I use the copy in the British Museum):

"Si bene vis fari, tu priscis utere verbis,
1470 Qualia doctiloqui quondam posuere poete.
Illi res omnes verbis lustrare quierunt.
Illa tamen verba statues, que noscere possunt
Omnes. Optima sunt, veterum que sunt noviora.
Que mage sunt vetera, sunt preponenda novellis.
1475 Vinum, quod quisque sua pridem sumpsit in ora,
non aliis tribui poterit de more decenti.
Sic, que cuiusque passim vulgantur ab ore,
Nomina non digna censentur rethore claro.
'Est consuetudo fandi certissima doctrix,'
1480 Ceu putat eximius orator Quintilianus.
Est mos cuique suus: rhetor bene rethora noscit,
Optimus orator est verbo doctus in omni.
Quod reliquos lateat, hoc est tibi cotidianum.
Rethor maneriem dicendi continet omnem.
1485 Sunt voces alique, que sunt a quoque relicte;
He quid designent, aliquem vix nosse putato.
Talibus orator non debet vocibus uti,
Qui nequit agnosci, numquid loqueretur aperte?
Quisque loqui doctus, lucenti voce fruetur.
1490 Adprime pulchre dicens Anthonius infit:
'Tangere non ausim quos dicunt esse poetas.
Hii michi non nota lingua dixisse videntur.'
Verborum nebulas reputavit ei fugiendas.
Ipse negare solet aliquos se scire poetas
1495 Aut oratores, ut eo laudatior esset,
Quo sine doctore valuit facundus haberi.
Scripta poetarum lege, luciditate bonorum.
Miris valde modis nos ornant metra poete,
Ut nos quisque putet artem retinere loquendi.
1500 Sic: 'Reor, o Soboles' dico; volgus: 'Puto, Fili.' "

time, he kept his distance from the humanists in order that he might
be praised as a self-made, eloquent man. If this interpretation is
correct, Schut provides us with a testimony of exceptional importance.
One can go even further and wonder if Haneron's statement was
perhaps elicited as a reaction against some enthusiastic reports
about studies in Italy by men who had been there, as the author of
the *Collatio de laudibus facultatum* (which, if the date of 1435 is correct,
Haneron must have heard) had been. I want to stress, however,
that this remains a hypothesis and not something established.

The end of Engelbertus's passage is also quite interesting, since
he recommends the reading of the *poetae* as a means of adorning
one's own style. This attitude may explain why the young Erasmus
admired him and why he was on good terms with a wandering
poeta, Stephanus Surigonus of Milan. Engelbert may have been a
bad writer, as Erasmus later said,[36] but he remains a remarkable
representative of a generation which was still steeped in mediaeval
traditions and forms, but which also recognised the value of the new
learning.

We must judge by the same principles the foundation of a chair
of eloquence at Louvain. From the first initiative in 1443 to the final
permission granted on 1 June 1447 by the humanist pope, Nicholas
V, some persons at Louvain—among them Petrus de Mera, who went
to Rome to negotiate the question—were driven by the desire to
keep academic instruction abreast of the latest developments in
Italy. Unfortunately, competent teachers were lacking, and the first
professor in the chair, Johannes Block, was much more interested
in mathematics than in the rhetorical works of Cicero, which he was
supposed to teach. None of his fifteenth-century successors would
achieve anything great while holding the chair of eloquence. Improvement came only in 1490 with the appointment of Johannes
Paludanus of Kassel (Flanders), later well known as a friend of
Erasmus and Thomas More and for his role in the foundation of the
Collegium Trilingue. It is not too much to say that more was done
for Latin by teachers in some colleges, such as the Lily (Viruli) and
later also the Pig (Dorpius), than by the holders of the chair of
eloquence.

------

[36] Desiderius Erasmus, *De conscribendis epistolis*, ed. Jean-Claude Margolin,
in *Opera Omnia Desiderii Erasmi Roterodami*, I, 2 (Amsterdam, 1971), 135-579, here
at 231.

III. The Founders of Humanism in the Low Countries

The period from 1455/60 until about 1485/90 marks the definite incorporation of a number of elements of Italian humanism into the general cultural milieu of the Low Countries. This does not mean, however, that Netherlandish humanism was a kind of duplicate or even a simple prolongation of the Italian. On the shores of the North Sea, interest in and admiration for the beauty and richness of Latin literature and ancient civilisation hardly ever led, during the fifteenth century, to a sustained practice of the study of the *humanae litterae* for their own sake or to a pursuit of a profane literature which would imitate the pagan glories in order to attain a similar immortality of fame. For aspirations of this sort, one has to wait until Janus Secundus and his *Basia* (1534). In the same way, the moral ideal of *humanitas* and the discussions either on various human virtues and qualities or on the general problem of the *vita activa* versus the *vita contemplativa* were almost never transplanted, except for the problem of *nobilitas*, which, in a limited way and in French translation, aroused the interest of the Burgundian court. Their places were taken by the ideal of (Christian) *pietas* and discussions on the *vita christiana*. Altering the title of the last great work of the French humanist, Guillaume Budé, one could define the transplantation of humanism to the Low Countries as a *transitus humanismi ad christianismum*. Except for the enthusiastic experiments of some young students (Erasmus!), the main purpose of the northern "humanists" was always the study of the *sacrae litterae* and, through them, a reformation of Christendom and of Christian (theological) studies. This was already stated by Rudolph Agricola, perhaps the most Italianised among the early northern humanists, who says explicitly (in his *De formando studio*):

> We must have regard for this [moral philosophy] first and foremost . . .
> By means of these [moral examples from the classical philosophers
> and poets] we make a step toward sacred literature, and we must direct
> our way of life to their teaching. . . . The rest of the things that have
> been handed down have something more or less of error mixed into
> them. . . . But sacred writings are very far removed from all error,
> and they alone lead us by a sure, solid path.[37]

---

[37] R. Agricola, *De inventione dialectica*, II, 193-201, here at 194-195: "Huius [= moralis philosophie] prima nobis et praecipua habenda est ratio . . . . Per haec [moral examples] gradus ad sacras literas faciendus est et ad illarum praescriptum dirigendus vitae nobis ordo . . . . Reliqua omnia aliorum tradita plus minusve erroris tamen habent admixtum aliquid . . . . At sacrae litterae tam longe ab omni errore remotae . . . sunt quae solae nos certa solida rectaque ducant via . . . ."

To these *litterae* the mature Erasmus decided to return, as he told John Colet in a letter of 1505. And even if the spell of the *humanae litterae* continued to attract him in later years, yet he ended his *Ciceronianus* with this profession of faith: "Here pupils are taught, here philosophy and eloquence are learned, so that we may know Christ and may celebrate his glory. This is the whole goal of erudition and eloquence." [38]

Nothing, of course, could have been more natural in a land so strongly influenced by mysticism and by the Modern Devotion. One is used to call the phenomenon just described "biblical" or "Christian" humanism, but in my opinion it would be better to speak of a "humanist Christianity." As a matter of fact, not the *humanae* but the *christianae litterae* were the final aim of these "humanists," to whom humanist studies and methods were only the means or the tools for the improvement and reformation of Christendom. The mystics had striven for the same goal by their mystical means.

Because the ultimate end was not the *humanae* but the *sacrae litterae*, we do not find poets imitating the profane themes of Catullus, Horace, or the Roman elegiacs, at least not before Remaclus Arduenna, an early sixteenth-century disciple of Fausto Andrelini. Stephanus Surigonus, a Milanese poet who tried to find an audience for his erotic epigrams at the Universities of Cologne and Louvain about 1472, met with no success and was greatly disappointed. A poet such as the German, Peter Luder (*fl.* 1450-60)—who was an exception in his own land, too—is not to be found at all in the Netherlands, where nearly all the intellectuals shared the opinion of the Carmelite of Ghent, Arnoldus Bostius: "Most modern poets seduce the eager ears but offer nothing true to the spirit." [39]

As a rule, interest in classical and humanist poetry for its own sake seems to have been rather limited. Two letters in Viruli's *Epistolares formulae* (first ed. 1474?) are typical in this respect. The subject of the first is "A friend counsels a friend to come to Louvain to teach the poetic arts," and it runs as follows:

---

[38] Desiderius Erasmus, *Dialogus Ciceronianus*, ed. Pierre Mesnard, in *Opera Omnia Desiderii Erasmi Roterodami*, I, 2 (Amsterdam, 1971), 581-710, here at 709: "Huc discuntur disciplinae, huc philosophia, huc eloquentia, ut Christum intelligamus, ut Christi gloriam celebremus. Hic est totius eruditionis et eloquentiae scopus."

[39] Philippus C. Molhuysen, "Cornelius Aurelius," *Nederlandsch Archief voor Kerkgeschiedenis*, new series II (1903), 1-35, here at 23: "Poetae moderni plurimi delectant, verum nihil spiritui conferunt."

I send you much honour in greeting! If you want instruction in T............
to teach the poetic arts, I know that never did Evander receive
Hercules, and never Achestes Anchises, so happily as those at Louvain
would receive you. I think that it would be very useful to you, because
the field is fertile, and there are few reapers.[40]

The friend, supposedly writing "ex Morino" (Viruli's native region
of Kassel), declines the offer:

I don't want to pursue these studies any more. It is foolish to pursue
what everyone else abandons. Already the Muses have grown pitiful.
Orpheus has died, Virgil and Homer, too. Lucan sings here and there
with an empty stomach. I cannot envisage that the Muses will ever
again rise up and sing happy songs, adorned with garlands.[41]

One could argue that these letters are school exercises on old,
stock themes. This is certainly true, but it is equally true that they
depict the real situation until the very end of the century, and that
Rudolph Agricola, when he had returned to Frisia from Italy, as
well as the young Erasmus, echoed the complaints of Viruli's correspondent. The chair of poetics at Louvain was founded only in 1477,
and for many years the professors had to come from Italy. Apart
from some isolated pieces, the first volume of *Carmina* ever published
by a man of the North who deserves the name of humanist, was that
of the Westphalian, Rudolphus Langius (1486).

The three decades with which we are now concerned (ca. 1460-
1490) are characterised by a conscious and outspoken confrontation
of the old, scholastic traditions, which remain very strong, with the
new ideals spreading very quickly from Italy. This confrontation,
felt as a "Conflictus Thaliae et Barbariei" by the young adepts of
humanism, was stimulated by a sustained exchange of persons and
books between the South and the North. The increasing number
of Italian humanists seeking employment outside the peninsula,
the growing political and cultural power of the Burgundian court,

---

[40] Carolus Viruli, *Epistolarum formulae* (Louvain, Joh. de Westphalia, s.a.),
fol. [e.8]ᵛ: "Honores plurimos pro salute. Si Lovanium venire velis lecturus
poeticas artes scio quod nunquam tam letus Herculem suscepit Evander aut
Achestes Anchisem quam te sint studentes omnes recepturi. Id tibi perutile
censeo quia frugifer illic campus est et pauci messores."
[41] *Ibid.*, fols. [p.7ᵛ-p.8ʳ]: "Neque in reliquum tempus multum his Musis insis-
tere curo. Stultum est id velle sequi quod ab omnibus deseritur. Misere iam
Muse gemunt; extinctus Orpheus est, extinctus Virgilius atque Homerus. Ieiunus
cantat Lucanus in ortis. Non video quod sic unquam Musae resurgent ut sertis
ornate leta carmina canant."

and, last but not least, the development of the printing press after 1473, were all factors which accelerated and multiplied the contacts. The economic prosperity of the Burgundian provinces and neighbouring countries also had favourable cultural consequences, such as a growing number of well-equipped libraries. All of this contributed to produce the first Netherlandish works which fully merit the qualification "humanist." At the end of this period, we find for the first time the optimistic statement that, at last, a rebirth of letters may be seen in the North. In the preface to his *De Natura Cantus*, dated 27 April 1496, Matthaeus Herbenus of Maastricht rejoices in the great flowering of humanism in the Rhineland, "though I don't know by what change in the heavens Literature has begun to be more sought after here than is usual in our age . . .," and he cites Trithemius, Reuchlin, Wimpheling, Brant, Celtis, Leontorius, and Rutgerus Sicamber as examples.[42] This text contrasts sharply with some complaints by Agricola, written about a decade earlier, that he did not find congenial men in the Netherlands.

Both Agricola and Herbenus looked at the situation in their native land with "Italianised" eyes. They were two of the many men who knew Italy through having spent long periods of time there. Just as in earlier generations, many Netherlanders continued to cross the Alps to study various subjects, such as canon law. Henricus Deulin (De Minorivilla), for example, who in 1470 became professor of eloquence at Louvain, had read law at Bologna.

Netherlanders also continued to enter the service of leading churchmen. One such was Henricus van Zomeren (ca. 1418-1472), who acted as secretary to Cardinal Bessarion from 1457 until 1460, when he was appointed professor of theology at Louvain. Friendly relations continued between the two men while both still lived, and, although Van Zomeren never became a champion of humanism at Louvain, it bears mentioning that in 1470 Bessarion sent him a copy of his *Adversus Platonis Calumniatorem*, which had been published at Rome in the previous year. On his side, the Louvain theologian dedicated to the cardinal a work on William of Ockham.

In addition to the traditional reasons for travelling to Italy, we now notice for the first time a new and distinctive one, the study

---

[42] *Herbeni Traiectensis de natura cantus ac miraculis vocis*, ed. Joseph Smits van Waesberghe, Beiträge zur Rheinischen Musikgeschichte, 22 (Cologne, 1957), 16: ". . . cum nesciam qua conversione coelorum litterae apud nostrates plus solito nostro aevo coli coeperint . . . ."

of the classics. Moreover, these students of the classics begin to participate, sometimes with great success, in the humanistic literary life at the Italian courts and universities. This combination of old and new can be found also, at a somewhat later date, in the career of Erasmus. He went to Italy to secure a doctorate in theology at Turin, but by far the greater amount of his time he spent working on classical authors and his own humanistic writings (the *Adagia!*) in such milieux as the humanistic circle around the Aldine press in Venice. Here he improved his knowledge of Greek and Greek literature, just as Agricola had done at Ferrara, thirty years before.

This seems an appropriate place to discuss the more important Netherlandish students of humanism in Italy between 1460 and 1490. One of the earliest may have been Cornelius de Mera (Van Meer) of Zeeland, whom we know only from a manuscript (Oxford Cod. Canon. misc. 452) containing a commentary on Porphyry's *Isagoge*, which he finished in Venice in the house of Iohannes Calderia on 20 January 1463. The list of really important students, however, begins in 1465/66 with the Italian journey of two Westphalians, Rudolphus Langius (ca. 1438-1519) of Münster and his friend, Count Maurice of Spiegelberg, who, according to H. Van der Velden,[43] did not actually accompany Langius but preceded him by two years (1463). Unfortunately, we know very little about what they did in the homeland of humanism.

The same is true of Langius's friend, Antonius Liber (Vrije) of Soest, who went to Pavia in 1468. In 1486 Langius returned to Italy, now accompanied by a young student from the region of Münster, Hermannus Buschius. About Buschius, who was to become one of the brilliant German humanists around 1500, we know for sure that he was for several years a pupil of Pomponio Leto.

If it is true that we cannot follow the tracks of Langius and Liber in Italy with sufficient detail, we are far better informed about the consequences of their Italian experience. Both men are central figures in the rise and development of humanist teaching in the northern Netherlands and Westphalia: Langius in his native town of Münster; and Liber, a much more peripatetic scholar, successively in Groningen, Emmerich, Cologne, Kampen, Amsterdam, and Alkmaar. They propagated, moreover, the works of Italian humanists, Langius those of Lorenzo Valla and Domizio Calderini, Liber those of Enea

---

[43] Henricus Eduardus J. M. Van der Velden, *Rodolphus Agricola (Roelof Huusman), een Nederlandsch humanist der vijftiende eeuw* (Leiden, 1911), 80, n. 1.

Silvio and Poggio, whose letters he included in an epistolary collection
for use in the schools.

An important circumstance contributed to the diffusion of the
learning these men got in Italy. With Langius and Liber, indeed, we
enter the famous circle of learned men from the northern area (Frisia-
Westphalia-Zwolle/Deventer), known as the Adwerth (now Aduard)
Academy from the name of a monastery west of Groningen, where
they used to meet under the abbacy of Henry van Rees (1449-1485).
The abbey had two Latin schools, one at the monastery itself and
the other at Bedum, a few miles to the northeast. Among the professors
is mentioned a certain "Emmanuel, bishop of Cremona, a learned
man of noble family. He was born a count but fled Italy because of
the disorders there and entered Adwerth, where he lived for more
than thirty years." [44] This man, whoever he may have been, along
with Langius, who was back at Adwerth by 1469, may have stimulated
the fervour of the academicians for humanist studies.

It would be exaggerated to compare this club of learned friends
to the much more famous Accademia Platonica of Florence; for it
certainly never reached that level, nor did it exercise a comparable
influence on the spread of humanism outside its own circle. Adwerth,
moreover, was much more concerned with religious discussions,
as is to be expected of an "academy" patronised by a northern abbey
and of which one of the leading members was Wessel Gansfort of
Groningen. Gansfort, too, went to Rome after long years of study
at Cologne, Heidelberg, and Paris. His stay (1471) was rather short
and does not have the humanist significance of those of his fellow
academicians, Johannes Canter and Rudolph Agricola. From the
beginning of his student days, Gansfort was interested in ancient
languages only as tools for biblical and theological studies. "He always
inclined toward theology," [45] says his old biographer, Hardenberg;
and the story goes that when his friend, Pope Sixtus IV, invited him
to ask a favour for himself, Gansfort replied: "I should like to have
a Greek and Hebrew bible from the Vatican Library." [46] This
answer typifies a man who wrote Latin with simple ease and elegance

---

[44] Wessel Gansfort, *Opera* (facsimile of ed. of Groningen, 1614; Nieuwkoop,
1966), p. *** 1v: "Emmanuel episcopus Cremonensis . . . homo doctus et nobilis
familia. Nam comes natus erat, sed propter seditiones Italicas profugit et Ad-
werdiam intravit, ubi supra triginta annos vixit."

[45] *Ibid.*, p. ** 3v: "Semper ad theologiam propendebat".

[46] *Ibid.*, p. ** 2r-v: "Rogo ergo ut mihi detis ex bibliotheca Vaticana Graeca
et Hebraea biblia."

- but only to foster his cherished *pia studia* A similar man may have
been the less important figure, Hadrianus van Echout, who died in
1499 as prior of the Carmelite house in Ghent, and who copied
various writings of the "Christian Virgil," Baptista Mantuanus,
while he was in Italy around 1476. Such men cared little for the
revival of the *humanae litterae*, and their unconcern left a clear mark
on the northern "academies" such as that of Adwerth—the membership of a man such as Agricola notwithstanding.

Agricola may be considered, indeed, one of the extremely rare
fifteenth-century Netherlanders who thoroughly assimilated humanism in its Italian form. It is not mere chance that he is the only one
to have been praised by a leading Italian humanist (Ermolao Barbaro)
as a man who had brought Germany to the same level of learning
as Italy or Greece. This Frisian, educated at Erfurt, Cologne, and
Louvain, arrived in Pavia probably in 1468, about the time when
Langius was on his way home. At the start he read law, like so many
others. Soon, however, just like Ovid, Petrarch, Boccaccio, Enea
Silvio, and so many others, both earlier and later, he became extremely
weary of juristic subtleties and turned his attention to the Roman
classics and the Italian humanists, among them Petrarch. Agricola
certainly felt himself a bit of a northern Petrarch, and his admiration
for the father of humanism materialised into the composition of a
life of his hero. The musically gifted son of the North assimilated
with great efficiency the secrets of harmonious and enchanting
Latin, which enabled him to compete with his Italian friends in
both prose and poetry. It was a rare foreigner in Italy who reached
such a level of competence, Janus Pannonius remaining the most
famous one. Among the men of the Low Countries, Agricola stands
out as nearly an isolated case. Closest to him come members of another
Frisian family, the Canters. Johannes Canter belonged to the Adwerth
Academy and is said to have spoken only Latin with his wife, his
children, and even his housemaid. About his sons there are traditions
of prodigious precocity, but most are uncertain and cannot be substan-
tiated. Andreas seems to have aroused the admiration of Sixtus IV
by a Latin speech; and Jacobus, who is better known as a scholar
and poet, was the first Netherlander to try his hand at an erotic
poem in the manner of the Italian humanists.

With some interruptions for trips back to Groningen, Agricola
stayed in Italy until 1479, first at Pavia and then, from about 1475, at
Ferrara. His motive for moving to the town of the Estes was the study

of Greek, for which there was no chair in the University of Pavia. Here appears a second aspect of Agricola's historical importance for northern humanism: a great many students from the Netherlands attended courses at the university of Ferrara, among them his friend and later fellow "academician," Wilhelmus Frederiks of Groningen. Agricola seems to have been the only one of them to engage himself wholly in humanist studies, and he is certainly unique in his ability to propagate the Greek language with some efficiency. In this respect he is the Coluccio Salutati of the Netherlands. He had a few forerunners, to be sure, such as Radulphus de Rivo (d. 1403), Joannes van Meerhout (d. 1476), and Wessel Gansfort. The first and also the second, who seems to have written a Greek grammar, remained isolated figures and were only very recently rediscovered. Gansfort is said to have learned some Greek from Byzantine monks at Cologne, but this learning influenced, if anything, only his own biblical studies. Agricola, though he wrote only a few works and cared little about their publication, at least aroused an enthusiasm for Greek in the director of the school at Deventer, Alexander Hegius, through whom the burning flame was transmitted to the generation of Erasmus. Agricola's translations of Plato, Isocrates, and Aphthonius were published before the end of the century (by Jacobus Canter) or shortly thereafter (by Petrus Aegidius and Alardus of Amsterdam) and mark the beginning of an intense activity of translation which involved figures no less important than Erasmus and Thomas More. Hegius's poem in praise of the study of Greek, awkward as it may be, gives expression to feelings very like those in some of Melanchthon's famous speeches.[47] It would never have been written, save for the message brought by Agricola from the South.

Compared to Agricola, Matthaeus Herbenus (1451-1538), a Walloon established at Maastricht, is a minor figure but one deserving more attention than he has received. History forgot him, largely because he did not find a link to a great man of the next generation, as Agricola was fortunate enough to do. Herbenus belongs to the humanism of the Meuse/Rhine area, but he worked in a remote border town which had neither a university nor an important library. He left for Rome in 1469 in the train of the papal legate, Onufrio, as noted above. Upon Onufrio's death (20 October 1471), Herbenus found a new protector in Niccolò Perotti, with whom he lived at Rome, Perugia, Bologna,

---

[47] *Alexandri Hegii . . . Carmina . . .* (Deventer, R. Paffraet, 1503), fol. D.3ᵛ. Cf. Johannes Lindeboom, *Het Bijbelsch Humanisme in Nederland* (Leiden, 1913), 80.

Ferrara, and perhaps also Venice, returning in 1480 to Maastricht, where he became rector of the school of St. Servatius. His modest literary output introduced into the Netherlands historiography and topography after the models of Leonardo Bruni and Flavio Biondo. The colophon of his *Diasynthetica (Syntax)* explicitly states that the work is "derived from the most learned teachers of grammar, Guarino and Niccolò Perotti, Archbishop of Santa Maria di Siponto and his own master." [48] This is so much more remarkable, because Herbenus also owes a great deal to Alexander de Villa Dei and to Anthonius Haneron (whom he apparently thought not worthwile to mention).

There were several other interesting Netherlanders in Italy, apart from the host of students who left no trace in history. We shall limit ourselves to two more names of outstanding importance, the Flemish printer, Dirk Martens (Theodoricus Martinus) of Aalst, and the Zeelander, Paulus of Middelburg, an influential astronomer. Both men represent essential aspects of humanist culture outside of the strictly literary and philosophical spheres. We do not yet know what induced Martens to travel to Italy, but it has been established that he learned the new technique of printing in the Venetian area, undoubtedly from or together with his fellow countryman, Gerardus de Lisa of Ghent, at Venice or Treviso. In the first book he printed alone, a *De Vita Beata* of Baptista Mantuanus (Aalst, summer 1474), he proudly announced: "Hoc opus impressi Martinus Theodoricus Alosti, qui *Venetum* scita Flandrensibus affero cuncta." [49] Martens borrowed from de Lisa a number of the features typical of the first books printed at Aalst in 1473 by himself and his partner, Johannes de Westphalia. It is worthwhile to recall the titles of these three books —the first printed in the Low Countries—because they are typical not only of the things Martens published throughout his career but also of the whole cultural situation of the land: [50]

---

[48] "ex eruditissimis Grammatice professoribus Guarino atque Nicolao Perotto Archiepiscopo Sipontino domino suo extracta." Matthaeus Herbenus, *De constructione substantivorum, adiectivorum, pronominum verborum, et de ordinibus eorundem, et de constructione coniunctionum prepositionum et interiectionum incipit libellus* (Deventer, Jac. de Breda, ca. 1490), fol. dDd.vi^v. I use the copy in the Stadsbibliotheek of Maastricht.

[49] *De vijfhonderdste verjaring van de boekdrukkunst in de Nederlanden.* Catalogus van de tentoonstelling in de Koninklijke Bibliotheek Albert I (Brussels, 1973), 121, No. 59. This colophon is reproduced in the catalogue *Dirk Martens 1473-1973* (Aalst, 1973), 260.

[50] These three volumes have been anastatically reprinted in Brussels, 1973, with an introduction by K. Heireman.

1) the *Speculum conversionis peccatorum* of Dionysius the Carthusian, who had died the year before;
2) *Manuale de salute sive de aspiratione animae ad Deum,* a mediaeval pseudo-Augustine; and
3) the famous short novel by Enea Silvio Piccolomini, *Historia de duobus amantibus.*

From 1473 until 1529, Martens was busy providing the people with pious readings and university students with humanistic books. His role at Louvain, where he soon established a shop in front of the university, and at Antwerp (1502-1512), was much the same as that of Richard Pafraet of Cologne at Deventer. But Martens's publications were much more significant, because he published not only classics and Italian humanists, such as Poliziano, Baptista Mantuanus, Ermolao Barbaro, Filippo Beroaldo, Sr., Pico, Filelfo, and Andrelini, as did Pafraet, but also Agricola, Dorpius, and, above all, many works by his good friend, Erasmus—not to forget the *Utopia* of Thomas More. He was, moreover, one of the first to produce textbooks for the study of Greek, such as Theodore of Gaza's grammar, and printed in 1518 the very first specimen of Hebrew printing from a Netherlandish press. Martens's role in the early stage of Netherlandish humanism may justly be compared with that of the Plantin press at the end of the sixteenth century, when this humanism culminated in the work of Lipsius and his contemporaries.

Whereas Martens learned his craft in Italy and brought his knowledge home, Paulus of Middelburg (1446-1533) went to Italy to exercise his profession, astronomy, following in this way in the footsteps of earlier men, such as Dominicus de Flandria. Paulus, however, did not work in a religious house or theological faculty but became a respected scholar at humanist courts, particularly at Urbino, where he became physician to Duke Federigo in 1480, and at Rome under Leo X. He received his first education at Bruges at about the time that some schoolmasters were quarrelling about who was the better grammarian, Priscian or Valla. Whether or not Paulus became acquainted at Bruges with some aspects of the new learning, remains an open question. After studying at Louvain, he soon became so disgusted with the ignorance reigning in his own country that he left for Italy. His few writings are all technical works, prognostications and treatises on the date of Easter; but he was in touch with the best representatives of a science which was renewing itself through humanist discoveries of ancient scientists. He knew Marsilio Ficino, Copernicus, and Jacobus de Spira, and J. C. Scaliger was his pupil. His success as a skilled astronomer at humanist courts is not astonishing. It is well known that astronomy and astrology appealed to the minds of many humanists, in Italy and elsewhere. The classical poem of Manilius, discovered by Poggio, was printed more often during the fifteenth century than it has been during the twentieth. Jovianus Pontanus wrote long astrological treatises and poems. That there was no less interest in the Netherlands can be shown by some poems in the *Silva Carminum* of Bartholomaeus Coloniensis and by the editorial work of Jacobus Canter, who published (1491) the *Liber astronomicus* of Guido Bonatus de Forolivio. And, after all, a famous conflict about the computation of the date of Easter pitted Paulus against Petrus de Rivo, professor of eloquence at Louvain.

Just when men from the Low Countries, such as Agricola, Herbenus, and Gerardus de Lisa, began to take their share in humanist studies and letters in Italy, an increasing number of itinerant *poetae et oratores* came to the Netherlands, some seeking a generous patron or a teaching job, others on official missions (Angelus de Curibus Sabinis, Ermolao Barbaro). Most of them appeared sooner or later at the universities, Cologne and Louvain, sometimes eventually finding their ways to Paris or England. A survey of those that came to Louvain during the second half of the fifteenth century may well illustrate their role and importance, but also the modest results of their visits. This is to be explained partly by the not always friendly reception they met, except in a narrow circle of fellow latinists, and partly by the poor intellectual quality of these wandering scholars. The best poets remained in Italy.

The first important Italian at Louvain was Raimundus de Marliano, professor of canon law from 1461 until 1463, after which date he devoted himself completely to the study of ancient Germanic topography in relation to the works of Caesar and Tacitus. Out of these studies he produced two works of classical scholarship, an *Index commentariorum C. Iulii Caesaris* [51] (a list of names of towns, rivers, and places) and its expanded version, *Veterum Galliae locorum . . . alphabetica desciptio, eorum maxime quae apud Caesarem in Commentariis sunt et apud Cornelium Tacitum*. This list enjoyed an enviable success and was printed several times in Italy, France, and Germany, the last

---

[51] (*Catalogus van de*) *Tentoonstelling Erasmus en Leuven*, Leuven, Stedelijk Museum, 17 nov.-15 dec. 1969 (Leuven, 1969), 149, No. 136.

time in 1606. Carolus Bovillus (Charles de Bovelles) used it in the composition of his work on the French language.[52] It is an attractive hypothesis that Marliano passed on his humanist enthusiasm to his successor, Robertus a Lacu (Van de Poel) of Ghent (d. 26 June 1483), who is known as one of the rare patrons of humanism at Louvain during this period. To him and to Carolus Viruli, Stephanus Surigonus, a Milanese Humiliate and wandering poet, addressed a long elegy, in which he complains about the complete lack of interest in poetry in Brabant:

> Tell me, Robert, why our crowned Apollo
>   And the Muses are hated here.
> I speak also to you, Charles, who scorns
>   Not our poetry—that two may share my burden.
>
> . . . .
> And yet this land does not bring forth outstanding bards,
>   Here Apollo remains hateful to man
> Yet you Brabantines are human beings!
>   Why then is there so much irreverence here?
> Brabant knows not the care of pious poets,
>   Who bear the whole of divine inspiration.[53]

These verses were written in 1472 at Louvain, where Surigonus arrived from Cologne in mid-July. He tried for a few months to stir interest among professors and students for a course in poetics—in vain. After a few weeks, he left for England to enter the service of William Caxton. His hope of entering the service of Charles the Rash as a court poet was also disappointed. Twice he tried to persuade Charles to commission an epic on the duke's martial deeds, but Charles was not interested.

---

[52] Charles de Bovelles, *Sur les langues vulgaires et la variété de la langue française — Liber de differentia vulgarium linguarum et Gallici sermonis varietate (1533)*, texte latin, traduction française et notes par Colette Dumont-Demaizière, Bibliothèque française et romane, D 5 (Paris, 1973), 104, 187-188.

[53] British Museum, Ms. Arundel 249, fols. 98v-99v:

> "Dic, Roperte, mihi cur noster comptus Apollo
>   Hic manet invisus Pyeridumque chorus.
> Te quoque qui nostram non spernis, Carole, Musam
>   Alloquor ut geminis sit labor iste meus.
>
> . . . .
> Non tamen egregios hec nutrit terra poetas:
>   Pluribus invisus Phebus et ipse manet.
> Vos tamen humani, quos dat Brabantia tellus!
>   Quid venit hic igitur impietatis amor?
> Pascere non novit sacros Brabantia vates,
>   Totus inest quibus spiritus aethereus!"

When Surigonus matriculated at Louvain the university had no chair of poetics. The chair of eloquence, founded in 1444, was successively held by Jan Block (1444-1453), Hugo van Rimen (1453-1460), Petrus de Rivo (1460-1470), and Henricus Deulin (1470-1490), all Netherlanders and all—except perhaps De Rivo—notorious failures in the field of eloquence. Their interests lay elsewhere, with mathematics or canon law. Whether or not Surigonus's visit eventually led to the establishment of a parallel chair of poetics, is difficult to say. There was certainly no direct connection, but men such as Viruli and A Lacu may have fostered the idea. Whatever the connection, the decision was taken five years after the Milanese poet's departure; and their bad experience with the chair of eloquence compelled the responsible authorities to look elsewhere for competent, serious candidates. Agricola was called first, but he preferred to continue his Greek studies at Ferrara. Having been refused by the only suitable Netherlandish candidate, the university pursued the only alternative course and appointed (January, 1478) an Italian. He was Lodovico Bruni of Acqui (b. 1434), whose current fame rested on the poems he had composed to celebrate the entry (August, 1477) of Maximilian of Austria into the Burgundian lands and his subsequent marriage at Ghent to the daughter of Charles the Rash. Bruni remained in office until 17 June 1486. He was a conscientious professor, and he continued to celebrate in poetry the chief events of Maximilian's reign. His work certainly improved his students' Latin without producing from their midst a real poet, though his presence may have stimulated such men as Adam Jordaens, then a monk at St. Martin's priory, and Judocus Beissel, a courtier of Maximilian.

Bruni's successor was Cornelius Vitellius of Cortona, an unstable man who remained at Louvain less than three years (1 February 1487-summer, 1489). Although he seems to have taught poetics satisfactorily, his visit left no concrete traces. The chair was vacant until February, 1493, when it was filled by a third Italian, Franciscus de Crema, who resigned early in 1499. The young Erasmus was his guest during a visit to Louvain in 1498 and found him to be an excellent humanist ("vir egregie litteratus"). This notice falls in the period of Erasmus's life when he still felt himself a *poeta*; and it is no wonder that he sought the hospitality of the professor of poetics at Louvain, just as in Paris he was on excellent terms with Andrelini, one of the most influential of all the Italians who came to the North to teach Latin poetry. Unlike the three Italian professors of poetics at Louvain, Andrelini did succeed in rousing a genuinely humanist poetical vocation in a Netherlandish student—Remaclus Arduenna of Florennes, who, however, belongs properly to the succeeding era.

With Franciscus de Crema closes the series of Italian professors of poetics at Louvain. He was followed—but only in 1505—by Balthasar Hockema, presumably a Frisian, who taught until 1510. Then the chairs of eloquence and poetics were united in the capable hands of a Fleming, Johannes Paludanus of Kassel, the well-known friend and host of Erasmus. The age of the Collegium Trilingue had nearly arrived, and natives of the Netherlands were now suited to the task of transmitting and adapting the Italian heritage, a subject to be treated below.

In order to map the increasing diffusion of humanism, especially from the 1470s onward, it is also important to study the composition of the northern libraries, in which the number of works by Italian humanists perceptibly increases. Additional evidence may be had from studying the lists of publications of the first printers in the Netherlands.

The most reliable information on the libraries has to do with private collections. Most catalogues of monastic and school libraries stem from the sixteenth or later centuries, so that it is nearly impossible to determine accurately which books entered the institutions before 1500. Scattered data, such as records of loans, purchases, and donations, do not provide sufficiently complete information, nor do the fragments of catalogues, such as the late fifteenth-century remnants of a wall catalogue from the house of Florens Radewijns at Deventer.[54] Judging by the two fragments of this catalogue, which introduces us to the library of one of the most important centres of the Modern Devotion, one would be inclined to deny any trace of interest in Italian humanism, even its moral and pedagogical literature. Precisely this class of literature, however, is richly represented in the library of the Modern Devotion at Sint Maartensdal, Louvain. To be sure, the Louvain catalogue is later in date, but what we know about men such as Adam Jordaens (d. 1494)

---

[54] P. F. J. Obbema, *Een Deventer Bibliotheekcatalogus van het einde der vijftiende eeuw. Een bijdrage tot de studie van laat-middeleeuwse bibliotheekcatalogi*, Archives et Bibliothèques de Belgique, Numéro spécial 8 / Archief en Bibliotheekwezen in België, extranummer 8, 2 vols. (Brussels, 1973).

justifies the hypothesis that at least some of these works were acquired before 1500.[55]

The most famous library in the Netherlands during the later fifteenth century was that of the dukes of Burgundy.[56] Credit for its shaping belongs in the first place to Philip the Good (1419-1467), who expanded the collection from 250 to 900 manuscripts, making it one of the most splendid libraries in Europe, which his son, Charles the Rash, enlarged still further. Humanism cannot be said to have been well represented in this collection, whose main weight lay with French literature, religious books, and French translations of the classics. Its composition confirms what we know from other sources, that the dukes and the nobles had little interest in Latin and the humanist cult of Latin, a point to which we shall return.

Some other interesting collections were gathered during the late fifteenth century, such as that of Bishop David of Burgundy and, at the very end of the century, the library of Sponheim, which was also the work of a single man, Abbot Trithemius. Such bibliophile abbots were not rare in the Low Countries, and two of them deserve to be mentioned. Jan III Crabbe was abbot of Ter Duinen on the Belgian coast from 1457 until 1488. Raphael de Marcatellis, a natural son of Philip the Good by an unknown mother, was abbot of St. Peter at Oudenburg from 1463 to 1478 and then of St. Bavo at Ghent until his death in 1508. The two men were friends and passed most of their time in Bruges. Crabbe, who was also on good terms with the Greek, Georgius Hermonymus of Sparta, at Paris, had a fine collection of Latin classics, including Cicero, Virgil, Sallust, Valerius Maximus, and Trogus/Iustinus, along with several works by Petrarch and Boccaccio (the *Genealogiae Deorum Gentilium*). De Marcatellis's library contained an amazing treasure of ancient, mediaeval, and humanist literature. We know it fairly well, because two lists of his books, still extant in the nineteenth century, were published. He owned nearly all important Roman authors and a fair number of Greek ones, the latter most likely in translations by Italian humanists. Mediaeval literature, apart from many philosophical, theological,

---

[55] Willem Lourdaux, *Moderne Devotie en Christelijk Humanisme. De geschiedenis van Sint-Maarten te Leuven van 1433 tot het einde der XVIe eeuw*, Universiteit te Leuven — Werken op het gebied van de geschiedenis en de filologie, 5th series, 1 (Leuven, 1967), 108-109.

[56] *La Librairie de Philippe le Bon. Exposition organisée à l'occasion du 500e anniversaire de la mort du duc*, Catalogue rédigé par Georges Dogaer et Marguerite Debae (Brussels, 1967). Also printed in Dutch.

and didactic works, is represented by the *Alexandreis* of Walter de Châtillon and, quite naturally, by the pseudo-Boethius *De disciplina Scholarium*, plus the *Doctrinale* of Alexander de Villa Dei. There is, finally, an astonishingly rich choice of humanist works, not only of the coryphaeuses, such as Petrarch, Boccaccio, Enea Silvio, Valla, Bruni, Filelfo, Tortelli, Ficino, and Pico, but also of several minor figures, including Francesco Nigri (*Opus cum epistolis multis et fabulis quamplurimis*), T. Livius de Forolivio [Frulovisiis] (*Orthographia*), Petrus Marsus (*Interpretatio in librum Officiorum Ciceronis*), and Octavius Cleophilus Phanensis (*Liber de coetu poetarum*). This unusual collection may have been at least partly due to the fact that de Marcatellis, became, through a subsequently marriage of his mother, a member of a great Venetian family and remained in contact with his Italian relatives. De Marcatellis did not focus his interest exclusively on Italy. Among his books we find a Latin version of Sebastian Brant's *Narrenschiff*, though it is unfortunately not indicated whether in Locher's version or that of Badius.

The propagation of humanism can also be noticed in more modest collections, some of which are known from testaments and post-mortem inventories. Several have been published, such as those of Nicolaus Clopper, Sr. (d. Brussels, 18 September 1472), a Burgundian courtier, and Jan Bayart, canon of Our Lady's chapter at Kortrijk in Flanders. The latter left 120 books, six of which may be classified more or less as humanist: *Diversa opera Fr. Petrarche* (No. 16), Boccaccio's *Genealogiae* (No. 19), *Diversa opuscula Pii papae* (No. 41), *Facetiae Poggi* (No. 59), *Epistolae familiares Aeneae Silvii poetae* (No. 81), and Boccaccio's *De mulieribus claris* (No. 98). We would not think of calling Bayart a humanist on the basis of this list—Petrarch's presence proves little, and the interest in Enea Silvio may be more in the pope than the poet—but it shows at least that Italian literature was penetrating even modest private libraries in the country towns.

The process of penetration was stimulated, of course, by the rapid development of printing. Most probably in 1473, while the Venetian printing industry was in crisis, the first shops were established in the Netherlands, at Utrecht (Niklaas Ketelaer and Gerard de Leempt) and at Aalst (Dirk Martens and Johannes of Westphalia). During the next few years the new art spread to Louvain (1474), Bruges (1474?), Brussels (1475), Gouda, Delft, and Deventer (1477), Oudenaarde and Hasselt/Overijssel (1480), Antwerp (1481), Ghent and Haarlem (1483), and Leiden (1484). Works by Italian humanists were only ıı ʍıʍıll ʝʍʍıʍıʍ ʍfı ılıʍ ıʍʍıl ıʍʍʝʍ ʍfı ılıʍʍ ʝʍʍʍʍ lʍıʍʝ ıʍıʝʍıʍʍ, even adding to them the editions of ancient classics. If we consider, however, the small number of "humanists" active in the Netherlands at that time, the figure may well be relatively high. These Latin books were printed almost exclusively at Louvain, Deventer, Utrecht, and Antwerp. Others were imported directly from Italy and France (Lyons and Paris) or were printed at Cologne and Münster, two centres—especially the former—which remained very important for humanistic publications. The concentration at Louvain, Deventer, and Antwerp was quite natural. Antwerp developed rapidly, at the cost of Bruges, into a cosmopolitan commercial centre, where the upper class began to turn interested attention to art and literature. In 1482 the town even invited Rudolph Agricola to become director of the Latin School, but the Frisian humanist declined this offer just as he had an earlier one at Louvain. Among the first Italian authors printed at Antwerp were Enea Silvio Piccolomini, *De duobus amantibus* (1484, 1488 "cum epistola retractatoria") and Poggio, *Facetiae* (1486, 1487). Among the weightier works, we find grammatical treatises, such as Perotti's grammar and Guarino's *De arte Diphthongandi* (1493), plus the omnipresent *Elegantiolae* of Dati, which were printed together with a work by Haneron at about the same time.

More numerous were the humanist publications produced at Louvain, the university town, and Deventer, where the Latin school under Hegius reached an unparalleled fame and attracted students from the whole land between Emden and Basel. It was also at Deventer (1488) and Louvain (1501) that Greek was printed for the first time in the Netherlands. These rather late dates make understandable Erasmus's complaint to a friend, Hermansz, in 1502 that no Greek books were available at Louvain.[57] Once again are revealed the limits of fifteenth-century humanism in the Netherlands, where the situation in 1500 was, in some respects, similar to that at Florence a century earlier.

The list of Italian humanist works printed in the Netherlands before about 1490 provides us with a fairly accurate idea of what appealed to the northern mind in that huge mass of Latin prose and poetry produced in Italy since the time of Petrarch. Beyond some occasional pieces, such as Barbaro's *Oratio ad Fredericum Imperatorem* pronounced at Bruges, the publications fall into two great classes:

---

[57] Allen, ep. 172, I, 381, ll. 13-14.

manuals of Latin; and treatises on moral problems. The manuals include Guarino, Valla, Perotti, Dati, and a few minor authors, such as Sulpitius Verulanus (*Opus grammaticum*, Deventer, 1489?) and the enigmatical Lucretius Bononiensis (*Tractatus de arte oratoria*, Deventer, 1485?). These theoretical works needed to be supplemented by examples of good Latin, for which purpose were published fables (Valla's Latin *Aesopus*, Deventer, 1486) and a great range of epistolary collections, including those of Bruni, Filelfo, Barzizza, and Enea Silvio. These books were probably used by advanced students who had already mastered the much simpler *Epistolares formulae* of Carolus Viruli and similar works.

The second class of literature met the traditional need for serious reading matter, thus prolonging, in a sense, the interest in the moral Petrarch, whose writings continued to be read. Authors published before 1490 at Louvain and Deventer include Petrarch himself (*Rerum Memorandarum libri*), Boccacio (*De claris mulieribus*), Baptista Mantuanus (*De Vita beata*, in a great many editions after 1490), Enea Silvio (*Epistola de fortuna*), Poggio (*De infelicitate principum*), Platina (*De honesta voluptate*), Maffeo Vegio (*Dialogus inter Alithiam et Philaleten, De felicitate et miseria*), Pier Paolo Vergerio (*De ingenuis moribus adolescentium*, printed with Basil's famous treatise on classical readings and Bruni's *Isagogicum* to Aristotle's *Ethics*), and, last, but not least, Lorenzo Valla, whose *De Vero Bono* was printed for the first time (1483, with his *De libero arbitrio* and *In Poggium apologus*) at Louvain in the shop of Rodolfus Loeffs. The *Historia de duobus amantibus* had the greatest commercial success, running through about fifteen editions between 1468 and 1490, at Cologne, Aalst, Louvain, Antwerp, and Leiden. This is absolutely exceptional, and one wonders whether this is to be explained by its erotic story —penned by a future pope—by its final moralising lesson, or by both. Whatever the answer, Piccolomini's novel stands, except for a few editions of Poggio's *Facetiae*, quite alone, since its natural context, the humanist love lyric, is completely absent before 1490. This only confirms Surigonus's experience in the early seventies and explains in part why the course of poetics at Louvain never awakened similar poetic impulses in the Netherlands. The only Italian *Carmina* printed in the Low Countries during this period were the poems of the inevitable Baptista Mantuanus and a collection of poems to the Holy Virgin by Sabellico, Tiphernas, and Vegio (Deventer 1486 and 1490). Perhaps Piccolomini's story fulfilled needs of the Latin-reading public similar to those satisfied by the *Cent Nouvelles Nouvelles* among French readers of the time.

We have pointed out the close connections between the humanistic publications and the centres of higher education. It is absolutely necessary, therefore, to examine the profound changes in the teaching of Latin, which, starting in the sixties and seventies, would revolutionise all grammatical instruction by the sixteenth century and, through grammar, the language of all learned literature and the sciences.

The old language pedagogy was based on the ancient grammars of Donatus and Priscian, whose authority was indisputable, on a series of mediaeval handbooks, among which ranked first and foremost Alexander de Villa Dei's *Doctrinale*, and, since the late thirteenth century, the so-called *modistae* or authors of the *modi significandi*. The latter, philosophical treatises on grammar, may have had some linguistic value, but they were completely unsuitable for teaching young children the basic notions of a foreign language. Another omnipresent work used until well into the sixteenth century—it was edited by Badius Ascensius—was the pseudo-Boethius, *De disciplina scholarium*. A collection of rules for student conduct rather than a grammar, its eccentric Latin exerted a bad influence on the styles of young latinists—as was correctly seen by the humanists around 1500.[58]

The earliest known witness to a reaction, under Italian influence, to this programme is Jan Van den Veren (Johannes de Veris), schoolmaster at Oudenburg near Bruges around 1463/65. This man, whose *studiorum curriculum* we (alas!) ignore, was a fervent adept of the new "Latin." In 1463 he sent one of his pupils, Jacobus Kervoet, to Louvain and secured him a place in Lily College, the very centre of Brabantine humanism at that time. The man is typified by the greeting he wrote above a letter to this student: "Jan Van den Veren sends to Jacob Kervoet, a student at Louvain wishes for instruction in Aristotelian subtleties and attaining Ciceronian eloquence." [59] In another letter he corrects some faults the young man had committed against the "elegantia." [60] More important is the grammatical dispute

---

[58] Jozef IJsewijn, "Alexander Hegius († 1498), *Invectiva in Modos Significandi*," *Forum for Modern Language Studies*, VII (1971), 299-318, here at 301-303.

[59] Gillis G. Meersseman, "L'épistolaire de Jean van den Veeren et le début de l'humanisme en Flandre," *HL*, XIX (1970), 119-200, here ep. XVII, pp. 152-153, at p. 152: "Johannes de Veris Jacobo Kervoet studenti Lovanii Aristotelicis imbui subtilitatibus et Tullianam assequi eloquentiam."

[60] *Ibid.*, ep. XXIX, pp. 178-179.

during the autumn of 1463 and summer of 1464, in which he opposed
Nicasius Weyts, an old chaplain of Our Lady's Church at Bruges,
who was much esteemed as a Latinist because, among other things,
he had made some versified inscriptions for the church.

De Veris's criticism of Weyts's style caused a long exchange
of letters, in which the schoolmaster rather pedantically corrects
some of Weyts's Latin expressions. The old man answers in a dignified
tone, proving his modesty and his learning:

> I know well, Johannes, I know my small learning, and I am also,
> well enough aware of my ignorance in many things, without your
> telling me about it. For who is so deprived of sense that he is able to
> avoid every vice with respect to eloquence, when even the most
> eloquent Cicero was charged with many such vices by his enemies, as
> witnesses Quintilian. Nor do I think, as our Walter [de Châtillon]
> does, that I am better than the Mantuan poet . . . But even our Jerome,
> a most eloquent and most Christian man, had to answer critics in
> each of his prefaces. Indeed, in the words of our fashioner of come-
> dies, the human race is so depraved that men see and judge another's
> vices more quickly than they do their own.[61]

De Veris, trying to justify his criticism, appeals in his reply to arguments, "which things I acquired by study and toil from the commentaries of Lorenzo Valla." [62] For him Valla's *Elegantiae*, long fragments
of which he quotes, have a much greater authority than Priscian. On
this point the two men parted, for Weyts sticks to the authority of
Priscian, whose rules he finds applied in such authors as Ovid and
Pius II and to whom he swore fidelity while at the Sorbonne. As
Weyts wrote to his friend, Basilius Wouters of Gistel, he did not like
those haughty innovators,

> wantonly fashioning for the ears new nonsense for the defacement,
> rejection, and ruin of our noble grammatical knowledge—though
> it bears no profit, honour, or beneficial fruit—except that it is

---

[61] *Ibid.*, ep. XXII, pp. 159-160, at p. 159: "Scio bene, Johannes, scio exiguitatem
ingenii; mee quoque ignorantie multipharie, te etiam non indicante, sat conscius
sum. Quis enim ita sensu orbatus, ut se putet universa eloquentie vicia posse
declinare, cum multa ipsi facundissimo Ciceroni a suis fuerint emulis, Quintiliano
teste, obiecta. Nec etiam nostro cum Galtero [= De Châtillon] arbitror me
meliorem esse Mantuano vate . . . . Sed et Jeronimus noster, vir tam disertissimus
quam christianissimus, suis singulis in prefationibus emulis respondere habebat.
Sed revera, nostro inquiente comico, adeo depravatum est genus humanum ut
aliena citius homines videant, et diiudicent quam sua."

[62] *Ibid.*, ep. XXIII, pp. 160-164, at p. 164: "que mihi studio et labore ex
commentariis Laurentii de Valle comparavi."

worthwhile to seem and to be called "Rabbi" above others, revealing their own arrogance..., and, what is even worse, they don't fear to measure up to the fundamental principles of the excellent grammarian, Priscian....[63]

Conflicts of this sort must have been frequent before the teaching of Latin underwent a complete renewal and the results of Italian scholarship (Valla, Perotti, Tortelli, Guarino, Barzizza) finally took the place of the mediaeval traditions. The situation was further complicated by the fact that, in the first stage, local teachers produced their own textbooks, which later were considered as barbarous as the mediaeval works, and, secondly, by the numerous attempts to modernize the *Doctrinale* in order to save in this way the old as well as the new.

Among the schoolbooks of local origin in use at the end of the century were the treatises of Haneron, especially his *Art of Letter-Writing* and his comprehensive *Syntax*, the short *Syntax* by Herbenus, and Viruli's *Examples of Letter Composition*. The latter booklet enjoyed a great, international success until it was peremptorily, and not quite justly, condemned by Erasmus and Bebel. It may be that Viruli got some help from Surigonus in composing it. In a poem to Viruli the Milanese humanist wrote: "Do not be reluctant to send our book, most kind father / I said 'our' because it is yours, too," which may indicate a form of collaboration.[64]

Be that as it may, Viruli already shows a certain acquaintance with Italian humanist work, as can be deduced from his insistence on writing *nichil* and *michi* instead of *nihil* and *mihi* ("It seems that the Ancients did not use the letter 'C'. But Leonardo of Arezzo, a trustworthy writer, advises that the 'C' ought to be used, adducing as witnesses Dante, Petrarch, Boccaccio, and Coluccio Salutati") and on writing *pulcer* ("thus Gasparino, a man of keen and charming disposition").[65] As with De Veris, we notice an attitude of deference

---

[63] *Ibid.*, ep. XXIV, pp. 164-165, at p. 164: "prurientes auribus nova inutilia cudentes in ipsius nobilis scientie grammaticalis suggillationem, detrectamen et ruinam, cum nullum exinde consequatur emolumentum, honorem seu fructum salutarem, sed dumtaxat opere pretium fore videri Rabbique pre ceteris vocari, suam propalantes arrogantiam..., verum quod et deterius, ipsius egregii grammatici Prisciani... fontalibus principiis obviare non verentes...."

[64] British Museum, Ms. Arundel 249, fol. 109ᵛ: "Ne pigeat nostrum, Pater optime, mittere librum / Id 'nostrum' dixi, cum sit et ipse tuus."

[65] Carolus Viruli, *Epistolares formulae*, fols. [p.7ᵛ-p.8ʳ]: "Vetustas forte C littera non utitur. Leonardus tamen Aretinus non futilis autor C poni consulit testes adducens Dantem, / Petrarcham, Bocacium et Collutium Salutatum." .. idemque vir acuti amenique ingenii Gasparinus".

towards the great Italian humanists, outweighing his respect for even the ancient authorities.

As was to be expected, efforts to modernize Alexander were concentrated in the Deventer/Münster area and at Louvain. Erasmus himself recognizes that Hegius and Sinthius at Deventer tried to remedy the most obvious faults of the *Doctrinale*.[66] The most lasting efforts at reform, however, came from the teachers and residents of the Lily College at Louvain, whose endeavours eventually merged into the famous grammar of Johannes Despauterius of Ninove (Flanders), who became a European authority for many generations and remained the basis of Latin grammars written in the Low Countries until the twentieth century. It is in this book that we find the reason why Alexander was not so peremptorily condemned as the *Antibarbari* might have led us to expect:

> Moreover, I am defending Alexander; and if he has erred, I think it ought to be attributed not to his fault but to that of the times, during which literary matters had nearly perished. He wanted neither to deceive young men nor to extinguish the Latin language, but to be of use to everyone; to whom, though he did not come up to the mark, we give great thanks.[67]

These are the same feelings of moral gratitude that Vives, at about the same time, expressed concerning Viruli.[68]

In the context of the renovation of grammar we must also place the unrelenting attacks on the *modistae* at Deventer and Münster and the origins of the humanist school theatre in the North. Italian and northern humanists agreed in condemning the philosophers of grammar, and Valla as well as Erasmus spoke of the *modi significandi* with scorn.[69] Hegius begins his *Contra modos significandi Invectiva* with this uncompromising statement: "They err who say that the knowledge of the *modi significandi* makes a grammarian." And the wise schoolmaster, with his great experience of children, adds: "Why don't the Italians teach boys the *modi significandi*, if not because they hold the

---

[66] Allen, I, 48. Cf. De Vocht, *HCT*, I, 80-81.

[67] Johannes Despauterius, *Commentarii grammatici* (Paris, 1537), 179: "Praeterea Alexandrum interim defendo: et siquid erraverit, non eius culpae, sed temporum, quibus res literaria paene interierat, adscribendum censeo. Neque enim adulescentulos decipere neque linguam Latinam extinguere, sed omnibus prodesse studuit. Cui, quamvis id assecutus non sit, magnas agimus gratias." Cf. M. A. Nauwelaerts, *Latijnse school*, 219.

[68] De Vocht, *HCT*, I, 98.

[69] Quoted by J. IJsewijn, "Alexander Hegius," 301-302.

boys too dear to teach them such useless and harmful things." [70] His colleague, Timannus Kemenerus at Münster, shared this opinion and tried to banish the *modi* from the comments on Alexander: "truly I could not allow good minds to be thus deceived and to wallow any longer in such ignorance." [71] These condemnations were not lightly made. A man such as Hegius knew the art of teaching languages to children; and it is an historical fact that the quality of Latin in the schools improved rapidly, once the new insights were generalised and applied in both the grammar schools and the university colleges.

One of the new didactic devices was the school theatre. It was developed successfully during this period by members of the academy of Pomponio Leto in Rome. Directly or indirectly, this may have had repercussions in the Low Countries. At any rate during the 1480s we hear for the first time of dramatic performances at Münster, Louvain(?), and Bruges. The curious thing is that shortly afterwards there is a gap in this young tradition (or in our records of it) from about 1488 until 1506/08. During these twenty years the only notice of humanist theatre connected with the Low Countries is the short piece, *Scornetta*, written by the Dutchman, Herman Knuyt van Slytershoven of Vianen (Utrecht) in 1494.[72] But this student work was written at Bologna and thus falls outside the local activities. Knuyt was one of those young foreigners who, in increasing numbers, participated in humanist literary life in Italy—not least in Bologna.

The following facts, ordered chronologically, have been established concerning the first dramatic efforts in the Low Countries: [73]

---

[70] *Ibid.*, 306, para. 1 and 4: "Qui dicunt modorum significandi noticiam efficere grammaticum falluntur." "Cur Itali non docent pueros modos significandi nisi quia eos cariores habent quam ut eis tam inutilia tamque noxia inculcent."

[71] *Ibid.*, 317, para. 3: "non potui sane pati bona ingenia sic decipi et turpiter errare diutius."

[72] Cf. Antonio Stäuble, *La Commedia umanistica del Quattrocento* (Florence, 1968), 99-100. Text edited by Johannes Bolte, "Zwei Humanistenkomödien aus Italien," *Zeitschrift für vergleichende Litteraturgeschichte und Renaissancelitteratur*, N.S., I (1887/88), 231-244.

[73] For Louvain, see *Henry VIII. A Neo-Latin Drama by Nicolaus Vernulaeus*, trans. and ed. with a *History of the Louvain Academic Theater* by Louis A. Schuster (Austin, 1964); *idem*, "The History of the Louvain Theatre," in *Acta Conventus Neo-Latini Lovaniensis*, Proceedings of the First International Congress of Neo-Latin Studies, Louvain 23-28 August 1971, eds. Jozef IJsewijn and Eckhard Kessler (Leuven and Munich, 1973), 589-593; *Gesamtkatalog der Wiegendrucke*, hrsg. von der Kommission für den Gesamtkatalog der Wiegendrucke, VII (Leipzig, 1938), coll. 361-362, nn. 8222-8225 ("Declamationes Lovanienses"). For Bruges, see Arthur C. De Schrevel, *Histoire du séminaire de Bruges*, 2 vols. (Bruges, 1895), I, 134; André Himpe, "Studie over het humanisme aan het

5 March 1480, Lily College, Louvain: "Per studiosos legum duos in Lilio tutelares ... acta declamatio 'Filii parentes suos aut alant aut vinciantur' ";

23 February 1481, Lily College, Louvain: a similar declamation on behalf of personal liberty for the students resident at the college, against official regulations;

29 January 1483, Lily College, Louvain: a third declamation on the question of whether the bees of a poor man have the right to gather honey from the flowers in a rich neighbour's garden;

18 October 1484, Bruges: the students of the Chapter School, directed by Godefridus Van Dommele, perform the first book of Virgil's *Aeneid*;

1485, Münster: publication of a play *Codrus* by Johannes Kerckmeister, "gymnasiarcha Monasteriensis";

before 1487, Bruges: performance of "commedie Luciani"; and

25 October 1487, Bruges: an unknown "comedy" (Terence?) performed at the Chapter School.

It is doubtful if the Louvain *declamationes* really belong to the history of school theatre. They are pieces in the (pseudo-) Quintilian tradition and exercises for law students much more than language training. On the other hand they have some structural similarities to Wimpheling's *Stylpho* (1480) which, though no real theatre either, is to be found on the first page of every history of humanist theatre in Germany. Its contents certainly make the second Louvain declamation a document of real cultural importance. In vigorous language, a student speaking in the name of the community pleads firmly the cause of personal liberty in conduct and in organising one's studies.[74] Only thus, it is said, will the students be worthy men, responsible in their deeds. This strongly suggests the spirit of humanism, and the declamation is certainly not a dull exercise on a stock theme, as the two others are. It allows us a glimpse into the state of fermentation of student minds in that crucial period of rapidly increasing Italian influence. Can it be mere chance that only two years later (1483) a printer at Louvain published Valla's *De Vero Bono* and *De Libero arbitrio*? This edition appears as a (commercial?) echo of the winter

---

Sint-Donaaskapittel te Brugge" (unpublished lic. diss., University of Ghent, 1941), 20. For Münster, see Johannes Kerckmeister, *Codrus. Ein neulateinisches Drama aus dem Jahre 1485*, ed. Lothar Mundt, Ausgaben deutscher Literatur des XV. bis XVIII. Jahrhunderts, Reihe Drama, III (Berlin, 1969), and the review by J. IJsewijn, in *Latomus*, XXX (1971), 179-181.

[74] This dialogue could also be a belated student reaction to the very severe regulations issued by Duke Charles the Rash on 3 January 1477.

debate in Lily College. Not so many years later the desire for *libertas* will be a fundamental characteristic of the great man of the age, Erasmus.

Nothing is known about the performances at Bruges which figure in the accounts of the Chapter of St. Donatian. As at Louvain, our next information is of a much later date (1524), when the Erasmian influence on the school programme was already very strong. The comedy of 1487 may have been a piece of Terence. Already a generation earlier, Nicasius Weyts knew this playwright thoroughly, and in 1524 he was again being staged.

The only real drama is Kerckmeister's *Codrus*, a dazzling piece of work. It is meant to be a defence of good Latin, a feature in which it runs parallel to the efforts of Langius to create humanist teaching at Münster. But the Latin of the students, who take the role of propagators of correct speech, is at least as awful and barbarous as, and at times even less understandable than that of Codrus, an old teacher whom they revile for his incorrect language. There is, moreover, no trace of Italian influence nor any allusion to the great renovators of the study of Latin. Although the *prologus* warns against "barbariem vite ac sermonis agrestis," it is itself a specimen of barbarism. Too little is known about its author, who probably was never in Italy but had heard something about renewal from Langius or his friends. One could compare this relationship with that between Hegius and Agricola, with the difference, however, that Hegius was a man of much greater ability.

One passage of the *Codrus*, awkward as it may be, is important as a humanist document—the long argument of Marcus to Codrus in scene 13. One of the first points he stresses is the importance of Greek for the study of good Latin: "Whence did you believe Latin diction arose, if it did not assume its essence and nature from oratory and poetry, gushing forth clearly from the Greek font." [75] At this date (1485) such words cannot but be an echo of Agricola's influence in the Westphalian region. It was at about the same time that Hegius wrote:

If you wish to learn grammar, learn Greek!
In order to write correctly, not wrongly, learn Greek!
If you do not know Greek, you ruin the names of things
. . . .

---

[75] J. Kerckmeister, *Codrus*, 61: "Unde Latinam dictionem ortam credis, si non ab oratoria poetisque vim et naturam sumpserit, que a Greco fonte liquidum est scaturier [sic!]."

The Pelasgian tongue forbids you to write faulty verses
. . . .
If you wish to learn rhetoric, learn Greek! [76]

A second point made by Marcus is that the new Latin grammar will enable them to read the Bible and to understand it without the immense mass of commentaries: "Can you gain a secure understanding of the Bible you read daily with yours [viz., mediaeval grammar] alone, with no other guide? By chance you may say: 'there are commentaries for it.' How about this? Would it not be better and more useful if you understood to a hair, as they say, without commentaries that which you daily read?" These commentaries, moreover, "are themselves so full of absurdities . . . that no one can adequately express it." [77] And not only the Bible is incomprehensible to the barbarians, for the same applies to the fathers of the Church (Augustine, Cyprian, Jerome), the early Christian poets, and the canon law. Here Kerckmeister rejoins the line which runs from Gansfort to Erasmus, wherein the renewal of Latin studies is ultimately directed not to its original intention, a better knowledge and restoration of the Roman classics, but to a renovation of biblical and theological studies. It would be wrong to assign this reorientation exclusively to men of northern Europe. Manetti and Valla, to name only two Italians, also applied their knowledge to improving the text of biblical writings. But the difference from Gansfort or even Erasmus is fundamental. For most of the Italian humanists their biblical studies remained purely philological and never overwhelmed their other interests.

To conclude this survey of the period 1460-1490, we want to describe in brief the situation of Latin literature in the Low Countries

---

[76] *Alexandri Hegii . . . Carmina* (Deventer, R. Paffraet, 1503), fol. D.3ᵛ (copy in the Koninklijke Bibliotheek, The Hague):

"Quisquis grammaticam vis discere, discito grece!
Ut recte scribas, non prave: discito grece!
Si grece nescis, corrumpis nomina rerum
. . . .
Lingua pelasga vetat viciosos scribere versus
. . . .
Quisquis Rhetoricen vis discere, discito grece!"

[77] J. Kerckmeister, *Codrus*, 62-63: "Num tua poteris tute sola [viz. mediaeval grammar], nulla duce reliqua, bibliam quam legis quotidie intelligere? Inquies forte: ad id commenta sunt. Quid? Nonne melius utiliusque si ad unguem, ut aiunt, sine commentis quod in dies lectitas intelligeres?"

at the time of Agricola. The description will necessarily be a rather
tentative one, because almost no preparatory work has been done in
this field, and many texts remain unpublished: a long *Carmen de
Morte* in the town library at Haarlem; [78] the *Mariad* of Cornelius Aurelius; [79] a number of poems by monks of Bethleem priory at Herent
(Louvain), preserved in the house's chronicle by Petrus Impens; [80]
and many other texts.

Because Latin poetry and prose formed one of the main concerns of humanists, and because they prided themselves on their
ability to compete with their Roman models, a study of the Latin
works produced in a country may well serve as a test of the level
attained by local humanism.

At first glance late fifteenth-century Latin poetry in the Low
Countries falls into two, well-distinguished classes: mediaeval
versificatio practised by monks and clerics; and humanist poetry
written by schoolmen and young students. It should be noticed
that contemporaries were conscious of this dichotomy, as we shall
show by examining texts by Nicasius Weyts and Bartholomaeus
Tungrensis.

To the first class belong the philosophical poems of Dionysius
the Carthusian, the pious verses of such monks as Thomas a Kempis
and Albertus Petri O.P. of Leiden, historical works such as the
anonymous *Liber Karoleidos* (1465/66) [81] and the *De ortu, victoria et
triumpho Domini Karoli ducis Borgundie moderni* by Simon Mulart of
Heinsberg, and the works of Bartholomaeus Macharii of Tongeren.
These sorts of versification survived even into the early sixteenth
century, as is shown by an anonymous poem on the great fire at
Harderwijk (1503).[82] These poems are characterised by the wholly
unclassical aspects of their language and metrical form. A few samples
of Mulart will demonstrate sufficiently their character:

---

[78] *Carmen de Morte*, Ms. in the Stadsbibliotheek of Haarlem, 183 D 2.

[79] Cornelius Aurelius, *Mariad*, Ms. in the Athenaeumbibliotheek Deventer, 31.

[80] Manuscripts: Vienna, Oesterreichische Nationalbibliothek, series nova
12816 and 12815; Abbey of Averbode, Gillis die Voecht, XV; Brussels, Rijksarchief, Kerkelijk Archief van Brabant, 14182; Brussels, Royal Library, Mss.
1278-1279 (3657).

[81] J. B. M. C. Kervyn de Lettenhove, *Chroniques relatives à l'histoire de la Belgique
sous la domination des ducs de Bourgogne* (*Textes latins*), 3 vols., (Brussels, 1876), III,
329-338.

[82] Hubert Silvestre, "Poème latin sur l'incendie d'Harderwijk (1503)," *HL*,
XXII (1973), 100-102.

v. 29 Hunc ego Burgund*um* Dominum laudo metuend*um*
       Rigmis et pros*is* versibus ecce me*is*
       Sicque tripart*ito* functurus provide st*ilo*
       Laudes huius pal*am* promere non desin*am*.
       Quedam long*avi* non inscius et brevi*avi*
       Sensus ut in me*tro* sit melior reli*quo*.

or

v. 920 Nobile cor fer*to*, te largum semper habe*bo*
       Meque tuum slav*um* sub agendis offero prompt*um*.
       O utinam modic*us* merear meritus fore serv*us*
       Ecclesiamque me*am* tibi commendo michi ca*ram* . . . .[83]

It would be hard to call such verses classical or humanist—and these
poets knew it! When Johannes de Veris criticised Nicasius Weyts
for styling himself *vates*, which according to De Veris meant *poeta*,
Weyts protested vigorously:

> I confess . . . that I am not a poet. Away with the idea that I am
> so mad—which I am not—that I dare to assert that I am or wish to
> be considered a poet. Indeed, I might strongly wish to be and to be
> held to be one; and, were it not that I am so old, I would strive to
> become one. Yes, it is true that I had inserted into some little verses
> that term "VATES," but not in the place of "POETA" since it is often
> interchanged with the term "VERSIFICUS" OR "VERSIFICATOR." [84]

Precisely the same attitude is seen in Bartholomaeus of Tongeren,
who repeatedly implores his readers' benevolence and visibly fears
the sarcastic criticism of "blasphemi," who can only have been
humanists. At the end of his *Carmina ad Mariam de Borgondia* he even
writes: "Lingua poetarum propicietur ei," and at the beginning
of his life of St. Servatius, he proclaims: "Rhetor et orator non
sum . . . ." In his *Carmina ad Sixtum papam quartum*, he styles himself,
"Bartholomaeus versificator," and in the second prologue of his
poems to Mary of Burgundy, which is "deprecatorius pro parte
salutantis," he explains his situation as follows:

---

[83] Petrus Cornelis Boeren, *Twee Maaslandse dichters in dienst van Karel de Stoute*
(The Hague, 1968), 199-200, 267.
[84] G. G. Meersseman, "L'épistolaire de Jean van den Veren," ep. XXV, p. 170,
and ep. XXVI, p. 172: ". . . fateor . . . me non esse poetam. Absit ut tanta
teneor dementia ut, quod non sum, me esse fateri ausim aut haberi velim. Esse
quidem summopere optarem et pro viribus ut forem, ni annorum tot obstarent
curricula, studerem. Verum equidem est me in nonnullis inseruisse versiculis
terminum illum VATE, non tamen pro POETA, cum se convertibiliter habeat
persepius cum illo termino VERSIFICO seu VERSIFICATORE."

Though unsuited, I am trying to write these things in this little book
The greatest things, which no poet can express.
I am not so great, I confess . . . .

. . . .
I haven't the writings material worthy of such heavenly things
    Nor can I bear the difficulties of metre for a long time. . .[85]

This is language a humanist poet would never have thought of
adopting. Compare what Surigonus wrote to Charles the Rash, the
father of Mary:

I am that bard by whom your names, great leader,
    Should be commemorated in verse.[86]

The humanist poet believes he can compete with the great *poetae*
of antiquity—whether this is true or false does not matter—and
consequently calls himself also "poeta." So did the young Erasmus
before he became "theologus." [87]

Sometimes the notion of "poeta" underwent a still greater narrow-
ing on an etymological basis, as we can read in a letter of Cornelius
Aurelius to Erasmus. Cornelius, interpreting "poesis" as "fictio,"
draws the conclusion:

therefore it is fitting that one may be thought a poet or at least one
skilled in poetry, who, either in intention or in reality, or in both, has
composed *a fictio*. If it is done otherwise. . . , it is not thought that
a poet has composed a poem, but that a versifier has composed a
verse.[88]

---

[85] Boeren, *Twee Maaslandse dichters*, 196, 111, 149, 167-168:

"Hec licet invalidus hoc scribere tempto libello,
    Que nullo poterint maxima vate cani.
Non ego sum tantus, fateor . . . .

. . . .
Codicibus careo tam celsa canentibus aptis
    Dissuetusque diu pondera ferre metri . . . ."

[86] British Museum, Ms. Arundel 249, fol. 106ᵛ:

"Ille ego sum vates a quo tua carmine vero
    Nomina sunt tanti commemoranda ducis."

[87] Jozef IJsewijn, "Erasmus ex poeta theologus, sive de litterarum instaurata-
rum apud Hollandos incunabulis," in *Scrinium Erasmianum*, 2 vols. (Leiden,
1969), I, 375-389.
[88] Allen, ep. 25, I, 111-112, here at p. 111, ll. 19-22: "consequens ergo est
ut ille poeta aut saltem poesim doctus censeatur qui vel in sententia, vel in facie,
vel in eorum utroque concinit fictionem. Quod si secum actum est . . ., non poema
poeta, sed versus versificator composuisse iudicatur."

Erasmus did not at all share this opinion, which reduced the number of poets to almost none.

There can be no doubt that the first poetry written in the humanist style in the Low Countries is to be sought in the Adwerth circle. One can easily distinguish two generations: that of Agricola and that of their pupils (including Erasmus)—neither produced poetry of exceptional quality. It seems as if the northern minds were refractory to the practice of refined verses, but the true reason for the poor quality of northern poetry is revealed perhaps in one of Agricola's letters. He says that in his homeland he felt himself thrown back into such cultural isolation, compared with his Italian experience, that words no longer came to fit in the harmony of a verse.[89] Adwerth and some correspondence with friends such as Hegius and Langius notwithstanding, this isolation was an inescapable and undeniable fact. It was the debt he had to pay for being the very first to introduce the new art he had learned in Italy:

> I, the first teacher of Latin and Greek poetry,
> first led the Germans into the camp of the Muses.[90]

This is the epigram under his portrait in Nicholas Reusner's *Icones* (1587), and rightly so. Agricola's friends knew it. Fridericus Maurus (Moorman) of Emden, director of the house of the Brethren of the Common Life at Münster, expressed to their common friend, Gansfort, his joy at Agricola's homecoming:

> Rudolph seeks his native soil, hurrah!
> Now, after such a long time, hurrah!
> The Frisian bard is returning, and from the lands of Italy
> He leads the Beotian chorus.[91]

Erasmus confirms in various places (such as in the letter to Johannes Sapidus [Witz] prefixed to his *Antibarbari*) that in his childhood—the

---

[89] R. Agricola, *Opera*, II, 187.
[90] "Primus ego Latiae cultor Graiaeque Camoenae
Germanos docui Musica castra sequi."

[91] H. E. J. M. Van der Velden, *Rodolphus Agricola*, 125:

> "Rodolphus patrios quaerit, io, Lares
> Iam post tempora, io, longa revisere
> Vates Frisius, ex finibus Italis
> Ducens Aonidum choros . . . ."

Cf. the welcome of Filippo Beroaldo, Sr., by Baptista Mantuanus in a poem of 130 verses, when he returned from France. *Opera Omnia Baptistae Mantuani* (Bologna, 1502), 98-101.

time of Agricola's return—"the *bonae litterae* were completely absent from the schools, ... for no honour added stimulus to one's natural inclinations—nay, rather, since all were deterred from these studies and forced into others." [92] Agricola's arrival caused a modest commotion in poetry. Soon the first humanist verses began to be printed, many more were written, and in the long run they overcame the traditional versification.

In 1483 and 1485 Agricola's *Anna Mater* and some other poems appeared at Deventer. Langius followed a year later with a first collection of *Carmina*, printed at Münster. Several years later, another member of the Adwerth circle, Paulus Pellantinus, a doctor who later composed an epicedium on Gansfort,[93] published at Zwolle his *Carmen lyricum de nativitate Domini nostri Jesu Christi*. Others, such as Alexander Hegius, were writing at the same time, though their work was posthumously published. These were the men of the older generation. But Hegius's school at Deventer became a kind of seminar for young student poets. Already about 1483, Erasmus seems to have written his eclogue. In the same letter to Sapidus he tells of himself that "not judgment, which I was then too young to have, but a certain sense of nature was gripping me, as though inspired to the rites of the Muses." [94] Perhaps the humanist of Rotterdam is here echoing a self-testimony of Petrarch, and perhaps he owed more to the atmosphere of Hegius's school than he was ready to admit. Be that as it may, very soon he and Gulielmus Goudanus (Hermansz) were eagerly practising the art of Latin verse. Erasmus would later (1497) edit Goudanus's *Silva Odarum* at Paris. In the meantime he had had a serious discussion with a third "Brother in Apollo," Cornelius Aurelius, concerning which topics they should treat in their poems. Aurelius had been very strict: Christian themes and no others. With some hesitation Erasmus accepted this rule,[95] as did the other poets—except for Jacobus Canter—until the moment

---

[92] Desiderius Erasmus, *Antibarbarorum liber*, ed. Kazimierz Kumaniecki, in *Opera Omnia Desiderii Erasmi Roterodami* I, 1 (Amsterdam, 1969), 1-138, here at p. 1: "prorsus exularent ludis literariis bonae litterae, ... cum nullus honos adderet ingenio calcar, immo cum passim omnes ab his studiis deterrerent et ad alia compellerent."

[93] Published in Wessel Gansfort, *Opera* (facsimile of edition of Groningen, 1614; Nieuwkoop, 1966), fols. *** 2r-*** 3v.

[94] D. Erasmus, *Antibarbarorum liber*, 1: "me tamen non iudicium, quod mihi tum per aetatem esse non poterat, sed naturae sensus quidam ad Musarum sacra velut afflatum rapiebat."

[95] J. IJsewijn, "Erasmus ex poeta theologus," *Scrinium Erasmianum*, I, 381-382.

when the teaching of Fausto Andrelini at Paris began to lure students, first of all Remaclus Arduenna. From that time onward there is a double current in the neo-Latin poetry of the Netherlands until the early nineteenth century: a pious one, which flourished mainly in the South and in the religious orders, such as the Augustinians and the Jesuits; and an erotic strain, including such figures as Secundus, Lernutius, Dousa, and Heinsius, which survived a long time in Holland and Frisia, the Protestant area.

In looking at some of the early attempts at humanist poetry, one is struck by a formal feature which denotes their novelty and the naive, almost pedantic, pride of their authors: they all take care not only to practise the more difficult lyric metres but also to announce precisely (in the titles of poems) the metre they are using, producing such titles as "Ode dicolos tetrastrophos sapphica hendecasyllaba" or "Ode dicolos distrophos altera versu dactylico hexametro heroico, altero item dactylica archilochio tetrametro catalectico." They sound like school exercises, which, for the most part, they are.

Agricola was also the link with the southern Netherlands. Because of his studies at Cologne and Louvain and his later travels in the service of the regime at Groningen, he knew the few humanists at Antwerp, Brussels, and Louvain, men such as Barbirianus the musician, Beisselius the courtier, and Jordaens the monk. To them he sent copies of his poems, and his example, combined with the influence of the new chair of poetics at Louvain, stimulated these men to try their own hands at poetical compositions.

Except for the friends of Agricola, poetic activity in the Low Countries was very limited. Only one other man deserves our attention, Matthaeus Herbenus of Maastricht. We have already seen how he came into contact with Onufrio and the poet, Angelus Sabinus, author of a long epic *De excidio civitatis Leodiensis libri sex* on the wars at Liège (1468).[96] Many years later, when he was back at Maastricht after a long stay in Italy, Herbenus set himself the task of making his friend's poem known among the leading men of his country and among his humanist friends. So he prepared copies of it for Henry of Bergen, bishop of Cambrai and best known as one of

---

[96] *Angeli de Curibus Sabinis . . . de excidio civitatis Leodiensis libri sex*, in *Veterum scriptorum et monumentorum historicorum, dogmaticorum, moralium amplissimo collectio*, eds. E. Martène and U. Durand, 9 vols. (Paris, 1724-33), IV, coll. 1379-1500. Analysis and extracts of the text by P. F. X. de Ram, *Documents relatifs aux troubles du Pays de Liège sous les princes-évêques Louis de Bourbon et Jean de Horne, 1455-1505* (Brussels, 1844), 235-260.

Erasmus's first patrons, and for Lambert d'Oupeye, chancellor of the prince-bishop of Liège. To the text of Angelus he added a short poem and a prologue in prose of his own making. The manuscript for d'Oupeye ends with short *argumenta* or summaries of each book, composed by Pascasius Berselius (d. May 1535), a Benedictine monk of St. Laurent's abbey near Liège.[97] This monk was one of the very first humanists at Liège, having learned Greek from Girolamo Aleandro (1514/16) and attended courses in the Collegium Trilingue at Louvain.

We have not yet discovered evidence of direct contacts between Agricola and Herbenus, but Beissel was their mutual friend. Herbenus was even less of a poet than Agricola and was thus hardly the man to stimulate new poetical vocations. His importance lies elsewhere: he may be considered the first Netherlander to have written history in the humanist manner. During the late fifteenth century, the Low Countries still produced a large number of historians who wrote in the mediaeval tradition and style, of whom only a few can be mentioned here: the great historian of the early phase of the Modern Devotion, Johannes Busch of Zwolle (1399-ca. 1480); the Westphalian polygraph, Werner Rolevinck (1425-1502); and the chroniclers of St. Laurent's abbey (Liège), Adrianus de Veteri Busco (Oudenbosch; until 1483) and Jan Peecks of Borgloon (1459-1516). It was especially the destruction of Liège (1483), on which Angelus Sabinus wrote his epic, that inspired many contemporary historical works, of which may be mentioned the *Compendiosa Historia de Cladibus Leodiensium* by Henricus de Merica (Van der Heyden; d. 1473), prior at Bethleem/Herent near Louvain. Henricus had connections with the early humanists at Louvain, and one wonders if they might have induced him to embellish his prose with poetical quotations from Horace and Virgil. This "literary" attitude is in contrast with that of a man such as Johannes Busch, who studiously cultivates an illiterate style. The prologue to his *Liber de Viris Illustribus* demonstrates that his teacher, the famous Johannes Cele of Zwolle, introduced him to classical historiography. Busch's stated motivation is quite classical: "Fame is so brief, limited to the span of a human life. Those who are celebrated in letters live forever," and he even

---

[97] Eugène Bacha, "Deux écrits de Mathieu Herbenus sur la destruction de Liège par Charles-le-Téméraire," *Bulletin de la Commission Royale d'Histoire (de la Belgique)*, LXXV (1907), 385-390, here at pp. 386-387.

quotes, though not explicitly, Cicero's famous definition of history in *De Oratore*, Bk. II: "Lastly, histories and writings are the witnesses to the times, the light of truth, the life of memory, life's instructors and the bearers of news of olden times" [98]—the very text which Pomponio Leto, writing half a century later at Rome, chose to begin his course on classical historiography. But Busch takes another path. Whereas an ancient or a humanist historian believed it an essential part of his task to write with great elegance, Busch avoids literary elegance and tells his readers: "Listen, therefore, not to lengthy but to forceful stories, not to false but to true things, neither spurning the simplicity of expression nor seeking the beauty of a polished style." He explains that the faithful do not want "sophistical words and poetic half-truths," and he will therefore omit speeches ("prolixis igitur diversarum arengarum interlocucionibus postpositis"),[99] which are indeed a distinctive feature of classical and humanist historiography. We can thus see that the reception of humanist principles was not only—and perhaps not so much—a question of knowledge, but much more of cultural attitudes.

Compared with the rich harvest of mediaeval historiography, the humanist counterpart before 1500 is more than modest, especially when one considers that next to oratorical and philosophical writings, history was the third great genre of classical and humanist prose.

Herbenus and Langius were nearly the only and certainly the first to try their hands at this genre, Herbenus being the more important because of the variety of his work. From Langius we have only a *Historia de urbis Hierosolymae excidio*, written in 1475/76 and printed around 1486. Herbenus also wrote an *Excidium* (this seems to have been a popular historical topic during these years!), a *Lamentabile Excidium Christianorum* of Euboea by the Turks. This short

---

[98] *Des Augustinerpropstes Iohannes Busch Chronicon Windeshemense und Liber de reformatione monasteriorum*, hrsg. von der Historischen Commission der Provinz Sachsen, bearb. von Karl Grube, Geschichtsquellen der Provinz Sachsen und angrenzender Gebiete, 19 (Halle, 1886; reprint, Westmead, Farnborough, Hants, 1968), 1: "Brevissima fama est, que humane vite spacio terminatur. Vivunt perhenni nomine, quos litere habent insertos . . . . Historie denique et scripture testes sunt temporum, lux veritatis, vita memorie, magistre vite et nuncie vetustatis. . . ."

[99] *Ibid.*, 3: "Accipite ergo non diserta, sed forcia [sic], vera non fucata, eloquii simplicitatem non spernentes nec politi stili venustatem requirentes . . . . sophistici sermones et poetice semivere locuciones . . . prolixis igitur diversarum arengarum interlocucionibus postpositis . . ."

work clearly reveals the influence of Sallust. It begins with a description of the ...., ... them to a lively account of the battles between Greeks and Turks, with successes and defeats on both sides, and stories of treachery and cruelty. As in every good classical history, climaxes are underlined by speeches, and at the end the numbers of casualties on both sides are given. The only non-classical element, perhaps a natural one in Herbenus's milieu, are some final considerations based on the prophecies of Isaiah and Jeremiah. As a whole the work is very readable, his Latin proving that Herbenus learned a lot in Italy, and he certainly merits the title of "first humanist historian in the Netherlands." He also wrote a *Descriptio tumultuarie factionis nuper habite inter principes Ferrarie*, a short account of the dynastic troubles at Ferrara (1476) concerning the succession of Niccolò d'Este. These few pages, written at Bologna, can be compared—*si parva licet componere magnis!*—to such works as the *Pactianae coniurationis commentarium* of Poliziano.[100] Herbenus's third Italian work is the *Oppugnatio oppidi Schrutensis* (in Albania), for which, as he writes, "I was informed by those who were in the town during the siege." [101] Herbenus wrote his greatest historical work under the influence of Flavio Biondo, whose grave he visited in Rome. Biondo had published a *Roma Instaurata*. Herbenus did the same for the antiquities of his adopted town by composing a highly interesting *Traiectum Instauratum*. In order to show by example the difference between a humanist and a mediaeval writer, we will quote a) the prologue of Herbenus's *Traiectum* and b) the dedication of Rolevinck's *De laude Antiquae Saxoniae nunc Westphaliae dictae* (1474), contemporary works of comparable scope. It should be noticed also that Rolevinck's style is much "purer" in his prologue than in the book itself, and that a comparison of the topics treated by the two authors—something that cannot be done here—would show other major divergences. The "Prologue" of Herbenus:

> Indeed, when any famous, memorable or magnificent thing happened in their state, those ancient and zealous men of literature were accustomed to acknowledge for posterity the authors of the deeds and their country, in their writings; whence a great many historians

---

[100] Angelo Poliziano, *Della Congiura dei Pazzi* (*Coniurationis Commentarium*), ed. Alessandro Perosa, Miscellanea erudita, 3 (Florence, 1958).

[101] "percunctatus sum ab his qui tempore obsidionis in oppido fuerant." For the *Lamentabile Excidium christianorum*, the *Descriptio . . . Ferrarie*, and the *Oppugnatio oppidi Schrutensis*, I use the volume conserved in the Stadsbibliotheek at Maastricht (s. l. et a.), which lacks numbering and signatures.

arose, who, when the others had made their country glorious by their deeds, preserved and praised the latter for posterity in their writings; from which—with by no means unequal glory, as Sallust bears witness, the state acquired both men of deeds and men of letters.

For Livy plainly describes what had been in Rome two thousand years ago, or from what founders the strength of the Empire and the City had sprung. If you wish to know by whom it was destroyed, Leonardo [Bruni] of Arezzo has laboriously gathered the knowledge from many ancient Greek and Latin histories. How Rome was then restored is recounted by Biondo, canon of St. John in the Lateran, whose tomb we saw at Rome. How the city of Jerusalem was restored after the Chaldaean devastation, the holy historian, Nehemias, tells in various passages. Having been influenced by the examples of these men, I thought it worthy—among my other difficult tasks— to describe in full not all the most ancient matters of the town, because that would be very difficult, but at least those things which repose in the memory of living men and which, whether imitated or completed, pertain to the city.[102]

And the "Dedication" by Rolevinck:

Since this fragile life is hedged in by very many irksome things and we are thus too little prepared for right living, this consistent advice of wise men from the past has endured: to what extent friends might mutually comfort one another by honorable, small joys, and how they might exchange those things which lighten a fatigued mind as seasonal gifts do. And though it is commended usually to neighbours, yet it is appreciated from strangers, and even more from those in exile— whom such great love draws together, so that, though they are far apart, they do not forget the benevolence of their friends and of their

---

[102] *Opuscules de Mathieu Herbenus, concernant les antiquités de Maestricht*, publiés par [P. F. X.] de Ram (Brussels, 1846), 5-6:

"Consueverunt prisci quidem illi atque studiosi litterarum viri cum praeclarum quidquam memorabile ac magnificum in eorum republica contigisset, ad authorum ejusmodi patriaeque laudem in scriptis suis posteris exhibere; inde erupit ingens historiographorum numerus, qui ut illi factis patriam suam gloriosam reddiderunt, hi scriptis ac commendatione laudanda illa facinora posteris suis tradidere; ex quo, haud dispari gloria, ut Salustius testatur, et actores et scriptores respublica consecuta est.

Quid enim Roma ante annorum duo millia fuerit, aut quibus authoribus vigor Imperii Urbisque creverit, Livius certissimus atque eloquentissimus historiographus plane describit. Per quos destructa sit, scire si cupias, Leonardus Aretinus nostris diebus ex multis antiquis Graecorum et Latinorum historiis, laboriosissime collegit. Quomodo deinde restaurata sit, Blondus, canonicus Lateranensis, cujus sepulcrum Romae vidimus, persequitur. Hierosolyma quomodo reformata fuerit post devastationem Chaldaicam, Nehemias sanctus historicus passim narrat. Horum exemplis ductus, inter molestas meas occupationes, factu dignum existimavi, non omnia antiquissima civitatis nostrae opera, quia difficillimum foret, perscribere, sed ea saltem quae in memoria viventium condita sunt, vel inchoata, vel perfecta et ad rempublicam pertinent."

dear ones. Hence this observance comes from a laudable custom, and the old proverb has confirmed that friendship would be as nothing, were it not conserved by freely giving. Our own people first learned this as they were scattered through the various parts of the world, often sending little gifts to their native land, as if renewing an old or native friendship. My own mind learned this according to its capacity and has been brought to maturity; but, since I have not the equipment for material gifts, it was incumbent on me to think about matters of the spirit, if at least I was competent, if I was able to write, if my style was pleasant. . . .

And, because he (as St. Gregory witnesses), who prepares himself for speaking of the things of the Lord by the piety of the faith itself, should begin his work from the scriptures, so that everything, as he puts it, might firmly lead back to the basis of divine authority—likewise, roused by this exhortation, I took up the following word for my theme, saying. . . .[103]

Herbenus's prologue clearly demonstrates his direct indebtedness to Italian humanist historiography. His own work also shows an interesting evolution. At first he wrote about contemporary events he witnessed in Italy (Ferrara). But then he began to think how unworthy of Christians it is to fight one another instead of uniting their forces against the Turks. Part of the preface to his history of the Euboean war is worth being reproduced here, because it shows that queer mixture of Christian pacifism and bellicosity against the Turks which also characterises the Erasmian attitude. We reproduce

---

[103] *Werner Rolevinck 1452-1502. Ein Buch zum Lobe Westfalens des alten Sachsenlandes. Der Text der lateinischen Erstausgabe vom Jahre 1474 mit deutscher Uebersetzung*, ed. Hermann Bücker (Münster/Westf., 1953), 4-6:

"Cum haec fragilis vita plurimis sit taediis circumsepta, et idcirco ad recte vivendum non parum praepedita, hoc inconcussum ab olim extitit sapientum consilium, quatenus alternatim honestis gaudiolis se mutuo amici refoverent et ea, quae fatigatum animum relevarent, quasi pro encaeniis affectuose transmitterent. Et quanquam plurimum commendatur istud apud vicinos, gratius tamen suscipitur ab extraneis, et adhuc gratissime ab exulibus, quos tantus amor perstringit, ut nec longe positi obliviscantur amicorum et carorum suorum benevolentiam. Hinc laudabili more exivit observantia haec, et vetus proverbium inoluit, quasi nihil sit amicitia, si non industriosa largitione conservetur. Didicerunt hoc nostri apprime nostrates per varia mundi climata dispersi, crebro ad patriam suam munuscula transmittentes, quasi pristinam ac nativam amicitiam renovantes. Didicit et hoc mens mea pro modulo suo et prompta est; sed cum mihi materialium encaeniorum apparatus non sit, de spiritualibus incumberet cogitari, si tamen facultas adesset, si sermo suppeteret, si oratio faveret . . . .

Et quia sancto Gregorio teste, qui in re Domini in ipsa fidei pietate se ad loquendum praeparat, operae pretium est a sacris scripturis exordia dicendi suscipiat, ut omne, quod loquitur, ad divinae auctoritatis fundamentum firmiter reducatur, ideo hac exhortatione provocatus, verbum, quod sequitur, pro themate assumpsi, dicens . . . ."

here the first half of the text from what seems to be a unique surviving copy, now in the town library of Maastricht:

> Since I am a little more at leisure for a few days, I thought it a good idea if I were to end this leisure and to turn, following the example of learned men, to some useful business; therefore, when I hear daily that men are preparing themselves for war, the material for writing about war is supplied. But you cannot may expect me to write approvingly about the wars of our leaders, so greatly praised by Christian people! For Cicero says truly in his oration defending Milo [cf. para. 13]: "In any free state at any time, the taking up of arms among the citizens is against the public good." For a state is damaged whenever even a wicked citizen is killed, because a member of the state is thus killed. To what purpose, then, do I write? So that I may clearly show how terrible are our leaders' wars within the common weal of Christendom. Such weighty Christian interests would be far better served, if all vicious hatreds and indignation were converted into friendship, for then would the whole weight of the Christian religion be turned against the common foe! Those who did this, I believe, would gain immortal names and undying crowns in heaven.[104]

For this discussion of Herbenus it should be clear that the quantity of humanist historiography was very small but important because of its novelty and its dependence on the Italian example. The same could be said of the other great genres, eloquence and philosophy. The *Collatio* by Snavel has been mentioned above as one of the very first attempts to speak in the humanist manner. It is, alas, impossible to follow the development of humanist rhetoric in the Low Countries, because almost no texts are preserved, except for a small corpus of speeches by Agricola. If we make a list of *orationes*, it is quite short, and it strikes one immediately that almost all are connected with Italy or Italians.

---

[104] *Lamentabile Excidium Christianorum* (see note 101 above): "Cum his diebus paucis paulo ociosior essem, praeclarum ratus si ipsum illud ocium aliquantisper pessundarem commutaremque exemplo studiosorum in honestum aliquod negocium, iccirco quom accipiam quottidie homines ad bella se parare, suggeritur materia belli scribendi. Neque tamen expectes ut aliquid de bellis nostrorum principum dicam, que a Christiano populo magnopere extollantur! Quippe ait Tulius in oracione pro Milone [cf. para. 13] verissime: 'In nulla unquam libera civitate ac populo arma suscepta esse inter cives non contra rempublicam.' Leditur enim respublica, quamcumque [sic! read: quandocumque] nefarius eciam civis occiditur, quia membrum civitatis occiditur. Quorsum hec? Ut ostendam videlicet bella nostrorum principum in sancta Christiana republica esse formidolosissima. Quanta enim melius se haberent res Christiane si, universis pravis odiis atque indignacionibus concordia sopitus, potenciam suam in Christiane religionis hostes converterent! Credo immortale nomen immarcessibilemque post hanc vitam in celo invenirent coronam . . . ."

8 October 1463· *Ad   Pium papam 2uum Guillelmi* [Fillaotro] *animum Tornacensis pro Christianorum expeditione in Thurcas elegans oratio.*[105]
The anonymous author, who composed this speech to be held by
the bishop of Tournai in his role of Burgundian ambassador,
strains himself to give his Latin a flavour of classical learning; and
its style is a mixture of classical structures and biblical wording.
Compared with Snavel there is some progress toward better classical
expression; but the anonymous writer cannot be said to have
already acquired the easy elegance of the better humanists. It goes
without saying that his attempt to write "Ciceronian" was dictated
by the presence of a humanist on the throne of Peter.

1 July 1471, Pavia: R. Agricola, *Oratio in laudem Matthiae Richili.*
This is the traditional speech in praise of a new rector of the university, held at the beginning of the academic year.

1 July 1473, Pavia: R. Agricola, *Oratio in laudem Pauli de Baenst.*

1 July 1474, Pavia: R. Agricola, *Oratio in laudem Johannis Dalburgii.*

Autumn 1476, Ferrara: R. Agricola, *In laudem philosophiae et reliquarum artium Oratio, dicta in studiorum ad hyemem innovatione.*[106]

The Frisian archhumanist, who translated the rhetorical textbook
of Aphthonius and wrote his own long treatise on the same subject
(*De inventione dialectica*), is the first Netherlander who really deserves
the humanist title of "orator." It was also one of the great ideals
of Agricola's life that his country might one day equal Italy, as one
can read in a letter to his friend, Langius, whom he hails as one of
those who will make his dream materialize:

> I am led to hope that some time we will rip away the ancient glory
> of haughty Italy and its (nearly stolen) reputation for eloquence,
> and that we will rid ourselves from the ignominy, based on which
> alone those Italians call us ignorant and ineloquent barbarians, the
> most savage of all peoples. I hope that our Germany becomes so
> erudite and learned that Latium itself will not be more Latinate.[107]

---

[105] H. V. Sauerland, "Rede des Burgundischen Gesandten und Bischofs von
Tournay Wilhelm Filastre in Sachen eines Kreuzzugs gegen die Türken, gehalten
zu Rom am 8. Oktober 1463 im öffentlichen Consistorium vor Papst Pius II,"
Römische Quartalschrift für christliche Alterthumskunde und Kirchengeschichte, V (1891),
352-363.

[106] R. Agricola, *Opera*, II, 138-143; Stuttgart, Württembergische Landes-
bibliothek, Cod. poet. 4° 36, fols. 323r-328r, and cf. Sottili, "I codici," *IMU*,
XIV (1971), 313-402, here at p. 363; Stuttgart, Württembergische Landes-
bibliothek, Cod. poet. 4° 36, fols. 328r-334r; R. Agricola, *Opera*, II, 144-159.

[107] R. Agricola, *Opera*, II, 178: "... in spem adducor fore aliquando ut priscam
insolenti Italiae et propemodum occupatam benedicendi gloriam extorqueamus,
vindicemusque nos et ab ignominia, qua nos barbaros indoctosque et elingues et
si quid est his incultius esse nos iactitant, exsolvamus, futuramque tam doctam
atque literatam Germaniam nostram, ut non latinius vel ipsum sit Latium."

That moment would come a generation later with Erasmus and, in the field of sheer eloquence, with Christophorus Longolius of Mechlin. Meanwhile Italy, speaking through a famous tetrastich by Ermolao Barbaro, [108] publicly recognised Agricola's talent, of which we possess a few more examples: an *Exhortatio ad Clerum Wormatiensem in synodo publico dicta* (Heidelberg, 1484); [109] a *De nativitate sive immensa natalis diei Jesu Christi laetitia* (Heidelberg, 1484); and a *Gratulatoria oratio pro Ioanne Camerario Dalburgio Vormaciensi Episcopo ac oratore . . . Philippi Comitis Palatini Rheni dicta Innocentio VIII P.M.* (Rome, 1485).[110] It is typical of Agricola that in the prooemium of the latter speech, composed only a few months before he died, we find the following excuse: "Moreover, I think that no pleasantness of speech, nor any polish or elegance in speaking, is or ought to be expected from any German." Even as a rhetorical exaggeration, these lines reveal a sense of inferiority which would be overcome only during the following century.

Yet another speech, held before Sixtus IV by a young Frisian, Andreas Canter, is now lost, so that we can no longer judge whether Sixtus was amazed by the real qualities of the "orator" or simply by his tender age.

Beyond these samples of northern eloquence on Italian soil, we have some information, though it is disappointingly small, about the situation of this art in the academic milieu at Louvain. The university was of course the ideal place for the development of Latin eloquence, for Latin *collationes* (as they were called in mediaeval Latin) or *orationes* were usual on various occasions: the statutes prescribed a *De Laude Facultatum* at the opening of each academic year (1 October). Alas, between the speech which may have been held by Professor Snavel in 1435 and the famous *Oratio* by Dorpius in 1513, none seems to have survived. A close comparison between these two pieces may, nevertheless, reveal the progress of humanism at Louvain, where in 1513 it certainly was still far from being the

---

[108] E. Barbaro, *Epistolae, Orationes et Carmina*, ed. V. Branca, II, 124. First published at the end of J. Beisselius, *Rosacea augustissime cristifere Marie corona* (Antwerp, G. Back, ca. 1498).

[109] Lewis W. Spitz and Anna Benjamin, "Rudolph Agricola's Exhortatio ad clerum Wormatiensem," *Archiv für Reformationsgeschichte*, LIV (1963), 6-14.

[110] R. Agricola, *Opera*, II, 276-289, and 163-171. The quotation from the latter reads: ". . . Arbitror autem orationis gratiam et quemvis eloquendi cultum atque splendorem ex homine Germano expectari magnopere neque posse neque debere. . . ."

dominant force as the coming troubles of the Collegium Trilingue would amply prove. Space precludes a detailed comparison, but we can point out that Snavel, in praising the faculties, followed the hierarchical order (theology, canon law, civil law, medicine, and arts), whereas Dorpius brings the arts and especially eloquence to the first place. In order to demonstrate the overall power of this art, he expatiates for several minutes on the brilliant career of Pius II, who owed all his successes to his skill as a perfect *orator.*

Visits of princes, diplomats, and other important persons provided further occasions for official addresses. It is a great pity that the *Oratio in Adventu Maximiliani Archiducis,* delivered in 1477 by a former professor of eloquence, Petrus de Rivo (Van der Beken), perished in a twentieth-century war before it could be edited from the Tournai manuscript. This loss leaves us with only two other texts, both in good Latin but not the work of a Netherlander. Their author is a Venetian, Antonius Gratiadei, professor of theology at Louvain. Best known is the short address in the name of the emperor Frederick III and his son, Maximilian, by which Gratiadei replied to the official greetings of the Venetian ambassador, Ermolao Barbaro, at Bruges, 3 August 1486. In this speech, Gratiadei extols Barbaro for his learning as the "Venetiarum et nostri saeculi decus." [111] It seems plausible that the emperor deliberately called upon an Italian to deliver his reply, thereby guaranteeing a good impression on a humanist such as Barbaro. The chair of poetics at Louvain being temporarily vacant (Bruni left the town on 17 June 1486), Frederick had to look for another "orator extemporalis"; and it was a happy coincidence that Gratiadei was also a Venetian, for the sound of spoken Latin could differ sensibly according to the origin of the speaker!

With Gratiadei our knowledge of fifteenth-century eloquence in the Netherlands breaks off. That so few texts have been preserved may be due partly to the small numbers of copies—they were rarely

---

[111] The oration by Ermolao Barbaro is published in his *Epistolae, Orationes et Carmina,* II, 110-120 (several extant versions); see also the additional note in Ermolao Barbaro, *De Coelibatu. De officio legati,* ed. Vittore Branca, Nuova collezione, 14 (Florence, 1969), 216-217. The answer of Antonius Gratiadei has recently been published by Jan Öberg, *Notice et extraits du Manuscrit Q 19 (XVIe s.) de Strängnäs,* Acta Universitatis Stockholmiensis, Studia Latina Stockholmiensia, 16 (Stockholm, 1968), 8-10. The author was not aware, however, of the existence of the editio princeps printed by Dirk Martens at Aalst in 1486 (about which see E. Barbaro, *Epistolae,* I, xxix-xxx, and *De Coelibatu,* 231-234).

printed—but also partly to the poor quality of their Latin, at least in the eyes of the next generations. For the latter, only one person, Agricola, was deemed worthy of attention and study. As for the others, there were now much better *oratores*, to begin with Erasmus, who delivered his *Panegyricus* for Philip of Burgundy at Brussels in 1504.

The amount of other prose—dialogues, treatises, letters—deserving of the qualification "humanist" is also very small for this period. Again we must single out Agricola with his *De inventione dialectica* and his interesting letters, which are sometimes small treatises. Such is the case of his *De formando studio* (1484), in which he traces for his Antwerp friend, Barbirianus, a detailed curriculum of humanist studies and condemns the traditional use of idle disputes, which kill in the bud the talents of the youth. A few other authors also deserve mention: Herbenus, who wrote his learned *De Natura Cantus ac miraculis vocis* (1496) with the express purpose of contributing his share to the unexpected revival of the *litterae* in the Rhineland; and Jacobus Canter, whose dialogue *De Solitudine* (1491?) still awaits an editor. A sample of Canter's work may illustrate how this Frisian already took an almost Italian delight in words and learned allusions without much content.

> The first book of a dialogue concerning solitude, by the most famous orator, Jacob Canter, a Frisian.
> Phi.: Greetings, O Hippolitus, half my life!
> Hyp.: And to you, Philodemus, greetings!
> Phi.: Aren't you that Hippolitus of ours?
> Hyp.: I surely am.
> Phi.: It is really you whom I see and embrace?
> Hyp.: For sure, it is I.
> Phi.: Then I do not have always to live in darkness, I see, as in a dark night, seeing that you, O Hippolitus, my light, are coming to meet me; for, since I first set eyes on you, the sun itself began to grow daily darker. Tell me, where are you going all alone?
> Hyp.: Ah! Where are you going alone, contrary to your custom?
> Phi.: By Hercules, I don't really know, my soul!
> Hyp.: Why is that you don't know?
> Phi.: Because, if I knew where I was going when I left home, I forgot it all when I caught sight of you approaching me.
> Hyp.: Nonsense!
> Phi.: No! Indeed (so that you'll believe me) for I, who often wander about, as they say, walking wherever I might come across you, look hither and yon for you as I walk. Thus, through a raging storm on a cloudy night, an alert sailor casts his eye everywhere, seeking a glimpse of the Dioscuri, brothers of Helen, or of Lycaon's bear. Thus I go about to all the nooks and crannies of the city, wandering

through crowds as well as into lonely places, seeking you until
at last I return home late at night, weary of wandering.[112]

Canter was perhaps not very representative of the men of the North.
He was, after all, the only one of his generation to practise erotic
poetry, making him almost the exact opposite of Wessel Gansfort.

Although Gansfort, on his return from Italy, was hailed by Antonius
Liber with these lines,

> Hail, O Wessel, O most distinguished fellow, hail
> Prince of literature and honor of the Muses . . . .
>
> . . . .
>
> Stay with us, O honor and decorum of the Roman tongue,
>   Stay, interpreter of Greek and Hebrew, too.
> You alone will be our Galen, and a second
>   Virgil; you alone will be our Cicero . . . .[113]

---

[112] Clm 4417ᵈ, fol. 1ʳ:

> "Incipit liber primus dyalogi de solitudine
> Domini Jacobi Canter Frisigene oratoris clarissimi.

Phi.: Salve, o Hyppolite, dimidium anime mee!

Hyp.: Et tu, Philodeme, salve!

Phi.: Non tu es ille noster Hyppolitus?

Hyp.: Ego!

Phi.: Non te video? Non te amplector?

Hyp.: Meipsum profecto.

Phi.: Non semper igitur mihi in tenebris (video) ac velut in obscura nocte
vivendum est, o Hyppolite, quandoquidem tu mihi, lux mea, te obvium
offers; quem ex quo tempore primum aspexi, sol ipse mihi obscurior
in dies videri coepit. Sed quo incomitatus, cedo, proficisceris?

Hyp.: Quo vero tu praeter morem solus?

Phi.: Nescio hercle ipse, anime mi!

Hyp.: Qui fieri potest ut nescias?

Phi.: Quia, et si quid domo egrediens quo proficiscerer animo concepi,
excidit omne mox ut te contra venientem aspexi.

Hyp.: Garris.

Phi.: Non! profecto quoniam (quod minus vereor credas) sepenumero in
incertum, ut aiunt, obambulo sicubi fortasse te vagus offendam, atque
obiter in omni parte lumina flecto si detur usquam oculorum atque animi
mei pabulo refici. Sic per nubilam in alto noctem, quum sevit tempestas,
oculos undique sollicitus nauta circumfert si quo Dioscuros Lacenae
fratres aut Lycaonis arcton videat. Nec secus ego pervia queque atque
invia urbis loca peragro et modo in frequentes cetus, modo in solitudinem
me confero videndi tui gratia; nec nisi supra valitudinem oberrando
defessus ad multam denique noctem domum redeo."

[113] Gansfort, *Opera*, 710:

> "Salve, o Wessele, o vir praestantissime, salve
>   *Littrarum* [sic!] *princeps* Pieridumque decus . . .
>
> . . . .
>
> Ergo age Romanae decus atque decentia linguae,
>   Interpres Graiae Hebraicaeque mane.
> Tu modo noster eris Galenus tuque secundus
>   Virgilius; Cicero tu modo noster eris . . ."

the categories we reserve for the leading humanists do not seem really to apply to him. Gansfort was certainly no Virgil, as poetry was the least of his interests unless it served his pious purposes: it is useful to have at hand such a passage as Virgil's description of Dido's wrath, "when you want to instill the fear of death, judgment, and Hell" (*Scala Meditationis* II. 10).[114] His mind is decidedly turned to theological and religious problems. A popular topic of Italian humanism, the *comparatio vitae activae et contemplativae*, is for him an exclusively religious problem; he turned it, symbolically enough, into a *comparatio Mariae Magdalenae et Marthae*.[115] He studied Cicero carefully and makes considerable use of Greek learning, but he does not look at the Greeks as lofty and perfect examples: "Some Greeks chatter aloud, extolling with puffed up cheeks that chiasmus of Demosthenes, which he used against Philip of Macedon. But they would marvel less if they could ponder closely the Lord's Prayer," is a typical passage with which he introduces his second book, *De oratione dominica*.[116] It is true that Gansfort writes a fairly good Latin, generally *stilo humili*, since he knew very well that the intelligence of many readers is not very great: "Hence it is true that there are few readers who understand the periods of Augustine and Cicero" (*Scala Med.* II. 20).[117] Solecisms such as "egressit" (*Scala Med.* I. 17) [118] may be due either to a *lapsus calami* or more probably to a phenomenon not unfamiliar to readers of humanist writings, the switch from deponent to active verb forms. All in all, Gansfort appears to us as a forerunner of the theologians of the later sixteenth century; their concern remained, quite naturally and normally, theological, but in the humanist's school they had learned to give a more classical and more elegant linguistic dress to their professional writings.

In all of this the direct link between Gansfort and the later theologians was, of course, Erasmus. Certainly, in the period under discussion, Erasmus felt himself much more *poeta et orator* than *theologus*.

---

[114] *Ibid.*, 233: "quando terrere voles de morte, de iudicio, de gehenna".

[115] It is the first part of the *Scala Meditationis*, in Gansfort, *Opera*, 194-225.

[116] Gansfort, *Opera*, 41: "Grande quidpiam Graeci crepitant et inflatis buccis chiasmum illum Demosthenis, quo in Philippum Macedonem utitur, efferunt. Sed minus mirarentur, si connexionem sanctae huius Dominicae orationis perspicaciter perpenderent . . . ."

[117] *Ibid.*, 240: "Hinc est ut ad periodos Augustini et Ciceronis pauci idonei lectores inveniantur."

[118] *Ibid.*, 216.

His name belongs here because his career as one of the great writers of humanist prose begins not only with such treatises as *De Contemptu Mundi* but also—what is more significant in the context of early humanism—with forceful pleas for the cause of the *bonae litterae* in the first version of his *Antibarbari* (ca. 1489),[119] the *Conflictus Thaliae et Barbariei*[120] (the title itself is a whole programme!), and even his abridgement of Valla's *Elegantiae*.[121] Later on his interests may have shifted to more specifically biblical studies, but he nonetheless always retained his love of the beautiful Latin form, and this ultimately affected the following generations of theologians and canonists.

In summary, if the harvest of humanist literature in the Low Countries up to the early 1490s is not very rich, its cultural significance far exceeds its quantity, because here were the modest beginnings of what was to become a predominant feature of sixteenth and seventeenth-century learning and literature. The ultimate results were perhaps much greater than what the generation of 1460-90 had dared dream of. Even Agricola was uncertain about their success, as he wrote to Liber:

> What, I say, shall we do? Shall we keep silent? By no means! Let us press forward more diligently and contend with the evils of the times; let us hasten to learn and to try with all our might to master those arts natural to humanity—to write and pass on even things which the ancients would not have scorned and things which posterity might disapprove, so that, if we achieve less, it will appear a fault of an age grown old and decadent rather than due to our own laziness.[122]

There were indeed serious reasons to doubt the final success of the attempt to win "Germania" for the humanist cause. Scholasticism, with bastions in the universities of Paris, Cologne, and Louvain, was certainly far stronger and more influential here than in Italy.

---

[119] James D. Tracy, "The 1489 and 1494 versions of Eramus's *Antibarbarorum liber*," *HL*, XX (1971), 81-120.

[120] D. Erasmus, *Opera Omnia*, ed. Joannes Clericus, 10 vols. (Leiden, 1703-06), I, 892-894.

[121] D. Erasmus, *Paraphrasis seu potius epitome in Elegantiarum libros Laurentii Vallae*, eds. Chris L. Heesakkers and Jan Hendrik Waszink, in *Opera Omnia D. Erasmi*, I, 4 (Amsterdam, 1973), 187-351.

[122] R. Agricola, *Opera*, II, 175: "Quid inquam faciemus? Tacebimus? Nequaquam! Sed nitamur diligentius atque cum temporum iniuria certemus; contendamus discere et vere ingenuas illas humanitatis artes toto nisu conemur amplecti excudereque aliquid et relinquere aut quod non sprevissent priores, aut quod non improbet posteritas, et ut (si quid minus fecerimus) non nostrae socordiae, sed senescentis et prope ruentis seculi vitium fuisse videatur."

The nationalistic incentive, moreover, to restore the country's ancient greatness by means of Latin—so evident in such figures as Petrarch and Valla—as well as the consciousness of Latin and the vernacular as two forms of one language and literature, could not operate in the North. Only a sensitivity to the beauty of classical Latin and the belief that this was spoiled by the mediaeval usages, could also be valid in a Germanic country. But this sensitivity was the privilege of the happy few, who were almost always to be found only in the classrooms. This explains the sharp sense of utter lone-liness felt by Agricola when he became a civil servant at Groningen upon his return from Italy. Groningen's magistracy could in no way be compared to that of Ferrara or another North Italian republic or principality. There was, moreover, little contact between the fifteenth-century humanists and vernacular culture in the Low Countries, except to a certain degree at the Burgundian Court at Brussels and Bruges. The period saw a keen revival of popular interest in the old mediaeval romances and epics, which affected even the Latin-reading public: a late thirteenth-century Latin version of the Dutch epic of Reynard the Fox was printed at Utrecht about 1473.[123] Literature in Dutch produced some of its finest late mediaeval works in the plays *Elckerlyc* and *Marieken van Nieumeghen*. Trans-lations from Latin, however, do not include humanist works—in this context Petrarch's *Griseldis* can hardly be considered a humanist work—but largely mediaeval legends and didactic treatises. Human-ists of the early sixteenth century tried to rework vernacular writings in classical Latin even before the vernacular authors began to pay closer attention to the learned literature: the best examples are the Latin versions of *Elckerlyc* by Christianus Ischyrius and Macro-pedius.[124]

This gulf established between the occasional humanists and the mass of the (literate) people was certainly a major hindrance to a broad diffusion, and thus a social strengthening, of the new Latin learning and literature. Only later, when a Latin-loving patriciate had developed in such towns as Antwerp, Ghent, The Hague, and

---

[123] *Reynardus Vulpes. De Latijnse Reinaert-vertaling van Balduinus Iuvenis*, ed. R. B. C. Huygens (Zwolle, 1968).

[124] *Vom Sterben des reichen Mannes. Die Dramen von Everyman, Homulus, Hecastus und dem Kauffmann nach Drucken des 16. Jahrhunderts*, trans. and ed. with introduction by H. Wiemken, Sammlung Dieterich, 298 (Bremen, 1965); R. Vos, "Elckerlyc — Everyman — Homulus — Der Sunden Loin ist der Toid," *Tijdschrift voor Neder-landse Taal- en Letterkunde*, LXXXII (1966), 129-143.

Amsterdam, did humanist culture obtain the indispensable social base for a full flowering.

Such a social base existed in the French-speaking parts of the Low Countries to a certain extent at the court of the Burgundian dukes. It was limited, however, by the outspoken predilection of the dukes and the nobility for the French language, which at once eliminated an essential feature of humanist studies, the cult of classical Latin. What then remained? In the first place, there was a certain influence of humanist ideas on writings on morals and politics. French authors in the service of the dukes translated Latin classics and some Italian humanists into French. A characteristic example both of the texts translated and the quality of the work is offered by Jean Miélot. In 1449 he had already made a French version of Buonaccorso da Montemagno's *Disputatio de Nobilitate*, which was still being printed at Bruges more than twenty-five years later. In 1450 he translated Aurispa's Latin version of Lucian's comparison of Scipio, Alexander, and Hannibal.[125] The dukes also appointed official (French) historiographers, as did many Italian states; and soon the German monarchs also had their Latin historians. But it must be stressed that the Latin culture of the Burgundian French authors, if judged by humanist standards of their day, is rather limited. We have a few Latin verses by Miélot and Jean Molinet;[126] but their quality is poor, and the poets sometimes prefer mediaeval rhymes to classical metres. There are other proofs of the superficiality of their command of Latin. When Molinet translated a text by Poliziano, for example, he confused the word *scipio* (stick) with the name Scipio, thus misunderstanding the entire passage.[127] Now *scipio* is

---

[125] David Cast, "Aurispa, Petrarch and Lucian: An Aspect of Renaissance Translation," *Renaissance Quarterly*, XXVII (1974), 157-173, here at p. 166.

[126] Gianni Mombello, "Quattro poesie latine di Jean Miélot," in *Miscellanea di Studi e Ricerche sul Quattrocento francese*, ed. Franco Simone (Turin, 1967), 211-240. Jean Molinet wrote a Latin and French epitaphium for Johannes Ockeghem; cf. *Johannes Ockeghem en zijn tijd*, Tentoonstelling gehouden in het Stadhuis te Dendermonde 14 november-6 december 1970, Oudheidkundige Kring van het Land van Dendermonde, Buitengewone uitgaven 24, p. 141.

For other Latin poems of Molinet, see Noël Dupire, *Etude critique des manuscrits et éditions des poésies de Jean Molinet* (Paris, 1932), passim.

[127] Pierre Jodogne, "La conjuration des Pazzi racontée par les chroniqueurs français et bourguignons du XVe siècle: Commynes, A. de But, Th. Basin, J. Molinet," in *Atti del Convegno su "Culture et politique en France à l'époque de l'Humanisme et de la Renaissance,"* Accademia delle Scienze di Torino, 29 marzo-3 aprile 1971 (Turin, 1974), 169-212, here at pp. 187, 207.

not a very unusual word; and, what is more, everyone who has read the more popular passages of Livy knows the word from the famous story of the Gauls' invasion of Rome under Brennus. Poliziano, of course, knew it, and his passage translated by Molinet is a clear example of humanist imitation of that page of Livy. Molinet, unaware of this and ignoring current Latin terms, shows in this way that his culture is hardly humanist. Compared to him, Jean Lemaire de Belges, a generation later, marks a definite progress. But even during the first decades of the sixteenth century, another courtier, Georgius Haloinus, regrets that his class, the nobility, has no interest in classical studies.[128] This attitude never changed very much. Years later Jean Bodin wrote his treatise on the state in French, because the nobles would not have understood it in Latin. This cannot have been but a serious limitation of humanist culture outside the schools and ecclesiastical circles.

IV. The Erasmian Age

Even at the very end of his life, Agricola did not feel sure that the humanist ideas would attain a final triumph over the mediaeval "barbarism" of his age.[129] A bare ten years later, however, Herbenus writes that the unbelievable did happen and that the *bonae litterae* were in full flower.[130] From the last decade of the fifteenth century onward, the number of authors who join the humanist cause increases rapidly, and so does the number and variety of humanist works published. We cannot describe in detail here the period between the first writings of Erasmus and the foundation of the Collegium Trilingue (1517) at Louvain, because to do so would swell beyond measure this study of the coming of humanism to the Netherlands and even overstep the subject itself. During this era, in fact, humanism begins its own development, depending less and less on Italian impulses alone. For this reason we will single out here only the main characteristics of this consolidation of northern humanism.

Because of the first successes, the humanists of Erasmus's age—though still a relatively small minority—felt much more confident

---

[128] Constant Matheeussen, "Een 16e-eeuwse aanval op de grammatica: de *Restauratio Linguae Latinae* van Georgius Haloinus (1533)," 2 vols. (unpublished doctoral dissertation, University of Leuven, 1974), II, 11-12.

[129] Letter to Liber, in R. Agricola, *Opera*, II, 174-175.

[130] *Herbeni Traiectensis de natura cantus* (cf. note 42 above), 16.

vis-à-vis both the "barbarians" and even the once venerated Italians.
The self-confident attitude against scholasticism is well enough
known in its more prudent, Erasmian form and in such violent
pamphlets as the *Epistolae Obscurorum Virorum* [131] and William
Nesen's *Dialogus bilinguium ac trilinguium*,[132] written at Louvain in 1519
at the heat of the fight for the Collegium Trilingue. But these are
late examples. Well before the turn of the century, Bartholomaeus
Coloniensis (ca. 1460-1514), a schoolmaster at Deventer under
Hegius and much admired by the young Erasmus, who described him
as "virum eruditione singulari ac poesis amantissimum," [133] wrote an
epigram entitled "In osores studiorum humanitatis." Found in his
Silva Carminum (first ed. 16 February 1491), it bears quoting in full:

> Babbling barbarism, you will sooner dethrone Boötes, Bear-keeper
>   From the pole of the northern world,
> Before you cast down from their twin-peaked mount
>   The learned, laurel-crowned chorus of Muses.
> If you do not cease molesting them with words, Apollo
>   Will crown you with a little donkey's ears.[134]

Bartholomaeus resorts to the use of an adynaton to express the total
superiority of humanism, conceived exclusively as Latin humanism.
He directs another epigram against a man who is more fluent in the
vernacular language than in Latin. One thinks of the attitude of some
extremists among the Italian latinists, but the sentiment is rather to
be connected with the views of Celtis, Euricius Cordus, and other
German poets, who consider writing in the vernacular an unworthy
activity by which even the most unlearned can diffuse their stupid
ideas. Bartholomaeus's view is as follows:

> Zoilus, what is the reason? Vernacular words flow
>   From your tongue in a torrent, like a river;
> Latin words, however, come slowly, at a tortoise's pace,
>   Flowing from your mouth only with great effort.

---

[131] Eduard Böcking, ed., *Ulrici Hutteni Equitis Operum Supplementum*, 2 vols. (Leipzig, 1864-70; reprint, Osnabrück, 1966).

[132] Text published by De Vocht, *HCT*, I, 544-574.

[133] Allen, ep. 28, I, 118, ll. 20-21.

[134] *Bartholomei Coloniensis Silva Carminum* (Deventer, 1505), fol. [A.v^r-^{v}]:

> "Garrula barbaries, prius Arctophylaca Booten
>   Orbis hyperborei cardine deiicies,
> Quam deturbabis de monte bivertice doctos
>   Musarum coetus laurigerosque viros.
> Hos si non cessas verbis obtundere, aselli
>   Aures temporibus figet Apollo tuis."

　　　The reason is clear: you learned the speech of the natives
　　　　　From you busy mother;
　　　But the eloquent language of bards who speak in Latin,
　　　　　That you neglected to learn.[135]

With the strengthening of the humanist forces, this self-confidence became more and more outspoken. In the end the northern humanists no longer admired indiscriminately their Italian forerunners. It is instructive in this respect to compare some student lines by Erasmus with a page of Vives's *De conscribendis epistolis*. Writing to a friend, Cornelius of Gouda, Erasmus asks: "Coming now to the Italians, who respected ancient eloquence more than Lorenzo Valla? than Filelfo? Who is more eloquent than Enea Silvio, Agostino Dati, Guarino, Poggio, or Gasparino?" [136] That Erasmus maintained this still unreserved admiration during his Paris years is shown by his friendship with Andrelini—certainly not the greatest of the Italian *poetae*.[137] He later became more critical, as did his French friend, Budé, who condemned the frivolous poetry imported from Italy, and as did Juan Luis Vives, the Spanish exile living in the Netherlands.[138] Vives passed in review the leading Italian humanists from Petrarch to his own day and found much to criticize: Petrarch certainly "shone like a little star amidst deep darkness," but he was nonetheless "prolix and morose in many difficult passages, and he

---

[135] *Ibid.*, fol. [A.v^v]:

　　　"Zoile, quid causae est? Vernacula verba citato
　　　　Gressu ex ore tuo fluminis instar eunt.
　　　Verba Latina meant tardae testudinis instar,
　　　　Quae magno nisu trudis ab ore tuo.
　　　In promptu causa est: vernarum tu didicisti
　　　　Linguam, quam mater sedula te docuit;
　　　Sed neglexisti facundam ediscere linguam
　　　　Vatum, qui norunt verba Latina loqui."

[136] Allen, ep. 23, I, 103-109, here at p. 107: "Ut autem ad Italos veniam, quid Laurentio Vallensi, quid Philelpho veteris eloquentiae observantius? Quid Aenea Sylvio, quid Augustino Datho, quid Guarino, quid Poggio, quid Gasparino eloquentius?"

[137] Lieve Tournoy-Thoen, "Faustus Andrelinus en Erasmus in het Parijse Humanistenmilieu rond 1500," *Handelingen der Koninklijke Zuidnederlandse Maatschappij voor Taal- en Letterkunde en Geschiedenis*, XXV (1971), 271-285.

[138] Maurice Lebel, *De Transitu Hellenismi ad Christianismus de Guillaume Budé — Le passage de l'Hellenisme au Christianisme*, texte traduit, accompagné d'index et présenté pour la première fois en français, Centre d'Études de la Renaissance de l'Université de Sherbrooke (Sherbrooke, 1973), 170.

drew much from the idle trash of his day." [139] Agricola had defended Petrarch against his Italian critics; but even Italian latinists of the late quattrocento, such as Paulus Cortesius, found fault with Petrarch's style.

Vives had other criticisms, among them that Gasparino "was the first to stutter Latin in Italy," and that Bruni was "still insufficiently cultivated." The two Filelfi have better styles, but they are "rather cold and empty in their ideas and lack charm in their constructions." Poggio is nothing more than "a chattering trifler and pettifogger," while Enea Silvio may be "of a happy personality" but is in any case "unhappy in his skill." Vives praises only a few men highly, among them Poliziano, while his judgment on Ficino is truly disconcerting: "Marsilio Ficino, that poor philosopher, meddled with these authors like a seagull with swans, and he wrote letters in an inelegant and difficult diction, trying to debate on Platonic themes." [140]

This more critical approach had profounder consequences than one might at first glance suspect. It was a decisive factor in averting northern minds from rhetoric and poetry as ends in themselves, at the very moment when Italian humanism became more rhetorical and poetical and less pedagogical and philosophical. A man such as the rhetorician, Christophorus Longolius of Mechlin (1488-1522), was exceptional, and his success in Italy is symptomatic. The others turned their attention to pedagogical, moral and social problems (Vives, Erasmus), to ecclesiastical history (Trithemius), to theology (Dorpius), or to biblical and patristic philology (Erasmus). Many passages in Erasmus's correspondence attest to a radical turn in this regard. In a long letter to John Colet, written at Paris towards the end of 1504, he underlines the theme repeatedly:

> Ah! I cannot tell you how I might speed myself to sacred literature by sails or on horseback, how all things weary me in so far as they either lead away from sacred literature or are remote from it. . . .

---

[139] *Joannis Ludovici Vivis Valentini Opera Omnia*, ed. Gregorius Majansius, 8 vols. (Valencia, 1782-90), II, 313: "velut stellula inter densissimas tenebras emicuit . . . prolixus ac plerisque locis morosus, difficilisque et multum trahens ex rubigine ac situ suorum temporum."

[140] *Ibid.*, 313: Gasparino "primus coepit in Italia Latine balbutire"; Bruni was "parum adhuc excultus"; the Filelfi are "sententiis inanes et subfrigidi, nec compositione satis grata"; Poggio is a "garrulus nugator et rabula"; Enea Silvio is "natura felix" but "infelix arte". On Ficino: "Admiscuit se his philosophaster Marcilius Ficinus, ut oloribus gravia, atque epistolas composuit ut de Platonicis quaestionibus disputaret, dictione invenusta et molesta."

> For, by whatever plan, I must arrange my time so as to have it entirely to myself for a few months, so that I may somehow draw myself away from the subjects I have treated in profane literature. . . .
> Wherefore I beseech you earnestly, help me to strive for sacred studies as best you can, and set me free from this literature which has already lost its savour for me.[141]

Even poetry and theatre were turned to the service of moral and religious ends, sometimes with the express aim of dispelling from the classroom the dangerous ancient and Italian poets. Cornelius Aurelius wrote his *Mariad*, a long series of elegies on the life of Christ, "when I learned that rotten (as Persius says) magpies had flown into the schools to the detriment of the Devout Brethren in Florentius's [Radewijns] house, and with acute spiritual danger to the townsfolk of Deventer, and that already the lips of simple folk there were beginning to be moistened, not to say polluted, by that horse-trough." [142]

At the same time the Carmelite of Ghent, Arnoldus Bostius (d. 1499), invited all his friends—including Conrad Celtis, Trithemius, Rutger Sicamber, and Robert Gaguin—to write hymns in honour of St. Joachim.[143] Hymns and moralising poems, nearly to the exclusion of other poetic forms, fill the volumes of many other poets around 1500: Petrus Burrus of Bruges (1430-1507), a canon of Amiens; Johannes Murmellius of Roermond (1480-1517); and Hermannus Buschius. Dramatic performances during the early sixteenth century also bring to the stage moral themes from the Bible or from classical and mediaeval sources with moralising tendencies (Hercules between Vice and Virtue, Griseldis). The first comedy of which we hear is a lost play by Reynerus Snoy of Gouda—"alterum litterarum Hollandicarum decus," according to Erasmus [144]—com-

---

[141] Allen, ep. 181, I, 403-406, here at pp. 404, 405, 406: "Dici non queat . . . quam velis equisque properem ad sacras litteras, quam omnia mihi fastidio sint qua illinc aut avocant aut etiam remorantur . . . ." "Quavis enim ratione mihi est elaborandum ut menses aliquot totus mihi vivam, quo me aliquando ab iis extri:em quae in litteris prophanis institui . . . ." "Quare te obsecro ut me a:l sacra studia vehementer anhelantem quoad potes adiuves atque ab hiis litteris, qua: .nihi iam dulces esse desierunt, asseras."

[142] Deventer, Athenaeumbibliotheek, Ms. 31, fol. 1ᵛ: "cum didicissem poetridas (ut Persius ait) picas cum Devotorum Fratrum domus Florentii dispendio tum animarum periculo Daventriensis oppidi scholis advolasse et iam incipere labra simplicium fonte prolui — ne dicam pollui — caballino . . .," ed. J. IJsewijn, "Erasmus ex poeta theologus," *Scrinium Erasmianum*, I, 385.

[143] Cf. Klaus Arnold, *Johannes Trithemius (1462-1516)*, Quellen und Forschungen zur Geschichte des Bistums und Hochstifts Würzburg, 23 (Würzburg, 1971), 103.

[144] Allen, ep. 190, I, 421-422.

posed on the subject of the Prodigal Son,[145] which was to be~~~~~~ ~~
~~~~~~~~~~ the~~~ of the school theatre. At about the same time Macropedius, by far the best Latin playwright in the Netherlands, began
composing on similar themes.

This moral and religious current was not just a product of a changed
attitude toward the Italian literati. One could even argue that there
was no change at all, as a religious current had always been present.
Though this is true, one cannot deny that such men as Erasmus and
Dorpius, at certain points in their careers, changed the direction of
their interests in a self-conscious manner. Often what remained of
Italian humanism were the pedagogical ideas (the heritage of
Quintilian, Isocrates, and Pseudo-Plutarch) and the renewed linguistic
forms of expression. The chief objects of interest, however, were
once again the Bible, the Church fathers, and the Christian life. Here,
beyond a doubt, lay the sharp difference with the great Italian humanists, for whom often enough Plato and Aristotle took the places
of Augustine and Jerome. In this light a reply of Barbaro to Bostius
assumes its true significance. Bostius had congratulated the Venetian
on his translation of Themistius and seized the opportunity to urge
him to translate Christian authors as well. Barbaro politely dismisses
the idea: "Moreover, as you urge me to turn my hand sometime to
Christian authors—Chrysostom, Gregory Nazianzen, Cyril, Athana-
sius, and Basil—as I cannot promise definitely to do it, I will not
refuse completely." [146]

Returning to the factors that favoured this preference for the
sacra studia among northern adepts of humanism, one must not
underestimate the roles of the Universities of Paris, Cologne, and
Louvain. Of old, Paris and Cologne were leading international
centres of scholasticism, and students and professors working
there could hardly escape the influence of their theological atmos-
pheres. In this regard, it is truly significant that, some time before
1500, Paris and Cologne also became international centres of humanist
learning. At Paris, Fichet and Gaguin had introduced both the
printing industry and a kind of humanist academy. Poets such as
Girolamo Balbi and Fausto Andrelini, while not artists of the first

---

[145] Bob de Graaf and Emilie de Graaf, *Doctor Reinerus Snoy Goudanus, Gouda ca. 1477-1st August 1537* (Nieuwkoop, 1968), 11: *Acolastus.*

[146] E. Barbaro, *Epistolae, Orationes et Carmina*, ep. LXXII, I, 91-93, here at p. 92: "Quod autem hortaris me ut ad christianos quoque auctores, Chrysosto-mum, Nazianzenum, Cyrillum, Athanasium, Basilium aliquando manus admoliar, ut hoc polliceri tibi omnino non possum, ita non plane pernego."

class but certainly greater than the professors of poetics at Louvain, exercised a tremendous influence on the students who came there from all over northern Europe. Even Greeks and many minor Italian figures, such as Franciscus Florius, found their ways to Paris, as did printers from the Netherlands, such as Petrus Caesar (De Keysere)—not to forget the Brabantine, Iodocus Badius Ascensius, whose *prelum Ascensianum* became one of the glories of the Parisian and humanist publishing industry. All of this means that by the beginning of the sixteenth century, Paris had taken the place formerly held by Italian universities in the literary formation of many northern and other European students, especially those from Spain, England, Flanders, and Germany. The same judgment applies, to a certain extent, to Cologne, where the Quentell printing firm and the presence of the Italian "pansophus," Peter of Ravenna, stirred much enthusiasm for humanist studies during the first decades of the century. The same role at Louvain was assumed by the Martens firm and the early teaching of Dorpius, but above all by the foundation of the Collegium Trilingue (1517), which marked the beginning of the great humanist age of the Brabantine university, lasting far into the seventeenth century. Finally, in the same vein, we may point to Juan Luis Vives, who never went to Italy, ignored much of contemporary Italian culture, and never became a great admirer of the Italian Renaissance.

As compared with the situation during the fifteenth century, the possibilities for humanist studies in the northern universities were undoubtedly much improved in the time of Erasmus. It goes without saying, however, that even for the most enthusiastic student of the *humanae litterae*, breathing daily the often paganising atmosphere of an Italian academic milieu was not quite the same as living in a stern scholastic centre of the North. Even if the masters were not a Pomponio Leto or the morose Standonck respectively, it remains true that, in Paris, Cologne, and Louvain, interest in the brighter side of life and the mere imitation of ancient art gave way more often than not to more serious occupations. The formal brilliance of Andrelini could hold the students for a time, but the effect seldom lasted longer than a few years. And even Andrelini finally forgot to sing at Paris about his Livia and turned to moralising maxims.

This coexistence of humanism and scholasticism in one place and sometimes, as an inevitable consequence, in one person is characteristic of northern Europe, though it cannot be said that it was entirely absent in Italy. One has only to recall how Giovanni Pico della Mirandola wrote his *Oratio de dignitate hominis* [147] in perfectly humanist Latin as an introduction to his *Theses*,[148] which are purely scholastic in both content and style. On the other side, extremists among the northern humanists could be induced to condemn serious scholars who, though they had great merits as humanists, happened to defend some scholastic standpoints. A notorious victim of such unjust attacks was Ortuinus Gratius of Deventer (ca. 1480-1542), a former student of Hegius. The number of classical and Italian humanists he knew, recommended, or edited is highly impressive. He wrote fluent Latin verse; and he procured an edition of Rolevinck's book on Westphalia, from which he expelled numerous barbarisms, such as "sitis bene ventus" ("be welcome"!), replacing them with genuine Latin expressions. He nonetheless became the main target of the slanderous shafts of the *Epistolae Obscurorum Virorum*. It is well to remember that many Italian humanists were no more friendly to one another—think of such men as Valla, Poggio, or Filelfo—and that in the homeland of humanism, too, the sharpest insults also were aimed at the alleged ignorance of the adversary. The main difference between North and South, then, remains the involvement of humanism with theology in the North, but not in Italy.

To round out this survey of northern humanism in the Erasmian age, we wish to point out the enormous broadening of its scope, activities, and European relations. It is true that humanism, by definition, was never shut within narrow national boundaries, because its language was the instrument of international contacts and exchanges of ideas. Ancient literature, moreover, was the common heritage of all the civilised peoples of Europe. As we pointed out above, fifteenth-century humanist studies in the Low Countries were the concern of a very few individuals. In the Erasmian age, however, humanist formation began slowly but steadily to take hold of the entire grammar school teaching in the Netherlands, and, as a logical consequence, of a broad range of academic and scientific life. The time was coming when jurisprudence, medicine, mathematics, and other disciplines would be practised by men trained as huma-

---

[147] Giovanni Pico della Mirandola, *De dignitate hominis. Lateinisch und deutsch*, eingeleitet von Eugenio Garin, Respublica Literaria, 1 (Bad Homburg v. d. H., Berlin, and Zurich, 1968).

[148] Giovanni Pico della Mirandola, *Conclusiones sive Theses DCCCC, Romae anno 1486 publice disputandae, sed non admissae*, ed. Bohdan Kieszkowski, Travaux d'Humanisme et Renaissance, 131 (Geneva, 1973). Cf. *HL*, XXIII (1974), 394-395.

nists, a transformation which would affect not merely the language of their writings but also their scientific methods, their teaching, and their research. Names such as Viglius, Vesalius, and Gemma Phrysius were to become and remain famous in the history of European culture, while those of their scholastic predecessors are, but for those of a few specialists, completely forgotten. The renewed direct contact with the ancient sources had revitalized the traditional *Septem Artes Liberales* and many other fields of human knowledge.

Much work toward such a profound renewal was accomplished during the first decades of the sixteenth century. Whereas their fifteenth-century forerunners had largely drawn from Italian books, men such as Erasmus, Vives, Dorpius, Torrentinus, Despauterius, and Petrus Pontanus now provided students with their own grammars and readers, including collections of fables, colloquies, and adages, and manuals of letter-writing and eloquence. The same was soon done for Greek by teachers and professors at Louvain, especially Adrianus Amerot and Nicolaus Clenardus. The outstanding quality of their work is proven by the lasting successes of such books as the *Aesopus Dorpii*,[149] the *Elucidarium Poeticum* of Hermannus Torrentinus, the colloquies of Erasmus and Vives, Erasmus's *Adages*, and the grammars of Despauterius and Clenardus. Down to the French Revolution and even later, much of educated Europe learned Latin, Greek, and classical antiquities from these manuals in their original or in adapted forms.

At the same time, these men inaugurated the great era of philology in the Netherlands. To be sure, Agricola had shown the way with his translations from the Greek and some philological work on the younger Pliny. His achievements gained wider notoriety only because of the editorial labours of Jacobus Canter, Alardus of Amsterdam, Petrus Aegidius, and Erasmus. Simultaneously translations, editions, commentaries, and anthologies multiplied on a hitherto unknown scale. It is only natural, and quite in accordance with the prevailing spirit in the North, that the Bible and patristic literature held pride of place in the interests of Netherlandish humanists. Accordingly, invaluable editions of the Bible, Augustine, Jerome, and other Christian writers appeared from the presses of international publishers

---

[149] Paul Thoen, "Aesopus Dorpius. Essai sur l'Esope latin des temps modernes," *Humanistica Lovaniensia*, XIX (1970), 241-316; idem, "Les grands recueils ésopiques latins des XVe et XVIe siècles et leur importance pour les littératures des temps modernes," in *Acta Conventus Neo-Latini Lovaniensis*, 659-679.

at Paris and Basel. To the more conservative members of the scholastic world it was not always evident that philologists had the right to pursue such studies, critical by definition, on sacred texts; and Erasmus, in his preface to Valla's *Adnotationes in Novum Testamentum*,[150] had to explain and justify this by asserting that philological work on the text of the Holy Scriptures was a normal area of research for the *grammaticus*. These editions and commentaries formed the necessary tools prepared for a renovation of Christendom and a reaction against its scholastic interpretation. The story of the new *pietas* surpasses the limits of the phenomenon of humanism and is not treated here.

We do have to look, however, at the new, international dimensions of the Latin school and literature of the Netherlands during the early sixteenth century. Whereas previous contacts had been nearly bilateral between Italy and the Netherlands, we now observe a rapidly growing network of multilateral relations and exchanges. Figures such as Erasmus and Trithemius and their European-wide connections are too well known to be repeated here. We want rather to show by looking at some minor authors that their position, though not the quality of their work and their lasting influence, was not exceptional but normal.

During the first decades of the century, one of the leading humanist poets was Remaclus Arduenna of Florennes. He was educated at Liège and Cologne and so was on friendly terms with other Rhenish humanists, such as Buschius, Gratius, and Johannes Cochlaeus. He went later to London and in 1512 to Paris, where he attended Andrelini's courses and came to know the first Scottish humanist poet, Jacobus Follisius (Foulis), with whom he exchanged some Latin poems. It is true that Remaclus, as a member of the court at Mechlin, held a favoured position from which to build a network of international relations. But we also have evidence that even modest schoolteachers aspired in their instruction to a broadly humanist openness to the world. We have, for example, the list of Latin plays performed in a grammar school at Ghent between 1512 and 1518 under the direction of Eligius Eucharius (Hoeckaert), who had been educated at Paris. The list comprises two ancient pieces, Plautus's *Captivi* and *Stichus*, and several modern dramas: one French, the comedy *Veterator* by Alexander Connibertus; one German,

---

[150] Allen, ep. 182, I, 406-412, here at p. 410.

Reuchlin's *Sergius*; one or more Italian plays, the *Dolotechne* of Bartolo-
meo Zamberti and a *Gravatomachia* [sic], which may be Verardi's
Granatae Obsidio; and an unidentified *Alithia*.[151] Eucharius himself
adapted Petrarch's *Griseldis* for the stage. It is fairly clear from this
programme that the spirit of this school at Ghent was anything
but provincial or conservative; and we have other evidence pointing
to the same frame of mind. Simon Grynaeus, the famous hellenist
of Basel, once visited Bruges and entertained there some educated
men of the school and the chapter of St. Donatian with a description
of his new edition of Aristophanes. A few months later, the schoolboys
performed the *Plutus* in a new Latin version by their master, Adrianus
Chilius, who explains that the existing version by the German,
Venatorius, did not satisfy his taste.[152] Such schoolmasters must
surely have exercised a stimulating influence on their pupils, whose
eyes they directed beyond the city walls to the exciting new world of
the *Respublica Litteratorum*.

Year by year the humanist teachers of the Low Countries increased
their level of participation in this *Respublica*. While in Italy Latin
literature was on the downgrade and was being replaced more and
more by Italian works, the number of *poetae et oratores* in the North
multiplied rapidly after 1500. In the area of poetry alone we find a
wealth of new genres and authors: Petrus Pontanus, a very versatile
writer who made a curious blend of Virgil, Baptista Mantuanus,
and Flemish folklore in his eclogues; Petrus Montanus and Gerardus
Geldenhauer, who wrote moralizing satires; and Jacobus Magdalius
of Gouda, who, among other things, published the first Christian
heroic epistle. Christian epic was attempted even before the turn of
the century by Jacobus Faber at Deventer, who wrote a *De Triumpho
Christi*, an example followed by Ortuinus Gratius in the four books
of his *Triumphus beati Job*.

There is little profit in extending this list further or in surveying
the prose works. It may suffice to point out the growing role of
Netherlandish humanists in the discussions about what constituted
good Latin style. Erasmus's *Ciceronianus* is the first culminating point
in these discussions, unending discussions in which Lipsius was one
day to be a protagonist.

---

[151] M. Grypdonck, "Eligius Houckaert. Een Schoolman uit het begin der XVIe
Eeuw," *De Gulden Passer*, XX (1942), 23-57; XXI (1943), 29-78, here at vol. XX,
pp. 43-44. Cf. Eligius Eucharius, *Grisellis* (Antwerp, 1519), fol. I.ii.r.

[152] Dirk Van Kerchove, "The Latin Translation of Aristophanes's PLUTUS by
Hadrianus Chilius, 1533," *HL*, XXIII (1974), 42-127.

So much is thus clear, that, during the first decades of the sixteenth century, the Italian heritage was thoroughly assimilated in the Netherlands by a solid intellectual minority, whose influence waxed steadily. This does not mean that reception was simple transplantation: the northern soil was too different from that of Italy. Roughly speaking, one can say that the heritage was transmitted and developed along the following lines.

1) The study of antiquity turned more and more into learned philology.

2) A northern counterpart of Italian civic humanism did not come into existence because of the greatly different political context and the rapid spread of the religious-political conflicts of the Reformation era, which absorbed a large part of the intellectual potential. A letter of Vives to Erasmus, written from London on 13 November 1524, bears eloquent testimony to this evolution: "I am astonished at how few editions of ancient texts are now coming out of Germany. Pieces for or against Luther have driven from the hearts of learned men all concern for other literature—so great is the pleasure of watching that fight." [153]

3) In literature, imitation of ancient style and genres increasingly prevailed and in the second half of the sixteenth century finally affected the whole of literary life in Dutch and French. But because most of the literati were clerics and schoolmen, Latin literature retained an overwhelmingly moralising and religious character. Profane literature in the sixteenth century was largely limited to a small number of courtiers and of patricians in the few large towns.

4) The influence of the classical revival in other arts under the influence of humanism is not perceptible in the Netherlands before the second quarter of the sixteenth century, when a few Italian architects began to work in the Low Countries. The art of the century during which humanism came to the Netherlands was Gothic. The Netherlands had no Alberti during this period.

As a final conclusion one can say that, during the entire period under discussion, humanism was the affair of a slowly growing but always limited number of students, teachers, and writers. Many of them did not view humanist studies as an end in itself but as a means

---

[153] Allen, ep. 1513, V, 576-577, here at p. 577, ll. 45-48: "Etiam miror tam raros nunc prodire veterum libros excusos in Germania. Ista vel pro Luthero vel in Lutherum excusserunt de pectoribus studiosorum omnem aliarum litterarum curam: tanta est spectandae pugnae istius dulcedo."

of improving theological studies and Christian life. For this reason, it is better perhaps to speak of humanist Christians than of Christian humanism. This is not merely a matter of terminology but an attempt to define the essential. In their eyes, the fundamental value was not so much a renascence of ancient literature as a renewal of Christian *pietas*, and here lies an abyss between them and the leading Italian *oratores et poetae*.

BIBLIOGRAPHY ON EARLY HUMANISM IN THE NETHERLANDS
SIGLA AND ABBREVIATIONS

GV = Alois Gerlo and Hendrik D. L. Vervliet, *Bibliographie de l'Humanisme des Anciens Pays-Bas, Avec un répertoire bibliographique des humanistes et poètes néo-latins,* Instrumenta humanistica, 3 (Brussels, 1972).

HCT = Henry de Vocht, *History of the Foundation and the Rise of the Collegium Trilingue Lovaniense, 1517-1550,* 4 vols., Humanistica Lovaniensia, 10-13 (Louvain, 1951-55).

HL = *Humanistica Lovaniensia.*

IMU = *Italia Medioevale e Umanistica.*

PT = *Petri Trudonensis catalogus scriptorum Windeshemensium,* editus cura W. Lourdaux et E. Persoons, Universiteit te Leuven — Publicaties op het gebied van de geschiedenis en de filologie, 5ᵉ reeks, deel 3 (Louvain, 1968).

J. IJsewijn, *Collatio* = 'Collatio de laudibus facultatum Lovanii saeculo XV (1435?) habita, nunc primum typis edita a J. IJsewijn et Pl. Lefèvre', in *Zetesis. Bijdragen op het gebied van de klassieke filologie, filosofie, byzantistiek, patrologie en theologie, door collega's en vrienden aangeboden aan prof. dr. Emile de Strijcker naar aanleiding van zijn vijfenzestigste verjaardag* (Antwerp-Utrecht, 1973), pp. 416-35.

Erasmus en Leuven, Catalogus = *(Catalogus van de) Tentoonstelling Erasmus en Leuven,* Leuven, Stedelijk Museum, 17 nov. - 15 dec. 1969.

J. IJsewijn, Henricus de Oesterwijck = Jozef IJsewijn, 'Henricus de Oesterwijck, the First Latin Poet of the University of Louvain (ca. 1430)', *HL,* XVIII (1969), 7-23.

I. SELECT BIBLIOGRAPHY ON EARLY HUMANISM IN THE NETHERLANDS

Johannes Gerardus Rijk Acquoy, *Het klooster te Windesheim en zijn invloed,* 3 vols (Utrecht, 1875-80; reprint: Amsterdam, 1968).

Stephaan Axters, *Geschiedenis van de vroomheid in de Nederlanden,* 4 vols (Antwerp, 1950-60).

Alois Bömer, 'Das literarische Leben in Münster vor der endgültigen Rezeption des Humanismus', in *Aus dem geistigen Leben und Schaffen in Westfalen* (Münster, 1906), pp. 119ff.

Petrus Nicolaas Maria Bot, *Humanisme en Onderwijs in Nederland* (Utrecht, 1955).

Benjamin De Troeyer, *Bio-bibliographia franciscana neerlandica saeculi XVI,* 2 vols (Nieuwkoop, 1969).

Id., *Bio-bibliographia franciscana neerlandica ante saeculum XVI,* 2 vols (Nieuwkoop, 1974).

Henry de Vocht, *History of the Foundation and the Rise of the Collegium Trilingue Lovaniense 1517-1550,* 4 vols, Humanistica Lovaniensia, 10-13 (Louvain, 1951-55).

Eugénie Droz, 'La première réforme scolaire à Munster en Westphalie', in

Ideen und Formen. Festschrift für Hugo Friedrich, herausgegeben von Fritz Schalk (Frankfurt/M. 1965). pp. 111-118.

Georg Ellinger, *Geschichte der neulateinischen Lyrik in den Niederlanden vom Ausgang des fünfzehnten bis zum Beginn des siebzehnten Jahrhunderts* (= Geschichte der neulateinischen Literatur Deutschlands im sechzehnten Jahrhundert, III, 1) (Berlin, 1933; reprint: Berlin, 1969).

Humanistica Lovaniensia, 1-23 (Louvain, 1928-1974).

Jozef IJsewijn, 'The Beginning of Humanistic Literature in Brabant', in *Nationale Erasmus-Herdenking. Handelingen* (Brussels, 1970) pp. 102-12.

Hermann Keussen, *Die Matrikel der Universität Köln 1389-1559*, 4 vols, Publikationen der Gesellschaft für rheinische Geschichtskunde, 8 (Bonn, 1892-1931).

Laurentius Knappert, 'Uit de geschiedenis der groote of Latijnsche School te Leiden', *Jaarboekje voor Geschiedenis en Oudheidkunde van Leiden en Rijnland* (Leiden, 1904).

Karl Krafft and Wilhelm Crecelius, *Beiträge zur Geschichte des Humanismus am Niederrhein und in Westfalen*, 2 vols (Elberfeld, 1870-75).

Johannes Lindeboom, *Het Bijbelsch Humanisme in Nederland* (Leiden, 1913).

Willem Lourdaux, *Moderne Devotie en christelijk humanisme. De geschiedenis van Sint-Maarten te Leuven van 1433 tot het einde der XVIe eeuw*, Universiteit te Leuven — Werken op het gebied van de geschiedenis en de filologie, 5e reeks, 1 (Leuven, 1967).

Jurjen Nanninga Uitterdijk, *Geschiedenis der voormalige abdij der Bernardijnen te Aduard* (Groningen, 1870; reprint: Groningen, 1973).

Marcel A. Nauwelaerts, *Latijnse school en Onderwijs te 's-Hertogenbosch tot 1629*, Bijdragen tot de geschiedenis van het Zuiden van Nederland, 30 (Tilburg, 1974).

Josef Bernhard Nordhoff, *Denkwürdigkeiten aus dem Münsterischen Humanismus. Mit einer Anlage über das frühere Press- und Bücherwesen Westfalens* (Münster, 1874). See also the important review by D. Reichling, *Pick's Monatsschrift für die Geschichte Westdeutschlands IV* (Trier, 1878), 486-515.

Regnerus Richardus Post, *The Modern Devotion. Confrontation with Reformation and Humanism* (Leiden, 1968).

Id., 'Het Sint-Bernhardsklooster te Aduard. Een bijdrage tot de geschiedenis der kloosters in de provincie Groningen', *Archief voor de Geschiedenis van het Aartsbisdom Utrecht*, XLVII (1922), 168-277; XLVIII (1923), 1-236.

Florus Prims, *Onze-Lieve-Vrouw-Priorij Korsendonk*, Campinia Sacra, 7 (Antwerp, 1947).

Dietrich Reichling, *Die Reform der Domschule zu Münster im Jahre 1500* (Berlin, 1900).

Edmond Reusens, Jos Wils and Arnold Schillings, *Matricule de l'Université de Louvain*, 10 parts in 15 vols, Académie Royale des Sciences, des Lettres et des Beaux-Arts de Belgique — Commission Royale d'Histoire, 32 (Brussels, 1903-1969).

Alphonse Roersch, *L'humanisme belge à l'époque de la Renaissance. Etudes et portraits*, 1e série (Brussels, 1910); 2e série (Louvain, 1933).

Michael Schoengen, *Die Schule von Zwolle von ihren Anfängen bis zu dem Auftreten des Humanismus* (Freiburg i.B., 1898).

Id., ed., *Jacobus Traiecti alias de Voecht, Narratio de inchoatione domus clericorum in Zwollis, met akten en bescheiden betreffende dit fraterhuis*, Werken uitgegeven door het Historisch Genootschap, gevestigd te Utrecht, 3e serie, 13 (Amsterdam, 1908).

Wolfgang Stammler, *Die deutsche Dichtung von der Mystik zum Barock, 1400-1600*, 2nd ed. (Stuttgart, 1950).

Hendrik Enno Van Gelder, *Geschiedenis der Latijnsche school te Alkmaar. Eerste gedeelte: De Groote School tot 1572* (Alkmaar, 1905).

II. BIBLIOGRAPHY OF PERSONS AND BIOGRAPHICAL DATA

ADORNO (Family):
Albert Derolez, 'Vroeg humanisme en middeleeuwse bibliotheken. De bibliotheek van de Adorne's en de Jeruzalemkapel te Brugge', *Tijdschrift voor Geschiedenis*, LXXXV (1972), 161-170.
Palémon Glorieux, 'Un chanoine de Saint-Pierre de Lille, Jean Adourne', *Bulletin du comité flamand de France*, XVIII (1971), 295-324.

ADRIANUS, Matthaeus (ca. 1475-post 1521):
HCT I, 241-55, 334-9, 369-75, 534-42.

AEGIDIUS, Petrus (= Peter Gillis) (1486-1533):
Marcel A. Nauwelaerts, 'Un ami anversois de More et d'Erasme: Petrus Aegidius', *Moreana*, XV-XVI (1967), 83-96.
Id., Aegidius Petrus, in *Nationaal Biografisch Woordenboek*, IV (1970), coll. 4-8.

AGRICOLA, Rudolphus (1444-1485):
GV, pp. 234-5, nn. 3055-64.
Marcel A. Nauwelaerts, *Rodolphus Agricola* (The Hague, 1963).
Id., 'Rodolphe Agricola et le pétrarquisme aux Pays-Bas', in *The Late Middle Ages and the Dawn of Humanism outside Italy. Proceedings of the International Conference Louvain May 11-13, 1970*, edited by Gerard Verbeke and Jozef IJsewijn (Leuven-The Hague, 1972), pp. 171-181.
Edzo Hendrik Waterbolk, *Een Hond in het Bad. Enige aspecten van de verhouding tussen Erasmus en Agricola* (Groningen, 1966).
Id., 'Deux poèmes inconnus de Rodolphe Agricola?', *HL*, XXI (1972), 37-49.

ALARDUS, Amstelredamus (1491-1544):
GV, p. 237, nn. 3085-90.

ALEANDRO, Girolamo (1480-1542):
Jules Paquier, *L'Humanisme et la Réforme. Jérôme Aléandre, de sa naissance à la fin de son séjour à Brindes (1480-1529), avec son portrait, ses armes, un facsimile de son écriture, et un catalogue de ses oeuvres* (Diss. Paris, 1900).
Ernest Jovy, *François Tissard et Jérôme Aléandre. Contribution à l'histoire des origines des études grecques en France*, 3 vols (Vitry-le-François, 1898-1913).
Jean Hoyoux, *Le carnet de voyage de Jérôme Aléandre en France et à Liège (1510-1516)*, Bibliothèque de l'Institut Historique Belge de Rome, fasc. XVIII (Brussels-Rome, 1969).

AMEROT, Adrianus (end 15th c.-d. 1560):
GV, p. 238, n. 3101.

ANDRELINI, Fausto (1462-1518):
The Eclogues of Faustus Andrelinus and Joannes Arnolletus, Edited by Wilfred P. Mustard (Baltimore, 1918).
Godelieve Tournoy-Thoen, 'Deux épîtres inédites de Fausto Andrelini et l'auteur du "Iulius Exclusus" ', *HL*, XVIII (1969), 43-76.
Id., 'Publius Faustus Andrelinus Foroliviensis. Leven, Werk en Kritische geannoteerde editie van de *Livia*', 2 vols (unpublished doctoral diss., Univ. of Leuven, 1973).

ANGELUS de Curibus Sabinis: cf. CURIBUS, Angelus de.

ANIANUS: cf. COUSSERE, Anianus.

ARDUENNA, Remaclus (ca. 1480-1524):
GV, p. 240, n° 3117. See also below: FOLLISIUS.
Henry de Vocht, *Jerome de Busleyden, Founder of the Louvain Collegium Trilingue.*

His Life and Writings Edited for the First Time in their Entirety from the
Unpublished Manuscripts, III, 5 (Cinrinhonie, 1950), pp. 218-22.

ARNALDUS de Bruxella: cf. BRUXELLA.

ARNOLDUS DE Gheel: cf. GHEEL.

AURELIUS, Cornelius, (= C. Goudanus = C. Gerardi) (ca. 1460-post 1523):
GV, p. 241, n⁰ 3123. Cf. J. IJsewijn, art. cited n. 87 above.
P. Debongnie, 'Corneille Gérard à Saint-Victor', *Nederlandsch Archief voor
Kerkgeschiedenis*, n.s. XVII (1924), 161-178.
Philippus C. Molhuysen, 'Cornelius Aurelius', *Nederlandsch Archief voor
Kerkgeschiedenis*, n.s., II (1903), 1-35, and IV (1907), 54-73.

AYMO de Poypone: cf. POYPONE, Aymo de.

AYTTA, Viglius ab (1507-1577):
GV, p. 242, nn. 3129-36a.

BADIUS, Judocus (1462-1535):
GV, p. 243, nn. 3142-45. See Addenda.

BALBUS, Hieronymus (ca. 1460-ca. 1535):
Percy Stafford Allen, 'Hieronymus Balbus in Paris', *The English Historical
Review*, XVII (1902), 417-28.
G. Rill, 'Balbi Girolamo', in *Dizionario Biografico degli Italiani*, V (Rome,
1963), 370-4.

BARBIRIANUS, Jacobus (Jacques Barbiriau) (d. 1491):
Florus Prims, *Antwerpiensia 1938 (Twaalfde Reeks). Losse Bijdragen tot de
Antwerpse Geschiedenis* (Antwerp, 1939), pp. 140-52.

BAYART, Jan (d.1481):
Albert Derolez, *Corpus Catalogorum Belgii. De middeleeuwse bibliotheekscatalogi
der Zuidelijke Nederlanden, I: Provincie West-Vlaanderen*, Verhandelingen
van de Koninklijke Vlaamse Academie voor Wetenschappen, Letteren
en Schone Kunsten van België, Klasse der Letteren, jaargang XXVIII,
nr. 61 (Brussels, 1966), pp. 128-37.
Raf De Keyser, 'Het boekenbezit en het boekengebruik in de seculiere
kapittels van de Zuidelijke Nederlanden tijdens de Middeleeuwen',
in *Studies over het boekenbezit en boekengebruik in de Nederlanden vóór 1600*,
Archief- en Bibliotheekwezen van België, Extranummer 11 (Brussels,
1974), 9-69 (p. 21).

BEISSEL, Judocus (ca. 1450-1505):
HCT I, passim.

BEKEN, Pieter van der: cf. RIVO, Petrus de.

BERCHEN, William of (1415/20-ca. 1481):
GV, p. 249, n⁰ 3208.
P. J. Begheyn, 'Willem van Berchen (1415/20-ca. 1481)', *Numaga*, XVIII
(1971), 224-228.
Wilhelmus de Berchen, *De nobili principatu Gelrie et eius origine*. E codice
archetypo, qui Noviomagi servatur, descripsit, vulgavit breviterque
annotavit Ludolf Anne Jan Wilt Sloet van de Beele ('s-Gravenhage,
1870).
De Gelderse kroniek van Willem van Berchen. Naar het Hamburgse handschrift
uitgegeven over de jaren 1343-1481 door Albertus Johannes De Mooy
(Arnhem, 1950).

BERGEN, Henry of (d. 1502):
Opus Epistolarum D. Erasmi, I, pp. 160-1.

BERSELIUS, Pascasius (ca. 1480-1535):
GV, p. 250, n⁰ 3218.
HCT I, 493-500.

BIONDO, Flavio (1392-1463):
Riccardo Fubini, 'Biondo, Flavio', in *Dizionario Biografico degli Italiani*, X (Rome, 1968), pp. 536-9.
BLOCK, Johannes (d. 1453):
HCT I, 116-8.
BOENDALE, Jan van (ca. 1282-1350):
Gerard Petrus Maria Knuvelder, *Handboek tot de geschiedenis der Nederlandse letterkunde*. Deel I, Vijfde, geheel herziene druk ('s-Hertogenbosch, 1970), pp. 244-5.
BOSTIUS, Arnoldus (1445-1499):
GV, p. 256, n⁰ 3279.
Eamon R. Carroll, *The Marian Theology of A. Bostius, o. carm. (1445-1499)* (Rome, 1962).
BOVIS, Joannes Leonardus De (De Bonis = Delbene?) (*fl.* ca. 1465):
Matricule de l'Université de Louvain, publiée par Joseph Wils, II (Brussels, 1946), p. 134.
BOVILLUS, Carolus (ca. 1478/9-1556):
Charles de Bovelles, *Sur les langues vulgaires et la variété de la langue française — Liber de differentia vulgarium linguarum et Gallici sermonis varietate (1533)*. Texte latin, traduction française et notes par Colette Dumont-Demaizière, Bibliothèque française et romane, D. 5 (Paris, 1973).
BRANT, Sebastian (1458-1521):
W. Gilbert, 'Sebastian Brant Conservative Humanist', *Archiv für Reformationsgeschichte*, XLVI (1955), 143-67.
Richard Newald, 'Sebastian Brant', in *Probleme und Gestalten des deutschen Humanismus* (Berlin, 1963), pp. 368-87.
José Jiménez Delgado, 'De Sebastiano Brant nobili scriptore Argentoratensi (1457-1521)', *Palaestra Latina*, XXXIX (1969), 97-108.
Id., ' "Stultifera Navis" pervulgata Sebastiani Brant satura', *Palaestra Latina*, XXXIX (1969), 145-54.
BRUGIS, Henricus de (*fl.* ca. 1450):
cf. *Epistolario di Guarino Veronese*, raccolto ordinato illustrato da Remigio Sabbadini, 3 vols (Venice, 1915-19; reprint: Turin, 1967), III, 512.
BRUNI, Ludovico (ca. 1434-1508):
HCT I, 163-66.
Erasmus en Leuven. Catalogus, pp. 145-6, nn. 130-1.
BRUXELLA, Arnaldus de (ca. 1430-ca. 1500):
Mariano Fava - Giovanni Bresciano, *La stampa a Napoli nel secolo XV*, Sammlung Bibliothekwissenschaftlicher Arbeiten, 32-33, 2 vols, (Leipzig, 1911-12; reprint: Nendeln/Liechtenstein-Wiesbaden, 1968), I, 47-56 and II, 67-87.
BRUXELLA, Radulphus de: cf. ZEELANDIA, Radulphus de.
BUDERICK, Arnoldus (d. 1444):
PT, pp. 23-7, n⁰ 14.
BURRUS, Petrus (1427/30-1505/7):
GV, p. 262, n. 3335.
BUSCH, Johannes (1399-1479):
PT, pp. 83-8, n⁰ 56.
BUSSCHIUS, Hermannus (1468-1534):
GV, p. 264, n⁰ 3347.
BUT, Adrianus de (d. 1488):
August Potthast, *Repertorium Fontium Historiae Medii Aevi II (Fontes A-B)* (Rome, 1967), p. 129.

CALIGATOR/CALICULA (Coussemaecker), Johannes (b. 1320):

[illegible] . . . *[illegible] Lovaniensium libri XIV*, 2 vols (Brussels, 1861), II, 700-701.

Wilhelm Berges, *Die Fürstenspiegel des hohen und späten Mittelalters*, Schriften des Reichsinstituts für ältere deutsche Geschichtskunde (Monumenta Germaniae historica), 2 (Leipzig, 1938), p. 348.

CAMPO, Heimericus de (d. 1460):

Rudolf Haubst, in *Lexikon für Theologie und Kirche*, V (1960), col. 320.

Zenon Kałuza, 'Trois listes des oeuvres de Heimeric de Campo dans le "Catalogue du Couvent Rouge" (Rouge Cloître)', *Mediaevalia Philosophica Polonorum*, XVII (1973), 3-20.

CANTER, Andreas, Jacobus and Johannes:

HCT I, 132-5.

CELE, Johannes (d. 1417):

Regnerus Richardus Post, *The Modern Devotion* (Leiden, 1968), passim.

CELTIS, Konrad (1452-1508): cf. *HL*, XXIII (1974), 398-399.

CHASTELLAIN, Georges (1405-1475):

Michel Prevost, 'Chastellain, Georges', in *Dictionnaire de Biographie française*, VIII (Paris, 1959), coll. 739-40.

Verdun Louis Saulnier, 'Sur George Chastelain poète et les rondeaux qu'on lui attribue', in *Mélanges de langue et de littérature du Moyen Age et de la Renaissance offerts à Jean Frappier* . . ., vol. 2 (Geneva, 1970), pp. 987-1000.

CLENARDUS, Nicolaus (1495-1542):

GV, p. 273, nn. 3427-32.

CLOPPER, Nicolaus, sr. (d. 1472):

Philippus C. Boeren, 'De bibliotheek van de Brusselse kanunnik Nicolaus Clopper sr. (1472)', *Het Boek*, N.R. XXX (1949-51), 175-225.

Raf De Keyser, 'Het boekenbezit en het boekengebruik in de seculiere kapittels van de Zuidelijke Nederlanden tijdens de middeleeuwen', in *Studies over het boekenbezit en boekengebruik in de Nederlanden vóór 1600*, Archief- en Bibliotheekwezen in België, Extranummer 11 (Brussels, 1974), 9-69 (p. 21).

COCHLAEUS, Johannes (1479-1549):

Martin Spahn, *Johannes Cochläus. Ein Lebensbild aus der Zeit der Kirchenspaltung* (Berlin, 1898; reprint: Nieuwkoop, 1964).

Brevis Germanie Descriptio (1512). Lateinisch und deutsch, Herausgegeben und übersetzt von Karl Langosch (Darmstadt, 1960).

COLUMBELLA, Antonio — de Recaneto: cf. RECANETO, Antonio.

COLONIENSIS, Bartholomaeus (1460-1514):

GV, p. 246, n⁰ 3169 (s.v. Bartholomaeus); p. 275, n⁰ 3452 (s.v. Coloniensis).

Bartholomaeus Coloniensis, *Epistola Mythologica. Humoreske aus der Zeit des deutschen Frühhumanismus*, Neu herausgegeben, mit Anmerkungen versehen und übersetzt von Dietrich Reichling (Berlin, 1897).

CORDUS, Euricius (1486-1535):

Epigrammata. Bücher I-III, herausgegeben von Karl Krause (Berlin, 1892).

Johannes Cornelis Arens, 'Descriptio per dialogismum: Revius en Euricius Cordus', *Spiegel der Letteren*, VI (1962), 133-134.

H. Vogel, *Euricius Cordus in seinen Epigrammen* (Inaug. Diss. Greifswald, 1932).

G. Wegemann, '*Der Humanist Euricius Cordus, 1486 bis 1535. Sein Leben und Wirken im Urteil der Nachwelt*' (Diss. dact. Erfurt, 1943).

CORNELIUS 1) Aurelius: cf. AURELIUS.

2) de Mera: cf. MERA, Cornelius de.

COUSSEMAECKER, Jan: cf. CALIGATOR, Johannes.

COUSSERE, Anianus (d. 1462):
Joannes Franciscus Foppens, *Bibliotheca Belgica*, 2 vols (Brussels, 1739), I, p. 63.
August Potthast, *Repertorium Fontium Historiae Medii Aevi* III (Rome, 1970), pp. 262-63.
CRABBE, Jan (1457-1488):
Nicolaas Huyghebaert, 'Trois manuscrits de Jean Crabbe, abbé des Dunes', *Scriptorium*, XXIII (1969), 232-242.
De vijfhonderdste verjaring van de boekdrukkunst in de Nederlanden. Catalogus van de tentoonstelling in de Koninklijke Bibliotheek Albert I (Brussels, 1973), pp. 21-23, n⁰ 13.
CREMENSIS, Franciscus (*fl.* ca. 1490):
HCT I, 173-4.
CROCKAERT, Petrus (1470-1553):
GV, p. 279, nn. 3492-3.
CURIBUS, Angelus de — Sabinis (d. between 1471 and 1500):
Giovanni Mercati, 'Le notizie del Sabellico e di Matteo Herben circa Angelo Sabino ed il poema *De excidio civitatis Leodiensis*', in *Ultimi contributi alla storia degli umanisti* II, Studi e Testi, 91 (Città del Vaticano, 1939), pp. 17-23.
DECANUS, Traiectensis: cf. HEES, Wilhelmus.
DESPAUTERIUS, Joannes (ca. 1460-1520):
GV, pp. 455-6, nn. 5315-6.
HCT I, 206-14.
DEULIN, Henricus — de Minorivilla (*fl.* ca. 1480):
HCT I, 128-9.
DIONYSIUS, Carthusianus (d. 1471):
GV, p. 286, nn. 3554-7.
Victor Scholderer, 'The Works of Dionysius Cartusianus', in *Fifty Essays in Fiftheenth- and Sixteenth-Century Scholarship*, edited by Dennis E. Rhodes (Amsterdam, 1966), pp. 271-4.
DOMINICUS de Flandria: cf. FLANDRIA, Dominicus de.
DORLANDUS, Petrus (1454-1507):
GV, p. 288, n⁰ 3574.
DORPIUS, Martinus (1485-1525):
GV, p. 288, nn. 3576-77a.
DOUSA, Janus, sr (1554-1609):
GV, p. 287, nn. 3568-69.
DOUSA, Janus, filius (1571-1596):
GV, p. 288, n⁰ 3570.
Jan Adrianus Van Dorsten, *Poets, Patrons and Professors. Sir Philips Sidney, Daniel Rogers and the Leiden Humanists* (Leiden, 1962).
DYNTER, Edmund van - (ca. 1382-1448):
Jozef IJsewijn, *Henricus de Oesterwijck*, 9-10.
Chronica nobilissimorum ducum Lotharingiae et Brabantiae ac regum Francorum auctore magistro Edmundo de Dynter in sex libros distincta, ... edidit ... Petrus Franciscus Xaverius De Ram, Publications de la Commission Royale d'Histoire de Belgique — Collection de chroniques belges inédites, 8, 4 vols (Brussels, 1854-60).
Cf. *Erasmus en Leuven. Catalogus*, p. 80, n⁰ 58.
EECHOUT, Hadrianus van (d. 1499):
Percy Stafford Allen, 'Letters of Arnold Bostius', *The English Historical Review*, XXXIV (1919), 225-36 (p. 226).

De vijfhonderdste verjaring van de boekdrukkunst in de Nederlanden Cataloo
(Brussels, 1973), p. 121, n° 59.

EUCHARIUS, Eligius (Hoeckaert) (ca. 1488-1544):
GV, p. 366, nn. 4389-90.

EUSTACHIUS, de Zichenis: cf. ZICHENIS, Eustachius de.

FABER, Jacobus (1473-d. post 1517):
GV, p. 329, n. 3999.

FABRI, Anselmus, of Breda (d. 1449):
Placide Lefèvre, 'Une lettre de Philippe le Bon en faveur de la création d'une
faculté de théologie à l'université de Louvain (10 novembre [1431])',
Ephemerides Theologicae Lovanienses, XL (1964), 491-494.
Jozef IJsewijn, *Collatio*, p. 417.

FICHET, Guillaume (1433-d. post 1490):
Franco Simone, 'Guillaume Fichet, retore ed umanista', *Atti della R. Accademia delle Scienze di Torino*, serie II, vol. 69, parte II (1938), 103-144.
Jacques Monfrin, 'Les lectures de Guillaume Fichet et Jean Heynlin d'après
le registre de prêt de la Bibliothèque de la Sorbonne', *Bibliothèque de
l'Humanisme et Renaissance*, XVII (1955), 7-23, 145-153.

FLANDRIA, Dominicus de (ca. 1425-1479):
Thomas Kaeppeli, *Scriptores ordinis praedicatorum Medii Aevi*, I (Rome, 1970),
pp. 315-16.
Alamanno Rinuccini, *Lettere ed orazioni*, a cura di Vito R. Giustiniani (Firenze,
1953), pp. 136-138.
Paul O. Kristeller, 'The Contribution of Religious Orders to Renaissance
Thought', *The American Benedictine Review*, XXI (1970), 1-55 (p. 40).

FLORIO, Francesco (ca. 1428-ca. 1490):
Gilbert Tournoy, 'De Latijnse prozanovelle in de Italiaanse Renaissance',
2 vols (Unpublished doctoral dissertation. University of Leuven,
1974), I, 317-345 and II, 189-247.
Lionello Sozzi, 'Petrarca, Tardif e Denys de Harsy (con una nota su Francesco
Florio)', *Studi Francesi*, XLIII (1971), pp. 78-82.

FOLLISIUS, Jacobus (James Foulis) (ca. 1485-1549):
Jozef IJsewijn and Douglas F. S. Thomson, 'The Latin Poems of Jacobus
Follisius or James Foulis of Edinburgh', *HL*, XXIV (1975) [in the press].

FRANCISCUS (Francesco), da Crema: cf. CREMENSIS.

FREDERIKS, Wilhelmus (ca. 1450-1527):
Johannes Lindeboom, *Het Bijbelsch Humanisme in Nederland* (Leiden, 1913),
passim.
Opus Epistolarum D. Erasmi, IV, ep. 1200, pp. 482-485.

GAGUIN, Robert (1431-1501/2):
GV, p. 335, nn. 4054-57.

GANSFORT, Wessel (ca. 1419-1489):
GV, p. 336, nn. 4064-69.
Wessel Gansfort, *Opera* (Groningen, 1614; reprint: Nieuwkoop, 1966).
Anne Jacob Persijn, *Wessel Gansfort, "De oratione dominica" in een dietse
bewerking* (Assen, 1964).

GARSIIS, Lodovico de (first half 15th c.):
HCT I, 131-132.

GEILHOVEN, Arnoldus (ca. 1480-1542):
PT, pp. 27-31, n⁰ 15.
Nicholas Mann, 'Arnold Geilhoven: an Early Disciple of Petrarch in the
Low Countries', *Journal of the Warburg and Courtauld Institutes*, XXXII
(1969), 73-108.

GELDENHAUER, Gerardus (1482-1542):
GV, p. 337, nn. 4074-78.
GEMMA, Frisius (1508-1555):
GV, p. 338, nn. 4086-90.
GERARDI: cf. AURELIUS.
GERARDUS de Lisa: cf. LISA, G. de.
GHEEL, Arnoldus de, Buscoducensis (ca. 1400-ca. 1460):
Emile Van Balberghe, 'Un manuscrit de la *Vitae Petrarchae* de Giannozzo Manetti (Bruxelles, 11466-78)', *HL*, XXII (1973), 77-82.
GIELEMANS, Johannes (d. 1487):
Franz Unterkircher, 'Maximilian I., "Dux Brabantinorum", im Historiologium Brabantinorum des Johannes Gielemans', in *Texts & Manuscripts. Essays Presented to G. I. Lieftinck*, 2 (Amsterdam, 1972), pp. 56-60.
GILLIS, Peter: cf. AEGIDIUS, Petrus.
GODEFRIDUS, de Traiecto: cf. TRAIECTO, Godefridus de.
GOUDANUS: cf. AURELIUS.
GRATIADEI, Antonius (d. 1491):
HCT I, 176-178.
Jan Öberg, *Notice et extraits du manuscrit Q 19 (XVIe s.) de Strängnäs*, Acta Universitatis Stockholmiensis — Studia Latina Stockholmiensia, 16 (Stockholm, 1968), pp. 8-12.
Joseph Bruno Marie Kervyn de Lettenhove, *Chroniques relatives à l'histoire de la Belgique sous la domination des ducs de Bourgogne (Textes latins)*, 3 vols, Académie Royale des Sciences, des Lettres et des Beaux-Arts de Belgique, Commission Royale d'Histoire, 12 (Brussels, 1870-76), III, 508-514.
GRATIUS, Ortuinus (1480-1542):
GV, p. 347, nn. 4182-4.
GROOTE, Geert (1340-1384):
Georgette Epiney-Burgard, *Gérard Grote (1340-1384) et les débuts de la Dévotion Moderne*, Veröffentlichungen des Instituts für europäische Geschichte Mainz, 54 (Wiesbaden, 1970).
Regnerus Richardus Post, *The Modern Devotion* (Leiden, 1968), passim.
GRUITRODE, Jacobus de (d. 1475):
Matthaeus Verjans, 'Jacobus van Gruitrode. Karthuizer (d. 1475), *Ons Geestelijk Erf*, V (1931), 435-470.
Cf. P. F. J. Obbema, *Een Deventer bibliotheekcatalogus van het einde der vijftiende eeuw*, Archief- en Bibliotheekwezen in België, Extranummer 8, 2 vols (Brussels, 1973), II, 159-160, 162-163, 166.
HAARLEM, Henricus de (d. 1496):
Dennis E. Rhodes, 'The Incunabula of Siena', in *Essays in Honour of Victor Scholderer*, edited by D. E. Rhodes (Mainz, 1970), pp. 337-348.
HALOINUS, Georgius (ca. 1473-1536):
GV, p. 359, n⁰ 4318.
Constant Matheeussen, 'Een 16e-eeuwse aanval op de grammatica: de *Restauratio Linguae Latinae* van Georgius Haloinus (1533)', 2 vols (unpublished doctoral diss., University of Leuven, 1974).
HANERON, Antonius (ca. 1400-1490):
HCT I, 120-124, 284-285.
Carlo Declercq, 'Oeuvres inédites d'Antoine Haneron', *De Gulden Passer*, VII (1929), 103-109.
Henri Stein, 'Un diplomate bourguignon du XVe siècle: Antoine Haneron', *Bibliothèque de l'Ecole des Chartes*, XCVIII (1937), 283-348.
Gerard Isaac Lieftinck, 'Antoine Haneron introduisant l'écriture humanistique

dans les Pays-Bas', in *Classical, Mediaeval and Renaissance Studies in Honor of B. L. Ullman*, II, (Rome, 1964), pp. 283-284.

George Duncan Painter, 'The Printer of Haneron', *Gutenberg-Jahrbuch*, 1967, 61-65.

Jozef Vindevoghel, 'Haneron Antoon', in *Nieuw Biografisch Woordenboek*, III (Brussels, 1968), coll. 374-377.

Critical Edition in preparation by Mrs Jacqueline IJsewijn-Jacobs.

HEES, Wilhelmus (= Willem van Heze = Decanus Traiectensis) (d. 1477):

Antonie Johannes Maria Kunst, 'De Utrechtse deken en de rede van "Cicero" ', *Jaarboekje van "Oud-Utrecht"*, 1965, 25-41.

Id., 'Die Lex XII Tabularum VIII, 26 und der Decanus Traiectensis', *Zeitschrift der Savigny Stiftung für Rechtsgeschichte, Romanistische Abteilung*, LXXXII (1965), 329-340.

Lotte and Wytze Hellinga, 'Wilhelmus Hees, Printer or Bibliophile?', in *Essays in Honour of Victor Scholderer*, edited by Dennis E. Rhodes (Mainz, 1970), pp. 182-195.

HEGIUS, Alexander (1433-1498):

GV, pp. 361-362, nn. 4343-47.

Jozef IJsewijn, 'Alexander Hegius (d. 1498), *Invectiva in Modos Significandi*', *Forum for Modern Language Studies*, VII (1971), 299-318. *HL*, XXIII (1974), 334.

Johannes Lindeboom, *Het Bijbelsch Humanisme in Nederland* (Leiden, 1913), pp. 70-81.

Ernst Wilhelm Kohls, 'Zur Frage der Schulträgerschaft der Brüder vom gemeinsamen Leben und zum Rektoratsbeginn des Alexander Hegius in Deventer', *Jahrbuch des Vereins für Westfälische Kirchengeschichte*, LXI (1968), 33-43.

Critical edition of his *Dialogi* and *Carmina* in preparation by Lawrence J. Johnson, Assistant Professor, Dept. of English, University of Texas at El Paso.

HEIMERICUS, de Campo: cf. CAMPO, Heimericus de.

HEINSIUS, Daniël (1580-1655):

GV, p. 362, nn. 4348-51.

HEINSIUS, Nicolaus (1620-1681):

GV, p. 362, nr. 4352-56a.

HENRICUS, de Brugis: cf. BRUGIS, Henricus de.

HENRICUS, de Haarlem: cf. HAARLEM, Henricus de.

HENRICUS, de Leuwis (van Leeuwen): cf. DIONYSIUS, Cartusianus.

HENRICUS, de Merica: cf. MERICA, Henricus de.

HENRICUS, de Oesterwijck: cf. OESTERWIJCK, Henricus de.

HENRICUS, van Zomeren: cf. ZOMEREN, Henricus van.

HENRY, of Bergen: cf. BERGEN, Henry of.

HERBENUS, Matthaeus, Traiectensis (1451-1538):

Herbeni Traiectensis de natura cantus ac miraculis vocis. Eingeleitet und herausgegeben von Joseph Smits van Waesberghe, Beiträge zur rheinischen Musikgeschichte, 22 (Köln, 1957).

Giovanni Mercati, 'Le notizie del Sabellico e di Matteo Herben circa Angelo Sabino ed il suo poema "De excidio civitatis Leodiensis" ', in *Ultimi contributi alla storia degli umanisti* II (Città del Vaticano, 1939), pp. 17-23.

Hubert Wouters, 'Mattheus Herbenus Traiectensis, een humanist van het eerste uur', in *Grensland en Bruggehoofd* (Assen, 1970), pp. 77-156.

G. J. M. Bartelink, 'Bemerkungen über die Quellen und Zitate in der Schrift "De Natura cantus ac miraculis vocis" von Herbenus Traiectensis', *HL*, XXI (1972), 51-64.

Opuscules de Mathieu Herbenus, concernant les antiquités de Maestricht, publiées par M. le chanoine Petrus Franciscus Xaverius De Ram (Brussels, 1846).

HERMONYMUS, Georgius (ca. 1450-ca. 1510):

Henri Omont, 'Georges Hermonyme de Sparta, maître de grec à Paris et copiste de manuscrits', *Mémoires de la Société d'Histoire de Paris et de l'Ile de France*, XII (1885), 65-98.

HERXEN, Dirc van (1381-1457):

Philippina Henriette Jacomina Knierim, *Dirc van Herxen (1381-1457), rector van het Zwolsche Fraterhuis* (Amsterdam, 1926).

Jan Deschamps, 'De dietse collatieboeken van Dirc van Herxen (1381-1457), rector van het Zwolse fraterhuis', *Handelingen van het 23e Vlaams Filologengencongres* (Brussel, 1-3 april 1959), 186-193.

HOECKAERT/HOUCKAERT, Elooi: cf. EUCHARIUS, Eligius.

HOCKEMA, Balthasar (*fl.* ca. 1505):

HCT I, 187-189.

HOUDELEM, Joris van (*fl.* ca. 1440):

Gerard Isaac Lieftinck, 'Antoine Haneron introduisant l'écriture humanistique dans les Pays-Bas', in *Classical, Mediaeval and Renaissance Studies in Honor of B. L. Ullman*, II (Rome, 1964), pp. 283-284.

HUGO van Rimen: cf. RIMEN, Hugo van.

IMPENS, Petrus (d. 1523):

PT, pp. 189-191, n⁰ 127.

ISCHYRIUS, Chr. (d. post 1536):

GV, p. 374, nn. 4474-77.

Vom Sterben des reichen Mannes. Die Dramen von Everyman, Homulus, Hecastus und dem Kauffmann nach Drucken des 16. Jahrhunderts, übersetzt, herausgegeben und eingeleitet von H. Wiemken, Sammlung Dieterich, 298 (Bremen, 1965).

R. Vos, 'Elckerlyc — Everyman — Homulus — Der Sunden Loin ist der Toid', *Tijdschrift voor Nederlandse Taal- en Letterkunde*, LXXXII (1966), 129-143.

JACOBUS, de Gruitrode: cf. GRUITRODE, Jacobus de.

JOANNES, Leonardus de Bovis: cf. BOVIS.

JOANNES, de Meerhout: cf. MEERHOUT, Joannes de.

JOANNES, Paludanus: cf. PALUDANUS, Joannes.

JOANNES, de Palude: cf. PALUDE, Joannes de.

JOANNES, de Los: cf. PEECKS, Jan.

JOANNES, de Veris: cf. VERIS, Joannes de.

JORDAENS, Adam (1449-1494):

PT, p. 1, nr. 1.

Jozef IJsewijn — Willem Lourdaux — Ernest Persoons, 'Adam Jordaens (1449-1494), an Early Humanist at Louvain', *HL*, XXII (1973), 83-99.

JORIS, van Oedelem: cf. HOUDELEM, Joris van.

KEMENERUS, Timannus (*fl.* beginning 16th c.):

Jozef IJsewijn, 'Alexander Hegius', 302, 315-318.

Joseph Frey, Die Thätigkeit Münsterischer Humanisten auf dem Gebiete der lateinischen Syntax', in *76. Jahresbericht über das kgl. Paulinische Gymnasium zu Münster i.W. (1895-96)* (Münster, 1896), pp. 1-17.

KEMPIS, Thomas a (d. 1471):

PT, pp. 202-211, n⁰ 138.

Thomas a Kempis en de Moderne Devotie. Tentoonstellingscatalogus (Brussel, Koninklijke Bibliotheek, 1971).

Bijdragen over Thomas a Kempis en de Moderne Devoten uitgegeven ter gelegenheid van de vijfhonderdste sterfdag van Thomas a Kempis († 1471) (Brussel-Zwolle, 1971).

Kᴇʀᴄᴋᴍᴇɪsᴛᴇʀ, Johannes (ca. 1450-ca. 1500):
Johannes Kerckmeister, *Codrus. Ein neulateinisches Drama aus dem Jahre 1485*, herausgegeben von Lothar Mundt, Ausgaben deutscher Literatur des XV. bis XVIII. Jahrhunderts, Reihe Drama III (Berlin, 1969).
Eugénie Droz, 'Les *Regule* de Remigius, Münster en Westph., 1485', in *Miscellanea T. de Marinis*, II (Città del Vaticano, 1964), pp. 265-280.
Id., 'La première réforme scolaire à Münster en Westphalie', in *Ideen und Formen. Festschrift für Hugo Friedrich*, hrsg. von Fritz Schalk (Frankfurt/M., 1965), pp. 61-78.

Lᴀᴄᴜ, Robertus a (Van De Poel) (d. 1483):
HCT I, 175.

Lᴀɴɢɪᴜs, Rudolphus (1438/9-1519):
Adalbert Parmet, *Rudolf von Langen. Leben und gesammelte Gedichte des ersten Münsterischen Humanisten. Ein Beitrag zur Geschichte des Humanismus in Deutschland* (Münster, 1869).
Wilhelm Crecelius, 'Epistolae Rudolfi Langii sex', in *Programm des Gymnasiums zu Elberfeld* (Elberfeld, 1876), pp. 3-12.
Karl Löffler, 'Rudolf von Langen', in *Westfälische Lebensbilder*. Hauptreihe, Band I (Münster, 1930), 344-357.

Lᴀᴜʀᴇɴᴛɪᴜs, physicus Noviomagus (*fl.* ca. 1450):
Jean Noël Paquot, *Mémoires pour servir à l'histoire littéraire des dix-sept provinces des Pays-Bas, de la Principauté de Liège et de quelques contrées voisines*, 3 vols (Louvain, 1765-1770), I, 584.

Lᴇᴍᴀɪʀᴇ, Jean, de Belges (1473-1515?):
Pierre Jodogne, *Jean Lemaire de Belges, écrivain franco-bourguignon*, Académie Royale de Belgique — Mémoires de la Classe des Lettres. Collection in-4°, 2ᵉ Série, XIII, 1 (Brussels, 1972).

Lᴇᴏɴᴛᴏʀɪᴜs, Conradus (ca. 1460-1511):
Georg Wolff, 'Conradus Leontorius. Biobibliographie', in *Beiträge zur Geschichte der Renaissance und Reformation — Joseph Schlecht* (München - Freising, 1917), pp. 363-410.

Lᴇʀɴᴜᴛɪᴜs, Janus (1545-1619):
GV, p. 384, nn. 4571-3.

Lᴇᴜᴡɪs, Henricus de (Leeuwen, Hendrik van):
cf. Dɪᴏɴʏsɪᴜs, Cartusianus.

Lɪʙᴇʀ, Antonius (Antonius Vrije) (d. 1506/7):
HCT I, 278.
Johannes Lindeboom, *Het Bijbelsch Humanisme in Nederland* (Leiden, 1913), pp. 68-70.
Wilhelm Crecelius, 'De Antonii Liberi Susatensis vita et scriptis commentatiuncula' in *Festschrift zur Begrüssung der XXXIV. Versammlung deutscher Philologen und Schulmänner zu Trier* (Bonn, 1879), pp. 139-149.

Lɪᴘsɪᴜs, Justus (1547-1606):
GV, pp. 388-390, nn. 4611-33.

Lɪsᴀ, Gerardus de (ca. 1440-d. 1499):
Augusto Serena, *La cultura umanistica a Treviso nel secolo decimoquinto*, Miscellanea di storia veneta, III, 3 (Venice, 1912), passim.
Victor Scholderer, 'A Fleming in Venetia. Gerardus de Lisa, Printer, Bookseller, Schoolmaster and Musician', *The Library*, 4th ser., X (1929), 253-273; slightly reworked in: Victor Scholderer, *Fifty Essays in Fifteenth- and Sixteenth-Century Scholarship*, edited by Dennis E. Rhodes (Amsterdam, 1966), pp. 113-125.

De vijfhonderdste verjaring van de boekdrukkunst in de Nederlanden. Catalogus van de tentoonstelling in de Koninklijke Bibliotheek Albert I (Brussels, 1973), pp. 112-117 (nn. 55-56) and passim.

LODOVICO, de Garsiis: cf. GARSIIS, Lodovico de.

LONGOLIUS, Christophorus (1488-1522):
GV, p. 391, nn. 4643-48.
Ernest Philip Goldschmidt, 'De Longueil's Letter on his Adventure in Switzerland, 1513', *Bibliothèque d'Humanisme et Renaissance,* XII (1950), 163-182.
Id., 'Jean des Pins et Longueil', *ibid.,* 183-189.
Giulio Vallese, *Da Dante ad Erasmo. Studi di letteratura umanistica* (Naples, 1962, 1966³), ch. 4: L'umanesimo al primo '500: da Cristoforo Longolio al "Ciceronianus" di Erasmo.
Robert Aulotte, 'Une rivalité d'humanistes: Erasme et Longueil, traducteurs de Plutarque', *Bibliothèque d'Humanisme et Renaissance,* XXX (1968), 549-573.

LOS, Johannes de: cf. PEECKS, Jan.

LUDER, Peter (d. post 1474):
Agostino Sottili, 'I codici del Petrarca nella Germania Occidentale I', *IMU,* X (1967), p. 412, n. 1.
Frank E. Baron, 'The Beginnings of German Humanism: the Life and Work of the Wandering Humanist Peter Luder' (unpublished diss., Berkeley, 1966).

MACHARII, Bartholomaeus Tungrensis (d. 1482):
Petrus Cornelis Boeren, *Twee Maaslandse dichters in dienst van Karel de Stoute* (The Hague, 1968).

MAGDALIUS, Jacobus (2nd half 15th c.-1520):
GV, pp. 394-395, n. 4682.
Gabriel Löhr, 'Der Kölner Dominikanerhumanist Jacobus Magdalius Gaudanus und seine *Naumachia Ecclesiastica*', *Archivum Fratrum Praedicatorum,* XVIII (1948), 281-302.

MACROPEDIUS, Georgius (ca. 1486-1558):
GV, p. 380, n⁰ 4534. Cf. below, Addenda.
Vom Sterben des reichen Mannes. Die Dramen von Everyman, Homulus, Hecastus und dem Kauffmann nach Drucken des 16. Jahrhunderts, übersetzt, herausgegeben und eingeleitet von H. Wiemken, Sammlung Dieterich, 298 (Bremen, 1965).
Rudolphus Cornelis Engelberts, *Georgius Macropedius:* Bassarus, *naar de editie Utrecht 1540 uitgegeven met inleiding en vertaling* (with a summary in English) (Tilburg, 1968).

MARCATELLI (family):
Gillis G. Meersseman, 'La raccolta dell'umanista fiammingo Giovanni de Veris "De arte epistolandi" ', *IMU,* XV (1972), 215-281 (pp. 251-257).
Alexandre Pinchart, 'Bibliothèque manuscrite de Raphaël de Mercatel, abbé de Saint-Bavon', *Le bibliophile belge,* VII (1872), 21-34.
Karel G. Van Acker, 'Marcatellis', in *Nieuw Biografisch Woordenboek,* II (Brussels, 1966), coll. 507-512.

MARLIANO, Raimundus de (ca. 1420-1475):
HCT, I, 135-138.

MARTENS, Dirk (1450-1534):
GV, p. 399, nn. 4736-39.
Tentoonstelling Dirk Martens 1473-1973 (Aalst, 1973).

MATTHAEUS van Mechlin: cf. MECHLIN, Matthaeus van.

MAUBURNUS, Johannes (d. 1501)
PT, pp. 118-125, nr. 82.
MAURICE, of Spiegelberg: cf. SPIEGELBERG, Maurice of.
MAURUS (Moorman), Fridericus (d. 1482):
  Henricus Eduardus J. M. Van der Velden, *Rodolphus Agricola* (*Roelof Huus-man*), *een Nederlandsch Humanist der vijftiende eeuw* (Leiden, 1911), pp. 124-128.
MECHLIN, Matthaeus van (*fl.* 1470):
  Cf. *IMU*, XVII/2 (1974), 64-65.
MEERHOUT, Joannes de (d. 1476):
  PT, pp. 126-129, nr. 83.
MENGHERS, Cornelius, of Zantvliet (d. 1461):
  August Potthast, *Repertorium Fontium Historiae Medii Aevi* (Rome, 1970), III, 651.
MERA, Cornelius de (*fl.* ca. 1460):
  Epistolario di Guarino Veronese, raccolto ordinato illustrato da Remigio Sabbadini, 3 vols. (Venice, 1915-19; reprint: Turin, 1967), III, 446.
MERA, Petrus de (d. ante 1.II.1485):
  HCT, I, 113-115.
MERICA, Henricus de (Van der Heyden) (d. 1473):
  PT, pp. 67-69, No. 43.
MIDDELBURG, Paulus de (1445-1533):
  Adolf De Ceuleneer, 'Paulus van Middelburg en de Kalenderhervorming', *Handelingen van het eerste Taal- en Geschiedkundig Congres* (Antwerp, 1910), 276-289.
  Dirk Jan Struik, 'Paulus van Middelburg 1445-1533', *Mededeelingen van het Nederlandsch Historisch Instituut te Rome*, V (1925), 79-118.
MIÉLOT, Jean (d. 1472):
  Gianni Mombello, 'Quattro poesie latine di Jean Miélot', in *Miscellanea di studi e ricerche sul Quattrocento francese*, a cura di Franco Simone (Turin, 1967), pp. 211-240.
MITHRIDATES, Flavius Gulielmus, Raimundus: cf. RAIMUNDUS, F. G.
MOLINET, Jean (1435-1507):
  Chroniques de Jean Molinet (1474-1506), publiées par Georges Doutrepont et Omer Jodogne, 3 vols. (Brussels, 1935-37).
  Pierre Jodogne, 'Molinet, Jean (1435-1507)', in *Dizionario critico della letteratura francese* (Turin, 1972), pp. 818-819.
  Noël Dupire, *Jean Molinet. La vie, les oeuvres* (Paris, 1932).
  Id., *Etude critique des manuscrits et éditions des poésies de Jean Molinet* (Paris, 1932).
MONET, Adrianus (= Adrianus Carthusiensis) (d. 1411):
  Nicholas Mann, 'New Light on a recently discovered manuscript of the "De remediis" ', *IMU*, XII (1969), 317-322.
MOORMAN, Frederik: cf. MAURUS, Fridericus.
MONTANUS, Petrus (1468-1507):
  GV, p. 409, nn. 4835-36.
MULART, Simon (d. 1474):
  Petrus Cornelis Boeren, *Twee Maaslandse dichters in dienst van Karel de Stoute* (The Hague, 1968).
MURMELLIUS, Johannes (1480-1517):
  GV, p. 412, nn. 4867-9.
OESTERWIJCK, Henricus de (*fl.* ca. 1430):
  Jozef IJsewijn, 'Henricus de Oesterwijck', pp. 7-23.

PALUDANUS, Johannes (d. 1525):
GV, p. 285, n⁰ 3542.
HCT I, 184-186, 188-190, 286-287.
PALUDE, Joannes de (d. 1418):
PT, p. 93, n⁰ 59.
PANNONIUS, Janus (1434-1472):
József Huszti, *Janus Pannonius* (Pécs, 1931).
R. Gerézdi, 'Ein mitteleuropäischer Dichter und Humanist', *Acta Litteraria Academiae Scientiarum Hungaricae*, V (1962), 384ff.
Id., 'Janus Pannonius', in *Italia ed Ungheria. Dieci secoli di rapporti letterari*, a cura di M. Horányi e T. Klaniczay (Budapest, 1967), pp. 91-112.
Veljko Gortan and Vladimir Vratović, *Hrvatski Latinisti*, I (Zagreb, 1969), pp. 151-224.
Tibor Kardos, 'Toni ed echi Ovidiani nella poesia di Giano Pannonio', in *Classical Influences on European Culture, A. D. 500-1500*, ed. R. R. Bolgar (Cambridge, 1971), pp. 183-194.
Munkái Latinul és Magyarul: Janus Pannonius élö emlékezetének halálának ötszázadik évforduloja alkalmából. Opera Latine et Hungarice: vivae memoriae Jani Pannonii quingentesimo mortis suae anniversario dedicatum (Budapest, 1972).
PAULUS de Zomeren: cf. ZOMEREN, Paulus de.
PAULUS of Middelburg: cf. MIDDELBURG, Paulus de.
PEECKS, Jan (= Johannes de Los) (b. 1459):
Johannis de Los ... Chronicon rerum gestarum ab anno MCCCCLV ad annum MDXIV, in: Petrus Franciscus Xaverius de Ram, *Documents relatifs aux troubles du Pays de Liège sous les princes-évêques Louis de Bourbon et Jean de Horne, 1455-1505* (Brussels, 1844), pp. 1-132.
PELLANTINUS, Paulus (*fl.* ca. 1480). Cf. Gansfort, *Opera*.
PETRI, Albertus, Leidensis (d. 1484/5):
Thomas Kaeppeli, *Scriptores Ordinis Praedicatorum Medii Aevi*, I (Rome, 1970), pp. 32-33.
PETRI, Gerlacus (d. 1411):
PT, pp. 45-51, n⁰ 32.
PETRUS, de Mera: cf. MERA, Petrus de.
PETRUS, de Rivo: cf. RIVO, Petrus de.
PETRUS, Ravennas: cf. RAVENNAS, Petrus.
POEL, Robert van de: cf. LACU, Robertus a.
POMERIUS, Henricus (1382-1469):
PT, pp. 62-67, n⁰ 42.
PONTANUS, Petrus (ca. 1475-post 1539):
GV, p. 261, n. 3321.
Paul Blondelle, 'De eclogen van Petrus Pontanus', *Haec olim*, XXIII (St. Lodewijkscollege, Brugge, 1973), 76-85.
POTTER, Dirk (ca. 1370-1428):
Gerardus Petrus Maria Knuvelder, *Handboek tot de geschiedenis der Nederlandse letterkunde*. Deel I, Vijfde, geheel herziene druk ('s-Hertogenbosch, 1970), pp. 308-311.
POYPONE, Aymo de (*fl.* ca. 1440):
IMU, XI (1968), 409-410.
PUBLICIUS, Jacobus Rufus (d. post 1473):
Agostino Sottili, 'Note biografiche sui petrarchisti Giacomo Publicio e Guinoforte Barzizza e sull'umanista valenziano Giovanni Serra', in *Petrarca 1304-1374. Beiträge zur Werk und Dichtung*. Herausgegeben von Fritz Schalk (Frankfurt am Main, 1975), pp. 270-286.

ᴿᴬᵁᴱᵂᴵᴶᴺˢ, Husum (d. 1400)¹

P. F. J. Obbema, *Een Deventer Bibliotheekcatalogus van het einde der vijftiende eeuw. Een bijdrage tot de studie van laat-middeleeuwse bibliotheekcatalogi*, Archives et Bibliothèque de Belgique, Numéro spécial 8 / Archief- en Bibliotheekwezen in België, extranummer 8, 2 vols (Brussels, 1973).

RADULPHUS/ROLANDUS de Rivo: cf. RIVO, Radulphus de.

RADULPHUS de Zeelandia: cf. ZEELANDIA, Radulphus de.

RAIMUNDUS, Flavius Gulielmus, Mithridates (d. 1525):
HCT I, 160-61.
Gustav Bauch, 'Flavius Wilhelmus Raimundus Mithridates, der erste fahrende Kölner Hebraist und Humanist', *Archiv für Kulturgeschichte*, III (1905), 15-27.

RAIMUNDUS de Marliano: cf. MARLIANO, Raimundus de.

RAVENNAS, Petrus (*fl.* ca. 1500):
Dietrich Reichling, *Ortwin Gratius. Sein Leben und Wirken. Eine Ehrenrettung* (Heiligenstadt, 1884; reprint: Nieuwkoop, 1963), pp. 19-28 and passim.
Charles G. Nauert, Jr., 'Peter of Ravenna and the "Obscure Men" of Cologne: a Case of Pre-Reformation Controversy', in *Renaissance Studies in Honor of Hans Baron*, edited by Anthony Molho and John A. Tedeschi (Firenze, 1971), pp. 607-640.

RECANETO, Antonio Columbella de (d. 1466):
HCT I, 129-31.

REES, Henry van (1449-1485).

REMACLUS: cf. ARDUENNA.

REUCHLIN, Johannes (1455-1522):
Hermann Goldbrunner, 'Reuchliniana', *Archiv für Kulturgeschichte*, XLVIII (1966), 403-410.
Ludwig Geiger, *Johann Reuchlin. Sein Leben und seine Werke* (Leipzig, 1871; reprint: Nieuwkoop, 1964).
Id., *Johann Reuchlins Briefwechsel*, Bibliothek des Literarischen Vereins, CXXVI (Stuttgart, 1875; reprint: Hildesheim, 1962).
Hugo Holstein, *Johann Reuchlins Komödien. Ein Beitrag zur Geschichte des lateinischen Schuldramas* (Halle a.S., 1888; reprint: Leipzig, 1973).
Id., 'Reuchlins Gedichte', *Zeitschrift für Literaturgeschichte und vergleichende Renaissance-Literatur*, N.F. III (1890), 128-136.
Johannes Reuchlin 1455-1522. Festgabe seiner Vaterstadt Pforzheim zur 500. Wiederkehr seines Geburtstages ... hrsg. von Manfred Krebs (Pforzheim, 1955).
J. Reuchlin, *Henno. Komödie*, Lateinisch und Deutsch, übersetzt und herausgegeben von Harry C. Schnur (Stuttgart, 1971).
Martin Sicherl, 'Zwei Reuchlin-Funde aus der Pariser National-Bibliothek' *Akademie der Wissenschaften und der Literatur (Mainz), Abhandlungen der geistes- und sozialwissenschaftlichen Klasse*, Jahrgang 1963, nr. 7 (Wiesbaden, 1963), 765-798.

RIMEN, Hugo van (ca. 1410-1460):
HCT I, 119-20, 124-5.

RIVO, Petrus de (Van der Beken) (d. 1499):
HCT I, 124-8.
Léon Baudry, *La Querelle des Futurs Contingents (Louvain, 1465-1475). Textes inédits par L.B.*, Etudes de philosophie médiévale, 38 (Paris, 1950).
Erasmus en Leuven, Catalogus, pp. 149 and 152-154, nn. 136-140.
Antonius Gerardus Weiler, 'Tussen Middeleeuwen en Nieuwe Tijd. Veranderingen in de Nederlanden: van Scholastiek naar humanisme', *Bij-*

dragen en Mededelingen betreffende de Geschiedenis der Nederlanden, LXXXVII (1972), 1-25.

RIVO, Radulphus/Rolandus de (d. 1401/3):
Cunibert Mohlberg, *Radulph de Rivo, der letzte Vertreter der altrömischen Liturgie*, Recueil de Travaux publiés par les membres des Conférences d'Histoire et de Philologie de l'Université de Louvain, 29 and 42, 2 vols (Louvain, 1911-15).
Erasmus en Leuven. Catalogus, pp. 316-317, n⁰ 293.

ROVELINCK, Werner (1425-1502):
Hermann Bücker, *Werner Rolevinck. Leben und Persönlichkeit im Spiegel des Westfalenbuches* (Münster/W., 1952).
Id., *Werner Rolevinck 1425-1502. De Laude antiquae Saxoniae nunc Westphaliae dictae/Ein Buch zum Lobe Westfalens des alten Sachsenlandes*. Der Text der Lateinischen Erstausgabe vom Jahre 1474 mit deutscher Uebersetzung, herausgegeben von H. B. (Münster/W., 1953).

RUTGER, Sicamber: cf. SICAMBER, Rutger.

RUUSBROEC, Joannes (1293-1381):
PT, pp. 131-38, n⁰ 86.

SANCTUS, Ludovicus (Heyligen?) from Beringen (1304-1361):
Giuseppe Billanovich, 'Tra Italia e Fiandre nel Trecento: Francesco Petrarca e Ludovico Santo di Beringen', in *The Late Middle Ages and the Dawn of Humanism outside Italy. Proceedings of the International Conference Louvain May 11-13, 1970*, edited by Gerard Verbeke and Jozef IJsewijn (Leuven - The Hague, 1972), pp. 6, 18.
Giuseppe Billanovich, 'Il Petrarca e gli storici latini', in *Tra latino e volgare, per Carlo Dionisotti*, 2 vols, Medioevo e Umanesimo, 17-18 (Padua, 1974), 67-145.
Marc Dykmans, 'Les premiers rapports de Pétrarque avec les Pays-Bas', *Bulletin de L'Institut Historique Belge de Rome*, XX (1939), 51-122.

SCHETS, Gaspar (1513-1580):
Opus Epistolarum D. Erasmi, ep. 2897, vol. X, pp. 346-348.

SCHUT, Engelbertus (ca. 1410-1503):
GV, p. 384, n⁰ 4577.
Jozef Noels, 'Leven en werk van Engelbert Schut' (unpublished lic. diss., Univ. of Leuven, 1970).

SECUNDUS, Johannes (1511-1536):
GV, p. 452, nn. 5278-5286ᵃ.
Leo Vander Elst, 'De "Basia" van de dichter-humanist Janus Secundus (1511-1536)', *Handelingen van de Koninklijke Kring voor Oudheidkunde, Letteren en Kunst van Mechelen*, LXXVI (1972), 87-150, and LXXVII (1973), 37-86.

SICAMBER, Rutger, de Venray (1456/7-d. post 1507):
PT, pp. 195-200, n⁰ 134.
Fr. Soddeman, *Rutgerus Sycamber de Venray, Dialogus de musica (um 1500)*, Beiträge zur rheinischen Musikgeschichte, 54 (Köln, 1963).

SNAVEL, Johannes (ca. 1405-d. post 1446):
J. IJsewijn, *Collatio*, pp. 416-418.
Id., 'New Evidence on Jan Snavel', *HL*, XXIII (1974), 382-384.

SNOY, Reynerus, Goudanus (ca. 1477-1537):
Bob and Maria Emilie de Graaf, *Doctor Reinerus Snoy Goudanus, Gouda, ca. 1477-1st August 1537* (Nieuwkoop, 1968).

SPIEGELBERG, Maurice of (ca. 1410-1483):
Henricus Eduardus J. M. Van der Velden, *Rodolphus Agricola (Roelof Huus-*

man), *Een Nederlandsch humanist der vijftiende eeuw* (Leiden, 1911), p. 00, n. 1.

STANDONCK, Jan (1443-1504):
Augustin Renaudet, *Humanisme et Renaissance*, Travaux d'Humanisme et Renaissance, 30 (Geneva, 1958), pp. 114-161.

SURIGONUS, Stephanus (d. post 1478):
HCT I, 159-60.
Renil Capelle, 'De humanist Stephanus Surigonus. Leven en publicatie van zijn werken' (unpublished lic. diss., Univ. of Leuven, 1967).

SYNTHEN, Johannes (ca. 1450-1533):
GV, p. 284, n⁰ 3533.
HCT I, 80-82.
Terrence Heath, 'Logical Grammar, Grammatical Logic and Humanism in Three German Universities', *Studies in the Renaissance*, XVIII (1971), 9-64.
Marcel A. Nauwelaerts, *Latijnse school en onderwijs te 's-Hertogenbosch tot 1629*, (Tilburg, 1974), p. 219.

SWILDEN, Petrus (*fl.* ca. 1450):
IMU, V (1962), p. 464.

TEDALDI, Francesco (ca. 1420-ca. 1490):
Paul O. Kristeller, 'Una novella latina e il suo autore Francesco Tedaldi mercante fiorentino del Quattrocento', in *Studi letterari. Miscellanea in onore di E. Santini* (Palermo, 1956), pp. 159-180.

THESSALIENSIS, Kempo (*fl.* beginning 16th c.):
HCT I, 199.

THOMAS a Kempis: cf. KEMPIS, Thomas a.

TORRENTINUS, Hermannus (ca. 1450-ca. 1520):
GV, p. 464, n⁰ 5403.
HCT I, 198-9.
Terrence Heath, 'Logical Grammar, Grammatical Logic and Humanism in Three German Universities', *Studies in the Renaissance*, XVIII (1971), 9-64.

TRAIECTO, Godefridus de (d. 1405):
Christian Klinger, *Godefridi de Traiecto Grammaticale. Untersuchungen und kritische Ausgabe*, Beiheft zum "Mittellateinischen Jahrbuch", 12 (Ratingen - Kastellaun - Düsseldorf, 1973).

TRITHEMIUS, Johannes (1462-1516):
Klaus Arnold, *Johannes Trithemius (1462-1516)*, Quellen und Forschungen zur Geschichte des Bistums und Hochstifts Würzburg, 23 (Würzburg, 1971).
Id., 'Ergänzungen zum Briefwechsel des Johannes Trithemius', *Studien und Mitteilungen zur Geschichte des Benediktiner-Ordens und seiner Zweige*, LXXXIII (1972), 176-204.
Johannes Trithemius, *De Laude Scriptorum — Zum Lobe der Schreiber*. Eingeleitet, herausgegeben und übersetzt von Klaus Arnold, Mainfränkische Hefte, 60 (Würzburg, 1973). English edition (Lawrence, Kansas, 1974).
Klaus Arnold, 'Johannes Trithemius und Bamberg: Oratio ad clerum Bambergensem', *Bericht des historischen Vereins für die Pflege der Geschichte des ehemaligen Fürstbistums Bamberg*, CVII (1971), 161-89.

VAN DER HEYDEN, Hendrik: cf. MERICA, Henricus de.

VERIS, Joannes de (b. ca. 1425):
Gillis G. Meersseman, 'L'épistolaire de Jean van den Veren et le début de l'humanisme en Flandre', *HL*, XIX (1970), 119-200.
Id., 'La raccolta dell'umanista fiammingo Giovanni de Veris "De arte epistolandi" ', *IMU*, XV (1972), 215-281.

VESALIUS, Andreas (1514-1564):
GV, pp. 470-79, nn. 5458-5570.
VETERI BUSCO, Adrianus de (Oudenbosch) (d. ca. 1482):
August Potthast, *Repertorium Fontium Historiae Medii Aevi, II (Fontes A-B)* (Rome, 1967), pp. 129-130.
VICTOR, Hugo (*fl.* ca. 1450):
IMU, VI (1963), 297: ms. 646 of the Bibl. Municipale of Saint-Omer.
VILLA DEI, Alexander: cf. below, Addenda.
VIGLIUS ab Aytta: cf. AYTTA, Viglius ab.
VIRULI, Carolus (ca. 1413-1493):
HCT I, 90-98.
VITELLI, Cornelio (ca. 1450-ca. 1500):
HCT I, 166-172.
VIVES, Juan Luis (1493-1540):
GV, pp. 480-2, nn. 5577-5607.
Vives' Introduction to Wisdom: a Renaissance Textbook. Edited by Marian Leona Tobriner (New York, 1968).
L. Vives, *De subventione pauperum*, a cura di Armando Saitta, Biblioteca di Studi superiori, Storia Moderna, 29 (Florence, 1973).
WERKEN, Theodoricus Nicolai, de Abbenbroek (*fl.* ca. 1440):
Roger Aubrey Baskerville Mynors, *Catalogue of the Mss. of Balliol College Oxford* (Oxford, 1963), pp. xxix-xxx; passim esp. 106, 313, 327 (Humanist treatises).
WEYTS, Nicasius (*fl.* ca. 1450):
Gillis G. Meersseman, 'L'épistolaire de Jean van den Veren et le début de l'humanisme en Flandre', *HL*, XIX (1970), 119-200.
WILDE, Jan de, of Bruges (1389-1419):
La Librairie de Philippe le Bon. Exposition organisée à l'occasion du 500e anniversaire de la mort du duc. Catalogue rédigé par Georges Dogaer et Marguerite Debae (Brussels, 1967), nn. 54, 222, 227, 229.
WILDE, Jan de (1360-1417):
Jacobus Meyerus, *Commentarii sive Annales rerum Flandricarum libri septendecim* (Antwerp, 1561), p. 212.
Antonius Sanderus, *De Gandavensibus eruditionis fama claris libri tres* (Antwerp, 1624), lib. II, p. 72.
Franciscus Sweertius, *Athenae Belgicae* (Antwerp, 1628), p. 486.
Joannes Franciscus Foppens, *Bibliotheca Belgica*, 2 vols (Brussels, 1739), II, 756.
Emile van Arenbergh, in *Biographie Nationale de Belgique*, X (Brussels, 1888-89), 447.
WILLIAM/WILLEM of Berchen: cf. BERCHEN, W. of.
WIMPFELING, Jakob (1450-1528):
Charles Béné, 'L'Humanisme de J. Wimpfeling', *Acta Conventus neolatini Lovaniensis*, edd. Jozef IJsewijn and Eckhard Kessler (Leuven - München, 1973), pp. 77-84.
WITTE, Jacobus, de Flandria necnon de Biervliet (*fl.* beginning 15th c.):
Remigio Sabbadini, *Giovanni da Ravenna, insigne figura d'umanista (1343-1408). Da documenti inediti*, Studi Umanistici, 1 (Como, 1924: reprint: Turin, 1961), p. 122.
Robert Weiss, 'Il codice oxoniense e altri codici delle opere di Giovanni da Ravenna', *Giornale storico della letteratura italiana*, CXXV (1948), 133-148 (pp. 142-144).

ZEELANDIA, Radulphus de, alias de Druxella (*fl. ca.* 1430):
Henricus Stevenson, *Codices Palatini Latini Bibliothecae Vaticanae* (Rome, 1886), p. 217 (cod. 608).

ZENDERS, Willem, of Weert (*fl.* ca. 1500):
Jozef IJsewijn, 'Alexander Hegius (d. 1498) "Invectiva in Modos Significandi" ', *Forum for Modern Language Studies*, VII (1971), 299-318 (p. 316).

ZICHENIS, Eustachius de (d. 1538):
Erasmus en Leuven. Catalogus, pp. 341-2, n⁰ 322. Cf. Addenda.

ZOMEREN, Henricus van:
HCT I, 126.
Léon Baudry, *La Querelle des Futurs Contingents (Louvain, 1465-1475). Textes inédits par L.B.*, Etudes de philosophie médiévale, 38 (Paris, 1950), passim, esp. pp. 21-23.
Erasmus en Leuven. Catalogus, pp. 152-154, n⁰ 140.

ZOMEREN, Paulus de (*fl.* 1486):
Franz Unterkircher, 'Maximilian I, "Dux Brabantinorum" im Historiologium Brabantinorum des Johannes Gielemans', in *Texts and Manuscripts. Essays Presented to G. I. Lieftinck*, 2 (Amsterdam, 1972), pp. 56-60.

ZUTPHEN, Gerardus of (*fl.* ca. 1500):
Terrence Heath, 'Logical Grammar, Grammatical Logic and Humanism in Three German Universities', *Studies in the Renaissance*, XVIII (1971), 9-64.

ADDENDA

GALLET-GUERNE, Danielle:
Vasque de Lucène et la Cyropédie à la cour de Bourgogne (1470). Le traité de Xénophon mis en français d'après la version latine du Pogge, Etude. Edition des Livres I et V. (Genève, 1974).

MACROPEDIUS, Georgius (ca. 1486-1558)
Alfred M. M. Dekker, 'Three Unknown "Cantilenae Martinianae" by Georgius Macropedius: a Contribution to the Study of the *Carmina Scholastica*', *HL*, XXIII (1974), 188-227.

SCHMIDT, P. G.:
'Jodocus Badius Ascensius als Kommentator', in: *Der Kommentar in der Renaissance*, hrsg. von A. Buck und O. Herding (Bad Godesberg, 1975), pp. 63-71.

VILLA DEI, Alexander de:
Das Doctrinale des Alexander de Villa Dei, kritisch-exegetische Ausgabe... von D. Reichling, Monumenta Germaniae Paedagogica, XII (Berlin, 1893).

ZICHENIS, Eustachius de:
Erasmi Roterodami Canonis Quinti Interpretatio.... édité... par J. Coppens (Brussel, 1975).

The *Panegyricus ad Philippum Austriae Ducem* of Erasmus (cf. above, p. 264) is edited by Otto Herding in *Opera Omnia Des. Erasmi Roterodami*, IV, 1 (Amsterdam, 1974), 3-93.

ENGLAND

ENGLAND AND THE HUMANITIES IN THE FIFTEENTH CENTURY

DENYS HAY

University of Edinburgh

The large subject of this study invites an answer, however tentative, to some questions which naturally arise in the mind of anyone reflecting on the matter. By the end of the fifteenth century we have in Thomas More (born 1478) the finest 'humanist' produced by England. Why had he no predecessor of stature? Why was he relatively isolated in his own day? How did the situation change so rapidly in the next generation? These queries are the more tantalising when we remember that the new learning had borne handsome fruit in Italy by 1400, and that traffic in men and ideas between England and Italy was more intense after the Schism (1378-1417) than it had been for a hundred and fifty years. The new ideas of the Italians were to be absorbed by the literate English (as by the literate among other European peoples) by the end of the sixteenth century, and it is worth pondering why the process of absorption took so long.

It is necessary to begin with some severe definitions if the argument is not to become vapid. Already the reader has encountered above two highly ambiguous expressions—humanist and literate. Any study which figures in a volume dedicated to Paul Oskar Kristeller must heed his strictures on the loose manner in which 'humanist' and 'humanism' are often used.[1] Humanist, either as noun or adjective, is less liable to abuse than humanism, at any rate by historians of the Renaissance period.[2] Certainly in the fifteenth and sixteenth centuries in both Italy and the North the word was applied primarily if not exclusively to the new type of Latin grammarian, the teacher of the humanities, the professor of 'humanity' as he was (and is) called in Scottish universities.[3] The new curriculum was geared to the 'cycle of scholarly disciplines, namely grammar, rhetoric, history, poetry,

---

[1] Kristeller has touched on these words and their meaning on several occasions. See especially *The Classics and Renaissance Thought* (Cambridge, Mass., 1955), 9-10 (reprinted as *Renaissance Thought*, New York, 1961).

[2] Note the temptation (especially in America?) to lengthen the adjective 'humanist' to the unnecessary Germanic 'humanistic'.

[3] Cf. below p. 366.

and moral philosophy' studied through the 'reading and interpretation' of the 'standard ancient writers in Latin and, to a lesser extent, Greek'.[4] When the slang Italian word *humanista* is recorded at the end of the fifteenth century it is clear that it is equivalent in meaning to the old term *artista*.[5] By a permissible extension we may apply the word also to those patrons of the practitioners of *literae humaniores* who themselves would have hardly stooped to teach or who only taught when driven to do so by dire necessity. We may therefore admit as a humanist one who practised, taught, promoted or comprehended with sympathy and approval the new educational and moral programme. 'Humanism' has, however, reasonable meaning for the Renaissance period only if it is similarly restricted, and is not used as a blanket term to cover every aspect of *quattrocento* life and learning. As a generic term for a system of education it is useful; as an invitation to confused assumptions about 'the dignity of man', of the 'humane' or 'human-centred' in anything approaching a modern connotation, it is best avoided. (I shall return shortly to the word 'literate').

That these remarks are not entirely superfluous may be seen when we turn to the standard and indispensable work by Roberto Weiss, *Humanism in England during the Fifteenth Century* (1940; 2nd ed., 1957; 3rd ed., 1967). Although the author begins with a statement not so very different from that given above he soon (as it seems to me) slips momentarily into a vaguer and more dangerous identification of 'humanism' as a 'cultural movement' which 'offered several advantages over scholasticism'. Provided we accept that the writer here alludes to two different pedagogical techniques we need not demur at the statement, even if it arouses our suspicions. But in fact Roberto Weiss immediately makes it clear that for him humanism was indeed an emotional or intellectual position affecting a man's total view of the world.

> In its attempts to unify all knowledge within a system of logic, scholasticism lacked flexibility and powers of adaptation, was difficult of application in particular instances, and left no room for romanticism [*sic*]. Humanism on the other hand with its leaning toward Platonism displayed a wider scope, greater elasticity, and less dogmatism and adherence to formulae, so that all this combined with its emergence

---

[4] Kristeller, *loc. cit.*

[5] Cf. P. O. Kristeller, *Studies in Renaissance Thought and Letters* (Rome, 1956), 553-583, and esp. 564-574.

as a distinct system at a time when scholasticism had practically
ceased to produce original speculation, rendered it very attractive to
those scholars who came into contact with it.[6]

It is exceedingly difficult to make sense of this passage but it should
be remembered when reading the detailed studies of patronage and
book collecting which form the substance of the book, for it would
have led one to expect some discussion of education in England in
both school and university, some analysis of social pressures. These
are not given by Weiss and obviously they cannot adequately be
covered in a short account such as this. But there does seem to be a
need for a brief response to the plan Weiss tries to sketch at the
beginning of his study, but did not really execute.

> Therefore in approaching English humanism it is important to con-
> sider the possible influence exercised not only by its scholarly, but
> also by its economic, political and social backgrounds, and to bear
> in mind the peculiarities common to intellectual movements in the
> making.[7]

In what follows I shall begin by comparing the Italian and the
English scene—social, political and cultural—at the turn of the fourteenth and fifteenth centuries. I shall then briefly examine Italian
cultural changes in the first half of the fifteenth century, treating this
as a critical period in the Italian Renaissance, when the major innovations (some of which had been made much earlier) firmly established
themselves. I shall then examine the contacts of Englishmen with
Italy at this time and try to piece together the degree to which they
were aware that change was in the Italian air. Finally I shall turn to
the later fifteenth and early sixteenth centuries. In the decades from
1470 onwards the pace at which Renaissance values were accepted in

---

[6] The revisions in this fundamental work are appended to the text in the second
and third editions; pagination is therefore not affected. In these addenda Weiss
refers to an important article by Kristeller, but he does not seem to have accepted
its relevance. He would have been the first to admit that he was primarily concerned with the development of classical studies as such and not with the 'Renaissance', a concept of which he certainly talked latterly in somewhat sceptical
terms. For all the implied criticism my dependence upon and respect for his
work will be apparent in what follows. His work entirely supersedes Walter
F. Schirmer, *Der Englische Frühhumanismus* (Leipzig, 1931). It will be long before
Weiss's book is superseded, but some useful additional material will be
found in the catalogue of the Bodleian Library exhibition, *Duke Humphrey and
English Humanism in the Fifteenth Century* (1970), with substantial introduction
and notes by Dr. Richard Hunt and Miss Tilly de la Mare.

[7] *Op. cit.*, p. 5.

the North quickened, not least because of minor but nonetheless influential changes in Italy.

I. ITALY AND ENGLAND: DIVISIONS AND UNITIES

Such a plan, it must be admitted, accepts in broad terms a contrast between Italy and the trans-Alpine world. Such a contrast can and must be drawn. But it will be apparent in what follows how profound also were the similarities. Indeed had they not been so it is impossible to imagine the ultimate transplantation of so much of Renaissance Italy to other parts of Europe: the transplantation took long to be effective, perhaps, but it could not have been effective at all had there been a fundamental opposition between Italy and her neighbours. And of course there was in the purely political sense no 'Italy' at all. If one talks of a European 'States-system' then the Italian participants are Milan, Florence, Venice, Naples, the Papacy and so on. A gulf separated Sicily from Piedmont far greater than that which separated the north of England from the South, or even those dividing England from Scotland or France.

This internal division in Italy, this absence of a centralised government comparable to those found in England, France, Castile and Aragon, was an old story and it was to persist for centuries to come. It perplexed and obsessed observers like Machiavelli and Guicciardini in the early years of the sixteenth century. It continues to bother, even torment, many Italian historians today—witness their approach in the monumental *Storia d'Italia* which has recently begun to appear from the publishing house of Giulio Einaudi in Turin.[8] Of course it is easy to exaggerate both the disunity of Italy and the unities of other countries. There had been a *rex Angliae* since 1200, but the *Angli* of of his earlier title were quite capable of tearing themselves in pieces— under Henry III, Edward II, Richard II, Henry VI, Charles I. In France, the *regnum Franciae* of the thirteenth century had to suffer not merely English attack, but devastating civil war in the fifteenth, sixteenth and seventeenth centuries—wars which had a markedly regional or provincial ingredient.[9] Moreover, if in Italy we find ourselves ignoring large areas—the south hardly enters the Renaissance story in the *quattrocento*, nor does Piedmont—so likewise in any ac-

---

[8] At the time of writing four volumes have appeared, 1, 2 and 5 in two parts (1972-73). See especially the contributions in vol. 1 by G. Galasso and Corrado Vivanti. The latter's title is 'Lacerazione e contraste'.

[9] Cf. Giulio Einaudi's shrewd remarks, *op. cit.*, I, xxii-xxiii.

count of 'pre-humanism' in England we find ourselves gravitating to the south and east of the country, and we would do this whatever aspect of change we were investigating. To that extent 'England' is almost as arbitrary or unreal a concept as 'Italy', although the natives of each region had no such hesitations in identifying those who came from the other. To that extent there were Italians even if there was no Italian state, and there were English even if their state was often weak and divided.

To a great extent the reception of Italian humanist and artistic methods and values occurred in northern Europe at about the same time and in somewhat similar ways. It is therefore helpful to keep in mind parallel developments in Germany (a land even more divided than Italy), France and other neighbouring countries. Among these must be included Scotland, and this not because from that day to this the foreigner confuses the component parts of the United Kingdom, but because in some ways the Renaissance had a more favourable climate in Scotland. The fifteenth century marks a high point in Scottish vernacular literature; and there were ecclesiastical, legal and educational changes which were conducive to the admission of new ideas. It was a Scottish king, James VI, who in 1603 became King also of England. In good humanist fashion James VI and I tried to name the new amalgam Great Britain.[10]

II. Anglo-Italian Contrasts

Any comparison of Italy and England in the age of Salutati and Chaucer must begin with the social scene, before proceeding to political institutions and practice, and the intellectual and artistic background. I shall start with the dissimilarities, as these have usually been stressed in earlier analyses.

At first sight society in Italy was dramatically different from what it was in England. Italy was a world of towns, big and little. The big towns, despite plague and prolonged economic recession, were much bigger and the small towns were infinitely more numerous than in England. Florence, Milan, Venice and Naples were all at least twice as populous as early-fifteenth century London, which had about 40,000 souls; and London was by far the biggest centre,

---

[10] Cf. S. T. Bindoff, 'The Stuarts and their Style', *English Historical Review*, LX (1945), 192-216; and my paper on 'The use of the term "Great Britain" in the Middle Ages', now reprinted in *Europe: The Emergence of an Idea*, 2nd ed. (Edinburgh, 1968), 128-144.

after which one dropped to a mere 10,000 at a few other important centres, York, Norwich, Coventry and Bristol. This was a reflection of the greater population and urban wealth of Italy and of the basically agrarian and village life of England. A distinction between town and country, between urban and bourgeois on the one hand and peasant and country gentleman on the other, marks this situation, even allowing that in Italian cities (as in cities everywhere) there were then large parks and gardens, long since built over. With this, perhaps even as a consequence of it, we must note a commercial and industrial activity in Italy which could not at the time be even remotely paralleled elsewhere. Admittedly this economic ferment was not universal in the peninsula. Florence, Milan, Venice and Genoa were in the fifteenth century, even if past their apogee, hardly typical of a land where the most numinous centre, Rome, was a collection of shabby ruins and the trade of Naples was largely controlled by Florentine bankers. Nevertheless the sophistication of the Italian businessman and his resources both technical and material made him appear a different animal to his northern counterpart, still pooling his slenderer capital, when engaged in long-distance trade, and with primitive methods of accounting. And the northern merchant in his Hanse was well aware of the difference, for the bankers of Tuscany were familiar figures, indeed rapidly becoming essential elements, in northern commerce. The English, especially in London and the bigger towns, had already exhibited their xenophobic sentiments.

In the English parliament there was a clumsy but unavoidable instrument through which much government had to operate and which, like the Crown, lent an air of unity to the public scene. Parliament by now an assembly with two houses, the lower consisting of elected gentry (lesser nobles in continental terms) and elected burgesses, the upper of the greater magnates (lords) and the greater clergy (prelates) passed statutes and voted money grants to the king. Apart from his irregular feudal revenue and the customs dues, the king was dependent on taxes voted in parliament and on subsidies voted by the clergy in their own assemblies. Constitutionalists like Fortescue and Commynes greatly admired the English parliament, but it undoubtedly prevented the king from tapping, as rulers did in France (and the Italian states), the real income of his subjects. This perhaps led to a certain sophistication in England. Budgeting a year ahead was important; it was scarcely found in the Italian hand-to-mouth financial arrangements. And we should not readily equate the Commons and Lords of England with the Estates (clergy, nobles, townsmen) of continental assemblies. Some elected representatives, the cream of the 'political class', governed in the Italian republics. Elsewhere the *parlamento* in Italy was a vestigial reminder of olden days, without real power and with no future. In one other field the contemporary observer might have detected a further political difference. The professional paid armies of France and England were larger and perhaps more loyal than the professional armies of the peninsula. This was perhaps a consequence of the Hundred Years War. It certainly derived strength from the stability of French and English dynasties; an element of allegiance entered the northern military situation which an Italian general like Francesco Sforza could scarcely feel for any of his employers; the sentiment was not even produced by two generations of Sforza rule as dukes of Milan. This military contrast was diminishing in the later fifteenth century, when many Italian states had standing armies of some kind—although this did not provide an 'Italian' force comparable to that of France.[11] And finally there is no doubt that the clergy outside Italy were subservient to their secular masters, and obedient to princely bidding. In Italy princes also tried to insist on control of the clergy but the pope was another prince with whom one sometimes had to make a deal.

This leads one to a consideration, necessarily somewhat longer, of the differences of a cultural kind between England and early Renaissance Italy. If religion may be subsumed under the rubric culture we may here notice at once the fire and colour of Italian devotion. The monastic life, withdrawn from the world, dependent on decent endowment and honest administration, was doubtless still practised with more success in England and the north than it was in Italy, where very many monasteries had collapsed into corruption and physical ruin. Episcopal control of diocesan discipline was likewise hardly to be found south of the Alps. Against this must be set the passionate devotion to the Holy Family (especially the Virgin) and the saints, the splendour of public worship in procession and at the great festivals, the repetition of mendicant excitement in the emergence in the 1360s of the Franciscan Observants.

---

[11] Cf. now Michael Mallett, *Mercenaries and their Masters: Warfare in Renaissance Italy* (London, 1974).

There is a tepidity about English religion in the later Middle Ages which makes the Italian seem perhaps unduly spiritual. There are no Bernardinos in London. There is little enough evidence even of Third Orders in England and even the quiet Brethren of the Common Life did not cross the North Sea. Parish rivalries in England were muted, compared with the violent polarisation of Mediterranean devotion. The Cathedral did not dominate so many cities; the Baptistery as such was unknown. With these differences, and closely related to them, was the relative wealth of the English secular clergy. This is most readily measured in episcopal income, but it covered the whole gamut of benefices. A fat clerical career was readily available in England and there was never difficulty in finding a poor curate or vicar to serve parishes which had lost most of the priests' stipend. In Italy there were parishes too poor to maintain any sort of priest; there were bishoprics with virtually no endowed income at all.

Probably more clergy in England (though still a small minority of the clerical order as a whole) went to universities than was the case in Italy, even allowing for the smaller English population. The universities to which they went were predominantly their own, Oxford and Cambridge. The days were nearly over when there was a substantial English nation in the Faculty of Arts at Paris; that had been killed by the long war, and it came to be called the German nation. Oxford and Cambridge not only educated clergy, which had been their main function from the start, but also an increasing number of laymen, anxious (as we shall see) for a little grammar and a year or two away from home, but not intending to put their university training to serious professional use. The courses were lengthy and, from a layman's point of view, singularly arid or inappropriate. We shall have to consider aspects of the scholastic scene later but it may be recorded here that to reach a bachelor degree at Oxford at the end of the fourteenth century the student usually spent four years in the schools; about three more years took him to a master's degree; if he aspired to the highest degree of all, the doctorate in Divinity, another seven or eight years were needed. Even if one began at the age of fifteen it was unlikely that one could finish before one was thirty. Wycliffe was over forty when he got his D.D. in 1372. Doctors of Divinity were at the apex of the educational ladder. In the English universities, as at Paris, theology was the senior discipline and the faculty of theology the senior faculty. For those who merely successfully survived the arts curriculum, a lush career opened out; 'churchmen, like their lay counterparts, were divided into the two nations of masters and men. The masters were the masters of arts'. [12]

Such a prolonged education needed money, so that in general it was the well-to-do clergy (apart from monks and friars) who were university trained. And the same can be said of the Italian university, save that the component of men in religious orders was conspicuously smaller: friars got their Divinity in one or other of their own convents; there were virtually no faculties of theology there in 1400. The prestige accorded in northern universities to theology was given in Italy to law and, to a much lesser degree, to medicine. Here again courses were long and expensive, young lawyers (as opposed to humbler notaries) tended to come from well-to-do families. How else could one afford a degree which, if one wished to be *Doctor utriusque juris*, doctor in both canon and civil law, took ten years— assuming one had adequate arts preparation to enter for a higher degree? Since young men reading law at the better Italian universities were about seventeen when they started they were often in their late twenties when they finished; there were, even at Bologna, short cuts but these were even more expensive. As with the northern doctor, the D.U.J. had the world at his feet.[13]

There is no disputing that we have here a difference between England and Italy which is of some cultural significance. The hierarchies of the professional élites were distinct. The young patrician on the road to high office and political prominence in Italy was trained in law, above all in Roman law. In England the practising lawyer was a common lawyer, trained not in Oxford or Cambridge but by a mixture of apprenticeship and teaching in the Inns of Court in London. Moreover, as we should notice in passing, this preeminence of the civil law was to pass from Italy to other northern countries, including Scotland, with the steady reception in these areas of Roman law. This did not in the end occur in England. There some canon law was taught at the universities until the Reformation, and a good deal of Roman law as well; the latter never had as much status at Oxford and Cambridge as Divinity, and we find a number

---

[12] K. B. McFarlane, *John Wycliffe and the Beginnings of English Nonconformity* (London, 1952), 14. And see *ibid.*, 19-21, for a succinct account of the Oxford university curriculum in the fourteenth century.

[13] A useful survey in Lauro Martines, *Lawyers and Statecraft in Renaissance Florence* (Princeton, 1968), 28-91.

of ambitious Englishmen reading civil law there as well as heading
for the schools of Bologna and Padua.[14]

The Latin formation of the M.A.s and theologians in the north
and of the lawyers in Italy was doubtless much the same in the
thirteenth and early fourteenth centuries: a solid foundation of
grammar and rhetoric. Already in the fourteenth century in Italy
we find some scholars inveighing against the law. Petrarch's aversion
to the legal training of his youth is well known, and this has a slightly
paradoxical air when one recalls how closely associated with an
interest in the classics were many lawyers of the time, many indeed
who were Petrarch's own admirers and correspondents.[15] Certainly
by the end of the century the number of lawyers and others who
had a higher command of classical Latin and a deeper understanding
of its possibilities for scholarship and art had begun to produce a
new situation in Italy, one which is not paralleled north of the Alps.
The D.D.s and B.D.s of the highest faculty in both Paris and Oxford
are still active as theologians and metaphysicians, but they are not
concerned to civilize their means of communication as the humanist
in Italy was. Nor should we place too much emphasis on university
training as a factor in promoting classical studies in Italy. It was
far more the way in which boys were taught Latin before going to
the university or in their training for the profession of notary.
Coluccio Salutati was a notary and had never been to a university.
One cannot find anyone remotely like him in the England of the
1380s and 1390s.[16]

Before the *Studia humanitatis* flowered after 1400 there was thus
far more evidence of changed attitudes to Latin literature to be
observed in Italy than elsewhere in Europe. Equally striking is the
extraordinary advance in the vernacular literature there during the
quattrocento. Dante, Petrarch and Boccaccio wrote much in Latin,
and much that was intensely original, but they were known to the
public in their own day and have been household words in Italy
ever since because of their Italian verse and prose. Only in England
have we two poets—Langland and Chaucer—who can (however

---

[14] See for students and for other English visitors, G. B. Parks, *The English
Traveller to Italy*, I (Rome, 1954).

[15] Roberto Weiss, *Il primo secolo del umanesimo italiano* (Rome, 1949).

[16] That is, no fourteenth-century product of an English 'business-school', as
such establishments have come to be called (*dictamen* in Latin and French, with
related drafting of conveyances, etc., and some accountancy), emerged as a good
scholar.

different their works are) bear comparison with the authors of the *Divine Comedy* and the *Trionfi*. No northern country could at the time match the prose of Boccaccio; we must remember that sophistication in prose is more demanding than in verse. It is surely not accidental that the three great Tuscans had each a remarkable talent in Latin composition. This cannot be said of the two English poets, and it is salutory to recall the gristly prose of *The Book of the Astrolabe* or 'The Persones Tale'. There seems little doubt that the more polished language of the Italian writers owed much to their better schooling in the classics.

There is thus a sharp enough contrast on the educational and literary fronts between Italy and England, or any other northern land. The same is true in art and architecture. The German or North French pilgrim to Rome or Palestine left behind him as he crossed the Alps a land of church spires and rural castles, and he entered a land where, despite the inroads of Gothic, the ancient basilica remained the basic pattern for a great church—indeed many of the cathedrals and collegiate churches were ancient enough in Italy— and where the magnate still had his town house as his fortress. So much has often been done later to destroy or remodel medieval Italian buildings that we may be in danger of overstressing differences: there is no doubt that the architects of Siena and Milan cathedrals were confidently copying French or Burgundian styles, and the same is true of scores of other thirteenth and fourteenth century churches. Medieval travellers seldom conveyed their reactions to novelties of an artistic kind, save in the case of curiosities such as the pavement in the Duomo in Siena. Yet the pervasive Romanesque and Byzantine survived, the coloured marble outside and the darkness within, and must have made the northern visitor conscious more of dissimilarity than of similarity even when he encountered churches expressly emulating styles with which he was familiar. And this must have been all the more the case when his eye fell on the painted decoration of altar or chapel or pulpit. Giotto and the Pisani have no contemporaries elsewhere on the Continent, let alone in England, who could match their accomplishments as painters and sculptors respectively, although it is arguable that the independent panel portrait was found in France before it emerged in Italy. Yet in the visual arts the late fourteenth century witnessed the dispersion all over Europe, Italy included, of the manner known to modern scholars as 'International Gothic'. Hence our comparison of England and Italy about

1400 has produced an area of shared experience. An Englishman who had admired the Wilton diptych would have found Lorenzo Monaco a sympathetic painter, or so it appears to one little qualified to generalise in the field of art history.

III. ANGLO-ITALIAN SIMILARITIES

There are many other similarities to record, many activities and assumptions common to the two countries. In turning to them now I shall deal with them, as before, under topics, economic and social, political, and those more general features of common culture to which we have been led by International Gothic. If Italy was a land of towns in some of which commerce and manufacturers had developed to an extent not found in other areas, it was also a country where, difficult as it may be to appreciate the fact, the vast majority of the population were peasants working in the fields and the hills. Moreover, one can see, though we seldom regard them, a rural 'aristocracy', who enter the records of the Romagna, or the Ligurian hinterland, or the kingdom of Naples as brigands and mercenary thugs, although for much of the class and for much of the time they cannot have been very different in their ambitions and enjoyments than the gentry and squirearchy of rural England. At all events their literary pleasures cannot have been very different—bawdy and lachrymose tales, many of them derived from the heroic cycles of Charlemagne and Arthur, and destined to provide, both in Italy and England, material for Renaissance epic. At a higher educational level, while the relative academic ratings of theology and law were undoubtedly as described above, there were of course many Italian theologians, the most able of whom often followed in the steps of Aquinas and Bonaventure to Paris. Likewise there were canonists and civilians in England: of the twenty-two archbishops of Canterbury and York whose pontificates fell in whole or in part into the fourteenth century, eight were doctors of civil law, four were doctors of both civil and canon law; only three were doctors of theology, two were M.A.s and four apparently had no degrees at all.[17]

---

[17] Figures taken, as later in this essay, from the new ed. of John Le Neve, *Fasti Ecclesiae Anglicanae 1300-1541*, 12 vols. (London, 1962-67). For comparison we may look at the degrees for which there is evidence held by cardinals created by the popes at Avignon: of the 66 for whom details are available (about half the total) 18 were theologians, 21 were canonists, 18 were civilians, and 7 D.U.J.s. Bernard Guillemain, *La cour pontificale à Avignon* (Paris, 1966), 217.

Again it is true that there was a unified central government in England, and in the fourteenth century war with Scotland and France did much to intensify the loyalties of his subjects to the king. English culture was gravitating ineluctably to a court and London was becoming a capital where litigation, administration and pleasure attracted nobles, gentry and burgesses from the whole land. Yet much of this political homogeneity is somewhat illusory. Great families dominated many country areas and the reign of the young king Richard II was to see a popular rebellion confined to the more advanced agricultural areas of south and east, and it was to culminate in his deposition and murder by magnates outraged by what they regarded as his high-handed and arbitrary rule. Italian politics may have been precarious at that time but none of his subjects deposed Giangaleazzo Visconti. If royal power existed throughout the realm of England it was often in practice exercised by, and to the advantage of, local potentates. So powerful is the model of monarchic unity that we forget these things, we forget Ireland, we assume that Edward I's conquest of Wales was at once effective and ignore the continuing independence or unruliness of the Marcher lords of the west and the north. All of this was reflected in the emergence of a mercenary or 'bastard' feudalism which has striking parallels with the *condotte* of Italy: a prince bought the services of soldiers for regular wages.

Nor can it be overlooked that, despite the different structures of the university curricula and despite the differing places occupied by the higher faculties of divinity and law, the substructure of fourteenth-century education was much the same everywhere. Basic Latin grammar was taught from Donatus and Priscian and from the glosses, commentaries and versifications derived from these authors, most pervasively the *Doctrinale* of Alexander de Villedieu. However wildly the pronunciation of language may have varied, Italians and Englishmen shared the same Latin grammar and more or less the same collections of authors—I refer to the run-of-the-mill scholar and student. Accidence and syntax do not lend themselves to regional variations and are resistant in the main to any fundamental alteration. What was to characterise humanist education was not the structure of elementary instruction in Latin, but the use to which it was put.

Italians, then, with the rest of the inhabitants of Western Europe, shared much the same economy, had much the same social and political arrangements, and were not too sharply distinguished by cultural attitudes. Even at the level of the vernacular a common substratum of *motifs* and traditional tales permeated all areas of Europe. Differences indeed there were, but an intellectual, Bishop Richard of Bury, diplomat author of the *Philobiblon*, could happily encounter Petrarch while he was on a mission to Avignon in 1333, as Geoffrey Chaucer seems to have done at Padua forty years later. Such contacts have sometimes been used to urge that there were men who belonged in some sense to the same 'movement'. It would be absurd to compare either of the Englishmen with Petrarch. Bury was an avid book-collector and admirer of scholarship, but his views on life and literature were conventional. Chaucer was a great poet, but entirely lacked Petrarch's philosophical and speculative interests, or his mastery of Latin. Nor can one regard as early 'humanists' the group of English mendicants about whom Miss Beryl Smalley has written so entertainingly in her *English Friars and Antiquity in the Early XIVth Century*.[18] What one can say is that in the fourteenth century there was a shared experience of religion, society and culture upon which subsequent development was to be based.

It is indeed this situation which makes the different routes taken in literature and the arts in England and Italy after about 1400 so very remarkable. That the two roads were later to join in the highway of early modern civilization makes the *quattrocento* contrasts all the more interesting and deserving of exploration.

IV. FIFTEENTH CENTURY CHANGE: ITALY AND ENGLAND

There is no doubt that Italy witnessed first the changes which we summarise in the term 'Renaissance'. It is, however, important to remember that the Renaissance, despite all its dramatic innovations was only gradually an Italian phenomenon, that is one affecting the peninsula more or less as a whole. It is necessary at the outset to set down the main stages in the development of new approaches in Italy so that they may be set against the time-table in England. I hope I may be forgiven for here summarising an argument which I have set out elsewhere at greater length.[19]

Perhaps it is as well to recall in broad outline the political scene.

---

[18] Oxford, 1960; see my review in *English Historical Review*, LXXVII (1962), 530-532.

[19] *The Italian Renaissance in its Historical Background* (Cambridge, 1961); the Italian translation has a revised bibliography. I do not repeat annotation in what follows.

The years of papal residence at Avignon (1305-78) had enabled or provoked the development of strong *signorie* in north Italy and the papal states. After the Schism (1378-1417) the re-established papacy managed with some set-backs to establish itself firmly in Rome, making the city a political centre of significance for the first time since the early thirteenth century. This precipitated a prolonged struggle for power in the Papal States, in turn involving Venice, Milan and Florence, to whose outcome rulers of the Kingdom of Naples, of whatever race, could not be indifferent. Until the 1450s there was a period of prolonged and bloody conflict. After 1454 and the establishment of the Italian League a period of uncertain equilibrium followed, to be ended by the death of the ruler of Naples in 1494 and the French invasion which followed. By the early sixteenth century the major powers of continental Europe had armies and political ambitions in the peninsula. It was against this background that there emerged the novel approaches to cultural and ethical problems which were in the end to be of such interest to the world at large.

The period of 'pre-humanism' in Italy contained some remarkable scholars and personalities. Petrarch was by far the greatest although Boccaccio in his Latin works was probably more accessible to other students, a more consistent exponent of new trends, and more immediately influential on scholarship. This period came to an end in the 1370s when Petrarch and Boccaccio both died and when Coluccio Salutati, notary and administrator, was appointed to be Chancellor of the republic of Florence. He it was (and again I use Voigt's extraordinarily perceptive phrase) who secured for humanism the right of citizenship in Florence. The 'new learning', one might say, had found an environment in which it was cherished—cherished, we must admit, for good reasons and for bad: because it was a weapon in the Florentine diplomatic armoury; because it was a comforting thing for worldly men to be told that they might be comfortable without being offensive in the eyes of God; because classical ideas chimed in with the art of Masaccio and Ghiberti, with the architecture of Brunelleschi; because it soon became chic to patronise the *studia humanitatis* even if one was not necessarily an adept.

With Coluccio and his successor, the chancellor Leonardo Bruni, we enter a remarkable period in Florentine history. The early decades of the fifteenth century see Florentines rewriting their history and rebuilding and redecorating their city. Much of this activity was provoked, it seems, by a desire to justify the cruel expense and prolonged efforts to withstand a series of political threats—from Milan, from Naples, from Milan again—which stretched out into the period when, after 1430, Cosimo de' Medici began to manage much of the political life of what remained, in a very important sense, a republic. These years witness an extraordinary flowering of humanist literature and of artistic achievement. It was perhaps natural that neighbouring states like Siena should react against Florentine manners and men. Other parts of the peninsula had little use for cultural accomplishments which were wrapped up in the envelope of republicanism. Yet in the 1440s and 1450s a bridge was being built between Florence and her neighbours. Cosimo de' Medici, the greatest patron of his dynasty as well as the shrewdest man of business, displayed the advantages of wealth and power by exhibiting his sympathy for books and ideas, for a new art and a new architecture. In his own day, as ever since, Florence laid claim to be the home of civilisation. This was a claim heard enviously by the other rulers of Italy. Medici power lay not only in a counting house and a vast commercial empire; it lay also with libraries and writers and with handsome new buildings. All of this could be readily adapted to bolster up the prestige and power of a prince as well as of a first citizen—indeed a prince had certain advantages in display over a Florentine subject who eschewed overt demonstrations of his magnificence. In 1450 Florence made peace with the Milanese. It was a sign perhaps that Florentine cultural primacy was coming to an end.

By the mid-fifteenth century the new art and the new humanities had begun to grow roots in the least propitious places. Small dynasties like the houses of Este and Gonzaga began to throw up great patrons and massive buildings. In Urbino, where a poor hill-top town in Umbria seemed to offer an inauspicious environment for advances in the arts, a successful *condottiere* Guidobaldo da Montefeltro built a superb modern palace and filled it with one of the most splendid collections of books and pictures. The papal court, meanwhile, was not only led by Nicholas V into plans for rebuilding St. Peter's and the Borgo, but heard the argument urged that the successor of St. Peter, far from being evangelically poor or stoically indifferent to riches, must himself be wealthy if he was to do proper justice to his role.

The final phase in Italian developments came with the penetration of humanist literature and (if the expression may be accepted) humanist art and architecture, into the great principalities of Italy—Milan, Naples and Venice. By now the doctrines of the active life and of service of the community had lost their republican overtones; even at Venice the Republic was a republic of 'nobles'. Now was the time when the ideas and the methods of the humanist, having penetrated Italy as a whole, could be more readily assimilated in neighbouring lands.

It has seemed desirable to take the broad outline of cultural development in Italy down to the end of the fifteenth century. It may be put in a few words as being centred in Florence, then in smaller courts, finally in larger ones; or as moving from a republican milieu to a princely one. We often still treat the Renaissance in Italy as a single movement, whereas it was diverse in both time and place. Diverse indeed far beyond what is revealed in the sketch offered above. Under Alfonso V, for instance, we find a king patronising some scholars, but as a centre of humanist activity with strong and continuous traditions Naples had to wait till the end of the century. Likewise (and this will be a factor to be encountered later in the evolution of the English scene) we must not regard Florence as dropping out of the race. Lorenzo de' Medici, while a lesser patron than his grandfather, was a lover of literature and continued to encourage the study and translation of Plato by Ficino and his friends. And far from slipping easily into a principate, after Lorenzo's death in 1492, Florence experienced a period of intense popular government: this was the age of Savonarola and Botticelli.

Before we turn to examine the situation in England we must identify the main features of the humanist programme. Expressed in a word this was (as we have seen the word itself implies) education.[20] It was a programme by which young men who would have public responsibilities were to be given training suited to their role in society. (This does not, of course, exclude a few prominent women being educated in this way, nor a large number of men who in the end became clergymen). The method of instruction was based on a thorough competence in Latin grammar and practice in using the language for speaking and writing. This last depended on an absorp-

---

[20] The works of W. H. Woodward remain basic expositions of the theory and (so far as we can assume it followed the methods of Guarino and Vittorino) the practice of the new curriculum: *Vittorino da Feltre and other Humanist Educators* (Cambridge, 1897); *Studies in Education during the Age of the Renaissance* (Cambridge, 1906). See also R. R. Bolgar, *The Classical Heritage and its Beneficiaries* (Cambridge, 1954).

tion of the precepts of the classical rhetorical writings of Cicero
and Quintilian; the main rhetorical practices had, of course, been
known and applied throughout the Middle Ages, but they were
now studied in the original theorists and with a new fervour for
civilised and stylish composition. All of this depended on a regular
study of the Latin classics and an emphasis on the moral teaching
of the philosophers, historians and poets. The prescription, it will
be seen, was a hard one. Boys had learned Latin in earlier centuries,
but only those destined for the Church had to take its study seriously
and even they were supposed to apply it not to the cultivation of
their moral or literary sensibilities but to the needs of devotion, of
scriptural exegesis, of liturgical observance and the business of the
Church. Now education was to be firmly structured in what were
regarded as the interests of the laity and so firmly did a 'classical'
curriculum become associated with the governing classes of Italy
and later of Europe that it is only in our own day that it is ceasing
to dominate the secondary schools. In my judgment there is no
doubt that the 'political class' of Florence, in the decades pivoting
on 1400, as later in the courtiers and gentlemen of Italy, took to the
new education because it was based on assumptions regarding
public and private morality more in keeping with their actual lives
than the traditional renunciation of life preached by Christian teachers.[21] A sympathy, conscious with the clever and instinctive with
the rest, drew more and more Italians of substance towards a plan
of learning based ultimately on an ethos that was compatible with
involvement in business public and private, and the rewards in
wealth and temporal honour which went with such involvement.
The world of Cicero and Livy, of Vergil and Ovid was an upper-
class world; the Latin of the Golden Age was designed for and
perfected by élites; all of this cemented the hold which the new
schoolmaster acquired over the teaching of men who mattered.

It must not be supposed that the humanists took over all instruction. For long the novel attitudes to literature and moral philosophy
made little impression on the university curriculum, although they
were not actively repulsed. Hence Aristotle stood unchallenged in
the universities, as he was to do until the seventeenth century. Side
by side with the cultivation of the new humanities at Florence,

---

[21] I must refer here to the seminal studies on the active life and the problem of
wealth contributed in 1938 by Hans Baron to *The Bulletin of the John Rylands Library*,
XX, 72-97, and *Speculum*, XIII, 1-37.

Ferrara, Mantua, or Venice, we have the unchallenged place of Justinian's code and digest, and of the Greek medical texts at Bologna, Pavia, Padua, Pisa. But more and more of the doctors of law or medicine were also steeped in the humanities and, like the gentry who were their social equals, ensured that their children had a classical education.

This then, from the viewpoint of ideas and pedagogical methods, was what the Italy of the fifteenth century had to offer Europe. In the fine arts and architecture a classicism no less imposing manifested itself, which I am not competent to do more than allude to. What did Englishmen find in this splendour which they could admire and use?

In England between 1399 and 1500 we are at first sight presented by an almost uninterrupted period of war, internal and external. It is the internal war (the Wars of the Roses) which appears to have been more damaging than the external war with France. The deposition of Richard II by Henry Bolingbroke in 1399, of Henry VI by Edward of York in 1461 and 1471, the murder of Edward's children by Richard III and the latter's defeat at Bosworth by the rank outsider Henry Earl of Richmond in 1485, who was to have two serious rebellions in his reign, are merely the highlights in a gruesome story. The divisions at the centre, the struggle for the throne itself, enabled thugs of all kinds noble and non-noble to practise brutality at the perimeter. Compared with such divisive forces the war with France exercised, as we have seen, a certain cohesive pressure: Agincourt was a tonic for distracted Englishmen; Henry V could become a hero-king. In any event (and much to the grumbling discontent of those who had done well in France) the English were evicted from all their conquests save Calais and the war petered out in 1453. Yet for all the treasure and blood squandered in France, for all the ruthlessness of the civil war at home (where the gentler conventions of chivalry and ransoms did not apply) one's overall impression of fifteenth-century England is one of promise rather than prejudice, to adopt C. L. Kingsford's celebrated title.[22]

---

[22] *Prejudice and Promise in Fifteenth Century England* (Oxford, 1925); there are good things in the rather disjointed contents, but none as good as the title. Two recent short books are full of interesting ideas: F. R. H. Du Boulay, *An Age of Ambition* (London, 1970); and J. R. Lander, *Conflict and Stability in Fifteenth-Century England* (London, 1969). Short but reliable accounts of the political and social background will also be found in A. R. Myers, *England in the late Middle Ages* (Harmondsworth, 1952), and George Holmes, *The Later Middle Ages* (Edinburgh, 1962).

War and economic stagnation did not prevent Henry VII being a stronger, more effective king than any of his predecessors save perhaps William I and Edward I. And when Henry VII died in 1509 he bequeathed his son a greater fortune than had ever been at the disposal of an heir to the throne. The machinery of central government steadily went on during the turmoil of the fifteenth century. Parliament met with such regularity that constitutional historians used to refer admiringly to the 'Lancastrian experiment'. More local rivalries were settled by due process of law than were settled by violence, which in any case was endemic in every part of Europe until the eighteenth century. The country gentleman wrote his letters even in the darkest days of the mid-century knowing that they would be delivered, and his estates, however widely scattered, were managed by men who had evidently never heard of the Wars of the Roses.[23] If the lack of 'governance' had been as bad as used to be alleged one would hardly expect landowners to have squandered fortunes not on defensible fortresses but on those comfortable mansions where crenellation was merely a status symbol.

The vast majority of the middle group in society, the 'Commons' of well-to-do burgesses and country squires, pursued its way more or less untroubled, but the changes in the dynasty and the fortunes of the very great have considerable interest for the cultural historian. There were features of Italian humanist activity very relevant to princes and great men, whether falling or rising in power. Likewise the sentiments which attracted the burgesses and minor nobility of Italy towards the new educational plan were far from absent in England or any other country of North Europe. Before examining how far these forces led to a quickening interest in the civilization of *quattrocento* Italy we must first briefly examine the points of contact between the two countries—and in doing so recall that to all intents and purposes the Italy we are dealing with excludes the Kingdoms of Naples and the duchy of Savoy.

V. ANGLO-ITALIAN CONTACTS

In his study of *The English Traveller to Italy* George B. Parks listed the following categories of visitors: kings and diplomats, clerics and pilgrims, soldiers and merchants.[24] (These categories overlap,

---

[23] On this see Kingsford, *Prejudice and Promise*, 33-34, 67-73. Too much emphasis has been put on the exceptional circumstances of the Paston family.

[24] Pp. 276-494.

a man who figures early as a student may later reappear as an envoy).
Few princes made the journey in the warring Middle Ages. Lionel
duke of Clarence married Violante Visconti in 1368, and died soon
afterwards. Bolingbroke, the future Henry IV, passed through
North Italy on his way as a pilgrim to the Holy Land in 1392-93.
Lord Rivers, Edward IV's brother-in-law, was in Italy, probably
as a pilgrim during a year of Jubilee (1475), and Edward IV's sister,
the dowager duchess of Suffolk, was in Rome in 1500, another
year of Jubilee. Far more important as a source of fruitful contact
than these episodic and aristocratic travellers were the professional
diplomats who, now that the pope was again an Italian and (after
1420, and more permanently since 1443) resident in Rome, maintained
English interests in the Curia. Many of these were Italians, as we
shall see, but the well-trained, if traditionally trained, professionals,
nearly all clerks with prelacies, listed by Parks contain the majority
of Englishmen who figure in the reception of Italian humanism in
fifteenth-century England.[25] To them must be added a small number
of English members of the Curia, whose limited literacy in Latin
and odd pronunciation aroused Flavio Biondo to adverse comment;[26]
a list of them would not be long but it would be worth compiling.[27]
Its most distinguished fifteenth-century member would be Adam
Moleyns, D.U.J., who served under Eugenius IV for about five
years (1430-1435). At any rate his written Latin passed muster.

If diplomacy took a fair number of distinguished men from
England to Italy for longish periods, business traditionally associated
with the Curia was drying up as a result of legislation against papal
provisions and the legal jurisdiction of Rome. Provisors and Praemunire were irregularly applied. Despite Provisors (1351 and later
reenactments) prelates continued to be technically 'provided' by
the pope and to pay common services; but they normally did this
through agents in Rome and lesser fry were prohibited from seeking
benefices through papal interventions. As for the Rota, a handful

---

[25] *Ibid.*, 301-303.

[26] F. Biondo, *Scritti inediti*, ed. B. Nogara (Città del Vaticano, 1927), 125,
in the 'De verbis Romanae locutionis'. Other non-Italians are censured along
with the 'Anglicos-Britannos . . . qui etsi litteras sciunt, adeo tamen rudes et
artis grammaticae aliarumque scientiarum aliquando ignari sunt . . . .' Their
defects are especially noticeable in 'latini sermonis . . . practicam'.

[27] The main reason why there were relatively few English curialists was that
there were no resident English cardinals before Bainbridge, and of course no
English popes; for similar reasons there are few English curialists in the Avignon
period: see the various tables in Guillemain, *La cour pontificale à Avignon*.

of English appeals are recorded (despite the statute of Praemunire)
throughout the fifteenth century—and some few litigants travelled
to Italy to supervise their Roman advocates.[28] Likewise a few Englishmen are found in the list of ordinations *apud sedem apostolicam*.[29]
There is small reason to suppose that these intermittent associations
with the learned *scriptores* had much cultural effect. Nor did the
much larger number of pilgrims contain many whose intellectual
formation was affected by a visit *ad limina*, though some of the agents
and ambassadors whose influence we must discuss shortly were
enrolled in the English college, the Hospice of the Holy Trinity
and St. Thomas of Canterbury in via Monserrato and in the various
fashionable confraternities patronised by foreign visitors.[30]

Mr. Parks's categories of soldiers and merchants are of small
interest to us; Italian merchants were far more prominent in England
than English merchants in Italy; English soldiers only figured to
any extent in the Italian wars of the fourteenth century. But with
students we deal with a group which was to prove much more alert
to cultural change, much quicker to transmit new ideas, and where
our information, although far from complete, is nevertheless based
on surviving graduation and other registers from Bologna, Padua
and other universities. There are gaps in these records but those
for Bologna seem sufficiently full for the later fifteenth century for
us to say with some confidence that English students were increasingly
switching their interest to civil law. Between 1451 and 1475 only
three Englishmen are recorded as graduating in civil law against
nine canonists; in the last quarter of the fifteenth century we find
thirteen civilians, fourteen canonists and four D.U.J.s.[31] A similar
impression is gained from the more fragmentary records of other
Italian universities.[32] On the other hand it will appear that the students
who were to prove most friendly to the new humanities were not
lawyers, but divines, so far as their training and qualifications were
concerned.

---

[28] I owe this information to the kindness of Mr. James Robertson.

[29] I hope to publish a study of curial ordinations.

[30] Parks, *The English Traveller to Italy*, 358-382. On the hospice see now B.
Newns, 'The hospice of St. Thomas and the English Crown', *The Venerabile*,
XXI (1962).

[31] Parks, *The English Traveller to Italy*, 625-627.

[32] *Ibid.*, 628-640; R. J. Mitchell, 'English students at Padua 1460-1475',
Transactions of the Royal Historical Society, 4th series, XIX (1936), 101-117; *id.*,
'English students at Ferrara in the fifteenth century', *Italian Studies*, I (1937),
74-82.

The traffic in Englishmen to Italy was balanced by visits of Italians
to England. These Italians were fewer in number but perhaps overall
more influential in stature. They have attracted much attention
from historians of humanism in England but we should remember
that most Italians who came to England came for professional
reasons (trade, diplomacy, ecclesiastical business) rather than as
students in search of learning or the support of cultivated patrons.
However much English scholastics such as Scotus and Ockham
were admired by Italian students of theology or philosophy, I cannot
find that there were many Italians at Oxford or Cambridge in the
fifteenth century;[33] the admiration felt for English scholastic thought,
which is reflected in well-known humanist jibes about British sophists
and so on [34] was nourished by books and not by the somewhat
unimpressive lectures of the English universities.[35] The Italian
merchant in England must have often been involved in the importation
of books and perhaps other objects of Italian origin, but such trade
is hard to document. What we do know is that the printed book
trade, although it was dominated by foreigners for half a century
after 1475, does not seem to have attracted Italian enterprise.[36]
Secular diplomacy, if we may judge by the earliest (ca. 1500) Venetian
relazione, was cool and calculating.[37] The ambassador made for the
men who mattered and they were important because they were
politicians, not because they were reputed to be intellectually eminent,
at any rate before Thomas More became chancellor. Castiglione's
visit of 1504 was, it appears, not a cultural occasion: [38] his influence
was to date from 1528 with the publication of *Il Cortegiano*.

---

[33] I count about a dozen Italians among the 60 foreign Dominicans sent to
study at Blackfriars in Oxford in the fourteenth and fifteenth centuries; see
appendices to W. A. Hinnebusch's paper on the subject in *Oxford Studies Presented
to Daniel Callus*, Oxford Historical Society, new series, XVI (1964), 101-134.
A. B. Emden in the introduction to his *A Biographical Register of the University of
Oxford to 1500*, 3 vols. (Oxford, 1957-59), I, xlii, says that only a few mendicants
came from abroad.

[34] E.g., in *Prosatori latini del quattrocento*, ed. Eugenio Garin (Milan, 1952),
60: Bruni's reference to 'britannicis sophismatibus'.

[35] A brief but suggestive survey of English writings known to Italian scholars,
a relatively unexplored field, in Parks, *The English Traveller to Italy*, 446-455.

[36] See below p. 350.

[37] *A Relation of . . . England*, ed. C. A. Sneyd (Camden Society, 1847).

[38] See the important revisions of Cecil B. Clough, 'Federigo Veterani, P.
Vergil's Anglica Historia and B. Castiglione's Epistola . . . ad Henricum Angliae
Regem', *English Historical Review*, LXXXII (1967), 772-783.

On the other hand, ecclesiastical diplomacy and the administrative business of the church did bring a number of persons to England who were humanists in the sense we have been using the term. None was a literary or scholarly figure of the first rank or even perhaps of the second. Poggio (if we may group him here), Piero del Monte, and lesser figures such as Simone da Teramo, Giuliano Cesarini and Gaspare da Verona; all these were in England in the early fifteenth century.[39] In the later fifteenth century papal emissaries were more important prelates as well as more thoroughly trained in the new educational manner of Italy: for example Giovanni and Silvestro Gigli, Adriano Castellesi, and (beyond 1500) Polydore Vergil and Piero Griffo.[40]

VI. English Patrons in the Fifteenth Century

By the time we reach the reign of Henry VII it is evident that there is a change in the official climate of opinion regarding the humanities. Before this is considered we must revert to the fifteenth-century environment and those Anglo-Italian contacts which bore fruit, however meagre. There are two sides to the matter. On the one hand we have a small group of wealthy English patrons whose personal learning is of less moment than their admiration for the learning of other people. On the other we have a smaller group of men whose talents reflected the new learning and who were fired to some extent by the novelties in the Renaissance programme of scholarship.

The wealthy English patrons are headed by a royal duke. Why Humphrey duke of Gloucester became enamoured of the new learning, even the degree to which he properly realised its novelty, must remain in some doubt.[41] He was vain and ambitious, knew France and the Low Countries and (through Italians such as the bishop of Bayeux, Zenone di Castiglione) must have been aware of the new learning such as it had filtered into France by this time.[42] The effectiveness of up-to-date Latin propaganda might have attracted him to the new style, although there was plenty of old-fashioned Latin and vernacular propaganda circulating in the Anglo-French

---

[39] Weiss, *Humanism in England*, 23-24.

[40] See now Michele Monaco, ed., *De officio collectoris in regno Angliae di Pietro Griffo da Pisa* (Rome, 1973), esp. 171-222 of the introduction.

[41] Weiss, *Humanism in England*, 39-70 and addenda; also the Bodleian exhibition catalogue, *Duke Humphrey and English Humanism*.

[42] Cf. below p. 333.

ambience which, one might have thought, would have carried more
influence than neo-classical panegyrics or hexameters.[43] At any rate
Humphrey had two Latin secretaries and used them as an Italian
prince would have done: for correspondence, administration and
flattery of Humphrey and his causes. He also accumulated contacts
with many important Italian scholars as well as a library containing
many humanist works commissioned or solicited by him, or sent
by hungry authors to the gullible Maecenas in faraway Britain. His
principal literary dogsbody was Tito Livio Frulovisi and Professor
Weiss regarded the life of Henry V written for Humphrey by Frulovisi
as the most influential of his many writings—but an influence exerted
rather in the sphere of historiography than in the classical revival
as such.[44] Certainly the poem the 'Humproidos' exalting Humphrey
himself passed at once into a deserved oblivion from which it has
only recently been partially recovered.[45] A more permanent inspiration for future scholars lay in his library. This is forever com-
memorated by the name 'Duke Humphrey' for part of the Bodleian
Library in Oxford. There is no doubt that Humphrey's collections
were very remarkable. His books included not only the classics
as known in the Middle Ages (and these were for the most part
the ones that mattered in the Renaissance) in new modern editions,
but also copies of recently discovered ancient texts. Even more
significant, he had a fair sample of the writings of Petrarch and his
successors. And he possessed not only the traditional Petrarch
(De remediis and so forth) but the more original Petrarch of the
letters and the Rerum memorandarum libri. He had Boccaccio's De
genealogiis deorum, Salutati's De laboribus Herculis, and probably other
humanist works of significance as well as a mountain of humanist
trivia.[46] Humphrey intended all his books for Oxford, but in the
end a number of them ended up in King's College Cambridge and
many were dispersed. The university library suffered in proportion

---

[43] For instance Le débat des herauts d'armes, ed. L. Pannier and P. Meyer, Société
des anciens textes français (Paris, 1877); A. Bossuat, 'La littérature de propagande
au XVe siècle: le mémoire de Jean de Rinel ... contre le duc de Bourgogne',
Cahiers d'histoire, I (Grenoble, 1956), 131-146.

[44] I paraphrase Weiss, Humanism in England, 44-45.

[45] Roberto Weiss, 'Humphrey duke of Gloucester and Tito Livio Frulovisi',
in Fritz Saxl. A Volume of Memorial Essays (Edinburgh, 1957), 218-227.

[46] On Humphrey's collection, see Weiss, Humanism in England, 62-67, with
related corrigenda and addenda, and the Bodley Library catalogue, Duke Humphrey
and English Humanism (1970).

as the colleges became effective teaching units.[47] It is however indisputable that his gifts to Oxford provided for a time the nucleus of a collection of classical and neo-classical texts the like of which did not exist elsewhere outside Italy.

Another nobleman of markedly less august origins who collected books and obedient humanist dependents was John Tiptoft, created earl of Worcester in 1449.[48] Another ambitious man, he coincided with the upheaval in England of the late 1450s and escaped from them to pilgrimage in Palestine and a visit of rather more than two years to Italy whence he returned (some thought) with an Italianate relish for tyranny. His scholarly aims were more personal than those of Humphrey: he had read arts at Oxford and later tried to be a humanist himself, as well as a patron of the many Italian scholars he met and of a few Englishmen like Free. His patronage was probably more important than the large collection of texts he accumulated, for these were in the event scattered after his execution in 1470. This did not mean that all his books were lost to English readers but it frustrated his intention of endowing Oxford and Cambridge in the manner of Duke Humphrey. His own talents as a Latinist are judged to be mediocre. His own tastes as reflected in his translations of Cicero (*De amicitia, De senectute*) and Buonaccorso da Montemagno (*De nobilitate*) were conventional.

Descending a further rung in the hierarchy of nobility we encounter the more imposing figure of William Gray or Grey, son of a north country knight and a daughter of the first Neville earl of Westmorland, nephew of a man who was successively bishop of London and Lincoln. Gray was well-connected, rich with benefices and a graduate of Oxford. From Oxford he went to Cologne to read theology (1442) and thence to Italy (1445) where he finally became a graduate in theology at Padua. He visited Florence, spent a few months attending Guarino's course at Ferrara and was then appointed royal proctor in Rome where he remained, with short visits back to England, until his final return in 1453 shortly before being given the see of Ely. And all the time—in Oxford, in Cologne, in Padua, Ferrara and Rome, and through the Florentine bookseller Vespasiano —Gray was buying books and on his death in 1478 they came to

---

[47] See *Duke Humphrey and English Humanism* and also the catalogue of another Bodley exhibition, *Oxford College Libraries in 1556* (1956), with an introduction by Dr. Neil Ker.

[48] Weiss, *Humanism in England*, 112-122 and refs.

his old college Balliol.[49] The collection is not remarkable from the humanist point of view. Gray was a theologian by training and by interest. But he bought books wherever they were good and interesting and in this way, especially during his Italian sojourn, he acquired a few classical texts and some *quattrocento* Italian writings. More important in the long run for literature was Gray's patronage for a few years in Italy of Niccolò Perotti and his encouragement of John Free. There is no evidence that his munificence was extended to these men as a matter of policy; he was a far more frequent benefactor of clergy who were neither humanists nor scholars.

Gray's career is strikingly paralleled in that of Robert Flemmyng. Another rich bishop's rich nephew, an Oxford man who later studied divinity at Cologne and Padua, another serious collector of books (bequeathed in the end to Lincoln College) he nevertheless is in many ways to be distinguished from Gray. He was without question attracted to the new learning. His attendance at Guarino's lectures was longer and less perfunctory than Gray's and he attained some competence in Greek, which he was at pains to keep up. There were Greek manuscripts in the collection given to Lincoln College, as well as a number of modern Latin versions of Greek classics, and the spread of his classical Latin texts was more extensive than Gray's; he had a copy of Valla's *Elegantiae*; he could employ 'a neat italic handwriting'. Even his embarking on a poetical eulogy of Sixtus IV and his Rome in the *Lucubraciuncula tiburtinae* (ca. 1477), bad though the verse is 'by Italian standards', represents a gesture which none of the patrons of scholarship and collectors of books previously mentioned could have attempted.[50]

Yet we must remember that, as with Gray, so with Flemmyng, divinity and books of a theological or liturgical character remained the prime interest. Lincoln College was devoted to divinity and I do not clearly understand what Weiss has in mind when he says of Flemmyng: 'As a "Maecenas" he contributed to the introduction of humane standards into Oxford, and to the bringing of theology into contact with neo-classicism'.[51] The one young English scholar whom any of these eminent personages directed towards the human-

---

[49] *Ibid.*, 86-95, and now the admirable account by R. A. B. Mynors, *Catalogue of the Manuscripts of Balliol College Oxford* (Oxford, 1963), introduction, xxiv-xlv.

[50] Weiss, *Humanism in England*, 86-95. Parks, *The English Traveller to Italy*, 601-606, gives a literal version of part of the poem.

[51] Weiss, *Humanism in England*, 105.

ities (apart from putting books on library shelves) was John Free.[52]
Free, after studying at Balliol, was sent by Gray, now bishop of Ely,
to work under Guarino at Ferrara in 1456; later on he was secretary
to Tiptoft. He undoubtedly became an accomplished scholar in both
Latin and Greek. His achievements, according to Weiss, place him
'beyond all doubt above every fifteenth-century English humanist
before the time of Grocyn and Linacre'.[53] While one cannot disagree
with this it is hard to see what consequences his career had for
literature and learning. He copied a few manuscripts (doubtless
more than the handful which have survived). He wrote a few formal
Latin letters and orations. He translated the Greek of Synesius's
satirical essay *On Baldness* into Latin. It is impossible to attribute
to him any lasting impression on the culture of his day in Italy or
England. His death at Rome in 1465 was hardly an intellectual
catastrophe. Weiss groups with 'the English pupils of Guarino'
(Gray, Tiptoft, Free) a more interesting man, John Gunthorpe,
about whom I shall say a word shortly.[54] For the rest the other
'English pupils of Guarino' seem to me somewhat idiosyncratic
characters who were touched with a love of books, enjoyed to some
extent the literary life, but in no sense were aware of the significance
of what was happening in Italy. It seems to me that we can apply
to all of them reflections similar to those of Sir Roger Mynors on
Bishop Gray:

> If we try to summarise the impression left on us by Gray as a patron
> of learning and a book-collector, we see at once that he was no renais-
> sance prelate-patron. He kept no tame humanists in his household,
> except Niccolò Perotti for a short time as a youth of eighteen. He
> received no dedications, except from the inexhaustible John Capgrave,
> who had been wooing Duke Humphrey a quarter of a century before.
> He was no great promotor of learning in others, except for his not
> very lavish support of John Free, whom he had decided to send to
> Italy as companion to one of his own nephews. . . . Nor was he
> specially devoted to the new learning. . . . It is the wide range and
> high standard of his original texts in philosophy and theology that
> is so impressive. . . . .[55]

It is hardly surprising that men brought up in the older mental
traditions should find it easier to assimilate what was familiar to

---

[52] R. J. Mitchell, *John Free. From Bristol to Rome in the Fifteenth Century* (London,
1955).

[53] Weiss, *Humanism in England*, 111.

[54] See below, p. 340.

[55] Mynors, *Catalogue*, xlv.

them. It was the Petrarch of the *De remediis* not the Petrarch of the *Secretum* which proved immediately comprehensible. It was the traditional morality purveyed by Bruni's translation of Aristotle's *Ethics* or *Politics* not (perhaps understandably) the much more explosive but domestic works such as the *Dialogue* against Vergerio or the history of Florence. Exactly the same kind of filter operated in the reception of Italian humanist writings in France, as has been shown by Professor Franco Simone.[56] To the incomprehensions inherent in this situation we should add hesitations due to a more positive hostility to all things Italian. King, Lords, Commons and clergy were at one in a generalised suspicion of the Italian—papal fiscality, papal rascality and the clever bankers who were the agents of rapacious Rome. In so far as the common lawyers were aware of a threat they too were resentful: Wycliffe had urged the superiority of the common law over the Roman law and so, later on, did Fortescue; Tiptoft's high-handed behaviour as High Constable was attributed to his having been corrupted by the law of Padua.[57] What was essential for a change in this situation was a conviction of the relevance of Italian experience among not merely a handful of rich eccentrics but among a larger and more continuously important group, the 'political' class of fifteenth and sixteenth-century England. The beginning of such a change can in fact be discerned. Its effects become more noticeable as the fifteenth century draws to an end.

VII. The Reception of the Renaissance in England: Preconditions

The traditional explanation for the spread of the Italian Renaissance to the rest of Europe is, of course, couched in terms of individual contacts, such as those alluded to in the previous pages. Gray and Flemmyng, later Linacre, Grocyn and Colet, brought back the humanities as though they were packets of seeds which had only to be scattered about in order to beautify England with peninsular pleasances. This seminal work was aided in the traditional tale by the diplomats (soldiers too in the case of France and Spain after the Italian wars began) who caught culture as others caught syphilis,

---

[56] For a synoptic and recent statement of his views, see *The French Renaissance* (London, 1961).

[57] Cf. H. D. Hazeltine's remarks in the introduction to S. B. Chrimes's edition of Sir John Fortescue, *De laudibus legum Anglie* (Cambridge, 1942), xvii-xviii.

that further contribution to western civilisation at this time which
was attributed to Italy. Shirwood, Sellyng, Pace are cases in point
of envoys and orators who spent time in Italy which they found
congenial.[58] This old 'explanation' went with a general assumption
that the Renaissance formed part of a period of human enlightenment—of exploration, intellectual adventure, religious reform—
which needed little justification or analysis.

An extension of this older view, or an elaboration of it, is the
emergence of the 'New Monarchy' and the 'Rising Middle Class'.
These myths—or 'models' as myths are called nowadays—were
part of the stock-in-trade of the first fifty years of this century and
still pop up, especially in works written by literary historians. It is
as though Henry VII (founder of the 'New Monarchy' in England)
would have been a better king if he had read Machiavelli's *Prince*,
as if the *Prince* contained information without which powerful
government would have been more difficult. I have already pointed
out that the early Tudors were extremely effective rulers, and no
lively prince in Europe but knew all that Machiavelli had to tell
him about winning friends and influencing people, about sweetness,
brutality and *virtù*. Machiavelli differed from earlier writers *de regimine
principum* only in analysing what princes had always done, not in
inventing new ways of ruling. And in northern Europe, where
princes were not hampered by the Italian urban complication of a
communal tradition, kings had in fact even less to glean from Renaissance Italy than Italians themselves.[59] As for the 'middle class'
this muzzy concept has been laughed out of court by Professor
Hexter: historians in England have used the term to cover the urban
bourgeoisie, the rural gentry (who were regarded as 'noble' in
continental lands) or the amalgam of both in the Commons. Regarding
their 'rise', they were rising (gentry and bourgeois) from as far
back as one can see. At any rate the gentry were, and the 'rise of
the gentry' is a kind of sentimental extension of the concept. They

---

[58] Cf. Weiss, *Humanism in England*, 149-159, and now the introduction by R.
Sylvester and F. Manley to their edition and translation of the *De fructu qui ex
doctrina percipitur* (New York, 1967). Pace awaits an adequate biography, but see
Jervis Wegg, *Richard Pace* (London, 1932).

[59] Cf. Allan H. Gilbert, *Machiavelli's Prince and its Forerunners* (Durham, North
Carolina, 1938), esp. 234; and the article by Felix Gilbert, 'The humanist concept
of the prince and the "Prince" of Machiavelli', *Journal of Modern History*, XI
(1939), 449-483.

were also falling. And bourgeois and gentlemen were to rise and
fall for centuries to come.[60]

What indeed is certain is that the basic tenets of the humanist
were as applicable north of the Alps as south. The doctrine that
the men who mattered should serve their community, their city,
their prince, and be properly educated with such service in mind,
did not need a Mediterranean environment in order to flourish.
But it did need a conviction that educated administrators and an
educated group of 'governors', to use Elyot's word, were essential
to efficient government at all levels. Of course educated administrators
were no new thing in Northern Europe and kings in England had
leaned heavily for many centuries on the clergy, the clerks, who
had been the only fully literate members of a society in which Latin
was used not only in the liturgy, not only in running the Church,
not only in international relations, but in many of the basic documents
of royal and noble life—the charters and other instruments conveying
title to land and other properties and privileges. These 'clerical
clerks' were rewarded by their masters with benefices as well as more
intermittent stipends. Such benefices were not directly heritable
since the clerks were technically celibate, although the greater
prelacies carried with them a vast amount of patronage, perfectly
legitimately exercised by bishop or abbot in the interest of members
of his family. In England this clerical basis of royal administration,
and of the administration of great and smaller lordships as well,
began to crumble in the fifteenth century. The laity were called in
to run the affairs of king, duke, great landowner, as well as of the
towns. Administration thus steadily came under lay control. Such a
process may be seen at work everywhere. It is one of the most
momentous transformations in European government and society.

VIII. Clerical and Lay Administrators

In the absence of detailed analysis of the process it seems likely
that what happened first was the emergence of a highly literate
group of nobles and gentlemen (or 'Commons', which included
the bourgeoisie, since we are concerned with the development in
England). These men were, at any rate from the thirteenth century,
acutely aware of the need for good management of their estates
(if they were landowners), of their business interests (if they were

---

[60] J. H. Hexter, *Reappraisals in History* (London, 1961), 26-44, 71-162.

merchants and tradesmen). It was the landlords who mattered
politically and socially and their literacy by the end of the fourteenth
century is hardly to be doubted, if by literacy we mean competence
in reading the vernacular, if not necessarily writing it. Some indeed
there surely were who neglected their stewards' accounts, who
rusticated in declining manors. But the men who got on, who were
active as sheriffs, commissioners for this and that, M.P.s and J.P.s,
were perfectly able to cope with the written word. So too, were
many of the women of this class, perhaps more so than some of the
men, for the women had often to manage the estates (or the businesses)
while the men were away for long periods. A smaller number consisted of men who had acquired some Latin: such a man was *bene
literatus* and indeed 'literacy', if the concept could have been conveyed
to the socially important men and women of the fourteenth and
fifteenth centuries, would have meant for them competence of some
sort in Latin grammar and the ability to read a Latin text. The late
K. B. McFarlane had an entertaining lecture on the education of the
nobility in the later Middle Ages.[61] He was certainly right in arguing
that a high proportion of them were very well educated. What he
wrote of the nobility can be applied *mutatis mutandis* at a considerably
lower social level,[62] even while admitting that the bulk of the population, consisting of peasants and artisans, had little need to read and
little or no ability to communicate in writing.

What then seems to have happened is that this educated lay group,
composed of rich and influential men, were anxious to have affairs
managed by men of their own sort, and so increasingly were princes.
Further, the aspiring man of business (in this slowly changing
climate of opinion) could make his way to the top without entering
the church. He could found a family and, with hard work and luck,
obtain lands in perpetuity rather than precarious prebends; in certain
circumstances he could become an earl, he and his descendants for
ever, rather than a bishop or even a cardinal for a life-time. Nor
should we ignore more honourable motives. A career and influence,
whether for the well-born or the relatively humble, had meant in
effect celibacy and some men who were otherwise gifted for public
life wanted to live honestly with the women they loved. The tension

---

[61] Printed posthumously in *The Nobility of Later Medieval England* (Oxford,
1972).
[62] See remarks on literacy in Sylvia Thrupp, *The Merchant Class of Medieval
London* (Chicago, 1948), 156-158, 161.

between the benefice and matrimony was a genuine one and we find traces of it in England at this time; the advance of lay administration removed it.[63] Without some such considerations it is, I believe, hard to account for the steady drift towards a new type of administration and, accompanying this change, towards a new type of education.

Why did the prince and the 'governors' further this steady change? At first sight it was hardly to their advantage. If one employed a clergyman he was in the main paid for out of the endowed income of the church, from the domestic chaplain and family 'clerk' who could hope for a family living or one solicited on his behalf by his master, up to the king's man who could in the end grow wealthy, even extremely wealthy (one thinks of William of Wykeham) out of royally-sponsored promotion in the church. Nor were such men inherently less able than their lay successors. Although their training was largely scholastic that discipline was in itself a rigorous exercise in marshalling arguments and remembering propositions: the syllogism had been perfected to a high degree, certainly being regarded as a more difficult exercise than the rules of rhetoric necessary only for polite letters and speeches. Moreover the clergyman-official could not treat his appointment as a property: he might feather his own nest but he could not transmit the nest to a legitimate son, or sell it to the highest bidder.

How able and alert such men could prove is illustrated from the careers of some of those reckoned by Professor Weiss as early 'humanists'. He discusses Thomas Bekynton, an Oxford don who became chancellor to Duke Humphrey, secretary to Henry VI, Keeper of the Privy Seal and bishop of Bath and Wells; this able man relished good Latin and acquired some humanist texts. Much the same can be said of Adam Moleyns; after his return from the papal Curia he became a busy servant of the Crown, clerk of the council, frequently on embassies, Keeper of the Privy Seal (1444), bishop of Chichester (1449).[64] At a much lower level Sir John Fastolf's secretary, William Worcester, had antiquarian leanings which faintly suggest those of Flavio Biondo; although there is no

---

[63] A good discussion of Italian material in Carlo Dionisotti, 'Chierici e laici', *Geografia e storia della letteratura italiana* (Turin, 1967), 47-63. On the English scene the careers of some men who in the end got wives and should be recalled: Lily and More. And so should the careers of some who remained 'celibate': Wolsey and Skelton.

[64] Weiss, *Humanism in England*, 71-75, 81-83, 189.

evidence that among the humanist texts he knew was the *Italia illustrata*, yet he indulged a taste for what would come to be called chorography, and he is not an entirely isolated figure as we can see if we recollect John Rous of Warwick.[65]

Such men, adaptable and intelligent though they were, had nevertheless grave disadvantages for their employers. As clergymen they were not readily pushed around or, when beneficed, stripped of their source of income. The parson had his freehold; the bishop might lose the Great Seal but not his see. I do not mean that in any significant sense the clergy had transcending loyalties to the Church, let alone to the pope. There are no Anselms or even Beckets in fifteenth-century Europe. The English clergy obeyed the king, in cathedral chapters they elected his nominee, in convocation they taxed themselves for his benefit. But while a peccant priest or bishop might be lynched (as Adam Moleyns was lynched by a mob of soldiers in 1450) you could not legally execute him save for treason: Archbishop Scrope of York had been so punished in 1405. The fall of Wolsey points a similar moral. He was replaced as chancellor by More but remained an extremely rich and powerful man, as cardinal archbishop of York, so powerful, indeed, that he proceeded secretly to continue with what was virtually his own foreign policy. This it was which led to his final arrest and presumably would have entailed a charge of treason. Yet if Wolsey had been less avid for power at the centre, less unable to relinquish his pivotal influence, he could well have remained an important, though not all-important, political personage.[66] Such protection and permanence was not afforded to a secular official. Wolsey's servant, Thomas Cromwell, a nobody like Wolsey, was a layman. He could become a millionaire earl. He could end up on the block, which terminated his political influence abruptly; but his son succeeded as Lord Cromwell. The trend towards the lay administration is slow in manifesting itself in the fifteenth century and its effects must not be exaggerated. Nevertheless we can point to the erosion of the clerical monopoly of administration from the fourteenth century, with its collegiate life

---

[65] K. B. McFarlane, 'William Worcester, a preliminary survey', *Essays presented to Sir Hilary Jenkinson* (London, 1957), 196-221; Worcester's *Itineraries* have recently been edited by John H. Harvey (Oxford, 1969). For Rous, see T. D. Kendrick, *British Antiquity* (London, 1950), 19-29; who also (pp. 29-33) discusses Worcester.

[66] A. F. Pollard, *Wolsey* (London, 1929), esp. chap. xii.

burdensome to men who were only technically clerks.[67] And in the new Signet Office we have a department which was staffed by laymen from the start.[68] Nor must it be thought that secular careers like this are novel in the fifteenth century. The fief in all its forms was the reward of military or administrative employment, even if by becoming hereditary the burdens of feudalism had become fiscal by the fifteenth century. Kings gave their intimates titles and (if they were poor) the wherewithall to maintain themselves. There are several social nonentities who became nobles as a result of their enterprise during the Hundred Years' War and related campaigns: there are the de La Poles of Hull, the earliest of the merchant magnates (and a rare enough breed for long enough). In short one climbed high by being an effective instrument of the Crown. 'The truth is', wrote K. B. McFarlane, 'that the aristocracy *was* in the main one of service, that it was entered by service and that acceptable service was the cause of promotion within it'.[69] The aristocracy, as another writer has recently pointed out, consisted in the main not of old families but of new families.[70] What I believe we find in the fifteenth century is a steady application of these pressures at a level lower than the peerage, and a consequent turning of the middle ranks of society to the acquisition of the means, mainly sound education, which enabled them to compete.

A quite different influence exerted itself, especially on the Crown and a few great men: competition with the administration and administrative techniques of Italy. When the Schism ended, especially from the mid-fifteenth century, Italy attracted intense diplomatic activity. In this England was naturally less concerned than the continental powers. But Rome was the diplomatic hub of Europe in the late fifteenth century, and we have seen how the King's proctors in the City were important men. This was to lead to even more

---

[67] Some interesting points bearing on this neglected problem in T. F. Tout, 'The English civil service in the fourteenth century', *Collected papers*, III (Manchester, 1934), 191-221. For the Statute 14 & 15 Henry VIII c.8, which permitted the six clerks in chancery to marry, cf. G. R. Elton, *The Tudor Revolution in Government* (Cambridge, 1953), 54, n. 1: 'a sign rather of the complete laicization of the secretarial offices than a beginning'.

[68] See my earlier essay, 'The Early Renaissance in England', *From the Renaissance to the Counter-Reformation . . . in honor of Garrett Mattingly*, ed. C. H. Carter (New York, 1965), 98-99 and refs.

[69] McFarlane, *Nobility*, 233.

[70] Du Boulay, *Age of Ambition*, 68.

important agents being accredited to Rome, until from the 1470s something like a permanent embassy was maintained there.[71] Regular contact with the Curia meant regular contact with humanists, for a large number were now employed by the pope in offices either important or honorific or venal or all three. (And, we may add, a fair number of them were laymen, including two well enough known about in England—Poggio and Flavio Biondo. Rome was a pioneer in selling offices and curialists, married or unmarried, lay or clerical, expert at conveying them *in favorem*). The orator or ambassador at Rome had to match in style, material and cultural, his hosts and the other orators who were engaged in both a *concours d'élégance* and a competition in eloquence; the rivalry sometimes reached the length of fisticuffs. Keeping up with the humanist Jones became a preoccupation of government not only in Rome but at home. The pope had a librarian with Platina in 1475 and his successors.[72] Henry VII had to have a librarian, and we find Latin secretaries in the English court and laureate poets if not poets laureate at about the same time.[73] If the prince was constrained to behave in the new manner so were those of his advisers who met foreign envoys or travelled on foreign missions. Henry VII employed John Gunthorpe on diplomatic work as Edward IV had done earlier. Another and more celebrated humanist ambassador was Richard Pace. Familiar though it may be, and regarded by McFarlane as *ben trovato*, the episode recounted in Pace's *De fructu* of the clodhopper gentleman, rapidly declining into anachronism, must be quoted:

> About two years ago, more or less, when I returned to my country from the city of Rome, I was at a banquet where I was unknown to most of the guests. After we had drunk a sufficient amount, one of them (I don't know who, but, as you could tell from his speech and appearance, he was no fool) began to talk about the proper education

[71] B. Behrens, 'Origins of the office of English resident ambassador at Rome', *English Historical Review*, XLIX (1934), 640-656; D. S. Chambers, *Cardinal Bainbridge in the Court of Rome 1509-1514* (Oxford, 1965). The above was written before I had seen William E. Wilkie, *The Cardinal Protectors of England. Rome and the Tudors before the Reformation* (Cambridge, 1974), but this proved to be a survey of the diplomatic policies of England with regard to the papacy from 1514 to 1534.

[72] The most recent and authoritative account is Jeanne Bignami Odier, *La Bibliothèque Vaticane de Sixte IV à Pie IX* (Città del Vaticano, 1973), chap. iii (pp. 20ff.). Chapter ii deals with the earlier and less permanent tenures of Giovanni Tortelli and Giovanni Andrea Bussi (Aleriensis).

[73] Weiss, *Humanism in England*, 122-127.

for his children, He thought first of all that he should find them a good teacher and that they should by all means attend school and not have a tutor. Now there happened to be a certain person there, a nobleman, or so we call them, who always carry horns hanging down their backs as though they were going to hunt while they ate. When he heard us praise learning, he became wild, overwhelmed with an uncontrollable rage, and burst out, 'What's all this stuff, buddy? To hell with your stupid studies. Scholars are a bunch of beggars. Even Erasmus is a pauper, and I hear he's the smartest of them all. In one of his letters he calls *tên kataraton penian*, that is, goddamn poverty, his wife and complains bitterly that he's not able to get her off his back and throw her in the ocean, *bathykêtea ponton*. God damn it, I'd rather see my son hanged than be a student. Sons of the nobility ought to blow the horn properly, hunt like experts, and train and carry a hawk gracefully. Studies, by God, ought to be left to country boys'.

At that point I wasn't able to keep myself from making some reply to the loudmouth in defense of learning. I said, 'I don't think you're right, my good man. For if some foreigner came to the king, a royal ambassador, for example, and he had to be given an answer, your son, brought up as you suggest, would only blow on his horn, and the learned country boys would be called on to answer him. They would obviously be preferred to your son, the hunter or hawker, and using the freedom that learning gives, they would say to your face, "We would rather be learned, and thanks to learning no fools, than to be proud of our stupid nobility" '.

Then glancing about him on all sides, he said, 'Who's this, talking to me like that? I don't know the man'. And when someone whispered in his ear who I was, he mumbled something to himself—I don't know what—and finding a fool to listen to him, he snatched up a cup of wine. Since he had no answer to give, he started to drink, and the conversation passed on to other things. And so I was saved not by Apollo, who saved Horace from a blowhard, but by Bacchus, who saved me from an argument with a madman, which I was afraid would go on a lot longer.[74]

The anecdote also neatly illustrates the inevitability for the humanist of a career in the service of the great or the usually much less welcome alternative of educating children—children who would in turn become either 'governors' or educators. Another tale, later in the book, declares that princes care nothing for theologians, and that theologians know nothing of the world and its ways.[75]

---

[74] *De fructu qui ex doctrina percipitur*, ed. and trans. F. Manley and R. S. Sylvester, 23-25, quoted by permission; and cf. the introduction, p. xxi; also McFarlane, *Nobility*, 228-229.

[75] *Op. cit.*, 83-85. For 'beggars' on p. 85, read 'mendicants'; the theologian is obviously a Dominican.

IX. INNOVATIONS IN EDUCATION

The expansion in secondary and the changes in university education in northern Europe in the later Middle Ages are well-attested facts and the invention of printing in the 1440s in the Rhineland is the most impressive of the many evidences of rising lay literacy. If printing spread with amazing speed—prior to the nineteenth century it is the only important technical innovation to cover the continent within a generation—it was because people could read and wanted books. This was because schools were numerous by the fifteenth century in many parts of the Continent. England was only exceptional because it was less populous, and so was proportionately less well supplied than were certain other areas of Europe.

Nevertheless England's schools were relatively plentiful in 1400 and multiplied steadily through the century. On this subject there has, of course, been much debate over A. F. Leach's contention that a large number of grammar schools were destroyed during the English Reformation, in particular with the suppression of the chantries after 1545. If Leach's arguments were based on exaggerated assumptions regarding the quantity and quality of schools associated with convents and chantries or chantry priests, his critics have probably erred in attributing too few establishments to the Middle Ages, and in emphasising too much the progressive influence of the Reformation.[76] The most recent work, based on a carefully compiled list of schools, prints a series of maps of which that for fifteenth-century England shows a remarkable spread of endowed and 'public' schools.[77] Admittedly these were often small and often in small places. But such schools were usually supplemented by more precarious institutions. If (for instance) the county of Northumberland had schools at Alnwick, Hexham and Norham, it is reasonable to suppose that at Newcastle upon Tyne it was possible for the townsfolk to find education suited to their needs, even though the endowed and public school apparently did not emerge until late in the six-

---

[76] A. F. Leach's researches remain extremely important. His *English Schools at the Reformation* (1896) has been particularly attacked: see Joan Simon's articles of 1955 and later and now her *Education and Society in Tudor England* (Cambridge, 1966), where there is a full examination of mid-Tudor developments (pp. 223-244). The most recent investigation of English education (to 1530) is Nicholas Orme, *English Schools in the Middle Ages* (London, 1973), a balanced and thorough study from which I have greatly benefited.

[77] Orme, *English Schools*, 216: 'Endowed schools found in England 1330-1530 and open to the public'.

teenth century.[78] There seems no doubt that our documentation
is very patchy, and that serious research may well multiply the
number of firmly established schools as well as those of a more
temporary character.

Expert opinion seems agreed that the fifteenth century sees a
marked step forward. Mr. Orme writes:

> The fourteenth century had seen the origin of the endowed schools;
> in the fifteenth they became at last a widespread and popular form
> of charity. It is here, and not in the age of the Reformation, that
> the great movement really begins by which during five centuries
> hundreds of private benefactors founded hundreds of endowed schools
> all over England, and thus effected one of the principal achievements
> of English civilization.[79]

Mrs. Simon, while regarding the Reformation period as the watershed,
nevertheless draws attention to 'the steady expansion of lay education
at various levels' in the fifteenth century.[80] Instructing the ignorant
was, after all, one of the traditional spiritual works of mercy and,
in centuries when the laity were steadily taking over intellectual
leadership, it was inevitable that schools should be an off-shoot
of lay devotion, whether by direct and independent endowment
or through gilds and chantries.[81] It is also highly significant that
William of Wykeham's foundation at Winchester (1382) and Henry
VI's at Eton (1440), while being initially intended to produce clergy
soon became a preserve of the lay nobles and gentry: the 'commoners'
began to take over before the Dissolution.

It is important to remember the developing provision of schools
in the England of the later Middle Ages, for it was in the old schools
that the new Renaissance educational methods were to take firmest
root, offering a pattern to the many new foundations of the mid-
and late sixteenth century. This was, of course, most plainly to be
seen in the case of St. Paul's School in London. In answer to the
chronic shortage of grammar schools in the capital, a concern which

---

[78] R. F. Tuck, 'The origins of the Royal Grammar School, Newcastle upon
Tyne', *Archaeologia Aeliana*, 4th series, XLIV (1968), 229-271.

[79] Orme, *English Schools*, 194.

[80] Simon, *Education and Society*, 56.

[81] See in general W. K. Jordan's works on charitable bequests and especially
the synoptic *Philanthropy in England 1480-1660* (London, 1959), 147, on the
'secularisation of the charitable impulse'. I am not convinced that the Protestant
reformation had much to do with this development: cf. Brian Pullan's work on
charity in an Italian town, *Rich and Poor in Renaissance Venice* (Oxford, 1971), and,
for schools in Venice, pp. 404ff.

had agitated the citizens for a century and more, Dean Colet lavishly refounded St. Paul's in 1509. His aim was a devout laity; his prescription, while encouraging good Latin, retained the old-standing suspicions of the unsettling effects of reading the pagan classics, especially the poets; but it was at this school that the classics were first to come into their own.

There are several signs that the period sees a new and more professional attitude to education. In 1448 William Byngham established a college at Cambridge called Godshouse, which has not unfairly been regarded as a kind of teachers' training college. It was intended to ground twenty-five scholars in advanced grammar; when qualified they were to work in grammar schools. In fact Godshouse was never as flourishing as intended but some of its purposes were taken over when it was absorbed into the Lady Margaret's foundation of Christ's College. The teaching at Godshouse comprised study of some of the classical authors but was not in any sense educationally adventurous. For a newer approach we have to turn to Magdalen College at Oxford, where William Wainfleet, bishop of Winchester and formerly provost of Eton, in 1480 added a grammar school. The first master appointed here was John Anwykyll who started the slow revolution in the teaching of Latin in England which was to be continued by John Stanbridge and John Holt, who both began their teaching careers at Magdalen College School, and by Colet and his schoolmasters, notably William Lily.[82] Interest in the humanities is evident, as we have noted, among a few wealthy and well-travelled gentlemen. It is also observable in much humbler folk, such as those discussed by V. H. Galbraith in dealing with 'John Seward and his circle'. In this we are shown a group of London schoolmasters who, in the early fifteenth century, are meeting for literary jollifications, swapping verses with somewhat laborious classical allusions and (it may be suspected) using epigrams and adages in a somewhat novel manner for educational purposes. The master whom these obscure *literati* revered was John Leland, 'flos grammaticorum', an Oxford schoolmaster whose contemporary reputation seems excessive.[83] These men had all to some degree felt

---

[82] A survey of the teaching of grammar in Orme, *English Schools*, 106-115.
[83] 'John Seward and his circle', *Medieval and Renaissance Studies*, I (1941-43), 85-104; R. W. Hunt, 'Oxford grammar masters in the later Middle Ages', *Oxford Studies Presented to Daniel Callus* (see n. 33 above), 163-193, where a sober appraisal, concluding with Leland, does not suggest much enlightenment.

the influence of the new humanities, yet it is surely significant that (save for Lily) their direct contact with Italy was minimal or non-existent.[84] The introduction into the grammatical teaching of the influence of Valla and Perotti reflected a willing acceptance of new methods by a few English teachers who shared instinctively a desire for a fresh approach. The steady increase in schools, the switch in endowments to secular purposes were to find instruments at hand for the reception of the humanist educational curriculum.

These developments owed little to the two universities, despite Godshouse and Magdalen College School. Of course Latin was basic to the arts courses at the University, but, though it was therefore easy to learn elementary Latin at Oxford and Cambridge there was no academic interest in the teaching of Latin as such. There were no chairs in poetry or rhetoric, and the later hostility of the older establishments to the new humanities is well known. On the other hand the 'university' as such was losing ground in the later Middle Ages to the colleges and this was to prove a most important change, for it facilitated both the penetration by laymen into the groves of Academe and the slow transformation of college curricula in ways which would have been resisted at university level. The establishment of new colleges permitted a rapid increase in the number of non-clerical 'commoners', and founders could introduce limitations on the character of the studies to be encouraged by their foundations which sometimes indicate an interest in innovation. Like the schools alluded to in the previous paragraphs, colleges were endowed as an act of piety. 'To maintain or "exhibit" a scholar or two at a school or university was a recognised "good work" long before the age of colleges'.[85]

The founders of late medieval colleges at the two English universities were predominantly clergymen who had risen high in the royal administration and had reaped the reward of at least a bishopric. At Oxford this generalisation admits of only one exception—Bishop Fleming of Lincoln, who founded (1429) the college of that name, was an ecclesiastical but not a royal politician. At Cambridge there are more exceptions: the great ladies who endowed Clare and Pembroke, Gonville who was beneficed well in return for stewardship of the lands of great men, Byngham of Godshouse (already mentioned),

---

[84] See below, p. 361.
[85] Hastings Rashdall, *The Universities of Europe in the Middle Ages*, eds. F. M. Powicke and A. B. Emden, 3 vols. (Oxford, 1936), III, 175.

the remarkable establishments of Corpus Christi (gilds, 1352) and St. Catherines (a provost of King's, 1475); and the colleges created by Henry VI (Kings and Queens, 1441 and 1448).

If Cambridge offers many exceptions it also offers a most remarkable example of royal association with the university. This was the establishment of the King's Hall as an off-shoot of the Chapel Royal by Edward II in 1317; Edward III with an endowment made the society into a college but the link between it and the world of administration did not weaken. Even when the recruitment of scholars ceased to be exclusively from the children of the Chapel Royal 'throughout the fourteenth and early fifteenth centuries a varying percentage of Scholars was drawn directly from this source or from the court circle'. I quote from the admirable account of Dr. Cobban. He goes on:

> Even after direct recruitment from the chapel had apparently ceased, the connection with the court continued and the college became to an ever-increasing extent a base for graduate fellows, especially for civil lawyers, who were frequently non-resident and were employed in various capacities in ecclesiastical and secular business.[86]

The concern of founders with the provision of public servants is occasionally expressed elsewhere,[87] but this is the only establishment which in effect made a college an adjunct of the royal household—the solid basis 'of the university-court nexus throughout the medieval period'.[88] In a way the arrangement reminds one of Wykeham's Winchester-New College connection, or of the Eton-Kings link which was to bring another royal foundation to Cambridge, for 'the chapel royal incorporated what may best be described as a sort of independent grammar school' and it was from this school that a considerable number then went on to the King's Hall.[89] How did these potential officials prepare themselves? In the main by the study of civil law. Dr. Cobban enables us to construct the following statement concerning the second degrees of scholars at the King's Hall over two half-centuries:

---

[86] A. B. Cobban, *The King's Hall within the University of Cambridge in the Later Middle Ages* (Cambridge, 1969), 13, n. 4.

[87] *Ibid.*, 22.

[88] *Ibid.*, 60-65. Dr. Cobban suggests that Wykeham's 'principal English model' was this Court-Cambridge relationship.

[89] *Ibid.*, 54-55.

	Total	M.A.	Civil Law	Canon Law	Theology
1350-1400	51	22	23	6	—
1400-1450	54	22	25	4	3

Equally important, of those entering the college in the first period less than a third proceeded to higher degrees; in the second period the proportion has risen to 45%.[90] This prominence of civil law is remarkable evidence of a preference among the ambitious and their patrons for this kind of training. If we repeat for the fifteenth century the simple arithmetic regarding the qualifications of the archbishops of Canterbury and York which we did for the fourteenth, we find out of a total of eleven names that six were civilians, one was a D.U.J., two were theologians and one was M.A.[91]

The lawyers of England were, however, common lawyers and their education was at the Inns of Court, not at the university. The history of the Inns at this time remains to be written [92] but it was clearly highly professional and in many ways resembled the lectures and disputations of the contemporary university. The Benchers and Readers of the Inns 'trained the students of the law and called them to the bar', each of the four Inns of Court and the smaller Inns of Chancery being organised on a collegiate basis. The resemblance to the university extended to the panoply of the Judges and Sergeants-at-law, whose position was, in Fortescue's words, 'no less worshipful and solemn than the degree of doctors'. It was, says Holdsworth, a rigorous apprenticeship which 'no doubt kept the practical, the argumentative, the procedural side of law prominently to the front'.

> At the same time we cannot say that it gave no opportunities for instruction in legal theory. It also produced Littleton and Fortescue. We may conjecture that the students had some opportunities for 'private reading', perhaps in the chambers of the elder lawyers; and to those whose minds are prepared by such reading suggestions thrown out in argument, and the quick play of mind upon mind, will often give hints as to the existence of difficult problems and clues to their solution. Moreover, we may remember that this mode of

---

[90] Loc. cit.

[91] And William Booth (York, 1452-64) is *magister*, which probably means an arts degree: Le Neve, *Fasti*, VI, 4.

[92] See Sir William Holdsworth, *A History of English Law*, 12 vols. (London, 1903-38), II, chap. V, II; and *Readings and Moots at the Inns of Court in the Fifteenth Century*, ed. Samuel E. Thorne, I (Selden Society, London, 1954); vol. II, in which fifteenth-century legal education is to be discussed is not yet published. An important contemporary witness is Sir John Fortescue, *De laudibus legum Anglie* (cf. above, n. 57).

instruction, if it began by making men pleaders, and continued by making them advocates and keen doctors, ended by making them judges.[93]

Nor was it the case that civil law was unknown to the young men in the Inns. Many of the better-off and the abler had read some law in the university before beginning their professional studies. The Inns had three further enormous advantages, which they only partially shared with Oxford and Cambridge. They were exclusively composed of laymen, whereas the undergraduate was still technically part of or associated with a clerical community. They accepted (as did the universities) students who did not intend to practise a profession but who stayed only for a portion of the course, who left (one might say) without graduating; but they gave such young men a smear or a deeper tincture of a subject which in a litigious age was of direct importance in everyday life to all men of any substance, and this could not be said of the traditional arts curriculum of the university. Finally the Inns had a location in the one big city in the land, the universities were tucked away in two little provincial centres. Doubtless the attractions of the capital were not all intellectual, but that probably mattered less than would appear; the boys at the university were far from all being swots. At London was the Court and the courts and the High Court of Parliament. When printing came it came to London first and foremost. Mrs. Simon may well be right to say

> It is usual to account the Elizabethan age as the time when the Inns of Court became leading educational establishments because they then attracted so many young gentlemen; but this influx and other pressures operated to undermine traditional forms of training, and it was rather before it took place, in the fifteenth century, that the Inns had their golden age as centres of legal education.[94]

At any rate, it was out of a spell at Oxford and professional training at Lincoln's Inn that there emerged the greatest English humanist, Thomas More.

X. Literature: Books and Libraries

If there are grounds in educational history for considering the pre-Reformation century as lively and receptive, so I believe there are in literature. Some aspects of literature are not impressive, it

---

[93] Holdsworth, *History of English Law*, II, 508.
[94] *Education and Society*, 55.

is true. Latin scholarship, before the last decade of the fifteenth century, when the new grammars and *vulgaria* began to appear, seem to have been in a low key, although until we have a history of English scholarship before the seventeenth century it is by no means certain what remains to be discovered and evaluated.[95] But one has the impression that literary historians are determined to regard the interval between Chaucer and Shakespeare as a period of almost unrelieved mediocrity in English. As a recent critic has neatly put it: 'it is possible to suggest that the "decline" of fifteenth-century literature is due to nothing so much as the historians' need for something of the sort between Chaucer and the Renaissance'.[96] It was part of C. S. Lewis's 'drab'; the Chaucerians were all in Scotland; the endless verses of Lydgate and Gower and the repetitive, slogging prose of Malory dominate the scene, relieved only by a handful of enchanting lyrics. 'The glory had departed'.[97] It is true that much fifteenth-century English prose and verse lacks sparkle, lacks the irony produced by the author regarding himself with interest: compare Malory's treatment of his heroes with Boiardo's or Ariosto's. But what the evidence does suggest is the rapidly growing public for books. In this England was on all fours with Germany and France. The scriveners were turning out manuscripts in the vernacular at an impressive rate. Some of the multiplying manuscripts were inherently fairly trivial, the *Brut* for example, (however important its continuations are for modern historians) or the works of John Shirley. But some were not. There are nearly 200 surviving manuscripts of the Bible in English (despite the slight danger that the possession of this could be awkward for anyone suspected of heresy) and over 80 manuscripts of all or part of Chaucer's *Canterbury Tales*. And how many copies of these popular works formerly existed but have now perished? Should not the quality of the reading public at any rate be partly judged on the older books

---

[95] For example, we have no adequate study of Reginald Pecock or Thomas Gascoigne; the *Loci e libro veritatis* of the latter was not published in its entirety by J. E. Thorold Rogers (1881). The only topic adequately covered is historiography in C. L. Kingsford's *English Historical Literature in the Fifteenth Century* (Oxford, 1913), which covers writings in both Latin and the vernaculars. It is a great pity that we do not have the revision of this which only K. B. McFarlane could have provided. There is an interesting comparison of two treatments of a critical question in J. M. Levine, 'Reginald Pecock and Lorenzo Valla on the Donation of Constantine', *Studies in the Renaissance*, XX (1973), 118-143.

[96] D. F. Pearsall, *John Lydgate* (London, 1974), 68.

[97] H. S. Bennett, *Chaucer and the Fifteenth Century* (Oxford, 1947), 96.

they read, as well as on current production? The production of the press, once the art arrived in 1475, bears out the popularity of an older literature. It also shows little or no humanist influence.

> Nearly half his (Caxton's) publications were of this [religious and didactic] kind (35 out of 77 original editions, or 56 out of 103 published items), and must have given him little anxiety. Indeed, nine of them ran into two or more editions—among them such substantial works as *The Golden Legend*, Maydeston's *Directorium Sacerdotum*, Mirk's *Liber Festivalis* and the pseudo-Bonaventura *The Life of Christ*. His other largest venture was the publication of various poetical works, but here again he ran only a small risk ... after Caxton had found a ready market for some of his little quartos of Chaucer or Lydgate's verses, he followed this up by the publication of *The Canterbury Tales* and the *Confessio Amantis* of Gower.[98]

Such a picture is more or less true of the first century of English printing as a whole: the volume of publication increases every year, but traditional tastes predominate.

Nevertheless the evolution of grammar school education noted earlier is reflected in the output of the press. Much of the old continued—Donatus, Alexander of Villedieu, John of Garland. But the new compilations of Anwykyll, Stanbridge and Whittinton also figure prominently.[99] If there are only two editions of Anwykyll's *Compendium* (1483), there are some fifty of Stanbridge's various works before 1530 and about four times as many of Whittinton's.[100] To this must be added a large importation of Latin educational works from continental presses. The *Short Title Catalogue* includes foreign-printed books designed for the English market. But it does not, of course, cover the books imported into England as a venture by merchants or booksellers, or at the request of a customer. From the beginning, it seems, sizeable quantities of such books were coming in, evidently mainly religious and educational.[101] An even better indication of the early trade in learned literature is found in early library catalogues, such as that for Syon Monastery, the first version of which apparently dated from 1504. In the catalogue

---

[98] H. S. Bennett, *English Books and Readers 1475-1557* (Cambridge, 1952), 17. Mr. Bennett in this work made good use of W. B. Crotch's edition of *The Prologues and Epilogues of William Caxton*, E. E. T. S. (1928).

[99] Bennett, *English Books*, 86-87.

[100] See *S.T.C.*, Nos. 23140-23199, 25444-25581. Many undated editions survive and exact figures are hardly worth attempting.

[101] Cf. H. R. Plomer, 'Importation of books into England in the fifteenth and sixteenth centuries', *The Library*, 4th series, IV (1923-24), 146-150.

as a whole (it was not continued after 1526) there are entries for nine printed items from England, and for 387 from the continent.[102] As was proper in a strict house of the Bridgettine Order, the contents (they are of the men's library, not the nuns') are predominantly liturgical, theological and grammatical—good, traditional material, although exhibiting, as will be noted, the influence of new ideas.

One can put a book in a library but one cannot ensure that anyone reads it, although we can be more sure when we have registers of the books lent out, such as the one Platina maintained for the library in the Vatican.[103] Hence library catalogues are by themselves perhaps a less certain guide to established taste than multiple copies for publication and sale. Yet one of the momentous changes in the laicization of literacy and life was not only the demand for books but the altered conditions for their preservation. One can now observe the creation of libraries of quite a novel kind. Great collections of manuscript books were nothing new. They are found in dozens of abbeys and friaries, even (as at Syon) in well-endowed nunneries; the two universities and their colleges had such collections, the latter becoming steadily more important, as already noted.[104] But with a literate gentry the gentleman's library became a possibility. The magnate was treating his home as a pleasure ground rather than as a centre of power: men of wealth made parks and comfortable country palaces; the bourgeoisie who could afford fresh air—'pastoralism' is Professor Du Boulay's word for it—had modest country houses.[105] Part of all this comfort included books and soon a library became part of a gentleman's equipment. When the literate, book-accumulating members of society had been clergy

---

[102] Ed. by Mary Bateson (Cambridge, 1898). Cf. p. viii: 'The English presses are very poorly represented'. On this library see further below, p. 365.

[103] E. Muntz and P. Fabvre, *La Bibliothèque du Vatican au XVe siècle* (Paris, 1887); Maria Bertola, *I due primi registri di prestito della Bibliotheca Apostolica Vaticana* (Città del Vaticano, 1932). Our information for England at this time is scanty. There is a register of borrowers (1440-1516) of the books bequeathed by Thomas Markaunt (d. 1439) to Corpus Christi College Cambridge, cf. J. O. Halliwell, in *Publications of the Cambridge Antiquarian Society*, quarto series, XIV, part 1, 16-20; F. M. Powicke, *The Medieval Books of Merton College* (Oxford, 1931), describes the system of *electio*, a distribution of books among members of the society, on pp. 12-18, and prints the pretty uninformative *electiones* from the fourteenth and fifteenth centuries (pp. 60-82). On borrowing see also Ernest A. Savage, *Old English Libraries* (London, 1911), 98-103.

[104] F. Wormald and C. E. Wright, eds., *The English Library before 1700* (London, 1958), 1-147; *Oxford Libraries in 1556* (cf. above, n. 47).

[105] *An Age of Ambition*, 51.

there was an inevitable dispersal of possessions, including books, at death. In this way college, monastic and other corporate libraries, as well as the relatives of testators, benefitted. And the impulse to donate to such institutions remained very strong indeed during the fifteenth century and indeed for much longer; it is not yet dead. But a great man, or even a man who had some secure income, might now bequeath his books to a son who added to them. Or he bequeathed not to a corporation of clergy but to some kind of 'public' library. Donors to the Library of the University of Cambridge, even if it was very small, were giving in some sense to a 'public' library; Duke Humphrey's munificent gift to Oxford—neglected though it soon alas became—is another example of the awareness of the need for public libraries; and so was the Guildhall Library, although its purpose was basically theological.[106] Far more is known about the institutional libraries of medieval England than about private collections,[107] especially those of laymen.[108] It seems undeniable that there were not very many of them, although inventories in wills do not become obligatory until 1521. No English collection exists comparable to the library assembled at Urbino by Duke Federigo da Montefeltro and we do not know what books were to be found in the great houses built by successful administrative operators like Sir Roger Fiennes (Hurstmonceaux) and Sir Ralph Cromwell (Tattershall). In any case the two greatest book collectors could in the end not look to a future for their families. Duke Humphrey died suddenly in 1447 *sine proliis legitimis* and John Tiptoft earl of Worcester was attainted and executed in 1470—one reason why his library was dispersed.[109] All one can say therefore is that conditions were ripe for the establishment of private lay as well as public libraries and there are hints of it among modest enough families, such as the Pastons, who 'were accustomed to turn to books for relaxation'. Their rumbustious ally Sir John Fastolf may not

---

[106] The Guildhall Library was begun about 1425. Two other public libraries, also theological in intention, were established later in the century at Worcester and Bristol. Orme, *English Schools*, 83-85.

[107] For institutional libraries, see N. R. Ker, ed., *Medieval Libraries of Great Britain*, second ed., Royal Historical Society (London, 1964).

[108] See the list in Savage, *Old English Libraries*, 274-285; and cf. Raymond Irwin, *The English Library* (London, 1964), 207. For 'catalogues' based on wills see Sears Jayne, *Library Catalogues of the English Renaissance* (Berkeley, 1956), and for the legislation of 12 Henry VIII cap. 5, see his introduction, p. 9.

[109] Weiss, *Humanism in England*, 118.

have had a room designated as a library but he kept a collection in
the Stewe House at Caister.[110]

Among these new buildings there is as yet no hint that Renaissance
architectural styles were admired by lay patrons. In ecclesiastical
buildings the final development of Gothic was reaching towards
its most elaborate perpendicular triumphs. Foreign influences, such
as they were, were Burgundian and German rather than Italian
in art and architecture. Where flimsy materials were concerned, the
decoration for *joyeuses entrées* and similar public displays, we deal
with the impermanent and ill-documented. But here too the country
was not without relevant experience.[111] In the limping meter of
Lydgate's middle English the verses describing the pageant of
Henry VI's entry into London in 1432 sound tawdry as well as
clumsy in comparison with the descriptions of (for instance) the
papal processions we find written up glowingly in Pius II's commentaries, or rehearsed efficiently in Burkard's *Diarium*, but the aim
and effects were not so dissimilar.

> And in the Cornhill anoon at his komyng
> To done plesaunce to his magestee,
> A Tabernacle surmontyng off beaute,
> Ther was ordeyned, be fful ffresch entayle,
> Richely arrayed with Ryall Apparayle.
>
> This Tabernacle off moste magnyficence,
> Was off his byldyng verrey Imperyall,
> Made ffor the lady callyd Dame Sapience;
> To-fore whos fface moste statly and Ryall
> Weren the seven sciences callyd lyberall . . .
>
> ffirst there was Gramer, as I reherse gan,
> Chief ffounderesse and Roote off all konnyng
> Which hadde a-fforn hire olde Precian . . . .

And so on. The whole inserted in a city chronicle, rejoicing in this
visible evidence that London was 'Citee of Cities, off noblesse
precellying, in they bygynnynge called newe Troye'.

> Suche Joye was neuer in the concistorie
> Made ffor the Tryumphe with all the surpluage,
> Whanne Sesar Julius kam home with his victorie;
> Ne ffor the conqueste off Sypion in Cartage . . . .[112]

---

[110] H. S. Bennett, *The Pastons and their England* (Cambridge, 1932), 112-113, and
Appendix, pp. 261-262.

[111] Sydney Anglo, *Spectacle and Pageantry in Early Tudor Policy* (Oxford, 1969),
54-56, 191, 195, 284-289.

[112] C. L. Kingsford, ed., *Chronicles of London* (Oxford, 1905), 105, 115.

XI. THE CROWN AND THE NEW CULTURE

To compare the poor sickly child Henry VI to Julius Caesar strikes one as absurd. The triumph of his entry into London after Henry VII's victory at Bosworth might well have seemed premature to contemporaries but we have no doubt that it was celebrated with new poetry as well as traditional decorum. Henry's laureate, who seems to have arrived in the country with him, tells us that, inspired by poetical frenzy, he recited publicly the verses carefully transcribed in his 'Vita Henrici VII'.

> Musa, praeclaros age dic triumphos,
> Regis Henrici decus ac trophaeum
> Septimi, lentis fidibus canora
>   Dic age, Clio
>
> Dicat arguta chorus ille sacro
> Voce cum Phaebo, cythara canente
> Grande certamen, ferat huncque regem
>   Semper ad astra

And much more besides.[113] That Henry's reign was inaugurated with a 'Carmen Sapphicum' was an omen. For it was in his reign that the humanities came to court and, equally important, began to be naturalised.

One must admittedly avoid the fallacy of thinking that in 1485 the 'Middle Ages ended' or (to quote an authority) 'Modern times as distinct from the middle ages had begun under the Tudors'.[114] Caution is indeed needed since every survey of English history makes a break in narrative or analysis at the accession of Henry VII and it is extremely hard to detach oneself from the assumption that with Henry and his successors we have a run up to, and then the fulfilment of, the Reformation and the Renaissance, regarded as conjoint moments of illumination. Sceptically though one must regard these old but tenacious propositions, associated as they are with other hoary absurdities I have mentioned earlier (New Monarchy, Rising Middle Class), there is no doubt that Henry VII's rule saw some remarkable innovations in English culture. That there had been a long period of preparation I have tried to show; that in concrete cases some positive developments antedate the Tudors is true; but the sense of a new atmosphere of patronage and the

---

[113] James Gairdner, ed., *Memorials of King Henry VII*, Rolls Series (London, 1858), 35-36; cf. Anglo, *Spectacle and Pageantry*, 8-10.

[114] Godfrey Davies, *The Early Stuarts* (Oxford, 1938), xix.

knowledge that this patronage was to have permanent connections
lends the decades on either side of 1500 a peculiar significance. Nor
was patronage alone responsible for change. We have solid evidence
for the spontaneous adoption of new ideas and new styles. Much of
this admittedly saw its flowering after Henry VII's death. Polydore
Vergil's *Anglica Historia*, for instance, was not published until
1534. But it had been commissioned by Henry VII.

The notion of Henry VII commissioning works of literature or
art is at first sight absurd, for another of the firm convictions of
scholarship, even fairly well-informed scholarship, is that the king
was the very model of parsimony. There has recently been considerable debate on this question, but the fact is that the king died
leaving both a fortune and a reputation for avariciousness.[115] His
adoption of foreign scholars was, in fact, an economical demon-
stration of taste compared with building, in which his activity was
modest—the Henry VI chapel at Westminster and continuing works
already begun at Windsor. Moreover the scholars were frequently
clergy who were rewarded, as of old, with benefices.

There was a purposefulness in the first Tudor's adoption of
Renaissance styles among his learned entourage which is not to be
accounted for in Henry's own upbringing. Princes had been well-
educated for long enough,[116] and it is perhaps indicative of the
hopes of his Tudor guardian, the earl of Pembroke, that some care
seems to have been taken over his training. Not a great deal seems
to be known about his tutors. Bernard André says that he heard
from one of them, Andrew Scott, since dead but then a student of
divinity at Oxford and a very well-trained scholar, that Henry's aptitude
for learning was remarkable. In his *Itinerary* Leland mentions in
passing the tomb in the collegiate church at Warwick of 'Hasely,
schole-mastar to Henry the 7 and Deane of Warwyke'. Edward
Hasely was, like Scott, an Oxford man.[117] After his accession their

---

[115] G. R. Elton, 'Henry VII: Rapacity and Remorse', *The Historical Journal*, I
(1958), 21-39; J. P. Cooper, 'Henry VII's Last Years Reconsidered', *ibid.*, II
(1959), 103-129; Elton, 'Henry VII: a restatement', *ibid.*, IV (1961), 1-29.
[116] An excellent short account in Orme, *English Schools*, 21-29.
[117] W. Busch, *England under the Tudors*, I (London, 1895), 319-320; André
'Vita', in Gairdner, *Memorials*, 13; John Leland, *Itinerary*, ed. Lucy Toulmin
Smith, 5 vols. (reprinted, London, 1964), V, 151, and cf. II, 42. Cf. also the
monumental work of A. B. Emden, *A Biographical Register* (above, n. 33), II,
883-884, and III, 1656.

pupil rapidly acquired those appurtenances of the princes who were his contemporaries which he lacked.

One office already existed, that of Secretary.[118] It had already attracted the services of some very well-trained scholars. Thomas Bekynton, royal secretary from 1438 to 1443, set the tone. This was *applied* learning, so to speak. In Professor Weiss's words, Bekynton 'conceived classical learning not only as an intellectual attainment but also as a thing of practical value'; and he attributes to Bekynton's influence the 'literary qualifications' of not fewer than six other royal servants and diplomats. Additional to Bekynton and his flock we find James Goldwell, a civil lawyer from All Souls who became Edward IV's secretary, proctor at Rome, bishop of Norwich (1472) and on his death (1499) bequeathed a remarkable collection of humanist books to All Souls. Under Edward IV the secretary becomes a very important person, and is a member of the Council. It was also Edward IV who appointed the first French secretary in the person of Oliver King. King was another lawyer: Eton and King's and later the university of Orleans. He was French secretary (1475-90) and then secretary to both Edward IV and his son (1480-83). Surviving Richard III's reign (uncomfortably) he became secretary once again with Henry VII, being rewarded successively with the bishoprics of Exeter and Bath and Wells. I have already alluded to the Signet Office, over which the secretary presided, and staffed by lay 'clerks' from its inception.[119]

On all this Henry VII built. The importance of the secretary steadily grew, though the mountainous *paperasserie* of his office has not survived as it was to do from the administration of Henry VIII's reign. (And doubtless Henry VIII's servants, and especially Thomas Cromwell, were a great deal more energetic and independent than his father's). The continuity of the Yorkist secretary King into the reign of the first Tudor is noteworthy. Councillors were

---

[118] See further my brief account 'The Early Renaissance' (above, n. 68).

[119] Weiss, *Humanism in England*, 74, 176-177; J. Otway Ruthven, *The King's Secretary and the Signet Office in the Fifteenth Century* (Cambridge, 1939); J. F. Baldwin, *The King's Council in England during the Middle Ages* (Oxford, 1913); A. R. Myers, *The Household of Edward IV: the Black Book and the Ordinance of 1478* (Manchester, 1959); *Dictionary of National Biography, sub nomina*. In general for administrative developments at this time see S. B. Chrimes, *An Introduction to the Administrative History of England* (Oxford, 1952), 241 and refs.; and G. R. Elton, *The Tudor Revolution*, chap. 1.

too expert to be squandered in factious changes of government [120] and the secretary as a councillor had what had become in effect a career appointment. King is the first secretary to be made a bishop while in office. When he is succeeded in 1500 by Thomas Ruthall the secretaryship had become in some sense 'public' and we are looking forward to the Cecils and Walsingham, although the term principal secretary of state does not become official until 1540. Ruthall (bishop of Durham 1509) like his immediate successors was a lawyer.[121] Equally noteworthy is the appointment in 1496 of Pietro Carmeliano as the first Latin secretary. Carmeliano, who came from Brescia or its neighbourhood, had been in England since 1481, and was a royal pensioner as early as 1486, probably being in royal employment well before then.[122]

The secretary (and *a fortiori* the Latin and French secretaries) was closely associated with diplomatic activity and diplomatic correspondence. No wonder then that the offices involved education and acquaintance with the Italian diplomatic style. Hence it comes as no surprise that to Thomas Ruthall was dedicated the oration of Pietro Griffo designed to be delivered to Henry VII.[123] Carmeliano edited some Italian diplomatic exchanges in elegant epistular form published by Caxton in 1483 (*S.T.C.* 22588). He celebrated the solemnities of the betrothal of the Archduke Charles with Princess Mary in 1507 (*S.T.C.* 4659). More important, he is the author of verses in Anwykyll's grammatical *Compendium* of 1483 and lent his name poetically to the English version of Dominic Mancini's *De Quatuor virtutibus* (*S.T.C.* 17242, 1523?), a popular poem combining neo-classical Latin with conventional moral ideas.[124]

The king's library had probably been organised at the instigation of Edward IV and on Burgundian models rather than Italian ones.

---

[120] J. R. Lander, 'Council, administration and councillors 1461-85', *Bulletin of the Institute of Historical Research*, XXXII (1959), 138-180.

[121] Pace's education in Italian universities may have resulted in a doctorate but this is far from certain. Cf. Wegg, *Pace*, chap. 1; Parks, *The English Traveller to Italy*, 317-318.

[122] Weiss, *Humanism in England*, 170-173; C. A. J. Armstrong, *The Usurpation of Richard III*, second ed. (Oxford, 1969), 4.

[123] *S.T.C.*, No. 12413; Monaco, *De officio*, 60. For dedications see the very helpful work by Franklin B. Williams, Jr., *Index to Dedications and Commendatory verses in English books before 1641* (Bibliographical Society, 1962). Ruthall is listed under 'Rontal'.

[124] *D.N.B.*, *sub nomine*; Williams, *Index to Dedications*, 33; and Armstrong, *Usurpation*, 19, n., who dates the Mancini book to about 1520 and discusses it (pp. 11-13).

Certainly 'the king's stay at Bruges in 1470 and 1471 must have been of signal importance, for it is with the Bruges and Ghent illuminators that the Edward IV books now in the Royal collection ... are associated'.[125] Equally telling, the first known royal librarians were Flemings, Quentin Poulet, librarian in 1492, and Giles Duwes, whose name occurs in 1509.[126] Compared with some of the princely accumulations on the continent, it was a very small library. But a librarian implies permanence and what the prince did was to be imitated by others. Very considerable libraries were to found in some English country houses by the middle of the sixteenth century.[127]

As I have indicated, attention had for long been paid to the education of the children of the royal family. This now took on a markedly humanist tincture. Henry VII's eldest child Arthur had as his tutors John Reed (later Warden of New College), André and Linacre, the latter at any rate being an outstanding humanist. Henry, the second son, and in the event to succeed, had as his teacher John Skelton, whose fame was to survive as an English poet, but whom contemporaries regarded primarily as a scholar, the translator of Cicero and Diodorus Siculus, already one of Henry VII's 'laureates'. Henry VIII in his turn was to provide his children with humanist instruction, the only difference being that the quality of the royal tutors increased immeasurably as the sixteenth century advanced; it was to include Cheke and Ascham.[128] Again, what the sovereign did was to be emulated by his subjects, though most of them had to rely on a good school rather than a good tutor.

Another development of Henry VII's reign lay in public and court spectacle. Processions and revels were not new but there seems little doubt that the first Tudor encouraged the use of display with a careful eye to its effects. Dr. Anglo has admirably discussed this subject and it is only necessary here to draw attention to the evidence

---

[125] Wright, *English Library*, 163.

[126] Wright, *loc. cit.*; and G. F. Warner and J. P. Gilson, *Catalogue of Western MSS. in the Old Royal and King's Collections*, I (London, 1921), xiii.

[127] Jayne, *Library Catalogues*, 93-103. The bulk of these collections consists in a relatively small number of books, mostly the possession of clergy and dons. But there are considerable libraries in lay hands: cf. Andrew H. Anderson's publication of the inventory of the collection of Lord Stafford (1556), *The Library*, 5th series, XXI (1966), 87-114.

[128] For the extraordinary programme of reading which André claimed Prince Arthur was subjected to by the time he was sixteen, see Gairdner, *Memorials*, 143. The prominence of the new grammarians is noteworthy: Guarino, Perotti, Pomponio Leto, Sulpizio and Valla; but the list of classical authors is also long.

he has assembled.[129] The stately and expensive entries into London and other centres, with their elaborate decoration, with the music and acting and stiff symbolic figures, gradually permit the introduction of classical motifs, not least the use of 'Britain' and 'British' as the theme of so much pictorial propaganda. The Welsh background here was provoking memories of Cadwallader and King Arthur; it was the Britain of Geoffrey of Monmouth. But it lent itself nicely to the rhythms of the poetasters of the court. Such decorative ceremonies, even if planned with courtly advice, were paid for by loyal subjects. They were a distinctly economical way of advertising. Court revels on the other hand had to be paid for and Henry was prepared for that. It seems that William Cornish was at work at court as early as 1501. It was his achievement to have introduced 'a multiform spectacle, combining music, poetry, débat, combat, scenic display and dance'.

> This complex spectacle was adopted during the early years of Henry VIII's reign—when Cornish, as Master of the children of the Chapel Royal, came to the fore as deviser of court entertainments—and is the direct ancestor of the mask which reached its apogee at the courts of James I and his son Charles.[130]

Cornish was, of course, in no sense a humanist, and we must not try to discern Milton's *Comus* in the early sixteenth century.

Skelton *was* a native and a humanist, a grammarian and rhetorician from Cambridge and Oxford, although he strikes one as a somewhat strange and exceptional individual. It is remarkable that so many foreigners thronged Henry VII's court and the influence of a substantial scholar like Vergil needs no stressing. But it is important not to exaggerate the deliberation behind Henry VII's patronage. It so happened that the uncle and nephew Giovanni and Silvestro Gigli who successively held the see of Worcester were humanists as well as useful to Edward IV and Henry VII, but they were in England because they were servants of pope and king; there is no reason to suppose that, when nominating Vergil as papal sub-collector, Adriano Castellesi intended to produce the main propagandist of the new dynasty. Nevertheless the humanists at court, however casually they had come there, were quick to demonstrate the value of up-to-date Latinity, and not only in panegyrics to members of the royal family but in invectives against foreign calumnies, as when in 1490

---

[129] Anglo, *Spectacle and Pageantry.*
[130] *Ibid.,* 118.

André, Cornelio Vitelli and Giovanni Gigli replied in kind to Gaguin's attack on England and her sovereign.[131]

XII. THE NATIVE HUMANIST

Gradually however native scholars and 'poets' would make the services of imported visitors unnecessary. Once a group of able English humanists emerged they were, by and large, very much better than the somewhat fly-blown foreigners who had failed to make a career at home, or sometimes (like Vitelli) anywhere. The great names in the roll-call of English humanists—Grocyn, Linacre, Colet, More—need have felt no sense of inferiority in the company of their continental contemporaries and, when all is said and done, the debt they owed to direct contact with Italian practice has probably been overstated; in the case of More it was, as I have said, non-existent. Yet the future of the humanities was hardly to be established by a handful of scholars however able and however highly placed. The basic importance of Henry VII's reign is that it saw the emergence of a new kind of secondary education which was to impress itself on the grammar school curriculum until the end of the nineteenth century, and even perhaps later.

The process is clear in general outline. The details are often obscure. One small point may be cleared out of the way. Greek in England, so long and so often made the test of what constituted humanist education, made precious little advance at this time.[132] It was never regarded as comparable in importance to Latin in Italy, so far as school teaching was concerned, and the same is true of Renaissance England. Only a handful of scholars took the study of Greek seriously, and when it came into school teaching it tended to be for higher forms. I believe it is therefore less important than some would have it to trace early Greek manuscripts in English libraries or to identify competence in the language. It is obviously of great interest that John Free's mastery of Greek was far above the average, polished as it was by the teaching of Guarino,[133] and it is equally interesting

---

[131] H. L. R. Edwards, *Skelton* (London, 1949), 43-45; L. Thuasne, ed., *Roberti Gaguini epistole et orationes*, 2 vols. (Paris, 1903), I, 81-87; one is reminded of the Brice-More controversy of 1513-20.

[132] Note the absurd observation of the editors of *Skelton's Diodorus Siculus* (E.E.T.S., 1957), in their foreword: 'At least one of us, and probably both, would now use that term [humanist] in a more restricted sense, confining it to true Hellenists'. Ignorance of the meaning of the term *umanista* cannot go further.

[133] R. J. Mitchell, *John Free*; Weiss, *Humanism in England*, 106-112.

that Prior William Sellyng of Canterbury, having learnt or perfected his Greek on visits to Italy, should have taught it in the convent about 1470.[134] But neither man seems to have made disciples, so to speak, and it is symptomatic of the irrelevance of the discipline that the Greeks Andronicus Callistus, George Hermonymos and Demetrius Cantacuzenos seem to have excited little patronage on their visits in the 1470s. John Serbopoulos, on the other hand, seems to have survived as a copyist of Greek texts at Oxford and Reading in the next decade and the survival of three manuscript copies of Gaza's Greek grammar in his hand in British libraries suggests, as Roberto Weiss wrote, 'the presence of a public anxious to learn Greek'.[135] But not, one imagines, a very large public.

The foundation of the Renaissance in England, as elsewhere in Europe, rested on the teaching of classical Latin as a preparation for an active participation in public affairs. The rapid penetration of Latin into the school curriculum begins in Henry VII's reign. It is largely an Oxford phenomenon in its initiation and closely connected with Waynfleet's school attached to Magdalen College. Some earlier evidence there is of the humanities at Oxford. Stefano Surigone, a humanist from Milan, who later contributed verses to Caxton's edition of Chaucer's Boethius (*S.T.C.* 3199, 1478?), was it seems teaching in Oxford in the 1450s and after and may have had some hand in inspiring Sellyng's humanist inclinations.[136] But the story essentially begins with Magdalen College school and its grammarians. Fortunately the story has been well told and its main monuments, the *vulgaria* of the teachers, are readily accessible.[137] The pupils and teachers of Magdalen School leavened English education and their direct influence can be first traced when Colet appointed a former Magdalen Demi (scholar) as first master of his reformed St. Paul's. Together with Colet himself, and with Erasmus as a further contributor, Lily produced a Latin grammar which swept all before it. Henry VIII later ordered a version of it to be used in place of all other similar works. Whittinton's and Stanbridge's grammatical writings were forgotten.

---

[134] Weiss, *Humanism in England*, 153-159.

[135] *Ibid.*, 145-147.

[136] *Ibid.*, 138; cf. Josephine W. Bennett, in *Studies in the Renaissance*, XV (1968), 70-91.

[137] R. S. Stanier, *Magdalen School* (Oxford Historical Society, 1940), with an admirably lucid picture of the old grammatical manner and the new; *The Vulgaria of John Stanbridge and the Vulgaria of Robert Whittinton*, ed. Beatrice White (E.E.T.S., 1932); William Nelson, ed., *A Fifteenth Century School Book* (Oxford, 1956).

Colet's aims in establishing his new St. Paul's were pious, as were those of most benefactors of education. That he himself was a devout and influential theologian, whose humanist approach to the scriptures owes something to Erasmus and Ficino, and much to the spirit of the *Nova devotio*, leaves one wondering how far he could have anticipated what would happen at his foundation. He had prescribed the Christian 'classics'—Juvencus, Lactantius and so on, with one or two devout moderns (Baptista Mantuanus and Erasmus). But within a generation this was all forgotten. St. Paul's, Eton, Winchester, and scores of lesser grammar schools such as that at Ipswich (set up by Wolsey, another former Magdalen teacher) were basing their teaching on Terence, Virgil, Cicero (especially the letters), Horace and Ovid; and of course the writers of modern dialogues, especially Erasmus. The total victory of the Renaissance curriculum in the humanities was accomplished by the mid-sixteenth century, so far as the secondary school was concerned. There were still Trojans holding out in Oxford University, but their ultimate defeat was assured and it had been largely because of the activities of an Oxford grammar school. 'Small Latin and less Greek' might perhaps be the result in most cases: but Latin and a bit of Greek and virtually nothing else was to be the pabulum of the grammar school-boy for generations to come.

We cannot associate this remarkable transformation with religious motives, nor attribute as much as was done in the past to the coincidence of Colet with the time when Ficino was the main intellectual force in Florence; the two men never met, although we now know that Colet studied carefully some of Ficino's writings.[138] It seems, indeed, very dubious if Ficino, on whom Paul Oskar Kristeller has shed so much light, would pass his own test for what constituted a humanist! The traditional association of Greek scholarship with the reformers is not in question, although it is important to remember that most of the leading Northern humanists adhered to the old religion. What does seem to be mistaken is the view (I quote the words of a well-known authority) that 'the progress of learning was intimately connected with the progress of the reformation. The study of Greek was now encouraged, now suspected, according to the royal attitude in ecclesiastical affairs'.[139]

The two English universities were cowed clients of the Crown

---

[138] Sears Jayne, *John Colet and Marsilio Ficino* (Oxford, 1963).
[139] J. D. Mackie, *The Earlier Tudors 1485-1558* (Oxford, 1952), 271-272.

after Wycliffe and were never more subservient than in the Tudor period. But it proved difficult to prevent innovation since the life of the places no longer lay in the university corporations themselves, but in the colleges. Even if Henry VII and his contemporaries could have forseen the Lutheran revolt and associated it with Humanity or Greek, such subjects might enter by the back door, so to speak. We have seen the explosive consequences of Magdalen College School. At Cambridge Alcock's foundation of Jesus college (1496), and Christ's (1505) and St. John's (1511), both inspired by that conventionally devout figure Henry VII's mother, the Lady Margaret Beaufort, all pointed the way towards change. Alcock's college had a grammar school attached, grammar teaching was also important at Christ's, where the Lady Margaret's confessor, Bishop Richard Fisher, was the first Cambridge man profoundly to affect the progress of humanist studies there. He not only introduced humanity into the curriculum, he sponsored Erasmus and Greek. At St. John's Fisher followed a similarly original line.[140]

It would be good to be able to measure the effect of these changes on the vernacular for it was only when the humanities really influenced English literature that the Renaissance in England came to full flower. There are hints and anticipations not merely in the somewhat laboured classical themes of early Tudor writers like Skelton and Barclay; much of such matter is correctly described by C. S. Lewis as 'Late Medieval'.[141] But occasionally the manner becomes arrestingly sharp. This is most often found in the *vulgaria* where the rigour of Latin composition lies close at hand. I believe that the late Professor Lewis was totally misguided when, having argued that it was false to regard neo-latinists as 'somehow more enlightened, less remote, less limited by their age, than those who wrote English',[142] he went on (a *tour de force*) to translate quotations from humanist Latin into sixteenth-century English. This is to misconceive entirely why writers chose to compose in Latin. They liked Latin because it had rules for spelling and composition, because one could attain a perfection and exactitude of expression in it as yet

---

[140] A first-class survey in M. H. Curtis, *Oxford and Cambridge in Transition* (Oxford, 1959), with some retrospective coverage of the early Tudor period (e.g., pp. 70-71). A more recent, wider ranging survey in Hugh Keearney, *Scholars and Gentlemen, 1500-1700* (London, 1970).

[141] *English Literature in the Sixteenth century excluding Drama* (Oxford, 1954), 120-156.

[142] *Ibid.*, preface.

unapproachable by northern vernaculars; they like it because it was glamorous; they liked it because it commanded an international public. Latin *was*, in short, 'more enlightened and less remote' than the angular and repetitive English of the time. In the end neo-classical Latin so worked on the vernacular that we reach the splendour of what Lewis called the 'golden English' of the later sixteenth century. Glimpses of it are found in the *vulgaria*. More's English prose points in the same direction. It seems to me that much remains to be done by scholars of English language and literature to enlighten us on the influence of Latin on English during the Renaissance.[143]

It is true that Professor Jones had displayed how competition with Latin led English writers to a profound dissatisfaction with their own 'uneloquent language',[144] but he does not discuss the pressure exerted by the new grammar school curriculum from the early sixteenth century. And the 'barrenness of the mother tongue' [145] was only partially fertilised merely by extending the vocabulary with new borrowings, the feature dealt with most thoroughly by students of English language in the late medieval, early modern period.[146] One book, however, does seem to me to touch on the heart of the matter. I quote Professor Ian A. Gordon:

> The effect of all this on the writing of English prose was everywhere apparent. One should perhaps speak of the effects in the plural, for the influence of humanist Latinity, though it was widespread and permanent, did not all tend in the same direction. At one end of the scale a fine classical Latinist like Sir Thomas More wrote English prose of Anglo-Saxon simplicity; at the other extreme the chronicler Edward Hall and Sir Thomas Elyot introduced Latinisms as strange as the Saxonisms that Pecock had unsuccessfully tried to naturalise.[147]

What is at issue is the whole swing, style and omnicompetence of a means of communication.

---

[143] Cf. my 'Early Renaissance', *ad fin.*, where I dig a 'couplet' of 'golden' English from a prose passage in the *vulgaria* edited by Professor Nelson (above, n. 137).

[144] Richard Foster Jones, *The Triumph of the English Language* (London, 1953), esp. 3-31. My colleagues Mrs. V. Salmon and Professor Angus McIntosh kindly allowed me to consult them on this subject.

[145] Jones, *Triumph of the English Language*, 70.

[146] For instance in the useful works by J. A. Sheard, *The Words We Use* (London, 1954); and Mary S. Serjeantson, *A History of Foreign Words in English* (London, 1935), 259-266. But note in the former the jejune account of the Renaissance (p. 242).

[147] *The Movement of English Prose* (London, 1966), 74; and see the whole section on 'The impact of humanist latinity', pp. 73-83.

Of one thing we can be sure. At the level of the availability of the classics the Englishman in the early Tudor period had, thanks to the printing press on the Continent, almost everything he required of ancient and modern scholarship; and, for good measure, medieval as well—we must remember that some of the greatest monuments of ancient thought were familiar parts of the medieval intellectual landscape. If one compares the availability of the Latin classics in medieval libraries, as tabulated by Dom David Knowles and Sir Roger Mynors [148] with those at the disposal of the Bridgettine fathers at Syon (1504-1526) one sees the scale of the change. Greek may still be thin on the ground. Latin and neo-Latin are plentiful. Here is Miss Bateson's summary of the books at Syon:

> Its strength lay in the Latin translations of the Renaissance; for instance Argyropoulos, Hermolaus Barbarus, Gaza, Marsilius Ficinus, G. Trapezuntios and Erasmus are well represented as translated from the Greek. The monastery kept pace with the new learning in its Latin Renaissance literature; Coluccio, Leonardo Bruni, Poggio, Bessarion, Platina, Poliziano, Pico della Mirandola, are here, but there are no books in Italian. Petrarch appears as a Latin writer on the penitential psalms, Boccaccio as the author of a dictionary of classical antiquities. Savonarola, *De virtute fidei* is there. Reuchlin represents the German humanists, but there are no books in German. From the English Renaissance, Colet's sermon to the clergy of St. Pauls is here, and Linacre's translation of Proclus. More is represented by the translation of Lucian . . . which he wrote with Erasmus.[149]

The 'hard core' of authors inaccessible in the early fifteenth century (Catullus, Lucretius, Pliny's *Letters* and Statius's *Silvae*) is not represented,[150] but the collection is still impressive. After all, as I have just observed, most of the main Latin authors of antiquity were known, if in indifferent texts, well enough in the Middle Ages and they were at Syon too, often in improved printed versions. This, let it be recalled, was a *monastic* library. To see what an English humanist could assemble the books of Grocyn may be adduced—a very choice collection indeed.[151] And for a glimpse of the wealth

---

[148] M. D. Knowles, 'The preservation of the classics', *English Library before 1700*, 136-137; R. A. B. Mynors, 'The Latin classics known to Boston of Bury', *Fritz Saxl . . . Essays*, 199-217 (an arrangement and commentary on material in the early fifteenth-century compilation of John Boston, monk of Bury St. Edmunds, *Cathologus de libris autenticis et apocrifis*).

[149] Edition cited above (n. 102), p. viii.

[150] Mynors, 'The Latin classics known to Boston of Bury', 217.

[151] Thomas Linacre's list, ed. Montagu Burrows in *Collectanea*, second series (Oxford Hist. Soc., 1890), 319-331; cf. Emden, *Biog. Reg. Oxford*, II, 828-830.

of material available to a man with money, a list of the books sold by the Oxford bookseller John Dorne in 1520 (the year after Grocyn died) has survived in his 'day-book'.[152] 'The English books are few compared with the Latin . . . Latin theology forms the bulk of the more important volumes sold, as might be expected, and next to that Latin classics'.[153]

It seems to me that by this date the humanities in England had reached the point of 'take-off', to use the economists' jargon. They were beginning to be self-supporting, and no longer needed to be propped up by royal or other high-level patronage. That such developments were to be seen at work all over northern Europe doubtless made Englishmen confident in the new ways they were gradually learning to tread. And in saying this one must on no account forget the Renaissance in Scotland.[154] England and Scotland were locked in political rivalry, but linked in 1503 in a dynastic marriage which was to lead a hundred years later to a Scottish king and his courtiers taking over in England. Already by 1500 there were three Scottish universities, each probably more in touch with the exciting changes on the Continent than the two universities (as opposed to their colleges) in England. At Aberdeen we have the first Renaissance university in 'Britain', as continental humanists indifferently called England or Scotland or both. The term 'humanity' in Scotland was to adhere to the professor of Latin.[155] It is perhaps equally important that in Scotland the early sixteenth century saw the steady reception of Roman law, in line perhaps with what some statesmen, including Henry VIII, may have wished to see south

---

[152] 'Day-book of John Dorn', ed. F. Madan, *Collectanea* (Oxford Hist. Soc., 1885), 73-177; corrections and additions by F. Madan with notes by H. Bradshaw, *Collectanea*, second series (cited above, n. 151), 463-517.

[153] 'Day-book', 75.

[154] Lewis, *English Literature in the Sixteenth century*, 66-119; J. Durkan, 'The beginnings of humanism in Scotland', *Innes Review*, IV (1953), 5-24; John Mac-Queen, *Robert Henryson* (Oxford, 1967), 1-23. None of these writers takes into consideration the effects on Scottish culture of the contemporary reception of Roman law, on which see Holdsworth, *History of English Law*, IV, 251, and, in general disappointingly, *Introductory Survey of the Sources and Literature of Scots Law, Stair Society*, I (1936). See also Lord Cooper, 'The central courts after 1532', *Stair Society*, XX (1958), 341-349. To an outsider it seems that the problem deserves much more scholarly attention than it has so far received.

[155] But the earliest case of a written example is 1564, according to the *Dictionary of the Older Scottish Tongue*, III, 175. The earliest English case of 'humanity' = Latin is 1483, according to the *O.E.D.*

of the Anglo Scottish border.[156] When James VI became also James I he came from a country where the grammar school was an official educational ideal. In both countries the curriculum was broadly the same: the curriculum of the Italian humanist of the fifteenth century. By the seventeenth century 'Great Britain' was to be joined to the Continent by cultural links stronger than any forged before.

---

[156] I am by no means sure that Maitland's argument that the English common law was seriously threatened in the early sixteenth century is as easily disposed of as his later critics have supposed: Holdsworth, *History of English Law*, IV, 252-263, whose views are repeated by many others. The nature of the new prerogative courts and concepts of equity both marry in with the establishment of chairs of civil law in sixteenth-century Oxford and Cambridge, the prestige of Doctors' Commons and the whole contemporary spirit of intelligent and modern government.

GERMANY

THE COURSE OF GERMAN HUMANISM

LEWIS W. SPITZ

Stanford University

Ode to Apollo

Phoebus, who the sweet-noted lyre constructed,
Leave fair Helicon and depart your Pindus,
And by pleasant song designated, hasten
    To these our borders.

You perceive how joyous the Muses gather,
Sweetly singing under a frozen heaven;
Come yourself, and with your melodious harp-strings,
    Gaze on these wastelands.

So must he, whom sometime a rude or rustic
Parent fostered, barbarous, all unknowing
Latium's splendors, choose you now as his teacher
    At writing verses.

Just as Orpheus sang to the old Pelasgians,
Orpheus, whom swift stags, beasts of savage custom,
Whom the lofty trees of the forest followed,
    Charmed by his plectrum.

Swift and joyous, once you forswore, and gladly,
Greece for Latium, passing the mighty ocean;
There you wished your delectable arts to broadcast,
    Leading the Muses.

Thus it is our prayer you may wish to visit
Our abode, as once those Italian reaches.
May wild tongue take flight, and may all of darkness
    Come to destruction.[1]

In these beautiful lines Conrad Celtis, christened by Friedrich von
Bezold the "German arch-humanist," called on Apollo to continue
his *itinerarium* beyond Italy to the lands across the Alps. In his inaugural address at the University of Ingolstadt he challenged the
youth of Germany to enter into cultural rivalry with the Italians.
"Take up again, O German men," he called, "that old spirit of yours

---

[1] The *Ode to Apollo*, trans. George C. Schoolfield of Yale University, is from
Conrad Celtis the German Arch-Humanist by Lewis W. Spitz (Cambridge, Mass.,
1957), 10, reprinted by permission of the Harvard University Press.

with which you so many times were a specter and terror to the Romans! " [2] To his friend the jurist, Sixtus Tucher of Nuremberg, Celtis wrote:

> When you read my writings, you will be convinced that I did not send them to you to display my poetic genius ..., but you will understand that I spared no trouble to accomplish a certain end. For if these efforts do not match those of the Italians, I wish to stimulate and awaken those men among the Germans who excel in learnedness and genius .... Then the Italians, most effusive in self-praise, will be forced to confess that not only the Roman imperium and arms, but also the splendor of letters has migrated to the Germans. [3]

Apollo did indeed leave the lands of the blue Mediterranean with their sun-bleached white marble classical remains and came to the frozen north under the septentrional stars. Especially the young men of the North responded to his melodious harp strings.

The culture of the North, however, could not be a Renaissance in the sense of a rebirth of classical antiquity such as Italy experienced in its springtime following its cultural lag of two centuries behind the great achievements of medieval France, for the Germans were not the Romans and did not have the artistic and architectural monuments, the learned notaries and *dictatores* who kept the memory of antiquity partly alive in even ordinary Italian minds. The culture of the North became rather a bookish culture more than a visual culture. Its characteristic Renaissance expression was that of humanism. Petrus Lotichius Secundus (1528-1560), a German poet, wrote from Italy: "Moreover, I am free of those hindrances which formerly kept me from studies: I am alone and live entirely for myself and my studies." [4] The Germans became students of the Roman and Greek authors and like the Italian *umanisti* they devoted themselves to the *studia humanitatis* because these complete and ornament man. Classical letters served as their measure and ideal.

No problem in intellectual history, Wilhelm Dilthey once observed, is so interesting as that of the changes which Renaissance humanism underwent as it crossed the Alps. The study of German humanism

---

[2] *Conradus Celtis Protucius Oratio in Gymnasio in Ingolstadt Publice Recitata cum Carminibus ad Orationem Pertinentibus*, ed. Hans Rupprich (Leipzig, 1932), 1-11.

[3] Konrad Celtis to Sixtus Tucher, Ingolstadt, 1491, in *Der Briefwechsel des Konrad Celtis*, ed. Hans Rupprich (Munich, 1934), 28 f., No. 15.

[4] "Careo praeterea iis molestiis, quae prius a studiis me avocabant: solus sum solique mihi et meis studiis rectissime inservio," cited by Karl Otto Conrady, "Die Erforschung der neulateinischen Literatur. Probleme und Aufgaben," *Euphorion. Zeitschrift für Literaturgeschichte*, XLIX (1955), 413.

is, in fact, studded with controversial issues, controverted interpretations, unresolved problems, great bodies of literature still
unexplored, and gaps in the material available for examination.
Werner Näf, the great Swiss biographer of Vadianus, once commented upon the need for scholarly editions of the humanists'
writings and new biographies of famous men as well as of men
undeservedly obscure.[5] Much work remains to be done. The present
study cannot pretend to provide lexicographical completeness in
such a limited space. It will have to be highly selective, seeking
to point up representative figures without dealing with even all the
important figures or categories. It will, therefore, be highly personal
in nature.

I. Problems of Origins, Nature, Continuity, and New Directions

Origins

History, said Lord Acton, should deal with problems and not
with periods. The first and one of the most vexing problems of
German humanism is that of its origins. Just as the origins of the
Italian Renaissance have been variously explained as to be found
in the native Roman soil, in French medieval or Provençal influence
or as resulting from the Byzantine or Greek influx, so the origins of
German humanism have been sought variously in northern sources
such as the Brethren of the Common Life, or the precocious court of
Charles IV, or in the Italian influence. The extent to which the roots
of German humanism were autochthonous and indigenous to the
North or were Italian in source is still a highly controverted issue.
R. R. Post in a highly revisionist work on the Brethren of the Common
Life argued vociferously against the position of Albert Hyma,
Augustin Renaudet and other scholars that the Brethren were heavily
into education and from the 14th century on (Groote d. 1384),
promoted the study of the "safe classics", and led dozens if not
hundreds of German students in the Rhineland and the North to an
appreciation of the classics.[6] While one might well argue that in his

---

[5] Werner Näf, "Aus der Forschung zur Geschichte des deutschen Humanismus," *Schweizer Beiträge zur Allgemeinen Geschichte*, II (1944), 214.

[6] R. R. Post, *The Modern Devotion. Confrontation with Reformation and Humanism*,
Studies in Medieval and Reformation Thought, III (Leiden, 1968). See the excellent review by Helmar Junghans, in *Luther-Jahrbuch*, XXXVII (1970), 120-127,
which says approximately what my own response to Post would have been, had
he lived, yielding some but not all on the points of controversy. See also the
outstanding article by H. Junghans, "Der Einfluß des Humanismus auf Luthers

detailed study Post was too literal minded and did not see the forest for the trees, a certain validity to his revisionism remains. Certainly the Italian influence upon the development of enthusiastic classicism was the critical determinant. One can still argue for the receptiveness and readiness of the northern soil, and one can play with the idea of a preestablished harmony between the non-dogmatic, non-speculative, education-minded pious Brethren and the non-dialectical, moral-philosophical, education-minded Italian humanists; but the great importance of the Italian Renaissance for the development of German humanism has become increasingly evident.

The early flowering of Renaissance culture at the Prague court of Emperor Charles IV was once hailed not only as the debut of the Northern Renaissance, but even heralded as the cradle in the North of the Renaissance itself.[7] But only a thin thread stretched by way of Emperor Maximilian's Vienna provides a tenuous tie between that early dawn and the mainstream of German humanist culture in the late fifteenth and early sixteenth centuries. The impact of Italian Renaissance culture upon the chief centers of German humanist culture can be traced more convincingly from the contacts provided by the great church councils in the early fifteenth century, the various

---

Entwicklung bis 1518," *Luther-Jahrbuch*, XXXVII (1970), 37-101, touching on these points. For Albert Hyma's interpretation see esp. his *The Christian Renaissance: A History of the "Devotio Moderna"* (Grand Rapids, Mich., 1924), and *The Brethren of the Common Life* (Grand Rapids, Mich., 1950). See also Kenneth A. Strand, ed., *Essays on the Northern Renaissance* (Ann Arbor, Mich., 1968), especially the articles by Julia S. Henkel, "School Organizational Patterns of the Brethren of the Common Life," pp. 35-50, and by Kenneth A. Strand, "The Brethren of the Common Life and Fifteenth-Century Printing: A Brief Survey," pp. 51-64. See the excellent pages on northern piety by Margaret E. Aston, "The Northern Renaissance," in Richard L. DeMolen, ed., *The Meaning of the Renaissance and Reformation* (Boston, 1974), 71-129, 82-90. W. Lourdaux has contributed important studies underlining the significance of the Brethren of the Common Life for northern humanism, emphasizing their work as critical editors of texts, men of letters with a well-developed aesthetic sense, whose reading included the works of the most important Italian humanists as well as of classical authors. See his *Moderne Devotie en Christelijk Humanisme* (Louvain, 1967) and his article "Dévotion Moderne et Humanisme Chrétien," in Professor G. Verbeke and Professor J. IJsewijn, eds., *The Late Middle Ages and the Dawn of Humanism Outside Italy*, Proceedings of the International Conference, Louvain, May 11-13, 1970 (Louvain, 1972), 57-77.

[7] Konrad Burdach, *Vom Mittelalter zur Reformation* (Halle, 1893); *Deutsche Renaissance: Betrachtung über unsere künftige Bildung* (Berlin, 1920); *Vom Mittelalter zur Reformation, Forschungen zur Geschichte der deutschen Bildung*, 6 vols. (Berlin, 1912-1939). See Wallace K. Ferguson, *The Renaissance in Historical Thought* (Boston, 1948), 306-311.

Italians who visited Germany, and the constant stream of German students who poured annually into Italy for a year or more of study—law for the most part—at Bologna, Padua, or some other university. The many political and ecclesiastical contacts of Italy and the Empire nourished the growth of humanism in the North during the fifteenth and sixteenth centuries.

The development of German humanism during the course of the fifteenth century ran parallel in many ways to that of French humanism, gaining steadily in strength from the conciliar epoch on down to its involvement with secular courts and the episcopal courts as well (a fact which is now more fully appreciated by scholars), followed later by urban centers and eventually by the universities, which only gradually came to appreciate the value and utility of humanist learning.[8] The role of cultivated noble women in the patronage of the new learning is also now more fully recognized. There is a revisionist point of view also on the conflict of humanism and scholasticism. Formerly historians placed full credence in the claims of the humanists, vociferously seconded by the reformers, that they were the youthful gladiators locked in deadly combat with fierce and deadly opponents, the scholastic doctors who fought for syllogistic logic and dialectical theology against the rhetoric, refined literature and enlightened religion of the humanists.[9] The humanists overdramatized their struggle, which often had more to do with a battle for endowment and professorial billets than with a sharply differentiated kind of learning or with an essentially different world view. The scholastic doctors were usually mute or fairly inarticulate in their defence against outrageous charges and were in general not given to taking the offensive against the new learning. Rather, in terms of humanist origins and the relation of the two approaches to studies, many mid-

---

[8] Franco Simone, *The French Renaissance, Medieval Tradition and Italian Influence in Shaping the Renaissance in France* (London, 1969). Of interest in this connection is Kurt Nyholm, "Das höfische Epos im Zeitalter des Humanismus," *Neuphilologische Mitteilungen*, LXVI (1965), 297-313.

[9] Charles Nauert, "The Clash of Humanists and Scholastics: An Approach to Pre-Reformation Controversies," *The Sixteenth Century Journal*, IV (April, 1973), 1-18; Charles Nauert, "Peter of Ravenna and the 'obscure men' of Cologne: A Case of Pre-Reformation Controversy," *Renaissance Studies in Honor of Hans Baron*, eds. Anthony Molho and John Tedeschi (DeKalb, Ill., 1971), 609-640. James H. Overfield, "A New Look at the Reuchlin Affair," *Studies in Medieval and Renaissance History*, VIII (1971), 165-207. Overfield has prepared an article for future publication which makes a very telling argument for the revisionist view on "Scholastic Opposition to Humanism in Pre-Reformation Germany."

and late fifteenth-century intellectuals can best be described as "half humanist" and "half scholastic" in outlook, as indeed much of the older scholarly literature described them. There was more of a blending and gradual transition than a real clash during the fifteenth century. The relation between them should not be understood retrospectively in the light of the Reuchlin controversy, itself often misunderstood, or by taking literally the thrusts of the satirical literature of the sixteenth century.

Nature

The great neo-Kantian philosopher and intellectual historian Ernst Cassirer reflected a very old romantic notion about German humanism as essentially folkish in nature, in contrast to that of Italy and France.[10] He saw the three humanisms as representing three basic types which only in their contrast brought out the ideal whole of the epoch. The Italian Renaissance produced a new relation to political reality which provided the basis and the means for a general intellectual change. In molding the state into a work of art there for the first time the modern personality in its wholeness became conscious of its creative energies, though still bound to the old Roman idea of *imperium*. Freed of this last restrictive factor the development of the concept of personality was the distinct achievement of the French Renaissance. Montaigne as the richest and most multi-faceted thinker of the epoch was not a statesman, poet, or philosopher, but a person whose essays present himself in his completely private form and individuality. In contrast to these tendencies of Italian and French humanism, German humanism, Cassirer explained, even in the renewal of antiquity still remained in close touch with folkish tendencies. Erasmus was praised as the restorer of the true rights of mankind, Hutten blended the humanist ideal with the cause of German freedom, religious enlightenment, and national consciousness. Humanism and the new concept of human culture was set in opposition to scholasticism which had darkened the picture of antiq-

---

[10] Ernst Cassirer, *Freiheit und Form. Studien zur deutschen Geschichte* (Berlin, 1922), 3-11. If the monumental study of medieval Latin thought and letters by Ernst Robert Curtius, *Europäische Literatur und Lateinisches Mittelalter* (Bern, 1948), can justifiably be criticized for not differentiating sufficiently between the various areas and traditions in depicting the unity and coherence of medieval culture, much Renaissance scholarship can justifiably be criticized for over-emphasizing the differences especially among the northern expressions of humanist culture and between Protestant and Catholic humanist learning.

uity and pure Christianity. Cassirer's analysis of German humanism was derived largely from the romantic tradition which was spawned in the early nineteenth century, a strange quirk for the great historian of the Enlightenment. The folkish nature of German humanism persisted almost as a cliché, especially in histories of literature, and crested in sickening waves with the *Blut und Boden* propagandistic writings of the National Socialist period. German humanism was characterized by the people's community spirit rather than by individualism. The extent to which German humanist culture was not merely particularist, local, spontaneous, and popular, but European, cosmopolitan, created or contrived, and specialized is now receiving renewed attention. In contrast to the romantics' assessment, favorable to medieval culture, which viewed the classical emphasis of humanism as an artificial, unnatural, Roman, overintellectual, formalistic, alien intrusion, necessarily absorbed and transformed by the force of folkish impulses, contemporary scholars are coming increasingly to recognize the classical influence, the simplicity, the formal sophistication, the rhetorical skill, and the European character of much literature of the German Renaissance. This new emphasis is being accompanied by a renewed attention to the literary aesthetic quality of German Renaissance letters and a tapering off of the philological linguistic approach.[11]

That German humanist literature was a bourgeois phenomenon providing a middle-class interlude between the medieval and the "courtly" values of the seventeenth century is one of the commonplaces of literary scholarship.[12] Its bourgeois character gave to German humanist literature its new direction. Even authors who were not personally of middle-class background adapted to the

---

[11] Harold Jantz, "German Renaissance Literature," *Modern Language Notes*, LXXXI (1966), 398-436, esp. 398-401. See Willi Flemming, *Das deutsche Schrifttum von 1500 bis 1700* (Potsdam, n.d.), 9: "So nahm die starke bürgerliche Kultur auch ein gut Stück bäuerlicher Gesundheit und Bodenverbundenheit in sich auf. Urkräfte des Blutes pochten in den Adern dieser Geschlechter und sangen sich im Lied volksmäßig aus, ergriffen die ewigen Erlebnisse des Menschenherzens wie die Sondererlebnisse der Einzelberufe. Ganz aus dem Alltag greift Fastnachtsspiel und Schwankerzählung, Schnurre und Anekdote die Menschentypen und Geschehnisse. Bürgerliche Tüchtigkeit wird in der Erzählung ernsthaft geschildert und propagiert."
[12] A. J. Krailsheimer, ed., *The Continental Renaissance 1500-1600* (Penguin Books, 1971), 351. See the very commendable recent survey, Barbara Könneker, "Deutsche Literatur im Zeitalter des Humanismus und der Reformation," *Neues Handbuch der Literaturwissenschaft*, ed. Klaus von See, *Renaissance und Barock* (II. Teil), eds. August Buck *et alii* (Frankfurt am Main, 1972), 145-176, 145.

378   LEWIS W. SPITZ

demands of this tendency. Marxist literary historians gladly embraced this general bourgeois assessment of humanist culture, refining it when being mindful of the orthodox historical time-table by labelling it "early-bourgeois." [13] During this phase in the development of capitalism, literature became the organ of the new collective self-consciousness. It is possible to haggle over the definitions and to niggle over specific instances, but in general the interpretation of the bourgeois character of humanist literature must be refined in two ways. First of all it must be acknowledged that many of the attitudes and virtues characterized as bourgeois had long been inculcated by the church and were appreciated by non-urban segments of society. The new literary expressions were in large measure derived from and blended with those of an earlier day, the play from the *Fastnachtsspiel*, for example. The German prose novel goes back to the inspiration of the nobility, its origins to be sought in the creations of Elisabeth of Nassau-Saarbrücken who translated four French verse novels into German prose novels between 1430 and 1440. Secondly, the so-called chivalric or courtly revival developed in a unique way only in the second half of the seventeenth century and constituted only a part of the literary scene during those decades. To allow a simple identification of humanist culture with bourgeois or urban middle-class values, however, would be to create a pseudomorph or caricature of the reality. Clearly the cities and especially the free imperial cities were important centers of humanist learning.[14] But the humanists themselves came from all segments of society,

---

[13] Ingeborg Spriewald, Hildegard Schnabel, Werner Lenk, Heinz Entner, *Grundpositionen der deutschen Literatur im 16. Jahrhundert*, Deutsche Akademie der Wissenschaften zu Berlin, Zentralinstitut für Literaturgeschichte (Berlin and Weimar, 1972), 45: "Die im Schoße der feudalen Gesellschaftsordnung sich vollziehenden ökonomischen Veränderungen der Umschichtungsprozesse im sozialen Gefüge und die damit verbundenen Umbrüche im geistig-ideologischen Bereich führten während der zweiten Hälfte des 15. Jahrhunderts zu einem massiven Anwachsen bürgerlicher Ansprüche gerade auch auf kulturellem Gebiet. Die allmähliche, wenn auch nur zögernd und sehr unterschiedlich sich vollziehende Zersetzung feudalen Denk- und Lebensformen, vor allem aber die einschneidenden Wandlungen im Bereich der sozialen Wirklichkeit und das neue Verhältnis des Menschen zu dieser Wirklichkeit implizierten eine Aufgabenstellung der Literatur, die von den gekennzeichneten Intentionen und Möglichkeiten der hochmittelalterlichen Dichtung qualitativ verschieden war." Strobach, *Geschichte der deutschen Literatur von den Anfängen bis zur Gegenwart*, by a scholarly collective of the DDR, vol. V (Berlin, 1963), Vorbemerkung.

[14] Bernd Moeller, *Imperial Cities and the Reformation. Three Essays* (Philadelphia, 1972), "German Humanists and the Beginnings of the Reformation," 19-38.

from peasants such as Celtis to nobles such as Hutten. Moreover, the patrons dwelt in episcopal palaces and courts as well as in patrician houses. The readers and enthusiasts were drawn from all occupations as the universities increasingly served as ladders of social mobility for the intellectually able. And this social mixture in the case of author, patron and audience persisted into the seventeenth century. In the case of the baroque poets, for example, it is the humanistic education and not the vocation which provides the social common bond. In terms of calling, those men of letters had no guild or corporate character, but their social base extended from Protestant ministers, judges, Latin teachers, university professors all the way to princely and city bureaucrats and medical doctors. It reached throughout the world of the half-cultured part-time academics who never graduated from the universities, the merchants, publishers, book dealers, apothecaries, lawyers, sextons, and teachers in the law schools.[15] It is clear that short of a very broad definition of bourgeois, the term has less applicability and utility than those who bandy it about assume.

Above all, the significance of the classical models for humanist letters must be reemphasized. The humanists, it is true, were Germans who happened to be writing in Latin. But that circumstance was determinative for the course of German literary culture. The introduction of classical forms, modes, and ideas was of critical importance not only for neo-Latin literature, but for the vernacular as well. German letters would have been severely retarded if they had not benefited from the inspiration and above all from the classical standards of the Renaissance.

Continuity

One of the great misreadings of German intellectual history is reflected in the average textbook account of German humanist culture in the sixteenth century. Every school child is told that there was an irreconcilable contrast between the Reformation and Renaissance humanism, which wilted away under the hot blasts of religious assertions and controversy. The old and unfortunately still standard picture is one of the feeble beginnings of humanist culture, a brief flowering between 1500 and 1520, and then total submersion with some revivification in the neo-classical during the *Aufklärung*. A

---

[15] Jörg-Ulrich Fechner, *Der Antipetrarkismus. Studien zur Liebessatire in Barocker Lyrik* (Heidelberg, 1966), 31.

completely revised assessment is in order. Sixteenth century German culture continued to be remarkably rich in classical letters and learning, in Greek and Hebrew as well as in Latin, paying tribute to the antique spirit as well as to classical form.[16] The reformers did not devote themselves exclusively to the propagation of their religious faith, but saw the place of the Reformation within the general cultural situation and were genuinely devoted to the cultivation of classical culture. Luther saw human society and higher culture as the "sphere of faith's works." Wittenberg became a center of neo-Latin letters. The Empire was fortunate in enjoying over a half a century of relative calm following the Peace of Augsburg, 1555, and the cultivation of letters and learning flourished in a benign climate.[17] The classic Dilthey and Troeltsch debate over the relation of the Renaissance and Reformation finds its local application with respect to German humanism and, when it is thought through in the light of all the knowledge now available regarding sixteenth-century German culture, must definitely be resolved in favor of the continuity of German humanism throughout the sixteenth century.[18]

The question of the termination of the Renaissance is intimately related to that of the continuity of German humanism through the Reformation period. With western Europe in mind, H. R. Trevor-Roper chose the year 1620 for the end of the Renaissance period.[19] A very good argument could be made for 1618 as a convenient date for the *terminus ad quem* of German humanism, for the Thirty Years' War had such a disruptive and depressing effect on German intel-

---

[16] Harold Jantz, *op. cit.*, 410-411. Jantz draws attention to the second volume of the second edition of Karl Goedeke's bibliography of German literature which records on pages 87-119 a selection of 273 neo-Latin poets of the time which reveals that a great part of the humanistic publication took place in Wittenberg precisely during the most active decades of the Reformation.

[17] See Heinz Liebing, "Die Ausgänge des europäischen Humanismus," *Geist und Geschichte der Reformation* (Berlin, 1966), 357-376; Lewis W. Spitz, "Humanism in the Reformation," in A. Molho and J. A. Tedeschi, eds., *Renaissance Studies in Honor of Hans Baron*, 641-662; Lewis W. Spitz, "Humanism and the Reformation," in Robert M. Kingdon, ed., *Transition and Revolution. Problems and Issues of European Renaissance and Reformation History* (Minneapolis, Minn., 1974), 153-188.

[18] Two key writings on the debate are available in translation, Wilhelm Dilthey, "The Interpretation and Analysis of Man in the Fifteenth and Sixteenth Centuries" and Ernst Troeltsch, "Renaissance and Reformation," in Lewis W. Spitz, ed., *The Reformation—Basic Interpretations* (Lexington, Mass., 1972), 11-43.

[19] H. R. Trevor-Roper, "Religion, the Reformation and Social Change," *The European Witch-Craze of the Sixteenth and Seventeenth Centuries and Other Essays* (New York, 1968), 2.

lectual as well as social life that it serves as a very convenient method and in every household. There is no utility whatsoever to the great scholar Georg Ellinger's artificial distinction between humanistic and neo-Latin literature, for the generic character of Latin letters remained too much the same.[20] Similarly it is not possible to mark the end of humanistic-neo-Latin culture at any such fixed date, for the continuity through mannerism and the baroque is obvious. While one is being arbitrary, then, one may as well be as audacious as Trevor-Roper and set the terminal point for purposes of discussion at 1620.

New Directions

Even after more than a century of serious scholarly study, the field of German humanism is far from closed out or its intellectual mines exhausted, for much work remains to be done. It will serve a useful purpose to point out limitations of our knowledge and new directions to be taken in order to place the present account of the course of German humanism into perspective.

The full story of the reception of Italian humanism in Germany is yet to be told, particularly the influence of less prominent figures such as the Carmelite general Baptista Mantuanus, beloved by humanists and reformers alike. The splendid survey by Willy Andreas is weak on beginnings, modest in scope, limited to the Reformation period, and insufficiently detailed. But no recent general work has superseded his. Moreover, the comprehensive literary histories are uniformly limited to letters and do not include in their purview the historical, political, philosophical and religious dimensions of humanism as one intellectual and cultural phenomenon.[21] The

---

[20] Georg Ellinger, "Neulateinische Dichtung Deutschlands im 16. Jahrhundert," Paul Merker and Wolfgang Stammler, eds., *Reallexikon der deutschen Literaturgeschichte*, II (Berlin, 1926/1928), 469-494; Georg Ellinger, *Italien und der deutsche Humanismus in der Neulateinischen Lyrik*, 3 vols. (Berlin, 1929-1933).

[21] Willy Andreas, *Deutschland vor der Reformation. Eine Zeitenwende*, 5th ed. (Stuttgart, 1948). See the brief observations of Jacques Ridé, "Deux grand synthèses sur l'Humanisme," *Études Germaniques*, XX (1965), 546-550, on Willy Andreas and Georg Voigt. The most thorough recent literary history, almost encyclopedic in nature, is that of the late Vienna scholar Hans Rupprich, *Die deutsche Literatur vom späten Mittelalter bis zum Barock*, Erster Teil, *Das ausgehende Mittelalter, Humanismus und Renaissance 1370-1520* (Munich, 1970), vol. IV/1 of Helmut de Boor and Richard Newald, *Geschichte der deutschen Literatur von den Anfängen bis zur Gegenwart*. The two most ambitious recent volumes are posthumous collections of essays, Michael Seidlmayer, *Wege und Wandlungen des Humanismus* (Göttingen, 1965), and Richard Newald, *Probleme und Gestalten des deutschen Humanismus* (Berlin, 1963), neither providing a comprehensive account.

influence and cross-fertilization between German and French humanism was lively and continuous, not only with Gaguin, Lefèvre, or
Budé, but through to mannerism, to Johann Fischart (1546-1590),
for example, whose *Gargantua* was related to, though in some ways
independent of, Rabelais, and to the Baroque.

The impact of patristic writings and of Christian antiquity upon
German humanism calls for a major study, now that more work
has been done on the patristic influence in Italian humanism. Far
beyond its obvious importance for Erasmus, that impact is of special
importance in the area where humanism and reform overlay and
interpenetrate through the sixteenth century.[22] The influence of the
pre-Socratic philosophers calls for precise assessment. Similarly the
continued influence of such medieval cultural figures as Bernard,
Jean Gerson, or of the Friends of God, Rhenish mysticism and
scholasticism requires further analysis.[23] Increased attention has
been paid in recent years to the dark underside of the Italian Renaissance, and similar studies of the irrational and occult aspects of
humanist thought in northern Europe would add completeness to
our picture and would make the emergence of the witchcraft craze
and other startling developments of the later sixteenth and seventeenth
centuries seem less astonishing.[24] Too often those suspect dimensions

---

[22] Paul Oskar Kristeller, "Studies on Renaissance Humanism during the Last
Twenty Years," *Studies in the Renaissance*, IX (1962), 20, stated that further study
of patristic influence on the Renaissance would be desirable. Charles Stinger,
"Humanism and Reform in the Early Quattrocento: The Patristic Scholarship
of Ambrogio Traversari (1386-1439)" (Stanford diss., 1971), and others have
since responded with monographic studies. This dimension of antique cultural
influences was scarcely appreciated by the Burckhardtians such as Ludwig Geiger,
Renaissance und Humanismus in Italien und Deutschland (Berlin, 1882). Among the
few monographs which take the patristic influence into account is Hans Jürgen
Schings, *Die patristische und stoische Tradition bei Andreas Gryphius* (Cologne and
Graz, 1966).

[23] An example of an admirable philological-literary study relating to mysticism
is Hermann Kunisch, "Die mittelalterliche Mystik und die deutsche Sprache:
Ein Grundriß," *Literaturwissenschaftliches Jahrbuch der Görres-Gesellschaft*, VI (1965),
37-90.

[24] Two recent studies which probe the underside of the Renaissance are Robert
S. Kinsman, *The Darker Vision of the Renaissance Beyond the Fields of Reason* (Berkeley
and Los Angeles, 1973), and Wayne Shumaker, *The Occult Sciences in the Renaissance.
A Study in Intellectual Patterns* (Berkeley and Los Angeles, 1973). See Lewis W.
Spitz, "Occultism and Despair of Reason in Renaissance Thought," *Journal of the
History of Ideas*, XXVII (1966), 464-469. H. C. Erik Midelfort, *Witch Hunting in
Southwestern Germany 1562-1684. The Social and Intellectual Foundations* (Stanford,
1972) reveals the popular depths of belief in witchcraft and offers some startling
revisionist explanations.

of the Renaissance world are passed over in what Eugenio Garin has called "a conspiracy of silence. A figure such as Agrippa of Nettesheim very naturally has attracted attention and Johannes Trithemius is being favored with new studies, but there are other lesser figures and there is a dimension of this sort in nearly all the representatives of humanist culture in the North.[25]

Another aspect of the revival of classical antiquity in the German Renaissance calling for further research is the new role of Roman law and its contribution to northern humanism. So far the exploration of this subject has been very much a one-man show, the work of that very distinguished scholar Guido Kisch, who has written on Erasmus, Zasius, Reuchlin, Melanchthon and others. Much work remains to be done on the significance of the revival of Roman law, the advance of the *mos gallicus* over the *mos italicus*, the significance of Italian law studies for the young German legists who returned to ecclesiastical and secular courts, to city secretariats and to universities.[26]

In the area of education many problems require explanation before a new general account can be undertaken. Otto Herding, the great scholar of German humanism at Freiburg University, has

---

[25] Charles Nauert, *Agrippa and the Crisis of Renaissance Thought* (Urbana, 1965). On Trithemius see the chapter on "Der Magier" in Klaus Arnold, *Johannes Trithemius (1462-1516)* Quellen und Forschungen zur Geschichte des Bistums und Hochstifts Würzburg, XXIII (Würzburg, 1971), 180-200, reviewed by Ulrich Bubenheimer in the *Zeitschrift der Savigny-Stiftung für Rechtsgeschichte, Germanistische Abteilung*, LXXXIX (1972), 455-459. Arnold recently translated and edited *Johannes Trithemius "De Laude Scriptorum" "Zum Lobe der Schreiber"* (Würzburg, 1973).

[26] Guido Kisch, "Forschungen zur Geschichte des Humanismus in Basel," *Archiv für Kulturgeschichte*, XL/2 (1958), 194-221; *Erasmus und die Jurisprudenz seiner Zeit* (Basel, 1960); *Zasius und Reuchlin* (Constance and Stuttgart, 1961); *Die Anfänge der juristischen Fakultät der Universität Basel, 1459-1529* (Basel, 1962); *Melanchthons Rechts- und Soziallehre* (Berlin, 1967). A recent study of a practicing humanistic jurist worthy of emulation is Hartmut Boockmann, *Laurentius Blumenau, Fürstlicher Rat, Jurist, Humanist* (Göttingen, 1964). R. C. Van Caenegem, "The 'Reception' of Roman Law: A Meeting of Northern and Mediterranean Traditions," M. G. Verbeke and J. IJsewijn, eds., *The Late Middle Ages and the Dawn of Humanism Outside Italy*, 195-204, offers a brief sketch in general terms of "reception" through the medieval and Renaissance periods. Thomas Burger, *Jakob Spiegel, Ein humanistischer Jurist des 16. Jahrhunderts* (Augsburg, 1973, a Freiburg i. Br. diss.), recounts the relation of the legist Spiegel, Wimpheling's nephew, to the leading humanists and to the Reformation. See the bibliographical study by Myron P. Gilmore, "The Jurisprudence of Humanism," *Traditio*, XVII (1961), 493-501, and his *Humanists and Jurists. Six Studies in the Renaissance* (Cambridge, Mass., 1963).

contributed more than any other specialist to the analysis of German humanist education. He has pointed to the need for distinguishing carefully the various genres of educational treatises. He has himself edited Wimpheling's *Adolescentia* and is doing further work on Socrates, Pseudo-Isocrates, and the early Greek influence on Erasmus and educational theory.[27] The comparison of German humanist with Italian educational treatises must be extended. The comparison of humanist with Reformation educational emphases on the classical curriculum, compulsory universal education, the role of teaching as a divine vocation, and the different concepts of calling of humanists and reformers, needs a major treatment. The impact of humanist-reformation education as represented by Johann Sturm's Strasbourg Academy upon French Calvinist as well as upon English secondary education is crying for a major comprehensive study.[28] While there have been several significant recent contributions to the history of humanism in the universities, going well beyond the justly famous studies of the venerable Gustav Bauch, including the monograph on the personal role played by Luther in promoting a humanist arts curriculum, much work remains to be done on the continued interplay of humanism and reform in the universities of both Protestant and Catholic areas of Germany into the seventeenth century.[29] The very number and regional spread of the universities suggests a difference in the nature of university influence than was true in England, for

---

[27] Otto Herding, "Zur Problematik humanistischer Erziehungsschriften. Textforschung und Menschenbild," *XIIe Congrès International des Sciences Historiques: Rapports.* III. *Commissions* (Vienna, 1965), 87-94. Otto Herding, *Jakob Wimpfelings Adolescentia* (Munich, 1965); "Der elsässische Humanist Jakob Wimpfeling und seine Erziehungsschrift 'Adolescentia'," *Zeitschrift für Württembergische Landesgeschichte*, XXII (1963), 1-18. See also Herding's *Jakob Wimpfeling/ Beatus Rhenanus, Das Leben des Johannes Geiler von Kaysersberg* (Munich, 1970), the review of which edition in the *Renaissance Quarterly*, XXVI/2 (Summer, 1973), 206-208, is a bit capricious and does not fully acknowledge the erudition and insight in evidence in the introduction.

[28] Pierre Mesnard, "La pédagogie de Jean Sturm et son inspiration évangélique (1507-1589)," *XIIe Congrès International des Sciences Historiques Rapports.* III. *Commissions* (Vienna, 1965), 95-110. A sample of the influence on the Melanchthon-Sturm approach to education on the French scene is provided by Claude Baduel's reform of the academy at Nîmes. Cf. Theodore W. Casteel, "The College and University of Arts in Nîmes: An Experiment in Humanistic Education in the Age of Reform" (Stanford diss., 1973).

[29] Representative recent studies are Gustav Benrath, "Die Universität der Reformationszeit," *Archiv für Reformationsgeschichte*, LXVII (1966), 32-51, and Gottfried Kliesch, *Der Einfluß der Universität Frankfurt auf die schlesische Bildungsgeschichte, dargestellt an den Breslauer Immatrikulierten von 1506-1648* (Würzburg, 1961).

example, with its concentration of university monopoly in London, Oxford and Cambridge.

If scholarly interest in German humanist expressions of cultural nationalism has noticeably cooled during the post-war years, the attention directed toward the religious thought of the humanists and the religious life and practices of the people has markedly increased.[30] There is a very natural bridge from the question of the religious positions of the humanists and the interrelation of humanism and the Reformation. Attention has been increasingly centered upon the influence of humanism on the magisterial and lesser reformers as well as upon the points of variance between humanism and reform. More scholarship also has been devoted to the transmission by the reformers of humanist cultural values to later generations.

At issue in the first instance is the question of the classical learning and humanist sympathies of the reformers, preeminently of Luther himself. Oswald Schmidt's limited and badly outdated work on the subject of Luther's knowledge of the classics needs to be superseded by a new study using the Weimar edition.[31] Secondly, Luther's relation to basic humanist disciplines such as rhetoric needs further detailed examination. Luther once wrote to Eobanus Hessus:

> Plane nihil minus vellum fieri aut committi in iuventute, quam ut pocsin et rhetoricen omittant. Mea certe vota sunt, ut quam plurimi sint et poetae et rhetores, quod his studiis videam, sicut nec aliis modis fieri potest, mire aptos fieri homines ad sacra tum capessenda, tum dextre et feliciter tractanda.[32]

---

[30] For example, Lewis W. Spitz, *The Religious Renaissance of the German Humanists* (Cambridge, Mass., 1963).

[31] Oswald G. Schmidt, *Luthers Bekanntschaft mit den alten Klassikern* (Leipzig, 1883). Wilhelm Pauck, "The Historiography of the German Reformation during the Past Twenty Years," *Church History*, IX (1940), 15, stated that the problem of Luther's relation to humanism needs a new and thorough investigation. Many of the older analyses must be rethought, such as Carl Stange, "Luther und der Geist der Renaissance," *Zeitschrift für systematische Theologie*, XVIII (1941), 3-27. For a solid discussion of Luther's appreciation of language, see Peter Meinhold, *Luthers Sprachphilosophie* (Berlin, 1958), esp. chap. 4 ("Die Abgrenzung vom Sprachverständnis des Humanismus"), pp. 28-38, showing how Luther defended the classical and biblical languages against the spiritualists or enthusiasts who believed that knowing the Scriptures in the vernacular sufficed and against the anti-humanists of the old church who held the Church to be the proper interpreter of the Scriptures. Luther held the revival of the languages to be further evidence of God working in history.

[32] *WA Br*, III, 50, 11. 25-39, No. 596: Luther to Eobanus Hessus, [Wittenberg], 29 March 1523. Peter Sandstrom, *Luther's Sense of Himself as an Interpreter*

Luther's involvement with rhetoric and other humanist modalities was far more extensive and intimate than has generally been recognized. For him also higher culture was a "sphere of faith's works" so that he could gladly and enthusiastically recommend humanist rhetoric and poetry. Luther's contemporaries and his admirers for the next three centuries were fond of calling Luther the "German Cicero." While the power of the Word was conveyed by the Holy Spirit, the power of speech is to be properly cultivated by every *vir doctus*, for man is, as the humanists held, characteristically a *Zoon logikon echon*, a living being having the power of speech. The way in which rhetorical principles affected Luther's hermeneutics in the combination of a christological and tropological interpretation requires further exploration.[33] For Luther, who repeatedly in his *Table Talks* cited the formula *Dialectica docet, Rhetorica movet*, saw the enthroning of rhetoric once again as the *regina artium* as a necessary prerequisite for a purified and affective theology. Luther's application

---

of the Word to the World (Amherst, Mass., 1961), is a clever little *Jugendarbeit* drawing some connections between rhetoric and the *verbum evangelii vocale* or the church as a "mouthhouse." See Reinhard Breymayer, "Bibliographie zum Thema 'Luther und die Rhetorik'," *Linguistica Biblica*, 21/22 (February, 1973), 39-44.

[33] Gerhard Ebeling, *Einführung in theologische Sprachlehre* (Tübingen, 1971), newly translated by R. A. Wilson as *Introduction to a Theological Theory of Language* (London, 1973), is not based upon a thorough awareness of the extensive scholarship in the secular rhetorical tradition, particularly with reference to the immediately relevant humanist culture. See the lengthy critique by Klaus Dockhorn, "Luthers Glaubensbegriff und die Rhetorik. Zu Gerhard Ebelings Buch *Einführung in theologische Sprachlehre*," *Linguistica Biblica*, 21/22 (February, 1973), 19-39. For a critique of Ebeling's "hermeneutical theology" as being "dated" along with Heidegger's obsolete philosophy, see Rüdiger Lorenz, *Die unvollendete Befreiung vom Nominalismus. Martin Luther und die Grenzen hermeneutischer Theologie bei Gerhard Ebeling* (Gütersloh, 1973). See also Dockhorn's article, "Rhetorik und germanistische Literaturwissenschaft in Deutschland," *Jahrbuch für internationale Germanistik*, III, no. 1, 168-185, esp. 178-179. Dockhorn traces the significance of rhetoric through the centuries down, in fact, to Nietzsche and Sartre. See Klaus Dockhorn, *Macht und Wirkung der Rhetorik*, Respublica Literaria. Studienreihe zur europäischen Bildungstradition vom Humanismus bis zur Romantik 2, eds. Joachim Dyck and Günther List (Bad Homburg, 1968). See the brilliant essay by Wesley Trimpi, "The Quality of Fiction: The Rhetorical Transmission of Literary Theory," *Traditio*, XXX (1974), 1-118, for the contribution of rhetoric to the continuity of literary theory. Wilfried Barner, *Barockrhetorik. Untersuchungen zu ihren geschichtlichen Grundlagen* (Tübingen, 1970), demonstrates the great importance of rhetoric for Baroque literature through the 17th century. Ulrich Nembach, *Predigt des Evangeliums. Luther als Prediger, Pädagoge und Rhetor* (Neukirchen-Vluyn, 1972), has a fascinating chapter on the sermon as oration in which (pp. 117-174) he analyzes Luther's sermons in relation to Quintilian's rhetorical principles, finding that Luther adopted Quintilian's *Volksberatungsrede* form and technique as the most appropriate and effective homiletical method.

of rhetorical principles has been demonstrated with respect to both
his treatise *On the Liberty of the Christian Man* and his *Sermon on the
Necessity of Sending Children to School.*[34] It is becoming increasingly
obvious that the great contrast between the reformer Luther and
the humanist Melanchthon, a cliché so dear to many writers, is on
this operative level of worldly culture and at the plane of maximum
contact with theology not really tenable.[35] It is to be hoped that the
major work on Luther and rhetoric promised by the distinguished
literary scholar Klaus Dockhorn will materialize and that a theologian
learned in Luther's exegetical and hermeneutical principles will
produce a complementary work taking this perspective fully into
account. What is said here of rhetoric could easily be repeated with
respect to moral philosophy, poetry, history, or virtually any other
humanistic discipline.

Thirdly, the final word on Luther's *Auseinandersetzung* with humanism embodied in Erasmus on the central theological issues has not
yet been spoken despite the volume of literature devoted to it.[36]
Actually, Luther's very radical existential theology clarified the
relation of theology to philosophy in a way not possible for the
sapiential theology of the Thomists or the prudential moralistic
theology of humanistic theologians, for it delineated the spheres
of the divine and human so clearly that each could rest more firmly
on its own base without confusing overlapping or hazardous over-
hangs.

The history of literature, poetry and prose, from the fifteenth to

---

[34] Birgit Stolt, *Studien zu Luthers Freiheitstraktat mit besonderer Rücksicht auf das
Verhältnis der lateinischen und der deutschen Fassung zu einander und die Stilmittel der
Rhetorik*, Stockholmer Germanistische Forschungen, 6 (Stockholm, 1969). Birgit
Stolt, "Docere, delectare und movere bei Luther. Analysiert anhand der 'Predigt,
daß man Kinder zur Schulen halten solle'," *Deutsche Vierteljahrschrift*, XLIV
(1970), 433-474.

[35] Thus Wilhelm Maurer, *Der junge Melanchthon zwischen Humanismus und Reformation*, I: *Der Humanist*; II: *Der Theologe* (Göttingen, 1967, 1969). So also Adolf
Sperl, *Melanchthon zwischen Humanismus und Reformation* (Munich, 1959). For a
bibliographical survey, Peter Fraenkel and Martin Greschat, *Zwanzig Jahre
Melanchthonstudium. Sechs Literaturberichte (1945-1965)* (Geneva, 1967), 72-77.

[36] See Friedrich Schenke, "Luther und der Humanismus," *Luther. Zeitschrift
der Luther-Gesellschaft*, XXXIII/2 (1962), 77-85, reexamines the theological issues
involved in the Luther-Erasmus exchange and rebuts the absurd assertion of
Friedrich Heer, who is all too frequently totally unreliable (*Die dritte Kraft*
[Frankfort, 1959]), that Luther's theocentrism undercuts the validity of *humanitas*.
Harry J. McSorley, C.S.P., *Luther Right or Wrong?* (New York and Minneapolis,
1969), discusses the Luther-Erasmus debate over free will, the issue which Luther
called the "hinge" and "jugular."

the seventeenth centuries has been favored with some excellent comprehensive treatments.[37] However, the argument has been made that the canon of approved authors was fixed by the nineteenth-century literary historians under romanticist influence. Other figures deserving to be more fully appreciated should be studied and rescued from neglect: Maternus Steyndorffer, author of the comedy *Ein hubsch Lustig und nutzlich Comödia* (Mainz, 1540); Johann Ditmar, *von der Heimfahrt und Beylager Des ... Herrn Friederich Wilhelms, Hertzogen zu Sachsen, etc.* (Jena, 1583); Philipp Camerarius, son of one Joachim and brother of the other, the author of genial essays the *Operae Horarum Subcisivarum Sive Meditationes Historicae* (1602 ff.), in German the *Historischer Lustgarten*; Ruprecht von Moshaim (1493-1543), Valerius Herberger (1562-1627), Leonhart Thurneysser zum Thurn (1530-1596). The three areas which are most neglected are those of fiction, the essay, and the sermon.[38] The relation of the lyric, music, and hymnody needs further exploration.[39] The continuity of the literary tradition from fifteenth century humanism into the age of the Baroque needs to be reemphasized.[40]

---

[37] Wolfgang Stammler, *Von der Mystik zum Barock 1400-1600* (Stuttgart, 1927), remains a standard work. The newer work edited by August Buck, *Renaissance und Barock*, I, *Neues Handbuch der Literaturwissenschaft*, ed. Klaus von See (Frankfurt am Main, 1972), places German literature into its European setting. Friedrich Gaede, *Humanismus-Barock. Aufklärung. Geschichte der deutschen Literatur vom 16. Jahrhundert* (Bern and Munich, 1971), is strong minded and independent in challenging older authorities (e.g., Ernst Curtius), in considering neo-Latin and the vernacular together, and in distinguishing counter-mainstream literature from the dominant mode. Heinz Otto Burger, *Renaissance, Humanismus, Reformation. Deutsche Literatur im europäischen Kontext* (Bad Homburg, 1969), offers a sprightly survey. The work of Hans Rupprich, *Vom späten Mittelalter bis zum Barock*, cited above is particularly notable for its thoroughness and for its inclusion of Catholic writers and Jesuit authors.

[38] Harold Jantz, *op. cit.*, 420-433.

[39] Hans Joachim Moser, "Renaissancelyrik deutscher Musiker um 1500," *Deutsche Vierteljahrsschrift für Literaturwissenschaft und Geistesgeschichte*, V, (1927), 381-412. This article, which Jantsch, *op. cit.*, 405, calls a "great new beginning," points the way to a reassessment of many lyrics which have long been viewed romantically as folksongs but which in reality are classical in structure, such as Luther's "Jesaia dem Propheten das geschah."

[40] Renata Hildebrandt-Günther, *Antike Rhetorik und deutsche literarische Theorie im 17. Jahrhundert* (Marburg, 1966), stresses the contribution of classical antiquity to literary theory. Richard Alewyn, *Deutsche Barockforschung: Dokumentation einer Epoche* (Cologne, 1965), includes essays which underline the contribution of German humanism to the baroque: Erich Trunz, "Der deutsche Späthumanismus um 1600 als Standeskultur," pp. 147-181, and Wolfgang Kayser, "Der rhetorische Grundzug von Harsdörffers Zeit und die gottesgebundene Haltung," pp. 324-335.

The whole question of the importance of printing for humanism and the Reformation is begging for a thorough and comprehensive study, for, from the first published book, Gutenberg's Constance Missal, and the Bible, printing became a major force with astonishing rapidity and continued to expand its production through the century. Only Italy rivalled Germany in the number of presses and productivity.[41] The German humanists heralded the invention of printing patriotically as a unique contribution of German culture that rivalled Italian achievements.

Enough has been said to suggest that, far from being a closed chapter for historical research, the course of German humanism is wide open to further study. The account which follows must be viewed then as partial in a two-fold sense. For it is a brief statement from one individual's perspective and it is provisional since many aspects of the total picture remain to be more thoroughly explored.[42] Fortunately a solid phalanx of well trained and highly endowed young scholars, German and American for the most part, is prepared to take up the pursuit of knowledge in this fascinating area of research. In the words of Vadianus, "Est enim amor omnium studiorum fomes".

---

[41] A great many very valuable studies have appeared, notably such articles as Maria Grossmann's "Wittenberger Drucke von 1502 bis 1517," Das Antiquariat, XVII (1964), 153(1)-156(4), 220(4)-226(10), and "Wittenberg Printing, Early Sixteenth Century", Sixteenth Century Essays and Studies (St. Louis, Mo., 1970), I, 54-74. Especially notable are Elizabeth L. Eisenstein, "The Advent of Printing and the Problem of the Renaissance," Past and Present, no. 45 (Nov., 1969), 27ff., and "The Advent of Printing and the Protestant Revolt: A New Approach to the Disruption of Western Christendom," in Robert M. Kingdon, ed. Transition and Revolution (Minneapolis, 1974), 235-270.

[42] See the excellent report on the current state of research by Dieter Wuttke, Deutsche Germanistik und Renaissance-Forschung. Ein Vortrag zur Forschungslage, Respublica Literaria. Studienreihe zur europäischen Bildungstradition vom Humanismus bis zur Romantik, eds. Joachim Dyck and Günther List, No. 3 (Bad Homburg, 1968), 1-46. A very useful recent bibliography is Günter Albrecht and Günther Dahlke, eds., Internationale Bibliographie zur Geschichte der Deutschen Literatur von den Anfängen bis zur Gegenwart (Berlin, 1969), Teil I: Von den Anfängen bis 1789. Karl Otto Conrady, "Die Erforschung der neulateinischen Literatur. Probleme und Aufgaben," Euphorion. Zeitschrift für Literaturgeschichte, XLIX (1955), 413-445, regrets the lack of new research works on the total complex of neo-Latin literature, for no one since Georg Ellinger has had the courage to undertake the study of the entire corpus and nexus of ideas. The questions which Ellinger posed in his article "Grundfragen und Aufgaben der neulateinischen Philologie," Germanisch-romanische Monatsschrift, XXI (1933), 1-14, have scarcely been answered.

II. The Early Phases

Antiquity knows of many encounters between the prophet or the philosopher and the king. The story is told that when King Alfonso of Naples once asked Gianozzo Manetti (1396-1459) what comprised the whole duty of man, he replied, "Intellegere et agere," to understand and to act. Johannes Regiomontanus (Koenigsberger), a representative of the natural scientific interest of the northern Renaissance, in the dedication to King Matthias Corvinus of his *Tabulae ac problemata primi mobilis* (ca. 1465) raised the question as to whether one should take the works of the ancients as one's guide or one's own experience. He answered that one should combine them, for experience alone is not adequate and to follow the ancients alone leads to life with the dead. The course of German humanism moved very rapidly away from the early preoccupation with the ancient dead for the sake of antique culture to an active engagement with real problems in the present. Whether the humanists were involved in religious enlightenment, cultural nationalism, ecclesiastical reformation, educational innovation, or literary production, they were not merely antiquarian but action-oriented and people-directed. The movement itself began with a fitful start, followed by a caesura and a second beginning, but then built up continuously and persisted well into the seventeenth century, and some would argue even into the age of the Enlightenment.

Traditionally the birth of the northern Renaissance has been associated with the Prague chancellery of Johann von Neumarkt, the chancellor of Emperor Charles IV (ruled 1346-1378). Johann von Neumarkt (ca. 1310-1380) was an admirer of Petrarch's Latin style and was inspired by the Roman patriotism of Cola di Rienzo. But aside from his own improved style, his contribution consisted of the transmission of two ancient writings ascribed to St. Augustine rather than of works by pagan authors. In that court milieu Johann von Tepl (ca. 1350-1414) (in the older literature he was known as Johann von Saasz after the city where he served as notary and rector of the Latin school for a good number of years) created the *Ackermann aus Böhmen*, the famous dialogue between a peasant whose wife had just died and death. The peasant challenges the right of death to steal away his wife. Death responds coldly and cynically, asserting his power over all that is in and of the world. The peasant derides death as mere negation whose power is limited for it depends upon the prior existence of life. God as judge concludes by commending both for disputing well and declares that the honor goes to the plaintiff and victory to death. In a letter written the evening before St. Bartholemew's Day, 1401, to an old friend Peter von Tepl, Johann described his dialogue as a rhetorical exercise, that is, it was a humanist piece similar to others that Johann von Neumarkt had made native to Bohemia. His concern with style was reminiscent of the work of the Prague court poet Heinrich von Mügeln some decades earlier. Experts have pointed to the probable influence of some pseudo-Seneca dialogues on the piece. The debate continues as to whether the *Ackermann* is medieval as a juridical, controversial dialogue rather than following the style of an antique Platonic dialogue, but it should be possible to agree that while the subject is as somber as a medieval *Jedermann*, in style it shows clear evidence of classical humanist influence.[43]

If the position of Johann von Tepl between the Medieval and Renaissance was ambiguous, the specific humanistic character of two other early fifteenth-century writers, Heinrich Wittenwiler and Oswald von Wolkenstein, is even more debatable. Wittenwiler's *Der Ring*, written before 1418, was basically a medieval work, half didactic and half a verse narrative, describing a world already in decline. A good portion relates a medieval *Schwank*, a form of Middle High German tale similar to the *fabliaux*. Oswald von Wolkenstein, a Tyroler, was a gifted lyric poet. He led an adventurous life, wandering about the world for some thirteen years preparing for knighthood. But Wittenwiler's work was not widely known, and, despite Wolkenstein's love of the world and of adventure, his life-style was more medieval than modern. These individuals can be considered progenitors of Renaissance humanism with even less plausibility than Johann von Tepl or the Prague court.

There is a real question as to whether the Prague beginnings can

---

[43] Heinz Otto Burger, *op. cit.*, 49-53. A good text edition is Johannes von Tepl, *Der Ackermann aus Böhmen*, ed. with a glossary and notes by M. O'C. Walshe (London, 1951). See also the article by Walshe, "Der 'Ackermann aus Böhmen', a Structural Interpretation," *Classica et Medievalia*, XV (1954), 130-145. The older classic scholarly treatment was Konrad Burdach, *Der Dichter des 'Ackermann aus Böhmen' und seine Zeit*, III, 2, *Vom Mittelalter zur Reformation* (Berlin, 1926, 1932). Among the more recent treatments of special value are Gerhard Hahm, *Die Einheit des "Ackermann aus Böhmen." Studien zur Komposition* (Munich, 1963); Renée Brand, *Zur Interpretation des "Ackermann aus Böhmen"* (Basel, 1944); Franz Bäuml, *Rhetorical Devices and Structure in the "Ackermann aus Böhmen"* (Berkeley, 1960); Ernst Schwarz, ed., *Der Ackermann aus Böhmen des Johannes von Tepl und seine Zeit* (Darmstadt, 1968).

with justice be considered the cradle of German humanism because of the virtual lack of direct influence and continuity within the Empire. A link does exist, although an indirect one, for the style of Charles IV's court influenced Emperor Maximilian and the connection with later German humanism may be a genuine, if tenuous, one over the route from Prague through Vienna.

The actual inception of a direct continuous movement is to be found rather in the Italian contacts which were accelerated anew by the church councils of the earlier fifteenth century. The councils of Constance (1414-1418) and Basel (1431-1449) gave the German churchmen an opportunity to see the rhetorically schooled Italians in action. Italian humanists and artists travelled north as ecclesiastical legates, diplomatic emissaries, lecturers on rhetoric and poetry in the universities, secretaries to northern princes and cities, and as business representatives. Poggio and Vergerio travelled in the Empire. Enea Silvio Piccolomini served as secretary at the court of the Habsburgs and wrote a description of Bohemia and of Germany in which he lauded the great cultural progress achieved under the aegis of the Roman church. Some of the stimulation came by way of a reaction to Italian superciliousness. Like Petrarch's letter to Urban V so critical of the French, Vespasiano's contemptuous remarks about those ultramontanes who lacked spirit, or Boccaccio's reference to the English as "thickheads", Sabellicus in his *Decades* ridiculed the Germans for lacking an early history and Antonio Campanus contrasted the Danube and the Tiber. One effect of Italian condescension, in the reaction also of later humanists such as Celtis who left Italy hurriedly in anger, was to stimulate a cultural rivalry which proved to be productive. There was throughout the fifteenth century a lively two-way traffic between Germany and Italy. Following the medieval student-wandering tradition, literally thousands of German students trekked down to Bologna or Padua to study Roman or canon law and sometimes acquired a taste also for classical Latin literature, although rarely for Renaissance art. On their return, they used their classical knowledge in order to ornament their festive orations and to add tone to their letters and diplomatic papers. Jurists and diplomats found classical literature to be a useful accoutrement professionally and led the way in the acquisition of antique Latin culture.

It is a matter of special interest to note the significant role of women in these early phases of humanism as author and patroness.

Countess Elisabeth of Nassau-Saarbrücken may justly be considered the originator of German prose novels. The daughter of Duke Frederick V of Lorraine, she was married in 1412 as a mere girl to Count Philip of Nassau-Saarbrücken. As his widow she governed while her sons were still minors. Between 1430 and 1440 she translated four French verse novels into German prose novels. In the best known of her prose novels, *Hugo Scheppel*, the hero, the illegitimate son of a butcher's daughter, strove to win the French crown. Although the background of the prose novels lay in the world of the nobility, this story differed in its greater naturalness, for its outcome depended upon a series of developments, not upon extraordinary qualities in the "hero" or upon divine intervention. The shift from verse to prose has by a long standing critical convention been viewed as a decline of a medieval form, but it can with equal justice be viewed as a step into Renaissance literature, for Italian authors even earlier and, be it said, more artistically had produced novels of this kind. Noble women of other courts encouraged early humanists in cultivating the new style. Eleanor, wife of Duke Sigismund of the Tyrol (1448-1480) did translations from French and had ties to the humanist-physician Heinrich Steinhöwel. The archduchess Mathilde communicated with Hermann von Sachsenheim, Jakob Pütterich von Reichertshausen, and Niklas von Wyle, pioneers of humanist letters in the fifteenth century.[44] The role of women enlarged during the sixteenth century as patrician families such as the Pirckheimers in Nuremberg educated their daughters.

After the primary contacts between German and Italian humanists in the first half of the fifteenth century, enthusiasm for the classics and for Italian humanist learning continued to mount. Italians continued to travel in the Empire, such as the Florentine Publicius Rufus from 1466 to 1467, who came to Erfurt, Leipzig, Cracow, Basel and other cities. Ecclesiastical rulers such as the Bishop of Augsburg, Peter von Schaumburg, and secular princes such as the

---

[44] Willi Flemming, *op. cit.*, 21. Since we shall not be returning to the specific theme of women's contributions, attention may be drawn to the book by Roland Bainton, *Women of the Reformation in Germany and Italy* (Minneapolis, 1971), and to his brief introduction to three papers, "The Role of Women in the Reformation," *Archive for Reformation History*, LXIII (1972), 141ff. On Eleanor, the sixth child of King James I of Scotland, who was the wife of Duke Sigmund of the Tyrol, see Morimichi Watanabe, "Humanism in the Tyrol: Aeneas Sylvius, Duke Sigmund, Gregor Heimburg," *The Journal of Medieval and Renaissance Studies*, IV (1974), 177-202, here at 186-188.

Count Palatine Frederick the Victorious and Margrave John the Alchemist in Franconia patronized humanist learning. A new generation of pioneers busied themselves like bees gathering Italian and classical lore, editing and translating, representing a stage of the primary accumulation of cultural material. Among a considerable number deserving of special notice are Niklas von Wyle, Heinrich Steinhöwel, and Albrecht von Eyb. These intermediaries served as cultural transmitters and were indispensable forerunners of the major figures who followed them. They cited the Italian humanists liberally and incorporated whole paragraphs and pages into their writings. Wyle, Eyb, and Peter Luder, for example, used the same passage from Leonardo Bruni in order to describe the content of the liberal arts. Hermann Schedel, the uncle of Hartmann Schedel, author of the Nuremberg chronicle, in his correspondence copied out whole passages from Petrarch, Poggio and Enea Silvio. Filelfo, Guarino, Poggio, Valla, Gasparino di Barzizza, and many others are excerpted and cited in addition to the even more popular Petrarch, Enea Silvio, and Bruni.

Niklas von Wyle (ca. 1410-1478), a schoolmaster in Zurich and from 1447 in Esslingen, a small city near Stuttgart, where he served as city-secretary and later as a diplomat in the princely employ, served the cause of cultural transmission through his pupils and by his translations of classical and Italian authors. He "transferred" Latin into German as his life's work, the first of these *Transzlatzen* being dated 1461. These translations, eighteen in all, done in part on direct commission from his patroness Mathilde, included writings of Petrarch, Poggio, and Aretino, Boccaccio's *Guiscardo and Sigismonda* and Enea Silvio's *Euriolus and Lucretia*. His tenth translation, the letter of Enea Silvio in which he commented on the cultural milieu of Germany, was of special importance for the elevation of the *nobilitas literaria* to the side of the nobility of birth. His aim was to Latinize German and to raise its formal level as a vehicle for literary expression and epistelography. Other translators were active such as Antonius von Pforr, Mathilde's chaplain and a Nuremberger who called himself Arigo and translated a part of the *Decameron*.

The Ulm physician Heinrich Steinhöwel (1412-1482/3) served Count Eberhard in Württemberg, Mathilde's son by her first marriage. He translated Rodericus de Arevato's chronicle of the world, the *Speculum humanae vitae* and some of Boccaccio, notably the *De claris mulieribus*, which he dedicated to Eleanor, wife of Duke Sigismund of the Tyrol. To her he also dedicated a highly successful *Empus*, done between 1474 and 1480, a collection of ancient fables and *facetiae* of Poggio and Petrus Alfonsi.

The role of lawyers in the introduction of humanist culture was significant. The Franconian Albrecht von Eyb (1420-1475) made an even greater contribution with his *Margarita poetica* (finished 1459, published 1472) in which he offered *florileges* drawn from the works of classical orators and poets.[45] He had studied law at Pavia, Bologna, and Padua. During the course of his legal studies he was attracted to Roman culture and to humanistic letters. Gregor Heimburg (ca. 1400-1472), for example, was born in the imperial city of Schweinfurt on the Main, attended the University of Padua, served as the representative of the elector of Mainz at the Council of Basel, and though he disclaimed literary merit of his own, he frequently cited Cicero, Juvenal, Terence and even Plato in Latin. Sigismund Gossembrot was similar to Heimburg in his classical interests. But Albrecht von Eyb was more productive in literature. His work was pragmatic and didactic, aimed at improving life, and as a schoolmaster of the people he at times substituted German names and popular phrases for foreign or difficult expressions. To his "Mirror of Morals" he added translations of three Latin comedies, Plautus's *Manaechmi* and *Bacchides* and Ugolino's *Philogenia*.[46] Around 1450 he did a book on marriage on the pattern of Franciscus Barbarus's *De re uxoria* (1415), using several Italian sources and including translations once again. He was less interested in Latinizing German than in transmitting the cultural and moral content of the classical and Italian humanistic writing to the people.[47] In that respect he pointed toward the didactic and pedagogical emphasis of later German humanism.

In assessing the early phases of German humanism it is necessary to come to terms with a giant figure of the century, Nicolaus Cryffs,

---

[45] The basic work is still Max Herrmann, *Albrecht von Eyb und die Frühzeit des deutschen Humanismus* (Berlin, 1893). Herrmann also edited the *Deutsche Schriften des Albrecht von Eyb* (Berlin, 1890). See also Joseph Hiller, *Albrecht von Eyb, a Medieval Moralist* (Washington, D. C., 1939). On the problematics of early humanism see Otto Herding, "Probleme des frühen Humanismus in Deutschland," *Archiv für Kulturgeschichte*, XXXVIII (1956), 344-389.

[46] See Karl Conrady, "Zu den deutschen Plautusübertragungen. Ein Überblick von Albrecht von Eyb bis zu J. M. R. Lenz," *Euphorion*, XLVIII (1954), 373-396; Max Herrmann, *Albrecht von Eyb*, 161-173, 356-397.

[47] *Ibid.*, 285-355, including a detailed analysis of his sources.

better known as Cardinal Nicholas Cusanus (1401-1464). The philosopher Leibniz considered Cusanus and Valla to be the two most brilliant men of the Quattrocento. Born in Cues on the Moselle, he studied at Deventer, then went to Padua where he studied law, Greek, Hebrew, mathematics, and astronomy. He lost the only legal contest he ever handled to Gregor Heimburg and is said as a consequence to have moved from the law to theology. He served as a representative of the Archbishop of Trier at the Council of Basel, as a convinced conciliarist, but he became disillusioned with the constant bickerings of the conciliarists and in 1437 he swung over to the papal side. He became a cardinal in 1448, bishop of Brixen in 1450, and retired to Rome in 1460. He was a true Renaissance man in his broad intellectual interests in philosophy, nature, and the classics, and he even discovered several classical manuscripts. Cusanus became a cultural hero, a symbol of philosophical achievement, influential in Italy as well as in Germany for his "Platonism" and *via negativa* speculation. But his place is rather on the metaphysical side of Renaissance thought and he does not belong to the mainstream of German humanism.[48]

The second half of the fifteenth century saw the founding of a whole new wave of universities by territorial princes and city councils: Freiburg im Breisgau (1457); Basel (1459), very early renowned for the study of Roman law; Ingolstadt (1472); Trier (1473); Mainz (1476); and Tübingen (1477). Then in 1502 Elector Frederick the Wise founded the University of Wittenberg. The universities old and new served as resting places for the wandering humanists who continued the medieval *Studentenwanderung* with a *Professorenwanderung*. Peter Luder, Samuel Karoch, and other Germans followed a similar pattern of wandering from university to university serving as guest lecturers in poetry and rhetoric. Luder (ca. 1415-1474) was born in Kislau in Franconia, studied in Italy, lectured subsequently in Heidelberg, Erfurt, Leipzig and elsewhere before entering the diplomatic

---

[48] The key book on Cusanus remains Ernst Cassirer, *Individuum und Kosmos in der Philosophie der Renaissance* (Leipzig, 1927). A. Meister, "Die humanistischen Anfänge des Nikolaus von Cues," *Annalen des historischen Vereins für den Niederrhein*, LXIII (1896), 1-26, on his early contacts with northern humanism. More recent is K. M. Volkmann-Schluck, *Nicolaus Cusanus* (Frankfurt, 1952). A fairly good summary is Henry Bett, *Nicholas of Cusa (1401-1464)* (London, 1932). The attempt to link Cusanus with Biblical humanism in an essential way is not persuasive, Herbert Werner Rüssel, *Gestalt eines christlichen Humanismus* (Amsterdam, 1940), 125ff.

service of Sigismund of Austria. Count Palatine Frederick I encour aged the new learning at Heidelberg. In 1456 at Heidelberg Luder, a hard-drinking, aggressive personality, announced that he would "deliver a public lecture on the *studia humanitatis*, that is, the books of the poets, orators, and historians." From 1456 to 1460 he played a very important role in advancing humanist learning at Heidelberg. There is a direct line from these early wandering humanists to Conrad Celtis and humanists of the high tide of humanism at the end of the century. One of Luder's most gifted and important students, Stephan Hoest, succeeded him in Heidelberg where he maintained that both scholastic philosophy and the *studia humanitatis* are necessary for the study of theology.[49]

During the second half of the fifteenth century printing presses were established in the commercial cities first of all, but then in university towns. The confluence of humanists and printers in the university environment was a fortuitous circumstance for the spread of German humanism, as we shall observe later.

Besides loose-living poets like Luder there were schoolteacher humanists such as Johannes Murmellius and Rudolf von Langen, scholastics such as Conrad Summenhart and Paul Scriptoris, and moralists such as Heinrich Bebel. The dominant characteristic of humanism during the last two or three decades of the fifteenth century was its practical, didactic, and moralistic nature. A pedagogical purpose directed toward an ethical end led the humanists to draw upon antique moral philosophy as well as upon religious sources. The cultivation of Ciceronian Latin in the city schools, now more under governmental than under monastic or ecclesiastical control, promised a generation of youths better schooled for humanist studies.

No doubt the most influential author of those decades was Sebastian Brant, whose great satire *The Ship of Fools* (1494) had an international impact, for it was translated into Latin by his pupil, the bumptious Jakob Locher, and from the Latin into various European languages. Brant (1458-1521) worked as a lawyer, from 1489 on as a professor

---

[49] On Luder, see Wilhelm Wattenbach, *Peter Luder, der erste humanistische Lehrer in Heidelberg* (Erfurt, 1869), Sonderdruck aus *Zeitschrift für die Geschichte des Oberrheins*, XXII (1869), 33-127, and Frank Baron, *The Beginnings of German Humanism: The Life and Work of the Wandering Humanist Peter Luder* (diss., University of California, Berkeley, 1966). On Karoch, see W. Wattenbach, "Samuel Karoch von Lichtenberg, ein Heidelberger Humanist," *Zeitschrift für die Geschichte des Oberrheins*, XXVIII (1876), 38-50. On Hoest, see Frank Baron, *Stephan Hoest. Reden und Briefe* (Munich, 1971).

in Basel, and from 1501 on as a city secretary in Strasbourg. He composed a collection of *varia carmina* (1498), moral, religious, and political in nature. He translated a collection of sayings from Cato, Facetus, Moretus, and others, and published a volume of perorations, highly didactic in nature. In 1502 Brant published an edition of Baptista Mantuanus's *Opus Calamitatum* with a commentary concluding that *astra inclinant, non necessitant*. His *Narrenschiff* was a classic in a rather long tradition of "ship of fools" literature, in clever verses needling the foibles and follies of all mankind. It has been a commonplace since the romantics to view the *Ship of Fools* as a medieval folkish work, but it was intended as a humanistic work and has a classical rhetorical structure, a blend of the new with the traditional. It was the first independent work of poetry in German so that Ulrich von Hutten later could rightly praise Brant as the new founder of German poetry.[50] Johann Geiler von Kaisersberg (1445-1510), the great moralistic pulpiteer, preached a series of sermons on the *Ship of Fools*.[51]

This satirical and pedagogical tradition persisted at Strasbourg with the work of Matthias Ringmann Philesius (1482-1511), who did translations of Caesar (1507), and of Johann Adolf Müling, the city physician, who did satires on the immorality, ignorance, and lack of culture of the clergy. Peter Schott (1460-1490), who belonged to an aristocratic Strasbourg family, wrote two extant works in humanistic Latin, *De mensuris syllaborum epithoma* and the *Lucubraciunculae*, which was edited by Jakob Wimpheling and published in 1498.[52]

---

[50] Edwin H. Zeydel, *Sebastian Brant* (New York, 1967), a biography; trans. and ed., *The Ship of Fools by Sebastian Brant translated into Rhyming Couplets with Introduction and Commentary* (New York, 1944). On the theme of fools and folly see Barbara Könneker, *Wesen und Wandlung der Narrenidee im Zeitalter des Humanismus. Brant. Erasmus. Murner* (Wiesbaden, 1966). Two studies by Ulrich Gaier merit special mention, *Studien zu Sebastian Brants "Narrenschiff"* (Tübingen, 1966), and "Sebastian Brant's *Narrenschiff* and the Humanists," *PMLA*, LXXXIII (1968), 266-270. Friedrich Zarncke's edition, *Sebastian Brants Narrenschiff* (Leipzig, 1854) was reprinted at Darmstadt, 1964. Dieter Wuttke, "Sebastian Brants Verhältnis zu Wunderdeutung und Astrologie," in Werner Busch, *et alii*, *Studien zur deutschen Literatur und Sprache des Mittelalters. Festschrift für Hugo Moser* (Berlin, 1974), 272-286, describes Brant as no Enlightenment figure, but bound by his times in his attitude toward wonders and astrology.

[51] See E. Jane Dempsey Douglass, *Justification in Late Medieval Preaching. A Study of John Geiler of Keisersberg* (Leiden, 1966).

[52] Murray A. and Marian L. Cowie, eds., *The Works of Peter Schott (1460-1490)*, I, University of North Carolina Studies in the Germanic Languages and Literatures, No. 41 (Chapel Hill, 1963).

But the most influential of this group was Jakob Wimpheling ('1450-1528), a humanist priest, a moralist, educator and German patriot. Wimpheling was born in Schlettstadt, the "pearl of Alsace," attended the Latin school of Ludwig Dringenberg, who had studied at Deventer and emphasized ethical-religious training in the manner of the Brethren of the Common Life. He went as a boy of fourteen to the University of Freiburg where he came under the influence of Geiler von Kaisersberg (1445-1510), sharp critic of vanity and worldly splendor. He studied further at Erfurt and Heidelberg, where he had some contact with the humanist circle of Bishop Johannes von Dalberg. He rose to become dean and rector of the university, then for fourteen years he served as cathedral preacher at Speyer, lived then in Strasbourg to be near Geiler, and retired to Schlettstadt for his closing years. Wimpheling's two major contributions as a humanist were as a playwright and as an organizer of a sodality. He was the author of *Stylpho*, a "prodigal son" play, a theme very popular in later sixteenth-century drama, with an unhappy ending. In Strasbourg he organized the *Sodalitas literaria Argentinensis*, a loose association of friends of the classics. He held Baptista Mantuanus to be the best poet of Italian humanism. The classics for him had only the provisional utility of enabling students the better to understand Christian writings. He wrote two educational works on education, the *Isidoneus*, concerned with Latin grammar and literature, and the *Adolescentia*, an omnibus volume containing materials from Petrarch, Vergerio, Baptista Mantuanus and other Italian humanists from classical and Christian authors, from Augustine to Thomas and Gerson, useful for ethical distinction.[53] In his *De Integritate* he attacked the concubinage and poor morals of the priests. Living on a frontier endangered by the French, he played the German patriot by arguing against Thomas Murner in favor of the German character of Alsace. The *Germania* and the *Epitoma rerum Germanicarum*, in which he and his friend Sebastian Murrho described the Rhine and its valley as a German stream, were patriotic and historical pioneering works contributing to the cultural nationalism of German humanism and the Reformation. Peter Schott was the granduncle and Wimpheling the teacher of Jacob Sturm, a leading Protestant councillor in Strasbourg. At Heidelberg Wimphe-

---

[53] The best edition is Otto Herding, *Jakob Wimpfelings Adolescentia* (Munich, 1965).

ling's paths crossed those of Rudolf Agricola the so-called "father of German humanism."

Agricola (1444-1485) stands at the border between the early phases of humanism and the high generation of humanists. If he had lived longer than the forty-one years allotted him, he might well have been the acknowledged leader of German humanism at high tide. He had a direct personal influence on the younger men and his major work on rhetoric was republished often during the sixteenth century and was influential from Italy to England. "It was Rudolf Agricola," Erasmus wrote, "who first brought with him from Italy some gleam of a better literature." [54] Agricola wrote a life of Petrarch to honor the "father and restorer of good arts", and many humanists considered the Dutch humanist the Petrarch of the North. He was educated at St. Martin's school in Groningen, Erfurt, and Louvain, and then spent ten years in Pavia and Ferrara. Returning to the North in 1479 he found that he "froze after the sun." After three years in Groningen he accepted the patronage of Elector Philip of the Palatinate and spent the last three years of his life in Heidelberg in close touch with the circle of Bishop Johannes von Dalberg, whom he accompanied on a trip to Rome to congratulate Innocent VIII on his election to the papacy. Agricola was a reticent author and his greatest impact was perhaps through the people such as Conrad Celtis, whom he inspired. His *De Formando Studio* laid out a humanist educational plan along the lines of Vergerio, Bruni or Vittorino's educational philosophy. His Christmas oration of 1484 and his *Exhortatio ad clerum Wormatiensem* [55] leave no doubt as to his deep and orthodox Christian faith.

His major work was an introductory manual for teachers in the arts course, *De Inventione Dialectica*, in which he taught the function of logic in marshalling arguments, *ars inveniendi*, useful in rhetoric which by effective style produces conviction and action, *ars iudicandi*. [56]

---

[54] "Letter to Joannus Botzhemius," Erasmus, *Opera*, I (Leiden, 1703), front matter.

[55] Lewis W. Spitz and Anna Benjamin, "Rudolph Agricola's *Exhortatio ad clerum Wormatiensem*," *Archive for Reformation History*, LIV (1963), 1-15. Johannes Janssen, *Geschichte des deutschen Volkes seit dem Ausgang des Mittelalters*, I, 1. abt., 4, A (Freiburg i. B., 1876), 51, already pointed to Agricola's religiosity, for he was even at one time pointed toward the priesthood, but it is absurd to suggest that anyone would necessarily be dependent upon Janssen for such an obvious fact about Agricola, least of all anyone familiar with the fervor of the *Exhortatio*.

[56] The best assessment of Agricola's place-logic is that of Walter Ong, S. J., *Ramus, Method, and the Decay of Dialogue* (Cambridge, Mass., 1958), 92-130. Neal

He presents two dozen topics, grounds for proofs, indicates how they are to be used, and demonstrates how rhetoric helps to achieve conviction in the hearer. The work is highly eclectic and draws materials from the entire Greek and Latin rhetorical tradition. It was translated into Italian, summarized in a handbook, republished often, and was particularly influential in England.

In the historical introduction to his *Ausführliche Redekunst*, Johann Christoph Gottsched described Friedrich Riedrer's *Spiegel der waren rhetoric, Usz Marco Tulio Cicerone, und andern getütsche* (Strassburg, 1509) as the first German rhetoric, first published in 1493, combining the medieval *ars dictaminis* teaching with ancient rhetoric. These books of rhetoric and epistelography remained popular throughout the sixteenth century and into the age of the baroque, when Johann Meyfart's *Teutsche Rhetorica* (1634) proved to be very popular. But Agricola's *De Inventione* towered above them all not only because it was in Latin, but because Philipp Melanchthon drew his own highly influential rhetorical teaching from the work and inspiration of Agricola, and he became the *praeceptor Germaniae*. Agricola marked the end of the preparatory stages and the advent of the mature generation of German humanism.

III. The High Generation

"I congratulate myself often on living in this glorious century in which so many remarkable men have arisen in Germany!" exclaimed Nikolaus Gerbellius in 1507.[57] The two decades following the turn of the century, 1500-1520, marked a special period in the course of German humanism. The preliminary steps had been taken in many fields of learning. Humanism was ensconced in episcopal and princely courts, in cities, and now in the universities as well. The Reformation was not yet underway. The humanists of this generation were devoted to three purposes, the further cultivation of the classics, the development of national culture and German freedom from foreign domination, and religious enlightenment. Nearly all parts of the Empire from Alsace to Silesia were involved in the movement, but there were four particularly vital centers which served as foci and inter-

---

W. Gilbert, *Renaissance Concepts of Method* (New York, 1960), 117 *et passim* places Agricola's rhetoric within the general context of Renaissance discussions of method.

[57] The basic book on Gerbellius remains Wilhelm Horning, *Der Humanist Dr. Nikolaus Gerbel, Förderer lutherischer Reformation in Strassburg (1485-1560)* (Strassburg, 1918).

sections of the humanist cross currents, Heidelberg, Vienna, Nuremberg and Erfurt.

The key figure in the Heidelberg circle was Bishop Johannes von Dalberg (1455-1503). His connections with Agricola, Wimpheling, Conrad Celtis, Johannes Reuchlin and a host of lesser men such as Dietrich von Pleningen (ca. 1420-1520), counselor to the Elector of the Palatinate and later to the Duke of Bavaria, who devoted himself to Seneca, made Dalberg an important force in the promotion of humanism.

The brightest planet to wander across the Heidelberg scene was Conrad Celtis (1459-1508), whom Friedrich von Bezold dubbed the "German arch-humanist." Celtis was the best lyric poet among the German humanists, and was crowned by Emperor Frederick III as the first German poet laureate upon the citadel at Nuremberg, April 18, 1487. His ambition was to be remembered as the German Horace. "Oh sacred and mighty works of the poets, you alone free all things from fate and lift up mortal ashes to the stars! ", he exclaimed.[58] Born in 1459 as the son of a peasant, Celtis ran away to school in Cologne, then moved to Heidelberg, known for its humanist learning, to Rostock, and to Leipzig. In 1487 he made a quick trip to Italy, seeing Venice, Padua, Bologna, Florence, and Rome. Angered at the airs of superiority of the Italians he hurried north to Cracow, Nuremberg, and Ingolstadt, where he taught as a frequently truant professor of rhetoric. At last he accepted the invitation of Emperor Maximilian to the University of Vienna in 1497, and there he founded the College of Poets and Mathematicians. He lies buried beneath the short tower of St. Stephen's Cathedral. To say that Celtis was the best poet among the German humanists is both to pay him tribute and to define the modest achievements of German humanism in poetry. In his *Amores* he celebrated in four books four of his loves symbolizing the four parts of Germany. In his *Odes* he rose occasionally to lofty levels in writing of love, life, and learning. His *Epigrams* were pungent and pointed. He called the Germans to cultural rivalry with the Italians and stirred up their national spirit. In 1500 he published a student edition of Tacitus's *Germania*. His descriptive book *Nuremberg* was to serve as an example for contributors from all parts of Germany to the *Germania Illustrata*, and his *Germania Generalis* was intended to be a preliminary to the

---

[58] *Quattuor Libri Amorum*, II, 9, lines 153f.

large topo-historical work on the Empire. In his *Inaugural Address* at Ingolstadt he called on the youth of Germany to take up the cultural rivalry with the Italians. Celtis organized Rhenish and Danubian sodalities of friends of humanism and encouraged the organization of many local sodalities to sponsor humanist writings and to carry out with local topo-historical descriptions the complete *Germania Illustrata*, modelled after Flavio Biondo's *Italia Illustrata*. Celtis's role as promoter of humanist culture was perhaps his greatest contribution.[59]

It was Maximilian I who invited Celtis to Vienna, the emperor who was the patron and darling of the humanists. Maximilian is habitually referred to in the literature as "der letzte Ritter," as though he were the last in a long line of important and frivolous rulers. Perhaps Johan Huizinga's picture of the decaying Burgundian court has been transferred, via the marriage with Mary, to the Habsburg court. But his talent for self-projection, his flair for the dramatic, his interest in art and letters—even to the point of commissioning Dürer to do the "Arch of Triumph" and of becoming personally involved in the *Heldenbuch*, the poetic allegory *Theuerdank* and the *Weiskunig*, which related his own daring deeds—his love for lavish display, and his respect for men of learning and support of the university, all suggest that he should really be considered the first in a long line of Renaissance rulers in the North whose lifestyle resembled that of the Italian princes, who played their role on a smaller stage. Maximilian made Vienna one of the lively centers of Renaissance culture in the early sixteenth century.[60]

[59] For Celtis, see Lewis W. Spitz, *Conrad Celtis the German Arch-Humanist* (Cambridge, Mass., 1957). The most exciting development in Celtis studies is the preparation by Dieter Wuttke, Klaus Arnold and others of a new scholarly edition of his works, superseding the various editions in the *Bibliotheca Scriptorum Medii Recentisque Aevorum*, ed. years ago by Ladislaus Juhász. Wuttke has found the manuscript prepared for use by the printer of Celtis's five books of epigrams; Arnold is working on a new edition of the *Norimberga*. See Dieter Wuttke, "Unbekannte Celtis-Epigramme zum Lobe Dürers," *Zeitschrift für Kunstgeschichte*, XXX (1967), 321-325; "Zur griechischen Grammatik des Konrad Celtis," *Silvae. Festschrift für Ernst Zinn zum 60. Geburtstag* (Tübingen, 1970), 289-303. Recent articles include Kurt Adel, "Konrad Celtis und Wien," *Österreich in Geschichte und Literatur*, X (1966), 237-244; Joseph Arno von Bradish, *Von Walther von der Vogelweide bis Anton Wildgans. Aufsätze und Vorträge aus fünf Jahrzehnten* (Vienna, 1965), 33-48: "Der 'Erzhumanist' Celtes und das Wiener 'Dichter-Kollegium' "; 49-62: "Dichterkrönungen im Wien des Humanismus."

[60] The first volume of a projected four-volume biography of Maximilian I has appeared. Hermann Wiesflecker, *Kaiser Maximilian I. Das Reich Österreich und Europa an der Wende zur Neuzeit*, I: *Jugend, burgundisches Erbe und Römisches Königtum*

Having followed Celtis down the Danube to Maximilian's Vienna we must return now to the upper Rhineland to take up the story there once again. The most intriguing friend of Celtis in that area was the learned and mysterious friend, Johannes Trithemius (1462-1516), Benedictine Abbot of Sponheim from 1506 on at Würzburg. A contemporary admirer, Arnold Wion, hailed him as the *orbis miraculum ac totius arca sapientiae*, though posterity has remembered him more for his association with the mysterious Dr. Faustus, who visited Sponheim, for his pious frauds, and for his friends in the Rhenish sodality. He was a monastic figure, a theological writer, a bibliophile, a historian, a hagiographer, the first theoretician of cryptography, and diligent epistelographer. But he also wrote in a monotonous style, was a dilettante though erudite, was fascinated with witchcraft, black magic, and demonology, and readily fabricated sources for the early history of the Benedictines and carried the Habsburg genealogy back to the Trojans. He wrote of himself in a fragmentary autobiography, *Nepiachus*, "quicquid in mundo scibile est, scire semper cupiebam ... Sed non erat in mea facultate satisfacere, ut voluissem, desiderio." Trithemius collected a great library of over two thousand volumes and a hundred Greek books. His *De scriptoribus ecclesiasticis* presented a bibliography of 963 authors. In his *Catalogus illustrium vivorum Germaniae*, written on Wimpheling's urging, he made his contribution to cultural nationalism. Even his fabrications, Hunibald and the Meginfrid, were related to this patriotic impulse.[61]

---

bis zur Alleinherrschaft, 1450-1493 (Munich, 1971), emphasizing the political, economic, and social forces within which Maximilian developed. On the Renaissance in Vienna, see Otto Rommel, ed., *Wiener Renaissance* (Vienna and Zurich, 1947); Conradin Bonorand, "Die Bedeutung der Universität Wien für Humanismus und Reformation, insbesondere der Ostschweiz," *Zwingliana*, XII (1965), 162-180; Peter von Baldass, *et al.*, *Renaissance in Österreich* (Vienna, 1966). Harold Jantz, *op. cit.*, 411-412, argues that Maximilian was the first of a new Renaissance order represented in Lodovico Ariosto's *Orlando Furioso*, which made use of the *Heldenbuch*, in Torquato Tasso's *Gerusalemme Liberata* (1581), Spenser's *Faerie Queene* (1590-96), and the like.

[61] Klaus Arnold, *Johannes Trithemius*, cited in note 25 above, is detailed, thorough, sound, and vastly superior to older biographies such as Oliver Legipont's *Vita* (1754) or Isidor Silbernagl's *Johannes Trithemius* (1868, 1885). It is reviewed by Ulrich Bubenheimer, *Zeitschrift der Savigny-Stiftung für Rechtsgeschichte, Germanistische Abteilung*, LXXXIX (1972), 455-459. Bubenheimer has contributed an interesting bit of new information on Trithemius's use of medieval sources, "Der Aufenthalt Burchards von Worms im Kloster Lobbes als Erfindung des Johannes Trithemius," in the same journal, vol. LXXXIX (1972), 320-337.

Humanist historical writings developed gradually during the fif teenth century out of roots in the medieval chronicles. The work of Felix Fabri (ca. 1441-1502) was still very much a part of ecclesiastical culture. Sigismund Meisterlin did an Augsburg chronicle (1456) and some thirty years later a Nuremberg chronicle. He showed historical critical sense, rejecting, for example, the myth of the Trojan origins of the Swabians. Lorenz Blumenau, who died in 1484, as the historian of the Teutonic Knights was influenced by Italian humanism, as was Matthias von Kemnat, the historian of Frederick the Victorious. But the most notable German historical production of the fifteenth century was the rightly renowned *Welt-chronik* (1493), which was published in Latin and German by Hart-mann Schedel, who was influenced by his uncle Hermann and his teacher Peter Luder in the direction of humanism. It became the most famous of the topographical historical works at which the Germans excelled.[62] The Renaissance myths of origins so prevalent in their works and only partially rejected were largely medieval in origin, but the humanist historians organized them and sought coherence. Later the Reformation historians, Carion, Melanchthon, Sebastian Franck, John Sleidan and others, were to make further critical progress but also to give a new theological dimension to their reading of history.[63]

The histories of the sixteenth century show a marked maturation. Johann Turmair or Aventinus (1477-1534) on the encouragement of Duke William IV wrote *The Annals of Bavaria* (1521).[64] In Nurem-berg the patrician Willibald Pirckheimer (1470-1528), a friend of Celtis and Albrecht Dürer, presided over humanist intellectual life. When his learned father Johann sent Willibald off to study in Italian universities he gave him this advice:

---

[62] Gerald Strauss, *Sixteenth-Century Germany: Its Topography and Topographers* (Madison, Wisc., 1959). On humanist historiography the old classics are still of great value. Paul Joachimsen, *Die humanistische Geschichtsschreibung in Deutschland*, 1: *Die Anfänge. Sigismund Meisterlin* (Bonn, 1895); and his *Geschichtsauffassung und Geschichtsschreibung in Deutschland unter dem Einfluß des Humanismus* (Leipzig and Berlin, 1910).

[63] See the outstanding volume by Frank L. Borchardt, *German Antiquity in Renaissance Myth* (Baltimore, 1971); and his articles, "The Topos of Critical Rejection in the Renaissance," *Modern Language Notes*, LXXXI (1966), 476-488; "Etymology in Tradition and in the Northern Renaissance," *Journal of the History of Ideas*, XXIX (1968), 415-429. For a review of Borchardt's book, see *Speculum*, XLVIII (1973), 733-736.

[64] Gerald Strauss, *Historian in an Age of Crisis: The Life and Work of Johannes Aventinus, 1477-1534* (Cambridge, Mass., 1963).

Audias lectiones in studiis humanitatis.
Item, ubi private leguntur et fit contributio.
Discas carmine facere.

He took the advice and studied both law and the classics in Italy. He could read and write Greek as well as Latin. He composed a history of the Swabian-Swiss war in which he had participated, in the humanist and classical tradition of doing contemporary history.[65]

The collection of historical sources and artifacts became a passion, as it had with Italians such as Cyriaco de' Pizzicolli of Ancona or Giovanni Aurispa. In Augsburg the city secretary Conrad Peutinger (1465-1547), who became a counselor of Maximilian I, was a highly influential legist and humanist. While a law student in Italy he became a devotee of classical learning. He collected art work, ancient coins, and classical manuscripts. Celtis presented to him the famous *Tabula Peutingeriana*, a military map of the Roman Empire.[66] A full discussion of humanist historiography would have to include the names of Albert Krantz, Nauclerus and Irenicus, and others. Historical writing, moving away from the medieval universal or world chronicle, became a vehicle for the expression of German cultural interest, inspired in part by the republication of Tacitus's *Germania*, altered then by the Reformation's reemphasis on the importance of ecclesiastical history.

This generation of mature humanism experienced the impact of Italian Neoplatonism. Just as Italian humanism went through its various literary and civic phases culminating in (or retreating to?) the Platonic revival in the second half of the *quattrocento*, so German humanism moved from a classical literary phase into a cultural nationalist and religious enlightenment phase, which included a

---

[65] Willehad Paul Eckert and Christoph von Imhoff, *Willibald Pirckheimer Dürers Freund im Spiegel seines Lebens, seiner Werke und seiner Umwelt* (Cologne, 1971), 138-172: "Schweizerkrieg." Johann's counsel is to be found in *Willibald Pirckheimers Briefwechsel*, Emil Reicke, ed., I (Munich, 1940), 29. See Hans Rupprich, "Pirckheimers Elegie auf den Tod Dürers," *Anzeiger der Phil.-hist. Klasse der österreichischen Akademie der Wissenschaften* (1956), no. 9, 136-150. The best succinct potrayal of Pirckheimer's intellectual and personal essence is that of Hans Rupprich, "Willibald Pirckheimer. Beiträge zu einer Wesenserfassung," *Schweizer Beiträge zur Allgemeinen Geschichte*, XV (1957), 64-110. See the charming commemorative volume of sources and essays, *Willibald Pirkheimer 1470/1970 Dokumente Studien Perspektiven Anläßlich des 500. Geburtsjahres herausgegeben vom Willibald-Pirkheimer-Kuratorium* (Nuremberg, 1970).

[66] Heinrich Lutz, *Conrad Peutinger. Beiträge zu einer politischen Biographie* (Augsburg, 1958).

substantial Neoplatonic component.[67] Giles of Viterbo, general of the Augustinian order, knew Marsilio Ficino in Florence and very probably saw Martin Luther on his 1510-1511 trip to Rome. He believed that the triumph of Platonic theology marked the return to a golden age. He was familiar with Pico's interpretations of the Cabala and corresponded with Johannes Reuchlin about the Cabala. His opening oration at the Fifth Lateran Council called for reform—men must be changed by religion, not religion by men. In his own person Giles linked together the worlds of Italian and northern humanism, of Renaissance and Reformation.[68] He is representative of many major Italian figures with close contacts with the Germans. The most popular of the Italian humanists among the Germans, judging impressionistically from the frequency of citation, were Valla, Ficino, Pico, and Baptista Mantuanus.

Ficino was respectful of the northerners and maintained personal contacts with various northern men of letters. He welcomed many to Florence, who came to see him or stopped on the way to Rome. In March, 1482, he welcomed a delegation of Duke Eberhard of Württemberg which included Johannes Reuchlin, Gabriel Biel, Ludwig Vergenhans, and Matthias Preninger, a canon lawyer. Ficino corresponded with Reuchlin, Vergenhans, and Preninger. Many young Germans interested in Greek learning came to Ficino for inspiration. Georg Herivart of Augsburg in later years cherished the memory of his visit with him in Florence. At Basel Paulus Niavus, the "German Filelfo", expounded on Ficino's writings. Konrad Pellikan was inspired by Ficino and Pico, whose interest in Hebrew led Pellikan to do the first guide to Hebrew studies in the North, *De modo legendi et intelligendi Hebraeum* (1501), before Reuchlin's *Rudimenta hebraica*. Froben and Auerbach published various works of Ficino. Among the northern humanists with a keen interest in Ficino's philosophy were Nicolaus Gerbel and Nicolaus Ellenbogen, a Benedictine prior who published an anthology from Plato, Peutinger, Celtis, Pirckheimer, Albrecht Dürer, Mutianus Rufus, Beatus Rhenanus, Trithemius, Agrippa of Nettesheim and many other figures of the Reformation generation, notably Zwingli.

---

[67] Lewis W. Spitz, "The *Theologia Platonica* in the Religious Thought of the German Humanists," *Middle Ages—Reformation Volkskunde. Festschrift for John G. Kunstmann* (Chapel Hill, 1959), 118-133.

[68] John W. O'Malley, S. J., *Giles of Viterbo on Church and Reform*, Studies in Medieval and Reformation Thought, V (Leiden, 1968), 5, 8, 139.

Pico's influence among the Germans was almost as powerful as that of Ficino. His theses on the Cabala and his stress on the importance of Hebrew letters were of critical importance for Christian Hebraism throughout the century, especially for Johannes Reuchlin. Moreover, Pico's philosophical goal of doing a grand synthesis of Plato and Aristotle appealed to the harmonizers such as Philipp Melanchthon, who once wrote, "Let us love both Plato and Aristotle." His defence of scholastic philosophy also found a sympathetic response in the North. His nephew Giovanni Francesco Pico spent years of exile in the Empire and became an intimate friend of German humanists and reformers. The knowledge of Hebrew was given added impetus by the Protestant emphasis on the importance of the biblical languages. By the end of the sixteenth century a knowledge of all three languages, Latin, Greek, and Hebrew, the triple linguistic tiara, was a very common achievement in the learned world. The importance of the Cabala, itself heavy with Neoplatonic philosophy, can best be seen in the thought of Johannes Reuchlin.

Johannes Reuchlin (1455-1522) studied at various northern universities. He read Cusanus and learned to know Ficino and Pico, as we have seen, on two trips to Italy. He served as chancellor to the duke of Württemberg for many years and his last years taught at Ingolstadt and Tübingen universities. Reuchlin believed that the most ancient wisdom was to be found in the Hebrew Cabala. Hebrew was more ancient than Greek, Moses centuries earlier than the Greek philosophers. He believed that Moses and the prophets had transmitted divine truths orally through the seventy wise men in a continuous tradition until they were embodied in the Jewish Cabala. "Marsilius produced Plato for Italy. Lefèvre d'Etaples restored Aristotle to France. I shall complete the number and . . . show to the Germans Pythagoras reborn through me!" he exclaimed. He believed the Cabalistic number-mysticism was related to the Pythagorean belief in the mysterious power and quality of numbers. In his works *De Verbo Mirifico* and the *De Arte Cabalistica* he sought to demonstrate that Cabalism and Pythagoreanism harmonized with Christian revelation and that Cabalistic messianism supported the Christian doctrine of the incarnation.[69]

---

[69] For a fuller account, see Spitz, *The Religious Renaissance of the German Humanists*, 61-80: "Pythagoras reborn." For a fine appreciation, see the commemorative volume, *Reden und Ansprachen im Reuchlinjahr 1955* (Pforzheim, 1956); and *Johannes Reuchlin 1455-1522. Festgabe seiner Vaterstadt Pforzheim* (Pforzheim, n.d.).

It is ironic that this Christian apologist who in his later years even stood firmly against the Reformation should have become the target of a ferocious assault by obscurantists. In 1506 a converted Jew named Pfefferkorn wrote *A Mirror for Jews* on the dangers of Hebrew books and argued for their confiscation. The Dominicans of the University of Cologne backed his demand. In 1509 Emperor Maximilian issued a decree ordering the Jews to turn in their books. Reuchlin ventured the opinion that Hebrew books should not be destroyed and thereby attracted to himself the lightning of Pfefferkorn who assaulted him with an outrageous pamphlet *The Hand Mirror*. Reuchlin detested controversy but replied in his own defense with *The Eye Mirror* and published a volume of testimonials in his behalf, *Letters of Famous Men*. The affair smouldered on and finally in 1520 the pope condemned Reuchlin's *The Eye Mirror*. Reuchlin's comment on Luther when the Reformation exploded was "God be praised that now the monks have found someone else who will give them more to do than I." [70]

The Reuchlin controversy galvanized into action Ulrich von Hutten, Crotus Rubeanus, and a phalanx of young humanists ready for the fray. Two strains came together in their polemic in behalf of Reuchlin, the critical and partially sceptical wit of Lucian and the spirit of cultural nationalism. As a knight Hutten belonged to a class that was rapidly losing its social utility and this loss of purpose played a role in Hutten's acerbic psychological set. Born in the fortress of Steckelberg, he was sent at the age of eleven to the monastery at Fulda. But at seventeen he fled, studied at Cologne, Erfurt, and Frankfurt an der Oder, where he took his A.B., then wandered

---

The scholarly world awaits the new eleven-volume edition of Reuchlin's *Sämtliche Werke*, edited by Hermann Greive, *et al.*, to be published by De Gruyter, Berlin, beginning with vol. 5 in 1975.

[70] James Harris Overfield, "Humanism and Scholasticism in Germany, 1450-1520" (diss., Princeton University, 1968), chapter 8, studies it against the background of the classical humanism-scholasticism conflict, arguing that the scholastics were not so actively opposed to humanism as the humanists and reformers alleged. Werner L. Gundersheimer, "Erasmus, Humanism and the Christian Cabala," *Journal of the Warburg and Courtauld Institutes*, XXVI (1963), 38-52, comments on the irony that Erasmus viewed the Cabala, i.e., Jewish anti-scholasticism, as more dangerous to Christendom than Scotism. That is to say, while Erasmus did not deny that cabalism had a well-established claim for scholarly attention, within the *letter* of humanism, he nonetheless felt that it was altogether antithetical to the *spirit* of his approach to learning. Clearly a mere scholastic vs. humanist antithesis is too simple a formula to catch all the counter-currents in the situation.

on to Leipzig, Greifswald, and Rostock. He devoted his life to poetics and polemics, excoriating the exploitation of the Germans by the Roman church, criticizing abuses, and stirring up the young to rival the Italians. The Reuchlin controversy was made to order for his polemical talents and in the *Letters of Obscure Men* he and Crotus Rubeanus published a devastating satire on the "obscurantists" of Cologne, addressing to them fake letters designed to mock their ignorance.[71] In 1517 he published an edition of Valla's *On the Donation of Constantine*, which proved so shocking to Luther. In his last years Hutten threw himself into the Reformation controversy with all the strength remaining. In a letter to Pope Leo X in December, 1520, he concluded with the biblical phrase: "Let us break their chains asunder and cast their yoke from us." He was too ill to play an active role in the Knights' Revolt of 1522 and died in August, 1523; he lies buried on the island of Ufenau where his grave was rediscovered only a few years ago. Both Hutten and Crotus Rubeanus had close ties to Mutianus Rufus, the canon of Gotha, who presided over the Erfurt school of humanists.

Erfurt was the first university in central and northern Germany to introduce humanist studies into its curriculum, and it was at Erfurt that the first books in that region containing Greek type were printed.[72] The university played a pivotal role in the development of humanism in the entire North and Northeast and was of critical importance for the Reformation because of Luther's study at Erfurt and the many close ties to Wittenberg. Hutten's co-author Crotus Rubeanus studied there and served as rector in 1520-1521. He and a university delegation of forty or more people met Luther at the city gates on the way to his ordeal at the Diet of Worms. He declared

---

[71] Thomas W. Best, *The Humanist Ulrich von Hutten. A Reappraisal of His Humor* (Chapel Hill, 1969); and Alga Gewerstock, *Lukian und Hutten. Zur Geschichte des Dialogs im 16. Jahrhundert* (Berlin, 1924, 1967). Walther Brecht explored the problem of authorship, *Die Verfasser der Epistolae Obscurorum Virorum* (Strassburg, 1904). Cf. Robert Herndon Fife, "Ulrich von Hutten as a Literary Problem," *Germanic Review*, XXIII (1948), 18-29. The best biography remains Hajo Holborn, *Ulrich von Hutten and the German Reformation* (New Haven, 1937), which superseded David Friedrich Strauss, *Ulrich von Hutten* (Leipzig, 1914; originally, 1871).

[72] Gustav Bauch, *Die Universität Erfurt im Zeitalter des Frühhumanismus* (Breslau, 1904) corrected the excessive enthusiasm and claims of F. W. Kampschulte's *Die Universität Erfurt in ihren Verhältnissen zu dem Humanismus und der Reformation*, 2 vols. (Trier, 1858). Erich Kleineidam, "Die Universität Erfurt in den Jahren 1501-1505," *Reformata Reformanda. Festgabe für Hubert Jedin*, 2 vols. (Münster, 1965), I, 142-195.

Luther to be the "judge of evil to see whose features is like a divine ⁙⁙⁙⁙⁙⁙⁙⁙." Eobanus Hessus, the young Erfurt poet, who became the leading poet among the evangelicals called out: "Rejoice, exalted Erfurt, crown thyself . . . for behold, he comes who will free you from disgrace."

The literary arbiter and key personality among the Erfurt humanists was the highly intellectual canon at nearby Gotha, Conrad Mutianus Rufus (1471-1526). From 1503 on Mutian was the leader of the humanists in Erfurt. Georg Spalatin was perhaps the first of his disciples, followed by Petreius Aperbacchus and Eobanus Hessus. From 1505-1506 an ever growing number of Erfurt students came to Mutian in Gotha for instruction and comradery, for he was now a canon at St. Mary's. Over the door of his house he had the words *Beata tranquillitas*, an epicurean haven, for as he wrote, "Tranquillitas dat vires ingenio." He was such a perfectionist and so tentative in his speculations that he wrote one book, a manuscript on rhetoric which Melanchthon declined to publish in later years because of its neglect of Greek rhetorical sources. His influence was rather, like that of Agricola, through the impact of his own person on his many pupils. Over six hundred letters survive from the years 1502 to 1525, despite his repeated admonition to Urban, a young Cistercian monk in the monastery of Georgenthal and his confidant, to tear up or burn letters compromising for their radical religious ideas. His influence in terms of caustic wit and acerbic commentary on abuses in the church was very pronounced on Hutten and Crotus Rubeanus, although scholars have long known that he did not himself personally contribute to the *Epistolae obscurorum virorum*.[73]

This remarkable man was born as Konrad Muth (Mutian) in Homberg, Hesse, the son of a prosperous patrician and a mother of noble family, which may have contributed to his aristocratic and elitist attitude toward the masses. As a red-headed boy (Rufus) he studied under Alexander Hegius at Deventer at the same time as Erasmus. At Erfurt he heard Celtis lecture on rhetoric and poetry, shortly after Celtis left Heidelberg in 1486 after the death of Agricola. Mutian spent seven years in Italy, 1495-1502, where he was completely won over by the Neoplatonism of Ficino and the eclectic thought of Pico. He was intrigued by late classical learning including religious mysteries and occult lore, devoting himself to the *studia*

---

[73] Walter Brecht, *Die Verfasser der Epistulae Obscurorum Virorum* (Strassburg, 1904), 4ff.; A. Bömer, ed., *Epistolae obscurorum virorum*, I (Heidelberg, 1924).

humanitatis for enjoyment not for professional advantage; "frui, non uti," as he put it. Though he became *doctor decretorum* in Ferrara, he was to choose a quiet life living on a small prebend as a canon rather than the pressures of the active life or the university. He brought from Italy a genuine enthusiasm for classical antiquity, which he apostrophized as a "virgo nubilis et formosa," a strong sceptical streak, and a bent for religious and philosophical speculation, for he considered himself to be a "priest both of Christ and of philosophy." His *religio docta* was universalistic, for he believed that there was *una religio in varietate rituum*. Like Ficino he compared the life of Christ with that of Apollonius of Tyana, for he had available Philostratus in the Aldine edition of 1504. In his private letters to Urban he denied that Christ was crucified in the flesh and held a "docetist" view of Christ as righteousness, love, and spirit rather than God truly incarnate. In some of his more extreme passages in which he confided arcane truths to Urban he described nature as a goddess in pantheistic phrases reminiscent of Celtis's nature enthusiasm. In August, 1505, he wrote to Urban, "Est unus Deus et una Dea . . . Sed haec cave ennuncies!" It is "our goddess the earth" who is "omnipares mater, augusta regia, diva, sanctissima." The many names for God and divine men, Jupiter, Sol, Apollo, Moses, Christ, Luna, Ceres, Proserpina, Tellus, Maria, are not only *nomina* of the nature-God, but also her *numina*. The sun is the "verus totius mundi animus." He is glad to be alive just as a man, wordly styles and titles aside. These excursions into natural religion (non-revelatory, non-Biblical, not exclusively Christian) were as radical as German humanism became. The ideas were clearly derivative from Florentine currents and their Neoplatonic and late classical antique sources. There is no reason to believe on the basis of his hints of dark secrets and admonitions to discretion that he had access to an arcane philosophy beyond these derivative notions from known sources. Nor did he develop these radical ideas into a systematic or coherent unified philosophy or natural theology. He seemed to be too uncertain or insecure to organize such thoughts into a coherent system, and they remained almost more poetic expressions than a philosophy, though he wished to be a philosopher rather than a poet. As a complex human being he held disparate ideas to be true on different levels. He was psychologically so bound by the received tradition and his clerical calling that he repeatedly took recourse to Christian piety, and did not merely return to Catholic orthodoxy in his old age.

He preferred St. Paul's epistles to the gospels, but his "Platoni" αναγεσις was a far cry from the Paulinism of that Augustinian professor at Wittenberg, who studied at Erfurt after Mutian's departure.[74]

One of the pioneers of humanist learning at Erfurt and at Wittenberg was Nicolaus Marschalk (1470-1525), who studied at Louvain and Heidelberg, and matriculated at Erfurt, where he studied with Mutian, taking an A.B. in 1492 and an M.A. in 1496.[75] He published a comparative study of Greek and Latin, *Orthographia*, a *Grammatica exegetica*, and a *Laus musarum*, printed on his own press. In the winter of 1502 he accepted Elector Frederick's call to the new University of Wittenberg, and there in 1504 he became *utriusque iuris doctor*, teaching in the liberal arts faculty while he studied law. On January 18, 1503, he delivered the commencement address for Wittenberg's inaugural session in which he praised classical studies for the foundation which they provide for the development of sound moral character. Marschalk moved on from Wittenberg, but his humanist influence lasted on. His pupil, Johannes Lang at Erfurt, gave Luther his earliest classical training. At Wittenberg between 1512 and 1517 Luther's interest in Latin, Greek, Hebrew, and the natural sciences as necessary subjects of study for well-educated clergy grew to the point that he led the way in the humanistic reform of the university. In 1510 Otto Beckmann delivered an oration at Wittenberg *In laudem philosophiae ac humaniorum literarum* and became a strong advocate of humanistic studies. It was to this Beckmann that Melanchthon dedicated his own inaugural address in 1518, *De corrigendis adolescentiae studiis*. So closely was the development of humanism at Erfurt and at Wittenberg interwoven.

One giant figure looms above the heads of all the German humanists of this high Renaissance generation, Desiderius Erasmus of Rotterdam, whose brilliant intellect dominated much of the intellectual

---

[74] See the scintillating pages of Heinz Otto Burger, *op. cit.*, 362-366; Willy Andreas, *op. cit.*, 518-520, Aufklärische Religionsphilosophie des Mutianus Rufus; Fritz Halbauer, *Mutianus Rufus und seine geistesgeschichtliche Stellung*, Beiträge zur Kulturgeschichte des Mittelalters und der Renaissance, 38 (1929); F. W. Krapp, *Der Erfurter Mutiankreis und seine Auswirkungen* (diss., Cologne, 1954); Lewis W. Spitz, *The Religious Renaissance of the German Humanists*, 130-154.

[75] Edgar C. Reinke and Gottfried G. Krodel, eds., *Nicolai Marscali Thurii Oratio habita albiori academia in Alemania iam nuperrima ad promotionem primorum baccalauriorum numero quattuor et viginti anno domim mccccciii* (St. Louis, 1967), 3-26 (introduction), 27-55 (text and translation). See also Gustav Bauch, "Wolfgang Schenk und Nikolaus Marschalk," *Zentralblatt für Bibliothekswesen*, XII (1895), 354-409.

life in the Empire from 1500 to 1520 and who lived in Basel and Freiburg for fourteen years. The Netherlands were still nominally part of the Empire, and Erasmus like Agricola and Hegius spoke of *Germania nostra* and spoke of "us" and "our people" with reference to the low Germans in general. He was important for the major humanist figures and reformers alike, be it Wimpheling, Pirckheimer, Reuchlin, Hutten, Mutian, Zwingli, or Melanchthon.[76] For no one, however, did Erasmus play a more important role than for Luther, for thanks to Erasmus he was able to make clear exactly where the line was to be drawn between the *philosophia Christi* and the *theologia crucis et passionis*.

IV. HUMANISM DURING THE REFORMATION ERA

Luther considered the Renaissance revival of learning a happy development preceding the coming of the Reformation just as John the Baptist once heralded the coming of Christ. Humanism made the Reformation possible, for the knowledge of the languages, the critical handling of sources, the attack on abuses, the national feeling, the war on scholasticism, and an army of young humanists who rallied to the evangelical cause were indispensable preconditions for the success of the Reformation. The Reformation in turn contributed to the continuity, the broadening of influence, the increase in classical learning, and the perpetuation of many humanist values into later centuries. A broad chasm did indeed separate evangelical theology from the religious assumptions of the classical world and from Christian humanism in the area of soteriology, in the sin/grace, law/gospel antinomies. But the reformers viewed worldly culture

---

[76] The discussion of Erasmus must be reserved to the section on Dutch humanism, but a few particularly relevant and recent titles may be cited here: J. Beumer, "Erasmus von Rotterdam und sein Verhältnis zu dem deutschen Humanismus mit besonderer Rücksicht auf die Konfessionellen Gegensätze," *Scrinium Erasmianum*, I, ed. J. Coppers (Leiden, 1969), 165-201; E. W. Kohls, "Erasmus und die werdende evangelische Bewegung des 16. Jahrhunderts," *ibid.*, 203-219; Augustin Renaudet, *Erasme et l'Italie* (Geneva, 1954); Gerhard Ritter, *Erasmus und der Deutsche Humanistenkreis am Oberrheim* (Freiburg i. B., 1937); James D. Tracy, "Erasmus Becomes a German," *Renaissance Quarterly*, XXI, (1968), 281-288; James D. Tracy, *Erasmus. The Growth of a Mind* (Geneva, 1972); Roland H. Bainton, *Erasmus of Christendom* (New York, 1969); Brian Gerrish, ed., *Reformers in Profile* (Philadelphia, 1967), 60-85; Richard L. De Molen, *Erasmus of Rotterdam. A Quincentennial Symposium* (New York, 1971); John C. Olin, *et alii*, eds., *Luther, Erasmus and the Reformation. A Catholic-Protestant Reappraisal* (New York, 1969); Georges Chantraine, S. J., *"Mystère" et "Philosophie du Christ" selon Erasme* (Namur and Gembloux, 1971).

also as a "sphere of faith's works" and were for the most part strong advocates of humanist learning, specifically in the universities and in the newly founded secondary schools. They broadened the base of learning by insisting upon a humanist curriculum on the arts level, on compulsory universal education for boys and girls, and upon the calling of the teacher as a lofty divine vocation.

Italian humanism also played a role in Wittenberg indirectly and directly.[77] Elector Frederick the Wise was determined to ornament his "Sparta" not only with new buildings such as the Castle and Castle church in Wittenberg or with the artistic work of Dürer, Cranach, and Vischer, but by building up the university in his capital city and by bringing teachers of the *humaniora*. He preferred peace to war, construction to destruction, learned humanist culture to barbarity. There were two literary sodalities in Wittenberg, the *Sodalitas Polychiana*, so named for Martin Pollich of Mellerstadt who was to became the first rector of the university, and the *Sodalitas Leucopolitana*, named for the town. To these sodalities belonged Matthäus Lupinus, Cuspinian's teacher, Bohuslas von Hassenstein, the Bohemian humanist, and Heinrich von Bünau, who was also a member of the Rhenish Sodality and a friend of Johannes von Dalberg, Trithemius, and Celtis.[78] The University of Wittenberg was the first German university founded without church permission. Emperor Maximilian in the founding letter gave the University the right to teach *scientiae, bonae artes* and *studia liberalia* as well as *theologia*. Mellerstadt came to Wittenberg from Leipzig and as rector in the early years favored humanism, though he later moved more deeply into Thomism. Johannes von Staupitz, the first dean of the theological faculty was not a humanist, but he was an open, reflective person who favored the renewal of the church.[79] Mellerstadt brought

---

[77] Maria Grossmann, "Humanismus in Wittenberg, 1486-1517," *Luther Jahrbuch*, 39 (1972), 11-30. Maria Grossmann, "Wittenberger Drucke von 1502 bis 1517," *Das Antiquariat*, XVII (1964), 153-157; XIX (1966), 220-226. E. G. Schwiebert, *Luther and his Times* (St. Louis, 1950), 268-274 (the pre-Lutheran Faculty), 275-302 (Triumph of Biblical Humanism in the University of Wittenberg). The old history of Walter Friedensburg, *Geschichte der Universität Wittenberg* (Halle, 1917), remains standard. The East German commemorative volume *450 Jahre Martin-Luther—Universität Halle-Wittenberg*, I: *1502-1816* (Halle, 1952), contains useful essays and underlines the initiative and important role of Luther in support of humanistic studies at Wittenberg.

[78] M. Grossmann, "Humanismus in Wittenberg," 17.

[79] David Steinmetz, *Misericordia Dei. The Theology of Johannes von Staupitz in its Late Medieval Setting* (Leiden, 1968), reveals Staupitz in the Augustinian tradition of viewing man as the instrument of God.

Hermann Buschius along from Leipzig, as the first professor of humanistic subjects. He had studied with Hegius at Deventer and with Rudolf Agricola and Rudolf von Langen in Heidelberg and spent several years in Italy. He is best known for his *Vallum humanitatis*, or defence wall for the *studia humanitatis* (1518). Marschalk was especially important for his emphasis on Greek language and literature, a tradition carried on by Trebelius, Andreas Carlstadt, Johannes Lang, who taught Luther, and Melanchthon.

But once again the Italian influence made itself felt, for three of the jurists who were strong advocates of humanism were inspired by Italian humanism. Peter of Ravenna and his son Vicentius were enthusiastic humanists. Johann von Kitzscher had been a member of the humanist circle of Cardinal Ascanio Sforza in Rome and was a friend of Filippo Beroaldo the elder. Christopher Scheurl, who came in 1507, was born in Nuremberg, studied in Heidelberg, and studied law and humanities in Bologna, spending nine years in Italy. He was elected rector three weeks after his arrival and on May 1 published a university catalog, *Rotulus doctorum Vittenberge profitentium*, in the manner of the Italian universities, which listed thirteen members of the arts faculty. In 1508 the *poeta laureatus* was made a member of the arts faculty. After he moved to Nuremberg Scheurl kept in close touch with Wittenberg as a friend of humanism and the Reformation.[80] Another key figure for the success of humanism in Wittenberg was Georg Spalatin, who had studied with Marschalk, Henning Goede, and Jodocus Trutvetter in Erfurt. Spalatin had come to Wittenberg in 1502 with Marschalk, left and returned to Wittenberg again in 1508 as a tutor to Johann Friedrich, the elector's nephew. The humanists clustered about him and he became a key liaison for Luther with the Elector.[81]

Initially the theological faculty at Wittenberg taught the *via antiqua*, Thomism and Scotism, but Elector Frederick brought the nominalist Jodocus Trutvetter from Erfurt in 1507 to broaden the approach and his student, Martin Luther, came soon after, though only for a year. When Luther returned to stay in 1511, humanism was well established in Wittenberg and the way prepared for his Biblical humanism, a return to the sources. The triumph over scholastic

---

[80] Maria Grossmann, "Humanismus in Wittenberg," 19-22; on the great importance of the library which Frederick assembled, pp. 26-28.

[81] See the exemplary biography by Irmgard Hösz, *Georg Spalatin, 1484-1545. Ein Leben in der Zeit des Humanismus und der Reformation.* (Weimar, 1956).

theology came, however, not with the victory of classical letters over scholastic philosophy, but through the return to the Scriptures led by the reforming circle of "Augustinians." Luther not only maintained a positive attitude toward classical culture, but, partially under the influence of Melanchthon, invested what time and energy remained for him during his later years to humanist studies, notably history, for he felt he had been deprived of these good things in his early years. He showed the initiative and played an important role in the major university reform of 1518 and encouraged Melanchthon, the *praeceptor Germaniae*, in his humanist and educational efforts.[82] Luther's confrontation with Erasmus over the theological issue of freedom of the human will to keep the law perfectly and to accept Christ as Savior of its own power did not prevent him from recommending to students Erasmus's humanist writings and did not lead him to discourage Melanchthon's continued correspondence with the prince of humanists. Luther could distinguish much more clearly than most Reformation scholars in our day between a right relationship with God of everlasting importance and the supreme benefits of culture for the very limited time allotted to man in the here and now.

The young Melanchthon, grand-nephew of Reuchlin, was a brilliant young humanist. At Tübingen in 1517 young Melanchthon had laid down a program for humanist studies in an oration *De artibus liberalibus*. Elector Frederick chose Melanchthon for the professorship of Greek in the arts faculty, a position he retained the rest of his life despite Luther's importuning him to take a chair in theology. Luther had wanted little Peter Mosellanus, but the wise elector fortunately prevailed. Melanchthon's inaugural address in 1518, *De corrigendis adolescentiae studiis*, developed the power of rhetoric and the function of dialectic in the service of rhetoric, the value of history and of moral philosophy.[83]

---

[82] Scholarship on the question of Luther's relation to humanism has moved well beyond the flat denial that Luther's early development was totally independent of the influence of humanism, Hans von Schubert, "Reformation und Humanismus," *Luther-Jahrbuch*, VIII (1926), 1-26. Perhaps the very best study is that of Helmar Junghans, "Der Einfluß des Humanismus auf Luthers Entwicklung bis 1518," *Luther-Jahrbuch*, XXXVII (1970), 37-101. See also Lewis W. Spitz, *The Religious Renaissance*, 237-293, and the bibliographical notes, pp. 345-354.

[83] The most convenient collection of Melanchthon's humanist writings is Robert Stupperich, ed., *Melanchthons Werke in Auswahl*, III: *Humanistische Schriften*, ed. Richard Nürnberger (Gütersloh, 1961), 29-42. Selections in English translation from the *De corrigendis* and the *In laudem novae scholae* (1526) are included in

It is true that Melanchthon was drawn by Luther's magnetic personality and powerful message to evangelical theology, distracted from the humanist program of 1518 to the authorship of the *Loci communes rerum theologicorum* of 1521. Now for Melanchthon the law of God shows the sinner his lost condition and is no longer a mere stimulus to virtue. Now philosophy is of no use as a preparation for theology or its handmaiden. Now antiquity is no longer the norm, but the Scriptures alone are the source of divine revelation.[84] His evangelical anthropology now coincides with Luther's view that the will is an *arbitrium servum* in matters of sin and grace. Nevertheless, the very form of the *Loci* is derived from the rhetorical topics and Erasmus heaped elaborate praise upon him for his effort, even though he considered the *Loci* to be competition for his own *Ratio seu methodus*. Melanchthon learned to differentiate the spheres of the human and divine in Luther's way, even though in later years he tended to blur the line and to fuzz up the picture. Many of his humanist writings and orations came after the *Loci* of 1521. In 1557, as a sixty year old professor, he ghost-wrote an oration for a beginner, Bartholomäus Kalkreuter, in praise of Erasmus.

Melanchthon was only the most prominent figure in a multitude of Reformation intellectuals who cultivated the classics and adopted humanistic literary forms.[85] Peter Mosellanus at Leipzig delivered a forceful *Oration Concerning the Knowledge of Various Languages Which Must Be Esteemed*. He proved to be an inspiration for Andreas Althamer, who became the leading reformer of Brandenburg-Anspach.

Lewis W. Spitz, "Humanism and the Reformation," in Robert Kingdon, ed., *Transition and Revolution* (Minneapolis, Minn., 1974), pp. 153-188, 167-175. Cf. Carl S. Meyer, "Melanchthon as Educator and Humanist," *Concordia Theological Monthly*, XXXI (1960), 533-540. On the humanistic and theological development of young Melanchthon, see especially Wilhelm Maurer, *Der junge Melanchthon zwischen Humanismus und Reformation*, I: *Der Humanist*; II: *Der Theologe* (Göttingen, 1969); Adolf Sperl, *Melanchthon zwischen Humanismus und Reformation* (Munich, 1959); Ernst Bizer, *Theologie der Verheißung. Studien zur theologischen Entwicklung des jungen Melanchthon (1519-1524)* (Neukirchen-Vluyn, 1964). A noteworthy thesis showing the mediating role of the humanistic reformer is by Judith Law Williams, "Philipp Melanchthon as an Ecclesiastical Conciliator, 1530-through 1541" (diss., University of North Carolina, 1973).

[84] Ekkehard Mühlenberg, "Humanistisches Bildungsprogramm und reformatorische Lehre beim jungen Melanchthon," *Zeitschrift für Theologie und Kirche*, LXV (1968), 431-444.

[85] For a fuller account which serves, however, merely as an introduction to the continuity of humanism through the Reformation era, see Lewis W. Spitz, "Humanism in the Reformation," A. Molho and J. A. Tedeschi, eds., *Renaissance Studies in Honor of Hans Baron*, 641-662.

Leipzig turned Lutheran after the death of Duke George and a
school of "evangelical humanists" developed, several of whom,
such as J. Lonicerus and Arnold Burenius, had studied with Mosellanus.

One of the greatest polymaths of the century, Joachim Camerarius
(1500-1574) studied at Leipzig, Erfurt, and Wittenberg, taught
history and Greek for several years at the Nuremberg gymnasium,
helped Melanchthon write the Augsburg Confession in 1530, led in
the reorganization of the University of Tübingen in 1535, and that of
Leipzig in 1541, where he spent most of his remaining years with
classical scholarship. He wrote more than one hundred and fifty
works and translated into Latin many Greek authors, such as Homer,
Sophocles, Lucian, and Demosthenes. His interest in history was
especially keen, and he delivered many orations praising classical
learning, for he believed that when combined with evangelical
faith, humanist learning made possible the fullest development of
man's humanity. Joachim's son with the same name carried on the
tradition in Saxony. His other son Philipp was a talented essayist
whose *Operae Horarum Subcisivarum Sive Meditationes Historicae*
(1602 ff.) or *Historischer Lustgarten* was translated into French and
into English as *The Walking Librarie* or *The Living Librarie*. A grand-
son, Ludwig, helped to negotiate the Peace of Westphalia.

Given Luther's emphasis upon the *verbum evangelii vocale* and the
response of the believer's *fides ex auditu*, the instrumental importance
of rhetoric gained a new dimension of significance during the Reformation era, despite the comeback staged by Aristotelian dialectic,
thanks again in part to Melanchthon. From Melanchthon's *De
Rhetorica libri Tres* (1519) and his *Encomion eloquentiae* (1523) on
rhetoric was firmly entrenched in the Protestant cultural tradition.
Camerarius did a very successful *Elementa rhetoricae* (Basel, 1541 and
later editions). Johann Sturm did a *De amissa dicendi ratione libri duo*
(Lyons, 1542) and other rhetorical works.

In history, too, the continuity from the fifteenth century through
to the seventeenth is very remarkable. Peter Luder in his Heidelberg
address had praised rhetoric and poetry but gave first place to history.
From Fabri, Meisterlin, Blumenau, Schedel, Celtis, Wimpheling,
Nauclerus, and Pirckheimer an unbroken succession of authors
adopted the humanist pragmatic approach to history, though the
Reformation historians took even greater pains to perceive the
footsteps of God in history. Luther read more history during his

later years and even prepared a chronology of universal history
for his own use. He wrote prefaces for the historical works' and
editions of Galeatius Capella, Lazarus Spengler, Georg Spalatin,
Robert Barnes and others. Melanchthon wrote his *Chronicon* based
on Carion's and the famous prefaces to Caspar Hedio's and Johannes
Cuspinian's histories. Sebastian Franck's German chronicle (1538)
was "intended to point out the true kernel and main themes of our
history," but not from a highly patriotic or nationalistic point of
view. He merely wished to make up for the previous neglect of
German history and to fill in the picture. Jacob Sturm in Strasbourg
was one of the patrons of Johann Sleidan (1506-1556), who wrote
the *Commentarii de statu religionis et rei publicae Germanorum Carolo
V. Caesare* on which he labored until just before his death and
which enjoyed a tremendous popularity. He saw the German nation
at its height under Charles V with a mission to the world. The learned
Jesuit Heinrich Schütz in 1761 did a critical commentary on all
the works which were dependent on Sleidan or related to his great
history.[86] Flacius Illyricus gave to Protestant historiography a
polemical cast with his *Catalogue of the Witnesses of Truth* (1556) and
the *Magdeburg Centuries* (1559ff.).[87] The historiographical line leads
directly to the "Centurions" of the seventeenth century and the
pragmatic secular and church historians of the eighteenth century,
to Veit Ludwig von Seckendorff and to Johann Lorenz Mosheim.

The focus placed upon the history of the early church and of the
Councils at the Leipzig debate in 1519 underlined the importance
of patristic studies and early church history.[88] Luther did a preface
for Georg Major's *Vitae Patrum* (Wittenberg, 1544). Melanchthon
wrote a "little patrology" in which he advised the reader as to how
Augustine, Ambrose, Origen and other teachers ought to be read.[89]
The *Catalogus Testimoniorum* of the church fathers figured promi-

---

[86] Werner Kögl, *Studien zur Reichsgeschichtsschreibung deutscher Humanisten* (diss.,
Vienna, 1972), 16-18, n. 37. Darrel Ashcraft is currently writing a Stanford
dissertation on Joachim Camerarius's understanding of history. See also Gerald
Strauss, "The Course of German History: The Lutheran Interpretation," A.
Molho and J. A. Tedeschi, eds., *Renaissance Studies in Honor of Hans Baron*, 663-686.
[87] Heinz Scheible, *Die Anfänge der reformatorischen Geschichtsschreibung. Melanchthon, Sleidan, Flacius und die Magdeburger Zenturien* (Gütersloh, 1966), offers the
texts of key prefaces.
[88] Donald J. Ziegler, ed., *Great Debates of the Reformation* (New York ,1969), 3-
34.
[89] *CR*, XX, 703ff.

nently in the confessional and apologetic writings of the time, continuing a tradition of serious scholarly interest in patristic literature begun by Ambrogio Traversari and the Italian humanists.[90] Georg Calixt (1586-1656) at Helmstedt serves as an instructive example of how a humanist view of history combined with an Aristotelian philosophy in a moderate orthodoxy could develop a theologian of an irenic and ecumenical disposition during the seventeenth century.[91]

"Education is a divine gift to be seized upon by all," exclaimed Luther. The reformers followed the humanists as strong advocates of education. Their primary motivation was clearly the religious need of literacy for the reading of the Scriptures. But that was not by any means the sole motivation. The phrase that recurs constantly is for the good of the church and of the commonwealth. In his famous treatise *Of the Upbringing and Education of Youth in Good Manners and Christian Discipline*, Zwingli carried on the humanist pedagogical tradition emphasizing along with religion the importance of virtue and honor. Luther's *Address to the Municipalities, Sermon on Keeping Children in School*, and other educational writings stressed the needs of the child, church, and society. The role of Melanchthon, Bugenhagen and other reformers in encouraging the founding of secondary schools, in reforming the system in Denmark, and in promoting a humanist liberal arts curriculum on the secondary and university levels was of crucial importance to the prospering of humanist learning down to the colleges of liberal arts and the university divisions of humanities and sciences of the present day. Johann Sturm's famous school in Strasbourg served as an inspiration and model for Claude Baduel, reformer of the academy in Nîmes, for Roger Ascham, the English educator, and for many others. In his *Vallum humanitatis* (1518) Hermann Buschius urged the thorough study of the classics in the schools. This emphasis was international and interconfessional, for the Catholic schools, preeminently those of the Jesuits as well as for Protestant schools. The Catholic Conrad

---

[90] The knowledge and use of patristic writings in the 16th century is a subject begging for a major study. A model for such a study is Peter Fraenkel, *Testimonia Patrum. The Function of the Patristic Argument in the Theology of Philip Melanchthon* (Geneva, 1961).

[91] Hermann Schüssler, *Georg Calixt. Theologie und Kirchenpolitik. Eine Studie zur Ökumenizität des Luthertums* (Wiesbaden, 1961), 35-39: "Humanistische Geschichtsbetrachtung."

Heresbach was typical rather than exceptional when at Freiburg he delivered an oration in praise of Greek letters.[92]

In poetry, drama, and prose the continuity with the early and mature phases of humanism is very impressive. The sixteenth century was remarkably rich in its emulation of classical Latin, Greek, and even Hebrew poetry. Salutati had declared poets to be "much more friends and open witnesses of the truth than the philosophers," a point on which the Germans were in tune with the Italians. A look at Karl Goedeke's bibliography of German literature reveals that of the selected 273 neo-Latin poets of the time a very large number of their humanist works were published in Wittenberg during the most active years of the Reformation.[93] This poetry had a strong moral and didactic emphasis, stressed the immortal fame of the poet, revitalized the religious component of life, and expressed a deep longing for a knowledge of the nature of things. But the unabashed eroticism of a Celtis is rarely found, although there is a deep strain of individualism and personalism, despite the adherence to classical forms. Some poets such as Eobanus Hessus (d. 1540) and Euricius Cordus (d. 1538) belonged to the old humanist circle but entered the new poetic guild. Laurentius Corvinus (d. 1527), Ursinus Velius (d. 1539), Georgius Logus (d. 1553), and Joachim Vadianus (d. 1551), the reformer of St. Gallen, carried over into the Reformation their humanist cultural concerns. Like Eobanus and Cordus, Jacobus Micyllus (d. 1558) and Joachim Camerarius (d. 1574) had belonged to Mutian's circle but were younger and clearly belonged to the new generation of Reformation humanist poets. The Wittenberg school of neo-Latin poetry included Georg Sibutus, Thiloninus Philhymnus, Andreas Crappen, Wolfgang Cyclopius, Johannes Eisenmann, and the Italian poet Richard Sbrulius. From the late 1520s on Melanchthon became the leader of a lively group of poets which included his son-in-law Georg Sabinus (d. 1560) and Johannes Stigel (d. 1562). A brash young poet Simon Lemnius (d. 1550), who roused Luther's anger by mocking older professors, produced a sensual *Amores* as

---

[92] The literature on the Reformation and education is enormous, although a truly thorough and well documented history is yet to be written. Of interest for the elementary level are the articles by Gerald Strauss, "Reformation and Pedagogy: Educational Thought and Practice in the Lutheran Reformation," pp. 272-293, and Lewis W. Spitz, "Further Lines of Inquiry for the Study of 'Reformation and Pedagogy'," pp. 294-306, in Charles Trinkaus and Heiko A. Oberman, eds., *The Pursuit of Holiness in Late Medieval and Renaissance Religion* (Leiden, 1974).

[93] Harold Jantz, *op. cit.*, 410.

well as harmless eclogues. Other members were Melchior Voln or Acontius (d. 1569), Johannes Gigos (d. 1581) and Georg Amilius (d. 1569). In Melanchthon's last years yet another generation of young humanists came forward, Friedrich Widebram (d. 1585), and the most talented of the group, Johannes Major (d. 1600). The greatest and most original of Germany's neo-Latin poets was Petrus Lotichius Secundus (1528-1560), whose four books of elegies, two books of carmina, and six eclogues were of the highest order, the elegies revealing a sensitive inner life. These poets experimented with various forms, lyrics, epics, eclogues, landscape descriptions (hodoeporicon), satires, and epigrams. The tie-in with hymns and religious song is worth noting. Two Swabian poets in the second half of the sixteenth century who were exceptional in depicting their personal inner life and experiences were Nathan Chyträus (1543-1598) and Nikodemus Frischlin (1547-1590). At the end of the sixteenth and early seventeenth century a group of poets known as the "Anakreontiker" which included Georg Rollenhagen, Julius Mynsinger the younger, and Jakob Fabricius copied Italian models, doing landscape poetry, shepherd poetry, and allegorical heroides.

At the beginning of neo-Latin poetry in Germany some of the less impressive Italian poets served as the models, Filippo Beroaldo the elder, Tifernas, Fausto Andrelini, half French, Octavius Cleophilus and above all Baptista Mantuanus. But gradually the influence of the better Italian poets made itself felt during the course of the century, Pontano, Poliziano, Sannazaro, Fracastoro, Bembo, and above all Flaminius. Religious fervor and deep personal feeling found expression in poetry that was good, if not the greatest. Many poets of the seventeenth century did both German and neo-Latin poetry, such as Martin Opitz (d. 1639), Johann Heermann, Fleming, Gryphius, Lauremberg and others. The Jesuit Jakob Bidermann carried on the neo-Latin tradition as did other Catholic poets. It is not possible to complete the roster or to develop the subject further, but enough has been said to document the importance of the Italian influence, to show the continuity between the early phases of German humanism and the Reformation century, and to suggest that literary life became a more powerful movement under the aegis of the Reformation than it had been before.[94] The romantics

---

[94] A major work on neo-Latin poetry during the second half of the 16th century into the baroque period needs to be done. Georg Ellinger provided the sketch drawn on extensively here, "Neulateinische Dichtung Deutschlands im

of the nineteenth century may have appreciated more deeply Hans Sachs and the indigenous German tradition so indebted to the *Meistergesang* and the medieval *Volksbuch* tradition, but it is hard to see how German letters of its golden age could have reached the splendor of Weimar without the input of Italian Renaissance classicism and the development of the Baroque.[95]

A similar double track between humanist drama and the folkish *Fastnachtsspiel* with its medieval roots ran parallel through the sixteenth century. The *Fastnachtsspiel* developed further during the fifteenth and sixteenth centuries as a dramatic form, originating from among the burghers as had the *Meistergesang* and running side by side with the religious dramas, where again there is a marked continuity through the Reformation era. It was cultivated by Hans Rosenplüt and Hans Folz in Nuremberg, and flourished especially in the Tyrol and at Lübeck. It developed from a primitive form of individual, unrelated speeches to dialogue.[96] While humanist drama no doubt owed something to the medieval tradition, the critical event was the discovery and widespread popularity of Terence.

---

16. Jahrhundert," Paul Merker and Wolfgang Stammler, eds., *Reallexikon der deutschen Literaturgeschichte*, II (Berlin, 1926/28), 469-494. His premature death prevented him from doing a complete work on the subject begun with his *Geschichte der neulateinischen Literatur Deutschlands im sechzehnten Jahrhundert*, 3 vols. (Berlin and Leipzig, 1929), on Germany and the Netherlands. Dr. C. Reedijk, *The Poems of Desiderius Erasmus* (Leiden, 1956), 19-24, provides a brief survey of German humanist poets. Gerald Gillespie, "Notes on the Evolution of German Renaissance Lyricism," *Modern Language Notes*, LXXXI (1966), 437-462, quite correctly argues (p. 437) that "because our sensitivity for rhythm and diction is historically conditioned, it is only a seeming paradox that, after Luther, 'really' native German verse sounds strange to us. The nature of German poetry was fundamentally altered by the end of the sixteenth century through the influence of Romance and ancient classical models."

[95] See Fritz Strich, "Hans Sachs und die Renaissance," *Festschrift für Hans R. Hahnloser*, E. J. Beer, ed. (Basel, 1961), 361-372; Barbara Könneker, *Hans Sachs* (Stuttgart, 1971); Eugen Geiger, *Der Meistergesang des Hans Sachs* (Bern, 1956); Archer Taylor, *The Literary History of Meistergesang* (New York, 1937).

[96] The important edition of Adelbert von Keller, *Fastnachtsspiele aus dem 15. Jahrhundert*, 4 vols. (Stuttgart, 1853-1858) has been reprinted in three volumes, Darmstadt, 1965. See also Eckehard Catholy, *Das Fastnachtsspiel des späten Mittelalters. Gestalt und Funktion* (Tübingen, 1961); M. J. Rudwin, "The Origin of German Carnival Comedy," *Journal of English and Germanic Philology*, 18 (1919), 402-454; Werner Lenk, *Das Nürnberger Fastnachtsspiel des 15. Jahrhunderts. Ein Beitrag zur Theorie und zur Interpretation des Fastnachtsspiels als Dichtung* (Berlin, 1966). Pamphilus Gengenbach in Basel in the years 1515 and 1516 adapted the *Fastnachtsspiel* to religious and moral ends. See Derek Van Abbé, "Development of Dramatic Form in Pamphilus Gengenbach," *Modern Language Review*, XLV (1950), 46-62.

The first school edition of Terence was published in Strasbourg in 1470. But the widespread use of Terence and of Plautus began in the 1490s. The actual start of humanist drama in Germany began with the presentation of original pedagogical dramatizations, with actual dramatizations of Terence's dramas done later. Credit for the first original drama goes to Wimpheling who wrote his *Stylpho* in 1480. Jakob Locher's *Historia de rege Franciae* was performed in one of the gardens of Freiburg University. He was a pupil of Celtis and of Sebastian Brant and developed his interest in theater during his studies in Italy in the 1490s, where he perhaps saw Verardi's *Historia Baetica* performed. German students at Italian universities did classical comedies. Locher also did the *Judicium Paridis*, in which he introduced the device of having a character on stage describe the approach of another off stage until his arrival. Johannes Reuchlin had his students perform his *Henno* in Dalberg's house on January 31, 1497, for the Heidelberg sodality. Reuchlin had previously written one comedy, the *Sergius*, mocking Holzinger, the chancellor of Duke Eberhard the younger, but Dalberg had advised against its performance. Celtis credited Reuchlin with being the founder of humanist comedy.[97]

In his *Ingolstadt Oration* Celtis praised the value of ancient drama and urged the German youth to initiate those public performances in which they "exhorted the spectators to virtue, piety, moderation, courage, and the patient endurance of all hardships." In Vienna during the winter semester of 1502/1503, Celtis directed the performance of the *Eunuchus* of Terence and the *Aulularia* of Plautus, the same two plays which his Cracow student Laurentius Corvinus, now at St. Elizabeth School in Breslau, had his students perform. The drama was a natural metier for Celtis, for it contained all the elements at which he excelled: display, festivity, and comradery. Some members of the Danubian Sodality presented on March 1,

---

[97] For German humanist drama see Wolfgang F. Michael, *Frühformen der deutschen Bühne* (Berlin, 1963), 67-86; *Das deutsche Drama des Mittelalters* (Berlin, 1971), which discusses in three chapters "Geistliches Drama," "Das weltliche Volksdrama," and "Das Humanistendrama," centering on the years 1440-1520, critically reviewed by Dieter Wuttke in the *Archiv für Reformationsgeschichte, Literaturbericht*, I (1972), 80, no. 293. See also Derek Van Abbé, *Drama in Renaissance Germany and Switzerland* (London and New York, 1961); Hening Brinkmann, "Anfänge des modernen Dramas in Deutschland. Versuch über die Beziehungen zwischen Drama und Bürgertum im 16. Jahrhundert," *Studien zur Geschichte der deutschen Sprache und Literatur*, II (Düsseldorf, 1966), 232-288; Leicester Bradner, "The Latin Drama of the Renaissance (1346-1640)," *Studies in the Renaissance*, IV (1957), 31-70.

1501, Celtis's first drama, the *Ludus Dianae* in Linz at the court of Maximilian and his Italian bride, Bianca Maria Sforza. It was done in the Italian style with a free use of classical forms and figures as in the festival plays, using rhetorical declamation and pantomime. In the *Rhapsodia* performed in Vienna he celebrated a minor victory of Maximilian against some Bohemian mercenaries during the Bavarian War of Succession in 1504.[98]

The reformers saw the great value of drama, combining as it did poetry, rhetoric, moral philosophy and the possibility of presenting Biblical as well as secular history both as popular theater and as school dramas for the youth. In the traditional *Fastnachtsspiel* some playwrights attacked abuses and developed Biblical themes. The Swiss Niklaus Manuel wrote a play on the "Ablaszkrämer" and also on "Vom Papst und seiner Priesterschaft". Burkard Waldi's "Parabell vam vorlorn Szohn" (1527) held up the pharisaism of the monks for criticism in the person of the prodigal son's older, self-righteous brother. In the 1530s in the Lutheran schools and parishes a widespread use of dramas developed with the prodigal son, Abraham, Tobias, Jacob, Susanna and the Elders, Esther and similar themes often repeated.[99] Like the evangelical hymns, these German dramas constituted a genuinely creative contribution of the Reformation. Two Dutchmen, Wilhelm Graphäus and Macropedius, first shaped Biblical materials into the classical model, thus uniting the formal interests of the humanists and the religious interests of the reformers. The school dramas appeared in the 1530s in Saxony and in Switzerland, done by Paul Rebhun, Heinrich Bullinger, Valten Voith, Hans Ackermann, Sixtus Birck and others.[100] Jacob Ruf and Bartholomäus Krüger depicted world history as a battle of God and Satan, like Luther and the pope. Thomas Naogeorgus in his *Pammachius* (1538) presented the history of the "devil's church" from the Donation of Constantine to the present, with Luther pushing it to destruction, but with the fourth act breaking off with the admonition that the

---

[98] Alfred Schütz, *Die Dramen des Konrad Celtis* (diss., Vienna, 1948). Lewis W. Spitz, *Conrad Celtis the German Arch-Humanist*, 72-82, 129-130, the playwright.

[99] Barbara Könneker, "Deutsche Literatur," 164-173. See Richard Froning, ed., *Das Drama der Reformationszeit* (Stuttgart, 1894; reprinted, Darmstadt, 1964). The old classic work is Hugo Holstein, *Die Reformation im Spiegelbilde der dramatischen Literatur* (Halle, 1886). On the Susanna theme, Robert Pilger, "Die Dramatisierungen der Susanna im 16. Jahrhundert," *Zeitschrift für deutsche Philologie*, IX (1880), 129-217.

[100] Hermann Palm, *Paul Rebhuns Dramen* (Stuttgart, 1859) was reprinted in Darmstadt, 1969.

audience must complete the destruction of that church which was not yet complete. Hans Sachs alone did over a hundred comedies and tragedies, but mostly on non-Biblical themes, using about all the material available in his day from the Bible to Homer, the Roman historians, or Boccaccio.[101] In Alsace Jörg Wickram wrote farces, although his prose novels were better known. The tradition persisted in lively form into the second half of the sixteenth century and into the seventeenth with the dramas of Nikodemus Frischlin (1549-1590), Johann Fischart (1546-1590), Georg Rollenhagen (1542-1609), author of the *Battle of Frogs and Mice* (*Froschmeuseler*), and others.[102] Luther had urged the performance of the plays of Terence in the schools and once reprimanded a Silesian schoolmaster for bowdlerizing his plays. As the century wore on the influence of Greek drama became increasingly powerful, especially in Strasbourg, which had the first permanent German theater. The history of sixteenth century drama closes with the work of Jacob Ayrer (1543-1605). This Nuremberg playwright wrote over a hundred tragedies, *Fastnachtsspiele*, and other works. He was very eclectic and drew on the materials of contemporary English plays as well as upon German humanist dramas and such authors as Hans Sachs, Frischlin, Wickram and others. A direct line runs from German humanist and Reformation drama to the great dramatist of the seventeenth century Andreas Gryphius (1616-1664), a Silesian who travelled in Italy as well as in the Netherlands and France, and wrote remarkable tragedies and comedies.[103]

From Saxony and Switzerland the school drama spread to other evangelical areas and was adopted in due course by Catholic authors such as the Swiss Hans Salat (1498-1561) and Wolfgang Schmetzl (ca. 1500-ca. 1560), who were fond of applying the prodigal son theme to Protestantism. Georgius Macropedius (1486-1558) from the Netherlands was also a Catholic. His play *Asotus* (1537) was on the prodigal son theme and his *Hecastus* (1539) was influenced by the morality play style of the *Jedermann*. He was influenced by Plautus. The Jesuits drew upon classical and humanistic sources for their famous school dramas, drawing strength from the medieval tradition

---

[101] Barbara Könneker, "Deutsche Literatur," 165-167. Edmund Goetze, ed., *Sämtliche Fastnachtsspiele*, 7 vols. (Halle, 1880-1887).

[102] Eli Sobel, "Georg Rollenhagen, Sixteenth-Century Playwright, Pedagogue, and Publicist," *PMLA*, LXX (1955), 762-780.

[103] Willi Flemming, *Andreas Gryphius. Eine Monographie* (Stuttgart, 1965), 194ff. on the influence of Italian comedy on Gryphius.

of church plays. Jesuit dramas were very rhetorical and the Jesuits regarded tragedies as representing a higher form of dramatic art than comedies. They contributed in turn to the achievements of the age of the baroque.[104]

It is not possible to develop here even an outline of prose literature during the course of the sixteenth and seventeenth centuries. Two general observations, however, are called for. One is that no artificial distinction should be made between neo-Latin and German prose literature during this period, for the borrowing of themes and techniques was extensive and many of the same authors wrote in both languages. Secondly, not only the positive and constructive, pragmatic and moralistic literature owed much to Renaissance letters, but also the satirical, negative, and critical literature, the grotesque, the "verkehrte Welt," was derived in part from the humanist literature of satire and folly.[105]

The humanist interest in the natural sciences was continued and reinforced during the Reformation era by both Protestants and Catholics. Luther and the Wittenberg reformers showed a lively interest in natural philosophy. The combination of the propagation of the faith with an interest in geography, alchemy, botany, zoology and the practice of medicine, which was often considered a part of pastoral care, was common. The *Schola Wittenbergensis* figures in the histories of medicine as a prominent school of medicine, and Luther and Melanchthon were listed as honorary members. The *uomo universale* of sixteenth-century Lutheranism was *historicus, philosophus,* and *medicus* as well as *theologus.*[106] Melanchthon's son-in-law, Kaspar Peucer (1525-1602), served as the elector's physician as well

---

[104] Of the many studies of Jesuit drama especially to be recommended are W. Flemming, *Geschichte des Jesuitentheaters in den Ländern deutscher Zunge* (Berlin, 1923); J. Müller, *Das Jesuitendrama in den Ländern deutscher Zunge vom Anfang (1555) bis zum Hochbarock (1665),* 2 vols. (Augsburg, 1930); N. Scheid, "Das lateinische Jesuitendrama im deutschen Sprachgebiet," *Lit. wiss. Jahrbuch,* V (1930), 1-96. The most significant Jesuit dramatists were Jakob Gretser (*Udo*), Jakob Pontanus (martyr and Biblical drama), Jakob Bidermann (*Cenodoxus,* 1609), the Vienna court dramatist Nikolaus Avancinus (*Pietas victrix*).

[105] See Friedrich Gaede's brilliant pages, *Humanismus. Barock. Aufklärung,* part 3, 79-114, "Verkehrte Welt, Realistische Literatur im 16. und 17. Jahrhundert."

[106] I owe this observation to Professor Manfred Fleischer of the University of California, Davis, who is currently at work on a study of the interrelationship between humanism and the Reformation in Silesia. See his article, "The Institutionalization of Humanism in Protestant Silesia," *Archiv für Reformationsgeschichte,* LXVI (1975).

as cultivating an interest in mathematics, astronomy, and theology. The achievements of Paracelsus in iatrochemistry were celebrated in the decades which followed and the tradition cultivated. A host of interesting sixteenth-century physicians and scientists await their biographers. Leonhard Rauwolf (b. 1535/40, died 1596), the Augsburg physician, studied at the University of Wittenberg, travelled widely in the Levant, and made remarkable contributions to botany. Many physicians and botanists studied at Wittenberg such as Valerius Cordus (1515-1544), Carolus Clusius, and Caspar Ratzenberg. The full story of the German Reformation and science is yet to be written.[107]

Just as eighteenth-century scholarship has become increasingly conscious of the dark underside of the Enlightenment and the loss of faith in reason especially during the second half of the century, so Renaissance scholarship has become increasingly aware of the "darker vision of the Renaissance," the non-rational, irrational, and suprarational events of the period 1300 to 1650 A.D. Not only was there a popular undercurrent of credulity, belief in the occult powers, resort to astrology, fear of demonic powers and witchcraft, but there was a strong component of these non-rational forces in the minds of many intellectuals and representatives of the social upper classes, humanists, reformers, princes, kings, and popes. This reassessment has been done most systematically for the Italian Renaissance, but some recent studies have pointed to new dimensions and new facets of the northern Renaissance and Reformation.[108] Early German humanism was already associated with the dark Faustian tradition.[109] Agrippa of Nettesheim (1486-1535), a sceptic and fideist, has been associated with a more general movement which was producing "a sense of debility, cultural decline, and decadence." [110] How thin the cultural veneer of humanist enlightenment actually was in the very area where it had prospered relatively

---

[107] Karl H. Dannenfeldt, *Leonhard Rauwolf, Sixteenth-Century Physician, Botanist, and Traveler* (Cambridge, Mass., 1968), 13-14. John Dillenberger, *Protestant Thought and Natural Science* (New York, 1960), explores the reception of Copernicanism over the subsequent century, but a detailed history of science and Protestantism remains to be written, one free of the polemics surrounding the debate about 1640, Puritanism and science, and other Weberian or Marxian hypotheses.

[108] Natalie Zemon Davis, *Society and Culture in Early Modern France* (Stanford, 1975). See also footnote 24.

[109] Dieter Harmening, "Faust und die Renaissance-Magie. Zum ältesten Faustzeugnis. (Johannes Trithemius an Johannes Virdung, 1507)," *Archiv für Kulturgeschichte*, LV (1973), 56-79.

[110] Charles G. Nauert, Jr., *Agrippa and the Crisis of Renaissance Thought*, 333.

early can be seen from the upsurge of witch hunting in Southwestern Germany, where in a period of 120 years there were more than 480 trials and 3,200 people executed for witchcraft. Ironically it was the fact that the upper classes, judges, and other establishment figures, were implicated as victims that led to the abating of the craze, though the opposition especially of evangelical preachers defending the sovereignty of God did help.[111]

A fusion of certain elements of Renaissance culture, Reformation theology, and the mystical and alchemical tradition occurred in the mind of Jacob Böhme (1575-1624), a not-so-simple shoemaker of Görlitz. The quintessence of his theosophy and natural philosophy was contained in his book *Aurora, oder Morgenrothe im Aufgang*, which had an enormous influence in Silesia, other parts of Germany, the Lowlands, and even in France and England down to the nineteenth century. His fellow countryman, Abraham von Franckenberg (1593-1652), helped to spread his ideas. Angelus Silesius (1624-1677), a Breslau physician, drawing inspiration from Johannes Tauler, the fourteenth-century mystic, and from Böhme, turned Catholic and produced two volumes of poetry, the *Heilige Seelen-Lust* (1657) and *Geistreiche Sinn- und Schlussreime* (1657), known in its second edition as *Der cherubinische Wandersmann* (1674).[112]

The pattern of cultural development diverged in art and music from the unity in evidence in German humanism under the presence of the Reformation. The visual arts after Albrecht Dürer clearly suffered.[113] But the tradition of music from Luther, who so warmly admired Ludwig Senfl and the Flemish composers, built up to

---

[111] An epochal book which has proved to be very stimulating for scholars in the field of intellectual and religious history is Keith Thomas, *Religion and the Decline of Magic. Studies in Popular Beliefs in Sixteenth and Seventeenth Century England* (London, 1971). Cf. Midelfort, cited in footnote 24 above.

[112] On Böhme, see Arlene A. Miller (Guinsburg), "The Theologies of Luther and Boehme in the Light of Their *Genesis* Commentaries," *The Harvard Theological Review*, LXIII (1970), 261-303; "Jacob Boehme from Orthodoxy to Enlightenment" (diss., Stanford, 1971), 720 pages. Erich Beyreuther, author of *Der geschichtliche Auftrag des Pietismus in der Gegenwart* (Stuttgart, 1963), has a very impressive knowledge of Böhme's impact upon thought in Pietism.

[113] Carl G. Christensen, "The Reformation and the Decline of German Art," *Central European History*, VI (1973), 207-232; Hans Rupprich, "Dürers Stellung zu den agnoëtischen und kunstfeindlichen Strömungen seiner Zeit," *Bayerische Akademie der Wissenschaften. Philosophisch-Historische Klasse Sitzungsberichte*, Jahrgang 1959, Heft 1, 3-31. A model of how artistic and literary cultural research should be pursued is Dieter Wuttke's article, "Methodisch-Kritisches zu Forschungen über Peter Vischer d. Ä. und seine Söhne," *Archiv für Kulturgeschichte*, XLIX (1967), 208-261.

the great hymnody of Paul Gerhardt (1607-1676) and the musical triumphs of Johann Sebastian Bach. The lifespan of Renaissance lyrics was long indeed and the romantic enthusiasm for the *Volkslied* and *Gesellschaftslied* as the major source of music must be radically revised.

Conrad Celtis boasted of the German inventor of printing, whom he could not name. Luther considered the printing press to be the last and greatest gift of God to man whereby the gospel would be disseminated to the ends of the earth. Printing not only served the cause of learning as its instruments for multiplying pages, but in important ways it changed the nature of the enterprise, of the way in which people thought and expressed themselves, and became a blender through which humanist and reformation thought fused as well as interacted. The sixteenth century was notable for the tremendous growth of private and public libraries, collections such as those of Frederick the Wise, that is, used by officials, professors, and the ruler himself. They invariably contained many humanist and classical as well as medieval and reformed theological writings.

Trithemius, like a very minuscle group of Italian humanists, set himself against the future. In his *De laude scriptorium Manuelium* he argued that parchment will last five times as long as paper (although paper cost only fifteen percent as much), that publishers are profit oriented and therefore many important books will not be printed and so lost (Trithemius a prophet!), and that printed books are less beautiful. But the days of the manuscript were numbered as the volume of printed books became virtually numberless. By 1520 all the major Latin authors had been published. Valla's *De Elegantiis Linguae Latinae* (1444) went through sixty editions between 1471 and 1536. Within two generations after the supreme invention there were presses in 250 towns, first of all in the commercial cities and then in the university towns. The leading German publishing centers during the early decades of the Reformation were Nuremberg, Wittenberg, Strasbourg, Augsburg, Magdeburg, Frankfurt, Basel and Zurich. Anton Koberger in Nuremberg kept twenty-four presses going and employed over a hundred workers. Just as in Italy, where printers and whole dynasties of publishers such as the Aldines were learned humanists, so also many of the German printers were learned men in their own right and advocates of humanism and reform. Pamphilus Gengenbach (d. 1524), for example, a printer and Meistersinger of Nuremberg, living later in Basel, adapted the *Fastnachtsspiel* to moral and religious ends.[114] He also published tracts of Eberlin von Günzburg, the most prolific and effective pamphleteer of the Reformation. Hans Lufft, one of Luther's favorite printers, became mayor of Wittenberg. A very large number of printers became evangelical preachers, possibly moved by the tracts they published and freed by the frequent bankruptcies of printing firms. If printing served humanism and reform, the humanists and reformers served publishing in turn. There was a steadily ascending curve in the volume of publications, but controversies triggered great upsurges in the number of books and pamphlets published. Like the Savonarola incident in Florence, the Reuchlin affair in Germany, the Carlstadt skirmish with the Thomists, the events of the Reformation opened the floodgates. The number of books published in Germany increased by ten times between the posting of the Ninety-Five Theses and the year 1524, which marked the high tide in the printing of religious and social treatises. On February 14, 1519, the humanist publisher Johannes Froben in Basel wrote to Luther:

> We sent six hundred copies of your collected works which I published to France and Spain. They are sold in Paris, read and appreciated at the Sorbonne. The book dealer Clavus of Pavia took a sizable number to Italy to sell them everywhere in the cities. I have sent copies also to England and Brabant and have only ten copies left in the storeroom. I have never had such good luck with a book. The more accomplished a man is, the more he thinks of you.[115]

The statistics tell an exciting tale of the proliferation and power of the press. Estimates vary, but a reasonable conjecture is that 40,000 titles were published in Europe during the fifteenth century. If the average edition numbered 250 volumes, and it may well have been closer to 300, there must have been a total of ten to twelve million incunabala published, many traditional medieval titles, but many also humanist and classical texts. By the year 1517 another ten million volumes were published, but by 1550 under the pressure of the Reformation 150,000 more titles had been published for a total of sixty million volumes.[116] Some 25,000 works were printed in Germany before 1500, not including broadsides and leaflets, but once

---

[114] Derek Van Abbé, "Development of Dramatic Form in Pamphilus Gengenbach," *Modern Language Review*, XLV (1950), 46-62.

[115] Froben to Luther, February 14, 1519, in *D. Martin Luthers Werke: Briefwechsel*, I (Weimar, 1930), 332.

[116] See Richard C. Coles, "The Dynamics of Printing in the Sixteenth Century," *The Social History of the Reformation*, Lawrence W. Buck and Jonathan Zophy,

the Reformation was underway the annual number rose to five hundred and then to a thousand. In Wittenberg alone over six hundred different works were published between the years 1518 and 1523, whereas in the British Isles the total for these years was less than three hundred.[117] Classical learning and religious thought no longer contributed exclusively to what Vico was to call "the conceit of the learned", but became the property of an ever broader range of the literate population. The French humanist Louis Le Roy rightly declared later in the sixteenth century:

> Besides the restoration of learning, now almost complete, the invention of many fine new things ... has been reserved to this age. Among these, printing deserves to be put first ... The invention has greatly aided the advancement of all disciplines. For it seems miraculously to have been discovered in order to bring back to life more easily literature which seemed dead.[118]

Luther, like Erasmus, was quick to see the power of the press, but he held that the message was still more powerful than the medium. In 1522 he wrote: "I have only put God's Word in motion through preaching and writing. The Word has done everything and carried everything before it."

V. Conclusion

In the first of his Martin Classical Lectures delivered at Oberlin College two decades ago, Paul Oskar Kristeller observed that "the Renaissance is a very complex period and it encompassed, just as do the Middle Ages or any other period, a good many chronological, regional, and social differences." [119] Our review of the *Itinerarium studii renascentium litterarum* to the North underscores the truth of Professor Kristeller's statement. German humanism was related by strong bonds of consanguinity to Italian humanism, and yet its historical development followed an independent course.

Italian humanism has been traditionally considered the fountainhead of all Renaissance humanism. The full development of humanism

---

eds. (Columbus, Ohio, 1972), 93-105; Elizabeth L. Eisenstein, "The Advent of Printing and the Protestant Revolt: A New Approach to the Disruption of Christendom," Robert M. Kingdon, ed., *Transition and Revolution* (Minneapolis, Minn., 1974), 235-270, has a useful bibliography, pp. 268-270; Rudolf Hirsch, *Printing, Selling and Reading, 1450-1550* (Wiesbaden, 1967).

[117] Harold Jantz, *op. cit.*, 418.

[118] Louis Le Roy, *De la vicissitude ou Varieté des Choses en L'Univers* (Paris, 1575), tr. J. B. Ross, *The Portable Renaissance Reader* (New York, 1965), 98.

[119] Paul Oskar Kristeller, *Renaissance Thought. The Classic, Scholastic, and Humanist Strains* (New York, 1961), 4.

in the other European countries has usually been attributed to the late fifteenth or to the sixteenth century at the very point when the movement in Italy itself had supposedly reached the end of the line.[120] Our review of the course of German humanism leads to the conclusion that whatever claims can be made for the indigenous or medieval roots of northern humanism, the influence of Italian humanism was the critical determinant during the early and the mature phases of German humanism in stimulating interest in classical culture as form and norm and in defining the cultural significance of the classical revival for the Germans. The tendency in some of the more recent scholarship to stress the native roots and the independent development of northern humanism, especially of Germany and the Low Countries and of France and England as well, must be very much attenuated. The distinctive Renaissance thrust, the classical revival, received its impetus from Italy in the fifteenth century, whatever the carry-over from earlier medieval renaissances in the North and the contribution of the Brethren of Common Life or the *via antiqua* may have been. Moreover, the influence of Italian humanism in the German speaking lands, as in the case of France, has been traced back to the early fifteenth century and even to the fourteenth, so that many of the "pre-humanists" in the North can be claimed as "humanists" with almost as much justice as the newly appreciated pre-Petrarchan forerunners of humanism in Italy.[121]

Just as the vitality of the Italian Renaissance and the creativity of Italian humanism especially in Florence and Venice is said to have lasted far beyond the *sacco di Roma* (1527), so German humanism, too, remained a powerful cultural force in alliance with the Reformation.[122] Partially subsumed under the religious drive of the Reformation, it received through the approbations of and amalgamation with the Reformation a broader, deeper, and long lasting impact

---

[120] Paul Oskar Kristeller, "Studies on Renaissance Humanism during the Last Twenty Years," *Studies in the Renaissance*, IX (1962), 8-9.

[121] *Ibid.*, 9. The claims made for the *via antiqua* as the cradle of humanism have long since been abandoned as argued by Heinrich Hermelink, *Die religiösen Reformbestrebungen des deutschen Humanismus* (Tübingen, 1907).

[122] Eric Cochrane, *Florence in the Forgotten Centuries, 1527-1800. A History of Florence and the Florentines in the Age of the Grand Dukes* (Chicago, 1973), maintains that the Florentines retained their creativity long after they had lost their position as the cultural leaders of Europe, although some reviewers of his work insist upon the great qualitative difference between the epigoni and the greats of the *Quattrocento*. William J. Bouwsma, *Venice and the Defense of Republican Liberty. Renaissance Values in the Age of the Counter Reformation* (Berkeley and Los Angeles,

through the sixteenth and seventeenth centuries. The study of the course of German humanism from the early fifteenth century to the seventeenth century demonstrates the tremendous continuity of that intellectual movement. The commonplace notion of a sharp break between Renaissance and Reformation so far as humanism in intellectual and cultural terms is concerned has proved to be a *fable convenue* which must be relegated to the historians' shelves of outmoded curiosities along with the idea of the Middle Ages as the dark ages or the Enlightenment as an antihistorical period.[123]

The Holy Roman Empire experienced over half a century of uneasy calm following the Peace of Augsburg in 1555, which gave to the German areas a distinct advantage over Italy, weighed down by Spanish control, and over France, torn for decades by religious wars and massacres. Neo-Latin publications, Greek and Hebrew studies, like natural science and education, made notable progress in Germany during the course of the sixteenth century. As early as the twelfth century the *carmina burana* expressed nostalgia for the good old days when *Florebat olim studium*. It was only natural for men later in the sixteenth century to look back on the early decades of Renaissance humanism and the heroic days of the Reformation as the good old days. In actual fact, the literary and linguistic achievements of the later sixteenth century are very noteworthy and in some ways marked the maturation of cultural efforts begun in an amateurish way early in the century.

There was perhaps a loss of verve and fire as the century moved on. Humanism became more a matter of classical study than of spontaneous expression or style of life. But this change must not be exaggerated and it was in some measure compensated for by the much broader spread of humanist learning as the century advanced thanks to the educational program which combined Renaissance humanist and reform goals. Cicero's intellectual definition of life, *docto homini et erudito vivere est cogitare*, gained the approval of a growing number of people drawn from all classes of society. This spread of humanism was less a result of a chance trickle-down process than it

---

1968), follows the development of Venetian republican consciousness from the relatively backward and inarticulate early Venetian Renaissance to the rich and sophisticated thought of late sixteenth and early seventeenth century writers such as Gasparo Contarini, Paolo Paruta, Enrico Davila, and Paolo Sarpi.

[123] Heinz Liebing, "Perspektivische Verzeichnungen. Über die Haltbarkeit der *fable convenue* in der Kirchengeschichte," *Zeitschrift für Kirchengeschichte*, III (1968), 289-307.

was the product of an educational system designed toward that end. Even the persistence of dialectic and the resurgence of Aristotle could not repress the humanist learned tradition of rhetoric, poetry, moral philosophy, history, Platonism, and natural philosophy. One is struck by the concatenation of influences from person to person, teacher to student, mind to mind. The spread of humanism to a reasonably broad segment of the German population began with the attendance of German youth at the Italian universities, increased as the German universities served as ladders of social mobility, and broadened as the reformers, Protestants and Jesuits alike, developed the gymnasium ideal of secondary education.

Renaissance humanism was an international phenomenon, and our survey has pointed to the many ties binding German to Italian, Dutch, French, and even English humanism. Many questions remain unanswered, and a library of books is yet to be written on unexplored aspects of this subject. One of the most intriguing questions begging for an answer is why, with the growing number of erudite and cultivated men, German humanism failed during the second half of the sixteenth century to produce any real genius comparable to those who made Elizabethan England a golden age from Spenser to Shakespeare.[124] Looking ahead from the year 1555 one might have expected Germany to take over the cultural leadership from Italy, with France and England following after, but just the reverse order actually occurred. Two centuries later, when German literature seemed doomed to tertiary status as imitative and unoriginal, it bloomed into the garden of Weimar genius just as French and English letters wilted away. Perhaps the centrifugal force of political particularism, the shift of economic activity to the Atlantic seaboard, the passing of the agonizing decades of religious struggle and the stalemate acknowledged and legalized by the Peace of Augsburg, the insistence on orthodoxies, or other considerations may be adduced as contributing factors. But the human spirit must not fare too well in this world, for creative genius responds to suffering and conflict and grows dull with overmuch prosperity. The German humanists such as Reuchlin were fond of quoting the line from Horace, *Exegi monumentum aere perennis*.[125] Compared with the golden age of the Italian Renaissance it was indeed a monument of bronze. But it also had a lasting quality, though it gave way in the end to the iron age of an industrial society.

---

[124] Harold Jantz, *op. cit.*, 435.
[125] Horace, *Carmina*, III, 30.

INDEX OF PERSONAL NAMES

Book titles appearing in the text are indexed under authors' names. Titles in the footnotes are not indexed.

INDEX OF PLACE NAMES

Names of places, schools, churches and religious houses are indexed; names of the major regions or countries of Europe treated in this book—England, Italy, Spain, France, Germany, the Low Countries—are not indexed.